REGISTERED PROGRAM SERIES

Retirement
PLANNING
AND EMPLOYEE BENEFITS
for Financial Planners
THIRD EDITION

Michael A. Dalton

Retirement PLANNING

AND EMPLOYEE BENEFITS

for Financial Planners

THIRD EDITION

Michael A. Dalton

YOUR MONEY EDUCATION RESOURCE.™

1000 RIVERBEND BLVD.
SUITE A
ST. ROSE, LA 70087
888-295-6023

Printed in the U.S.A.

ISBN: 0-9748945-4-0
Custom Edition for The College for Financial Planning ISBN: 0-9748945-5-9

Library of Congress Card Number: 2005924261

ABOUT THE AUTHOR

Michael A. Dalton, Ph.D., JD, CPA, CLU, ChFC, CFP®

- Former Chair of the Board of Dalton Publications, L.L.C.
- Former Senior Vice President, Education at BISYS Group
- Teaches personal financial planning at Georgetown University's Executive Certificate in Financial Planning Program
- Provides litigation support for NASD securities arbitration and as an expert in securities litigation.
- Associate professor of Accounting and Taxation at Loyola University in New Orleans, Louisiana
- Ph.D. in Accounting from Georgia State University
- Juris Doctorate from Louisiana State University in Baton Rouge, Louisiana
- MBA and BBA in Management and Accounting from Georgia State University
- Former board member of the CFP Board's Board of Examiners, Board of Standards, and Board of Governors
- Former member (and chair) of the CFP Board's Board of Examiners
- Member of the Financial Planning Association
- Member of the *Journal of Financial Planning* Editorial Advisory Board
- Member of the *Journal of Financial Planning* Editorial Review Board
- Member of the LSU Law School Board of Trustees (2000 - Present)
- Author of *Dalton Review for the CFP® Certification Examination: Volume I – Outlines and Study Guides, Volume II – Problems and Solutions, Volume III - Case Exam Book, Mock Exams A-1 and A-2 (1st - 8th Editions)*
- Author of *Estate Planning for Financial Planners (1st - 3rd Editions)*
- Author of *Retirement Planning and Employee Benefits for Financial Planners (1st - 3rd Editions)*
- Co-author of *Dalton CFA® Study Notes Volumes I and II (1st - 2nd Editions)*
- Co-author of *Personal Financial Planning: Theory and Practice (1st - 3rd Editions)*
- Co-author of *Personal Financial Planning: Cases and Applications (1st - 4th Editions)*
- Co-author of *Cost Accounting: Traditions and Innovations* published by West Publishing Company
- Co-author of the *ABCs of Managing Your Money* published by National Endowment for Financial Education

ABOUT THE CONTRIBUTING AUTHORS

Randal R. Cangelosi, JD, MBA
- Practicing litigator throughout Louisiana, in commercial law and litigation, wills and trust litigation, environmental law and litigation, medical malpractice defense, and insurance law and litigation
- Has successfully defended numerous corporations, businesses, and doctors in jury and judge tried cases throughout Louisiana
- Juris Doctorate from Loyola University New Orleans
- Master of Business from Loyola University New Orleans
- BS in Finance from Louisiana State University
- Member of the American & Federal Bar Associations
- Member of the New Orleans and Baton Rouge Bar Associations
- Former Chairman of New Orleans Bar Association, Community Service Committee
- Former Chairman of New Orleans Bar Association, Food and Clothing Drives
- Co-author of *Personal Financial Planning: Theory and Practice (1st - 3rd Editions)*
- Co-author of *Professional Ethics for Financial Planners*

Kristi M. Tafalla, JD, MS, ChFC, CFP®
- Attorney and Personal Financial Planner specializing in Income Tax and Estate Planning
- Teaches estate planning, income tax planning, and comprehensive case course through various CFP Board-Registered Programs as well as comprehensive reviews for the Certified Financial Planner designation
- Former Director of Product Development, Advanced Designations for BISYS Education Services
- Juris Doctorate from Louisiana State University in Baton Rouge, Louisiana
- Masters of Science in Accounting with a Tax Specialty from the University of New Orleans
- Bachelors of Civil Law from Louisiana State University in Baton Rouge, Louisiana
- Bachelors of Business Administration in Accounting from Loyola University, New Orleans
- Member of the American Bar Association (Sections: Real Estate; Probate and Trust; Income Tax; Family Law; Business Law)
- Member of the Texas, Louisiana, New Orleans, Baton Rouge, and Dallas Bar Associations
- Member of the Financial Planning Association
- Contributor *Estate Planning for Financial Planners (1st - 3rd Editions)*
- Contributor *Personal Financial Planning: Theory and Practice (1st - 3rd Editions)*
- Contributor *BISYS Review for the CFP® Certification Examination: Volume I - Outlines and Study Guides, Volume II - Problems and Solutions, Volume III - Case Exam Book, Mock Exams A-1 and A-2 (5th - 8th Editions)*

ACKNOWLEDGEMENTS & SPECIAL THANKS

We are most appreciative for the tremendous support and encouragement we have received throughout this project. We are extremely grateful to the instructors and program directors of CFP Board-Registered programs who provided valuable comments on the first, second, and third edition. We are fortunate to have dedicated, careful readers at several institutions who were willing to share their needs, expectations, and time with us. We also owe a debt of gratitude to all the reviewers and students who have read and commented on the first two editions.

We owe a special thanks to two key professionals, Randall C. Martinez, MS, CPA, CFP® and Chris White, MBA, CFP® for their significant contribution of time and effort with this project.

Randall Martinez is a Personal Financial Planner specializing in personal financial planning, estate, and individual income tax planning. He teaches retirement planning, estate planning, and income tax planning through various CFP Board-Registered Programs as well as comprehensive reviews for the Certified Financial Planner designation. Mr. Martinez has a Masters of Science in Accounting with a Tax Specialty from the University of New Orleans and Bachelors of Accountancy degree from Loyola University, New Orleans. Mr. Martinez provided a significant contribution to the first two editions of this text. His thoughtful reading, rewriting, and editing of various sections throughout the book, as well as writing and developing Key Concepts, Quick Quizzes, Discussion Questions, Multiple Choice Problems, and instructor materials were extremely valuable.

Chris White teaches the financial planning program to financial service professionals, attorneys, insurance agents, CPAs, and others working to attain their CFP® certification at Xavier University in Cincinnati. He is also vice president of the National City Private Client Group, a board member, and the 2006 president of the Greater Cincinnati Chapter of the Financial Planning Association and an instructor for comprehensive reviews for the CFP® Certification Examination. Mr. White has an MBA with a concentration in Taxation from Xavier University and a B.S. in Accounting from the University of Cincinnati. After using the 2nd Edition in his retirement planning course, he provided invaluable feedback on where improvements could be made for the 3rd edition. He also meticulously reviewed the 3rd edition of the text and provided many valuable suggestions for improvements.

Thanks also to John McCammon, CJ Guenzel, Kevin Dalton, Karen Robinson, Gary Knoepfler, and Casey Cadella for their manuscript reviews and thoughtful feedback. Their thorough editing, detailed calculation reviews, helpful suggestions for additional content, and other valuable comments, improved this edition. To each of these individuals we extend our deepest gratitude and appreciation.

Developing a textbook that is aesthetically pleasing and easy to read is a difficult undertaking. We would like to pay special thanks to Robin Meyer and Donna Dalton who typed and formatted the entire text. This book would not have been possible without their extraordinary dedication, skill, and knowledge. We also extend our thanks to Barry Kerrigan and Del LeMond of Desktop Miracles for designing the cover and the sidebar artwork used throughout the text.

We have received so much help from so many people, it is possible that we have inadvertently overlooked thanking someone. If so, it is our shortcoming, and we apologize in advance. Please let us know if you are that someone, and we will make it right in our next printing.

PREFACE

Retirement Planning and Employee Benefits for Financial Planners is written at the graduate and undergraduate level for students interested in acquiring an understanding of retirement planning from a professional financial planning viewpoint. The text is intended to be used in a Retirement Planning course as part of an overall curriculum in financial planning. The text is also intended to serve as a reference for practicing professional financial planners. It was designed to meet the educational requirements for a Retirement Course in a CFP Board-Registered Program. Through this text, the author hopes to convey his knowledge and enthusiasm for retirement and financial planning with a user-friendly approach to learning the topic at hand.

Special Features

A variety of tools and presentation methods are used throughout this text to assist in the learning process. Some of the features presented in this text that are designed to enhance the readers' understanding and learning process include:

- **Key Concepts** – At the beginning of each subsection are study objectives, or key concepts, each stated as a question. To be successful in this course, you should be able to answer these questions. So as you read, guide your learning by looking for the answers. When you find the answers, highlight or underline them. It is important that you actually highlight/underline and not just make a mental note, as the action of stopping and writing reinforces your learning. Watch for this symbol:

- **Quick Quizzes** – Following each subsection you will find a Quick Quiz, which checks and reinforces what you read. Again, actually write in the text, answer each question, and then check your answers supplied at the bottom of the quiz. If you missed any and do not understand why, flip back to that section and review it until you do. Watch for this symbol:

- **Examples** – Examples are used frequently to illustrate the concepts being discussed and to help you understand and apply the concepts presented. Examples are identified in the margin with the following symbol:

- **Exhibits** – The written text is enhanced and simplified by using exhibits where appropriate to promote learning and application. Exhibits are identified with the following symbol:

- **Know The Numbers** - Several chapters contain a "Know the Numbers" box at the beginning of the chapter, which is designed to alert you of the important numbers that will be discussed throughout that chapter.

- **Key Terms** – Key terms appear in **boldfaced type** throughout the text to assist in the identification of important concepts and terminology. A list of key terms with definitions appear at the end of each chapter.

- **End of Chapter Questions** – Each chapter concludes with a series of discussion and multiple choice questions that highlight the major topics covered in the chapter. The questions test retention and understanding of important chapter material and can be used for review and classroom discussion.

- **Glossary** – A compilation of the key terms identified throughout the text is located at the end of the book.

Special Note on Estimated Numbers – Numbers that require annual indexing were estimated throughout the text for future years not released by the Internal Revenue Service or the Department of Labor at the time of printing. These estimated numbers are marked with a † for easy identification. We have taken great care to determine the indexing method for each of these numbers and expect minimal, if any, modifications through 2007. In the event that there are any changes, we will provide updates on our website at www.money-education.com.

Table of Contents

3. QUALIFIED PLAN OVERVIEW

3. APPENDIX: SPECIAL TOPICS OF QUALIFIED PLANS

4. QUALIFIED PENSION PLANS

5. PROFIT SHARING PLANS

6. STOCK BONUS PLANS AND EMPLOYEE STOCK OWNERSHIP PLANS

7. DISTRIBUTIONS FROM QUALIFIED PLANS

8. INSTALLATION, ADMINISTRATION, AND TERMINATION OF QUALIFIED PLANS

9. IRAS AND SEPS

10. SIMPLES, 403(b) PLANS, AND 457 PLANS

11. SOCIAL SECURITY

12. DEFERRED COMPENSATION AND NONQUALIFIED PLANS

13. EMPLOYEE BENEFITS: FRINGE BENEFITS

14. EMPLOYEE BENEFITS: GROUP BENEFITS

Introduction to Retirement Planning

INTRODUCTION

Retirement planning and employee benefits are difficult but fascinating areas of study because, while complex, they provide tremendous career and intellectual opportunities for a wide variety of interested parties. Most individuals are interested in achieving financial security. This typically means achieving financial independence so that they are able to maintain a desired lifestyle without employment income. To become financially independent one may have to forgo some immediate consumption to provide an opportunity for discretionary funds to grow and accumulate over time, as well as avoid catastrophic financial occurrences that could result in financial dependence. Retirement planning and employee benefits play an essential role in satisfying the need to save for future consumption.

Employers are keenly interested in the areas of retirement planning and employee benefits because they consider and select benefit plans. Therefore, they are impacted by both the current and future benefits costs and the limitations of such plans. Employees are also interested since benefits are a generally considered a part of overall compensation. Another large group interested in this area of study is the diverse group of professionals and members of the financial services industry because of the professional opportunities and the sheer dollar size of retirement assets in the market. Lastly, the U.S. Government has a public, social, and tax policy interest in the area. When the government wants to promote social policy, such as health care benefits, it frequently utilizes tax policy to encourage plan selectors to adopt the programs desired by the government.

Be forewarned, the topics of study are neither simple nor entirely intuitive. Determining funding requirements for retirement requires an in-depth understanding of life expectancies, work life expectancies, retirement life expectancies, the projection of inflation and investment returns, and the determination of expenditure needs for particular persons far in advance of their occurrence. When a person reaches retirement age, the optimal distribution amount must be determined given a probability element that the distribution amount will provide sufficient income to maintain the retiree's lifestyle for the entire retirement period while having little or no risk of being depleted during the retiree's life.

A vast amount of study is needed to initially master the subject of qualified retirement plans because of the complexity of the federal legislation controlling the area. In addition, as one might expect, the rules governing qualified retirement plans are frequently changing by new legislation. Therefore, the current rules and optimal choices today may change at any time. Thus, continuing study in the area is essential to maintain and improve your skill level. Tax-advantaged plans, other than qualified plans, are also government created or approved, have similar complexities, and also run the risk of change.

This text also deals with Social Security legislation and its benefits and employee benefits, both of which are large and complex topics. Furthermore, after the implementation of employee benefit plans, the costs and benefits, as well as the employee censuses (age, income, length of services, etc.) do not remain static. Therefore, there will always be a need for monitoring, making changes, or terminating plans. As a result, one must learn the myriad of federal rules and stay current with changes in law and practice to become a master of the retirement planning field.

INTERESTED PARTIES

EMPLOYEES

Retirement plans and employee benefits provide an essential role in the pursuit of financial security. Retirement plans, whether employer or employee funded, offer employees an opportunity to accumulate assets that can later be used to provide a stable standard of living and financial security during retirement.

Funding of retirement benefits has changed significantly over the last thirty years. Years ago, most employers provided employees with a retirement benefit, typically in the form of a fixed pension that would continue for the life of the retiree. Over time these plans, which were noncontributory by employees and costly to employers, have been replaced by plans that place more funding reliance on employees and shift the investment risk and responsibility to employees. The most well known and common of these plans are the 401(k) plan, the SEP, and the SIMPLE, all of which will be discussed in-depth throughout the text.

As employer funding has decreased and as life expectancy has increased, employees have begun to realize the importance of planning for retirement in hopes of achieving financial independence through their own savings and investments. Employees are also becoming more interested in risk management benefit plans (health insurance, disability insurance, life insurance, and long-term care insurance) because they are beginning to understand the risk and potential negative financial impact of a catastrophic event on their financial security. While it is the employer's responsibility to communicate employer-sponsored employee benefit and retirement plans provided to employees so that the employees have an opportunity to fully understand the benefits, the employee must take an active role in choosing and evaluating among benefits available.

Many employees view retirement plan benefits and employee benefits (where employer contributions are present) as a part of their overall compensation package. For example, employees realize that premiums paid for group health insurance are generally less costly than premiums paid for an individual plan with the same coverage and exclusions. Employees also realize that to the extent the employer contributes to the payment of such premiums, this value is not included in the employee's taxable income and, therefore, is less costly to the employee, who would have to purchase health insurance with after-tax dollars without such a plan.

Unfortunately, not all workers are covered by employee benefit plans, nor are they covered by retirement plans sufficient to produce adequate retirement income. While 65 percent of full-time employees of employers with 100 or more employees were covered by one or more employment based retirement plans in 2003, only 35 percent of full-time workers in small private companies or institutions (99 or less workers) were covered by a retirement plan.[1] Consider that even with these dismal statistics, the covered employees may not be adequately covered.

Meanwhile, Americans' overall confidence in their ability to retire comfortably is extraordinarily high. The 2003 retirement confidence survey by the Employee Benefit Research Institute, the American Surveys Education Counsel, and Matthew Greenwald and Associates indicates that over 70 percent of workers are "somewhat" to "very confident" that they will have sufficient assets to live comfortably throughout retirement.

CONFIDENCE SURVEY

EXHIBIT 1.1

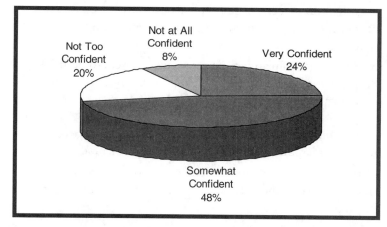

Not Too
Confident
20%

Not at All
Confident
8%

Very Confident
24%

Somewhat
Confident
48%

The study lists three factors to explain why Americans have such a high confidence level about their ability to retire comfortably.
1. They do not really know how much it will cost to retire.
2. They are mentally postponing retirement.
3. They are unaffected by investment market declines because they have no money in the investment markets.

The study also revealed that employee's spend more time planning vacations than planning for retirement, save blindly without knowing how much to save, do not know the normal retirement age for receiving full Social Security benefits (51 percent think they are eligible before they actually are), and have given little thought to the need for health or long-term care insurance during retirement.

---

1. US Department of Labor, Bureau of Labor Statistics "Employee Benefits in Private Industry in the United States, 2002 - 2003" Bulletin 2573, January 2005.

The study also points out the following myths and realities:

> *Myth:* 70 percent of respondents say they plan to work during retirement.
>
> *Reality:* Only 28 percent of retirees actually work during retirement.
>
> *Myth:* 25 percent of respondents want to retire at age 65 and 25% want to retire at age 66.
>
> *Reality:* The average worker retires at age 62. 40 percent of retirees retired early (before age 65) for some reason that was beyond their own control (50 percent due to health and 23 percent due to changes in employment).
>
> *Myth:* 39 percent of respondents think that retirement needs are ≤ 60 percent of pre-retirement income. 50 percent of workers expect to need 70 percent of pre-retirement income. Less than 20 percent of respondents expect to need 80 percent or more of pre-retirement income to maintain their lifestyle in retirement.
>
> *Reality:* Financial planners expect average retirees to need 70-80 percent of pre-retirement income to maintain their pre-retirement lifestyle.
>
> *Myth:* Only 13 percent of respondents expect Social Security to be their largest single source of retirement income.
>
> *Reality:* 44 percent of current retirees report that Social Security is actually their largest single source of retirement income.

The study illustrates how generally uninformed employees are about retirement planning, retirement plans, employee benefits, pension plans, and Social Security. Unfortunately, even where employer-sponsored retirement plans exist, many are self-reliant plans requiring the participant to determine both the amount to save and which investments to choose from those offered.

The optimism reported in the survey is ill founded, and the need for assistance in the form of competent financial advice regarding this entire area cannot be overemphasized.

EXHIBIT 1.2

- Employees view benefits as part of overall compensation.
- Employees would rather pay costs with pretax dollars.
- Employees generally understand retirement plans and employee benefits are part of their overall financial plan.
- Employee confidence regarding their ability to retire comfortably is high, but inconsistent with reality.
- Employees generally do not really know the cost of retirement.

EMPLOYERS

Employers view employer-sponsored retirement plans and employee benefits as an overall part of compensation costs. Employers are sensitive to the fact that once these plans are put into place, it is the employer that will have to manage these costs in the future, in spite of increasing rates of inflation associated with some of these benefits. The U.S. Chamber of Commerce reports that employee benefits cost employers an additional 39 percent over other wage expenses in 2001. The most common benefits offered by employers included health insurance, paid vacation, holiday benefits, and retirement and life insurance benefits. The largest share of employee benefit costs was medical premiums at 11 percent of total gross payout.[2]

Below is an example of how basic employee benefits including health, life, and disability insurance; a 401(k) match; and reasonable vacation, personal, and holiday time can increase employer payroll costs. In this case, the employer paid the employee a $40,000 salary and incurred $12,068 in additional benefits. These costs vary depending on the benefits offered, the age of the employee (insurance), and the salary received. Keep in mind there may be other benefits provided by the employer, such as worker's compensation insurance and unemployment taxes.

EXAMPLE 1.1

	Amount	% of Compensation
Salary	**$40,000**	
Social Security	$3,060	7.65%
Health Insurance Premiums Paid	$4,800	12.00%
Life and Disability Insurance Premiums Paid	$700	1.75%
401(k) Employer Match	$1,200	3.00%
Vacation Time - 10 Days	$1,538	3.85%
Personal Time - 5 Days	$769	1.92%
Holiday Time - 8 Days	$1,231	3.08%
	$12,068	**30.17%**

2. U.S. Chamber of Commerce, January 31, 2003 Press Release, "Benefits Account for More Payroll Costs."

The reasons that employers establish employee benefits and retirement plans are principally business related. Such plans have a positive impact on the ability to recruit, hire, and retain qualified employees. The two leading reasons employers do not sponsor such plans are affordability and a lack of faith that such plans would have a positive effect on production and profitability.

Unfortunately most small business owners are no more well informed about retirement plans and employee benefits than the workers they employ. There are a number of retirement plans that cost the employer little or nothing and would greatly benefit both the owner and the employees. Such plans are widely available but unknown or not understood by the small business owners. Approximately one-third of small business owners have never heard of a SIMPLE plan, which has low costs and a positive impact on retirement planning.

Larger employers are more likely to have a wide variety of employee benefits and a retirement plan than small employers. These employers have human resource departments, which help select and administer employee benefit and retirement plans. The human resource departments make use of outside professional institutions and experts in plan selection, plan communication, and plan administration. The professionals include actuaries, pension experts, ERISA attorneys, employee benefit consultants, investment advisors, and plan administrators.

| EXHIBIT 1.3 | COMMON EMPLOYER PERSPECTIVES OF RETIREMENT PLANS |

- Employers view retirement plans and employee benefits as part of overall compensation costs.
- Employee benefit expenses may add an additional 30% - 40% to payroll costs.
- Employers use employee benefit plans to recruit, hire, and retain qualified workers.

PROFESSIONALS AND INSTITUTIONS

There are a wide array of professionals and experts providing services in the areas of retirement planning, retirement plans, and employee benefits. There are also large financial institutions that manage plan assets (investments), administer plans, and communicate plan information to plan participants. Professionals within these financial institutions include personal financial planners who assist individuals and small business owners; actuaries whose primary role is in defined benefit or target benefit pension plans; pension experts and ERISA attorneys who assist in plan selection or creation, implementation, and communication; valuation experts who are used to value closely-held stock used in retirement plans; pension administrators who manage plan assets and communicate plan information to participants; Certified Public Accountants and other tax preparers who file required tax compliance reports; insurance planning professionals; and investment advisors who may advise either employers, plan participants, or both.

Major financial institutions play a role in the retirement plan area by providing prototype plans for the convenience of customers, taking assets under management, and serving as custodians of assets. These institutions may also provide employee benefit plans and include insurance companies, banks, investment houses, and mutual fund companies.

Because of the complex nature of the entire field, any of these experts may only be an expert in a small portion of the whole field. However, it is essential that financial planners have a solid working knowledge of all of the areas and understand what each expert contributes so they can advise both employees and employers accordingly.

PROFESSIONALS AND INSTITUTIONS INTERESTED IN RETIREMENT PLANNING

EXHIBIT 1.4

INTERESTED PROFESSIONALS

- Actuaries
- Pension Consultants
- Valuation Experts
- Financial Planners
- Employee Benefit Consultants
- ERISA Attorneys
- Certified Public Accountants
- Plan Administrators
- Insurance Professionals

INTERESTED INSTITUTIONS

- Banks
- Mutual Funds
- Insurance Companies
- Wirehouses and Brokerage Firms

According to the Federal Reserve Bank, there was approximately $10.7 trillion in tax-deferred accounts in 2001 with new annual contributions of approximately $400 billion, which shows why so many financial institutions and professionals are keenly interested in this area. The $10.7 trillion includes Individual Retirement Accounts (IRAs), SEP IRAs, Roth IRAs, employee-sponsored defined contribution plans, state and local government plans, private and federal defined benefit plans, and annuities.

TAX-DEFERRED DOLLARS 2001

EXHIBIT 1.5

IRAs (including rollovers)	$2.4 Trillion
Defined Contribution Plans	$2.4 Trillion
State and Local Government Retirement Plans	$2.2 Trillion
Private Defined Benefit Plans	$1.8 Trillion
Federal Defined Benefit Plans	$0.8 Trillion
Annuities	$1.1 Trillion
TOTAL	**$10.7 Trillion (rounding)**
	2001 Federal Reserve Board

In particular, 401(k) plan assets have risen from $385 billion in 1990 to $1.75 trillion in 2001. The largest amount of the money (44%) was invested in mutual funds.

GOVERNMENT

The U.S. Government has a fundamental interest in employer-sponsored private retirement plans and privately-sponsored employee benefit plans. The government, as sponsor of the Social Security program and its benefits (retirement, disability, and survivorship) and health care benefits for retirees over 65 through Medicare, is greatly concerned that Social Security contributions (funded through payroll taxes) may be insufficient to meet already promised benefits. The government has a vested interest in promoting employee benefits such as employer-sponsored health care plans and retirement plans to mitigate the risk of more people ending up in the public welfare system. The government uses tax policy to make retirement plans and employee benefit plans attractive enough that a large number of employers will adopt them.

Keep in mind, however, that what the government gives out with one hand, it may take back with the other. Consider when studying these areas that while there are advantages to all these plans, usually in the form of tax relief, there are also disadvantages, usually in the form of compliance and costs. Specifically, as it relates to retirement plans, the $10.7 trillion in assets combined with the $400 billion annual contribution is expected to grow by 12 percent per year and may produce tax revenues of as much as $80 trillion from 2003 to 2040 (assuming a 30% tax rate). Both the Department of Labor and the Internal Revenue Service play an important role in these areas as does the quasi-governmental entity, the Pension Benefit Guaranty Corporation (PBGC).

| EXHIBIT 1.6 | GOVERNMENT PERSPECTIVE OF RETIREMENT |

- The government promotes social changes through tax legislation.
- The government sponsors the Social Security and Medicare systems, which act as a safety net for individual workers.
- The government has a vested interest in taxing deferred accounts.

PERSPECTIVE OF THE TEXT

The perspective of this text will be of a professional financial planner who is providing professional services to workers and employers in the following areas:
- retirement funding;
- retirement plan selection;
- Social Security benefits; and
- employee benefits.

In order to provide the highest level of service to the client, the financial planner must have a thorough knowledge of retirement funding and forecasting. The planner must also have a working knowledge of which qualified plans are appropriate for large employers given the goals and the employees census; which qualified plans are appropriate for small to medium size businesses; and which qualified plans are appropriate for single or few employee professionals.

The general financial planner needs to know the advantages and disadvantages of qualified plans and other tax-advantaged plans. The planner needs to know when to use a nonqualified plan and how nonqualified plans fit into an employer's executive compensation plan.

Financial planners need a deep understanding of the retirement, disability, and survivorship benefits provided by Social Security and the benefits provided by Medicare to properly advise clients of the government sponsored safety net programs and to determine the gaps that need to be filled to meet client goals or needs.

OVERVIEW OF TEXT

EXHIBIT 1.7

- Chapter 2 discusses the mechanics and issues surrounding the funding of retirement needs.
- Chapters 3 through 8 describes qualified plans, with Chapter 3 providing a critical overview of the standard rules relating to qualified plans.
- Chapters 4 through 6 provide a more in depth analysis of each of the qualified plans, including pension plans, hybrid plans, profit sharing plans, 401(k) plans, stock bonus plans, and ESOPs.
- Chapter 7 identifies and discusses rules and strategies related to distributions from qualified plans.
- Chapter 8 provides insight into plan installation, administration, and termination.
- Chapters 9 and 10 focus on other tax-advantaged plans that are not qualified but provide many of the benefits of qualified plans.
- Chapter 11 discusses Social Security.
- Chapter 12 describes and discusses deferred compensation plans, stock option plans, and planning for executive compensation.
- The last two chapters, 13 and 14, discuss employee fringe benefits, employee group benefit plans, and the taxation of such plans.

Introduction to Retirement Funding

FACTORS AFFECTING RETIREMENT PLANNING

Individuals face many decisions regarding retirement planning. In particular, they must decide what retirement means to them. Does retirement simply mean withdrawing from the workforce when financially able, or does it mean particular changes in lifestyle and family situations? For most, it is a major lifestyle change resulting from a major shift in how they spend their time, money, and energy.

Adequate retirement planning requires an understanding of the factors that affect retirement planning and the proper interrelationship of these factors. While this chapter discusses the major factors, it does not include all the factors that affect retirement planning. The major factors are the remaining work life expectancy (RWLE), the retirement life expectancy (RLE), the savings amount and rate, the annual income needed (needs) during retirement, the wage replacement ratio (WRR), the sources of retirement income, inflation expectations, investment returns, and other qualitative factors.

The resultant retirement plan, using these factors, must produce sufficient income at retirement to ensure that a comfortable preretirement lifestyle is maintained throughout the retirement period. A discussion of each factor, its associated risks, and the calculations essential to retirement planning (capital needs analysis) is presented below.

REMAINING WORK LIFE EXPECTANCY (RWLE)

Work life expectancy (WLE) is the period of time a person is expected to be in the work force. This time period, generally 30 - 40 years, is essential in retirement planning because it is the period when one saves and accumulates for retirement. Increasing or decreasing the work life expectancy impacts the time period over when individuals save for retirement. The United States has seen a substantial decline in the overall WLE in the last several years primarily due to individuals pursuing advanced education, which delays their entry into the workforce, and early retirement, which hastens their exit from the workforce.

Historically, normal retirement age was 65 mainly because Social Security designated it as such, and other employer-provided retirement plans followed suit. With changes in retirement plan distribution rules over the last two decades, the trend has moved toward an earlier retirement age. On the other hand, the retirement age to begin receiving Social Security benefits has increased over the past several years and looks like it will continue to increase over the next few years. The average retirement age was slightly under 62 between 2000 and 2005, indicating that individuals are either becoming more reliant on their own personal savings for retirement and less reliant on Social Security or that people are being forced to retire earlier for either health or employment reasons.

The concept of early retirement arose because of heightened awareness and preparedness for the financial aspects of retirement planning and the substantial economic wealth that many individuals accumulated through wise investment decisions. This early retirement trend is illustrated in Exhibit 2.1.

EXHIBIT 2.1   **MEDIAN RETIREMENT AGE FROM 1965-2005**

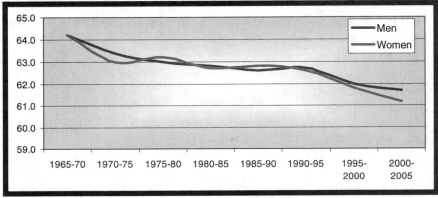

Source: U.S. Bureau of Labor Statistics

Key Concepts

Underline/highlight the answers to these questions as you read:

1. What are the major factors affecting retirement planning?

2. Define work life expectancy and retirement life expectancy.

3. When will most clients retire?

4. Explain the work life expectancy/retirement life expectancy dilemma.

Exhibit 2.1 illustrates that the retirement age has steadily declined over the last 35 years, with some individuals now retiring before age 62. Exhibit 2.2 focuses on the percentage of individuals in the U.S. that actually retire between the ages of 62 and 65 inclusively, identified as area A on the graph. The chart shows that 93 percent of U.S. residents retire between ages 62 and 65. It is important for financial planners to understand this because it can give them a good benchmark to use when calculating retirement needs. The planner must also realize that seven percent of these individuals do not retire between 62 and 65. Thus, the planner needs to talk with the client to determine when the client is going to retire.

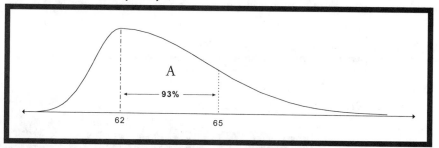

A is the area between ages 62 and 65 and represents 93% of the area under the curve.

The **remaining work life expectancy (RWLE)** is that work period that remains at a given point in time before retirement. For example, a 30-year-old client who expects to retire at age 65 has a RWLE of 35 years. Determining the RWLE is important for the financial planner because it tells the planner the remaining number of years the client has to save for retirement.

RETIREMENT LIFE EXPECTANCY (RLE)

Retirement life expectancy (RLE) is the time period beginning at retirement and extending until death. Currently, many retirees live 20 to 30 years in retirement. However, this was not always the case. In 1900, the average life expectancy for a newborn child was 47 years, and many individuals worked as long as they were able. The concept of retirement, as we know it today, did not exist. Exhibit 2.3 presents data depicting the increase in life expectancy from 1980 to 2001.

Although statistical data is not available for the current year, 2001 data can provide the financial planner a good understanding of how long a person may live in their RLE. Individuals born today are expected to live on average 77.2 years. Assuming a person retires at age 65, they will be in the RLE for 20 years on average because the average life expectancy for 65 year olds is 20 years. The problem is that the average life expectancy is just that - an average. 50 percent of 65 year olds are expected to live longer than 20 years. For instance, a person who was 65 in 2001 could expect to live 20 more years, thus reaching the age of 85 years old. However, if the individual happened to be 75,

Quick Quiz

Highlight the answer to these questions:

1. Approximately 93% of individuals retire between ages 60 and 62.
   a. True
   b. False

2. The RLE is the time period beginning at retirement and extending until death.
   a. True
   b. False

3. As the RLE increases because of early retirement, there is generally an increased need of funds to finance the RLE and a shortened WLE in which to save and accumulate assets.
   a. True
   b. False

False, True, True.

then he could expect to live to be 86.5 years old (11.6 additional years beyond age 75). Thus, the older an individual gets, the more likely they are to live beyond the average age of 77.2, which was expected at birth. Proper planning is needed because if the retired individual lives longer than he and his financial planner prepared for, there is a risk of running out of money.

| EXHIBIT 2.3 | LIFE EXPECTANCY AT BIRTH (U.S. 1950-2002) |

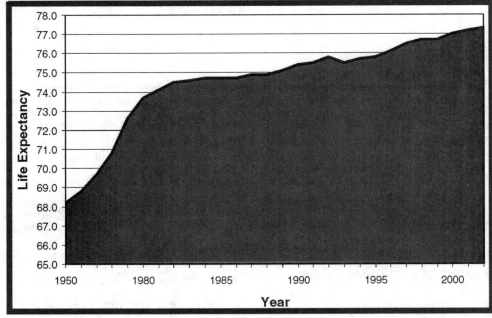

Source: www.cdc.gov

THE WLE AND THE RLE RELATIONSHIP

It is important that the financial planner understand the WLE and the RLE relationship. Since there is a fixed time between life and death, each period of time moves inversely with the other. If the WLE increases or decreases, the individual must shorten or lengthen the pre-work life expectancy (PWLE) or RLE. Each period is inversely related to the other. Thus, the planner must estimate each period to determine the ability to save and the need for retirement. In addition, when clients have been unable to save adequately, the planner can alter the periods in order to meet the client's needs. For example, if a client is unable to meet the needed retirement goal at 62, the planner can discuss lengthening the WLE and shortening the RLE in order to meet the retirement need. Exhibit 2.4 visually depicts this relationship.

| EXHIBIT 2.4 | THE WLE/RLE DILEMMA |

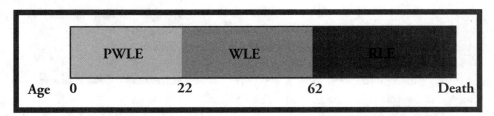

The area to the left of WLE represents the prework life expectancy (PWLE), which continues until the person enters the work force on a full time basis. Generally, the PWLE ends between ages 18 - 26, with the average age at 22. The middle area, the work life expectancy (WLE), represents the period of working years prior to retirement. This period begins at the end of the PWLE and ends at the beginning of retirement. The retirement life expectancy (RLE) usually begins around age 62 and ends around age 85 but may continue beyond age 100. Notice that as the RLE period increases due to early retirement and longer life expectancy, there is an increased need to finance the RLE and a shortened WLE in which to save and accumulate assets. Careful planning is needed long before the attainment of the desired retirement age to meet the funding requirements for a financially secure retirement.

SAVINGS AND INVESTMENT ISSUES

The savings amount, the savings rate, the timing of savings, and investment decisions are important concepts in retirement planning. If people were adequately saving for retirement beginning at an early age (25 - 35), they would need to save about 10 to 13 percent of their gross annual income and invest in a broad portfolio of growth investments over their entire work life to adequately fund the retirement goal. They would need to be ever mindful of investment returns and inflation to ensure sufficient savings and accumulations. Unfortunately, as demonstrated below, most of our society saves at a much lower savings rate than is necessary to adequately fund retirement, is not investment savvy, and is insensitive to the impact of inflation.

Key Concepts

Underline/highlight the answers to these questions as you read:

1. What are the savings and investment concepts that are important to retirement planning?

2. Why is it important to begin to save early for retirement planning?

3. Why is it important to understand investment decisions and their consequences in retirement planning?

4. How is inflation relevant to retirement planning?

THE SAVINGS AMOUNT

If individuals do not begin at an early age, then they must save a greater amount of their gross earnings to compensate for the missed years of contributions and compounding of investment returns. Exhibit 2.5 illustrates the amount individuals must save if they choose to begin saving for retirement later.

EXHIBIT 2.5

REQUIRED SAVINGS RATE FOR RETIREMENT
(ASSUME $0 OF ACCUMULATED SAVINGS AT THE BEGINNING AGE)

Age Beginning Regular and Recurring Savings*	Savings (as percent of gross pay) Rate Required to Create Appropriate Capital*
25 - 35	10 - 13%
35 - 45	13 - 20%
45 - 55	20 - 40%**

*Assumes appropriate asset allocation for reasonable-risk investor through accumulation year; also assumes normal raises and an 80 percent wage replacement ratio at Social Security normal retirement age and includes Social Security retirement benefits.
** At age 55 the person will have to delay retirement until age 70.

Exhibit 2.5 illustrates a major problem with delaying retirement savings. Namely, the need to save large amounts because there is less savings time to accumulate a sufficient amount of capital to retire. Saving requires foregoing current consumption, and most individuals find it difficult to decrease consumption by 20 to 30 percent, especially when they have been accustomed to maintaining a certain standard of living.

As an alternative to Exhibit 2.5, consider Exhibit 2.6, which assumes that each person is saving 10 to 13 percent of gross pay, including any employer retirement plan contributions. Assuming that the person saves 10 to 13 percent and also has an investment account balance equal to what they need at each age, they are making adequate progress toward the goal of financial security. If the person does not have the appropriate investment assets or is saving less, the problem will eventually surface. Therefore, both investment assets and savings issues are relevant.

EXHIBIT 2.6

BENCHMARK FOR INVESTMENT ASSETS AS A PERCENTAGE OF GROSS PAY

Age	Investment Assets as a Ratio to Gross Pay Needed at Varying Ages
25	0.20 : 1
30	0.6 - 0.8 : 1
35	1.6 - 1.8 : 1
45	3 - 4 : 1
55	8 - 10 : 1
65	16 - 20 : 1

The benchmarks as calculated consider incomes between $50,000 and $250,000, inflation at approximately two to three percent, a balanced investment portfolio of 60/40 equities to bonds returning five percent over inflation, a savings rate of 10 to 13 percent of gross pay and a wage replacement ratio of 80 percent of gross pay. To the extent that any of these assumptions are incorrect for a particular person, the results may be misleading and require a specific personal calculation. These benchmarks are only a beginning.

Note that Exhibit 2.6 illustrates that a person planning to retire at age 65 will need investment assets approximately 16 to 20 times the preretirement gross pay. A person at age 55 who plans to retire at 65 will need investment assets equal to eight times their current gross pay and will need to continue to save 10 to 13 percent of gross pay, including any employer contributions to achieve adequate retirement funding. More precise calculations are addressed throughout this chapter. This is only a benchmark, although it works well for incomes at $50,000 to $250,000, inflation at two to three percent, and a balanced portfolio earning about five percent over inflation.

Assume Beth, age 45, comes to you and is currently earning $100,000 per year. She has $300,000 (3x) of investment assets (cash, mutual funds, retirement funds, etc.), not including personal use assets (equity in personal residence) and is saving $10,000 of her gross pay (10%.) Beth is concerned about making adequate progress towards her retirement goals. Assuming that Beth is invested in an appropriate portfolio, she appears to be making adequate progress. Beth's investment assets are three times her gross pay, and she is saving ten percent of her gross pay for her retirement.

SAVINGS RATE

The **savings rate** identifies the average savings amount in the U.S. based on consumption. The savings rate is interpreted as personal saving as a percentage of disposable personal income. According to the Bureau of Economic Analysis, the personal savings rate has declined significantly since the 1980s. In fact, the personal savings rate fell to an all time low of 1.2 percent in 2004. Exhibit 2.7 illustrates this sharp decline. The growth in personal expenditures may be the cause of the drop in savings over the past few years and suggests that individuals are not saving enough for retirement. This low savings rate identifies a major concern for all planners. Recall, that in order to meet just the retirement goal, a savings rate of 10 to 13 percent of gross pay over a long period is necessary.

U.S. PERSONAL SAVINGS RATE (1982-2004)

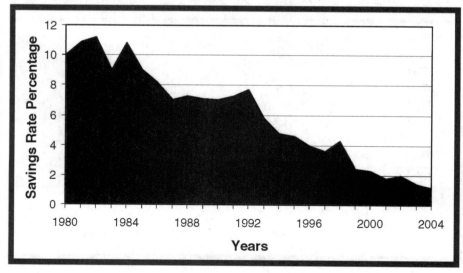

TIMING OF SAVINGS

The earlier a person saves, the greater the number of future compounding periods available prior to retirement. A greater number of compounding periods leads to a lower required savings rate and a larger accumulation of capital at retirement. When savings is delayed, the power of compounding is lost and individuals must compensate by saving a greater percentage of their disposable income.

EXAMPLE 2.2

Lori saves $2,500 a year from age 25 until age 34 inclusively and invests in an account earning eight percent annually. Lori stops investing at age 34, but does not withdraw the accumulation until age 65. Lori's accumulation at age 65 is $393,588 even though she only deposited $25,000. In contrast, Peter saves $2,500 a year from age 35 until age 65 inclusively and invests in a similar account to Lori, earning eight percent annually. Even though Peter saved $52,500 more than Lori, he will have accumulated $85,223 less than Lori at age 65. The deposits and balance at age 65 for Lori and Peter are presented in Exhibit 2.8.

EXHIBIT 2.8

TIME/SAVINGS EXAMPLE (ACCUMULATION AT AGE 65)

	Lori	Peter
Total Invested (OA)	$25,000	$77,500
Balance at 65	$393,588	$308,365
Earnings Rate	8%	8%

While Peter invested more than three times as much as Lori, Lori has 22 percent more than Peter at age 65. This result demonstrates the power of compound earnings over the longer period of 41 years versus 31 years. Exhibit 2.9 illustrates this phenomenon graphically.

EXHIBIT 2.9

EXAMPLE ACCUMULATION OF UNEQUAL DEPOSITS OVER VARYING TIME PERIODS

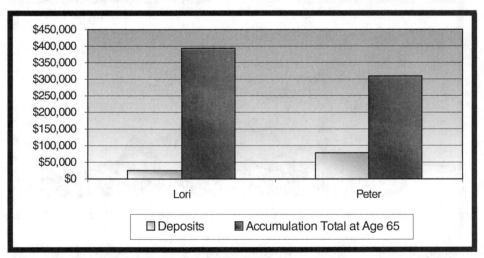

INVESTMENT DECISIONS

A fundamental understanding of investment decisions and their consequences is essential to successful retirement planning. All asset classes do not have the same historical investment returns or risks. When planning for retirement, it is important to have a historical perspective of investment returns and risks for a wide variety of asset classes. Exhibit 2.10 provides a 70 year perspective on historical investment returns, inflation-adjusted returns, and risk as measured by standard deviation.

HISTORICAL RETURNS, INFLATION-ADJUSTED RETURNS, AND STANDARD DEVIATION OF ASSET CLASSES (1932 - 2003)   EXHIBIT 2.10

Asset Class	Historical Returns	Inflation-Adjusted Returns	Standard Deviation	Real Return After-Tax and Inflation
Small-Capitalization Stocks	12	9	30	5.4
Large-Capitalization Stocks	10	7.5	20	4.5
Fixed-Income Securities (Corporate)	5	2.5	8	1
Treasury	4.6	2.1	4	1
Consumer Price Index (CPI)	3	N/A	4	N/A

Exhibit 2.10 illustrates the need to choose investments wisely for inclusion within a portfolio based on the risk and return of the asset class. You should notice that after inflation, real economic returns are extremely low for fixed-income securities and Treasuries, and these returns are further reduced after considering the effects of taxation. This suggests that the only way to have real investment growth in an investment portfolio over a long term is to invest at least some portion of the portfolio in common stocks. Common stocks also provide the best hedge against inflation (the loss of purchasing power).

When investors are young, their investment portfolio should be dominated by common stocks because, due to long time horizons, young investors can generally afford the risk. As persons near retirement, their asset allocation generally shifts so that it becomes less risky while still maintaining some growth component to mitigate against the risk of inflation.

Quick Quiz

Highlight the answer to these questions:

1. Our society tends to save at a rate that is adequate for retirement planning.
   a. True
   b. False

2. Fixed-income securities generally provide the best hedge against inflation and loss of purchasing power.
   a. True
   b. False

3. Individuals must consider the impact of inflation when projecting retirement needs.
   a. True
   b. False

False, False, True.

The selection of an expected portfolio return begins with an analysis of risk tolerance. Risk tolerance has two components, ability and willingness. If both are high, the risk tolerance will be high. If both are low, the risk tolerance will be low. A mismatch of ability and willingness to tolerate risk suggests a need for education. The selected risk tolerance and expected portfolio return leads to an asset allocation. There is evidence that asset allocation explains about 90 percent of the returns to a portfolio. The asset allocation decision has as its intent either an expected return for a given level of risk or the lowest risk for a given expected return.

INFLATION

Inflation causes a loss of purchasing power. If a retiree has a fixed retirement income beginning at age 65 and inflation is three percent, the retiree has a loss of purchasing power of 26 percent in 10 years, 45 percent in 20 years, and 59 percent in 30 years. While Social Security retirement benefits are inflation adjusted, many private pension plans are not. Thus, the financial planner must consider the impact of inflation when projecting retirement needs and advise clients to save accordingly. Exhibit 2.11 illustrates the decline in purchasing power over a 50-year period of a $100,000 fixed income associated with a three percent inflation rate.

| EXHIBIT 2.11 | IMPACT OF INFLATION |

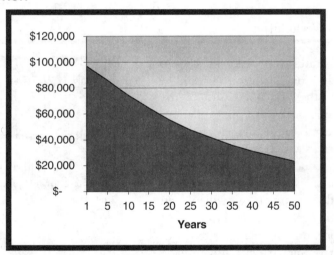

As illustrated, in year 10 the $100,000 has lost purchasing power by 26 percent. After 10 years, one can only buy $74,409 worth of items using $100,000 of today's dollars. More disturbing is the fact that in year 50, the same person would only be able to purchase $22,811 worth of assets for that same $100,000. Imagine the client that expected to have a carefree retirement in 50 years with the $100,000 income they have today.

How much money and/or income does a person need to be financially independent? Most persons entering retirement intend to maintain the same lifestyle they had immediately prior to retirement. Clients generally do not radically reduce their expenses during retirement unless it is necessary. When preparing a retirement budget, the budget should have similar expense categories and amounts as the preretirement budget with a few adjustments. There are expenses that may increase and those that may decrease as a person moves into the retirement phase of life. Expenses that may decline in retirement include: (1) the elimination of costs associated with employment (certain clothing costs, parking, some meal costs); (2) the elimination of mortgage costs if the mortgage debt is scheduled to be repaid by retirement; (3) the elimination of costs of children (tuition, clothes); (4) the elimination of payroll costs—FICA; and (5) the elimination of savings because the plan will require the use of accumulated savings. For some persons, retirement can bring increased spending on travel and other lifestyle changes. Some retirees are at risk for increases in health care costs. Exhibit 2.12 presents lists of potential decreasing and increasing costs when entering retirement.

Key Concepts

Underline/highlight the answers to these questions as you read:

1. List the common factors that increase and decrease retirement income needs.

2. What is the wage replacement ratio?

3. Identify the two alternative methods for calculating the wage replacement ratio.

4. How is WRR calculated utilizing the two applicable methods?

BALANCING INCREASING AND DECREASING RETIREMENT INCOME NEEDS

EXHIBIT 2.12

DECREASING INCOME NEEDS:

- Reduced Social Security payments
- Reduced need to save
- Reduced work related expenses
- House mortgage may be paid off
- Automobile insurance may be reduced
- Possible lifestyle adjustments (less cars, less entertainment, etc.)

INCREASING INCOME NEEDS:

- Rising cost of health care and increased medical expenses
- Increasing expenditures and/or gifts to relatives
- Rising property taxes (due to inflation)
- Possible lifestyle changes (more travel, second home, clubs, hobbies, activities, etc.)

PLANNING FOR RETIREMENT - PRETAX OR AFTER-TAX

It is possible to plan for retirement needs either on a pretax or an after-tax basis. Most financial planners who are not certified public accountants (CPAs) plan in pretax dollars believing that a pretax approach is what their clients best understand. The assumption with the pretax approach is that clients are more likely to know their gross income rather than to know their net after-tax cash flow. Therefore, planners establish retirement plans pretax with the expectation that the clients will simply pay whatever income taxes they have out of their gross retirement income, similar to what clients do during preretirement years. Many CPAs think in terms of after-tax dollars and, therefore, plan for retirement on an after-tax basis. After-tax planning assumes that income taxes are paid before other retirement needs. Planning can be effective either way as long as the client and the planner understand the pretax or after-tax planning choice. Throughout the text, we generally use a pretax approach.

WAGE REPLACEMENT RATIO (WRR)

The **wage replacement ratio (WRR)** is an estimate of the percent of annual income needed during retirement compared to income earned prior to retirement. The wage replacement ratio or percentage is calculated by dividing the amount of money needed on an annual basis in retirement by the preretirement income. For example, if a client in the last year of work (prior to retirement) makes $100,000, and that client needs $80,000 in the first retirement year to maintain the same preretirement lifestyle, the wage replacement ratio (WRR) is 80 percent (80,000 ÷ 100,000).

CALCULATING THE WAGE REPLACEMENT RATIO

There are two alternative methods to calculate the wage replacement ratio—the top-down approach and the bottom-up approach (also called the budgeting approach).

Top-Down Approach
The top-down approach is frequently used with younger clients where expenditure patterns are unlikely to remain constant over time. As clients approach retirement age, a more precise wage replacement ratio should be calculated using a budgeting approach. The top-down approach estimates the wage replacement ratio using common sense and percentages.

| EXAMPLE 2.3 | To illustrate the top down approach, assume a 40-year-old client earns $50,000 a year, pays 7.65 percent of his gross pay in Social Security payroll taxes, and saves 10 percent of his gross income. If we assume that any work-related savings resulting from retirement are expected to be completely off-set by additional spending adjustments during retirement and that the client wants to maintain his exact preretirement lifestyle, we would expect that the client would need a wage replacement ratio of 82.35% (100% - 7.65% - 10%). |

$50,000	=	100.00%	of salary in % terms
(5,000)	=	(10.00%)	less: current savings in % terms
(3,825)	=	(7.65%)	less: payroll taxes in % terms (not paid in retirement)
$41,175	=	82.35%	wage replacement ratio in % terms

The client is currently living on 82.35 percent of his gross pay. The remaining 17.65 percent is paid to FICA taxes and savings. Therefore, the 82.35 percent is a reasonable estimate, or proxy, of the amount necessary, as a percentage of current income, to maintain the (current) preretirement lifestyle.

Quick Quiz

Highlight the answer to these questions:

1. The WRR is an estimate of the percentage of annual income needed during retirement compared to income earned prior to retirement.
   a. True
   b. False

2. The two methods for calculating WRR are the top-down approach and the budgeting approach.
   a. True
   b. False

True, True.

Bottom-Up (Budgeting) Approach

The bottom-up approach used to calculate the wage replacement ratio is also called the budgeting approach. It is often used with older clients because as a person nears retirement age, it is possible to examine the actual current expenditure patterns of the person and to more accurately forecast the retirement expenditure patterns. In cooperation with the client, the planner can determine which costs in the current (preretirement) budget will change (plus or minus) in the retirement budget, allowing the planner to determine a wage replacement ratio with greater precision than the top-down approach of estimating retirement needs.

Assume you had two clients, Amy and Bill, that had identical income and expenses each year. Amy and Bill each make $120,000 in preretirement income. Amy has arranged her financial affairs in such a way that she will have no mortgage payment or car payment while in retirement. Bill, on the other hand, expects to continue to have both a mortgage payment and a car payment throughout the majority of his retirement years. Both of them expect some expenses to decrease during retirement. The following chart illustrates that while Amy will need a 64.75 percent WRR, Bill will need a 84.75 percent WRR. The difference is due to Bill's $18,000 annual mortgage payments and $6,000 annual car payments.

EXAMPLE 2.4

	CLIENT AMY & BILL	CLIENT AMY	CLIENT BILL
	Current Budget	**Retirement Budget**	**Retirement Budget**
Income (Current) Budget	$120,000	**	**
Expenses:	Current	Retirement	Retirement
Income Taxes (28%)	$33,600	$33,600	$33,600
Food	5,400	5,400	5,400
Utilities/Phone	6,000	6,000	6,000
Mortgage	18,000*	0	18,000
Social Security Taxes	2,500	0	0
Health Insurance	2,000	2,000	2,000
Auto Insurance	1,200	1,200	1,200
Entertainment	6,000	6,000	6,000
Clothing	4,000	2,500	2,500
Auto Maintenance/Operation	1,000	750	750
Auto Payment	6,000	0	6,000
Church	2,400	2,400	2,400
Savings	12,000	0	0
Miscellaneous	19,900	17,850	17,850
Total Expenses (Needs)	**120,000**	**77,700**	**101,700**
Wage Replacement Ratio (WRR)		**64.75%**	**84.75%**

* Note that the mortgage of both is 15% of current income before retirement but 0% for Amy and 18% of needs for Bill after retirement.
** The current budget at retirement will be equal to the needs.

Does a person really need the same wage replacement percentage dollar amount or purchasing power amount throughout the entire retirement period? The answer is generally no. There are indications that consumption slows somewhat as people age. The 70 to 80 percent wage replacement ratio is probably most appropriate from the beginning of retirement regardless of age until the retiree reaches the late 70s. It appears that a person's consumption past the age of 80 declines primarily due to limited mobility. While this may be correct for society at large, certain individuals will incur dramatic medical costs during the latter part of their retirement period. Therefore, while most who study retirement expenditures would suggest a consumption function similar to the one provided in Exhibit 2.13 below, such a model may or may not apply to a particular individual.

EXHIBIT 2.13

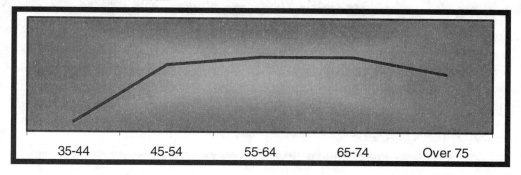

| 35-44 | 45-54 | 55-64 | 65-74 | Over 75 |

Many expert financial planners conclude that most clients need approximately 70 to 80 percent of their preretirement current income to retire and maintain their preretirement lifestyle. While many clients would fall into this range, there are also those particularly frugal clients who may need as little as 40 percent of their preretirement income and others who may need substantially more than the 80 percent wage replacement ratio (usually due to corporate perks which are no longer received during retirement).

ADJUSTMENTS FROM PRERETIREMENT INCOME TO RETIREMENT INCOME NEEDS

EXHIBIT 2.14

From Preretirement Income to Retirement Income Needs Adjustments to Expenditures	
Adjustments which decrease income needs:	Amount or Percent Saved
• No longer pay Social Security taxes	7.65% to 15.3%
• No longer need to save	10% to 15%
• No longer pay house mortgage	Maybe
• No longer pay work-related expenses	*
• Auto insurance may be reduced	*
• Possible lifestyle adjustments	*
Adjustments which may increase income needs:	
• Increasing cost of health care	*
• Lifestyle changes	*
• Increase in travel	*
• Second home	*
• Clubs and activities	*
• Expenditures on family/gifts/grandchildren	*
• Increased property taxes	*
*Amounts must be estimated for each individual	

Exhibit 2.14 presents common adjustments from preretirement to retirement in terms of estimated percentages. Notice that most of the adjustments in Exhibit 2.14 will be client-specific.

SOURCES OF RETIREMENT INCOME

Most retirees rely on a combination of funds to finance retirement, including Social Security, private and company-sponsored retirement plans, income from personal retirement plans, and income from personal savings. These sources of funds are intended to complement each other to provide adequate retirement income. Exhibit 2.15 shows the average percent of income for the average retiree in 2002 from each of these sources.

EXHIBIT 2.15 **RETIREMENT INCOME SOURCES**

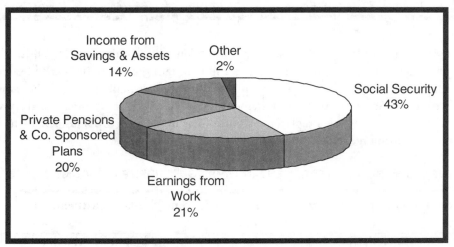

Source: Social Security Administration

Notice that the average retiree receives 43 percent of their income from Social Security. Social Security will only provide a wage replacement ratio of 11 to 16 percent for a worker with income of $200,000 (see Exhibit 2.17). Therefore, such a worker will need to look to other sources of funds to make up the amount of the short-fall in wage replacement to maintain their desired lifestyle.

 *Key Concepts*

Underline/highlight the answers to these questions as you read:

1. Identify the main sources of retirement income.

2. How does Social Security factor into retirement income?

3. Discuss the importance of personal savings to an individual's retirement income needs.

SOCIAL SECURITY

Social Security provides a foundation of retirement income. Social Security covers almost all occupational groups (except 25 percent of state and local government employees) with retirement benefits adjusted for inflation. It is considered the safety net of a secure income, but for most income levels, it is not by itself a sufficient source of income replacement during retirement. According to the Social Security Administration, 91 percent of individuals aged 65 or older received Social Security benefits in 2001. As Exhibit 2.16 illustrates, Social Security was the major source of income for 65 percent of retired individuals, and it was the only source of income for 20 percent.

Percentage of Retired Individuals Receiving Social Security Benefits by Relative Importance to Total Retirement Income

EXHIBIT 2.16

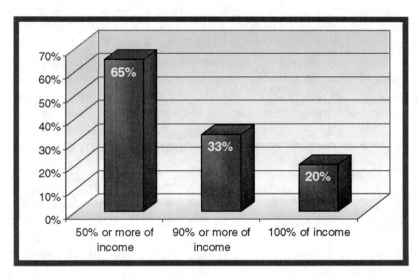

Source: Social Security Administration, Fast Facts and Figures about Social Security, June 2003

Most middle to higher income individuals planning for retirement should, therefore, consider Social Security as a foundation rather than depending on Social Security retirement income as their main source of retirement income. Social Security retirement benefits provide a wage replacement ratio ranging from less than 20 percent (for high-income earners) to approximately 80 percent (for low-income earners who have a same age, nonworking spouse). As illustrated in Exhibit 2.17, Social Security is an adequate wage replacement for lower wage earners but is clearly inadequate to provide sufficient replacement income for middle-to-upper-wage earners. (The Social Security system and the Social Security benefits are covered in detail in Chapter 11.)

Social Security as a Wage Replacement Percentage (For Individuals Having Various Earnings)

EXHIBIT 2.17

Current Earnings	Wage Replacement Ratio Provided by Social Security*	With Same Age, Nonworking Spouse
$13,100	52%	78%
$20,000	41%	62%
$25,000	37%	56%
$28,924	35%	53%
$35,000	33%	49%
$46,663	30%	45%
$72,100	25%	38%
$100,000	21%	31%
$200,000	11%	16%

Estimated based on single person at normal retirement age 2003. Average wages were $33,252 in 2002.
A same age, nonworking spouse would receive 50 percent of the benefits of the covered worker.

PRIVATE PENSION AND COMPANY-SPONSORED RETIREMENT PLANS

Private pension plans are the second source of retirement income. According to the Employee Benefit Research Institute, of the 151.3 million workers in 2002, 80.7 million worked for an employer or union that sponsored a pension or retirement plan, and 63.2 million participated in the plans (a 41.8 percent participation rate considering all workers). Private retirement plans provided by employers are covered in Chapters 3 through 6. Qualified retirement plans have dramatically changed over the last few years from employer-sponsored and funded plans to employer-sponsored but employee self-reliant plans, increasing the emphasis on personal savings as the primary source of retirement income for middle-to-upper-wage workers.

Quick Quiz

Highlight the answer to these questions:

1. Retirees generally rely on Social Security, private pension plans, and personal savings to fund their retirement income.
   a. True
   b. False

2. Social Security is an adequate wage replacement for most individuals.
   a. True
   b. False

3. Personal savings is the source of retirement income most influenced by the individual.
   a. True
   b. False

   True, False, True.

PERSONAL ASSETS AND SAVINGS

Personal assets and savings is the third source of retirement income and is the one source that has traditionally been the most influenced by the individual. This is a more difficult way to accumulate savings for retirement because of the lack of tax deductions or tax deferrals on earnings. However, personal savings can be a significant source of retirement income, as the more personal savings put aside for retirement, the larger the accumulation at retirement and the larger the retirement income for the individual.

Exhibit 2.7 illustrated the significant decrease in the personal savings rate since 1990. As illustrated, the savings rate has fallen from 7.9 percent of disposable income in 1990 to 3.8 percent in 2002.

Whenever a retiree has income from invested assets, it can mean a substantially higher overall retirement income. The median income of those retirees with asset income is more than twice as large as the income of retirees with no asset income. As the two pie charts in Exhibit 2.18 illustrate, retirees without personal asset income are concentrated in the lowest income categories. Notice in Exhibit 2.18 that of retirees having income from personal assets and savings, 33 percent have income of $30,000 or more, while of retirees without personal assets and savings, only six percent have income of $30,000 or more in retirement. There is a noticeable difference between retirees who have income from personal assets and those that do not.

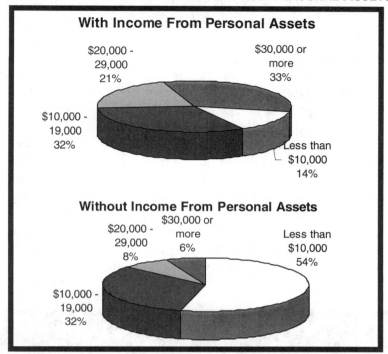

With Income From Personal Assets

$20,000 - 29,000 — 21%

$30,000 or more — 33%

$10,000 - 19,000 — 32%

Less than $10,000 — 14%

Without Income From Personal Assets

$20,000 - 29,000 — 8%

$30,000 or more — 6%

Less than $10,000 — 54%

$10,000 - 19,000 — 32%

Source: Social Security Administration

QUALITATIVE FACTORS IN RETIREMENT – ADVISING CLIENTS

Qualitative factors associated with retirement may be more important than the financial or quantitative factors. Qualitative factors include: involuntary versus voluntary retirement, emotional and psychological factors, such as loss of esteem with loss of job and boredom in retirement, and the decision to relocate or to do things that were postponed during the work life (i.e., travel or pursue another vocation).

The best overall advice financial planners can give their clients is for the client to have a strong support system, have a well-planned qualitative side to retirement, and have a system in place to maintain ego and self-esteem. Many persons in our culture define themselves by what they do at work.

Key Concepts

Underline/highlight the answers to these questions as you read:

1. Why are qualitative factors important considerations in retirement planning?

2. What are some of the common factors that negatively affect retirement planning, and what impact do they have on the planning process?

The mere act of going to work may be a ritual or a habit that provides that person with a sense of self worth and with a reason to live. A trusted colleague at the workplace may be a source of support and personal gratification. Voluntary retirement, even when well planned, means change—and change is difficult.

Involuntary retirement, if perceived as undesirable, can have a devastating emotional impact on an individual including shock, anger, and denial. Financial planning professionals need to recognize the emotional state of clients and realize that when someone is emotionally troubled, major decisions (financial or otherwise) are sometimes best delayed. Rather than abruptly making important financial decisions, it may be better to do the minimum financial maneuvering during a grieving period. Such grieving may last for a period of a year or longer. Trying to optimize the financial situation when the client is emotionally unable to determine his or her goals or priorities is probably counterproductive and may add stress to the situation.

A client's decision to relocate after retirement (for example, move to another state) should be carefully considered over a long period of planning. Some retirees do not realize that when they move, they will have a completely new environment to adjust to, as well as a substantial loss of their former support system of friends and family. Someone considering moving should conduct a trial transition over a number of years, spending increasingly longer periods at the desired location. This gradual adjustment will help determine if what the retiree believes will actually enhance retirement will, in fact, be true. Persons considering retiring abroad will encounter even more change, thereby necessitating even more detailed planning.

SUMMARY OF FACTORS AFFECTING RETIREMENT PLANNING

Financial planners may encounter clients who subjectively "feel" they are financially secure because they have a good job and/or a good net worth. If a good job is lost through premature death, disability, lay off, job termination, unexpected illness, etc., or if net worth decreases dramatically, the client's financial security is impaired. Thus, the actual determination of financial security is objective rather than subjective. Regardless of how people feel subjectively, in the real, objective world, there is a certain quantitative percentage of people who will become disabled, die untimely, or become unemployed.

Other complications that affect the retirement planning process include at least two societal issues. Our society has become more mobile with the traditional family unit deteriorating. Having lost the close connection to family, older persons may not be able to depend on family to provide retirement assistance. Thus, there is a greater need for financial independence for each individual. Additionally, because our society seems to place more value on youth than on age and wisdom in the workplace, retirees have less chance of being hired for part-time employment, which could supplement retirement income.

Many people begin planning for retirement too late in life and save too little to effectively meet retirement capital accumulation needs. Some people do not give retirement funding a thought until they are in their forties. Even when people do save, many of them make poor investment choices and, therefore, have poor investment returns.

Inflation reduces an individual's purchasing power. To recipients of fixed incomes, inflation is like a progressive tax which causes declining purchasing power.

Exhibit 2.19 lists the factors that frustrate effective retirement planning and the negative impact associated with each factor.

FACTORS THAT NEGATIVELY AFFECT RETIREMENT PLANNING AND THEIR IMPACT ON THE PLANNING PROCESS

EXHIBIT 2.19

Factors	Impact
Reduced WLE	Insufficient savings period
Increased RLE	Increases capital needs
Reduced family reliance	Fewer alternatives in retirement
Reduced ability to work	Fewer alternatives in retirement
Planned too late	Fewer compounding periods
Low savings rate	Unable to meet capital requirements
Inflation	Reduces purchasing power
Poor earnings rate and asset allocation	Unable to meet capital requirements

Long-term financial security does not happen automatically. It requires careful planning, a clear understanding of the quantification of the goal, and identification and management of the risks that are present. Retirement planning requires the collection and projection of data and must be conducted meticulously and conservatively.

RISKS TO FINANCIAL INDEPENDENCE

There are many risks on the way to achieving financial independence. Selected risks are identified in Exhibit 2.20. It is a wise idea to save early, save a sufficient amount, invest prudently, and not underestimate retirement needs or the impact of inflation.

EXHIBIT 2.20   SUMMARY OF SELECTED FACTORS AFFECTING RETIREMENT PLANNING

FACTOR	RISK	MITIGATOR
Work Life Expectancy (WLE)	Shortened due to untimely death, disability, health, unemployment	Life insurance, disability insurance, health insurance, education, training, experience
Retirement Life Expectancy (RLE)	Lengthened	Adequate capital accumulation
Savings rate, amount, and timing	Too low and too late	Save enough; start early
Inflation	Greater than expected	Conservatively estimate inflation and needs
Retirement needs	Underestimated	Use wage replacement estimators
Investment returns	Inadequate to create necessary retirement capital	Knowledge of and investments in broad portfolio of diversified investments and proper asset allocation
Sources of retirement income	Overestimation of Social Security benefits, private pension plans, or personal income (or adverse changes in taxation of such income)	Conservatively estimate and plan for such income, as well as, monitor income projections and tax policy

CAPITAL NEEDS ANALYSIS

Capital needs analysis is the process of calculating the amount of investment capital needed at retirement to maintain the preretirement lifestyle and mitigate the impact of inflation during the retirement years. It uses objective and subjective criteria to determine retirement income needs. There are three methods for analyzing capital needs: the basic annuity method, the capital preservation model, and the purchasing power preservation model.

ACCURATE ASSUMPTIONS

Before calculating the capital needs analysis, the planner must first make several assumptions. Assumptions are made for the wage replacement ratio, the work life expectancy, the retirement life expectancy, inflation, earnings, Social Security, and any other benefits. If these assumptions are inaccurate, the projection using those

Key Concepts

Underline/highlight the answers to these questions as you read:

1. What is capital needs analysis and why is it important in retirement planning?

2. What are the three most common methods for analyzing capital needs?

3. How do each of these methods differ?

4. What assumptions must be made in capital needs analysis?

assumptions will be flawed. The wage replacement ratio should be calculated carefully, especially for a client near retirement. Estimating life expectancy usually begins with the IRS tables and is conservatively estimated at 90 - 93, due to the risk of outliving retirement money. Where family history indicates a particularly long life expectancy, that age should be increased. The estimate of the work life expectancy is critical, as one less year of work means one less year of saving and one more year of retirement funding. Conversely, working one additional year may make an otherwise unworkable retirement plan work quite nicely due to the additional year of savings, the additional year of earnings accumulation, and one less year of consumption.

The assumptions regarding inflation and earnings rates are essential ingredients in capital needs analysis. Historical data is available for inflation; however, future inflation is hard to predict. Perhaps the best estimate is the inflation rate for the most recent few years. Earnings rates are dependent on the client's asset allocation and the markets but can be estimated for a well-diversified portfolio over a long period. It is wise to conservatively estimate inflation (up a little) and conservatively estimate earnings (down a little). Such estimation provides a little conservatism in case one or more of the assumptions are not realized. Social Security benefits and pension benefits that are inflation protected should be carefully determined and documented. The retirement plan and capital needs analysis can be adjusted on an annual basis as information becomes more certain.

BASIC PLANNING – ANNUITY METHOD

The annuity method is the simplest way to determine retirement needs. The annuity method assumes the individual saves for a period of time, begins taking distributions at retirement, and then dies without money on the projected life expectancy date. The following steps are used to determine the capital necessary at the beginning of retirement to fund the retirement period:

1. Calculate WRR. Determine the wage replacement ratio (WRR) today using one of the two methods identified earlier (top-down or budgeting).
2. Determine gross dollar needs. Determine the wage replacement amount in today's dollars from Step 1.
3. Determine net dollar needs. Reduce the result from Step 2 by any expected Social Security benefits in today's dollars or other benefits that are indexed to inflation.
4. Calculate preretirement dollar needs inflated. Inflate the result from Step 3 to the retirement age at the CPI rate to determine the first annual retirement payment.
5. Calculate capital needed at retirement age. Calculate the present value at retirement of an annuity due for an annual payment equal to the result from Step 4 over the full retirement life expectancy (estimate life expectancy conservatively at 90 - 93), and use the inflation-adjusted earnings rate. It is important to note that a conservative approach should be used when estimating the life expectancy, as this will allay any short fall in funding.

To determine the amount to save during the work life expectancy, discount the capital needed at retirement using the savings rate, being mindful as to whether the client is expected to save annually or more frequently and whether the client is expected to save under an annuity due or an ordinary annuity scheme.

EXAMPLE 2.5	Jordan, age 42, currently makes $70,000. Her wage replacement ratio is determined to be 80 percent. She expects that inflation will average 3 percent for her entire life expectancy. She expects to earn 9.5 percent on her investments and retire at age 62, possibly living to age 90. She has sent for and received her Social Security benefit statement, which indicated that her Social Security retirement benefit in today's dollars adjusted for early retirement is $15,000 per year. It is reasonable to subtract the Social Security benefit from today's needs because they are inflation adjusted.

1. Calculate Jordan's capital needed at retirement at age 62.

Step 1	80% WRR		
Step 2	($70,000 x 0.80)	=	$56,000 Total needs in today's dollars
Step 3			- 15,000 Less Social Security in today's dollars
			$41,000 Annual amount needed in today's dollars
Step 4	N	=	20 (62 - 42)
	i	=	3% (inflation)
	PV	=	$41,000 (Step 3)
	PMT	=	0
	FV	=	74,050.56 (Step 4) First year needs for retirement
Step 5	N	=	28 (90 – 62)
	i	=	6.3107 [(1 + earnings rate/1 + inflation rate) – 1] x 100
			[(1.095 ÷ 1.03) – 1] x 100
	FV	=	0
	PMT_{AD}	=	$74,050.56 (from Step 4) this is also an annuity due
	$PV_{AD@62}$	=	$1,022,625.84 (Step 5 - amount needed at age 62)

Note: the math in this example assumes you use unrounded numbers throughout the calculation. If you clear your calculator at each step and enter a rounded number, your results will be slightly different.

2. Calculate the amount she must save monthly, at month end (an ordinary annuity), assuming she has no current savings to accumulate the capital needed for retirement at age 62.

$FV_{@62}$	=	$1,022,625.84 (from Step 5)
N	=	240 (20 years x 12 months)
i	=	0.79167 (9.5% ÷ 12)
PV	=	0
PMT_{OA}	=	$1,436.43 (monthly savings necessary) at month end

3. Calculate the amount she must save monthly, at month end, assuming she has $50,000 in current retirement savings.

$FV_{@62}$	=	$1,022,625.84
N	=	240
i	=	0.79167
PV	=	- $50,000
PMT_{OA}	=	$970.36 (monthly savings necessary) at month end

To mitigate against the risk of the assumptions being overly optimistic, the planner can make use of a capital preservation model or a purchasing power preservation model rather than a simple annuity model to determine capital needs. These two additional models help to overcome the risks of the pure annuity model (primarily the risk of running out of money).

ADVANCED FINANCIAL PLANNING – CAPITAL PRESERVATION MODEL (CP)

The basic capital needs analysis is a **pure annuity concept,** generally prepared on a pretax basis. The annuity concept means that if all of the assumptions happen exactly as expected, the person will die exactly at the assumed life expectancy with a retirement account balance of zero. There is a substantial risk that many clients could outlive their assets using an annuity approach. Therefore, they may actually need more money at retirement. Two models used to mitigate the risk of outliving money are the capital preservation model and the purchasing power preservation model. The **capital preservation model** assumes that at life expectancy, as estimated in the annuity model, the client has exactly the same account balance as he did at retirement. The purchasing power preservation model assumes that the client will have a capital balance of equal purchasing power at life expectancy as he did at retirement. In spite of any conservatism that the planner may have built into the annuity model with their assumptions, it is always possible that one or more of their assumptions will be unrealized.

The capital preservation model maintains the original capital balance needed at retirement for the entire retirement life expectancy.

Quick Quiz

Highlight the answer to these questions:

1. Capital needs analysis is the process of calculating the amount of investment capital needed at retirement to maintain the preretirement lifestyle.
   a. True
   b. False

2. The annuity method assumes that the individual will die at the expected life expectancy with a retirement account balance of zero.
   a. True
   b. False

3. The capital preservation model and the purchasing power preservation model are used to mitigate the risk of outliving retirement funds.
   a. True
   b. False

True, True, True.

| EXAMPLE 2.6 |

Recall that the amount needed for Jordan at age 62 calculated from Example 2.5 was $1,022,625.84. If we discount that amount at the expected earnings rate of 9.5 percent, then we can determine the additional amount of capital necessary to leave an estate of $1,022,625.84 at life expectancy.

N	=	28
i	=	9.5
$FV_{@90}$	=	\$1,022,625.84 (amount at life expectancy)
PMT	=	0
$PV_{@62}$	=	\$80,560.37
\$1,103,186.21	=	\$80,560.37 + \$1,022,625.84
		(amount needed for capital preservation model)

Thus, the capital preservation model will require an additional \$80,560.37 at retirement more than the pure annuity model but will reduce the risk of running out of money (superannuation). Such an increase in capital will also require that savings be increased in calculations 2 and 3 in the Jordan example (Example 2.5).

The chart below compares the Capital Preservation Model with the Annuity Method for our example.

	Capital Preservation Model		Annuity Model	
	No Savings **Calculation 2**	**Savings** **Calculation 3**	**No Savings** **Calculation 2**	**Savings** **Calculation 3**
$FV_{@62}$	\$1,103,186.21	\$1,103,186.21	\$1,022,625.84	\$1,022,625.84
N	240	240	240	240
i	0.79167	0.79167	0.79167	0.79167
PV	0	- \$50,000	0	- \$50,000
PMT_{OA}	\$1,549.59	\$1,083.52	\$1,436.43	\$970.36

Even though the capital preservation model requires additional savings of \$113 per month, it mitigates against many of the risks in the traditional capital needs annuity approach.

ADVANCED PLANNING – PURCHASING POWER PRESERVATION MODEL (PPP)

An even more conservative approach to capital needs analysis is the **purchasing power preservation model**. This model essentially maintains the purchasing power of the original capital balance at retirement.

Again recall Example 2.5, the capital balance of $1,022,625.84 is used as the future value, and then the entire calculation made in the original capital preservation model is repeated. By doing this, the $1,022,625.84 is simultaneously inflated at the rate of inflation and discounted at the earnings rate.

N	=	28
i	=	6.3107
FV	=	$1,022,625.84
PMT_{AD}	=	$74,050.56 (amount needed the first year of retirement)
$PV_{@62}$	=	$1,206,939.24
		capital needed for purchasing power preservation model

The additional accumulation at retirement using a purchasing power model is $184,313.40 greater than the pure annuity approach.

The answers to calculation 2 and 3 in the Jordan example would again change. The chart below compares the Purchasing Power Model with the Annuity Method for our example.

	Purchasing Power Model		Annuity Model	
	No Savings Calculation 2	**With Initial Savings** Calculation 3	**No Savings** Calculation 2	**With Initial Savings** Calculation 3
$FV_{@62}$	$1,206,939.24	$1,206,939.24	$1,022,625.84	$1,022,625.84
N	240	240	240	240
i	0.79167	0.79167	0.79167	0.79167
PV	0	- $50,000	0	- $50,000
PMT_{OA}	$1,695.33	$1,229.25	$1,436.43	$970.36

	Annuity Model	Capital Preservation Model	Purchasing Power Preservation Model
Capital needed at retirement (calculation 1)	$1,022,625.84	$1,103,186.21	$1,206,939.24
Monthly savings with no initial balance (calculation 2)	$1,436.43	$1,549.59	$1,695.33
Monthly savings with $50,000 initial balance (calculation 3)	$970.36	$1,083.52	$1,229.25

SENSITIVITY ANALYSIS, SIMULTATIONS, AND MONTE CARLO ANALYSIS

As one might expect, small changes in the assumptions regarding earnings, inflation, life expectancy, and retirement funding needs can have a dramatic impact on the retirement plan. One of the problems with capital needs analysis performed in the traditional way is that financial planners use deterministic (assumes the estimate is predetermined as opposed to probable) estimates for each of the variables (needs, inflation, portfolio returns, life expectancies, etc.). While these point estimates help the planner create a plan for the client, it is unrealistic to think that these variables are really predictable to an exact deterministic point (given) rather than that they may vary. Generally, point estimates used in deterministic models are the mean expectancy, for example 10.4 percent returns on large capitalization common stocks. While it is true that over the last 78 years large-cap stocks' average returns were 10.4 percent, there were only six years out of 78 when the actual return was close to the mean. In 41 years it was greater and in 31 years it was less by a considerable margin. It is unlikely that for any period going forward the investment return will replicate that historical return. A plan that only uses deterministic assumptions is likely to produce results that may range far from the original forecast. The planner can employ techniques to help begin to understand the effect of the range of probable outcomes for each variable in a plan. These techniques include range estimates, sensitivity analysis, and simulations such as Monte Carlo analysis.

Key Concepts

Underline/highlight the answers to these questions as you read:

1. Explain how sensitivity analysis is used.

2. What is a Monte Carlo Analysis?

Range Estimates

Using range estimates allows the planner to project what outcome will occur if we use a range of assumptions (e.g., 2.5% to 3.5% inflation) for a variable as opposed to a mean expectation (three percent inflation). A range estimate approach helps to produce multiple outcomes that will allow us to gain some insight into the impact of a change in one variable or changes in a set of variables. Range estimate assumptions are usually conducted around the mean estimate, both lower and higher than the mean point estimates. If a planner wanted to rotate the assumed coefficient of the variable toward the risk of an adverse outcome (e.g., an investor who is more concerned with down side losses than upside potential returns may use semivariance analysis or alternatively, the number of months returns that were less than T-bill returns), the technique to employ is sensitivity analysis rather than range estimating.

Sensitivity Analysis

Sensitivity analysis consists of rotating each variable assumption toward the undesirable side of the risk to determine the impact of a small change in that variable on not achieving the overall plan. Small deviations in one variable may significantly impact the entire plan. For example:

1. One additional year of employment often makes the retirement plan work because there is one more year of savings, one more year of earnings accumulation, and one less year of consumption. The opposite is also true that one less year of work may destroy an otherwise achievable plan.
2. Small changes in the spread between the earnings rate and the inflation rate can have a significant impact on a plan, both positively and negatively.
3. A small increase in inflation can have a large negative impact on an otherwise achievable retirement funding plan.

Understanding the importance of each individual variable and the risk involved if there is a change from the assumed number to a more conservative number allows the planner to use sensitivity analysis to build a slightly worse case scenario and then determine the impact of these more conservative assumptions on the overall plan.

EXAMPLE 2.8

Recall the assumptions given in the Jordan annuity calculation (Example 2.5). The left columns below identify the given variables while the right columns below identify alternative variables that could be used.

Deterministic Example 2.5 Selected Assumptions		Sensitivity Analysis Conservative Assumptions
N	20 years to retirement	• Try 19 years
i	3% inflation	• Try 3.5% inflation
PV	$41,000 current needs	• Try $42,000 needs
PMT	$0	
FV	$74,050.56 future needs	

Deterministic Example 2.5 Selected Assumptions	
N	28 years in retirement
i	$[(1.095 \div 1.03) - 1] \times 100 = 6.3$
PMT_{AD}	$74,050.56 future needs
$PV_{@62}$	$1,022,625.84 needed at retirement
FV	$0

Sensitivity Analysis Conservative Assumptions
• Try 30 years in retirement
• Try a real rate of 5.75 instead of 6.3
• Try $80,745 as a future needs payment

Notice that slightly more conservative assumptions were used for the sensitivity analysis than were used in the original example in order to determine the robustness or alternatively the sensitivity of the previously calculated solution. If the retirement plan was recalculated using all of the sensitivity analysis assumptions previously identified, Jordan would need $200,000 more at retirement than originally expected, an increase of 20%.

Solution with Conservative Assumptions Using Sensitivity Analysis	
N	19 years to retirement
i	3.5 inflation
PV	$42,000 current needs
PMT	$0
FV	$80,745 future needs
N	30 years in retirement
i	5.75 real rate of return
PMT_{AD}	$80,745 real payment (future dollars)
$PV_{@62}$	$1,207,472 (compared to $1,022,625) needed at age 62
FV	$0

Approximately $160,000 of the change was caused by the inflation assumption being 3.5 percent instead of three percent.

Simulations and Monte Carlo Analysis

There is uncertainty associated with any retirement funding projection. The assumptions can be analyzed using the latest retirement planning software packages that incorporate simulations, such as Monte Carlo Analysis (MCA). As illustrated below, most retirement projections are based on fixed (deterministic) assumptions. While useful during retirement planning, the projections do not account for variations. A **Monte Carlo Analysis** is a mathematical tool that can be used to illustrate the unpredictability of the "real" world and its effects on an individual's retirement plan. MCA uses a random number generator for inputs into a software package that will provide an output with specific probabilities of outcomes. MCA provides insight into the most likely outcome but also provides other possible outcomes. It allows for a variety of alternative assumptions, in particular changes in investment rates of return, the variability of inflation, adjustments to life expectancy, and many other market-condition scenarios. Such a method is invaluable to the planner, as it allows the planner to observe a large number of projections illustrating a potential range of future outcomes based on changing variables. Various software programs are available that allow the planner to run simulations projecting various scenarios, and, therefore, the probability that the individual's retirement plan will be successful.

Quick Quiz

Highlight the answer to these questions:

1. Sensitivity analysis eliminates the risk of retirement planning.
   a. True
   b. False

2. Monte Carlo analysis predicts particular events.
   a. True
   b. False

3. Simulations allow for an unlimited number of simultaneous ranging variables.
   a. True
   b. False

False, False, True.

A simulation calculates multiple scenarios of a model by repeatedly sampling values from probability distributions for uncertain variables. Traditional range estimates calculate outcomes on a best case, expected case, and worst case basis. Sensitivity analysis allows the model user to manipulate variables usually one at a time or one set of variables at a time. Simulations allow for an unlimited (or very large) number of simultaneous ranging of variables, possibly leading to more insight into the problem and the impact of interacting variables.

Because retirement is frequently 20 - 30 years or longer and there are many historical patterns of investment returns for selected 20 - 30 year periods, the planner simply does not know what the market conditions will be when the client retires, nor does the planner know the pattern of market returns that will follow a particular retirement date. Monte Carlo Analysis help us to understand the possibilities and probabilities. However, Monte Carlo Analysis cannot predict particular events. An excellent discussion of the problems with Monte Carlo Analysis was written in the Journal of Financial Planning by David Rawrocki (November 2001, Article 12) and is summarized in Exhibit 2.22.

SELECTED PROBLEMS WITH MONTE CARLO ANALYSIS

EXHIBIT 2.22

- Assumes normal distributions, serial independence, and linear relationships for investment returns (none of which are true).
- Stock returns are not normal distributions - kurtosis is higher than expected. (Stock returns are actually **lepto-kurtic**.)
- Means and standard deviations for stock returns vary over time rather than remain static.
- Many Monte Carlo Analysis ignore tax consequences.

While Monte Carlo Analysis is a tool and an interesting exercise, it has not yet proven its value in terms of significant additional benefit. As with most financial planning, retirement planning is a process that includes regular monitoring and adjustments to the plan as needed. Clients should visit their planner regularly (at least annually) to modify and update their retirement plan to adjust for changes in the preselected variables so that their retirement objectives can be met.

Key Terms

Capital Needs Analysis - The process of calculating the amount of investment capital needed at retirement to maintain the preretirement lifestyle and mitigate the impact of inflation during the retirement years.

Capital Preservation Model (CP) - A capital needs analysis method that assumes that at client's life expectancy, the client has exactly the same account balance as he did at the beginning of retirement.

Lepto-Kurtic - A distribution that appears to be normal but has more area under the two tails than a normal distribution (i.e. fat tails).

Monte Carlo Analysis - A mathematical tool used to calculate the success of an individual's retirement portfolio using changing variables.

Purchasing Power Preservation Model (PPP) - A capital needs analysis method that assumes that at a client's life expectancy, the client will have a capital balance with purchasing power equal to the purchasing power at the beginning of retirement.

Pure Annuity Concept - The basic capital needs analysis approach, which is generally prepared on a pretax basis.

Remaining Work Life Expectancy (RWLE) - The work period that remains at a given point in time before retirement.

Retirement Life Expectancy (RLE) - The time period beginning at retirement and extending until death; the RLE is the period of retirement that must be funded.

Savings Rate - The average savings amount in the U.S. based on consumption.

Sensitivity Analysis - A tool used to understand the range of outcomes for each variable in a retirement plan by rotating each variable toward the undesirable side of the risk to determine the impact of a small change in that variable on an overall plan.

Wage Replacement Ratio (WRR) - An estimate of the percent of income needed at retirement compared to earnings prior to retirement.

Work Life Expectancy (WLE) - The period of time a person is expected to be in the work force, generally 30-40 years.

DISCUSSION QUESTIONS

1. List some of the major factors affecting retirement planning.

2. Define work life expectancy.

3. Define retirement life expectancy.

4. What is the median retirement age for individuals in the U.S.?

5. Explain the work life expectancy/retirement life expectancy dilemma.

6. List the major savings and investment concepts that are important to retirement planning.

7. Explain the importance of beginning a retirement savings plan early.

8. Explain the importance of understanding investment decisions and their consequences in retirement planning.

9. How is inflation relevant to a retirement plan?

10. Why does an individual's needs increase or decrease during retirement?

11. List some of the common factors that increase an individual's retirement income needs.

12. List some of the common factors that decrease an individual's retirement income needs.

13. Define the wage replacement ratio.

14. What is the most common estimate range in percentage terms for the wage replacement ratio?

15. Describe why a person may or may not need the same wage replacement percentage dollar amount or purchasing power amount throughout their entire retirement period.

16. List the two alternative methods for calculating an individual's wage replacement ratio.

17. How is the WRR calculated utilizing the top-down approach?

18. How is the WRR calculated utilizing the budgeting approach?

19. List the three most common main sources of an individual's retirement income.

20. Explain how Social Security affects an individual's retirement income.

21. Describe the importance of personal savings to an individuals' retirement income needs.

22. List some of the qualitative considerations that are important in retirement planning.

23. List some of the common factors that negatively affect retirement planning.

24. Explain capital needs analysis and its importance for retirement planning.

25. List the three most common methods for analyzing an individual's capital needs.

26. Identify the main assumptions made while completing capital needs analysis.

27. Describe how Monte Carlo Analysis can be used in retirement planning.

28. Explain how the Annuity Method calculates retirement needs.

29. What assumption does the capital preservation model make to mitigate the risk of an individual outliving their retirement savings?

30. Why is sensitivity analysis important to retirement planning?

MULTIPLE CHOICE PROBLEMS

1. Which of the following expenditures will most likely increase during retirement?

    a. Clothing costs.
    b. Travel.
    c. FICA.
    d. Savings.

2. Shirley, a 35-year-old client who earns $45,000 a year, pays 7.65 percent of her gross pay in Social Security payroll taxes, and saves eight percent of her annual gross income. Assume that Shirley wants to maintain her exact preretirement lifestyle. Calculate Shirley's wage replacement ratio using the top-down approach (round to the nearest %) and using pre-tax dollars.

    a. 70%.
    b. 80%.
    c. 84%.
    d. 90%.

3. Andy would like to determine his financial needs during retirement. All of the following are costs he might eliminate in his retirement needs calculation except:

    a. The $200 per month he spends on drying cleaning for his work suits.
    b. The $1,500 mortgage payment he makes that is scheduled to end 5 years into retirement.
    c. The FICA taxes he pays each year.
    d. The $2,000 per month he puts into savings.

4. Cindy has the following expenses during the current year:

	EXPENSE	AMOUNT
1.	Health Care	$800
2.	Savings	$4,000
3.	Travel	$500
4.	Gifts to Grandchildren	$1,000

    Which of these costs would you expect to decrease during Cindy's retirement?

    a. 2 only.
    b. 2 and 4.
    c. 1 and 3.
    d. 1, 2, 3, and 4.

5. Angie, a self employed dentist, currently earns $100,000 per year. Angie has always been a self proclaimed saver, and saves 25% per year of her Schedule C net income. Assume Angie paid $13,000 in Social Security taxes. Angie plans to pay off her home at retirement and live debt free. She currently spends $25,000 per year on her mortgage. What do you expect Angie's wage replacement ratio to be at retirement based on the above information?

   a. 37.00%.
   b. 59.70%.
   c. 65.30%.
   d. 84.70%.

6. Which factors may affect an individual's retirement plan?

   1. Work life expectancy.
   2. Retirement life expectancy.
   3. Savings rate.
   4. Investment returns.
   5. Inflation.
      a. 1 and 2.
      b. 1, 2, and 3.
      c. 1, 2, 3, and 4.
      d. All of the above.

7. Marsha and her twin sister Jan, both age 25, each believe they have the superior savings plan. Marsha saved $5,000 at the end of each year for ten years then let her money grow for 30 years. Jan on the other hand waited 10 years then began saving $5,000 at the end of each year for 30 years. They both earned 9% on their investment and are 65 years old today and ready to retire. Which of the following statements is correct?

   a. Both strategies are equal as they have equal account balances at age 65.
   b. Marsha's strategy is better because she has a greater account balance at age 65.
   c. Jan's strategy is better because she has a greater account balance at age 65.
   d. Neither strategy is better because Jan has a greater account balance but Marsha contributed less.

8. Lindsay saves $3,000 per year, for ten years, at the end of each year starting at age 26 and ending at age 35. She invests the funds in an account earning 10% annually. Lindsay stops investing at age 35, but continues to earn 10% annually until she reaches the age of 65. In contrast, Garner saves $3,000 per year at the end of the year between the ages of 36 and 65 inclusively and invests in a similar account to Lindsay, earning 10% annually. What is the value of Lindsay's and Garner's separate accounts at age 65?

	Lindsay	Garner
a.	$710,861	$387,212
b.	$710,861	$493,482
c.	$834,296	$387,212
d.	$834,296	$493,482

9. Kwame and Omarosa, both age 40, have $80,000 of combined retirement assets. They both expect to retire at the age of 65 with a life expectancy to 100 years old. They expect to earn 10% on the assets within their retirement accounts before retirement and 8% during their retirement. If they did not make any additional contributions to their account and they receive a fixed monthly annuity benefit for life, what is the monthly benefit (annuity due) amount they will receive during retirement?

   a. $4,775.30.

   b. $4,984.20.

   c. $6,115.60.

   d. $6,156.37.

10. Bobby would like to retire in 11 years at the age of 66. He would like to have sufficient retirement assets to allow him to withdraw 90% of his current income, less Social Security, at the beginning of each year. He expects to receive $24,000 per year from Social Security in today's dollars. Bobby is conservative and assumes that he will only earn 9% on his investments, that inflation will be 4% per year and that he will live to be 106 years old. If Bobby currently earns $150,000, how much does he need at retirement?

   a. $1,955,893.

   b. $2,049,927.

   c. $3,011,008.

   d. $3,155,768.

11. Bowie, age 52, has come to you for help in planning his retirement. He works for a bank, where he earns $60,000. Bowie would like to retire at age 62. He has consistently earned 8% on his investments and inflation has averaged 3%. Assuming he is expected to live until age 95 and he has a wage replacement ratio of 80%, how much will Bowie need to have accumulated as of the day he retires to adequately provide for his retirement lifestyle?

    a. $726,217.09.
    b. $784,314.45.
    c. $1,050,813.28.
    d. $1,101,823.40.

12. Assuming the same facts as above, approximately how much must Bowie save at the end of each year, from now until retirement, to provide him with the necessary capital balance assuming he has a zero balance today?

    a. $67,163.98.
    b. $70,424.36.
    c. $72,537.10.
    d. $76,058.31.

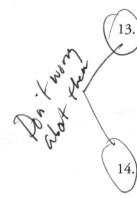

13. Utilizing the facts given in question #11, how much more will Bowie need at retirement to have the same amount at his death as he will have (calculated in #11) at his retirement?

    a. $82,897.54.
    b. $86,921.69.
    c. $109,496.29.
    d. $230,545.40.

14. Utilizing the facts given in question #11, how much more will Bowie need at retirement to have the same amount at his death with an equal purchasing power as he will have (calculated in #11) at his retirement?

    a. $82,897.54.
    b. $86,921.69.
    c. $109,496.29.
    d. $230,545.46.

15. Which of the following statements is false?

    a. To be more conservative in planning for an individual's retirement, extend the individual's life expectancy.

    b. A Monte Carlo Analysis uses a random number generator to provide the financial planner with an array of possible outcomes utilizing the same fact pattern.

    c. A sensitivity analysis helps the financial planner determine the single most effective factor in a retirement plan.

    d. The capital preservation model assumes that at life expectancy the client will have exactly the same account balance as he did at retirement.

Qualified Plan Overview

INTRODUCTION

Employers have many choices when deciding to select a retirement plan to benefit their company and its employees. Each retirement plan has unique benefits and characteristics, but if the plan is to be a **qualified plan**, it must follow a standard set of rules and requirements to attain a "qualified" status under Internal Revenue Code (IRC) Section 401(a). Once a plan has achieved qualified status, provided it maintains the qualified status per section 401(a), the plan sponsor and the participants will benefit from tax deferral, asset protection, and several other advantages as discussed throughout this chapter and Chapters 4, 5, and 6.

To help understand the unique advantages of each available qualified retirement plan and the specific requirements for the plans to attain qualified status, the universe of available qualified plans can be segregated into four categories. Each of these four categories can be defined because of its specific combination of certain qualities, benefits, and rules. First, qualified plans are divided between **pension plans** and **profit sharing plans** and then further divided into **defined benefit** and **defined contribution** qualified plans. This categorization is depicted at Exhibit 3.1. (Note that "defined benefit" and "profit sharing" are category titles as well as plan names.)

As Exhibit 3.1 illustrates, a qualified plan will always possess the characteristics of either a pension plan or a profit sharing plan combined with the characteristics of either a defined benefit plan or a defined contribution plan. For example, a money purchase pension plan is defined as having the qualities, advantages, disadvantages, and requirements of both a pension plan and a defined contribution plan, whereas a cash balance pension plan has the qualities of a pension plan and a defined benefit plan.

Know The Numbers

	2005	2006[*]	2007[*]	2008[*]
Covered Compensation	$210,000	$215,000[†]	$220,000[†]	$225,000[†]
Defined Benefit Maximum Limit	$170,000	$175,000[†]	$180,000[†]	$185,000[†]
Defined Contribution Maximum Limit	$42,000	$43,000[†]	$44,000[†]	$45,000[†]
401(k) Etc. Limit	$14,000	$15,000	$15,000[†]	$15,500[†]
Highly Compensated Employee	$95,000	$95,000[†]	$100,000[†]	$100,000[†]
Key Employee	$135,000	$135,000[†]	$140,000[†]	$140,000[†]
Social Security Wage Base	$90,000	-	-	-

Numbers that require annual indexing were estimated throughout the text for future years not released by the Internal Revenue Service or the Department of Labor at the time of printing. These estimated numbers are marked throughout the text with a † for easy identification.

EXHIBIT 3.1   QUALIFIED PLANS

Pension Plans (4 Types)		Profit Sharing Plans (7 Types)	
DEFINED BENEFIT PENSION PLANS (2 Types)	Defined Benefit Pension Plans Cash Balance Pension Plans	Profit Sharing Plans Stock Bonus Plans Employee Stock Ownership Plans	**DEFINED CONTRIBUTION PROFIT SHARING PLANS** (All 7)
DEFINED CONTRIBUTION PENSION PLANS (2 Types)	Money Purchase Pension Plans Target Benefit Pension Plans	401(k) Plans Thrift Plans New Comparability Plans Age-Based Profit Sharing Plans	

PENSION PLANS V. PROFIT SHARING PLANS

Historically, a retirement plan paid benefits to retired employees until death. Some retirement plans continued the payment of retirement benefits even after the employee's death until the surviving spouse's death. The employee usually did not contribute to the plan or bear any responsibility for investment decisions or the management of the plan or plan assets. The employee was simply promised a guaranteed benefit at retirement. Over the past 20 years, however, the number of these types of plans (noncontributory defined benefit) has decreased substantially as some employers did not fulfill the promise of paying the retirement benefit and as employees began changing jobs frequently throughout their work life. In fact, from 1985 to 2005 the number of defined benefit pension plans has decreased from 112,000 to 30,000. Changing jobs even a few times in a lifetime could result in significantly limiting the growth of retirement benefits payable from these old plans, which require many years of continuous service to the same employer to attain the expected benefit.

Key Concepts

Underline/highlight the answers to these questions as you read:

1. Explain the reason for the change from pension plans to profit sharing plans.

2. From a global perspective, what are the differences between defined benefit and defined contribution plans?

With the decline of these "guaranteed" type plans, commonly known as defined benefit pension plans, came the addition of profit sharing plans. Under profit sharing plans, plan participants usually became responsible for the management of the plan's assets (investment decisions) and sometimes even responsible for personal contributions to the plan (contributory plans). The profit sharing plan also changed the employer's funding requirement and began to permit, subject to limitations, in-service withdrawals from qualified plans and investment in the employer's securities. Exhibit 3.2 contrasts the basic differences between pension and profit sharing plans, which are discussed further in Chapters 3, 4, 5, and 6.

THE DIFFERENCES BETWEEN PENSION PLANS AND PROFIT-SHARING PLANS

EXHIBIT 3.2

CHARACTERISTIC	PENSION PLAN	PROFIT-SHARING PLAN
Legal promise of the plan	Paying a pension at retirement	Deferral of compensation and taxation
Are in-service withdrawals permitted?	No	Yes (after two years) if plan document permits
Is the plan subject to mandatory funding standards?	Yes	No
Percent of plan assets available to be invested in employer securities	10%	Up to 100%
Annual contribution limit	25%*	25%
Must the plan provide qualified joint and survivor annuity and a qualified pre-survivor annuity?	Yes	No

The limit for defined benefit plans may be higher if actuarially required.

DEFINED BENEFIT V. DEFINED CONTRIBUTION

As illustrated in Exhibit 3.1, qualified plans can be further divided into defined benefit plans and defined contribution plans. All defined benefit plans are pension plans, but some defined contribution plans are also pension plans with the remainder being profit sharing plans. The primary differences between the categorization of the plans as defined benefit or defined contribution are the assumption of the investment risk, the allocation of plan forfeitures, coverage under the Pension Benefit Guaranty Corporation (PBGC), the calculation of the accrued benefit or account balance, and the availability to grant credit for prior service. Each of these differences are illustrated in Exhibit 3.3 and discussed in detail below.

Quick Quiz

Highlight the answer to these questions:

1. Pension plans are currently much more common than profit sharing plans because individual workers stay longer with one employer and, therefore, can receive more insurance.
   a. True
   b. False

2. All pension plans are defined benefit plans.
   a. True
   b. False

False, False.

| EXHIBIT 3.3 | CHARACTERISTICS OF DEFINED BENEFIT V. DEFINED CONTRIBUTION PLANS |

CHARACTERISTICS	DEFINED BENEFIT	DEFINED CONTRIBUTION
Who assumes the investment risk?	Employer	Employee
How are forfeitures allocated?	Reduce plan costs	Reduce plan costs or allocate to other participants
Is the plan subject to Pension Benefit Guaranty Corporation (PBGC) coverage?	Yes (except professional firms with less than 25 employees)	No
Does the plan have separate investment accounts?	No, they are commingled	Yes, they are usually separate
Can credit be given for prior service?	Yes	No

Since pension plans can be either defined benefit or defined contribution (all profit sharing plans are defined contribution plans), the differences are more fully discussed in Chapter 4.

ADVANTAGES OF QUALIFIED PLANS

The U.S. government offers several income tax advantages to both the employers and the employees who elect to maintain and participate in a qualified retirement plan. The plan must be designed and adopted in a fashion "approved" by the government, and the plan must meet certain requirements enumerated in IRC section 401(a). Most of these requirements are established to ensure that any qualified plan is designed to protect and benefit rank-and-file employees. As distinguished from the senior executives and owners, the rank-and-file are those employees such as the factory workers, counter clerks, mechanics, staff accountants, associate attorneys, etc. The government's primary intention for the IRC requirements of Section 401(a) is to prevent employers from adopting qualified retirement plans that solely benefit executives and owners of

Key Concepts

Underline/highlight the answers to these questions as you read:

1. Explain the matching principle between expenses and income and its application to qualified retirement plans.

2. How does the imposition of payroll taxes on contributions impact qualified retirement plans?

3. How are the investment earnings within a qualified plan taxed?

the business. When a plan meets the qualification requirements and is considered a "qualified plan" under section 401(a), the employer and the plan participants will benefit from income tax deferrals, payroll tax savings, and federally provided creditor asset protection. Each of these advantages is discussed below. The trade-off for the tax advantages of qualified plans is compliance, including vesting, funding, eligibility, non-discrimination testing, IRS reporting, and employee disclosure.

TAXATION OF CONTRIBUTIONS TO PLANS

Income Tax

In almost all cases in the field of income taxation, when one individual or entity has a tax deductible expense, another entity or individual will have taxable income. This concept is referred to as the matching principle and is prevalent throughout the IRC. Consider an office supply store that sells office supplies to a publishing company for $600. The office supply store has revenue, or taxable income, of $600 subject to its costs, and the publishing company has a tax deductible expense of $600. This matching of income and expense especially holds true when an employer pays employees' wages, salaries, or bonuses for performance of services. The employees have taxable income, and the employer has a tax deduction for the same amount. This is referred to as the matching principle because of the matching of income and deductions.

> Carla works 40 hours a week at Best Feed Supply for $6.00 per hour. In addition, if Carla sells more than 200 pounds of feed during the week, she receives a bonus of $200. In a week that Carla works 40 hours and sells 300 pounds of feed, Carla has taxable income of $440 (($6.00 x 40) + $200), and Best Feed Supply has a tax deductible wage expense of $440.

EXAMPLE 3.1

Contributions by employers to qualified plans, however, do not have to comply with this "matching" of taxable income with tax deductible expense. An employer may deduct an amount up to 25 percent (or as actuarially determined for defined benefit plans) of the total compensation paid to its employees as a contribution to a qualified plan. The employer will immediately have an income tax deductible expense, but the employee will not have taxable income related to the plan contribution (until the funds are later distributed from the plan). This "mismatch" of income and expense is provided for in the IRC as a governmental incentive to entice employers to establish and fund qualified retirement plans for their employees. This mismatch is unprecedented as it reduces the current tax revenue for the U.S. Treasury and defers the taxation of the funds until the participant receives a distribution from the qualified plan. Because of this tax benefit and its potential abuse, the government has established and continues to establish certain limits for funding and deducting contributions to qualified retirement plans to minimize the reduction of tax revenue and to ensure that a substantial portion of the benefits are available to rank-and-file employees.

Quick Quiz

Highlight the answer to these questions:

1. Contributions to qualified retirement plans follow the IRC matching principle of the inclusion of income and the deduction of the expense at the same time.
   a. True
   b. False

2. The employer and employee are each responsible for their share of payroll taxes on the employee's compensation.
   a. True
   b. False

3. Distributions from a qualified retirement plan are generally taxable as ordinary income.
   a. True
   b. False

False, True, True.

EXAMPLE 3.2

Computer Connection, a regular C Corporation, employs fifteen service technicians, each earning $40,000 salary per year. The sole-shareholder of Computer Connection, Jason, who is also a service technician and employee, pays himself $120,000 per year. For 2006, Computer Connection contributed 20 percent of each employee's salary to a qualified profit sharing plan. For 2006, Computer Connection will have a deductible business expense for contributions to the profit sharing plan of $144,000 ((15 x $40,000) x 20% + 20% x ($120,000)). Neither the employees nor Jason will have any taxable income related to the contribution to the qualified profit sharing plan, but any distributions from the plan will be taxable as ordinary income (and may be subject to penalties) to the recipients at the time of distribution.

Payroll Taxes

In addition to income taxes, an employee who receives compensation for services rendered to an employer also incurs **payroll taxes** equal to 6.2 percent for Old Age Survivor and Disability Insurance (OASDI) on his compensation up to $90,000 for 2005 and 1.45 percent for Medicare tax on 100 percent of the employee's compensation. The employer is also required to match any payroll taxes paid by the employee creating a combined total payroll tax of 12.4 percent for OASDI up to $90,000 and 2.9 percent for Medicare.

However, when the employer makes a contribution to a qualified retirement plan on behalf of its employees, that contribution is not subject to payroll tax even though the contribution was on account of services rendered. This payroll tax savings acts once again to entice employers to fund qualified retirement plans and to view the combination of a qualified retirement plan and an employee's salary as part of an overall compensation package. Since the employee is not subject to payroll taxes on the contribution to a qualified retirement plan either, a total savings of up to 15.3 percent (12.4% OASDI and 2.9% Medicare tax) on the contribution may be realized. In Example 3.2, the alternative would have been to pay the $144,000 to the employees as additional salary instead of making the contribution to the qualified retirement plan. In that case, both the employer and the employee would have paid payroll taxes up to 15.3 percent on the $144,000.

If Butcher Block paid its two employees $50,000 each in wages and did not contribute to a qualified profit sharing plan for the year, Butcher Block would incur payroll taxes relating to the wages of $7,650 ($100,000 x 7.65%). Butcher Block's employees would have also incurred payroll taxes of $7,650 for total payroll taxes of $15,300.

EXAMPLE 3.3

As a comparison, if Butcher Block would have paid its 2 employees $45,000 each in wages and contributed $5,000 to a qualified profit sharing plan for each employee, Butcher Block would incur total payroll taxes relating to the wages and profit sharing plan contribution of $6,885 ($90,000 x 7.65%). In this case, Butcher Block's employees would also only incur $6,885 of payroll taxes for a total of $13,770 of payroll taxes. The combined payroll tax savings would be $1,530 ($15,300-$13,770); however, Butcher Block's employees received total payments for services rendered equal to $50,000, $45,000 as cash compensation and $5,000 in contributions to a qualified profit sharing plan. Note that even at the time distributions are taken from the qualified profit sharing plan, the distributions will not be subjected to any payroll taxes. The $1,530 of payroll tax is permanently avoided.

EXAMPLE 3.4

The payroll tax exclusion for contributions to qualified retirement plans does not pertain to employee elective pretax contributions to retirement plans such as 401(k) or 403(b) plans. Therefore, if an employee defers income by making a pretax elective deferral contribution into a 401(k) or 403(b) plan, then amounts deferred by the employee will be subject to payroll taxes. However, if these employee contributions have employer-matching provisions, or the employer is making other contributions (such as profit sharing), the employer-matching contribution is not subject to payroll taxes. Note that 403(b) plans are generally not qualified plans and will be discussed later in the text.

<table>
<tr><td>**EXAMPLE 3.5**</td><td>Joseph earns $166,667 and is a participant in his employer-sponsored 401(k) plan that offers a 75 percent match for contributions up to three percent of salary. Joseph elects to defer three percent of his salary, or $5,000, into the qualified 401(k) plan, and his employer matches the contribution with a $3,750 (75% x $5,000) contribution into the plan. Joseph's contribution of $5,000 is subject to payroll taxes, but the employer's contribution of $3,750 is not subject to payroll taxes. Note that because Joseph's earnings are in excess of the Social Security wage base and the OASDI of 6.2 percent is only paid on compensation up to the Social Security wage base, the employer is only saving the Medicare tax portion of 1.45 percent on the matching contribution to Joseph's 401(k) plan. However, in other cases where the employee's earnings are below the Social Security wage base, the employer is saving the full payroll taxes of 7.65 percent of the compensation.</td></tr>
</table>

TAX DEFERRAL OF QUALIFIED PLAN EARNINGS AND INCOME

Assets contributed to a qualified retirement plan are held in a tax exempt trust by a fiduciary, the plan sponsor, or an appointee of the plan sponsor. The plan assets are invested per the direction of the fiduciary or the employee (as determined at the creation or by amendment of the qualified plan), and the earnings on the plan investments are not subject to current income tax.

<table>
<tr><td>**EXAMPLE 3.6**</td><td>Mark's employer contributed $4,000 to a money purchase pension plan on his behalf. The funds were invested in a mutual fund that earned $300 in income during the year. The $300 is paid to Mark's money purchase pension plan account and reinvested in the mutual fund. Neither Mark nor his employer will currently recognize any taxable income from the $300 of income from the mutual fund.</td></tr>
</table>

When funds are distributed from the qualified retirement plan, the recipient of the distribution will have taxable income. With a few exceptions (as discussed below), the entire distribution will be taxed at the recipient's ordinary income tax rate at the time of the distribution regardless of whether the plan distributes cash, municipal bonds, Treasury bonds, or even stocks with "built-in" or unrealized capital gains.

ERISA PROTECTION

Because of various abuses by plan sponsors, Congress enacted the **Employee Retirement Income and Security Act (ERISA)** in 1974 to provide protection for an employee's retirement assets, both from creditors and from plan sponsors. Title I of ERISA ensures the employee's right to receive their dedicated benefits, and is enforced by the Department of Labor.

Anti-Alienation Protection

Because a qualified plan is designed to provide individuals with income at their retirement, ERISA provides an **anti-alienation** protection over all assets within a qualified retirement plan. This anti-alienation protection prohibits any action that may cause the plan assets to be assigned, garnished, levied, or subject to bankruptcy proceedings while the assets remain in the qualified retirement plan. Assets in a retirement plan covered by ERISA can only be seized to pay federal tax liens. This protection is to ensure that the individual has income at retirement.

Key Concepts

Underline/highlight the answers to these questions as you read:

1. What protection does ERISA provide to participants in qualified plans?

2. Describe the special taxation options available for lump-sum distributions.

George has $4,000,000 in qualified retirement plan assets. George's business failed and George personally filed for federal bankruptcy (Chapter 7). At the time of the bankruptcy filing, George had assets totaling $250,000 and debts totaling $650,000. The court awarded George's creditors $0.38 on the dollar and relieved George of any remaining creditor claims. This left George with nothing except his qualified retirement plan assets. Because of the ERISA afforded anti-alienation protection, the court could not award any of George's $4,000,000 of qualified retirement plan assets to his creditors. George will continue to have full rights over the assets of his qualified retirement plan.

EXAMPLE 3.7

Nicole Brown Simpson's family and Ron Goldman's family won a civil judgment that exceeded $30 million dollars against O.J. Simpson in 1997. However, most of O.J.'s remaining assets (after the trial and his subsequent bankruptcy) were qualified retirement plan assets that are protected under ERISA. Because of the ERISA protection, the Brown and Goldman families have been unable to collect any of the $30 million dollar judgment even though the value of O.J.'s retirement assets could pay some of the judgment.

EXAMPLE 3.8

Once the funds are distributed from a qualified retirement plan, the distributed assets are no longer protected by ERISA. Additionally, qualified retirement plan assets are not protected from alienation due to a **qualified domestic relations order** (QDRO - a court order related to divorce, property settlement, or child support) a federal tax levy, or from a judgment or settlement rendered upon an individual for a criminal act involving the same qualified plan. Because they are not qualified retirement plans, Individual Retirement Accounts (Traditional, Roth, SEP, or SIMPLE) are not afforded the same anti-alienation protection under ERISA, but they may be afforded similar protection under the particular state law of the plan creator and in some instances are provided protection under Federal Bankruptcy law (discussed in Chapter 9).

Protection from Employers

ERISA provides the laws, rules, and enforcement provisions to protect employees from abuse and misuse of the qualified plan by employers as plan sponsors. Specifically, but not limited to, employers are prohibited by ERISA from discriminating against employees based on the benefits payable to the employee under the plan, from substantially altering the plan document without appropriate approval and notice, and from managing the qualified plan in a manner that is not in the best interest of the qualified plan participants and their beneficiaries.

SPECIAL TAXATION OPTIONS FOR LUMP-SUM DISTRIBUTIONS

As briefly discussed above (and fully discussed in Chapter 7), the full value of a distribution from a qualified plan is usually subject to ordinary income tax at the date of the distribution (except for the return of a participant's adjusted taxable basis from certain types of after-tax contributions). However, in certain circumstances, when an employee takes a lump-sum distribution from a qualified plan, that **lump-sum distribution** may be eligible to receive favorable income tax treatment. A lump-sum distribution is a complete distribution of a participant's account balance within one taxable year on account of death, disability, attainment of age 59½, or separation from service. Specifically, a lump distribution may be eligible for ten-year forward averaging, pre-1974 capital gain treatment, or net unrealized appreciation treatment (discussed in detail in Chapter 7). The beneficial tax treatment of these distribution options is intended to lower the overall income tax payable by the distribution recipient (but also functions to increase the tax revenue for the current administration by encouraging the participant to take a full distribution rather than just the yearly annuity amount needed during retirement). It is important to recognize that due to various changes in the tax laws over the years, these lump-sum distribution options do not always create the lowest overall income tax and may not be the best choice for taxpayers eligible for this option.

Quick Quiz

Highlight the answer to these questions:

1. ERISA protects qualified plan assets from all creditors.
   a. True
   b. False

2. One disadvantage of a qualified plan is that it does not protect the employee from the employer's wrong doings.
   a. True
   b. False

3. A lump-sum distribution from a qualified retirement plan may be eligible for special income tax treatment.
   a. True
   b. False

False, False, True.

Only lump-sum distributions from qualified plans qualify for the ten-year forward averaging taxation option. Distributions, even distributions of the full account balance, from an IRA, SEP IRA or SIMPLE IRA do not qualify as lump-sum distributions for purposes of ten-year averaging and taxed at ordinary income tax rates.

ADVANTAGES OF QUALIFIED PLANS

Advantages to the Employer
• Contributions are currently tax deductible
• Contributions to the plan are not subject to payroll taxes
Advantages to the Employee
• Availability of pretax contributions
• Tax deferral of earnings
• ERISA protection
• lump-sum distribution options (ten-year averaging, NUA, Pre-1974 capital gain treatment)

DISADVANTAGES OF QUALIFIED PLANS

- • Limited contribution amounts
- • Contributions cannot be made after money is received
- • Distributions are usually has limited investment options
- • No or limited access to money while an active employee
- • Distributions usually taxed as ordinary income (Basis = $0)
- • Early withdrawal penalties may apply
- • Mandatory distributions at age 70½
- • Only ownership permitted is by the account holder
- • Cannot assign or pledge as collateral
- • Cannot gift to charity without income tax consequences
- • Limited enrollment periods
- • Considered to be an IRD asset

QUALIFICATION REQUIREMENTS

To benefit from the advantages of qualified plans, the IRC imposes requirements regarding eligibility, coverage, vesting, and plan funding limits for employers sponsoring qualified retirement plans. These requirements exist to protect the rank-and-file employees and to ensure that qualified plans are not being used solely to provide additional benefits to owners and senior executives of the employer.

Key Concepts

Underline/highlight the answers to these questions as you read:

1. What are the eligibility rules for qualified plans?

2. Explain the special two-year election for eligibility in a qualified plan.

3. How are tax exempt educational institutions encouraged to establish qualified plans?

PLAN DOCUMENT

When a qualified plan is adopted, the terms of the plan are identified and described in the plan document. In order for the plan to maintain its qualified status, the plan document and the administrator of the plan must be consistent with the IRC qualification requirements, which are discussed in this chapter. In some cases, the plan adopters may choose between several options (such as vesting schedules and loans) and still maintain their qualified status. These selections must be identified and described in the initial plan document and the plan document must be amended if different options are later selected. The plan document will be discussed in more detail in Chapter 8.

ELIGIBILITY

A qualified retirement plan must provide rules regarding when an employee becomes eligible for participation in the plan. The IRC provides **standard eligibility requirements** that state that an employee must be considered eligible to participate in the plan after he has completed a period of service with the employer extending beyond the later of either the date on which the employee attains the age of 21 or the date on which the employee completes one year of service (defined as a 12 month period in which the employee works at least 1,000 hours). Any employer-provided qualified retirement plan may be more generous and provide that an employee is eligible to participate before one year of service or before the attainment of age 21, but this generally only occurs with 401(k) plans because a majority of contributions to 401(k) plans consist of employee elective deferrals and, thus, may only cost the employer a minimal matching amount. In fact, a plan that requires an employee to attain any age or term of service less than the standard eligibility requirements of the IRC will meet the eligibility requirements necessary to be a qualified retirement plan.

Note that an eligible employee is not automatically a participant in the qualified retirement plan. As discussed below, other provisions of the plan may limit an employee's participation in the plan. The eligibility rules requiring age and service are established to ensure that employers are not requiring excessive years of service by employees or only allowing older employees to be eligible for the plan.

Plan Entrance Date

The eligibility rules could create an administrative burden for employers, requiring them to track eligible employees each day of the year. However, the IRC provides an elective grace period for the employer that states that even if an employee meets the requirements for eligibility listed above, an employer can make the employee wait until the next **plan entrance date** after the date the employee meets the eligibility requirements. The employer is allowed to follow this plan entrance date rule as long as the next available entrance date is not more than six months after the date of eligibility as determined above. Because of this rule, most qualified retirement plans establish two plan entrance dates per year so that no eligibility date requires an employee to wait more than six months to enter the plan once the eligibility requirement has been met. However, a qualified retirement plan with quarterly or monthly entrance dates will also meet the grace period requirement because it is more generous than twice per year and would always meet the six month requirement set by the IRC.

Helium Limited operates a money purchase pension plan on behalf of its employees. The plan has entrance dates of January 1 and July 1 of each year. On April 12, 2006, Bob turned 21 years old and celebrated three years of service. On November 15, 2006, Cathy, age 25, celebrated her one-year anniversary of employment. Helium Limited considered Bob a participant in the plan at July 1, 2006 and Cathy a participant in the plan at January 1, 2007. Both employees were required to wait for entrance into the qualified retirement plan past their exact eligibility date, but neither was required to wait for more than six months past their exact eligibility date. Thus, the plan meets IRC entrance requirements.

1/1/2006	7/1/2006	1/1/2007
Entrance Date	Entrance Date	Entrance Date
	Bob enters plan	Cathy Will
		Enter Plan

4/12/2006	11/15/2006
Bob turned 21 years old and celebrated 3 years of service.	Cathy's 1 year anniversary

Special Eligibility Rules
Two Year, 100 Percent Rule

As an exception to the above eligibility rule, a qualified retirement plan could require that an employee complete two years of service to be eligible for participation into the qualified retirement plan. When an employer elects this special requirement for its qualified retirement plan, there are consequences. The plan must provide the plan participants with 100 percent immediate vesting of their accrued benefit or account balance upon completion of two years of service for the retirement plan to be considered qualified under Section 401(c). With this exception, the employer may still require that the employee attain the age of 21. Thus, such a plan would have an age 21 and two years of service requirement.

EXAMPLE 3.10	Doctor's Resource sponsors a stock bonus plan (a qualified plan) that requires that its employees be 21 and complete two years of service before being considered eligible to participate in the stock bonus plan. To retain qualified status for the stock bonus plan, Doctor's Resource's stock bonus plan must provide its plan participant's with a 100 percent immediate vested account balance after completing two years of service. Therefore, any employer contributions to the plan will be automatically fully vested for the employee as of age 21 and 2 years of service.

The special **two-year eligibility election** is not available for 401(k) plans because most of the contributions to 401(k) plans are employee elective deferral contributions. As will be discussed in Chapter 5, a 401(k) plan may have employer-matching contributions, but these employer contributions usually account for a smaller portion of the total 401(k) account balance compared to the employee elective deferral contributions. Because the government wants to provide employees with the maximum ability to save for their retirement and the 401(k) plan provides the employees with such a device, the government statutorily prohibits 401(k) plans from requiring two years of service for eligibility.[1]

---

1. IRC Section 401(k)(2)(D).

Educational Institution

A tax-exempt educational institution with a qualified retirement plan maintained exclusively for its employees may delay eligibility in its qualified retirement plan until the later of the employee attaining age 26 or the completion of one year of service. The IRC allows for this delayed age requirement to provide an incentive for tax-exempt institutions to establish and fund qualified retirement plans to benefit their employees. Otherwise, a tax-exempt institution is unlikely to establish a qualified plan for its employees because the tax-exempt institution does not benefit, by nature, from the tax deductions created by the contributions to a qualified retirement plan. From the organization's standpoint, a contribution to a qualified plan only creates additional costs to maintain the plan. It does not create additional tax deductions as a tax-exempt educational institution does not pay tax on its earnings. The organization's age requirement of 26 allows the tax-exempt educational institution, most of whose employees are teachers, the ability to deny eligibility to those new teachers that do not spend many years with the school. As discussed above, the employer could be more generous and consider employees eligible before attaining age 26 and one year of service, but unless the employer permits eligibility based on the general rule of completing one year of service and attaining the age of 21,

Quick Quiz

Highlight the answer to these questions:

1. Using the standard eligibility rules, an employee must be allowed to enter a qualified plan on the day they attain the age of 21 and have completed one year of service.
   a. True
   b. False

2. If a company elects the two year eligibility rule, they can still require the employee to attain the age of 21 before being eligible for participation to the qualified retirement plan.
   a. True
   b. False

3. Tax-exempt educational institutions can require participants to attain the age of 26 before being eligible to participate in the qualified retirement plan.
   a. True
   b. False

False, True, True.

the employees must be 100 percent vested in their account balance or accrued benefit after meeting the eligibility requirements of age 26 if that eligibility requirement is selected.

A qualified profit sharing plan of a tax-exempt high school permits its employees to be eligible for the profit sharing plan after completing six months of service and attaining the age of 20. The qualified retirement plan follows a three-year cliff-vesting schedule. In this case, the profit sharing plan retains its qualified status under Section 401(a) even though participant account balances are not 100 percent vested after they complete one year of service because the plan did not increase the age requirement for eligibility to 26.

EXAMPLE 3.11

EXAMPLE 3.12

A tax-exempt middle school sponsors a qualified money-purchase pension plan. To be considered eligible for the money purchase pension plan, the employees must complete one year of service and attain the age of 24. Because the money-purchase pension plan does not permit eligibility based on the general rule of completing one year of service and attaining the age of 21, the money purchase pension plan must provide 100 percent vesting to participant's accrued benefit.

COVERAGE

As described above, an employer is only required to consider those employees that meet the eligibility requirements (age and years of service) for participation in the plan. In addition, all employees covered under a collective bargaining agreement and nonresident alien employees who do not perform services in the U.S. are also excludable from the plan.[2] All other employees, those deemed **nonexcludable**, must be considered for participation in the qualified plan. However, even after this determination, an employer is not required to adopt a plan that benefits each and every nonexcludable employee. In fact, many employer-provided plans are designed to benefit only select classes of the nonexcludable employees, and provided the employer's selection of the beneficial class is not discriminatory (as defined below), the employer-provided plan may still be considered qualified if it meets the IRC coverage tests described below.

Key Concepts

Underline/highlight the answers to these questions as you read:

1. Which employees may be excluded from a qualified plan?

2. Which employees are highly compensated?

Participation in a qualified retirement plan counts as coverage in the plan. Specifically, an employee is **covered** under a qualified retirement plan when he receives a benefit from the plan. For example, if the qualified retirement plan is a profit sharing plan, the employee is considered covered if he receives a contribution to his profit sharing plan account for the year. If the plan is a defined benefit plan, the employee is covered if the employee accrues a benefit for the plan year. Also, an employee who makes an employee elective deferral contribution under a 401(k) arrangement or an employee who receives a forfeiture allocation is considered covered under a qualified retirement plan.

Nondiscriminatory

The selection of the class of nonexcludable employees who will benefit under a qualified retirement plan must be reasonable and established based on the facts and circumstances of the business under objective business criteria. A few classifications considered reasonable are those based on whether the employee is hourly or salaried, the geographic location of the employee, or the employee's job description. For example, many law firms will completely exclude their associate attorneys while some businesses will exclude their commissioned sales people from coverage under the qualified retirement plan. In these examples, the employers are excluding all

---

2.   IRC Section 410(b)(3).

employees who share a job description from coverage, and provided the exclusion is uniform, the exclusion will be treated as nondiscriminatory. If, however, an employer bases coverage on age (other than according to the eligibility rules discussed above), sex, or any other non-business determination such as color of hair, eyes, or an employee's height, the classification will be considered discriminatory and the retirement plan will be disqualified thereby losing the tax benefits of qualified status.

When selecting the criteria to determine which employees benefit from the qualified retirement plan, an employer should always consider that a retirement plan is part of an employee's overall compensation package and should be viewed as a method of attracting, rewarding, and retaining employees. For example, if an employer chooses not to benefit those employees in the Atlanta office, the employees within that office may seek employment with competing employers in the local market who offer retirement plan benefits to its Atlanta employees. In this case, the former employer may lose qualified employees to its competitor. The cost of the lost employees will most likely far outweigh the cost of covering the employees under a qualified retirement plan.

Coverage Tests
The ability to determine which employees benefit under a qualified retirement plan is further governed by the requirements of the IRC that state that a certain number of nonhighly compensated employees (defined below) must benefit from the plan for the plan to retain its qualified status. Specifically, to be qualified, the retirement plan must meet one of the three following tests (1) the general safe harbor test, (2) the ratio percentage test, or (3) the average benefits test. (As discussed below, a defined benefit plan must also satisfy another coverage test known as the 50/40 test.) Each of these tests only considers those nonexcludable employees (as defined above), and each employer-provided retirement plan must only satisfy one of these tests (except defined benefit plans which must also satisfy the 50/40 test) to meet the coverage requirements of the IRC.

Highly Compensated Employees
For purposes of several coverage test calculations, all of the nonexcludable employees are further segregated into two classifications, **highly compensated** (HC) and **nonhighly compensated** (NHC). The definition of a highly compensated employee provided by the IRC is an employee who is either:
- A more than five percent owner (defined below) at any time during the plan year or preceding plan year, or
- An employee with compensation in excess of $95,000 for the prior plan year (2005) ($95,000[†] for 2006, $100,000[†] for 2007, and $100,000[†] for 2008).

Notice that under this definition, an employee who meets either one of these requirements is considered a highly compensated employee. So, any owner with more than a five percent interest is a highly compensated employee, even if his compensation is the lowest of any employee.

5-Percent Owner Defined

Although the term "5-percent owner" seems relatively self-explanatory, it is actually a bit more complicated. The IRC defines a "5-percent owner" as anyone who owned more than five percent of a company's stock or capital.

In addition to direct ownership, the family attribution rules direct that an individual is considered as owning the shares of stock of certain relatives, including stock owned by:[3]

1. Spouse;
2. Children;
3. Grandchildren;
4. Parents.

Ownership of corporations, partnerships, estates, and trusts can also be attributed to individuals in the determination of whether one meets the definition of a 5-percent owner.

EXAMPLE 3.13	Harold, his wife Wanda, and his son Steve, each own one-third of the stock of the Great Corporation. For purposes of determining the amount of stock owned by Harold, Wanda, or Steve, the amount of stock held by the other members of the family is added together. Thus, for coverage testing, each of them is deemed to own 100 percent of the stock of the Great Corporation.
EXAMPLE 3.14	Bob, his wife Wilma, his son Sam, and his grandson (Sam's son) George, own the 100 outstanding shares of BWSG, Inc. stock, each owning 25 shares. Bob, Wilma, and Sam are each considered as owning 100 shares of BWSG, Inc. George is considered as owning only 50 shares (his own and his father's).
EXAMPLE 3.15	Jeanette and her husband Don started Trophy Shop, Inc. many years ago. Together they owned 95% of the business and their only employee at that time, Cheryl, owned the remaining 5%. Don died last year and left his shares to Jeanette. Jeanette wanted to give up a majority of her responsibilities at the trophy shop and spend more time with her grandchildren. In the current year, Jeanette sold all but a 5% interest to Cheryl. Jeanette now owns 5% of the business and Cheryl owns 95%. Cheryl recently had a baby and no longer wants to work full time. Cheryl and Jeanette each receive a salary of $50,000 for the limited amount of work they do. Cheryl hired Delano, a successful salesman, to run the day-to-day operations and grow the business. Delano's

---

3.   IRC Section 318(a).

salary is $120,000. Which of the three employees are considered highly compensated based on the qualified plan rules?

EMPLOYEE	SALARY	OWNERSHIP % CURRENT YEAR	OWNERSHIP % LAST YEAR
Jeanette	$50,000	5%	95%
Cheryl	$50,000	95%	5%
Delano	$120,000	0%	0%

In this example, all three individuals are considered highly compensated for the current year. Even though Jeanette does not own more than 5% in the current year, she is considered highly compensated because she owned greater than 5% last year. Cheryl is highly compensated because she is a greater than 5% owner in the current year. Delano is highly compensated because his income exceeds the compensation test for the current year.

Highly Compensated Election
An employer election is available to reduce the number of employees considered highly compensated. This election allows an employer to only count those employees whose compensation is in excess of the dollar limit as highly compensated if that employee is also in the top 20 percent of all paid employees as ranked by compensation. This exception will not exclude employees who are more than five percent owners because such employees will be considered highly compensated based on ownership. An employer would consider this election when it would reduce the number of highly compensated employees as compared with the general highly compensated definition. An employer's overall goal is to reduce the number of employees classified as highly compensated and, thus, have more nonhighly compensated employees because the plan will be more likely to pass the coverage test.

Quick Quiz

Highlight the answer to these questions:

1. Qualified plans can exclude employees who are non resident aliens that do not perform services in the US.
   a. True
   b. False

2. A qualified plan can exclude as a class all women from the plan.
   a. True
   b. False

3. A person who earns $70,000 during 2006 is highly compensated for the 2007 plan year.
   a. True
   b. False

True, False, False.

EXHIBIT 3.6   **DETERMINATION OF HIGHLY COMPENSATED**

Owner Employees	Nonowner Employees
Either An owner of > 5% for current or prior plan year *or* Compensation in excess of $95,000 for 2005* for prior plan year	Compensation in excess of $95,000 for 2005* for prior plan year

* If special employer election is made, add "and in top 20% of employees ranked by salary."

EXAMPLE 3.16

Desk Emporium has the following 10 employees.

EMPLOYEE	SALARY	OWNERSHIP %
A	$200,000	65%
B	$125,000	35%
C	$110,000	-
D-J	$30,000	-

Utilizing the general definition of highly compensated (greater than five percent owner or compensation greater than $95,000 for 2005), employee A and B would be highly compensated because both are greater than five percent owners of Desk Emporium. Employee C would also be considered a highly compensated employee because his salary is in excess of $95,000 for 2005. So, in this example, three of the 10 employees would be considered highly compensated.

If Desk Emporium elected to only count those employees as highly compensated if they were also in the top 20 percent of employees ranked by compensation, only employees A and B would be considered highly compensated. Employee C would not be considered highly compensated because he is not an owner of the company and if ranked by salary, C is not in the top 20 percent. In a company with 10 employees, only the top two ranked by salary would be considered as in the top 20 percent. In this case, employee C is ranked third by salary and is therefore not considered highly compensated. By making the election, Desk Emporium was able to reduce the number of highly compensated employees to two of the 10 employees. In a situation like this, the employer would make the 20% election and reduce the number of highly compensated employees to help pass the coverage tests.

DESK EMPORIUM HIGHLY COMPENSATED TEST				
	General Rule		**20% Election**	
Employee	**> 5% Owner**	**> \$90,000 Compensation**	**>5% Owner**	**Top 20% (ranked by compensation)**
A	✓	✓	✓	✓
B	✓	✓	✓	✓
C		✓		
D				
E				
F				
G				
H				
I				
J				

Key Concepts

Underline/highlight the answers to these questions as you read:

1. What is the general safe harbor test for coverage in a qualified plan?

2. What is the ratio percentage test for coverage in a qualified plan?

3. What is the average benefits test and its component parts?

4. What is the defined benefit 50/40 test?

General Safe Harbor Coverage Test

The **general safe harbor coverage test** is a straightforward test that considers the number of nonhighly compensated employees covered by the qualified retirement plan. A qualified retirement plan satisfies the general safe harbor coverage test if the plan benefits 70 percent or more of the nonexcludable, nonhighly compensated (NHC) employees. Notice that this test only considers the nonhighly compensated employees, often called the rank-and-file, to determine the percent covered by the plan. The safe harbor test is not concerned with the percentage of highly compensated employees covered by the retirement plan.

EXAMPLE 3.17

Gerard's Automotive has 125 employees. 100 of the employees are nonexcludable and 25 of those are highly compensated (75 are nonhighly compensated). The company's qualified profit sharing plan benefits 21 of the highly compensated employees and 55 of the nonhighly compensated employees. The profit sharing plan meets the general safe harbor coverage test because it benefits 73.33 percent (55/75) of the nonhighly compensated eligible employees.

General Safe Harbor Coverage Test			
	Nonexcludable employees	**Covered**	**(%) Covered**
NHC	75	55	73.33%
HC	25	21	N/A
Total	100	76	General Safe Harbor Test % of NHC covered = 73.33 ≥ 70%

Only those employees considered nonexcludable were considered for the calculation of the safe harbor coverage test, but the plan does not cover each of those nonexcludable employees. In fact, 20 (75-55) of the nonexcludable NHC employees and four (25-21) of the nonexcludable HC employees are not covered by the plan. All of these employees meet the eligibility rules of the qualified retirement plan yet are not covered under the plan. Provided that the selection of the beneficial class was based on a nondiscriminatory classification (for example, the plan only benefits Gerard's Automotive's mechanics), the plan will satisfy the safe harbor coverage test because it covers at least 70 percent of the NHC employees. If an employer only has HC employees, the plan will automatically meet the coverage test.

Ratio Percentage Test

In the event a plan does not meet the safe harbor coverage test, the plan must meet one of two other coverage tests available or risk disqualification. The first of these two is the ratio percentage test. The **ratio percentage test** compares the percentage of covered nonhighly compensated employees to the percentage of covered highly compensated employees. A plan satisfies the ratio percentage test if the plan covers a percentage of nonexcludable nonhighly compensated employees that is at least 70 percent of the covered nonexcludable highly compensated employees. The coverage percentage of each class is calculated simply by dividing the number of covered employees from that class by the total number of nonexcludable employees of that class. After these calculations are performed, the percentage of covered nonhighly compensated employees divided by the percentage of covered highly compensated employees equals the plan's ratio percentage test. If this percentage is at least 70 percent, the retirement plan satisfies the ratio percentage test.

EXAMPLE 3.18

A qualified profit sharing plan covers 60 of the 100 (60%) nonexcludable NHC employees and 40 of the 50 (80%) nonexcludable HC employees. This profit sharing plan's ratio percentage is 75 percent (60%/80%), and, thus, satisfies the ratio percentage test.

Ratio Percentage (%) Test			
	Nonexcludable Employees	Covered	(%) Covered
NHC	100	60	60%
HC	50	40	80%
Total	150	100	
Ratio %Test $= \dfrac{\%\text{ of NHC Covered}}{\%\text{ of HC Covered}} = \dfrac{60\%}{80\%} = 75\% \geq 70\%$ Pass			

In this example, the plan would not pass the general safe harbor coverage test because the plan only covered 60 percent (not 70 percent) of the nonhighly compensated employees. Remember, the plan only has to pass one test and this one passed the ratio percentage test.

A qualified profit sharing plan covers 40 percent of the nonexcludable (80 out of 200) NHC employees and 60 percent of the nonexcludable HC employees (30 out of 50). The plan's ratio percentage is 66.67 percent (40%/60%), failing the ratio percentage test. The plan also fails the safe harbor test because the plan does not cover ≥ 70% of the NHC.

EXAMPLE 3.19

Ratio Percentage (%) Test			
	Nonexcludable Employees	Covered	(%) Covered
NHC	200	80	40%
HC	50	30	60%
Total	250	110	
Ratio %Test $= \dfrac{\%\text{ of NHC Covered}}{\%\text{ of HC Covered}} = \dfrac{40\%}{60\%} = 67\% \leq 70\%$ Fails			

If a qualified plan fails to meet all of the coverage tests, it is subject to disqualification. The above plan has failed two tests, but gets a chance to pass the third test (the average benefits test).

Average Benefits Test

The third coverage test, the **average benefits test**, determines whether the plan adequately benefits the nonhighly compensated employees compared with the benefits received by the highly compensated employees and determines whether the employee classification is nondiscriminatory. As such, the average benefits test actually consists of the following two tests:
- The average benefits percentage test, and
- The nondiscriminatory classification test.

A plan must pass both of these two tests, as described below, to be considered as passing the average benefits test and fulfilling the coverage requirement. If a plan does not pass both of these tests, it fails the average benefits test and must pass either the requirements of the general safe harbor coverage test or the ratio percentage test to satisfy the coverage requirements.

Average Benefits Percentage Test
A retirement plan satisfies the **average benefits percentage test** if the following ratio is at least 70 percent.

$$\frac{\text{Average Benefit Percentage of Nonhighly Compensated Employees}}{\text{Average Benefit Percentage of Highly Compensated Employees}} \geq 70\%$$

The average benefit percentage of each class of employees is determined by first calculating the benefit percentage for each nonexcludable employee. To do this, the benefit provided to each nonexcludable employees is divided by that employee's annual compensation (i.e., an employee who has a $100,000 salary and receives a $10,000 benefit has a 10 percent average benefit). A benefit percentage is also determined for each nonexcludable employee who does not benefit from the plan (thus, a benefit percentage of 0%). The calculated benefit percentages are then summed according to the employee's class (HC or NHC) and an average is calculated to determine the average benefit percentage. As expressed in the above formula, the average benefit percentage for the nonhighly compensated employees is then divided by the average benefit percentage of the highly compensated employees to arrive at a ratio that must be equal to or greater than 70 percent for the plan to pass the average benefits percentage test portion of the average benefits test.

EXAMPLE 3.20

Employee	Status	Salary	Benefit	Benefit %	Avg %
A	HC	$150,000	$15,000	10%	10.00%
B	HC	$100,000	$10,000	10%	
C	NHC	$50,000	$3,000	6%	5.33%
D	NHC	$50,000	$5,000	10%	
E	NHC	$50,000	$0	0%	

HC = Highly Compensated
NHC = Non Highly Compensated

$$\frac{\text{NHC\%}}{\text{HC\%}} = \frac{5.33\%}{10.00\%} = 53\% \text{ Fails Average Benefits Percentage Test}$$

EXAMPLE 3.21

Waggaman's Meat Market employs 400 people and sponsors a money purchase pension plan for its employees. Of the 350 nonexcludable employees, 50 are HC employees and 300 are NHC employees. The HC have a calculated average benefit percentage of 10 percent, and the NHC have a calculated average benefit percentage of eight percent. This money purchase pension plans satisfies the average benefit percentage test of the average benefits test because the ratio of the average benefit of the nonhighly compensated (8%) to the average benefit of the highly compensated (10%) is 80 percent (8%/10%), which is greater than the requirement of 70 percent. This plan must also satisfy the nondiscriminatory classification test to satisfy the average benefits test.

Average Benefit Percentage (%) Test		
	Nonexcludable Employees	Average Benefit %
NHC	300	8%
HC	50	10%
Total	350	

$$AB\%\,Test = \frac{\%\ of\ NHC\ Covered}{\%\ of\ HC\ Covered} = \frac{8\%}{10\%} = 80\% \geq 70\%$$

Nondiscriminatory Classification Test

The second requirement of the average benefits test is the nondiscriminatory classification test. To satisfy this requirement, the method in which an employer chooses employees to cover under a qualified plan must meet both of the following requirements:

- The classification must be reasonable and established, based on the facts and circumstances of the business, under objective business criteria that identify the category of employees who benefit under the plan (i.e. hourly or salaried, geographic location), and

- The classification must be nondiscriminatory. In order for the classification to be nondiscriminatory, the plan must meet one of the following two tests:

1. **Safe harbor test.** A plan satisfies the safe harbor test for a plan year if and only if the plan's ratio percentage is greater than or equal to the employer's safe harbor percentage. The employer's safe harbor percentage is equal to 50 percent, reduced by ¾ of a percentage point for each whole percentage point that the percentage of nonexcludable nonhighly compensated employees exceeds 60 percent of the employer's total employees. (See chart and examples below.)

2. **Facts and circumstances test.** To meet this test the plan's ratio percentage must be greater than or equal to the unsafe harbor percentage and the classification must satisfy a factual determination. The unsafe harbor percentage of an employer is 40 percent, reduced by 3/4 of a percentage point for each whole percentage point that the nonhighly compensated employee concentration percentage exceeds 60 percent. However, in no case is the unsafe harbor percentage less than 20 percent. (See chart and examples below.) A classification satisfies a factual determination if and only if, based on all the relevant facts and circumstances, the Commissioner finds that the classification is nondiscriminatory. No one particular fact is determinative. Included among the facts and circumstances relevant in determining whether a classification is nondiscriminatory are the following:

- The underlying business reason for the classification. The greater the business reason for the classification, the more likely the classification is to be nondiscriminatory. Reducing the employer's cost of providing retirement benefits is not a relevant business reason.
- The percentage of the employer's employees benefiting under the plan. The higher the percentage, the more likely the classification is to be nondiscriminatory.
- Whether the number of employees benefiting under the plan in each salary range is representative of the number of employees in each salary range of the employer's workforce. In general, the more representative the percentages of employees benefiting under the plan in each salary range, the more likely the classification is to be nondiscriminatory.
- The difference between the plan's ratio percentage and the employer's safe harbor percentage. The smaller the difference, the more likely the classification is to be nondiscriminatory.
- The extent to which the plan's average benefit percentage exceeds 70 percent.

| EXHIBIT 3.7 | NONDISCRIMINATORY CLASSIFICATION TEST |

Must Meet Both Requirements
1. Classification must be reasonable and established based on the facts and circumstances of the business under objective business criteria, and
2. Nondiscriminatory Classification

- **Safe Harbor Test.**

Meets the following test:

$$\frac{\% \text{ of NHC Covered}}{\% \text{ of HC Covered}} \geq \left[50\% - \left(0.75\% \times \left(\frac{\# \text{ of NHC}}{\# \text{ of Eligible Employees}} - 60\% \right) \right) \right]$$

Or

- **Facts and Circumstances Test.**

Commissioner finds the classification nondiscriminatory and it meets the following test:

$$\frac{\% \text{ of NHC Covered}}{\% \text{ of HC Covered}} \geq \left[40\% - \left(0.75\% \times \left(\frac{\# \text{ of NHC}}{\# \text{ of Eligible Employees}} - 60\% \right) \right)^{*} \right]$$

* But not less than 20%

| EXAMPLE 3.22 |

Teddybear Productions has 200 nonexcludable employees, of whom 120 are nonhighly compensated employees and 80 are highly compensated employees. Teddybear Production maintains a plan that benefits 60 nonhighly compensated employees and 72 highly compensated employees.

The plan's ratio percentage is 55.56%, which is below the percentage necessary to satisfy the ratio percentage test.

$$\frac{\% \text{ of NHC Covered}}{\% \text{ of HC Covered}} = \text{Ratio Percentage}$$

$$\frac{(160 / 120 = 50\%)}{(72 / 80 = 90\%)} = 55.56\%$$

Teddybear Production's nonhighly compensated employee concentration percentage is 60 (120 ÷ 200) percent, thus their safe harbor percentage is 50 percent and its unsafe harbor percentage is 40 percent. While the calculations are provided below, the safe and unsafe harbor percentages can be found in Exhibit 3.7.

$$\frac{\# \text{ of NHC}}{\# \text{ of Eligible Employees}} = \text{Nonhighly Compensated Employee Percentage}$$

$$\frac{120}{200} = 60\%$$

$$\text{Safe Harbor Percentage} = \left[50\% - \left(0.75\% \times \left(\frac{\# \text{ of NHC}}{\# \text{ of Eligible Employees}} - 60\% \right) \right) \right]$$

$$\text{Safe Harbor Percentage} = \left[50\% - \left(0.75\% \times \left(\frac{120}{200} - 60\% \right) \right) \right]$$

Safe Harbor Percentage = 50%

$$\text{Unsafe Harbor Percentage} = \left[40\% - \left(0.75\% \times \left(\frac{\# \text{ of NHC}}{\# \text{ of Eligible Employees}} - 60\% \right) \right) \right]$$

$$\text{Unsafe Harbor Percentage} = \left[40\% - \left(0.75\% \times \left(\frac{120}{200} - 60\% \right) \right) \right]$$

Unsafe Harbor Percentage = 40%

Because the plan's ratio percentage (55.56%) is greater than the safe harbor percentage (50%), the plan's classification satisfies the safe harbor test. Since the average benefit percentage test was also met, the plan will meet the coverage test.

EXAMPLE 3.23

Assume the same facts as above except that the plan benefits only 40 nonhighly compensated employees. Now the plan's ratio percentage is 37.03 percent.

$$\frac{(40\,/120 = 33.33\%)}{(72\,/80 = 90\%)} = 37.03\%$$

Under these facts, the plan's ratio percentage (37.03%) is below the unsafe harbor percentage (40%) and is considered discriminatory.

EXAMPLE 3.24

Assume the same facts above except that the plan benefits 45 nonhighly compensated employees. The plan's ratio percentage is 41.67 percent.

$$\frac{(45\,/120 = 37.50\%)}{(72\,/80 = 90\%)} = 41.67\%$$

Under these facts, the plan's ratio percentage (41.67%) is above the unsafe harbor percentage (40%) and below the safe harbor percentage (50%). The plan will fail the nondiscriminatory classification test unless the Commissioner determines that the classification is nondiscriminatory after considering all the relevant facts and circumstances.

EXHIBIT 3.8

Nonhighly compensated employee concentration percentage *	Safe harbor percentage	Unsafe harbor percentage
0-60	50.00	40.00
61	49.25	39.25
62	48.50	38.50
63	47.75	37.75
64	47.00	37.00
65	46.25	36.25
66	45.50	35.50
67	44.75	34.75
68	44.00	34.00
69	43.25	33.25
70	42.50	32.50
71	41.75	31.75
72	41.00	31.00
73	40.25	30.25
74	39.50	29.50
75	38.75	28.75
76	38.00	28.00
77	37.25	27.25
78	36.50	26.50
79	35.75	25.75
80	35.00	25.00
81	34.25	24.25
82	33.50	23.50
83	32.75	22.75
84	32.00	22.00
85	31.25	21.25
86	30.50	20.50
87	29.75	20.00
88	29.00	20.00
89	28.25	20.00
90	27.50	20.00
91	26.75	20.00
92	26.00	20.00
93	25.25	20.00
94	24.50	20.00
95	23.75	20.00
96	23.00	20.00
97	22.25	20.00
98	21.50	20.00
99	20.75	20.00

* This is the total number of nonhighly compensated employees as a percentage of total eligible employees.

The Nondiscriminatory classification test is provided to guarantee that a plan truly provides benefits to a substantial group of the nonexcludable nonhighly compensated employees. If this nondiscriminatory test were not part of the average benefits test, it would be possible to satisfy the average benefits percentage test by benefiting only a very small group of nonhighly compensated employees with a substantial benefit. For example, if an employer chose to only provide a benefit to the janitors and the executives, the classification would satisfy the general nondiscrimination rule discussed above because it is a classification based on job description. The employer could then provide the janitors with a benefit sufficient enough to satisfy the average benefits percentage test, and the plan would be considered qualified. This second nondiscriminatory classification test (the plan ratio percentage) is included to protect against a classification selection such as this by requiring the employer to provide a benefit to at least a certain number of nonexcludable nonhighly compensated employees.

For a plan to satisfy the average benefits test, it must actually satisfy three tests, the average benefits percentage test and the two nondiscriminatory classification tests. If the plan satisfies all three of the average benefits tests, it will satisfy the coverage requirements and it will not be required to satisfy the general safe harbor coverage test or the ratio percentage test. Otherwise, if a plan does not pass the average benefits test, it must pass either the general safe harbor test or the ratio percentage test for it to satisfy the coverage requirement.

A retirement plan is required to pass only one of these three coverage tests (general safe harbor, ratio percentage test, or average benefits test) to be a qualified retirement plan. Once it is determined that the plan passes one of these tests, the coverage requirement is met and no other test is performed. It is possible for a plan to fail one test and still meet the requirements of another and, thus, pass the coverage requirements.

EXHIBIT 3.9	COVERAGE TESTS SUMMARY

A retirement plan must annually satisfy at least one of the following tests to be considered a qualified retirement plan.*	
General Safe Harbor Test	% of NHC covered $\geq 70\%$
Ratio% Test	$\dfrac{\% \text{ of NHC Covered}}{\% \text{ of HC Covered}} \geq 70\%$
Average Benefits Test (Both Tests)	1. Average Benefit% Test $\dfrac{\text{AB\% of NHC}}{\text{AB\% of HC}} \geq 70\%$ 2. Nondiscriminatory Test
* A defined benefit plan must also pass the 50/40 test described below.	

Defined Benefit 50/40 Test

A defined benefit plan must satisfy the **50/40 coverage test** in addition to one of the other three coverage tests described above. The 50/40 coverage test requires the defined benefit plan to benefit on each day of the plan year the lesser of 50 nonexcludable employees or 40 percent of all nonexcludable employees. In the case of a defined benefit plan that has four or fewer nonexcludable employees, the plan must benefit at least two employees (or if there is only one nonexcludable employee, that employee must benefit from the defined benefit plan). This 50/40 coverage test does not segregate the calculation between the highly compensated and the nonhighly compensated.

EXAMPLE 3.25

A defined benefit plan sponsored by an employer with 125 nonexcludable employees must benefit at least 50 of the employees. This is calculated by determining the lesser of 50 employees or 40 percent of the employees. In this case, either calculation provides a requirement of exactly 50 employees. Note: A plan does not ever need to cover more than 50 employees to meet this test, but must still pass one of the previously discussed coverage tests.

EXAMPLE 3.26

A defined benefit plan sponsored by an employer with 100 nonexcludable employees must benefit at least 40 employees. The determination is calculated by determining the lesser of 50 employees or 40 percent of the employees – in this case 40 employees. (0.40 x 100 employees)

EXAMPLE 3.27

A defined benefit plan sponsored by an employer with three nonexcludable employees must benefit at least two employees. The determination is calculated based on the rule that states that a plan with less than four employees must benefit at least two of the employees.

EXAMPLE 3.28

A defined benefit plan sponsored by an employer with 5,000 nonexcludable employees must benefit at least 50 employees. The determination is calculated by determining the lesser of 50 employees or 40 percent of the employees – in this case 50 employees is less than 2,000 employees (40 percent of 5,000).

A defined benefit plan must satisfy either the general safe harbor test, the ratio percentage test, or the average benefit test and must also satisfy the 50/40 rule to satisfy the coverage requirements imposed by the IRC.

EXAMPLE 3.29

Walker Brothers sponsors a defined benefit plan for its employees. Walker Brothers has 200 employees, 20 of which are excludable because they do not meet the age and service requirements set forth in the plan document. 15 of the non-excludable employees are HC, and the remaining 165 are NHC employees. 10 of the HC employees are covered under the defined benefit plan, and 150 of the NHC employees are covered under the defined benefit plan. The average benefit percentage for the HC is 15 percent, and the average benefit percentage for the NHC is six percent. The selection of the covered class is determined to be nondiscriminatory. To be considered as passing the coverage test, Walker Brothers' defined benefit plan must pass either the general safe harbor test, the ratio percentage test, or the average benefits test and must also pass the 50/40 coverage test.

Employees	Nonexcludable	Covered	% Covered	AB%
NHC	165	150	90.91%	6%
HC	15	10	66.67%	15%
Total	180	160		

Coverage Test	Required to Pass	Plan Specific	Pass/Fail
Safe Harbor Test	$\geq 70\%$ of NHC covered	90.91% of NHC covered	Pass
Ratio% Test	$\dfrac{\% \text{ of NHC Covered}}{\% \text{ of HC Covered}} \geq 70\%$	$\dfrac{90.91\%}{66.67\%} = 136.36\%$	Pass
Average Benefits Test	$\dfrac{\text{AB \% of NHC}}{\text{AB \% of HC}} \geq 70\%$	$\dfrac{6\%}{15\%} = 40\%$	Fail
50/40 Test	Plan must cover the lesser of: • 50 Employees • 40% of Employees	Plan covers 160 Employees	Pass

Note: Since the plan passed the safe harbor test, it does not have to pass the ratio percentage test or the average benefits test. However, because it is a defined benefit plan, it is required to also pass the 50/40 test.

VESTING

Historically, some employers would require their employees to attain many years of service for the employee to **vest** or receive ownership of employer benefits (employer contributions and the earnings on those contributions) provided by a retirement plan. The stringency of these requirements reduced the employer's final cost of providing the benefit to its employees because the employee did not receive the otherwise full benefit as determined without meeting the vesting requirement. In other words, the employer would segregate and deduct the

employer contribution made on behalf of the employee to the plan each year as determined under the plan document, but unless the employee continued employment for a period of time equal to or greater than the vesting requirement, the employee would only receive a portion, if any, of the intended benefit. The loss of benefit upon termination would act as an incentive for employees to continue employment with the plan sponsor. Often, if the employee terminated employment before retirement, the employee would not receive any benefit at retirement. If the benefit was not paid to the participant, it was forfeited. In this case, the employer used these "forfeited" funds to contribute to the remaining employee's future benefits; thus, reducing the employer's future retirement plan costs (the expense of funding the employee's benefit). The IRC continues to allow qualified retirement plans to maintain a vesting requirement but limits the number of years of service required by the employer for an employee to fully vest in the employer contributed benefits and associated earnings.

All of an employee's elective deferral contributions to a qualified plan and the earnings attributable (pro-rata) to the employee's elective deferral contributions are not subject to any vesting requirements, and those contributions and earnings are always 100 percent vested in the employee's account. These funds are always the employee's funds because they are part of a salary reduction plan and were always owned by the employee.

The IRC requires that the employer's contributions and the earnings attributable (pro-rata) to the employer's contributions follow a vesting schedule that provides a vested benefit to the employee at least as rapidly as a 5-year cliff vesting schedule or a 3 to 7 year graduated vesting schedule (detailed in Exhibit 3.10). Also, when a plan is considered a top-heavy plan (defined below) or when the employer's contributions are made as part of a matching contribution (such as in a 401(k) plan), the employee's accrued benefit or account balance under the plan must vest at least as rapidly as a 3-year cliff or a 2 to 6 year graduated vesting schedule. The vesting schedules defined here do not replace or modify the 100 percent vesting requirements for a plan that elects the two years of service for eligibility (as discussed above).

A **cliff vesting schedule** provides an employee full rights to the plan's assets immediately upon the passage of a certain number of years of service, usually three years or five years. A **graduated vesting schedule** provides an employee with full rights to a certain percentage benefit (less than 100%) after completing a certain number of years of service and provides the employee with an additional percentage for each additional years of service. The most common cliff and graduated vesting schedules are illustrated in Exhibit 3.10.

A plan must also vest an employee 100 percent in any accrued benefit or account balance when the employee attains normal retirement age (for vesting purposes, normal retirement age is specified by the plan or the later of the employee becoming age 65) or upon termination of the plan.

EXHIBIT 3.10   **STANDARD GRADUATED, CLIFF, TWO-YEAR, AND TOP-HEAVY VESTING SCHEDULES**

YEARS OF SERVICE	STANDARD		2-YEAR ELIGIBILITY ELECTION	TOP-HEAVY PLAN (OR) EMPLOYER MATCH		EMPLOYEE CONTRIBUTIONS
	3 TO 7 YEAR GRADUATED	5-YEAR CLIFF		2 TO 6 GRADUATED	3-YEAR CLIFF	
1	0	0	0	0	0	100%
2	0	0	100%	20%	0	100%
3	20%	0	100%	40%	100%	100%
4	40%	0	100%	60%	100%	100%
5	60%	100%	100%	80%	100%	100%
6	80%	100%	100%	100%	100%	100%
7	100%	100%	100%	100%	100%	100%
8	100%	100%	100%	100%	100%	100%

EXAMPLE 3.30

Marcus has been employed by Blue Cliff Supply Stores for two years. After meeting the plans eligibility rules, he is a benefiting participant of Blue Cliff's qualified profit sharing plan, which consists of employer contributions only and follows a 5-year cliff vesting schedule. The current balance of Marcus' profit sharing plan is $14,000. The $14,000 will be forfeited if Marcus terminates employment before reaching five years of service. Any forfeited funds will then be used by the plan to either reduce current plan costs or to increase the benefit provided to remaining participants.

EXAMPLE 3.31

Craig has attained four years of service with Stone Corporation. Over those four years, Craig has received contributions to a qualified profit sharing plan in the amount of $60,000. If the plan follows a 3 to 7 year graduated vesting schedule, Craig has a vested account balance of $24,000 (40% of $60,000).

Vesting Schedule Options

Vesting schedules exist to ensure that nonhighly compensated employees will benefit under the plan and that it does not require an unreasonable amount of time to become vested. The employer may always elect to provide the employee with a vested benefit faster than the 5-year cliff or 3 to 7 graduated vesting schedule (or even the 3-year cliff or 2 to 6 year graduated vesting schedules for a top-heavy plan). For example, the plan may vest an employee's benefit 100 percent after four years of service, or the vesting schedule may be based on a 1 to 4 graduated vesting schedule. When an employer elects a faster vesting schedule, however, the vested benefit must always be comparatively better than one of the approved vesting schedules and cannot provide a greater vested percentage as compared to one of the schedules in some years and in other years fulfill the requirement by providing a greater vested percentage as compared to other vesting schedules. The chart below lists several examples of permitted vesting schedules and non-permitted vesting schedules that do not follow the general 3 to 7 year graduated or 5-year cliff vesting schedules.

The following chart illustrates various sample vesting schedules and whether they meet the qualified plan vesting requirements.

EXAMPLE 3.32

Years of Service	Permitted 3-7 Graduated	Permitted 5-Year Cliff	Permitted Schedule (A)	Not Permitted Schedule (B)	Permitted Schedule (C)	Not Permitted Schedule (D)
1	0%	0%	5%	5%	0%	0%
2	0%	0%	10%	10%	5%	5%
3	20%	0%	20%	15%	10%	20%
4	40%	0%	60%	60%	15%	30%
5	60%	100%	80%	80%	100%	60%
6	80%	100%	100%	100%	100%	80%
7	100%	100%	100%	100%	100%	100%

The permitted vesting schedules are at least as rapid as either the 3 to 7 year graduated vesting schedule or the 5-year cliff vesting schedule. Whereas, the "not-permitted" vesting schedules provide a vesting schedule that is at least as rapid in some years than one of the schedules and at least as rapid as other vesting schedules in other years. Specifically, Permitted Vesting Schedule A provides a greater vested percentage in every year compared to the 3 to 7 year graduated vesting schedule. Not Permitted Vesting Schedule B provides a greater vested percentage than the 5-year cliff vesting schedule in years 1 to 4, but in years 5 to 7 its vesting schedule is only as rapid as the 3 to 7 year graduated vesting schedule. To provide a vested benefit at least as rapid as the permitted vesting schedules, Schedule B must be compared in a blended fashion to both the 3 to 7 year graduated and the 5-year cliff; thus, is not a permitted vesting schedule. Vesting Schedule C provides a greater vested percentage in each year as compared to the 5-year cliff; therefore it meets the requirements and is considered a permitted vesting schedule. Vesting Schedule D meets the requirements compared to the 5-year cliff for years 1 to 4 and then only meets the requirements for years 5 to 7 in comparison to the 3 to 7 year graduated vesting schedule. Since Vesting Schedule D does not meet the minimum vesting requirements of either schedule, it is not a permitted vesting schedule.

Quick Quiz

Highlight the answer to these questions:

1. Employee contributions to a qualified retirement plan are always 100% vested.
   a. True
   b. False

2. Employees who attain the normal retirement age as defined by their qualified retirement plan must be fully vested in that retirement plan.
   a. True
   b. False

3. An employee meets the requirement of attaining one year of services if they work 1,000 hours in the first six months.
   a. True
   b. False

True, True, False.

Years of Service

As illustrated in Exhibit 3.10, employees earn a certain percentage benefit based on the applicable vesting schedule and after the employee attains a certain number of years of service. The **years of service** determination is based on the number of years, defined as a 12-month consecutive period with at least 1,000 hours worked for the employer. The determination is based on the employee's beginning date of employment and not on the date the employee becomes eligible to participate in the plan. For example, an employee who has worked 1,200 hours within a 12 month period has attained one year of service for purposes of vesting even though they may have just become eligible to participate in a qualified retirement plan that follows the general eligibility rule. This means that an employee will generally be accruing years of service from the beginning of employment even though he is not eligible for the plan.

It is important to note that an employer does not have to count for purposes of vesting: (1) years of service the employee acquired with the employer before reaching the age of 18 if the employee was not participating in the plan at that time, (2) years of service the employee attained before the employer-sponsored a qualified plan, or (3) years of service the employee attained during years when he did not contribute to an employee-contributory qualified plan.[4] If the employer desires, the employer can count any of these otherwise excludable years towards the employee's vesting requirement as long as all employees are treated the same.

---

4.   IRC Section 411(a)(4).

Taters Restaurant sponsors a defined benefit plan that does not permit employee contributions. Brian has been employed by Taters Restaurant for the past five years and has an accrued benefit to date under the plan of $20 per month at retirement. The Tater Restaurant's defined benefit plan is considered top-heavy and follows the least generous graduated vesting schedule. If Brian terminated his employment with Taters Restaurant today, he would be entitled to a benefit of $16 ($20 x 80%) per month at his retirement, an 80 percent vested accrued benefit. Taters Restaurant follows the 2 to 6 year graduated vesting schedule and not the 3 to 7 graduated vesting schedule because Taters Restaurant's plan is considered top-heavy (see below for more information on top-heavy plans).

EXAMPLE 3.33

The employees of Tax Heaven are given the opportunity to contribute to a 401(k) plan after six months of continuous service. As part of the benefit, Tax Heaven matches employee elective deferral contributions with an amount equal to 25 percent. The plan maintains the least generous graduated vesting schedule for the employer matching contributions. Mike has four years of service with Tax Heaven and has contributed $18,000 to his 401(k) account over those four years. Mike has received $4,500 (25% of $18,000) of employer matching contributions to the 401(k) plan, has earnings of $9,500, and has a current balance of $32,000. As of today, Mike has a vested balance of $29,440 as illustrated in the chart below.

EXAMPLE 3.34

Calculation of Mike's vested account balance:

CONTRIBUTIONS		VESTED PERCENTAGE	VESTED BALANCE
Employee	$18,000	100%	$18,000
Employer	4,500	60%*	$2,700
Total Contributions	$22,500		
EARNINGS ($32,000 - $22,500 = $9,500)			
Employee	$9,500 \times \dfrac{18,000}{22,500} = $7,600	100%	$7,600
Employer	$9,500 \times \dfrac{4,500}{22,500} = $1,900	60%*	$1,140
	$9,500		
Total Account Balance	**$32,000**	**Total Vested Balance**	**$29,440**

* Employer matching contributions for a 401(k) must vest at least as rapidly as 2 to 6 year graduated or 3-year cliff vesting schedules.

TOP-HEAVY PLANS

The **top-heavy** rules were designed to ensure that qualified plans that primarily benefit owners and executives of the company must also provide some minimum level of benefits for the rank-and-file employees. The top-heavy requirements are most commonly applicable to small employer plans, age-based profit sharing plans, and any other plans that provide the owners and executives with a disproportionate level of benefit from the plan. Most often the top-heavy rules are not applicable because the benefits provided to the non-key employees are generally greater than the required minimums of the top-heavy rules. A plan is considered top-heavy under either of the following two definitions:

- A defined benefit plan is considered top-heavy when the present value of the total accrued benefits of key employees (defined below) in the defined benefit plan exceeds 60 percent of the present value of the total accrued benefits of the defined benefit plan for all employees.

- A defined contribution plan is top-heavy when the aggregate of the account balances of key employees in the plan exceeds 60 percent of the aggregate of the accounts of all employees.

When a qualified retirement plan is determined to be top-heavy, the plan must: (1) use top-heavy vesting schedules and (2) provide a minimum level of funding to non-key employees. These top-heavy provisions attempt to ensure that non-key employees are actually benefiting from the qualified retirement plan and that the key employees are not benefiting in a disproportionate way.

Key Employee

A **key employee** is any employee who is any one or more of the following:
- A greater than five percent owner, or
- A greater than one percent owner with compensation in excess of $150,000 (not indexed), or
- An officer (defined below) with compensation in excess of $135,000 for 2005 ($135,000[†] for 2006, $140,000[†] for 2007, and $140,000[†] for 2008) as determined last year.

EXAMPLE 3.35	John owns five percent of the stock of Market Resources, Inc. and receives an annual salary of $110,000. Even though John is an owner, he is not considered a key employee because his ownership percentage is not greater than five percent, and even though he is a greater than one percent owner, his income is not greater than $150,000.

EXAMPLE 3.36

Maurice is an officer of Whinny National Bank. He earns $500,000 per year in annual compensation. Maurice is a key employee because he is an officer with compensation in excess of the limit.

Officer

Whether an individual is an officer shall be determined upon the basis of all the facts, including the source of his authority, the term for which elected or appointed, or the nature and extent of his duties. Generally, the term officer means an administrative executive who is in regular and continued service.

An employee who merely has the title of an officer but not the authority of an officer is not considered an officer for purposes of the key employee test. Similarly, an employee who does not have the title of an officer but has the authority of an officer is an officer for purposes of the key employee test.

No more than 50 employees can be treated as officers. If the number of officers, as defined above, exceeds 50, then only the first 50 ranked by compensation will be considered officers under the key employee definition.

Top-Heavy Vesting

A qualified retirement plan must provide a vested benefit to its employees as least as rapidly as either the 3 to 7 year graduated vesting schedule or the 5-year cliff-vesting schedule. If the qualified retirement plan is top-heavy, the plan must accelerate the vesting from the standard vesting schedules to either a 2 to 6 year graduated or a 3-year cliff vesting schedule. The employer may provide a vesting schedule that provides a vested benefit to its employees faster than that required by the top-heavy rules, but the employer must utilize a vesting schedule that is always comparatively more rapid than one of the permitted vesting schedules.

Top-Heavy Funding

The sponsor of a top-heavy plan must also provide its non-key employees with a minimum level of funding. The amount of the minimum level of funding depends on whether the plan is a defined contribution plan or a defined benefit plan. These differences are discussed below.

Minimum Funding for Defined Contribution Plans

A defined contribution plan that is considered top heavy must provide each of its nonexcludable, non-key employees a contribution equal to at least three percent of the employee's compensation. The benefit is payable to all eligible employees of the plan sponsor. An exception to the three percent minimum funding requirement occurs when the largest funding made on behalf of all key employees is less than three percent.[5] In this case, all of the non-key employees must receive a minimum benefit equal to the funding for the key employee.

---

5. IRC Section 416(c)(2)(B)(i).

EXAMPLE 3.37

The qualified profit sharing plan of MakeUps, LLP is considered top-heavy for the year. James, a plan participant, has annual compensation equal to $65,000, James is not a key employee. The minimum amount that MakeUps, LLP must contribute to the qualified profit sharing plan on James' behalf is $1,950 ($65,000 x 3%) assuming that they contribute at least 3% to key employees.

EXAMPLE 3.38

Erasers, Inc. sponsors a qualified age-based profit sharing plan. For the plan year, Eraser made contributions to its two key employees of one percent of compensation to Key Employee A and two percent of compensation to Key Employee B based on the formula provided under the plan document. The qualified profit sharing plan is top-heavy; therefore, all eligible nonexcludable, non-key employees must receive at least a two percent contribution to the qualified age-based profit sharing plan on their behalf because this is the largest funding percent made to a key employee (Employee B).

Quick Quiz

Highlight the answer to these questions:

1. An officer with compensation of $120,000 is a key employee.
   a. True
   b. False

2. Qualified plans that are considered top-heavy must use a 3 to 6 year graduated vesting schedule or a 3-year cliff vesting schedule.
   a. True
   b. False

False, False.

Defined Benefit Plan

A top-heavy defined benefit plan must provide a benefit to its non-key employees equal to two percent per the employee's years of service multiplied by the employee's average annual compensation over the testing period.[6] A participant's testing period shall be the period of consecutive years (not exceeding 5) during which the participant had the greatest aggregate compensation from the employer.[7] The maximum top-heavy requirement is a minimum benefit of 20 percent (or 10 years of service at two percent each year) of the employee's average annual compensation for the period of consecutive years not exceeding five. If the employer's benefit funding equation provides a greater percentage than the minimum funding level calculated for the year, the employer's funding equation will be used to determine the employee's benefits. See Example 3.39 for an illustration of a possible funding schedule compared with the minimum funding requirements of top-heavy plans.

---

6.   IRC Section 416(c)(1).
7.   IRC Section 416(c)(1)(D).

Boudreaux, Kadeaux, and Thibodeaux Corporations sponsor defined benefit plans providing benefits based on years of service and an employee's average annual salary. Boudreaux, Kadeaux, and Thibodeaux provide benefits of 1%, 1.5%, and 3% respectively for each year of service.

EXAMPLE 3.39

DEFINED BENEFIT PLANS ACCRUED BENEFIT PERCENTAGE AFTER YEARS OF SERVICE - MINIMUM FUNDING FOR TOP-HEAVY PLANS				
	Funding Schedules			Minimum Funding Requirement for Non-Key Employees if the Plan is Top-Heavy (D)
Years of Service	Boudreaux Corp. (A)	Kadeaux Corp. (B)	Thibodeaux Corp. (C)	
1	1.0%	1.5%	3.0%	2.0%
2	2.0%	3.0%	6.0%	4.0%
3	3.0%	4.5%	9.0%	6.0%
4	4.0%	6.0%	12.0%	8.0%
...				
10	10.0%	15.0%	30.0%	20.0%
11	11.0%	16.5%	33.0%	20.0%
12	12.0%	18.0%	36.0%	20.0%
13	13.0%	19.5%	39.0%	20.0%
14	14.0%	21.0%	42.0%	20.0%
15	15.0%	22.5%	45.0%	20.0%
* Beyond 20%, the top-heavy rules no longer apply.				

If the plans are top heavy, Boudreaux Corp. and Kadeaux Corp. must provide a benefit of 2.0% per year of service up to 20% (D) for non-key employees, rather than the 1.0% (A) and 1.5% (B) per year of service, as defined in their plan documents. Notice that in Year 14, the funding schedule for non-key employees of Kadeaux Corp. reverts back to the original schedule (B). Key employees with Boudreaux Corp. and Kadeaux Corp. will not be impacted and will simply receive the benefits provided for in their plans (A) and (B). Thibodeaux Corp. benefits are more generous than those provided by the top-heavy rules; therefore, the top-heavy rules would not apply and both key and non-key employees would receive benefits as provided under their plan.

EXAMPLE 3.40

Entertainment Hourly, Inc. sponsors a defined benefit plan for its employees. The plan benefit formula is 1.5 percent multiplied by the employee's years of service multiplied by the average of the employee's three highest consecutive years of compensation. The plan is determined to be top-heavy for the year. Charlotte, a participant of the plan, has been employed by Entertainment Hourly, Inc. for eight years. Under the current benefit formula, Charlotte should have an accrued benefit in the defined benefit plan of 16 percent (2% x 8 years) times her three highest consecutive years of compensation. The defined benefit plan funding formula is based on two percent times years of service in this case because the defined benefit plan is considered top-heavy and the benefit provided under the plan is less than that provided by the top-heavy rules.

EXAMPLE 3.41

A defined benefit plan's benefit formula is 25 percent of an employee's average three highest consecutive years compensation at retirement. The plan has been determined to be top-heavy for the year. An employee with 30 years of service and an average three highest consecutive years of compensation of $40,000 has an accrued benefit equal to $10,000 (25% x $40,000). In this case, the top-heavy formula is not applicable because it would have only provided the employee with a 20 percent benefit (the minimum funding formula always tops out at a 20 percent benefit). When the plan benefit formula provides a greater benefit than the top-heavy benefit formula, the plan benefit formula is used.

Case Study 1

In the case of Snyder v. Elliot W. Dann Co., Inc., top heavy minimum benefits were at issue.[1] In the case, Snyder, a vested participant in an employee pension plan, filed a lawsuit against the Plan, its administrators, and its fiduciaries seeking, among other things, minimum top-heavy benefits.

The court first addressed whether the Plan was top heavy. Section 416(c) of the Internal Revenue code of 1986 and Section 7.3 of the Plan provided that a member of the Plan who was not a "key employee" was entitled to a "top-heavy minimum benefit," also referred to as a "minimum annual pension," equal to the product of two percent of compensation multiplied by his or her "years of service."[2] The Plan was deemed to be "top-heavy" because the present value of the cumulative accrued benefits under the plan for key employees exceeded 60 percent of the present value of the cumulative accrued benefits under the plan for all employees. Snyder was not a "key employee" as defined by 26 U.S.C. Section 416(i)(1) and Section 2.18 of the Plan.

The court next addressed whether Snyder was entitled to top heavy minimum benefits for his last incomplete year of service. Dann Co. conceded that Snyder was entitled to top-heavy minimum benefits under the Plan for prior years, but contested his claim for his final year of employment on the basis that Snyder did not complete a "year of service." Snyder had been actively employed by defendant Dann Co. during all of 1984 and 1985. Snyder resigned from his employment on September 15, 1986, but he continued to render service to Dann Co. on a regular basis through December 15, 1986.

Snyder submitted evidence indicating that he conducted extensive efforts, including series of telephone conferences, correspondence, and meetings that culminated in a property sale on December 10, 1986, which generated a fee of $475,000 to Dann. Co., one half of which was paid to Snyder on December 15, 1986. The court reasoned that because Snyder was compensated on a commission basis, he may be considered employed for Plan purposes through the final date of his remuneration. Because Snyder put forth sufficient evidence to establish his claim that he worked past September 1986 and into December 1986, the court granted top-heavy minimum benefits for all three years at issue including 1986.

---

1. Snyder v. Elliot W. Dann Co., Inc., 854 F.Supp. 264 (S.D.N.Y. 6/8/1994).
2. See 26 U.S.C. Section 416(c)(1)(A)-(B).

EXHIBIT 3.11 **TOP-HEAVY PLAN SUMMARY**

	Defined Benefit Plan	Defined Contribution Plan
Definition	More than 60% of the total accrued benefits of the defined benefit plan are for the benefit of key employees.	More than 60% of the total account balances of the defined contribution plan are for the benefit of key employees.
Funding	Must be at least 2% x years of service x compensation factor	3% minimum to all eligible employees or less if less provided to the key employees
Vesting	The plan participant's benefits must vest at least as rapidly as a 2 to 6 year graduated vesting schedule or a 3-year cliff vesting schedule.	

ACTUAL DEFERRAL PERCENTAGE/ACTUAL CONTRIBUTION PERCENTAGE

Any qualified plan that includes a cash or deferred arrangement (CODA), such as a 401(k) plan, must also satisfy each of the two following tests:

- The Actual Contribution Percentage (ACP) Test for employer matching contributions (and employee after-tax contribution), and
- The Actual Deferral Percentage (ADP) Test for employee elective deferrals.

Key Concepts

Underline/highlight the answers to these questions as you read:

1. What is the covered compensation limit for qualified plans?

2. What are the plan limits for defined benefit plans?

3. What are the plan limits for defined contribution plans?

4. What are the plan limits for combined qualified plans?

Both of these tests compare the benefits derived from the CODA plan by the nonhighly compensated employees to the benefits attributable to the highly compensated employees to ensure that the plan is not benefitting the highly compensated employees by an impermissible disproportionate amount.

As these tests are specific to CODA type plans, the requirements of the ADP and ACP tests are explained and discussed in detail in Chapter 5.

PLAN LIMITATIONS ON BENEFITS AND CONTRIBUTIONS

To retain its qualified status and to benefit from the qualified plan advantages discussed earlier, an employer-sponsored qualified plan is limited in the benefits and/or contributions that it is permitted to provide to its employees. The various types of plans (defined benefit or defined contribution) have different methods by which the plan's benefits are provided to its participants. A defined benefit plan promises a definable payment at retirement whereas a defined contribution plan provides a contribution to a plan for each year of employment or at least on a regular basis. For this reason, the contribution limits differ for each type of plan. Defined benefit plans limit the distributions provided at retirement, and defined contribution plans limit the annual contributions to each employee's account for the year.

Covered Compensation

The benefits payable under a qualified plan are based on the employee's compensation from the employer. However, the maximum amount of compensation that can be considered for the plan year is $210,000 for 2005 ($215,000[†] for 2006, $220,000[†] for 2007, and $225,000[†] for 2008), and is referred to as the **covered compensation limit**. Before applying any of the rules or limitations discussed below, the covered compensation limit must be taken into account. For example, an employee whose compensation is $350,000 for the year may only consider a covered compensation limit of $210,000 for 2005. As such, any plan funding formula that requires the use of the employee's compensation cannot consider any compensation amount above the covered compensation limit.

Defined Benefit Plans

As will be fully discussed in Chapter 4, a defined benefit plan is designed to provide a benefit to an employee at normal retirement age, approximately age 65, and will not provide the employee with any benefit during the term of employment or prior to his separation from service with the employer. As such, the employer determines when designing the plan the amount of benefit desired to provide to employees for this future date. The statutory requirements generally limit the employer to providing an employee with the following maximum annual expected benefit at retirement:

The lesser of:

- $170,000 for 2005 ($175,000[†] for 2006, $180,000[†] for 2007, and $185,000[†] for 2008) or

- 100 percent of the average of the employee's three highest consecutive years compensation during the time of plan participation (considering the covered compensation limit).

Accordingly, the greatest annual amount an employee can expect to receive as a benefit from a defined benefit plan will never exceed $170,000 (adjusted periodically for inflation) or the average of the employee's three highest consecutive years compensation. A defined benefit plan may always provide a lesser benefit based on its formula but can never provide a greater benefit than $170,000 per year for 2005.

Trinity Audio has employed Ronald for 12 years. Trinity Audio operates a defined benefit plan that provides a benefit to its employees equal to one percent per year of service of the average of employee's three highest consecutive years compensation. Ronald has earned $275,000, $325,000, and $350,000 for the past three years, his highest consecutive years of compensation. The maximum benefit Trinity Audio can provide Ronald with at retirement considering the plan formula and the 2005 covered compensation of $210,000 is $25,200 (1% x 12 x $210,000) annually.	**EXAMPLE 3.42**

To ensure that qualified retirement plans do not benefit only certain employees with very few years of plan participation, an individual who participates in a defined benefit plan for less than 10 years must reduce the calculated maximum benefit by 10 percent for every year of participation less than 10.[8] For example, an individual with an average compensation for his three highest consecutive years of $60,000 and six years of plan participation would be allowed a maximum benefit under a defined benefit plan of $36,000 ($60,000 – (40% x $60,000)).

Distributions from defined benefit plans should begin at the normal retirement age of the employee. However, employers may provide in the plan document that the benefit be payable to the employee before the normal retirement age, perhaps as a method to encourage early retirement. In these situations where the benefit payments begin prior to normal retirement age, the calculated maximum benefit is actuarially reduced to an equivalent maximum benefit for the payment year. Other circumstances may create the need for an employer to establish an incentive to continue employment past the normal retirement age and allow the employee to accrue additional benefits in the defined benefit plan. Accordingly, where an individual's benefit payments begin after the normal retirement age, the maximum payment can be actuarially increased to an equivalent maximum benefit for the payment year. The depth and detail of these actuarial calculations are reserved for an advanced course in retirement planning.

EXAMPLE 3.43

Jose, age 68, has been employed by Whole Drinks Store for 39 years. He began employment as a grocery clerk and is now the President of the company. Jose has calculated that under the company's defined benefit plan, he will receive $170,000 per year after his retirement. However, because Jose has continued to work past his normal retirement age, his benefit will be increased to an amount actuarially equivalent to what it would have been if he had taken it at his normal retirement age.

Defined Contribution Plans

Similar to the defined benefit plan, the defined contribution plan also has a maximum benefit it may provide to its participants. However, the maximum benefit of a defined contribution plan is the maximum amount that may be contributed to an employee's defined contribution account for the year, not the amount payable to the employee at retirement as in the case for defined benefit plans. This "annual additions limit" is a statutory ceiling which consists of employee deferrals, employer matching contributions, employee discretionary contributions, and employee after-tax contributions.[9]

In general, the maximum contribution to a defined contribution plan is the lesser of:
- 100 percent of an employee's compensation for the plan year or
- $42,000 for 2005 ($43,000[†] for 2006, $44,000[†] for 2007, and $45,000[†] for 2008).[10]

Only those employees whose compensation is less than $42,000 (2005) are affected by the percentage limitation of 100 percent of compensation. For example, an employee whose compensation for the plan year is $30,000 could potentially receive a $30,000 contribution to a

---

8. IRC Section 415(b)(5).
9. IRC Section 415(c).
10. Does not include the catch-up contribution for those 50 and older, which is $4,000 in 2005. Therefore, the limit for these individuals is $46,000.

defined contribution plan. However, an employee whose compensation for the plan year is $150,000 could only receive a maximum $42,000 contribution to a defined contribution plan in 2005.

The maximum contribution is an aggregate amount consisting of:
- The employer contributions to the plan, plus
- The employee contributions to the plan, plus
- Any forfeiture allocated from a non-vested employee who terminated employment during the year.

The maximum contribution discussed here should not be confused with the employer's maximum tax-deductible amount of 25 percent of the employer's total compensation paid (discussed below).

Employer Contributions to the Plan

The total employer contributions to a defined contribution plan include any mandatory contributions, discretionary contributions, and matching contributions. If the employer maintains multiple defined contribution plans, the limit is based on the aggregate of all contributions to all of the qualified retirement plans.

Employee Contributions to the Plan

The total employee contributions to a defined contribution plan include any mandatory contributions, elective deferral contributions, and any after-tax contributions. The maximum employee elective deferral, as discussed in Chapter 5, is included within the defined contribution account maximum annual contribution. Catch-up contributions made by the participant are not limited by the $42,000 for 2005 limit and could allow an individual that was over the age of 50 to have contributions over $42,000 for 2005.

Forfeitures from Non-Vested Employees

If an employee terminates employment prior to being fully vested, the employee's benefits or a percentage of the employee's benefits will be forfeited and may then either be used to reduce future plan costs or increase the other plan participants' account balances. Any **forfeiture** allocated to an employee's defined contribution plan account during the year is included as a contribution to the plan when determining the maximum annual limit.

Pretzels, Inc. sponsors a defined contribution plan for its employees. Ashley, a long-term employee, with compensation of $135,000 for 2005, has received a $33,500 profit sharing plan contribution and $2,000 of forfeiture allocations. Ashley could still defer $6,500 ($42,000 - $33,500 - $2,000) in the 401(k) plan to maximize her annual contribution limit of $42,000 for the plan year.

EXAMPLE 3.44

	DEFINED BENEFIT	**DEFINED CONTRIBUTION**
Covered Compensation	$210,000 for 2005	$210,000 for 2005
Maximum Benefit	Lesser of: • $170,000 for 2005 or • Average of 3 highest consecutive years of compensation	Lesser of: • 100% of compensation or • $42,000 for 2005

EXHIBIT 3.12 MAXIMUM PLAN LIMITATIONS

EXHIBIT 3.13 COORDINATION OF MAXIMUM DEFINED CONTRIBUTION LIMIT

Employer Contributions
+ Employee Contributions
+ Plan Forfeitures
―――――――――――――――
= Lesser of $42,000 or 100% of compensation

Employer Contribution Limit

In addition to the limits per employee as detailed above, another limit applies to the maximum tax deductible amount allowed by an employer. Generally, an employer cannot deduct contributions to defined contribution plans in excess of 25 percent of the employer's total covered compensation. Covered compensation includes the compensation up to $210,000 (2005) for all those employees included in the plan. The 25 percent rule does not apply to defined benefit pension plans because the employer is required to fund the defined benefit plan to the minimum funding standard determined by the actuary.

Multiple Plan Limitations

In the case of an employer who maintains both a defined benefit plan and a defined contribution plan, the funding limit set forth is also combined. The maximum deductible amount is the greater of:

- 25 percent of the employer's total covered compensation paid or
- The required minimum funding standard of the defined benefit plan (as discussed in Chapter 4).

Because of the defined benefit plan minimum funding standards and its mandatory funding requirements, the defined benefit plan must always be funded with the required minimum funding standard. If this amount is less than 25 percent of the employer's total compensation paid, a contribution for the difference can be made to the defined contribution plan.

Mary's Carpentry Supplies (MCS) operates a defined benefit plan and a defined contribution plan. The annual covered compensation for MCS is $1,000,000. The actuary has determined that a contribution of $120,000 must be made to the defined benefit plan. In this case, MCS can make a profit sharing plan contribution on behalf of its employees up to $130,000 (($1,000,000 x 25%)-$120,000) for the current year.

EXAMPLE 3.45

Consider the same facts as above except that the actuary determined that a contribution of $400,000 had to be made to the defined benefit plan. In this case, MCS cannot make a contribution to the profit sharing plan because the $400,000 contribution exceeded 25% of MCS aggregate compensation, or $250,000, but they can still deduct the $400,000 contribution to the defined benefit plan.

EXAMPLE 3.46

Quick Quiz

Highlight the answer to these questions:

1. The covered compensation limit for 2005 is $210,000.
   a. True
   b. False

2. The defined benefit plan limit is $170,000 for 2005.
   a. True
   b. False

3. The defined contribution plan limit is the lesser of 25% of compensation or $42,000 for 2005.
   a. True
   b. False

True, False, False.

EMPLOYEE PLANS COMPLIANCE RESOLUTION SYSTEM (EPCRS)

If a qualified plan does not meet any one of the necessary requirements discussed throughout this chapter, the plan could lose its qualified status and its tax-favored status. In this case, the employer will lose their tax deductions for contributions to the plan, and the employees (usually only highly-compensated and key employees) would be taxed on the value of the plan's assets, including any earnings in their accounts.

To avoid the total loss of its tax advantages, a plan sponsor may voluntarily correct any problems with its qualified plan following the **Employee Plans Compliance Resolution System** (EPCRS) before two years from the end of the plan year in which the problem occurred. By voluntarily correcting the problem, the IRS will be more lenient and, provided the plan sponsor retroactively benefits all employees as if the problem had not occurred, will more likely than not allow the continuance of the plan's qualified status.

Key Terms

Anti-Alienation - An ERISA afforded protection for qualified plans that prohibits any action that may cause a qualified plan's assets to be assigned, garnished, levied, or subject to bankruptcy proceedings. Exceptions to the anti-alienation rule apply for tax levies and QDROs.

Average Benefits Percentage Test - One requirement of the average benefits coverage test that requires the average benefit percent of the nonhighly compensated employees to be at least 70 percent of the average benefit percentage of the highly compensated employees.

Average Benefits Test - A qualified plan coverage test that determines whether the plan adequately benefits the nonhighly compensated employees by comparing the benefits received by the nonhighly compensated to the benefits of the highly compensated employees and also determines whether the employee classification is nondiscriminatory. The test consists of the Average Benefits percentage test and the nondiscriminatory classification test.

Cliff Vesting Schedule - A vesting schedule that provides the participant's full rights to the plan's assets immediately upon the passage of a certain number of years.

Covered Employee - An employee who benefits from a qualified plan during the year.

Covered Compensation Limit - The maximum employee compensation that may be considered for contributions to qualified plans or the accrual of benefits to a qualified plan. For 2005, the covered compensation limit is $210,000.

Defined Benefit Plan - A qualified retirement plan that provides its participants with pre-determined calculated benefits at retirement.

Defined Contribution Plan - A qualified retirement plan that provides its participants the benefit of tax-deferred growth for contributions to the plan.

Employee Plans Compliance Resolution System (EPCRS) - The system provided by the IRS that allows plan sponsors to voluntarily correct any disqualifying actions within two years of the plan year end in which the problem occurred.

Employee Retirement Income and Security Act (ERISA) - An act enacted by Congress in 1974 because of various abuses by plan sponsors to provide protection for an employee's retirement assets, both from creditors and from plan sponsors.

50/40 Coverage Test - A coverage test applicable only to a defined benefit pension plans that requires the plan to cover for every day during the plan year the lesser of 50 employees or 40% of all eligible employees.

Forfeiture - The nonvested portion of an employee's account balance or accrued benefit at his termination date.

Key Terms

General Safe Harbor Test - A coverage test that requires the employer to cover at least 70% of the nonhighly compensated employees.

Graduated Vesting Schedules - A vesting schedule that provides an employee with full rights to a certain percentage (less than 100%) of benefits after completing a number of years of service and provides the employees with an additional percentage for each additional years of service.

Highly Compensated Employee - An employee who is either a more than 5 percent owner at any time during the plan year or preceding plan year, or had compensation in excess of $95,000 for the prior plan year (2005). A special election can be made to count only those employees whose compensation is in excess of $135,000 and are in the top 20% of employees as ranked by compensation.

Key Employee - Any employee who is a greater than five percent owner, a greater than one percent owner with compensation in excess of $150,000 (not indexed), or an officer with compensation in excess of $135,000 (2005).

Lump-Sum Distribution - A complete distribution of a participant's account balance within one taxable year on account of death, disability, attainment of age 59½, or separation from service. Lump-sum distributions from qualified plans are eligible for special taxation options.

Nonexcludable - An employee who must be considered as eligible to participate in a qualified plan.

Officer - An administrative executive who is in regular and continued service and has the executive authority normally associated with an officer.

Payroll Taxes - The combination of OASDI and Medicare tax paid by an employee and employer on an employees compensation.

Pension Plan - A qualified retirement plan that pays a benefit, usually determined by a formula, to a plan participant for the participant's entire life during retirement.

Plan Entrance Date - The date an eligible employee becomes a participant in a qualified plan.

Profit Sharing Plan - A plan established and maintained by an employer to provide for the participation in profits by employees or their beneficiaries.

Qualified Domestic Relations Order (QDRO) - A court order related to divorce, property settlement, or child support.

Qualified Plan - A retirement plan that meets the qualifications of IRC Section 401(a).

Key Terms

Ratio Percentage Test - A coverage test that compares the ratio of nonhighly compensated covered by a retirement plan to the ratio of highly compensated covered by the plan. The comparative ratio must be at least 70%.

Standard Eligibility Requirements - IRC eligibility rules for participation in a qualified plan. Provides that an employee must be considered eligible to participate in the plan after completing a period of service with the employer extending beyond either the date on which the employee attains the age of 21 or the date on which the employee completes one year of service (1,000 hours of service within 12 months).

Top-Heavy - Rules that were designed to ensure that plans established primarily to benefit the owners and executives of the company also provided some minimum level of benefits for the rank-and-file employees.

Two-Year Eligibility Election - A special election that overrides the standard eligibility requirements and permits the employer to only consider those employees who have two years of service as eligible to participate in a plan. If the employer elects the two year requirement, than the employer must also provide 100% vesting at the completion of two years of service.

Vest - To give an employee rights to employer contributions and earnings in their retirement plan benefits.

Year of Service - 1,000 hours of service for an employer within 12 months.

1. Describe the historical change from pension plans to profit sharing plans.

2. Describe the overall differences between defined benefit and defined contribution plans.

3. Explain the matching principle of expenses and income and its impact on qualified plans.

4. What are payroll taxes and how do they impact qualified retirement plans?

5. How are contributions to, earnings within, and distributions from qualified plans taxed?

6. Describe the anti-alienation protection afforded to qualified plans.

7. How are assets of a qualified plan protected for employees from the employer?

8. List the special taxation options available for lump-sum distributions.

9. Explain the standard eligibility rules for qualified plans.

10. What is the "Two-Year" eligibility rule?

11. Explain how eligibility rules are used to encourage tax-exempt educational institutions to sponsor qualified plans.

12. Which employees may be excluded from a qualified plan?

13. Define "highly compensated."

14. Describe the general safe harbor coverage test.

15. Describe the ratio percentage coverage test.

16. Describe the average benefits test and its component parts.

17. Describe the defined benefit 50/40 coverage test.

18. Explain the available vesting schedules for qualified plans.

19. Define "years of service" for qualified plans.

20. Define a "top-heavy qualified plan."

21. Define "key employee."

22. How are the vesting and funding requirements of a qualified plan affected by it being a top-heavy status plan?

23. What is the current covered compensation limit?

24. What is the maximum annual benefit that may be provided to an employee from a defined benefit plan?

25. What is the maximum allowable contribution to a defined contribution plan for 2005?

26. How is the funding limit calculated when an employer maintains both a defined benefit plan and a defined contribution plan?

1. Which of the following is not an example of a qualified retirement plan?

    a. ESOP.

    b. Age-based profit sharing plan.

    c. ESPP.

    d. 401(k) plan.

2. Dole Electronics, a C Corporation, has 5 employees. The company sponsors a profit sharing plan and contributed 10% of employee compensation for the current year to the plan. The company has the following employee information. There is no state income tax and federal withholding is 15% of gross pay.

EMPLOYEE	GROSS SALARY	PROFIT SHARING CONTRIBUTION
Andy	$50,000	$5,000
Candy	$40,000	$4,000
Mandy	$30,000	$3,000
Sandy	$20,000	$2,000

    Which of the following statements is true?

    a. Dole Electronics will not be able to take a deduction for the contribution to the profit sharing plan.

    b. After payroll taxes and with holdings, Andy will only receive $38,675 in take home salary.

    c. Dole electronics will pay total payroll taxes of $11,781.

    d. Candy must include the $4,000 contribution to the profit sharing plan made on her behalf in her gross income for the current year.

3. Steve has a qualified plan with an account balance of $2,000,000. In which of the following circumstances would a third party be able to alienate the assets within Steve's qualified plan?

    1. A QDRO in favor of a former spouse.

    2. A federal tax levy.

    3. Creditors in a personal bankruptcy.

    a. 3 only.

    b. 1 and 3.

    c. 1 and 2.

    d. 1, 2, and 3.

4. Barry's Graphic Arts Studio sponsors a qualified profit sharing plan. The plan requires employees to complete one year of service and be 21 years old before entering the plan. The plan has two entrance dates per year, January 1st and July 1st. Assuming that today is December 15, 2006 and the Studio has the following employee information, which of the following statements is correct?

EMPLOYEE	AGE	START DATE
Barry	35	1/1/2005
Del	34	8/1/2005
Karen	24	6/1/2006
Jenn	18	5/1/2005

    a. Two people have entered the plan.

    b. The qualified plan must provide participants with 100% vesting upon entering the plan because of the eligibility requirements of the plan.

    c. Del has not yet entered the plan.

    d. Jenn entered the plan on July 1, 2006.

5. Organic Inc. sponsors a qualified plan that requires employees to complete one year of service and be 21 years old before entering the plan. The plan also excludes all commissioned sales people and all other allowable exclusions allowed under the code. Which of the following employees could be excluded?

    1. Sarah, age 32, who has been a secretary for the company for 11 months.

    2. Andy, age 20, who works in accounting and has been with the company for 23 months.

    3. Erin, a commissioned sales clerk, who works in the Atlanta office. Erin is 25 years old and has been with the company for 4 years.

    4. George, age 29, who works in the factory. George has been with the company for 9 years and is covered under a collective bargaining agreement.

        a. 1 only.

        b. 1 and 3.

        c. 1, 2, and 4.

        d. 1, 2, 3, and 4.

6. Which of the following people would be considered a highly compensated employee for 2005?

    1. Kim, a 1% owner whose salary last year was $128,000.

    2. Rita, a 6% owner whose salary was $42,000 last year.

    3. Robin, an officer, who earned $80,000 last year and is the 29th highest paid employee of 96 employees.

    4. Helen, who earned $109,000 last year and is in the top 20% of paid employees.

      a. 1 and 4.

      b. 1, 2, and 4.

      c. 1, 3, and 4.

      d. 1, 2, 3, and 4.

7. Wanka Factory has 100 nonexcludable employees, 10 of whom are highly compensated. Eight (8) of the 10 highly compensated and 63 of the 90 nonhighly compensated employees are covered under Wanka's qualified plan. The average accrued benefits for the highly compensated is 4% and the average accrued benefit for the nonhighly compensated is 1.5%. Which of the following statements is true regarding coverage?

    1. The plan passes the ratio percentage test.

    2. The plan passes the average benefits test.

      a. 1 only.

      b. 2 only.

      c. Both 1 and 2.

      d. Neither 1 nor 2.

8. Cheque Company has 100 eligible employees and sponsors a defined benefit pension plan. The company is unsure if they are meeting all of their testing requirements. How many employees (the minimum) must be covered by Cheque Company's defined benefit pension plan for the plan to conform with ERISA?

      a. 40.

      b. 50.

      c. 70.

      d. 100.

9. Billy's company sponsors a 401(k) profit sharing plan with no employer match, but the company did make noncontributory employer contributions because the plan was top heavy. Billy quit today after six years with the company and has come to you to determine how much of his retirement balance he can take with him. The plan uses the least generous graduated vesting schedule available. What is Billy's vested account balance?

	EMPLOYER	EMPLOYEE
CONTRIBUTIONS	$2,000	$2,000
EARNINGS	$600	$600

    a. $2,600.
    b. $4,160.
    c. $4,680.
    d. $5,200.

10. WHR, LLC sponsors a defined contribution plan. Vaughn, age 44, has compensation of $150,000 for the year. WHR has made a $15,000 profit sharing plan contribution on Vaughn's behalf and $4,000 of plan forfeitures were allocated to Vaughn's profit sharing plan during the year. How much can Vaughn defer into his CODA plan (401(k)) to maximize his annual contributions to the qualified plan for 2005?

    a. $14,000.
    b. $18,000.
    c. $19,000.
    d. $23,000.

11. SJ, Inc. covered the following employees under a qualified plan.

    1. Joan, a 9% owner and employee with compensation of $30,000.

    2. Lind, a commissioned salesperson with compensation of $150,000 last year (the highest paid employee).

    3. Reilly, the chief operating officer, with had compensation of $100,000 last year but was not in the top 20% of paid employees.

    4. Garner, the president, who was in the top 20% of paid employees with compensation of $145,000.

Assuming the company made the 20% election when determining who is highly compensated, which of the following statements is correct?

    a. Exactly three people are key employees.

    b. Exactly two people are highly compensated.

    c. Lind is a key employee but is not highly compensated.

    d. Reilly is neither highly compensated nor a key employee.

12. Which of the following vesting schedules may a top-heavy plan use?

YEARS OF SERVICE	(A)	(B)	(C)	(D)
1	5%	10%	0%	0%
2	10%	20%	0%	0%
3	15%	45%	0%	20%
4	20%	65%	100%	40%
5	60%	100%	100%	60%
6	100%	100%	100%	80%
7	100%	100%	100%	100%

13. Charles earns $400,000 per year at Home Cleaning Services, Inc. where he has been employed for the last ten years. Home Cleaning Services sponsors a defined benefit plan that provides its employees with a benefit equal to 1.5% per year of service of the employees final compensation. At the current time, what is Charles' retirement benefit payable from the defined benefit plan?

    a. $31,500.

    b. $60,000.

    c. $170,000.

    d. $210,000.

14. Milton, age 38, earns $170,000 per year. His employer, Dumaine Consulting, sponsors a qualified profit sharing 401(k) plan and allocates all plan forfeitures to remaining participants. If in the current year, Dumaine Consulting makes a 20% contribution to all employees and allocates $4,000 of forfeitures to Milton's profit sharing plan account, what is the maximum Milton can defer to the 401(k) plan in 2005?

    a. $0.

    b. $4,000.

    c. $14,000.

    d. $18,000.

15. Mouse Emporium sponsors a qualified defined benefit pension plan and a qualified profit sharing plan. Mouse's annual covered compensation is $2,000,000 and the actuary has determined that a $600,000 contribution must be made to the defined benefit plan for the year. If Mouse would like to contribute the maximum to their defined contribution plan for the year, how much could Mouse contribute to the defined contribution plan?

    a. $0.

    b. $42,000.

    c. $100,000.

    d. $500,000.

Appendix:
Special Topics of Qualified Plans

LEASED EMPLOYEES

Qualified and other tax-advantaged retirement plans, such as SEPs and SIMPLEs, have specific guidelines as to which persons must benefit under the plan. Generally, only an employee of the sponsor organization will benefit under the plan. Independent contractors and temporary or leased employees are usually not covered by a company's retirement plan. However, there are specific rules that determine when a leased employee must be treated as an employee for purposes of the plan. If these rules were not in place, a company could simply hire temporary employees (leased employees) to fill the majority of positions within the company and avoid having to provide them with retirement benefits. This would create the illusion of a nondiscriminatory plan while, in fact, such a plan would be discriminatory. To avoid this possibility, the IRC provides guidance on who are to be considered leased employees and the employer's (sponsor) requirements as it relates to these employees.

Any person who provides services to the employer and is not an employee will be considered a leased employee if the following criteria are met:
- The services provided are pursuant to an agreement between the employer and a leasing organization;
- Such person has performed services for the employer on a substantially full-time basis for a period of at least one year; and
- Such services are performed under the primary control of employer.[11]

The significance of these rules is that leased employees must be considered a common law employee for purposes of meeting coverage rules, top-heavy rules, contribution and benefit rules, as well as a variety of other rules.[12]

EXAMPLE 3.47

ABC company, sponsor of a qualified plan, hires a receptionist, Diana, through a temporary service and employs Diana for a period in excess of one year. In such a case, Diana is treated the same as any employee of the organization for certain requirements related to qualification of the retirement plan. For example, Diana must be considered for purposes of meeting the coverage rules if she was otherwise eligible (e.g., 21/1). Although the general rule is that only 70 percent of

---

11. IRC Section 414(n)(2).

12. IRC Section 414(n)(3) states that a leased employee is considered an employee for purposes of the following code sections: Sections 401(a)(3), (4), (7), (16), (17), and (26); Section 408(k); Section 408(p); Section 410; Section 411; Section 415; Section 416; Section 79; Section 106; Section 117(d); Section 120; Section 125; Section 127; Section 129; Section 132; Section 137; Section 274(j); Section 505; and Section 4980(B).

the non-highly compensated employees must be covered, the addition of Diana may cause the plan to violate the coverage rules.

The IRC provides that if certain requirements are met (safe harbor rules) by the leasing organization, someone meeting the rules defining a leased employee will not have to be treated as an employee. The leased employee(s) must be covered by a plan that is maintained by the leasing organization and the leased employee(s) do not represent more than 20 percent of the employer's non-highly compensated work force. However, the plan that is sponsored by the leasing organization must also meet certain requirements, including:

- The plan must be a money purchase pension plan with a nonintegrated employer contribution rate for each participant of at least 10 percent of compensation;
- Such plan provides for full and immediate vesting; and
- Each employee of the leasing organization (other than employees who perform substantially all of their services for the leasing organization) immediately participates in such plan.[13]

Although the above rules provide a safe harbor for an employer who uses leased employees, the requirements are so stringent that they are unlikely to be met.

CONTROLLED GROUP

There are a variety of tax benefits that are available to corporations and other taxable entities, such as lower tax brackets, expensing of depreciable business assets (IRC Section 179), and tax deductions for contributions to qualified plans. Except for the controlled group rules under IRC Section 1561, savvy business owners could double or even triple these and other tax benefits by splitting current companies into two or three companies and still maintaining complete ownership. The controlled group rules cause multiple entities that are commonly owned to be treated as one entity for purposes of certain tax limits and tax benefits. These rules are intended to prevent business owners from simply splitting a company into separate companies with identical ownership so as to double or even triple certain benefits that are provided under the Internal Revenue Code.

However, fully understanding the controlled group rules may allow a family to structure entity ownership in such a way as to avoid falling within the controlled group rules; thus, being able to benefit by having multiple entities.

The Internal Revenue Code (specifically IRC Section 414(b)) also provides that companies belonging to a controlled group be treated as a single employer for purposes of qualified plans, specifically for purposes of:

- IRC Section 401 – qualification
- IRC Section 404 – deductions
- IRC Section 410 – participation
- IRC Section 415 – contribution and benefit limitations
- IRC Section 416 – top-heavy rules

---

13. IRC Section 414(n)(5).

Therefore, companies belonging to a controlled group must comply with the qualification rules, participation rules, and the other rules relating to qualified plans as if the companies were a single employer. In the event that such businesses fail to meet these requirements, the qualified plan(s) will be subject to disqualification. In addition to the rules for qualified plans, the rules under IRC Section 408(k) relating to Simplified Employee Pensions (SEPs) are also subject to the same limitations.

WHAT IS A CONTROLLED GROUP

A controlled group consists of two or more commonly owned corporations. These commonly owned entities generally take one of two forms. A controlled group will be classified as a parent-subsidiary group or as a brother-sister group. However, a group of related entities may be classified as a combined controlled group of corporations.

Parent-Subsidiary Controlled Group

A parent-subsidiary controlled group of businesses consists of a group of entities with common controlling ownership and a common parent. A controlling interest generally implies an 80 percent ownership interest. However, for purposes of IRC Section 415 (limitation on contributions and benefits), the 80 percent limit is reduced to 50 percent. The following examples will help to illustrate the point.

P corporation owns stock representing 80 percent of the total combined voting power of all classes of stock entitled to vote of S corporation. P is the common parent of a parent-subsidiary controlled group consisting of member corporations P and S.

EXAMPLE 3.48

Assume the same facts as above. Assume further that S owns stock representing 80 percent of the total value of shares of all classes of stock of T Corporation. P is the common parent of a parent-subsidiary controlled group consisting of member corporations P, S, and T. The result would be the same if P, rather than S, owned the T stock.

EXAMPLE 3.49

L Corporation owns 80 percent of the only class of stock of M Corporation, and M, in turn, owns 40 percent of the only class of stock of O Corporation. L also owns 80 percent of the only class of stock of N Corporation, and N, in turn, owns 40 percent of the only class of stock of O. L is the common parent of a parent-subsidiary controlled group consisting of member corporations L, M, N, and O.

EXAMPLE 3.50

Brother-Sister Controlled Group

A brother-sister controlled group consists of two or more companies that share common owners. There are two tests that must be met for a group of entities to be considered a controlled group: the 50 percent test and the 80 percent test. Two or more entities are a brother-sister controlled group if the same five or fewer persons who are individuals, estates, or trusts own stock possessing:

- At least 80 percent of the total combined voting power of all classes of stock entitled to vote or at least 80 percent of the total value of shares of all classes of the stock of each corporation; and
- More than 50 percent of the total combined voting power of all classes of stock entitled to vote or more than 50 percent of the total value of shares of all classes of stock of each corporation, taking into account the stock ownership of each such person only to the extent that such stock ownership is identical with respect to each such corporation.

These tests are best understood through an example.

EXAMPLE 3.51

Assume that individuals A, B, C, D, and E own corporations P, Q, R, S, and T as follows. Are these corporations or some of these corporations considered a controlled group? The answer to this question depends on whether or not both the 80 percent test and the 50 percent test are met.

	CORPORATIONS					
Individuals	**P**	**Q**	**R**	**S**	**T**	**Identical Ownership**
A	55%	51%	55%	55%	55%	**51%**
B	45%	49%	-	-	-	**45%***
C	-	-	45%	-	-	
D	-	-	-	45%	-	
E	-	-	-	-	45%	
Total	100%	100%	100%	100%	100%	
(P & Q only)						

The 50 percent test is met for all five corporations (P through T). However, corporations R, S, and T are not members of a controlled group because at least 80 percent of the stock of each of the corporations is not owned by the same five or fewer individuals whose ownership is considered for purposes of the 50 percent test. Only corporations P and Q are classified as a controlled group in the above example.

Consider the following example:

EXAMPLE 3.52

Individuals	SCENARIO 1		SCENARIO 2		SCENARIO 3	
	P	Q	P	Q	P	Q
A	100%	-	80%	20%	70%	30%
B	-	100%	20%	80%	30%	70%
C	-	-	-	-	-	-
D	-	-	-	-	-	-
E	-	-	-	-	-	-
Total	100%	100%	100%	100%	100%	100%

Clearly, Companies P and Q in Scenario 1 are not a controlled group. A owns 100 percent of the stock of Company P, while B owns 100 percent of the stock of Company Q. In Scenario 2, the 80 percent test is met, however, the 50 percent test is not met. A has 20 percent common ownership of Companies P and Q and B has 20 percent common ownership of Companies P and Q. Thus, the identical ownership is 40 percent, not the required greater than 50 percent. In Scenario 3, both tests are met, which means that Companies P and Q are members of a brother-sister controlled group.

AFFILIATED SERVICE GROUPS

Affiliated service groups are groups of entities that perform services together on a regular basis. The importance of affiliated service groups to retirement planning is that the entities that constitute an affiliated service group are treated as one organization or entity for purposes of the qualified plan rules. Prior to these rules, elaborate structures of entities could be established to provide higher qualified plan benefits to certain groups of owners at the expense of the rank-and-file employees. The affiliated service group rules were enacted to prevent such abuses.

A classic example of an affiliated service group is a two person law firm that is structured as a partnership with two corporations as the partners. Each corporation is solely owned by an individual attorney, who is also the only employee of such corporation. The three organizations, the partnership and the two corporations, constitute the affiliated service group.

An "affiliated service group" is particular type of group of related employers. The affiliated service group designation refers to two or more organizations that have a service relationship and, in some cases, an ownership relationship.[14] There are three types or categories of affiliated service groups, including A-Organization groups, B-Organization groups, and management groups.

---

14. IRC Section 414(m).

A-Organization Groups

An A-Organization (A-Org) group consists of two or more entities.[15] One entity, referred to as a First Service Organization (FSO), may be any type of entity, including a partnership, corporation, or LLC.

However, if it is a corporation, it must be a professional corporation.[16] The second entity, referred to as an A-Organization, must have an ownership interest in the FSO and must regularly perform services for the FSO or must be regularly associated with the FSO in performing services for third parties.[17]

Both the FSO and the A-Org must be service type organizations, meaning that capital is not a significant income producing factor of the firm.[18] Capital is a significant factor if a substantial portion of the total income of the firm results from the use of capital in the business. Examples of capitally intensive businesses include manufacturing and distribution companies.

Based on this definition of an A-Org Group, the law firm in the above example is an affiliated service group. The partnership is the FSO, with the corporations being the A-Organizations. Each of the A-Orgs regularly performs services for the FSO.

> A doctor is the 100% shareholder of Corporation X, a medical corporation that specializes in sports injuries. He also owns a 40% interest in Corporation Y, which performs such medical diagnostic services as X-rays and MRIs. The doctor regularly refers patients to Y for such services. Under the attribution rules of Section 318(a)(3), the doctor's 40% ownership interest in Corporation Y is attributed to Corporation X. The corporations are regularly associated in providing medical services to patients; thus, constitute an affiliated service group. Under the A-Org test, Corporation Y is the FSO and X is the A-Organization. Y has ownership interest in X and the organizations regularly perform services for patients.

---

15. Note that the "A" in A-Org refers to the last letter in the code section, IRC Section 414(m)(2)(A).
16. A professional corporation is a corporation that provides professional services. Examples include accountants, actuaries, architects, attorneys, chiropodists, chiropractors, medical doctors, dentists, professional engineers, optometrists, osteopaths, podiatrists, psychologists, and veterinarians. Prop. Treas. Reg. Section 1.401 (m)-l(c).
17. Includes ownership due to attribution under IRC Section 318.
18. Prop. Treas. Reg. Section 1.414(m)-2(f)(1).

B-Organization Groups

A B-Organization (B-Org) group consists of an FSO and at least one B-Organization.[19] The B-Organization must derive a significant portion of its business from the performance of services for the FSO, or for an A-Organization related to that FSO; perform services for the FSO or A-Organization that are the type historically performed by employees; and be owned at least 10 percent by persons who are highly compensated employees of the FSO or A-Organization.[20] The B-Organization does not have to be a service organization, as defined above for the A-Org group.

The IRS prescribes two safe harbors to determine whether a B-Organization derives a significant portion of its business from performing services for the FSO or A-Organization. The safe harbors are based on receipts. If neither safe harbor applies, then the determination is made on a facts and circumstances basis. The two safe harbors are the service receipts safe harbor test and the total receipts safe harbor test. These are described below.

Service Receipts Safe Harbor Test

The B-Organization's services are not considered significant if its "service receipts percentage" is less than five percent. The service receipts percentage is the ratio of the gross receipts derived from services the B-Organization performs for the FSO and/or the A-Organization to the total gross receipts derived from all services performed.

Total Receipts Safe Harbor Test

The B-Organization's services are considered significant if its "total receipts percentage" is 10 percent or more. The total receipts percentage is the ratio of the gross receipts derived from services the B-Organization performs for the FSO and/or the A-Organization to the total gross receipts (whether or not service related).

> Jones, an attorney, is a 25% shareholder in a law firm. Jones also has a 25% interest in corporation X, which provides word processing and other clerical and secretarial services. The law firm engages the services of corporation X on a regular basis. X derives at least 10% of its gross receipts from this relationship. The law firm and corporation X constitute an affiliated service group. The law firm is the FSO and Corporation X is a B-Organization with respect to the FSO because it performs services that are historically performed by employees; it meets the total receipts safe harbor test; and Jones, who is an HCE of the law firm, owns at least 10% of X.

EXAMPLE 3.53

---

19. Note that the "B" in B-Org refers to the last letter in the code section, IRC Section 414(m)(2)(B).
20. Highly compensated employees as defined in IRC Section 414(q). Note, the attribution rules of IRC Section 318 apply to IRC Section 414(q).

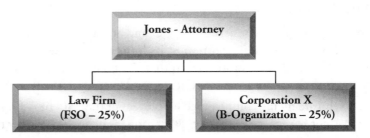

MANAGEMENT GROUPS

A management group consists of a recipient organization and a management organization. To be an affiliated service group, the management organization's principal business must be the performance of management functions on a regular and continuing basis for the recipient organization.[21]

> Mike is the former owner of Company P. He sells his interest in the company but continues to provide management consulting services to Company P through a new wholly owned entity, Company Q. Company Q provides management functions to P on a regular basis with all of the income for Company Q derived from Company P. Companies P and Q constitute an affiliated service group.

Unlike the A-Org groups and the B-Org groups, there is no ownership requirement. In the above example, there was no ownership between Company P and Company Q. Company Q simply provided management functions to Company P as its primary business.

How is principal business established? While there is apparently no objective test in the determination of what constitutes a principal business, a reasonable approach is to evaluate total income or revenue. If more than 50 percent of the income is derived from a single source, it is likely that there is an affiliated service group.

EXAMPLE 3.55

> Assume the same facts as above except that Company Q also provides management functions to 2 other businesses (total of 3) and that the revenue received from each of the companies is approximately equal. In this case, there is not an affiliated service group. Since no one company is the principal business of Company Q, there is no affiliated service group.

Impact of a Management Group Organization

In practice, most management organizations are adversely affected. Typically, the management organization employs mostly highly compensated employees, while the recipient organization employs mostly non-highly compensated employees. If the management organizations establishes a qualified plan, then it must be tested for coverage (IRC Section 410(b)) considering the employees of the management organization and the recipient organization. As a result, the

---

21. IRC Section 414(m)(5).

management organization either has to join the plan of the recipient organization or must maintain a plan that provides similar benefits as the recipient organization plan.

IMPACT OF AFFILIATED SERVICE GROUPS

As with the controlled group rules, when a group of companies are classified as an affiliated service group, the group of companies is treated as a single employer for purposes of qualified plans rules. The qualified plan rules that are impacted include eligibility, coverage, vesting, non-discrimination (including ADP and ACP), contribution/benefit limits under IRC Section 415, top-heavy rules, and other rules.

SEPARATE LINE OF BUSINESS

Eligible employees within the same company are generally required to be treated uniformly as it relates to qualified retirement plans. However, companies that maintain separate lines of business may be permitted to treat the employees of one line of business different than employees of another line of business.[22]

Usually, a separate line of business will have a separate organizational unit, separate accounting, separate employee group, and separate management. A firm can provide different benefits, including qualified retirement plan benefits, to employees of a separate line of business than to other parts of a business. This provision may allow a firm to reduce company expenses.

For an employer to treat various parts of a business as separate lines of business requires there to be a valid business purpose and that certain rules are met. The employer must have at least 50 employees within a line of business and notify the Secretary (IRS) that such line of business is going to be treated as a separate line of business for purposes of IRC Section 129(d)(8) and 410(b). Form 5310-A (Notice of Merger or Consolidation, Spinoff, or Transfer of Plan Assets or Liabilities; Notice of Qualified Separate Line of Business) is used to notify the IRS that a company intends to maintain separate lines of business. In addition, such lines of business must meet certain guidelines prescribed by the Secretary or the employer must receive a determination letter permitting the line of business to be treated as a separate line of business.

Certain safe harbor provisions will satisfy the previous requirement of meeting prescribed guidelines established by the Secretary.[23] A line of business will meet the safe harbor requirements if the percentage of highly compensated employees is not less than one-half and not more than twice the percentage that highly compensated employees are of all employees of the employer. There are also a variety of administrative safe harbor rules that will permit a separate line of business.

---

22. IRC Section 414(r).
23. IRC Section 414(r)(3).

BREAK IN SERVICE RULES

In some cases an employee may leave their job and return at a later time. This may occur because an individual quits and then is later rehired, or the individual may take a leave of absence due to the birth of a child or for military service. These types of leaves from the employer may create what is referred to as a "break in service." The consequences of a break in service depend on the length of time the employee is away, whether their retirement benefit was fully vested, and, in some cases, the reason that the employee took the leave.

A one year break in service is defined as a "calendar year, plan year, or other 12-consecutive-month period designated by the plan (and not prohibited under regulations prescribed by the Secretary of Labor) during which the participant has not completed more than 500 hours of service."[24] In the case of a plan utilizing the elapsed time method, the term "1-year break in service" generally means a 12-consecutive month period beginning on the severance from service date or any anniversary thereof and ending on the next succeeding anniversary of such date.

EXAMPLE 3.56

Fischer and Company maintains a qualified plan. The plan requires 2 years of service to become eligible for the plan. Paul was hired on January 1, 2005 and works 40 hours per week. Paul takes a leave of absence from February 1, 2006 to December 31, 2006 to care for his aging father. Paul returns to work January 1, 2007. Since Paul only worked 160 hours in 2006 a one year break in service occurred for 2006.

In general, a qualified plan must count all of the employee's years of service for eligibility purposes since the employee's date of hire. However, for an employee who has incurred a 1-year break in service, years of service completed before such break are not required to be taken into account until the employee has completed one year of service after his return to service.[25] In addition, if a plan requires two years of service before an employee can enter the plan, then the plan can, if properly elected in the plan document, disregard years of service before a "one year break" in service.

EXAMPLE 3.57

In the example above, Paul had one year of service before he had a one year break in service. Since the plan requires two years of service for eligibility the plan is not required to take into account Paul's service for 2005. Thus, when Paul returns back to work in 2007 his years of service for eligibility will start over.

If an employee is already eligible for the qualified plan then a break in service can affect the employee's vesting in the plan. In the case of a nonvested participant who has incurred a 1-year break in service, years of service completed after such break are not required to be taken into

---

24. IRC Section 411(a)(6)(A).
25. IRC Reg. Section 1.411(a)-6.

account with regard to vesting if the employee has the greater of five consecutive one year breaks in service or the participant's years of service before the break.

EXAMPLE 3.58

Fischer Company maintains a qualified plan. The plan utilizes a calendar year 5-year cliff vesting schedule. Paul was hired on January 1, 2005. After 3 years of service Paul separated from service. One year later Paul returns to Fischer Company and reenters the plan. If Paul completes one year of service after reentering the plan then the plan must credit Paul for his previous years of service. Thus, when Paul has completed one year of service after reentering the plan, he will have 4 years accumulated toward meeting the vesting requirement.

EXAMPLE 3.59

Assume instead Paul returns five years later instead of one year later. Since Paul has five one year breaks in service, the plan is not required to credit Paul for his previous years of service. Therefore, when Paul has completed one year of service after reentering the plan, he will only have 1 year towards the 5 year requirement.

In the case of a participant in a defined contribution plan who has incurred a 1-year break in service, years of service completed after such break are not required to be taken into account for purposes of determining the nonforfeitable percentage of the participant's right to employer-derived benefits that accrued before the break if the employee has five consecutive one year breaks in service or receives a distribution of the account balance.

EXAMPLE 3.60

Fischer Company maintains a defined contribution plan. The plan utilizes a calendar year 2 to 6 year graduated vesting schedule. Paul was hired on January 1, 2005. After 3 years of service Paul separated from service with a vested balance of 40% that was not distributed from the plan. One year later Paul returns to Fischer Company and reenters the plan. If Paul completes one year of service after reentering the plan, then the plan must credit Paul's pre-break in service account for years of service after the break. Thus, Paul's account balance will be 60% vested in all funds in the account at his initial separation. In addition, the contributions made by Paul after he reenters the plan will benefit from the prior years of service. Thus, when Paul has completed one year of service after reentering the plan, he will also be 60% vested in that year's contributions.

EXAMPLE 3.61

Assume instead Paul returns five years later instead of one year later. Since Paul has five one year breaks in service, the plan is not required to credit Paul's pre-break in service account for years of service after the break. Thus, the 60%

unvested portion in his pre-break account is forever lost. In addition, contributions made after Paul's return do not benefit from Paul's prior service. Therefore, when Paul has completed two years of service after reentering the plan, he will only be 20% vested in his post break account balance.

For purposes of determining the employee's accrued benefit under a plan, the plan may not disregard service due to distribution unless the plan provides an opportunity for the participant to repay the full amount of the distribution after returning to service. A defined benefit plan can also require the repayment to include interest no greater than 120% of the federal midterm rate on the first day of the plan year that the repayment occurs. The plan provision required may provide that such repayment must be made in the case of a withdrawal because of separation from service, before the earlier of 5 years after the first date on which the participant is subsequently re-employed by the employer, or the close of the first period of 5 consecutive 1-year breaks in service commencing after the withdrawal; or in the case of any other withdrawal, 5 years after the date of the withdrawal.

EXAMPLE 3.62	Fischer Company maintains a defined contribution plan. The plan utilizes a calendar year 2 to 6 year graduated vesting schedule. Paul was hired on January 1, 2005. After 3 years of service Paul separated from service with a vested balance of 40%, which was distributed from the plan. One year later Paul returns to Fischer Company and reenters the plan. Since Paul took the distribution from the plan, the plan does not have to credit Paul for post break service unless he repays the distribution.

Employees wanting to take a leave of absence should carefully examine their plan document so that they do not inadvertently and unnecessarily lose retirement benefits.

MILITARY SERVICE

If an employee leaves employment for qualified military service and is then reemployed after such service, then the employee is treated as not having incurred a break in service. The term "qualified military service" means any service in the uniformed services (as defined in Chapter 43 of Title 38, United States Code) by any individual if such individual is entitled to reemployment rights under such chapter with respect to such service. Each period of qualified military service served by an individual is, upon reemployment, deemed to constitute service with the employer maintaining the plan for the purpose of determining the nonforfeitability of the individual's accrued benefits under such plan and for the purpose of determining the accrual of benefits under such plan.

There is no requirement for the employer to make contributions to the military employee's defined contribution plan while they are on active duty. However, once the military employee returns from military duty and is reemployed, the employer must make the employer contributions that would have been made if the military employee had been employed during the period of military duty. If employee contributions are required or permitted under the plan, the employee has a period equal to three times the period of military duty or five years, whichever ends first, to make up the contributions. If the employee makes up the contributions, the employer must make up any matching contributions. There is no requirement that the employer contributions include earnings or forfeitures that would have been allocated to the employee had the contributions been made during their military service.[26]

The military employee must be permitted to make the maximum amount of elective deferrals that the individual would have been permitted to make under the plan during the period of qualified military service if the individual had continued to be employed by the employer during such period and received compensation. The maximum compensation amount is reduced for any elective deferrals actually made during the period of qualified military service. An employee's compensation (for purposes of elective deferrals) during qualified military service is deemed to be the compensation the employee would have received during the period if the employee were not in qualified military service based on the rate of pay the employee would have received from the employer. If the compensation the employee would have received during such period was not reasonably certain, then the employee's compensation is deemed to be the employee's average compensation from the employer during the 12-month period immediately preceding the qualified military service (or, if shorter, the period of employment immediately preceding the qualified military service).

MATERNITY/PATERNITY LEAVE

For vesting and eligibility purposes, an employee who is absent from work due to pregnancy or the birth or adoption of a child is treated as having completed the number of hours that would have been credited but for the absence up to 501 hours of service. The credit for hours of service during the absence is only for determining if a break in service has occurred.[27]

> Donna works for Mad Scientist Inc. 10 hours a week. Mad Scientist Inc. has a qualified plan and Donna participates in the plan. For the current year Donna worked 36 weeks and was on maternity leave for 16 weeks. While Donna only worked 360 hours for the year, for purposes of the break in service rules she is credited with the 160 hours she would have worked had she not been on maternity leave. Therefore, Donna will not have a break in service since she is deemed to have worked 520 hours for the year.

EXAMPLE 3.63

---

26.   http://www.dol.gov/vets/usc/vpl/usc38.htm#4318
27.   http://www.irs.gov/retirement/article/0,id=135692,00.html

Qualified Pension Plans

INTRODUCTION

The traditional **pension plan** pays a formula-determined benefit beginning at retirement, usually in the form of an annuity, to a plan participant for the participant's remaining life. In some cases, a lump sum option may be available. Historically, pension plans were offered by many employers; however, over the last 30 years, many employers have converted their pension plans to profit sharing plans in an attempt to reduce employers' costs, eliminate mandatory funding requirements, and shift the investment responsibility to the employees.

The legal promise of a pension plan is to pay a pension. There are defined benefit pension plans, including both defined benefit and cash balance pension plans, that are characterized by annual funding requirements, actuarial needs, Pension Benefit Guaranty Corporation (PBGC) insured benefits, and investment risk retained by the employer. There are also two defined contribution pension plans characterized by separate individual accounts, investment risk borne by the participants, and no insured benefits. All of these issues will be discussed in this chapter.

PENSION PLANS (4 TYPES)	
DEFINED BENEFIT PENSION PLANS (2 TYPES)	Defined Benefit Pension Plans
	Cash Balance Pension Plans
DEFINED CONTRIBUTION PENSION PLANS (2 TYPES)	Money Purchase Pension Plans
	Target Benefit Pension Plans

Recall from Chapter 3, there are numerous limits that qualified plans must comply with including contribution limits, limits on distributions, limits on covered compensation and other. Many of these limits are illustrated below in the "Know The Numbers" table.

Know The Numbers				
	2005	**2006**	**2007**	**2008**
Covered Compensation Limit for Qualified Plans	$210,000	$215,000[†]	$220,000[†]	$225,000[†]
Defined Benefit Maximum Limit	$170,000	$175,000[†]	$180,000[†]	$185,000[†]
Defined Contribution Maximum Limit	$42,000	$43,000[†]	$44,000[†]	$45,000[†]
401(k) SARSEP, 457, 403(b)	$14,000	$15,000	$15,000[†]	$15,500[†]
PBGC Monthly Benefit at Age 65	$3,801.14	-	-	-
PBGC Yearly Benefit at Age 65	$45,613.68	-	-	-

Traditional defined benefit pension plans continue to exist today but are primarily used in mature, well established companies (often publicly traded) that have not changed to profit sharing plans. The PBGC pays monthly retirement benefits to approximately 518,000 retirees in 3,479 pension plans that no longer exist.[1] Some companies that traditionally had pension plans have also introduced profit sharing plans as an additional or alternative retirement benefit arrangement. Fewer new pension plans are being established today because employers have shifted the retirement planning burden from the employer to the employee. This trend is illustrated in Exhibit 4.1. However, most governmental agencies continue to have pensions plans (although these are not qualified plans) as the predominant form of retirement benefit, but the benefits payable from these pension plans have been reduced through the years. Many governmental agencies have begun to include profit sharing type plans in conjunction with the traditional pension plan in an attempt to shift some of the responsibility for retirement funding and planning to the individual employee through self-reliant contributory plans.

Traditional pension plans promise a certain defined benefit amount available at the time of a participant's retirement. This benefit, the present value of which can be calculated at any given time during the employee's service, is most commonly based on a combination of the participant's years of service with the company and the participant's salary. A participant's salary for these purposes is usually defined as the participant's final salary, the average of the participant's highest salaries, or the average of the participant's salaries over his career. If, however, a career average salary is used in the formula, there will be a significant loss of purchasing power

1. www.pbgc.gov/publications/factshts/factpbgc.gov

when the benefit is received compared to the final salary method. An example of a common pension plan benefit formula is illustrated below:

$$\begin{array}{c} 1.5\% \\ \text{per year} \end{array} \times \begin{array}{c} \text{\# of} \\ \text{Years of} \\ \text{Service} \end{array} \times \begin{array}{c} \text{The Average of the 3} \\ \text{Highest Consecutive} \\ \text{Years Salary} \end{array} = \begin{array}{c} \text{Annual Pension} \\ \text{Benefit Amount} \end{array}$$

PENSION PARTICIPATION RATES 1979-1999

EXHIBIT 4.1

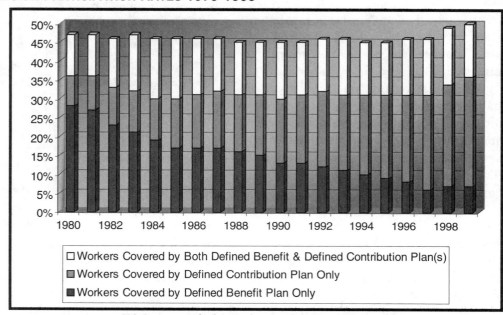

U.S. Department of Labor, Employee Benefit Security Administration

EXAMPLE 4.1

Assume that Eric works for ABC company, which sponsors a a defined benefit plan with a benefit formula of 1.5% times the years of service times the final salary. Assuming that Eric worked for ABC for 40 years and that his final salary is $100,000, he would be entitled to an annual benefit of $60,000 per year (1.5% x 40 x $100,000) during retirement. If Eric were to live for 30 years in retirement, ABC would have to pay a total of $1.8 million in retirement benefits to Eric.

There are many possible variations for the benefit formula of a pension plan; resulting in a promise to pay the employee a defined benefit during retirement. Generally, pension plans do not include employee contributions (**noncontributory plans**). However, it is possible, especially in a not-for-profit or governmental institution, to have a defined benefit plan with mandatory employee contributions. In the case of a noncontributory plan, the full funding burden is on the employer. The plan document defines the formula that will be used to determine the pension benefit.

does not allow employee deferrals.

PENSION PLAN CHARACTERISTICS

An employer who establishes a pension plan promises to pay a defined benefit to an employee. In some cases, the funds necessary to pay benefits are not available at the employee's retirement. Usually, this occurs due to the employer's bankruptcy, cash flow problems, poor investment decisions, or some combination of the above. In any case, the employee did not receive the promised retirement benefit. As a result of the employer's promise to pay a retirement benefit and the employee's reliance on this expected retirement benefit, the government established several requirements to increase the likelihood that a pension plan has the funds required to pay the promised defined benefit at the employee's retirement.

Key Concepts

Underline/highlight the answers to these questions as you read:

1. Explain the mandatory funding requirement and how it is different for defined contribution plans and defined benefit plans.

2. Define an "in-service withdrawal."

3. What are the investment limitations for pension plans?

Specifically for qualified pension plans, the government requires mandatory annual funding, disallows in-service withdrawals, limits the investment of the plan assets in the employer's securities, and limits the investment of the plan assets in life insurance. Each of these requirements is designed to provide protection for the employee's promised benefit. In addition, the **Pension Benefit Guaranty Corporation (PBGC)** was established to provide additional protection to lower-wage participants of defined benefit plans. The PBGC is discussed in more detail later in this chapter.

EXHIBIT 4.2 **PENSION PLAN REQUIREMENTS**

> 1. Mandatory annual funding
> 2. Disallowed in-service withdrawals
> 3. Limited investment in employer securities 10% limit
> 4. Limited investment in life insurance

Hardship distributions, does not include loans

MANDATORY FUNDING

The **mandatory funding** requirement sets forth an amount, or a range of amounts in the case of a defined benefit plan, that must be contributed to the pension plan by the employer each plan year. The mandatory funding requirements implement quantitative standards to help ensure that the future benefits promised by the defined benefit formula in the plan document are sufficiently funded and that the employer only deducts (shelters from tax) the amount necessary to fund the future promised defined benefit. There is a balance between insuring that the promised defined benefits are properly funded and limiting the employer's ability to overfund these plans simply as a means to shelter current taxable income.

The calculation of the mandatory funding requirement differs for defined benefit pension plans and defined contribution pension plans, but in either case, the employer is required to fund the plan with the determined amount (or within a range of amounts for defined benefit pension plans) regardless of the current investment market situation. The application of the mandatory funding standard requirement for both defined benefit pension plans and defined contribution pension plans is described below.

Defined Benefit Plans

A **defined benefit plan** is a plan that focuses on the benefit payable to participants during retirement. Based on those expected payments, an actuary determines the amount of current funding necessary to drive that future benefit. The mandatory funding requirements of a defined benefit pension plan, either a defined benefit plan or a cash balance pension plan, require that the plan sponsor fund the plan on an annual basis with an amount within the range provided by an actuary (whose services are required annually). The range provided by the actuary is statutorily defined in the IRC as an amount that is between the maximum accumulated funding deficiency and the full funding limitation.

The funding range calculated by the actuary utilizes employee census information (i.e. age, sex, life expectancy, expected mortality rates, market interest rates, employee turnover, disability, and salary growth) to determine the actuarial equivalent in today's dollars of providing the defined pension benefit promised at each employee's retirement. The employer must fund the plan with an amount within the range for the plan year. The calculation of this funding range is discussed in detail below.

Defined Benefit Plan A has assets with a fair market value of $500,000.

Defined Benefit Plan B has assets with a fair market value of $300,000.

Defined Benefit Plan C has assets with a fair market value of $700,000.

Each pension plans' actuary has determined that the funding range for each defined benefit plan is between $450,000 and $600,000.

EXAMPLE 4.2

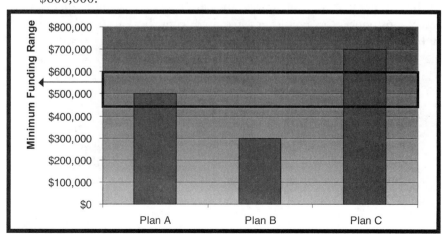

Plan A has assets with a fair market value greater than the maximum accumulated funding deficiency amount of $450,000 but less than the full funding limitation amount of $600,000; therefore, the plan sponsor may choose to make a tax deductible contribution of up to $100,000 ($600,000 - $500,000) to the plan or chose not to make a contribution to the plan. The sponsor of Plan B must contribute at least $150,000 ($450,000 - $300,000) to the plan to meet the maximum accumulated funding deficiency but may contribute up to $300,000 ($600,000 - $300,000) to maximize their tax deduction and reach the full funding limitation. The plan sponsor of Plan C may not make a deductible contribution to the plan for the current year because the fair market value of the plan's assets exceeds the full funding limitation.

Defined Contribution Plans

There are two types of **defined contribution pension plans**, money purchase pension plans and target benefit pension plans. The mandatory funding requirements for a defined contribution pension plan, either a money purchase pension plan or a target benefit pension plan, require that the plan sponsor fund the plan annually with an amount as defined in the plan document.

EXAMPLE 4.3	An employer who establishes a money purchase pension plan requiring a 17% annual contribution must make an annual contribution of 17% of each employee's salary to the money purchase pension plan to meet the mandatory funding requirement.

Underfunding

The plan sponsor of a pension plan that does not meet the mandatory funding requirements may apply to the IRS for a funding waiver. The IRS grants the waiver in most cases when the employer is temporarily experiencing hardships that limit the availability of funding and when not waiving the requirement would negatively impact the interests of the plan participants. For example, if the requirement was not waived, the company may become bankrupt. The funding waiver merely postpones the employer's required contribution (as determined under the mandatory funding requirements) but does not eliminate the funding requirement of the plan. In fact, the employer will be required to fund the plan with the "waived" amount and any additional amounts that accrue during the waiver period.

EXAMPLE 4.4	If an employer receives a waiver to fund the plan when the funding requirement contribution is $40,000 and the employer has not funded the $40,000 by the following year, the employer will be required to fund the plan with the $40,000 and also fund the current year's determined mandatory funding amount.

Long periods of poor performance in the equity market cause many plans to become underfunded, but the underfunded status may change because of reversing market conditions.

DISALLOWANCE OF IN-SERVICE WITHDRAWALS

An **in-service withdrawal** is any withdrawal from the plan while the employee is a participant in the plan other than a loan (which requires a defined term, interest accrual, and repayment provisions as discussed in Chapter 7). Because the fundamental promise of a pension plan is to pay the employee a benefit at retirement, the plan cannot permit in-service withdrawals or would risk not having enough money to pay the benefit. Any such provision would be inconsistent with the promise to pay the pension benefit at retirement. Plan loans are not in-service withdrawals because they are required to be paid back. Although loans are allowed by the IRC, most pension plans do not permit plan loans because the contributions are primarily funded by the employer.

LIMITED INVESTMENT IN EMPLOYER SECURITIES

The assets of a pension plan may be invested in the securities of the employer plan sponsor provided the aggregate value of the employer securities does not exceed 10 percent of the fair market value of the pension plan assets at the time the employer securities are purchased. Employer securities are any securities issued by the plan sponsor or an affiliate of the plan sponsor, including stocks, bonds, and publicly traded partnership interests.

The purpose of this limitation is to protect the ability of the plan to pay the promised retirement benefit. The value of the plan sponsor's securities are tied to the value of the company. If the company performs poorly, its securities will likely decrease in value. In the case where there was no limit on investment in the employer's securities, the defined benefit plan assets would also decrease substantially. This decrease would subsequently create a large funding requirement from the same employer that is in financial difficulty (the cause of the plan's decrease in value).

If the company is struggling financially and the pension plan assets were heavily invested in the employer's securities, several problems would occur. The company would already have cash flow problems due to the financial situation and the reduction in the plan assets attributable to the decrease in the company's stock price would further exacerbate the cash flow struggle by increasing the minimum amount necessary to fund the plan. Therefore, it is not reasonable to have a significantly large percentage of plan assets in a pension plan invested in employer securities. The 10 percent limitation of investment of a pension plan's assets in the employer's securities is designed to protect the employer's promise to pay a pension to the employee.

In addition, a significant exposure to any one security is inconsistent with the concept of asset allocation and portfolio diversification. A basic understanding of asset management and portfolio management supports the notion of limiting the exposure to the employer's securities to promote risk reduction through diversification in the investment portfolio.

LIMITED INVESTMENT IN LIFE INSURANCE

One exception to the retirement benefit promise is the ability to use the assets of the pension plan to provide incidental death benefits to a participant beneficiary through the purchase of life insurance. In fact, any qualified plan may purchase life insurance (subject to these limitations). As long as life insurance is not the primary focus of the pension plan, the government allows this

Life Insurance needs to be an incidental benefit.

See: 25% Test or 100 to 1 Ratio Test

exception from the ultimate retirement benefit promise because the death benefit of the life insurance policy is payable to the employee's spouse and other survivors at the employee's death. The beneficiaries of the policy are usually the same beneficiaries who would receive the remainder of the employee's retirement benefits at the employee's death; therefore, purchasing life insurance allows the employee to leverage the amount he will leave to his survivors in the event of his untimely death. However, premiums paid by the employer for the life insurance policy are taxable to the employee at the time of payment. As discussed in Chapter 7, the employee will have an adjusted taxable basis in the plan at the time of distribution for the amounts paid for life insurance premiums.

Whether the life insurance is the primary focus of the qualified plan or is an incidental death benefit is determined by a series of tests that limit the amount of life insurance coverage provided by a qualified plan or the cost of the life insurance provided by the plan. To maintain its qualified plan status, a qualified plan that includes life insurance must pass either the (1) 25 percent test or (2) the 100 to 1 ratio test.

Quick Quiz

Highlight the answer to these questions:

1. A pension plan that is unable to deposit the mandatory funding amount may apply for a one time waiver eliminating the funding needed for that particular year.
   a. True
   b. False

2. Pension plans do not allow in-service withdrawals.
   a. True
   b. False

3. Pension plans may only invest in 15 percent of the employer stock.
   a. True
   b. False

False, True, False.

25 Percent Test (Defined Contribution)

Term = 25%
Whole Life = 50%

The 25 percent test consists of two tests, a 25 percent test and a 50 percent test. The one used depends upon the type of life insurance provided by the plan. If a **term insurance** or **universal life insurance** policy is purchased within the qualified plan, the aggregate premiums paid for the life insurance policy cannot exceed 25 percent of the employer's aggregate contributions to the participant's account. If a **whole life insurance policy** is purchased within a qualified plan, the aggregate premiums paid for the whole life insurance policy cannot exceed 50 percent of the employer's aggregate contributions to the participant's account. In addition, for any permanent life insurance policy, the entire life insurance policy must be converted to cash or an annuity at or before retirement. In the case of term insurance, the policy cannot be maintained in a qualified plan after retirement. The IRS treats whole life policies different from term and universal life policies. Term and universal policies must meet the 25 percent rule while whole life policies must meet the 50 percent rule, and the mortality cost alone cannot exceed 25 percent of the contributions. In general, the 25%/50% rule will be applied to defined contribution plans, including defined contribution pension plans. A qualified plan that meets the 25 percent test (either the 25 percent test or the 50 percent test) does not have to meet the 100 to 1 ratio test to retain its qualified status.

EXAMPLE 4.5

Joe is a participant in a qualified plan sponsored by his employer. The employer has made aggregated contributions for Joe of $100,000. His plan holds a $90,000 term life insurance policy on his life. The total premiums that have been paid for the policy are $4,000. Because this is a term life insurance policy, the premiums paid cannot exceed $25,000 ($100,000 x 25%) per the 25% test. Since the premiums for this policy have been $4,000, the plan meets the 25% test.

100 to 1 Ratio Test *(D.f. Benefit)*

Face amount ~~cannot~~ *to accrued monthly benefit cannot exceed 100:1.*

A defined benefit plan may have life insurance in the plan and retain its qualified status by meeting the 100 to 1 ratio test, which provides limits based on the benefits provided by the life insurance protection rather than the cost of the life insurance protection. Specifically, the 100 to 1 ratio test limits the amount of the death benefit of life insurance coverage purchased to 100 times the monthly-accrued retirement benefit provided under the same qualified plan's defined benefit formula. It is quite common to use the 100 to 1 ratio test for a defined benefit pension plan because of the ease of calculating the monthly accrued retirement benefit. Most qualified defined contribution plans, including pension and profit sharing plans, will use the 25%/50% tests. Although, if the defined contribution plan benefit is an annuity, it would be possible to use the 100 to 1 ratio test (unusual). In any case, the objective of these rules is to insure that life insurance death benefits are incidental to the retirement benefit and not the primary focus of the plan.

Employer cost of LF is taxable to employee.
- Deductible to employer as compensation paid.

EXAMPLE 4.6

As a participant in her employer's defined benefit plan, Becky has accrued a retirement benefit of $4,000 per month. Based on the 100 to 1 ratio test, the plan is limited to utilizing plan assets to purchase life insurance up to a face amount of $400,000 ($4,000 x 100).

412(i) plan

A "section 412(i) plan," set forth in IRC Section 412(i), is a specific type of defined benefit pension plan that is funded entirely by a life insurance contract or an annuity. The employer claims tax deductions for contributions that are used by the plan to pay premiums on an insurance contract covering an employee. The plan may hold the contract until the employee dies or it may distribute or sell the contract to the employee at a specific point, such as when the employee retires.

The typical candidate for this type of plan is a sole proprietor with only a few employees. The 412(i) plan allows greater contributions to the plan than a traditional defined benefit plan because of the need to fund the life insurance or annuity. In addition, the plan is easier to explain to employees because the insurance/annuity is fixed and provides less risk due to the certainty of the insurance/annuity. The plan is also less costly than a traditional defined benefit plan. Because of the exclusive use of life insurance or annuities as a funding vehicle, no actuarial calculations are necessary, reducing administrative requirements and associated expenses. Unfortunately, the plan does not provide alternative investment choices; thus, sacrificing the opportunity for significant short term appreciation. In addition, the employer does not have much flexibility with regard to plan design and the plan cannot permit loans.

Although originally thought to be beneficial, some planners have determined the plans generally are not growth or cash flow beneficial. The lack of growth potential for 412(i) plans often overshadows the ability for greater funding. In addition, 412(i) plans have been the focus of IRS controversy over the last few years, prompting narrowing regulations and rulings. While 412(i) plans may initially appear beneficial to defer taxes, costs and cash flow requirements have slowed their growth. Caution should be taken when considering this type of plan.

DEFINED BENEFIT PENSION PLANS v. DEFINED CONTRIBUTION PENSION PLANS

The defined benefit pension plan and the cash balance pension plan are defined benefit pension plans whereas the money purchase pension plan and the target benefit pension plan are defined contribution pension plans. Each of these plans share the characteristics attributable to pension plans but differ between the categorization of defined benefit and defined contribution. The primary differences between the two categorizations of the plans include the following:

- the use of an actuary (annually or at inception);
- assumption of the investment risk (to the employer or to the employee);
- the disposition of plan forfeitures (reduce plan costs or allocate to remaining employees);
- coverage under the **Pension Benefit Guaranty Corporation (PBGC)**;
- the use of Social Security integration (offset or excess);
- the calculation of the accrued benefit or account balance;
- the ability to grant credit for prior service for funding; and
- the use of commingled versus separate, individual investment accounts.

THE ACTUARY

Defined benefit and cash balance pension plans require the use of annual actuarial services to determine the proper funding of the plan. The target benefit pension plan uses actuarial assumptions only at the inception of the plan and does not require annual actuarial work. The money purchase pension plan has no need for actuarial services because the annual contribution is predefined in the plan documents.

ACTUARY

EXHIBIT 4.3

Plan Type	Actuary Needed
Defined Benefit & Cash Balance	Annually
Target Benefit	At Inception Only
Money Purchase Pension Plan	Not Used At All

The **actuary** makes assumptions about future inflation, wage increases, life expectancy of the assumed retirees, investment returns on plan assets, mortality rates for retirees, and forfeitures resulting from termination. Each of these assumptions has an impact and relationship to plan costs and plan funding.

ACTUARY ASSUMPTIONS AND RELATIONSHIP TO PLAN COSTS

EXHIBIT 4.4

	Direct Relationship			Indirect Relationship		
	Expected Inflation	Expected Wage Increases	Life Expectancy	Expected Investment Returns	Expected Mortality	Expected Forfeiture / Employee Turnover
Change	↑	↑	↑	↑	↑	↑
Impact on Plan Costs	↑	↑	↑	↓	↓	↓

Inflation affects plan costs directly and includes such costs as actuarial services, any employee's office, telephones, supplies, and the cost of providing summary plan documents of the plan. As wages increase, plan costs increase because benefits are almost always paid as an annuity derived from a formula that includes some measure of the last or highest salaries. Because the pension is a life or joint life annuity, any increase in life expectancy will increase plan costs. On the indirect side, plan costs are reduced by better investment returns than what was assumed. If the retiree's mortality rate increases faster than expected, payouts are lessened and plan costs are reduced. In addition, if there are more forfeitures than originally expected, plan costs are reduced because forfeitures in defined benefit plans must be used to reduce future plan costs.

Key Concepts

Underline/highlight the answers to these questions as you read:

1. How does the investment risk differ for defined contribution plans compared with defined benefit plans?

2. How are forfeitures treated in defined benefit and defined contribution plans?

3. Which types of qualified plans are covered by the PBGC?

4. How is the accrued benefit of a defined benefit plan calculated?

5. Which qualified plans allow credit for prior service?

INVESTMENT RISK

A defined benefit pension plan is designed to pay a promised benefit to a plan participant at the participant's retirement, whereas a defined contribution pension plan only guarantees that contributions based on a defined formula will be made to the plan per the plan document. In other words, the participant in a defined contribution plan is entitled to the value of the defined contribution plan account balance at his retirement, including any investment gains or losses. The participant in a defined benefit plan is entitled to the promised defined benefit at his retirement, regardless of investment performance. Consider employees A and B who earn equal salaries, are the same age, and have the same length of service. Each will receive exactly the same pension benefit as calculated under any one of the defined benefit funding formulas at their retirement. If, however, A and B were participants in a defined contribution plan, they would have each received the same contribution each year to their defined contribution accounts, but their individual investment performance may vary widely resulting in different account balances at their retirement due to choices they make regarding the investment of the plan assets. Because of the nature of the benefit to be provided (a promised benefit or a promised contribution), the investment risk while the plan assets are within the qualified plan is borne by the plan sponsor for a defined benefit pension plan and generally borne by the individual plan participant for a defined contribution pension plan.

| | EXHIBIT 4.5 | **INVESTMENT RISK** |

Plan Type	Burden of Investment Risk
Defined Benefit & Cash Balance	Employer
Target Benefit & Money Purchase Pension Plan	Employee

Defined Benefit Plan

The plan sponsor of a defined benefit plan must ensure that the guaranteed benefit as provided under the plan document is available to pay the employee at the time of the employee's retirement. After meeting the mandatory funding standards as required for all pension plans (as discussed above), the plan assets are invested and will experience investment returns dependent upon the investment selections made by the plan sponsor or investment manager. If the plan's investments experience positive returns and the assets grow to a level exceeding the plan's mandatory funding requirement, the plan is said to be overfunded, and the employer benefits from the excess growth by being able to offset the required funding amount for future years by the excess growth. Conversely, if the value of the plan's assets decrease, the employer is responsible for contributing additional amounts to maintain the mandatory funding requirement. Any deficiency in funding is the employer's responsibility regardless of how low the value of the plan's assets have decreased in comparison to the minimum required funding amount determined by the actuary.

If an employer funds a defined benefit pension plan with the required mandatory funding for the current year of $100,000, and subsequently the fair market value of the pension plan assets declines in value to $60,000, the employer is required to contribute an amount equal to the loss and fund the plan at least to the determined mandatory funding standard amount.	**EXAMPLE 4.7**
If employer funded a defined benefit pension plan with the mandatory funding standard amount of $100,000 for the current year and the fair market value of the pension plan assets grow to $180,000, the plan sponsor could utilize the growth of the assets to offset future plan funding requirements. If in the subsequent year, the mandatory funding amount was $190,000, the employer would only be required to contribute $10,000 to meet the requirement. Any excess investment growth will reduce the employer's future plan costs.	**EXAMPLE 4.8**

One advantage for the participant of a defined benefit pension plan is that he does not bear any of the investment risk. His benefit is guaranteed to be the amount determined by the benefit formula in the plan document.[2] The fact that the employer bears this investment responsibility is viewed as a disadvantage for the employer because it is required to fund whatever amount is determined by the actuary to meet the mandatory funding requirements. This funding requirement increases the cost of providing retirement benefits to employees in years when the market performs poorly and disrupts the projected cash flows of the employer.

Within the last few years, several Fortune 500 companies' defined benefit pension plans that had not required any employer contributions to meet the mandatory funding requirements in several years, required large contributions to meet the mandatory funding standards because of the continuously poor performing investment market. In the summer of 2003, General Motors' defined benefit pension plan was so underfunded that they issued bonds worth $17 billion. The proceeds were solely directed to fund the deficiency in its pension plan.

---

2. Assuming the company has the requisite funds to pay the benefit.

Defined Contribution Pension Plans

The investment risk of plan assets within a defined contribution pension plan is generally borne by the participant in the plan. To a large extent, the plan sponsor's responsibility ends after the contribution required in the plan document is made to the defined contribution plan account on behalf of the plan participant. As such, if the value of the investments in the account increase, the plan participant benefits from all of the increase in the account value. Conversely, if the value of the account decreases, the plan participant bears sole responsibility and risk for this decrease. The employer is not required to subsequently contribute any additional amounts to make up for the decline in value of the account.

Defined contribution pension plans require the employer to fund the plan annually per the plan document, but the employer is not required to continuously maintain any minimum value in the individual participant's account. After the employer contribution is made, a defined contribution pension plan generally allows the individual employee participant to select investments. A poor performing investment market will not affect the employer's cash flows in the same way it might be affected under a defined benefit pension plan.

The shift from defined benefit pension plan to defined contribution pension plan has generally resulted in a shifting of the investment risk to employees, who may not be in the best position to manage their own investments.

EXAMPLE 4.9	Amelia's Flight School sponsors a 15% money purchase pension plan. In the current year, Amelia's contributed $15,000 to the plan on behalf of Joann. If the value of the $15,000 contribution decreases to $10,000 in the subsequent year, Amelia's is not responsible for the loss. If Joann is still employed by Amelia's at the end of the subsequent year, Amelia's must make another contribution of 15% of covered compensation on Joann's behalf for that subsequent year.

ALLOCATION OF FORFEITURES

When an employee terminates employment from an employer before he is fully vested (discussed in Chapter 3), those benefits allocated to the employee that are not vested are known as **forfeitures**. For a defined benefit pension plan, the forfeited funds can only be used to reduce future plan costs for the employer. The forfeitures within a defined benefit plan cannot increase the benefit of any other plan participant, nor may the forfeited funds be allocated for any other purpose. The plan sponsor of a defined contribution pension plan, however, can choose to utilize plan forfeitures in one of two ways, either to reduce future plan costs or the forfeitures can be allocated to other remaining participants in a nondiscriminatory manner; thus, increasing the participants' account balances. Including any forfeitures, the total contributions to a plan participant of a defined contribution plan are limited to the maximum annual contribution as discussed in Chapter 3.

EXAMPLE 4.10

Tony has an accrued benefit from his employer's defined benefit plan equal to $6,000 per month at retirement. However, based on the plan's vesting schedule, Tony has a vested accrued benefit equal to $4,800 per month at retirement. If Tony terminates employment today, the $1,200 of non-vested assets in the defined benefit plan will be used to offset future plan costs.

EXAMPLE 4.11

Carmela has a defined contribution pension plan account balance equal to $100,000, but she is only 20% vested in the plan. If Carmela terminates employment today, the non-vested amount of $80,000 could be allocated to the other plan participants or it could be used to reduce plan costs.

FORFEITURES

EXHIBIT 4.6

Plan Type	Forfeitures
Defined Benefit & Cash Balance	Must Reduce Plan Costs
Target Benefit & Money Purchase Pension Plan	Can Reduce Plan Costs or Allocated to Remaining Participants

PENSION BENEFIT GUARANTY CORPORATION INSURANCE

The **Pension Benefit Guaranty Corporation (PBGC)** was established in 1974 when President Gerald R. Ford signed the Employee Retirement Income Security Act (ERISA) into law. The PBGC acts, just as its name implies, to guarantee pension benefits. It is a federal corporation that acts as an insurance provider to maintain the benefits promised to employees by their defined benefit pension plans. The plan sponsors of defined benefit and cash balance pensions plans pay premiums for the insurance coverage, but the PBGC only provides plan participants with a limited retirement benefit in the case the plan completely or partially terminates with an unfunded or underfunded liability.

The PBGC does not insure defined contribution pension or profit sharing plans, nor does it insure defined benefit pension plans of professional services corporations with 25 or fewer participants. The PBGC does insure all other defined benefit plans at an annual cost to the plan sponsor of $19 per plan participant and $9 per $1,000 of plan underfunding for the year.[3]

---

3. The current premium payment has been the topic of Congressional meetings over the last several years and is expected to increase in the future.

EXAMPLE 4.12

Daniel is one of three partners in SueMe Law Corporation, which employs five other attorneys and 6 staff members. A defined benefit plan sponsored by SueMe would not be covered by the PBGC because it is a professional services corporation with less than 25 participants.

EXAMPLE 4.13

ABC has a defined benefit pension plan with 1,000 participants and it has unfunded liabilities payable to the plan of $2 million dollars. The PBGC insurance premium is $19,000 ($19 x 1,000) + $18,000 ($9 per $1,000 of underfunding) for a total of $37,000.

EXHIBIT 4.7 **MAXIMUM PBGC GUARANTEE FOR 2005**

	Guarantee Limit at Age 65	Guarantee Limit at Age 62	Guarantee Limit at Age 60	Guarantee Limit at Age 55
Monthly	$3,801.14	$3,002.90	$2,470.74	$1,710.51
Yearly	$45,613.68	$36,034.80	$29,648.88	$20,526.12

In the case that a defined benefit plan terminates or partially terminates with an unfunded amount, the calculation of the benefit payment is not equal to the calculation under the terminated plan document. Instead, the PBGC benefits have a maximum limit that is indexed to inflation. As discussed in Chapter 3, a defined benefit pension plan may provide a benefit to a plan participant with a maximum of $170,000 for 2005 ($175,000[†] for 2006, $180,000[†] for 2007, $185,000[†] for 2008) at retirement. However, the maximum benefit paid to plan participants at retirement by the PBGC is $45,613.68 per year for 2005. This lower amount can create a significant deficiency in expected retirement benefits for employees with higher compensation levels. Earning the maximum benefit based on the pension plan document does not equate to the plan participant earning the maximum under a plan managed by the PBGC. The payment from the PBGC is based upon (1) the form of the benefit as payable under the terminated plan, (2) the participant's age, and (3) any amounts that PBGC recovered from the employer in the case that the plan was underfunded.

EXAMPLE 4.14

In April of 2003, the PBGC became the trustee of the defined benefit pension plan for the US Airways pilots. Many of these pilots had salaries in excess of the covered compensation limit and had accrued benefits at their retirement equal to the maximum defined benefit pension plan amount, $170,000 for 2005 ($175,000[†] for 2006, $180,000[†] for 2007, $185,000[†] for 2008). However, under the PBGC payout guidelines, these same pilots would only receive the maximum of $45,613.68 for 2005. That amount would then be actuarially reduced if they retired prior to age 65, which is quite common given mandatory retirement at age 60 for pilots. If the pilot retired at age 60 the annual benefit would only be $29,648.88 for 2005.

PBGC INSURANCE

EXHIBIT 4.8

Plan Type	PBGC Insurance
Defined Benefit & Cash Balance	Yes
Target Benefit & Money Purchase Pension Plan	No

BENEFITS - ACCRUED BENEFIT/ACCOUNT BALANCE

At any given time, based on the provisions of each specific plan, a plan participant has accrued a benefit within his qualified pension plan. How the accrued benefit is calculated depends upon the type of plan sponsored by the participant's employer. A participant in a defined benefit plan has an accrued benefit roughly equal to the present value of the expected future payments at retirement (discussed further below). Whereas, a participant in a defined contribution plan has an accrued benefit equal to the account balance of the qualified plan consisting of any combination of employer and employee contributions plus the earnings on the respective contributions reduced by any non-vested amounts.

Accrued Benefit

A defined benefit plan is subject to the mandatory funding requirement as calculated by an actuary. An employee who terminates participation in the plan, usually through termination of employment before full retirement age, will be entitled to a benefit payable from the plan equal to the retirement benefit earned to date. This benefit is the actuarial equivalent of the benefit that would have been provided to the participant had the participant waited until retirement to receive the payments. As each plan document will detail the plan benefit formula (as discussed below), the calculation of the participant's accrued benefit utilizes all information at the date of termination. Communicating the value of the accrued benefit to the participants of a defined benefit plan is difficult because participants generally do not understand the funding process and the plan benefit formula. Also, an employee who is far from retirement and whose accrued benefit is quite small, will likely not grasp the true value of the ultimate benefit.

Account Balance

Calculating the accrued benefit for the participant in a defined contribution plan is usually much easier than calculating the accrued benefit for the participant of a defined benefit plan because the benefit in a defined contribution plan is simply the participant's account balance reduced by any non-vested amounts. The participant's account balance is the sum of the employer contributions to the plan and the employee contributions to the plan plus or minus any investment earnings or losses. This balance is communicated to the plan participants with periodic investment statements. These statements explain to the participants the exact amount of any plan benefit.

EXHIBIT 4.9 BENEFITS

Plan Type	Benefits
Defined Benefit & Cash Balance	Accrued Benefit
Target Benefit & Money Purchase Pension Plan	Account Balance

CREDIT FOR PRIOR SERVICE

At the creation of a retirement plan, every employee's accrued benefit or account balance is zero. However, an employer who establishes a defined benefit plan may elect to give employees credit for their service prior to the establishment of the plan. A defined benefit plan can easily incorporate the prior years of service into the defined benefit formula. If the plan is established in the current year, an owner who is also an employee can give himself credit for all of his years of service since the inception of the company. Granting **credit for prior service** must be nondiscriminatory but in any case may benefit an older owner employer who does not have many long-term employees. The benefit of giving himself credit for his prior years of service may outweigh the additional cost of giving the other short-term employees credit.

EXAMPLE 4.15

Danny started Dirty Day Car Wash 12 years ago. His company is finally profitable, and he would like to establish a defined benefit plan to benefit himself and his employees. The plan will provide the employees with a benefit equal to 1.5% x years of service x final salary. If Danny elects when he establishes the plan to give credit for prior service, immediately Danny's benefit would be based on 12 years of service; however, the plan must then count prior years of service for all employees. Alternatively, Danny could choose not to count prior years of service in the calculation of the benefit, but then his benefit would only be calculated on years of service after the establishment of the defined benefit plan.

A defined contribution plan cannot grant credit for prior service.

EXAMPLE 4.16

Washboard Industries, Inc. established a defined contribution plan today that provides for a 20% of compensation annual contribution to all of its employees. As a defined contribution plan, contributions can only be made to participants' accounts based on compensation for plan years after the establishment of the plan.

EXHIBIT 4.10

Plan Type	Credit for Prior Service
Defined Benefit & Cash Balance	Yes
Target Benefit & Money Purchase Pension Plan	No

INTEGRATION WITH SOCIAL SECURITY - PERMITTED DISPARITY FOR DEFINED BENEFIT PLANS

Permitted disparity (often referred to as Social Security Integration) is a technique or method of allocating plan contributions or benefits to employees that provides higher contributions to those employees whose compensation is in excess of the Social Security wage base for the plan year. All qualified pension plans may utilize permitted disparity (Social Security integration) as a method of allocating benefits to plan participants. Permitted disparity allows the qualified plan to consider the Social Security benefits that will be provided to plan participants in the calculation of the participant's accrual of benefit or contribution amount.

The two primary parts of the Social Security system are OASDI (Old Age Survivor Disability Insurance) and Medicare taxes. Both employers and employees each contribute to the system through FICA payments that consist of 6.2 percent for OASDI and 1.45 percent for Medicare. The OASDI portion of 6.2 percent applies to income up to the Social Security wage base ($90,000 for 2005), while the Medicare portion applies to all income with no limit. In effect, the Social Security system does not consider income that exceeds the wage base for purposes of retirement benefits. Therefore, an individual who earns $100,000 will be treated exactly the same as someone who earns $1,000,000 for purposes of retirement benefits and for purposes of the amount of income that is subject to the 6.2 percent tax.

Consider Employee A who earns $90,000 for 2005 and Employee B who earns $180,000. In this case, their employer will make a 6.2 percent contribution to the governmental retirement plan (OASDI) on 100 percent of Employee A's income and only a 3.10 percent contribution on Employee B's total income. Stated another way, the 6.2 percent contribution or payment applies to 100 percent of Employee A's income and only 50 percent of Employee B's income. Social Security taxes are only paid on earned income up to the wage base and Social Security benefits are only based on Social Security covered earnings. However, because of this disparity in treatment for lower and higher paid workers in the Social Security system, the IRC permits qualified plans to provide higher contributions or benefits to employees with income that exceeds the Social Security wage base.

The two methods of permitted disparity are the offset method and the excess method. Defined contribution plans are only permitted to utilize the excess method (see Chapter 5), whereas defined benefit plans can utilize the offset method or the excess method (discussed below).

Excess Method – Defined Benefit Pension Plans

The excess method provides an increased percentage benefit, referred to as the excess benefit, to those plan participants whose earnings are in excess of an average of the Social Security wage bases over the 35 year period prior to the individual's Social Security Retirement Age. This average is called the covered compensation limit, which is $46,344 for 2005.[4] The covered compensation limit can be found in an annual Revenue Ruling from the IRS.

The increased percentage benefit only applies to income that exceeds the covered compensation limit and is limited to the lesser of (1) 0.75 percent per year of service or (2) the benefit percentage for earnings below the covered compensation limit per year of service. This additional benefit only applies up to 35 years. Therefore, the maximum increase in benefits for compensation over the covered compensation limit is 26.25 percent, which is found by multiplying 0.75 percent by 35 years.

Give higher income employees More money

Def. contrib can only use excess method.

EXAMPLE 4.17

Katy is a participant of Button World's defined benefit pension plan, earns $50,000 per year, and has been employed with Button World for 30 years. The base funding formula for Button World's defined benefit plan is 1 percent per year of service multiplied by final salary. Under this formula, Katy would have a benefit equal to $15,000 (1% x 30 x $50,000).

In addition, Button World also provides an additional benefit of 0.75 percent per year of service for income that exceeds the covered compensation limit. Assuming that the covered compensation limit is $40,000, Katy would be entitled to an additional benefit of $2,250 (0.75% x 30 x $10,000). Therefore, by integrating the plan with Social Security, Katy

---

4. Revenue Ruling 2004 - 104.

receives $2,250 more during retirement than she would have received if the plan had not been integrated.

Offset Method – Defined Benefit Pension Plans

To provide an increased benefit to those individuals whose earnings are in excess of the covered compensation limit, the offset method applies a benefit formula to all earnings and then reduces the benefit on earnings below the covered compensation limit. It simply takes a different approach compared to the excess method, which provides additional benefits for earnings above the covered compensation limit. The reduction of the benefit is limited to the lesser of (1) 0.75 percent per year of service up to 35 years or (2) 50 percent of the overall benefit funding percentage per year of service. As with the excess method, the total reduction is limited to 26.25 percent of the earnings below the covered compensation limit.

Give lower income employees less money.

EXAMPLE 4.18

Consider the same facts as above except that Button World's defined benefit funding formula is 1.75 percent per year of service multiplied by final salary and includes an offset reduction that reduces the benefit for earnings below the covered compensation limit by 0.75 percent. In this case, Katy would receive a benefit equal to $17,250 [(1.75% x 30 x $50,000)-(0.75% x 30 x $40,000)].

The above examples were designed to illustrate that the same outcome could be reached whether you followed the excess benefit method or the offset method. However, the important concept is that defined benefit plans can be structured in such a way as to provide higher benefits to those employees who have compensation above the Social Security wage base.

INTEGRATION

EXHIBIT 4.11

Plan Type	Method of Integration
Defined Benefit & Cash Balance	Excess or Offset
Target Benefit & Money Purchase Pension Plan	Excess Only

Commingled v. Separate Individual Investment Accounts

Defined benefit pension plans use commingled investment accounts but send individual summaries to participants of what benefits they have accrued to a certain date. Most defined contribution plans, including target benefit and money purchase pension plans, utilize separate, individual investment accounts and require that the individual participant invest their own retirement assets. In some cases in a defined contribution plan, the employer will direct the investments or hire an outside investment advisor to manage the investments, in which case the funds will be commingled. However defined contribution plans will maintain separate accounting for all partnerships in the plan.

EXHIBIT 4.12 **COMMINGLED V. SEPARATE ACCOUNTS**

Plan Type	Accounts
Defined Benefit & Cash Balance	Commingled
Target Benefit & Money Purchase Pension Plan	Usually Separate

EXHIBIT 4.13 **SUMMARY OF CHARACTERISTICS OF DEFINED BENEFIT PENSION PLANS V. DEFINED CONTRIBUTION PENSION PLANS**

Characteristic	Defined Benefit Plans	Defined Contribution Plans
Actuary (Annually)	Yes	No (Target Benefit at Inception)
Investment Risk Borne by	Employer	Employee
Treatment of Forfeitures	Must Reduce Plan Costs	Reduce Plan Costs or Allocate to Other Plan Participants
PBGC Insurance	Yes	No
Credit for Prior Service	Yes	No
Social Security Integration	Offset or Excess	Excess Only
Separate Investment Accounts	No - Commingled	Yes - Separate (Usually)

DEFINED BENEFIT PENSION PLANS

The various qualified retirement plans have been initially divided in pension and profit sharing type plans and further subdivided into defined benefit and defined contribution plans. Beyond the requirements and characteristics detailed above, the defined benefit pension plan is unique compared to the other pension plans.

ESTABLISHING THE FORMULAS FOR BENEFITS

To determine the retirement benefit provided by a defined benefit pension plan, first the plan funding and allocation formula must be established. The IRC offers several ways of calculating the participant's ultimate retirement benefit, but the most common benefit formulas are (1) the flat amount formula, (2) the flat percentage formula, and (3) the unit credit formula.

Flat Amount Formula

A defined benefit pension plan that provides its participants with a benefit calculated under the **flat amount formula** provides each participant with an equal dollar benefit at retirement. The formula provides an amount that each plan participant will receive at retirement, such as $250 per month. The formula is not based on years of service with the employer or based on the participant's salary. From the highest paid plan participant to the lowest paid plan participant, each participant will receive the same amount at retirement.

A plan that utilizes the flat amount formula protects the employer from having to provide increased benefits as salaries increase. Such a plan does not provide the participant with any incentive to attain additional years of service with the employer because the benefit will not increase with any additional years of service beyond the minimum number required to receive the benefit. This formula is used more commonly in union plans and collective bargaining agreements.

An employer wishing to utilize a defined benefit plan to improve employee retention would generally not choose a flat amount formula. Also, highly paid employees, usually the persons selecting the qualified plan for the employer, are unlikely to choose a flat amount formula because as a proportion of income, they would benefit less than the lesser paid employees. However, a flat amount formula may be used in combination with a unit credit formula or some other benefit formula.

Flat Percentage Formula

The **flat percentage formula** provides all plan participants with a benefit equal to a specific percentage of the participant's salary, usually the final salary or an average of the participant's highest salaries. The percentage remains the same throughout participation in the plan and does not increase based on additional years of service or age. The flat percentage formula will provide a plan participant with an increasing benefit as salary increases simply based on the fact that the benefit will be calculated based on the increased salary. Usually the participant must attain a required minimum number of years of service to be eligible to receive the benefit. This type of benefit formula is not widely used because it does not give credit for long service. However, flat percentage formula can be used to provide benefits to older owners who are attempting to fund defined benefit plans with larger amounts of additional cash flow.

Unit Credit Formula

When a defined benefit plan utilizes both a participant's years of service and salary to determine the participant's accrued benefit, the plan is using a **unit credit formula**. Unit credit formulas provide a fixed percentage of a participant's salary multiplied by the number of years (the unit) the participant has been employed by the employer. Examples include two percent per year of

Key Concepts

Underline/highlight the answers to these questions as you read:

1. What are the common funding allocation methods for a defined benefit plan?

2. How are participant accounts treated within a defined benefit plans?

3. Which age group benefits more from the establishment of a defined benefit plan?

service multiplied by the participant's annual compensation or 1.5 percent per year of service multiplied by the average of the participant's three highest annual consecutive salaries. A unit credit formula gives credit for both a participant's term of employment and salary in the awarding of the benefit. A participant without substantial years of employment will not accrue a benefit comparable to his annual salary. Generally, a unit credit formula is more likely to retain employees than the flat amount formula or the flat percentage formula. The unit credit formula approach is widely used in defined benefit pension plans.

EXAMPLE 4.19

CE Corporation uses a unit credit formula for calculation of benefits as follows:

$$2\% \text{ per Year} \quad \times \quad \text{\# of Years of Service} \quad \times \quad \text{The Average of the 3 Highest Consecutive Annual Salaries}$$

Kevin, Brian, Jimmy, and Michael are retiring this year. Each person's benefit is calculated below based on their years of service and compensation.

	Years of Service	Average of 3 Highest Years of Compensation	Annual Benefit	Wage Replacement Ratio
Kevin	28	$100,000	$56,000	56%
Brian	30	$120,000	$72,000	60%
Jimmy	40	$150,000	$120,000	80%
Michael	33	$60,000	$39,600	66%

EXHIBIT 4.14 **SUMMARY OF DEFINED BENEFIT PLAN FUNDING FORMULAS**

Funding Formula	Benefit Calculation	Example	Comments
Flat Amount Formula	Flat amount per month	$250 per month	No incentive for participants to continue employment after attaining maximum flat amount
Flat Percentage Formula	Flat percentage based on compensation	10% of compensation per year at retirement	Incentive to increase compensation through raises but not to continue employment after attaining a desired benefit
Unit Credit Formula	Benefit determined on a combination of service and compensation	2% x years of service x average 3 highest consecutive years of pay	Incentive to attain additional years of service and additional compensation to increase ultimate benefit

COMMINGLED ACCOUNTS

Even though a participant in a defined benefit pension plan may have a calculated accrued benefit, a defined benefit pension plan does not have separate accounts for each participant. All of the assets of a defined benefit plan are managed as a group and it is impossible to segregate any individual participant's funds. Benefits are simply paid from the pool of assets.

YOUNGER/OLDER

A defined benefit pension plan is generally considered to benefit older participants because at the creation of the plan, the largest percent of the overall contribution to the plan will be attributable to the older participant(s). Older employees entering the plan will also require higher accrued benefits because of less compounding periods to retirement.

ELIGIBILITY/COVERAGE/VESTING

Defined benefit plans follow the eligibility, coverage, and vesting rules, which are described in Chapter 3 for all qualified plans.

DISTRIBUTIONS

Distributions from defined benefit pension plans are subject to the rules for distributions from qualified plans described in Chapter 7.

CASH BALANCE PENSION PLAN

A **cash balance pension plan** is a defined benefit pension plan that shares many of the characteristics of defined contribution plans but provides specific defined benefits. From the participant's perspective, a cash balance pension plan is a qualified plan that consists of an individual account with guaranteed earnings attributable to the account balance. However, the account that the employee sees is merely a hypothetical account displaying hypothetical allocations and hypothetical earnings. The accounts are hypothetical because the cash balance pension plan assets are managed by the plan sponsor in the same manner as a defined benefit pension plan. This commingled account consists of the assets that will be used to fund the benefits promised to the plan participants on their account statements.

[handwritten margin note: FAVORS YOUNGER WORKERS]

[handwritten margin note: Guarantee a minimum return]

Because the cash balance pension plan is a defined benefit pension plan, it is subject to all of the requirements of defined benefit plans and pension plans. Most notable of these requirements, the plan sponsor of a cash balance pension plan is subject to mandatory funding (the guarantee that the participant will have a benefit at retirement), insurance from PBGC, and the investment risk of the plan's assets.

Underline/highlight the answers to these questions as you read:

1. Explain how participant accounts are treated in cash balance pension plans.

2. Which age group usually benefits the most from the establishment of a cash balance pension plan?

3. Define "interest rate whipsaw" with regard to cash balance pension plans.

CONTRIBUTIONS AND EARNINGS

When a cash balance pension plan is established, the plan sponsor develops a formula to fund the cash balance hypothetical allocation. Usually, the promised funding is based on a percentage of a participant's salary, such as four percent of salary, and earnings on the contributions are guaranteed to be at least a fixed amount, such as two percent earnings per year, or may be tied to a variable rate, such as the U.S Treasury Bond rate. The contributions may be integrated with Social Security to produce a higher benefit percentage to those participants who earn a salary above the Social Security wage base or may be based on a combination of age and years of service – thus rewarding participants for longer service.

In any case, the participant receives a statement each year detailing the additions to his account equal to the promised contribution and the promised earnings for the plan year. This statement communicates the participant's benefit to the employee in an understandable format, but this account statement only portrays a hypothetical account. The value detailed to the participant is the benefit that will be payable to the participant based on the funding formula set forth in the plan document by the plan sponsor but not until the participant's retirement.

The plan sponsor does not fund a cash balance pension plan with the full benefit as detailed by the participant's hypothetical account; instead, the plan sponsor will fund the cash balance pension plan with the actuarial equivalent of the benefit (allocations plus earnings) that will be payable from the cash balance pension plan to the participant at the participant's normal retirement age. This actuarial equivalent is calculated by an actuary (whose services are required annually) considering mortality, disability, turnover, and salary growth.

Like all defined benefit plans, the plan sponsor is responsible for the investment performance of the plan's assets and earnings. The benefit, as determined under the plan document, will be payable to the participant at retirement regardless of the plan's true earnings, whether greater than or less than the benefit provided by the plan formula.

Note that some plans will credit the participant with the earnings in excess of the guaranteed minimum amount but can never credit the participant with less than the guaranteed minimum amount.

QUASI-SEPARATE ACCOUNTS

A cash balance pension plan does not have separate accounts for each participant even though the plan participant receives a statement detailing a separate account in his name. A cash balance pension plan consists of a commingled account that has a value equal to the actuarial equivalent of the present value of the expected future benefits that will be paid from the cash balance pension plan to the participants (the promised contribution and earnings).

YOUNGER/OLDER

A cash balance pension plan is generally more beneficial for younger participants because the formula is generally based on the number of years the participant is employed by the plan sponsor with a guaranteed rate of return. Younger participants have more years of contributions and earnings than older participants.

ELIGIBILITY/COVERAGE/VESTING

The cash balance pension plan follows the rules and requirements for eligibility, coverage, and vesting, which are described in Chapter 3.

DISTRIBUTIONS

The available and required distribution options of qualified plans are discussed in Chapter 7, but of particular concern for lump-sum distributions from cash balance pension plans is the guaranteed interest rate used to determine the value of the participant's accrued lump-sum value. In some cases, where the hypothetical earnings credit rate is greater than the interest rate required by ERISA (to calculate the lump-sum payment), the required payment to the participant will be greater than provided under the plan benefit formula.

Quick Quiz

Highlight the answer to these questions:

1. Participants in a cash balance pension plan have separate accounts.
   a. True
   b. False

2. The establishment of a cash balance pension plan generally benefits the younger employees more than the older employees.
   a. True
   b. False

False, True.

To determine the value of the lump-sum payment, first calculate the annuity that the participant would have received had he continued employment through retirement is calculated using the interest rate provided under the plan document. This is the hypothetical account balance. Second, the present value of this annuity is then calculated utilizing the interest rates provided under ERISA, usually a rate tied to the 30-year Treasury rate. The participant entitled to a lump-sum distribution must be paid the greater of the present value calculated under the ERISA rate or the hypothetical account balance. A cash balance pension plan with interest credits tied to the same rate provided by ERISA or with a rate lower than the ERISA rate would not experience a difference in the calculation value of the lump-sum distributions. But those cash balance pension plans that utilize a higher (more generous) guaranteed earnings rate credit under the above formula may be required to provide a lump-sum payment greater than the payment calculated under the plan document. This effect on the distribution is sometimes referred to as "interest rate whipsaw." The whipsaw results in terminating employees being paid amounts far in excess of their hypothetical account balance. This, of course, is detrimental to the plan and plan sponsor.

Victor, age 35, is 30 years away from retirement. His employer sponsors a cash balance pension plan, and Victor's accrued benefit from this cash balance pension plan utilizing an 8% earnings credit is $400 per month for 20 years at his retirement. If Victor were to terminate employment today	**EXAMPLE 4.20**

and the ERISA provided rate was 6%, his lump-sum benefit would be calculated as follows:

ERISA Method	
PMT	$400
i	0.5 (6/12)
FV	0
N	240 (12 x 20)
PV	$55,832
FV	$55,832
i	0.5 (6/12)
N	360 (12 x 30)
PMT	0
PV	$9,270

Plan Method	
PMT	$400
i	0.6667 (8/12)
FV	0
N	240 (12 x 20)
PV	$47,822
FV	$47,822
i	0.6667 (8/12)
N	360 (12 x 30)
PMT	0
PV	$4,373

In this example, Victor would have to be paid the $9,270 as his lump-sum distribution determined under the ERISA method. Notice that the $4,373 would have produced an annuity for 240 months at retirement of $400 while the $9,270 invested for 30 years at 8% would produce an annuity of $848.

As discussed in the next section, the whipsaw result is controversial and discussions are under way between the IRS and Congress to resolve the issue.

CONVERSIONS TO A CASH BALANCE PLAN

A cash balance "conversion" occurs when an employer changes from a traditional pension plan into a cash balance plan. Current law does not prevent companies from converting to cash balance plans. The law does prevent an employer from taking away or reducing the value of a pension benefit that has already been earned by a worker; whether or not there is a cash balance conversion.[5] A cash balance plan conversion has no effect on current retirees.

During the 1990s, a number of companies converted their defined benefit plans into cash balance plans, prompting charges from older workers that the change violated age-discrimination laws. The Treasury proposed regulations in December 2002 to address this issue. The proposed regulations provided guidance under the statutory age-discrimination rules for all qualified plans, including cash balance pension plans. The proposed regulations set forth specific conditions under which cash balance plans and cash balance conversions would not be considered to violate these age-discrimination rules. Thousands of comment letters were submitted on the proposed regulations, including comments from older and longer-service employees who stated that they had been adversely affected by cash balance conversions. Other comments set forth employer

---

5. http://www.ustreas.gov/press/releases/js172.htm.

concerns that the regulations would create issues for certain traditional defined benefit plans that had not previously been considered age-discriminatory.

Section 205 of the Consolidated Appropriations Act, 2004, Pub. L. 108-199, eliminated funding to implement the proposed age-discrimination regulations or any regulations reaching similar results. Additionally, the Act required the Secretary of the Treasury propose legislation providing transition relief for older and longer-service participants affected by cash balance conversions. In response, the Treasury set forth a proposal addressing cash balance plans and conversions to cash balance plans. The legislative proposal would require companies converting to cash balance plans to protect current employees through a five-year "hold harmless" period and would prohibit any benefit wear-away. The proposal also would provide rules under which cash balance formulas would not be considered age-discriminatory. The proposal would eliminate the "whipsaw" effect, which acts as a cap on the interest credits that cash balance plans can provide to workers. This would permit companies to give higher interest credits, allowing larger retirement accumulations for workers.[6] The proposal would provide similar rules for other types of hybrid plans and hybrid plan conversions.[7]

In July of 2004, the Treasury withdrew the proposed age-discrimination regulations issued in December 2002 to provide Congress an opportunity to review and consider the Administration's legislative proposal and to address cash balance and other hybrid plan issues through legislation. Currently, the law is unsettled on this topic. Many companies converting to a cash balance plan are allowing employees to elect to be treated under the new plan or be grandfathered into the old plan to avoid lawsuits in the interim. Until further legislation has been promulgated, employers should be mindful of these issues when considering converting from defined benefit to cash balance plans.

Case Study 1

In Cooper v. IBM Personal Pension Plan, a class action was filed against the IBM Personal Pension Plan ("IBM Plan").[1] Various plaintiffs claimed that IBM's defined benefit plan violated the age discrimination prohibitions of ERISA.[2] Plan amendments were made that converted the IBM defined benefit plan to a cash balance plan. The court calculated that a 49-year-old employee with 20 years of service would accrue $8,093 in age-65 annuity benefits in 2000 under that employer's cash balance plan, an additional $622 in benefits in 2001, and $282 per year in benefits by 2010.[3] Thus, the employee's benefit accrual is reduced for each year he ages.

1. Cooper v. IBM Personal Pension Plan, 274 F.Supp.2d 1010 (S.D.Ill. July 31, 2003).
2. Employee Retirement Income Security Act, 29 U.S.C. Sections 1001-1461.
3. Cooper, 274 F.Supp.2d at 1021-22.

---

6. http://www.ustreas.gov/press/releases/js1132.htm
7. http://www.irs.gov/irb/2004-27_IRB/index.html

The court acknowledged that a defined benefit plan violates ERISA's age discrimination prohibition if "an employee's benefit accrual is ceased, or the rate of an employee's benefit accrual is reduced, because of the attainment of any age."[1] The court explained that the theory that cash balance plans violate this provision is based on a series of premises. The court said that when evaluating defined benefit plans, ERISA directs that accrued benefits are calculated in terms of "an annual benefit commencing at normal retirement age,"[2] or in other words, in terms of a traditional annuity beginning at age 65. In order to apply this definition to a cash balance plan, the current hypothetical balance in an employee's account must be translated into the equivalent age-65 annuity that those sums could purchase. The court reasoned that age discrimination arises because money contributed to a younger employee will be worth more (when expressed as an annuity starting at age 65) than the same amount of money contributed to an older employee because the contribution to the younger employee will have more years to accrue interest before normal retirement age.[3] Stated another way, if any employer contributes the same amount to an employee's cash balance account every year, the value of those annual benefits when expressed as an annuity starting at age 65 decreases with every passing year.[4] This inevitably results in a declining benefit accrual rate as an employee ages, an apparent violation of ERISA.

The court ultimately ruled that IBM's cash balance plan conversion was a violation of ERISA because it impermissibly discriminated against participants based on age. Under the ruling of the case, all cash balance plans per se violate the ERISA age discrimination provision by virtue of their design. Interestingly, there are other cases in the federal case law that lead to a different result. See for example Eaton v. Onan Corp., 117 F.Supp.2d 812, 817 (S.D.Ind.2000)(finding cash balance plan did not violate ERISA); see also Campbell v. BankBoston, N.A., 327 F.3d 1, 9-10 (1st Cir. 2003) (noting problems with the age discrimination theory to attack cash balance plans).

1. 29 U.S.C. Section 1054(b)(1)(H)(i). See also Cooper, 274 F.Supp.2d 1010, 1021-22.
2. 29 U.S.C. Section 1002(23)(A).
3. Cooper, 274 F.Supp.2d at 1021.
4. Cooper, 274 F.Supp.2d at 1021-22.

MONEY PURCHASE PENSION PLANS

Mandatory funding

A **money purchase pension plan** is a defined contribution pension plan that provides for a contribution to the plan each year of a fixed percentage of the employees' compensation. Specifically, the employer promises to make a contribution to the plan for the plan year, but the employer is not required to guarantee a specific retirement benefit. The limitations and characteristics of money purchase pension plans are discussed below.

CONTRIBUTION LIMIT

As a defined contribution plan, money purchase pension plans are limited in the amount of contributions that an employer can make on behalf of the participants. An employer cannot deduct contributions to the plan in excess of 25 percent of the employer's total covered compensation paid. As discussed in Chapter 3, a defined contribution plan is limited in the contribution to the plan each year on behalf of each participant to the lesser of 100 percent of the participant's compensation or $42,000 for 2005 ($43,000[†] for 2006, $44,000[†] for 2007, $45,000[†] for 2008). This limit is an aggregate per person limit for all contributions to defined contribution plans for the year and includes employer contributions, employee contributions, and any forfeitures allocated to a participant's account for the year.

The funding formula of the money purchase pension plan is stated in the plan document. A common funding formula is a percentage of a participant's salary, which is like the cash balance pension plan but without the promise of a guaranteed earnings rate. For example, a money purchase pension plan might promise a contribution of 10 percent of each participant's salary per year. Or, the plan may be integrated with Social Security (as detailed in Chapter 5) or otherwise designed in such a way to provide disproportionate contributions to a certain class of participants, perhaps based on a combination of age and years of service.

SEPARATE ACCOUNTS

When the employer makes a contribution on behalf of each participant to a money purchase pension plan, the contribution is made to a separate account on behalf of each participant. As such, the participant knows exactly the value of his benefit from the stated value on the account statement – allowing the plan benefits to be communicated to the plan participants easier than with a defined benefit pension plan.

The plan sponsor can choose to manage the funds of each participant but usually does not do so. The plan usually requires that participants manage their own investments. In either case, each employee retains his own separate account.

YOUNGER/OLDER

A money purchase pension plan, like all defined contribution plans, benefits younger participants more than older participants because of the increased number of contributions and compounding periods. The younger participants will have the benefit of receiving more contributions to the account over time and the benefit of the tax-deferred growth. An older participant simply has fewer years to accumulate assets within the retirement plan.

IMPACT OF THE ECONOMIC GROWTH AND TAX RELIEF RECONCILIATION ACT OF 2001 (EGTRRA 2001)

After the enactment of EGTRRA 2001, most employers interested in establishing a defined contribution plan would establish a profit sharing plan instead of a money purchase pension plan. Before EGTRRA 2001, employers could deduct contributions to money purchase pension plans up to 25 percent of the total employer's compensation paid but could only deduct contributions to profit sharing plans up to 15 percent of the total employer's compensation paid. Under these old limits, some employers (especially single practitioner professionals) would establish two plans, a money purchase pension plan and a profit sharing plan. Commonly, the employer would set the funding limit of the money purchase pension plan at 10 percent (the mandatory component) and would have discretionary contributions to the profit sharing plan up to 15 percent for a total 25 percent limit. This combination of the pension plan and the profit sharing plan is known as a Tandem Plan and would provide the employer with the maximum deductibility for contributions to employee retirement plans with the greatest flexibility in the funding for the plans. With the Tandem plan, the employer was only required to make a 10 percent contribution to the money purchase pension plan each year, but because the profit sharing plan contributions are discretionary, the employers' contributions to the profit sharing plan only have to be "substantial and recurring" allowing the employer to forego contributions in certain years (discussed fully in Chapter 5).

Quick Quiz

Highlight the answer to these questions:

1. A plan sponsor cannot deduct more than 25 percent of their covered compensation as a contribution to a money purchase pension plan.
   a. True
   b. False

2. Each participant has a separate account in a money purchase pension plan.
   a. True
   b. False

3. The establishment of a money purchase pension plan generally benefits older employees more than younger employees.
   a. True
   b. False

4. EGTRRA 2001 increased the popularity of money purchase pension plans.
   a. True
   b. False

True, True, False, False.

EGTRRA 2001 increased the contribution limit for profit sharing plans to 25 percent and created an equal deduction limit for both defined contribution pension and profit sharing plans of 25 percent. Employers now wishing to establish a defined contribution plan will likely establish a profit sharing plan because they will be able to deduct the maximum amount in any given year (25 percent of employer compensation), but the contribution will not be mandatory as is the case of money purchase pension plans. Consequently, some employers with money purchase pension plans converted their plans to profit sharing plans (or terminated their money purchase pension plans) to avoid the future mandatory funding requirements.

ELIGIBILITY/COVERAGE/VESTING

The money purchase pension plan is subject to all of the eligibility, coverage, and vesting rules applicable to defined contribution pension plans, which are described in Chapter 3.

DISTRIBUTIONS

Chapter 7 describes the distribution options, availability, and requirements for all qualified plans.

TARGET BENEFIT PENSION PLANS

A special type of money purchase pension plan, known as a **target benefit pension plan**, determines the contribution to the participant's account based on the benefit that will be paid from the plan at the participant's retirement. The plan formula may be written to provide a contribution to each participant during the plan year that is actuarially equivalent to the present value of the benefit at the participant's retirement. An actuary is required at the establishment of the target benefit pension plan, but unlike a defined benefit plan or a cash balance pension plan, an actuary is not required on an annual basis. The actuary will create a funding formula for participants entering the plan at various ages. Once established, the funding formula is generally not recalculated for changes in assumptions. The target benefit pension plan considers the formula as the "target," the benefit the employer hopes the employee will have at retirement. Instead of funding the plan with the amount necessary to attain the target and ensuring that the target is met, the employer promises a contribution to the participant's individual account based on the original actuarial assumptions. Once the contribution has been made, the participant is responsible for choosing investments. Like any defined contribution plan, the participant, at retirement, is entitled to the plan balance regardless of its value, be it greater than or less than the intended target benefit.

Key Concepts

Underline/highlight the answers to these questions as you read:

1. List the benefits of a target benefit pension plan.

2. What are the eligibility and coverage rules for a target benefit pension plan?

[handwritten note: Considers age and salary]

The actuarial equivalent contribution will vary from participant to participant because of age and salary differences. In fact, the contribution will be greatest for the oldest participants because the discounting period (contribution date to retirement date) is less than the discounting period for younger participants. Accordingly, target benefit pension plans are utilized to disproportionately benefit older participants because the target benefit funding formula will allocate a greater contribution to the older participants.

Quick Quiz

Highlight the answer to these questions:

1. A target benefit pension plan is a defined benefit pension plan.
   a. True
   b. False

2. Target benefit pension plans have the same coverage and eligibility rules as money purchase pension plans.
   a. True
   b. False

False, True.

The target benefit pension plan is a form of money purchase pension plan; consequently, the target benefit pension plan is subject to all of the same contribution, eligibility, coverage, vesting, and distribution limitations as the money purchase pension plan. Mainly due to the increase of the profit sharing deductibility limits to 25 percent under EGTRRA 2001, target benefit pension plans have lost some of their attractiveness. Instead, employers are establishing age-weighted profit sharing plans (see Chapter 5) so that the contributions to the plan each year are discretionary rather than mandatory but still favor older employees.

EXAMPLE 4.21

Ken, a business owner, is age 50 and earns $210,000 per year. The company's target benefit plan has a benefit formula equal to 134.92% of compensation reduced by 1/25th for each year of participation less than 25 years. The plan also benefits Melissa, an employee age 25 earning $25,000 per year. The first year contribution is determined as follows, assuming a normal retirement age of 65 and 8% interest:

	Business Owner	**Employee**
Age	50	25
Compensation	$210,000	$25,000
Target Benefit	$170,000	$33,730
Actuarial Factor for age	2.338	0.304
PV of Benefit	$397,460	$10,254
Factor	0.1075	0.0812
Theoretical Contribution	$42,727	$833
Annual Additions Limit (100% or $42,000)	$42,000	$25,000
Top-Heavy Minimum (3% of Compensation)	$0	$750
Actual Contribution	$42,000	$833
Contribution Rate	20.00%	3.33%
Percent of Contribution	98%	2%

* The benefit for the business owner is 134.92% x $210,000 x (15 ÷ 25) = $170,000.

** The benefit for the employee is 134.92% of $25,000 = $33,730.

The plan permits the benefits to be principally contributed to Ken, the owner. The target benefit plan can still be used to reduce overall plan costs. However, as you will see in Chapter 5, profit sharing plans allow contributions up to 25% of covered compensation and discretionary funding. In some cases, age-based profit sharing plans and new comparability plans can produce similar results to the target benefit plan without the mandatory funding and compliance issues.

Key Terms

Actuary - An expert professional who makes quantitative calculations and assumptions about inflation, wage increases, life expectancy of the assumed retirees, investment returns on plan assets, mortality rates for retirees, and forfeitures resulting from termination in order to determine funding for a retirement plan.

Cash Balance Pension Plan - A defined benefit pension plan that shares many of the characteristics of defined contribution plans but provides specific defined benefits based on a mandatory contribution and earnings rate.

Credit for Prior Service - To give employees credit for years of service (with the plan sponsor) prior to the establishment of the qualified plan.

Defined Benefit Plan - A qualified retirement plan that provides its participants with pre-determined formula-based benefits at retirement.

Defined Contribution Plan - A qualified retirement plan that provides its participants the benefit of tax-deferred growth for contributions and earnings in the plan.

Flat Amount Formula - A benefit formula of a defined benefit pension plan that provides each of its participants with an equal dollar benefit at retirement.

Flat Percentage Formula - A benefit formula of a defined benefit pension plan that provides all plan participants with a benefit equal to a fixed percentage of the participant's salary, usually the final salary or an average of the participant's highest salaries.

Forfeitures - The percentage or amount of a participant's accrued benefit that was not vested in the employee at the employee's termination from the plan sponsor. The forfeited amount stays with the plan and may be allocated to the other plan participants or reduce future plan costs.

In-Service Withdrawal - Any withdrawal (from a qualified retirement plan) while the employee is a participant in the plan, not a loan.

Mandatory Funding - An amount or percentage that must be contributed to a qualified pension plan by the employer each plan year.

Money Purchase Pension Plan - A defined contribution pension plan that provides for mandatory employer contributions to the plan each year of a fixed percentage of the employees' compensation. The employer does not guarantee a specific retirement benefit.

Noncontributory Plans - Qualified retirement plans that do not include employee contributions.

Pension Benefit Guaranty Corporation (PBGC) - Established in 1974 when President Gerald R. Ford signed the Employee Retirement Income Security Act (ERISA) into law. The PBGC guarantees qualified pension benefits. It is a federal corporation that acts as an insurance provider to maintain the benefits promised to employees by their defined benefit pension plans.

Key Terms

Pension Plan - A qualified retirement plan that pays a benefit, usually determined by a formula, to a plan participant for the participant's entire life during retirement. May be defined benefit or defined contribution and requires mandatory funding and allows no in-service withdrawals.

Target Benefit Pension Plan - A special type of money purchase pension plan that determines the contribution to the participant's account based on the benefit that will be paid from the plan at the participant's retirement rather than on the value of the contribution to the account. Requires an actuary at inception.

Unit Credit Formula - A benefit formula of a defined benefit pension plan that utilizes a combination of the participant's years of service and salary to determine the participant's accrued benefit.

Whole Life Insurance Policy - A permanent life insurance policy that guarantees that the policy will remain in force as long as the premium is paid. The life insurance policy has a cash account that grows tax deferred.

1. Explain the mandatory funding requirement and its impact on defined contribution plans and defined benefit plans.

2. Define "in-service withdrawal."

3. Explain the investment limitations for pension plans.

4. Compare the investment risk of defined contribution plans to the investment risk of defined benefit plans.

5. Compare the treatment of forfeitures within defined benefit plans and defined contribution plans.

6. What is the PBGC and what plans are covered by the PBGC?

7. How is a participant's accrued benefits calculated for defined benefit and defined contribution plans?

8. List and describe the common funding formulas of a defined benefit plan.

9. How are participant accounts treated in defined benefit plans?

10. Which age group generally benefits the most from the establishment of a defined benefit pension plan?

11. List the advantages of cash balance pension plans.

12. Which age group generally benefits the most from the establishment of a cash balance pension plan?

13. What is the contribution limit for money purchase pension plans?

14. How are participant accounts treated in money purchase pension plans?

15. Which age group generally benefits the most from the establishment of a money purchase pension plan?

16. What impact did EGTRRA 2001 have on money purchase pension plans?

17. List the characteristics of a target benefit pension plan.

MULTIPLE CHOICE PROBLEMS

1. Which of the following is not a characteristic of pension plans?

    a. Mandatory funding.
    b. In-Service withdrawals.
    c. Limited investment in life insurance.
    d. A limit of 10 percent investment in the employer's securities.

2. Which one of the following statements is not true for a defined benefit plan?

    a. A defined benefit plan favors older age entrants.
    b. In-Service Withdrawals are permitted from defined benefit plans.
    c. The maximum retirement benefit payable from a defined benefit plan is the lesser of 100 percent of the participant's compensation or $170,000 for 2005.
    d. A defined benefit plan with 100 employees is required to pay PBGC insurance premiums.

3. If a participant's accrued benefit from a qualified defined benefit pension plan is $2,000 per month, what is the maximum life insurance death benefit coverage that the plan can provide based on the 100 to 1 ratio test?

    a. $0.
    b. $2,400.
    c. $200,000.
    d. $240,000.

4. Which of the following statements regarding defined benefit plans is true?

    a. A defined benefit plan can allocate forfeitures to other plan participants.
    b. A defined benefit plan can use forfeitures to reduce future plan costs.
    c. A defined benefit plan cannot give credit for prior service.
    d. Each participant of a defined benefit plan has an individual account.

5. Which of the following actuarial assumptions is not used by the actuary who determines the mandatory funding range for a defined benefit plan?

    a. Mortality.
    b. Turnover.
    c. Divorce rate.
    d. Disability rate.

6. Which of the following is not a common defined benefit plan funding formula?

 a. Flat amount formula.

 b. Flat percentage formula.

 c. Unit credit formula.

 d. Excludible amount formula.

7. Which of the following statements is true?

 a. A cash balance pension plan usually benefits older employees the most.

 b. A defined benefit plan promises a contribution to a hypothetical account each year for a plan participant.

 c. Cash balance pension plan participants may take a withdrawal from the plan during employment with the plan sponsor.

 d. A cash balance pension plan does not have individual separate accounts for each participant.

8. Which of the following statements regarding the plan sponsor of a money purchase pension plan is correct?

 a. The plan sponsor is required to make an annual contribution to the plan.

 b. The excess earnings of a money purchase pension plan are returned to the plan sponsor.

 c. The plan sponsor generally bears the investment risk of the plan assets.

 d. A plan sponsor with fluctuating cash flows would adopt a money purchase pension plan.

9. Which of the following statements regarding EGTRRA 2001 is false?

 a. EGTRRA 2001 increased the employer's deductible contribution limit for profit sharing plans to 25 percent of employer compensation.

 b. After the enactment of EGTRRA 2001, money purchase pension plans adoptions have increased.

 c. Many Tandem Plans were terminated and/or converted after the enactment of EGTRRA 2001.

 d. Prior to EGTRRA 2001, an employer could deduct contributions to a money purchase pension plan up to 25 percent of employer covered compensation.

10. Of the following statements regarding target benefit pension plans, which is true?

    (a.) A target benefit pension plan is a money purchase pension plan with a funding formula that considers age and salary.

    b. The plan sponsor of a target benefit pension plan guarantees that the participant will receive an amount, expected to be the "target benefit" amount, at his retirement.

    c. Plan participants of a target benefit pension plan do not have separate accounts.

    d. The plan sponsor guarantees an earnings rate for the contributions made to target benefit pension plans.

11. Which of the following pension plans would allocate a higher percentage of the plans' current cost to a certain class or group of eligible employees?

    1. Defined benefit pension plan.

    2. Target benefit pension plan.

    3. Money purchase pension plan with permitted disparity.

      a. 1 only.

      b. 1 and 2.

      c. 2 and 3.

      (d.) 1, 2, and 3.

12. A defined benefit pension plan has a funding formula equal to 1% x years of service x final salary. If Jim's final salary is $600,000 and Jim has earned 30 years of service, what is Jim's retirement benefit in 2005?

    a. $51,000.

    (b.) $63,000.

    c. $170,000.

    d. $180,000.

$1\% \times 30 \times Cap$ (Max covered comp.)

$2006 = \$220,000$

13. Accent, Inc. sponsors a 25% money purchase pension plan for its eligible employees. Carlos earns $200,000, Kevin earns $60,000, Kelly earns $250,000, and Rick, who is ineligible, earns $27,000. What is Accent's required deductible contribution for the year? All employees are under age 50.

    a. $99,000.

    b. $105,750.

    c. $117,500.

    d. $134,250.

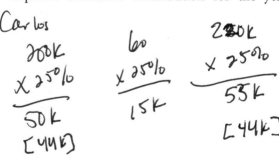

14. Bobby is the owner of Ideal Mechanics, Inc., and he would like to establish a qualified pension plan. Bobby would like most of the plan's current contributions to be allocated to his account. He does not want to permit loans and he does not want Ideal to bear the investment risk of the plan's assets. Bobby is 47 and earns $300,000 per year. His employees are 25, 29, and 32 and they each earn $25,000 per year. Which of the following qualified pension plans would you recommend that Bobby establish?

    a. Defined benefit pension plan.

    b. Cash balance pension plan.

    c. Money purchase pension plan.

    d. Defined benefit pension plan using permitted disparity.

15. Which of the following statements regarding target benefit pension plans is true?

    a. A target benefit pension plan cannot allocate plan forfeitures to remaining plan participant accounts.

    b. Target benefit pension plans may not be established after 2001.

    c. Assuming equal salaries, a target benefit pension plan would allocate a higher percentage of its current contributions to an older employee.

    d. A target benefit pension plan may always exclude any participant who has not attained the age of 26 and completed one year of service.

Profit Sharing Plans

PROFIT SHARING PLANS

Profit Sharing Plans (7 Types)
Profit Sharing Plans
Stock Bonus Plans
Employee Stock Ownership Plans
401(k) Plans
Thrift Plans
Age-Based Profit Sharing Plans
New Comparability Plans

The term profit-sharing plan is defined in Treasury Reg Section 1.401-1(b) as follows:

A **profit-sharing plan** is a plan established and maintained by an employer to provide for the participation in profits by employees or their beneficiaries. The plan must provide a definite predetermined formula for allocating the contributions made to the plan among the participants and for distributing the funds accumulated under the plan after a fixed number of years, the attainment of a stated age, or upon the prior occurrence of some event such as layoff, illness, disability, retirement, death, or severance of employment. A formula for allocating the contributions among the participants is definite if, for example, it provides for an allocation in proportion to the basic compensation of each participant. A plan (whether or not it contains a definite predetermined formula for determining the profits to be shared with the employees) does not qualify under section 401(a) if the contributions to the plan are made at such times or in such amounts that the plan in operation discriminates in favor of officers, shareholders, persons whose principal duties consist in supervising the work of other employees, or highly compensated employees. For the rules with respect to discrimination, see Section

1.401-3 and 1.401-4. A profit-sharing plan within the meaning of section 401 is primarily a plan of deferred compensation, but the amounts allocated to the account of a participant may be used to provide for him or his family incidental life accident or health insurance.

Know The Numbers

	2005	2006	2007	2008
Covered Compensation Limit	$210,000	$215,000[†]	$220,000[†]	$225,000[†]
Defined Contribution Maximum Limit	$42,000	$43,000[†]	$44,000[†]	$45,000[†]
401(k), SARSEP, 457, 403(b) Catch Up	$4,000	$5,000	$5,000[†]	$5,000[†]
401(k), SARSEP, 457, 403(b) Employee Deferral Limit	$14,000	$15,000	$15,000[†]	$15,500[†]
Highly Compensated Employee	$95,000	$95,000[†]	$100,000[†]	$100,000[†]
Social Security Wage Base	$90,000	-	-	-

EXHIBIT 5.1 BASIC DIFFERENCES BETWEEN PENSION PLANS AND PROFIT-SHARING PLANS

CHARACTERISTIC	PENSION PLAN	PROFIT-SHARING PLAN
Legal Promise of the Plan	Paying a pension at retirement	Deferral of compensation and thus tax deferral
Are in-service withdrawals permitted?	No	Yes (after two years)
Is the plan subject to mandatory funding standards?	Yes	No
Percent of plan assets allowed to be invested in employer securities	10 percent	100 percent
Employer annual contribution limit of covered compensation	25 percent	25 percent*

* Increased from 15 percent by the EGTRRA 2001 for years after 2001.

Profit-sharing plans allow employers to make contributions to a qualified plan on behalf of employees of the company. A pure profit sharing plan is a noncontributory plan (employees do not contribute). As with all qualified plans, earnings within a profit sharing plan are not taxed until the funds are distributed from the plan. Because profit sharing plans are not subject to mandatory funding requirements, contributions can be, and generally are, made on a discretionary basis from year to year. However, contributions must be made to participant's accounts on a nondiscriminatory basis. In other words, contributions cannot discriminate against the rank-and-file employees for the benefit of shareholders, officers, and highly compensated employees.

Although contributions must be made on a **nondiscriminatory** basis, there are types of profit sharing plans and techniques available to financial planners that can be used to allocate larger contributions to the shareholders, officers, and highly compensated employees. Among these techniques are age-based profit sharing plans, integrated plans, and new comparability plans. The use of such plans and techniques is permitted by the IRS because they are within the anti-discrimination permissible limits.

Key Concepts

Underline/highlight the answers to these questions as you read:

1. Define "profit sharing plan" as per Treasury Regulation 1.401-1(b).

2. Identify the key differences between pension and profit sharing plans.

3. When is the deadline for establishing and funding profit sharing plans?

4. What is the maximum annual contribution to profit sharing plans considering the covered compensation limit?

CONTRIBUTIONS AND DEDUCTIONS

As with all qualified plans, profit-sharing plans must be established by December 31st of the year for which the employer will be contributing to the plan. However, contributions can be made to the plan as late as the due date of the company tax return (including extensions).

> XYZ partnership, a calendar year taxpayer, wants to establish a profit sharing plan for the year. They must do so by December 31 of that year. However, they can fund the plan after December 31, but no later than October 15 of the next year assuming that they have properly filed all extensions for their tax return.

EXAMPLE 5.1

Contributions to profit sharing plans are generally discretionary but funding must be "substantial and recurring." Contributions can be in the form of employer stock, but proxy voting rights remain with the plan trustee. A plan that does not make any contributions for an extended period of time risks disqualification.

Although most contributions to profit sharing plans are tied to profits of the company, there is no requirement that a company must contribute to the plan in a year in which it has profits nor is there a prohibition against contributions to the plan in years in which the company does not have profits.[1]

Profit sharing plans have an employer plan contribution limit of 25 percent of covered compensation. **Covered compensation** is considered the compensation of all eligible employees.[2] Therefore, if an employer's total covered compensation paid to its employees is $1,000,000, then the largest income tax deduction that can be taken for contributions to the plan is $250,000 ($1,000,000 x 25%).[3]

In some cases, an employer may contribute more than the permitted 25 percent. In such a case, the employer will currently deduct the 25 percent (on the tax return) and may carry forward the contribution amount in excess of the 25 percent limit and deduct this amount in a future year. However, the amount carried forward when added to the contribution made for the future year cannot exceed 25 percent. Additionally, the employer is required to pay a 10 percent excise tax on the portion of the contribution that exceeds 25 percent of covered compensation for the current year.

ALLOCATIONS

Standard Allocations

A profit sharing plan must provide a definite predetermined formula for allocating plan contributions to employee's accounts. The standard method of allocating contributions to a profit sharing plan is to simply allocate the contribution based on a percentage of each employee's compensation. Example 5.2 illustrates this method.

---

1. The determination of whether the plan under which any contributions are made is a profit sharing plan shall be made without regard to current or accumulated profits of the employer and without regard to whether the employer is a tax-exempt organization. IRC Section 401(a)(27).
2. The compensation considered cannot exceed the compensation limit for each covered employee - $210,000 for 2005 ($215,000[†] for 2006, $220,000[†] for 2007, and $225,000[†] for 2008).
3. The overall plan limitation does not include employee 401(k) deferrals.

There are 7 employees (A-G), ages 25-55 with compensation
ranging from $30,000 to $200,000.

EXAMPLE 5.2

STANDARD PROFIT SHARING ALLOCATION					
Employee	Age	Covered Compensation*	Contribution Percent	Overall Contribution	Percent of Total Contribution
A (owner)	55	$200,000	11%	$22,000	42%
B	45	$60,000	11%	$6,600	13%
C	40	$60,000	11%	$6,600	13%
D	35	$50,000	11%	$5,500	11%
E	30	$40,000	11%	$4,400	8%
F	25	$35,000	11%	$3,850	7%
G	25	$30,000	11%	$3,300	6%
		$475,000		$52,250	100%
* Recall that there is a covered compensation limit.					

In this example, each employee receives a contribution of
11% of their covered compensation. The 11% was selected
by the employer based on what the employer wanted to contribute to the plan ($52,250). Note that the percentage
could have ranged from 0% to 25%. Assuming that
employee A is the owner as well as an employee, A receives a
contribution of $22,000 or 42% of the total plan contribu-
tion.

This methodology benefits the highly compensated
more than the non-highly compensated in terms of
absolute dollars but is nondiscriminatory with regard
to percentages because the contributions are based
on a straight percentage of total covered
compensation.

Permitted Disparity (Social Security Integration)

Permitted disparity (often referred to as **Social
Security Integration**) is a technique or method of
allocating plan contributions to employee's accounts
that will provide higher contributions to those
employees whose compensation is in excess of the
Social Security wage base for the plan year. In the
standard allocation example, all plan participant's
received a contribution of 11 percent of their covered
compensation. However, an integrated (permitted

Key Concepts

Underline/highlight the answers to
these questions as you read:

1. Identify the methods available for allocating contributions and their key
characteristics.

2. How can forfeitures be used in plan
contributions?

3. Identify the eligibility requirements for
profit sharing plans.

Do double but
not more than
5.7%

disparity) formula will provide an even higher percentage contribution for the higher compensated employees (those above the Social Security wage base) when compared to lower compensated employees (those below the Social Security wage base).

For defined contributions plans, such as profit sharing plans, an integration level is chosen by the plan sponsor (employer). This integration level is typically the Social Security wage base, which is $90,000 for the year 2005.[4] There are two profit sharing plan contribution rates established, the base contribution percentage rate and the excess contribution percentage rate. The base rate is applied on income earned up to the integration level, while the excess rate is applied to income earned above the integration level but below the maximum covered compensation limit for the year, $210,000 for 2005. The excess rate is generally 5.7 percent higher than the base rate.[5] The excess rate is limited to the lesser of twice the base rate or a difference of 5.7 percent. In other words, the excess rate can never be greater than two times the base rate, nor can it be more than 5.7 percent greater than the base rate. Consider the following table:

Base Rate	Excess Rate	Maximum Disparity
1.0%	2.0%	1.0%
2.0%	4.0%	2.0%
3.0%	6.0%	3.0%
5.0%	10.0%	5.0%
5.7%	11.4%	5.7%
8.0%	13.7%	5.7%
10.0%	15.7%	5.7%
12.0%	17.7%	5.7%

Assume that Tantalus sponsors an integrated plan that provided for a 10 percent base contribution percentage and an excess contribution percentage of 15.7 percent. If Dave earns $50,000, he would receive a contribution of $5,000 (10% x $50,000). If Mike earned $200,000 and the Social Security wage base was $90,000, then Mike would receive a contribution of $26,270 [10% x $90,000 plus 15.7% x ($200,000 - $90,000)]. It is important to understand that integration has increased Mike's contribution by $6,270 over a straight 10 percent plan. This higher contribution is a result of the higher excess contribution rate for compensation above the integration level. An illustration of an integrated profit sharing plan is provided in Example 5.3.

---

4. The integration level may be less than the Social Security wage base; however, if so, the excess percentage will be reduced.
5. If the base rate is less than 5.7 percent, then the excess rate cannot be more than twice the base rate. If the base rate is equal to or greater than 5.7 percent, then the excess rate can be no more than 5.7 percentage points greater than the base percentage rate. In addition, if the integration level is not at the Social Security wage base, then the 5.7 percent rate will generally be lower.

Consider the same facts as Example 5.2 (they want to contribute about $52,000), except with an integrated profit sharing plan and a base contribution rate of 9.6% (the excess rate is 15.30% (9.6 + 5.7 = 15.3)).

EXAMPLE 5.3

Employee	Covered Comp	Base Comp	Excess Comp	Base Cont 9.6%	Excess Cont 15.3%	Total Cont	Percent of Comp	Percent of Total Cont
A (Owner)	$200,000	$90,000	$110,000	$8,640	$16,830	$25,470	12.74%	49.10%
B	$60,000	$60,000	$0	$5,760	$0	$5,760	9.60%	11.10%
C	$60,000	$60,000	$0	$5,760	$0	$5,760	9.60%	11.10%
D	$50,000	$50,000	$0	$4,800	$0	$4,800	9.60%	9.25%
E	$40,000	$40,000	$0	$3,840	$0	$3,840	9.60%	7.40%
F	$35,000	$35,000	$0	$3,360	$0	$3,360	9.60%	6.48%
G	$30,000	$30,000	$0	$2,880	$0	$2,880	9.60%	5.55%
Totals	$475,000	$365,000	$110,000	$35,040	$16,830	$51,870		100.00%

INTEGRATED PROFIT SHARING PLAN

Base compensation ($)– represents compensation up to the integration level, $90,000 for 2005.

Excess compensation ($)– represents compensation above the integration level, over $90,000 for 2005 but below the covered compensation limit, $210,000 for 2005.

Base contribution ($)– represents the contribution for compensation up to the integration level (9.6% in this example).

Excess contribution ($)– represents the contribution for compensation above the integration level (rate of 15.30%) and below the covered compensation limit.

Total contribution ($)– represents the sum of the base contribution and the excess contribution. The total amount contributed ($51,870) is close to what would have been contributed using a standard allocation ($52,250). This amount was chosen by management as what they could afford to contribute to the plan.

In this example, the base rate equals 9.6%. Therefore, all employees will receive a contribution of 9.6% of compensation earned up to $90,000, the integration level for 2005. Notice that the column "Percent of Comp" is the same for employees B through G; all have a contribution of 9.6% of their compensation. None of them have compensation above the integration level, so none will have a contribution at the higher excess contribution rate of 15.3%.

Because employee A has compensation in excess of the integration level, he will have a contribution for the base compensation and an additional contribution for the excess compensation. His base contribution equals $8,640 ($90,000 x 9.6%), while his excess contribution equals $16,830[($200,000 - $90,000) x 15.30%]. His excess contribution is for the $110,000 of compensation over the integration level.

Notice that in this example, the company has contributed $51,870 to the plan and the owner A receives an allocation of $25,470; whereas in the first example, the total contribution was $52,250 and A received $22,000. Integration has allowed the owner to reduce the overall contribution to the plan by $380 and to increase his contribution by $3,470 or 1.74% (12.74% - 11.00%). The $3,470 has come from reducing the contributions of B-G from 11% to 9.6% each to reflect that the employer contribution to Social Security is part of the overall retirement plan. Without using integration, the excess earnings over the wage base would not be considered.

Although the integration level is generally equal to the Social Security wage base, it can be reduced to allow for larger amounts of income to be subject to the higher excess rate. However, as the integration level is reduced, so is the maximum difference between the base rate and the excess rate. If the integration level is less than the Social Security wage base, but more 80 percent of the wage base, then the 5.7 percent is reduced to 5.4 percent. If the integration level is less than or equal to 80 percent of the wage base and greater than 20 percent of the wage base, then the 5.7 percent is reduced to 4.3 percent. At 20 percent or less, the rate remains at 5.7 percent.[6]

If the integration level is more than:	But not more than:	The 5.7% factor is reduced to:
80% of taxable wage base	Amount less than the taxable wage base	5.4%
20% of taxable wage base	80% of taxable wage base	4.3%
Zero	20% of taxable wage base	Not reduced - remains at 5.7%

Integration is generally used when the owner wants to increase or skew the contributions toward higher paid employees or himself. Social Security integration is not considered discriminatory because +the employees who are receiving the excess contributions are not receiving Social Security retirement contributions on their wages that are in excess of the Social Security wage base.

6. Treas. Reg. Section 1.401(l)-2.

Age-Based Profit Sharing Plans

Age-based profit sharing plans use both age and compensation as the basis for allocating contributions to an employee's account. An age-based plan is chosen when the employee census is such that the owner or key employee is older than most or all other employees and the company wants to tilt the contribution toward those older employees. The concept of using an age-weighting formula in the allocation of benefits is based on a theory of comparable benefits for employees at normal age retirement (usually 65). Because older employers are closer to normal retirement age, current contributions must be higher relative to younger employees. While this result initially appears to be discriminatory when comparing the current contributions to the plan, it seems relatively fair after comparing the ultimate benefits derived from the plan at the time of the employee's retirement.

It is possible that employees may perceive an inequity in the contributions to the plan under a age-based profit sharing formula. For example, if two employees are performing the same duties and are paid the same salary but are of different ages, the older employee will receive a higher current contribution to the plan than the younger employee. An illustration of an age-based profit sharing plan is provided in Example 5.4.

There are seven employees (A-G), ages 25-55 and with compensation ranging from $30,000 to $200,000.

EXAMPLE 5.4

				AGE-BASED PROFIT SHARING PLAN		
Employee	Age	Covered Comp	PV of $1	Allocation Factor (age-weighted compensation)	Percent of Total Contribution	Dollar Contribution
A (Owner)	55	$200,000	0.4423	$88,457	0.755305	$39,465
B	45	$60,000	0.1956	$11,737	0.100218	$5,236
C	40	$60,000	0.1301	$7,806	0.066650	$3,482
D	35	$50,000	0.0865	$4,326	0.036937	$1,930
E	30	$40,000	0.0575	$2,302	0.019652	$1,027 *
F	25	$35,000	0.0383	$1,339	0.011436	$598 *
G	25	$30,000	0.0383	$1,148	0.009802	$512 *
		$475,000		$117,114	1.000000	$52,250

* Note that this plan is most likely a top-heavy plan. Therefore, employees E, F, and G would have to be allocated 3% of their salary $1,200 ($1,050 and $900 respectively). This would reduce the amount available to the owner or increase the overall cost of the plan.

The initial step in calculating the contribution under an age-based profit sharing plan is to determine the present value of one dollar of benefit at the normal retirement age, usually age 65. For example, to determine this present value factor for employee A, the following calculation is performed:

FV = 1.0

N = 10 (65–55) difference in age from normal age retirement 65

i = 8.5 (employer selected interest rate)

Pmt = 0

PV = 0.44229 (the contribution factor for this employee)

The term (N) is determined by subtracting the current age from the normal retirement age. In this case, the employee (A) has 10 years until he attains the age of 65. The interest factor is generally permitted by the IRS to be between 7.5% and 8.5%. This calculation results in a present value of 0.4423, which means that for employee A to receive a benefit of $1.00 at age 65, the plan sponsor would have to contribute $0.4423 today.

Notice that the factor decreases for younger age participants reflecting the longer period until retirement. For example, employee C's factor is 0.1301 whereas employee E's factor is 0.0575. The result is that contributions will be higher for those employees who are older because the factor will increase each year for each employee as they approach retirement.

The next step in the calculation is to weight the present value factor by the employee's compensation to arrive at an age-weighted compensation. For employee A, the allocation factor equals $88,457 ($200,000 x 0.4423). Once this process is completed for each employee, the resulting allocation factors are used to pro rate the total contribution to the plan to the individual employees. Employee A's allocation factor over the total age-weighted compensation equals 75.53 percent ($88,457 ÷ $117,114), a significantly higher contribution percentage relative to the other employees. The percentage of total contribution is then multiplied by the total dollar contribution to the plan ($52,250).

The age-weighted profit sharing formula provides an amazing result. The owner, employee A, increases his allocation of the $52,250 contribution from $22,000 in our first example to $39,465 (recall that the 2005 limit for any particular employee is $42,000). This method of allocating contributions works extremely well when the owner is older than the other employees and when his compensation is relatively high. We could even calculate the total amount of employer contribution to the plan necessary to give A the maximum contribution for profit sharing plans in 2005 of $42,000 ($42,000 ÷ 75.5305% = $55,606.68). As illustrated in Exhibit 5.2, the owner employee can allocate a high percentage of the total contribution to his account balance utilizing the two available options illustrated if the census data were as presented.

COMPARISON OF STANDARD, INTEGRATED, AND AGE-BASED PROFIT SHARING PLANS   EXHIBIT 5.2

Technique for Plan Contributions	Allocation of Contribution to Owner	Total Employer Contribution to Plan	Owner's Percentage of Contribution	Impact of the Change Over Standard Allocation
Standard Allocation	$22,000	$52,250	42.11%	N/A
Permitted Disparity (Integration)	$25,470	$51,870	49.10%	+ 15.77%
Age-Weighted Plan	$39,465	$52,250	75.53%	+ 79.4%
Age-Weighted - Maximum contributions to owner	$42,000	$55,607	75.53%	+ 90.91%

Unfortunately, most business owners are unaware of the availability of these favorable contribution methods for a retirement plan. This provides financial planners and pension experts who are knowledgeable with an opportunity to add significant value to the professional/client relationship.

New Comparability Plans

A **new comparability plan** is generally a profit sharing plan in which contributions are made to an employee's account based on their respective classification in the company as defined by the plan sponsor (employer). The contributions for the "owner" category classification will always be higher than the contributions for other employee classifications. To meet the nondiscrimination rules, new comparability plans, like age-based profit sharing plans, must comply with the cross-testing rules.[7] In the usual case of new comparability plans, the owners classification generally receives $42,000 for 2005 (the maximum) and all other classifications receive less.

Quick Quiz

Highlight the answer to these questions:

1. Permitted disparity is a method of allocating plan contributions that allows the employer to make contributions only to highly compensated individuals because they do not receive Social Security.
   a. True
   b. False

2. Age-based profit sharing plans use both age and compensation as the basis for allocating contributions to employee accounts.
   a. True
   b. False

3. New Comparability plans are safe, flexible plans that allow the employer to allocate all benefits to the owner.
   a. True
   b. False

False, True, False.

These plans are more expensive administratively and are under careful scrutiny by the IRS. The IRS has issued final regulations impacting cross-tested plans that are effective January 1, 2002.[8] These regulations restrict the flexibility of plan design and are reducing (although not eliminating) the benefits of cross-tested plans.

Other Allocation Methods

A highly compensated owner can fund his plan with the annual additions limit, $42,000 for 2005, using profit sharing plans with or without a cash or deferred arrangement. In many cases, the use of a cash or deferred arrangement (CODA) may enable an owner to reach the maximum contribution limit of $42,000 (2005) with a lower total employer contribution.

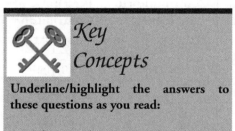

Key Concepts

Underline/highlight the answers to these questions as you read:

1. What are the vesting schedules available for profit sharing plans?

2. When are distributions allowed from profit sharing plans?

Forfeitures

When employment is terminated and the employee has funds in a profit sharing plan that are not 100 percent vested, the employee will forfeit the amount that is not vested. **Forfeitures** for a profit sharing plan may either be used to reduce plan contributions or be reallocated to the remaining participant's accounts.[9] However, any such reallocation of the forfeiture amounts must not be discriminatory in favor of highly compensated employees, owners, or officers.

Forfeitures can be allocated to remaining employees' accounts based on account balances as long as the allocation method does not discriminate. Alternatively, the forfeitures could be allocated on current year compensation – the same as normal contributions to the plan. Forfeitures cannot be reallocated to participants' accounts that have already reached their annual additions limit for the year. Therefore, an owner who has managed to have current contributions of $42,000 for 2005 made to his account will likely consider having forfeitures reduce current contributions to the plan. A forfeiture policy of reallocation can be combined with integration or an age-based approach to assist the owner in receiving the maximum contribution allowed.

EXAMPLE 5.5

George has a $30,000 balance and is 80% vested in his profit sharing plan when he terminates employment. In this example, George's vested balance in the profit sharing plan is $24,000 and he will forfeit the remaining $6,000. This forfeiture could be used to reduce future plan contributions. For example, the $52,250 contribution to the age-based profit sharing plan in the previous example could be reduced to $46,250 ($52,250 - $6,000). Alternatively, in the previous example demonstrating the profit sharing plan that utilized

---

7. Cross-testing rules dictate testing of defined contribution plans based on the expected benefits to be received by employees at retirement.

8. Treas. Reg Section 1.401(a)(4)-8(b)(2)(i).

9. IRC Section 401(a)(8).

the standard allocation formula, the $6,000 could be distributed to the remaining participants with $2,526 (200,000/475,000 x 6,000) allocated to employee A. In this case, employee A, the owner, would have total contributions to the profit sharing plan in the amount of $24,526 ($22,000 + $2,526) rather than the $22,000.

ELIGIBILITY

Profit sharing plans are subject to **standard eligibility** rules of other qualified plans. Therefore, the standard eligibility of age 21 and one year of service will generally apply to profit sharing plans. As discussed before, plan sponsors may always relax the eligibility requirements.

In addition, profit sharing plans may also require a two year waiting period before the employee is eligible; however, all contributions must then be 100 percent vested. The two year eligibility rule is not a common choice for most businesses due to the 100 percent vesting requirement.

VESTING

The vesting rules for profit sharing plans are the same as for other qualified plans. The standard 5-year cliff vesting and the graduated 3 to 7-year vesting apply unless the plan is top-heavy. In the case of a top-heavy plan, the vesting period is shortened to a 3-year cliff or a 2 to 6 year graduated vesting. As discussed before, the plan sponsor is always permitted to be more generous but may not exceed these vesting requirements.

Quick Quiz

Highlight the answer to these questions:

1. A profit sharing plan can require the participants to wait three years before entering the plan, but all contributions must then be 100% vested.
   a. True
   b. False

2. Profit sharing plans must use a 3-year cliff vesting schedule or a 2 to 6 year graduated vesting schedule.
   a. True
   b. False

3. Profit sharing plans may permit in-service withdrawals after a participant has attained two years of service in the plan.
   a. True
   b. False

False, False, True.

DISTRIBUTIONS

Generally, profit sharing plans do not permit employees to receive distributions from the plan except upon termination, hardship, disability, or retirement. However, profit sharing plans may permit in-service withdrawals after the participant has fulfilled two years of service in the plan. Chapter 7 fully explains the taxation of distributions from qualified plans and the application of any penalties for early withdrawal.

CASH OR DEFERRED ARRANGEMENTS (CODA) [401(k) PLANS]

Employee deferrals are made.

A **cash or deferred arrangement (CODA)**, generally referred to as a 401(k) plan, is a feature that attaches to certain types of qualified plans to create a contributory component. Specifically, a CODA is permitted with profit sharing plans and stock bonus plans.[10] The CODA permits employees to defer a portion of their salary on a pretax basis to the qualified plan, thereby reducing their current income tax liability. These employee elective deferral contributions are tax-deferred - meaning that the earnings are not subject to income taxation until such time as the employee takes a distribution from the plan. It is referred to as a cash or deferred arrangement because employees are given the option to receive their current salary in cash (in their payroll) or make an elective deferral contribution into the 401(k) plan.

Key Concepts

Underline/highlight the answers to these questions as you read:

1. What are the general characteristics of cash or deferred arrangement?

2. List the advantages for employees to have a 401(k) plan.

3. Which type of entities may establish a 401(k) plan?

401(k) plans are attractive to employers because these plans are employee self-reliant plans and provide a means of establishing a qualified retirement plan for employees without requiring the employer to make contributions to the plan (although employer contribution matches are an option and are common).

| **EXHIBIT 5.3** | **ADVANTAGES OF 401(k) PLANS** |

TO EMPLOYEES	TO EMPLOYERS
Shelter current income from taxation in a qualified plan.	Minimal expense.
Self-directed investments.	No annual contribution commitment required.
Earnings grow tax-deferred until distributed.	

CODA plans are the most popular type of newly installed qualified retirement plans today. Cash or deferred arrangements are so prevalent because employers have begun to shift from plans in which the employees are dependent on the employer for the funding of retirement benefits to plans in which the employees are dependent on themselves for the funding of retirement benefits. Employers can provide contributions to such plans (usually in the form of a match based on the employee's deferral) but, as with any profit sharing, such employer contributions are discretionary.

---

10. Could also be a pre-1974 money purchase pension plan.

ESTABLISHING A 401(k) PLAN

As with any qualified plan, plan sponsors may use prototype plans (see Chapter 8) or custom designed plans to establish a cash or deferred arrangement. Because these cash or deferred arrangements are qualified plans, the procedures to establish one are similar to other qualified plans. However, there are certain differences in terms of which entities can establish CODAs.

Which Entities May Establish a 401(k) Plan?

Only certain types of entities are permitted to establish and sponsor a 401(k) plan. Employers, such as corporations, partnerships, LLCs, and proprietorships can establish such a plan. In addition, for years after 1996, tax-exempt entities are permitted to establish 401(k) plans. Traditionally, tax-exempt entities (such as 501(c)(3) organizations) have established tax sheltered annuities (403(b) plans), but today, these entities may establish either the traditional TSA (403(b))or a 401(k) plan. Over the past few years, these two types of plans have become very similar in nature. A governmental entity may no longer establish a 401(k) plan;[11] however, certain grandfathered government plans that were in existence prior to May 6, 1986 may continue to be maintained.

Quick Quiz

Highlight the answer to these questions:

1. A tax exempt organization cannot establish a 401(k) plan.
   a. True
   b. False

2. Employers can establish 401(k) plans with minimal expense.
   a. True
   b. False

3. Governmental entities can not establish 401(k) plans today.
   a. True
   b. False

False, True, True.

A 401(k) plan is typically a profit sharing plan (although it may be arranged as a stock bonus plan) that permits employees to make contributions from their salary to the plan on a pretax basis.

Entities Which May Establish a 401(k)
Corporations
Partnerships
LLCs
Proprietorships
Tax-exempt entities

Because of its qualified status, 401(k) plans must comply with the rules discussed in Chapter 3 regarding eligibility, coverage, nondiscrimination, vesting, etc. However, some of the rules that relate to 401(k) plans are somewhat different than the standard rules relating to qualified plans. These differences are discussed below.

---

11. IRC Section 401(k)(4)(B).

ELIGIBILITY

401(k) plans, like other qualified plans, have rules regarding who is eligible to participate in the plan. As you recall, the standard eligibility rules for qualified plans are that the employee must have attained the age of 21 and worked **one year of service** (defined as 1,000 hours within a 12 month period).[12] The exception to the one year of service rule is that an employer may make an employee wait two years to enter the plan if upon entrance into the plan, all benefits are fully vested. However, an employee cannot be required to complete more than one year of service as a condition of participation in a section 401(k) arrangement.[13] The reason for this is that the employee elective deferral contributions are already 100 percent vested.

As with any qualified plan, the eligibility rules may always be more liberal to benefit the employees but cannot be more restrictive.

Once the eligibility requirements are met, the employee will enter the plan upon the next plan entrance date. As discussed in Chapter 3, most qualified plans have two entrance dates to meet the qualification requirement, which limits the vesting period to six months after eligibility.

Key Concepts

Underline/highlight the answers to these questions as you read:

1. What are the eligibility rules for 401(k) plans?

2. Describe how entrance days work for 401(k) plans.

3. Identify the participation rules and negative elections.

EXAMPLE 5.6

Dirk, age 35, has just taken a job at Advanced Technologies, which sponsors a 401(k) plan that requires one year of service and has entrance dates on January 1st and July 1st. If Dirk started work on February 15th, 2005, he will be entering the plan on July 1, 2006.

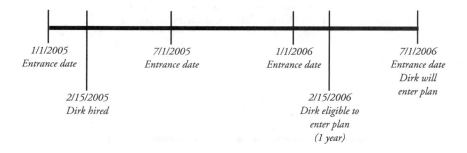

---

12. Rule is generally referred to as "21 and 1."
13. IRC Section 401(k)(2)(D).

VESTING

The vesting requirements for 401(k) plans are different than the vesting requirements of other qualified plans. Contributions to 401(k) plans consist of employee elective deferrals and if applicable, employer matching contributions. If the 401(k) is sponsored in conjunction with a profit sharing plan or stock bonus plan, contributions to those plans are considered separate from the 401(k) plan contributions. For vesting purposes, all employee deferral contributions and the earnings on those contributions are always 100 percent vested. The employer matching contributions and the earnings on the employer match must vest under a schedule at least as generous as the top-heavy vesting schedules of 2 to 6 year graduated or 3-year cliff. The contributions to the profit sharing plan or stock bonus plan must vest according to the rules discussed in Chapter 3, either a 3 to 7 year graduated vesting schedule or a 5-year cliff vesting schedule (2 to 6 year graduated and 3-year cliff if the profit sharing plan is top-heavy).

EXAMPLE 5.7

The total balance of Wallace's 401(k) profit sharing plan is $200,000. Of this balance, $60,000 is attributable to employer profit sharing plan contributions and $40,000 is attributable to earnings on the employer profit sharing plan contributions. $39,000 consists of Wallace's elective deferral contributions to the 401(k) plan and $21,000 is the earnings on Wallace's elective deferral contributions. The remainder of the balance consists of employer matching contributions and the earnings on the employer match. If the 401(k) profit sharing plan is not top-heavy and follows the least generous graded vesting schedule and Wallace has completed two years of service with his employer, what is his vested balance in this 401(k) profit sharing plan?

To calculate this, first separate all of the contributions to determine the proper type of vesting schedule to use with each type of contribution, and then apply the appropriate vesting percentage.

Profit Sharing Plan		Vested %		Vested Amount
Employer contribution	$60,000	0%	3 to 7 graduated vesting	$0
Earnings	$40,000	0%	3 to 7 graduated vesting	$0
Total	$100,000		Vested profit sharing plan	$0
401(k) Plan				
Wallace contribution	$39,000	100%	Employee deferral contribution	$39,000
Earnings	$21,000	100%	100% vested	$21,000
Employer matching contributions and earnings	$40,000	20%	Employer match follows 2 to 6 year graduated vesting	$8,000
Total 401(k)	$100,000			
			Vested Account Balance 401(k)	**$68,000**

PARTICIPATION

Employee enrollment meetings are typically held after the creation of a 401(k) plan to inform the employees of the plan details and to encourage participation in the plan.[14] These educational meetings also help the plan sponsor to comply with their IRC Section 404(c) fiduciary requirements. The most popular form of election under a CODA is a salary reduction agreement in which the employee agrees to reduce compensation in exchange for the elective deferral contribution into the plan. The salary reduction agreement may apply to current salary; to a salary increase; or to a bonus, commission, or other form of compensation for services. The employee's election to defer is generally made as a percentage of income or a dollar amount that will be contributed to the plan for the current year and usually directs the funds to be invested in a specific manner.

Quick Quiz

Highlight the answer to these questions:

1. The 401(k) eligibility rules are not the same as profit sharing plans.
   a. True
   b. False

2. A 401(k) must have at least 4 entrance dates.
   a. True
   b. False

3. A negative election is an election the employee can make that states they want to participate in the plan.
   a. True
   b. False

True, False, False.

EXAMPLE 5.8

Sam agrees (elects) to reduce her $50,000 salary by 20% ($10,000) if the funds are deposited in the 401(k) plan. She receives a W-2 showing taxable compensation of $40,000 with the remainder ($10,000) of her salary contributed to the 401(k) plan. Typically, she will choose how the funds are invested – whether stocks, bonds, cash, or other investments.[15] Plans that provide for employee self-

---

14. Participation is encouraged for the benefit of the employee and for ADP/ACP testing.

direction of plan assets generally permit the employees to change their investments on a regular basis, in many cases on a daily basis.

EMPLOYEE CONTRIBUTIONS

Contributions to 401(k) plans can be made as employee elective deferral contributions, employee after-tax contributions, employer matching contributions, employer profit sharing contributions, or employer contributions used to solve an ADP/ACP problem (discussed below).

Employee Deferrals

Employee elective deferral contributions are limited per year to the amounts in the following table:

401(k) ANNUAL ELECTIVE DEFERRALS LIMITS

EXHIBIT 5.4

Cash or Deferred Arrangements*			
Year	Annual Elective Deferral Limit	Catch-Up Contributions **	Total Elective Deferral
2005	$14,000	$4,000	$18,000
2006	$15,000	$5,000	$20,000
2007	$15,000†	$5,000†	$20,000†
2008	$15,500†	$5,000†	$20,500†

The same limits apply to SARSEPs, 403(b) Plans, and 457 Plans.
**Age 50 or older.*

Tax Impact

Besides the mere accumulation of benefits towards retirement, funds deferred in a 401(k) plan are not currently subject to federal income tax and are not currently subject to state income tax. This tax deferral reduces current tax payments and allows for greater compounding of the funds contributed and the earnings over time.

Although employee elective deferrals are not subject to income tax, these deferral amounts are subject to payroll taxes. This means that the employee and the employer must pay payroll taxes on the employee elective deferral amounts contributed to a 401(k) plan. This will result in a Form W-2 that has different amounts in the various boxes on the form.

---

15. While most 401(k) plans provide for self-direction, some plans may provide for outside management of the plan assets.

EXHIBIT 5.5   W-2 EXAMPLE

a Control number 30096	22222	Void ☐	For Official Use Only ► OMB No. 1545-0008		

b Employer identification number (EIN) 35-1234567		1 Wages, tips, other compensation 136,000.00	2 Federal income tax withheld 34,000.00

c Employer's name, address, and ZIP code	3 Social security wages 90,000.00	4 Social security tax withheld 5,580.00

Best Employer
99 Company Drive
City, GA 12345

5 Medicare wages and tips 150,000.00	6 Medicare tax withheld 2,175.00
7 Social security tips	8 Allocated tips

d Employee's social security number 35-1234567	9 Advance EIC payment	10 Dependent care benefits

e Employee's first name and initial Best	Last name Employee	11 Nonqualified plans	12a See instructions for box 12 C 81.28

Best Employee
100 Best Drive
City, GA 12345

13 Statutory employee ☐ Retirement plan ☒ Third-party sick pay ☐	12b D 14,000.00
14 Other	12c
	12d

f Employee's address and ZIP code				
15 State GA	Employer's state ID number 9876543210	16 State wages, tips, etc. 136,000.00	17 State income tax 6,800.00	18 Local wages, tips, etc.	19 Local income tax	20 Locality name

Form **W-2** **Wage and Tax Statement**   **2005**   Department of the Treasury—Internal Revenue Service

Copy A For Social Security Administration — Send this entire page with Form W-3 to the Social Security Administration; photocopies are **not** acceptable.

For Privacy Act and Paperwork Reduction Act Notice, see back of Copy D.

Cat. No. 10134D

Do Not Cut, Fold, or Staple Forms on This Page — Do Not Cut, Fold, or Staple Forms on This Page

Notice, in the Form W-2 above, Medicare wages (box 5) represents the total income for the employee. Subtracting the 401(k) deferral of $14,000 (box 12b) from Medicare wages results in the taxable wages found in box 1. Box 4 (Social Security tax withheld) equals 6.2 percent of box 3 (Social Security Wages) and box 6 equals 1.45 percent of box 5 (Medicare wages). Recall that the Medicare tax applies to all wages, while the Social Security tax (OASDI) is limited to the Social Security wage base ($90,000 for 2005). (Box 12a indicates the taxable component of the insurance premiums for the employee's group term life coverage.)

Employer Deposits of Employee Deferrals

Employee elective deferrals must be deposited and segregated from the employer's assets by the earliest date that is reasonably possible. However, the segregation of the funds must be completed by the 15th day of the month following the deferral from the employee's compensation. It is important to note that the 15th day is not a safe harbor. The employer has a responsibility to deposit the funds as soon as it is reasonably possible.

Catch-Up Contributions

Employees who are at least 50 years old may increase their elective deferral limit by up to $4,000 for 2005 ($5,000 for 2006, $5,000[†] for 2007, and $5,000[†] for 2008). The additional deferral is called a **"catch-up" contribution** and allows those nearing retirement to increase their deferral contributions to improve their financial situation for retirement.

In 2006, the employee elective deferral catch-up contribution may increase an employee's deferral limit by 33 1/3 percent from $15,000 to $20,000. In addition, these employee deferral catch-up contributions are not limited by plan limits, limits on annual accumulations, or by the ADP/ACP testing (discussed below). In other words, as long as the plan provides for equal treatment among participants (both HC and NHC), there are virtually no restrictions on using these catch-up contributions for employees 50 and older.

Employee deferrals are included as part of the employee's annual funding limit of the lesser of 100 percent of income or $42,000 for 2005. However, the catch-up contributions do not count against this limit and, therefore, allow a participant who is age 50 and older to increase the maximum contributions to qualified plans to $46,000 for 2005.

Key Concepts

Underline/highlight the answers to these questions as you read:

1. Identify the methods employees can contribute to 401(k) plans and the applicable deferral contribution limits.

2. What is the income tax impact of 401(k) employee deferral contributions?

3. When must the employer deposit employee deferral contributions into the 401(k) plan?

4. Discuss the application of the catch-up contribution rules and the limits on catch-up contributions.

> Andrea, age 50, has a salary of $120,000. She chooses to defer $18,000 for 2005 into the 401(k) plan. The employer may also contribute up to $30,000 ($120,000 x 25%) to the plan. However, the employer's contribution will be limited to $28,000 due to the maximum annual contribution limit. In total for the year, Andrea would have contributions to qualified plans totalling $46,000 ($42,000 + $4,000 catch-up).

EXAMPLE 5.9

Employee After-Tax Contributions - Thrift Plans

Although not as popular as in the past, some 401(k) plans still permit employees to make after-tax contributions to the plan. These types of contributions have typically been called **thrift plan** contributions and were utilized by those persons who wanted to save more than the elective deferral limit or more than the amount allowed under the ADP/ACP test (discussed below). Any earnings on the after-tax contribution grow tax free until distribution just as the earnings on pretax contributions. As will be discussed in Chapter 7, these after-tax contributions (Thrift Plan) give the plan participant an adjusted taxable basis in their 401(k) plan.

Roth Contributions (Roth Accounts)[16]

Effective for years after December 31, 2005, 401(k) plans may allow participants to make Roth contributions to the qualified plan. These employee elective deferral contributions will consist of after-tax dollars, as with contributions to Roth IRAs, and qualified distributions that are attributable to these Roth contributions will be non-taxable and not subject to penalties. The qualified distribution rules for these Roth 401(k) accounts are the same as those for qualified distributions from Roth IRAs (discussed in Chapter 9).

Quick Quiz

Highlight the answer to these questions:

1. The employee 401(k) deferral limit increases only at the rate of inflation.
   a. True
   b. False

2. Employee deferral contributions to 401(k) plans are subject to payroll taxes at the time of contribution.
   a. True
   b. False

3. An employer is not required to deposit the employee's 401(k) deferral contributions until the 15th day of the month following the deferral.
   a. True
   b. False

4. As a maximum, an individual over 50 years old can defer $18,000 in 2005 to a 401(k) plan.
   a. True
   b. False

False, True, False, True.

Qualified plans that adopt these types of contributions are required to adopt separate accounts and maintain separate record keeping for these Roth contributions and earnings allocable to the contributions. The same limits that apply to employee pretax deferrals also apply to Roth contributions.

Contributing to Roth accounts provides many advantages. The contribution limit in 2006 increases to $15,000, which is significantly higher than the limits for contributions to traditional IRAs (discussed in Chapter 9). Contributions to individual Roth IRA accounts are also limited based on an individual's adjusted gross income (AGI). The Roth accounts within a 401(k) plan do not have such income limitations, so an individual with an AGI in excess of the limit would be able to fund a Roth through a Roth 401(k) account, but not a Roth IRA.

EMPLOYER CONTRIBUTIONS

Matching Contributions

Employers and plan sponsors often provide a matching contribution based on the **employee deferral contributions** to the 401(k) plan. These **employer matching contributions** act as an incentive for plan participants to defer larger portions of their compensation than they may have otherwise contributed. Examples of methodologies for matching contributions are:

- 50 percent match up to six percent of compensation. If an employee contributes six percent or more of his compensation, the employer would match with a three percent contribution.

---

16. IRC Section 402A.

- Dollar-for-dollar match up to four percent. For every dollar of employee elective deferral, the employer will contribute (match) equally up to four percent of the employee's compensation.

In 2005, Rita elects to defer 8% of her $40,000 salary to a 401(k) plan. Her employer matches 50% of her deferral up to a maximum of 6%. For the year, Rita contributes $3,200 and her employer contributes 3%, or $1,200, for a total contribution of $4,400.

If Rita is attempting to maximize her employee deferral contributions, she can elect to defer $14,000, and if she is age 50 or over, she can elect to defer the catch-up of $4,000. Rita's total deferral contribution to the 401(k) plan would be $18,000. Her employer would match $2,400 (6% x $40,000) for a total of $20,400 or 51% of her salary. Rita's W-2 income would be $22,000, although she and her employer would pay payroll taxes on the full $40,000. The employer match would not be subjected to payroll taxes.

While employee elective deferral contributions are always 100 percent vested, employer matching contributions must vest at least as rapidly as either a three-year cliff vesting schedule or a 2 to 6 year graduated vesting schedule. These are the same maximum vesting schedules that are required for top-heavy plans. Remember, plan sponsors can always be more generous by reducing years of service requirements for employees to achieve full vesting but may not extend the vesting period. Some matching contributions are applied simultaneously with employee deferral contributions. Other plans may require active employment as of December 31 to qualify for the employer match, so matching contributions occur after year end.

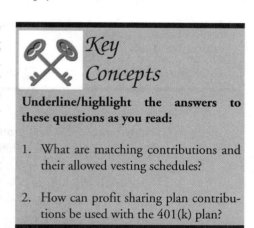

Key Concepts

Underline/highlight the answers to these questions as you read:

1. What are matching contributions and their allowed vesting schedules?

2. How can profit sharing plan contributions be used with the 401(k) plan?

Profit Sharing (Stock Bonus) Contributions

Because 401(k) plans consist of a CODA attached to a profit sharing plan or stock bonus plan, employers may also make a contribution to the profit sharing (or stock bonus) plan. These contributions are often referred to as the non-elective employer contribution. The employee elective deferral contributions do not count against the plan contribution limit of 25 percent, so large contributions can be made as a non-elective profit sharing contribution. The total contributions to qualified plans for the year is still limited to $42,000 per person for 2005 ($46,000 if the participant is age 50 and over).

The following example illustrates how profit sharing contributions, employee deferral contributions, and catch-up contributions work in unison. This example also illustrates how the annual additions limit works in harmony with the 401(k) limit and plan contribution limit.

EXAMPLE 5.11

Assume that each employee wants to maximize his employee deferral contributions and the employer is making a 25% of employee compensation contribution to a profit sharing plan on behalf of each employee.

Consider Employees A through D with compensation ranging from $30,000 to $210,000. Also assume that each employee is over the age of 50.

PROFIT SHARING, ELECTIVE DEFERRALS, AND CATCH-UP CONTRIBUTIONS				
	Employee A	**Employee B**	**Employee C**	**Employee D**
Salary	$30,000	$100,000	$150,000	$210,000
Catch-up contribution	$4,000	$4,000	$4,000	$4,000
401(k) deferral	$14,000	$14,000	$4,500	$0
P/S contribution (25%)	$7,500	$25,000	$37,500	$42,000
Total contributions	**$25,500**	**$43,000**	**$46,000**	**$46,000**

Notice if you assume the employer is going to make a 25% contribution, that will limit the elective deferral for C and D but will not affect the catch-up contribution.

The profit sharing contribution is assumed to be 25% of the employee's salary limited to the annual additions limit of $42,000, as in the case of Employee D. The 401(k) deferral is assumed to be limited to the lesser of the difference between the annual additions limit or the maximum deferral for the year. In the case of Employee A, he can not reach either the $42,000 limit or 100% of his annual compensation because of how the limits work together. Notice that because the profit sharing contribution for Employee C is so high, he is only allowed to defer $4,500 in the 401(k) plan. In the case of Employee D, the profit sharing contribution is limited to the $42,000 limit and thus he is unable to contribute to the 401(k) plan with the exception of the catch-up contribution.

EXAMPLE 5.12

Now assume that each employee maximizes his employee deferral contributions, and then the employer makes the maximum profit sharing plan contribution.

	Employee A	Employee B	Employee C	Employee D
Salary	**$30,000**	**$100,000**	**$150,000**	**$210,000**
Catch-up contribution	$4,000	$4,000	$4,000	$4,000
401(k) deferral	$14,000	$14,000	$14,000	$14,000
P/S contribution	$7,500	$25,000	$28,000	$28,000
Total Contributions	**$25,500**	**$43,000**	**$46,000**	**$46,000**

In this case, the profit sharing contributions are limited for C and D rather than the employee deferral contributions, but each employee (C and D) still reaches the maximum contribution to qualified plans for the year.

NONDISCRIMINATION TESTING

All qualified plans are required to meet certain nondiscrimination tests, but qualified plans that maintain a CODA must also meet two special nondiscrimination tests known as the actual deferral percentage test (ADP) and the actual contribution percentage test (ACP).

Negative Elections

A negative election clause in a 401(k) plan can assist a plan in meeting the special nondiscrimination test. With a negative election, an employee is deemed to have elected a specific employee deferral, such as four percent of compensation unless the employee specifically elects out of such deferral election in writing. This type of election has been approved by the IRS and can help increase employee participation in the plan.[17]

The negative election can apply to both current employees as well as recently hired employees or employees who meet eligibility requirements.

Quick Quiz

Highlight the answer to these questions:

1. Matching contributions vest at either a 2 to 6 year graduated vesting schedule or a 5-year cliff vesting schedule.
   a. True
   b. False

2. A catch-up contribution can allow an eligible employee to defer more than the annual additions limit of $42,000 for 2005.
   a. True
   b. False

False, True.

---

17. Rev Rul 2000-8.

EXAMPLE 5.13

After one year of service, Adrian meets the eligibility requirements for the ABC company 401(k) plan. The plan provides for a negative election in which the employer will deposit five percent of participants' compensation to the 401(k) plan. If Adrian earns $40,000, the plan sponsor will contribute $2,000 of her compensation to the plan unless she affirmatively elects to increase or decrease the contribution.

ACTUAL DEFERRAL PERCENTAGE TEST (ADP)

The **Actual Deferral Percentage (ADP)** test limits employee elective deferrals for the highly compensated employees (HC) based on the elective deferrals of non-highly compensated employees (NHC). A qualified plan with a CODA does not fail the ADP test simply because all eligible employees are highly compensated.[18]

IRC Section 401(k)(3) states that the actual deferral percentage for eligible highly compensated employees for the plan year is limited by the actual deferral percentage for all other eligible employees for the preceding plan year and must meet either of the following tests:

- Test 1: The actual deferral percentage for the group of eligible highly compensated employees is not more than the actual deferral percentage of all other eligible employees multiplied by 1.25 (the 1.25 requirement).
- Test 2: The excess of the actual deferral percentage for the group of eligible highly compensated employees over that of all other eligible employees is not more than two percentage points, and the actual deferral percentage for the group of eligible highly compensated employees is not more than the actual deferral percentage of all other eligible employees multiplied by 2 (the 200% / 2% test).

Although the ADP test above appears rather convoluted and difficult to follow, the test can be interpreted rather easily with the following charts.

ADP SCHEDULE	
If the ADP for NHC Employees is:	**The Permissible ADP for HC Employees is:**
0% to 2%	2 times ADP for NHCs
2% to 8%	2% plus ADP for NHCs
8% and over	1.25 times ADP for NHCs

---

18. IRC Section 401(k)(3).

The Rule	ADP of NHC	ADP Limit for HC
2 times ADP of NHC	1%	2.00%
	2%	4.00%
Plus 2 percentage points of ADP of NHC	3%	5.00%
	4%	6.00%
	5%	7.00%
	6%	8.00%
	7%	9.00%
	8%	10.00%
1.25 times ADP of NHC	9%	11.25%
	10%	12.50%
	11%	13.75%
	12%	15.00%
	13%	16.25%
	14%	17.50%
	15%	18.75%

As indicated in the above charts, the elective deferral contributions of the highly compensated employees are limited based on the elective deferrals of the nonhighly compensated employees. Generally, the current plan year ADP for the highly compensated employees is tested against the ADP of the nonhighly compensated employees for the prior plan year. Using this approach will generally minimize excess contributions by highly compensated employees. In other words, knowing the ADP for the nonhighly compensated employees for the prior plan year will allow the highly compensated employees to comply with the ADP test for the current plan year.

Key Concepts

Underline/highlight the answers to these questions as you read:

1. What are the ADP tests, and how are they calculated?

2. What remedies are available if a company fails the ADP test?

3. What are the safe harbor rules?

Plans can choose either the Current Year Method or Prior Year Method for ADP testing. The Prior Year Method calculates the maximum permissible deferral for highly compensated employees by using the nonhighly compensated employee's ADP from the previous year. Although the highly compensated employees have less certainty in knowing their deferral limits by using the Current Year Method, this approach may give the highly compensated employees a slightly higher deferral ceiling. The Current Year Method also provides more flexibility to the plan sponsor in the event of ADP failures.

In the first year of a 401(k) plan or the year that such plan is established, there is obviously no prior year on which to base the ADP for the highly compensated employees. In the first plan year, the ADP for the nonhighly compensated employees will be either three percent (as provided for in the regulations) or the actual ADP for the current year.[19]

How is the ADP Calculated?

To determine whether the requirements of the ADP test have been met, the first step is to separate the eligible employees into highly compensated and nonhighly compensated groups. The only employees included in the calculation are those who meet the eligibility requirements of the 401(k) plan. It is important to note that this also includes those employees that have met eligibility but have chosen not to defer any of their compensation.

Next, calculate the actual elective deferral ratio (ADR) for each of the eligible employees by dividing the elective deferral contribution by the employee's compensation. Once the ADR is determined for each eligible employee, the amount of the ADP is calculated by averaging the ADRs for the employees within each group (HC or NHC). Once the ADP for each group is determined, they are compared to determine that the qualified plan complies with either the 1.25 test or the 200%/2% test.

EXAMPLE 5.14

Boo Company sponsors a 401(k) plan with ten eligible employees. Each employee can defer up to 70 percent of their compensation limited to the annual deferral limit. The employees made the following deferral elections:

Basic Data				
Employee	Ownership	Compensation	Elective deferral	ADR
A	60%	$200,000	$11,000	5.5%
B	30%	$140,000	$9,800	7.0%
C	5%	$100,000	$10,000	10.0%
D	3%	$80,000	$8,000	10.0%
E	2%	$50,000	$2,500	5.0%
F	-	$30,000	$3,000	10.0%
G	-	$25,000	-	0.0%
H	-	$25,000	$1,000	4.0%
I	-	$25,000	-	0.0%
J	-	$20,000	$500	2.5%

---

19. Treas. Reg. Section 1.401(k)-1(g)(11).

Employee	Alternative A HC definition without election*		Alternative B HC definition with election*	
	HC	NHC	HC	NHC
A	5.5%		5.5%	
B	7.0%		7.0%	
C	10.0%			10.0%
D		10.0%		10.0%
E		5.0%		5.0%
F		10.0%		10.0%
G		0%		0%
H		4%		4%
I		0%		0%
J		2.5%		2.5%
Average	7.5%	4.5%	6.25%	6.0%

Election to include only top 20% of employees as determined by compensation as HC.

Who is highly compensated in the example?

- Employee A and B are clearly highly compensated because of their ownership percentage.

- Employee C is highly compensated based on his income of $100,000. However, if the definition for highly compensated included the election of being in the top 20 percent of paid employees, then Employee C would be NHC. Although Employee C owns 5% of the company, he is not a "5% owner" because he is not a <u>more</u> than 5% owner of the company.

- Employees D through J are all NHC employees.

Alternative A and Alternative B demonstrate the difference of treatment depending upon whether the top 20% election is made or not.

Following Alternative A (without the top 20% election), the ADP of the HCs is 7.5%, while the ADP for the NHCs is 4.5%. Referring to the table above, with the NHCs ADP equal to 4.5%, the ADP for the HCs should be no greater than 6.5% - two percentage points more than the ADP for the NHCs. Therefore, the plan fails the ADP test.

See the discussion below for remedies.

HC	NHC
ADP of HC - 7.5	ADP of NHC must be equal to 6.5 = 4.5% + 2%

Following Alternative B (with the top 20% election), the ADP of the HCEs is 6.25%, while the ADP for the NHC employees is 6.0%. Based on these figures, the plan complies with the ADP test. Notice that in this example, the difference between passing the ADP and not passing is how the plan defined the definition of highly compensated. By electing the top 20% of paid employees, Employee C shifted from the HC category to the NHC category. This example illustrates one reason an employer might choose the 20% election as the definition of highly compensated.

Failing the ADP Test

If the ADP test is not met, then there has been an excess elective deferral contribution by the highly compensated. An excess contribution occurs when the HCs defer more than is permitted under the ADP test. When this happens, there are four alternative remedies that the plan may use to bring the plan into compliance:

- corrective distributions;
- recharacterization;[20]
- qualified non-elective contributions (QNEC); or
- qualified matching contributions (QMC).

If a plan does not meet the ADP test, there are two explanations on why the plan did not meet the nondiscrimination test:

- The highly compensated employees deferred too much, or
- The non-highly compensated employees deferred too little (or some combination of the two).

This is a question of whether the "glass is half full or half empty." As stated above, the negative election is often used to entice participation and increase the deferral for the NHC. In either case, the plan must be corrected to meet the ADP test by either reducing the HC employees elective deferral contributions or by increasing the NHC employees elective deferral contributions. Corrective distributions and recharacterizations are methods to reduce the HC employees elective deferrals, while QNECs and QMCs are methods to increase the ADP of the NHC employees.

---

20. IRC Section 401(k)(8)(A).

When there are excess contributions, the 401(k) plan must correct the situation within 2.5 months (75 days) after the plan year for which the contributions were made. If the correction is not made, then the employer is subject to a 10 percent penalty on the excess deferral contribution amount. In addition, if the correction is not made within twelve months, the plan may be deemed disqualified.

If the employer chooses to use a QNEC, or QMC, then these contributions can be made beyond the 2.5 month period.

Corrective Distribution

When a plan fails the ADP test, the most common method of correcting the situation is to reduce the elective deferrals of the HCs by distributing or returning funds to the HCs. This distribution is referred to as a **corrective distribution** because it corrects the elective deferrals with regard to the ADP test. Corrective distributions must be completed within 2½ months after the end of the plan year; otherwise, a 10 percent excise tax is imposed on the amount that should have been distributed.

Recall Alternative A of the Boo Company example above in which the ADP for the HC was 7.5% while the ADP for the NHCs was 4.5%. With the NHC's ADP equal to 4.5%, the ADP for the HCs must equal 6.5%. Therefore, the plan would have to distribute enough from the HCs to reduce the ADP to 6.5% from 7.5%. The leveling method is used to determine the total excess contributions based on the dollar amount of the deferrals.

EXAMPLE 5.15

	Employee A	Employee B	Employee C	Total
Initial deferral	**$11,000**	**$9,800**	**$10,000**	
First reduction <1>	-$1,000	$0	$0	-$1,000
Net	$10,000	$9,800	$10,000	
Next reduction <2>	-$200	$0	-$200	-$400
Net	$9,800	$9,800	$9,800	
Final reduction <3>	-$933	-$933	-$933	-$2,799
Corrected deferral (level)	**$8,867**	**$8,867**	**$8,867**	**-$4,199**
Initial deferral – corrected deferral = Corrective distribution	$2,133	$933	$1,133	$4,199*

Rounded

Under the leveling method, the elective deferral of the HC employee with the highest deferral, Employee A is reduced by the amount, <1> necessary to reduce the deferral to the highest deferral to the next highest dollar deferral, $10,000. The process continues to reduce to the next highest deferral,

<2>. If the total excess contribution is not fully allocated, the process continues, <3>, until the full amount is distributed.

HC Employees	Compensation	Elective deferral	Corrective distribution	Corrected deferral	ADR
A	$200,000	$11,000	$2,133	$8,867	4.43%
B	$140,000	$9,800	$933	$8,867	6.33%
C	$100,000	$10,000	$1,133	$8,867	8.87%
Total			$4,199	ADP =	6.54%

This process results in Employee A reducing his deferral by $2,133, Employee B reducing his deferral by $933, and Employee C reducing his deferral by $1,133. Averaging the ADR for each HC employee results in an ADP of 6.54% rounded to 6.5% – a deemed acceptable level.

In addition to the excess contributions being returned to the HC employees, any earnings on those contributions must also be returned or distributed to the HC employees.

Tax Treatment of Corrective Distributions

Corrective distributions are intended to properly adjust the HC's deferral amount. Therefore, if the HC deferred too much, the corrective distribution results in a lower deferral. However, the distribution may be taxable in the year in which the deferral was taken or the following year, depending on when the distribution is received by the HC.

If the distribution is received within 2½ months after the plan year end, then the distribution will be taxable to the HC in the year in which the deferral was taken. In effect, it is as if the HC deferred the proper amount. However, if the distribution is received after the 2½ month period, then it is taxable in the following year. Thus, the HC would have received a larger deduction than should have been allowed in one plan year and more income the next.

EXAMPLE 5.16

Randy defers $10,000 in the current year. However, after the ADP test is calculated, Randy is determined to have deferred $2,000 more than permitted under the test. Therefore, Randy needs to receive a corrective distribution of the $2,000 by March 15 of the next year. If this happens, then the $2,000 will be included in Randy's taxable income for the previous year. If the distribution is received after March 15 of the next year, then it is taxable to Randy in the next year and the employer must pay a 10 percent penalty on the amount not distributed within 2½ months after the plan year end, in this case $2,000.

Recharacterization

If a plan fails the ADP test, the plan sponsor may choose to recharacterize the excess deferrals (pretax) as after-tax employee contributions. This **recharacterization** must be completed within 2½ months after the end of the plan year, at which time these recharacterized contributions are taxable to the employee.[21] If the excess contributions are not recharacterized within 2½ months of the plan year end, then the employer is subject to a 10 percent excise tax (penalty) on the amount of excess contributions (the amount that should have been recharacterized).

One potential problem with recharacterization is that the pretax contributions that are recharacterized to after-tax contributions may cause the plan to fail the actual contribution percentage (ACP) test. The ACP test is the exact same mathematical test as the ADP test except that instead of testing employee elective deferrals (actual deferral percentage, ADP), it tests employer matching contributions and employee after-tax contributions (actual contribution percentage). In addition, these after-tax contributions will be counted against the employee's annual additions limit of the lesser of $42,000 for year 2005 or 100 percent of compensation.

Qualified Non-Elective Contributions

An employer may choose to make a **qualified nonelective contribution (QNEC)** to NHC employees CODA plan accounts to increase the ADP of the NHC employees for purposes of passing the ADP test. The QNEC is made by the employer without regard to any elective deferral election made by the employee, so the contribution is made on behalf of all eligible employees. The contribution is treated as if deferred by the employee and therefore is included in the calculation of the ADP test to increase the ADP of the NHC. Since the contribution is treated as an employee elective deferral, it is also 100 percent vested in the employee.

> The ADP of the HC employees is six percent and the ADP of the NHC is 3.75%. To pass the ADP test, the NHC employees must have an ADP at least equal to 4%. To increase the ADP of the NHC, the plan sponsor may elect to make a QNEC to all eligible employees that will increase the ADP of the NHC to 4%. Whatever amount of QNEC contributions is made will be considered 100% vested in the NHC employees.

EXAMPLE 5.17

---

21. These after-tax employee contributions would then be subject to the ACP test.

Qualified Matching Contributions

A **qualified matching contribution (QMC)**, like a QNEC, increases the ADP of the NHC employees. However, unlike the QNEC, the QMC is only made to those eligible employees who had elected to defer during the plan year. Essentially, the QMC is an additional match from the employer to increase the deferral percentage of the NHC. Because the contributions are treated as being made by the employee, the QMC is 100 percent vested.

EXAMPLE 5.18

The ADP of the NHC employees was 6% for the plan year, and the ADP of the HC employees was 8.20% for the year. To pass the ADP nondiscrimination test, the plan sponsor would make QMC to all NHC employees who had elected to defer during the plan year to increase the ADP of the NHC to 6.20%. Those employees who had not deferred during the year would not receive any QMC. The QMC is 100% vested in the employee.

ACTUAL CONTRIBUTION PERCENTAGE (ACP)

The **actual contribution percentage test (ACP)** is calculated just like the ADP test except that instead of testing the employee elective deferral contributions, the ACP test calculates a contribution percentage based on the sum of the following:

1. Employee after-tax contributions, and
2. Employer matching contributions.

After calculating the ACP for both NHC employees and HC employees, the two are compared using the same scale as the ADP test. If the plan does not pass the ACP test, the same corrective measures as used for the ADP test are used to either reduce the ACP of the HC or increase the ACP of the NHC.

SAFE HARBOR 401(k) PLANS

Plans that provide for a CODA are subject to the nondiscrimination rules discussed above as well as the top-heavy rules discussed in Chapter 3. For many employers and plan sponsors, the annual testing required to comply with these rules is administratively burdensome and costly. Fortunately, the IRC provides a safe harbor provision whereby the employer is not required to comply with the ADP test, the ACP test, or the top-heavy testing if the plan meets the safe harbor test.

An election must be made 60 days prior to the beginning of the plan year to convert a 401(k) plan to safe harbor status. To comply with safe harbor status, the plan must provide a minimum contribution that must be immediately 100 percent vested. The permissible contributions can either be a three percent minimum non-elective contribution or a matching contribution (discussed below). Under the non-elective contribution, all eligible employees would receive a 100 percent vested contribution equal to three percent of their compensation from the employer.

If the employer elects to use a match rather than the non-elective contribution, the standard safe harbor match formula requires the employer to match 100 percent of the first three percent of employee elective deferrals and 50 percent of employee elective deferrals greater than three percent and less than five percent.

SAFE HARBOR MATCH	
Employee Elective Deferral	**Employer Safe Harbor Match**
0%	0.0%
1%	1.0%
2%	2.0%
3%	3.0%
4%	3.5%
5% or more	4.0%

Alternatively, the employer can provide for any formula that is at least as generous as this formula and satisfy the safe harbor provisions. A common formula found in many CODA safe harbor adoption agreements is a match of 100 percent up to four percent of compensation. This formula is slightly more generous than the one discussed above and is easier to communicate to employees.

Although matching contributions or non-elective contributions are required to be 100 percent vested, safe harbor plans allow the employer to avoid the ADP test, the ACP test, and the top-heavy rules and thus have become quite popular over the last few years.

PLAN LOANS

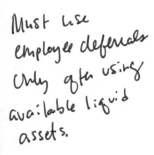 (handwritten: See pg. 285 - pg. 287)

Although distributions to employees are generally not permitted until retirement or termination, qualified plans are permitted to make loans to plan participants. However, plan loans must be made available to all participants and beneficiaries on an effectively equal basis, must be limited in amount, must be paid back within a certain time period, must bear a reasonable rate of interest, must be adequately secured, and the administrator must maintain proper accounting for the loans. Although any qualified plan could establish a loan provision, they are generally only found in CODA type plans, such as 401(k) plans and 403(b) plans. Chapter 7 includes a full discussion of the rules related to qualified plan loans.

DISTRIBUTIONS

Participants of 401(k) plans can generally take distributions from the plan following the same rules as provided to other qualified plans (discussed in Chapter 7). However, all CODA type plans, including 401(k) plans, provide that in addition to the normal distribution options, plan participants may take distributions for hardships. Specifically, distributions may occur after:

Key Concepts

Underline/highlight the answers to these questions as you read:

1. Under what circumstances may individuals take distributions from their 401(k) plan?

2. Define "hardship distributions."

- The retirement, death, or separation of service of the participant;
- The termination of the plan without the establishment of another plan;
- Certain acquisitions of the company or company assets;
- The attainment of age 59½ by the participant; or
- Certain hardships.

Distributions on account of any of these items are taxable as ordinary income to the extent the participant does not have an adjusted taxable basis in the 401(k) plan and may also be subject to a 10% penalty. The full distribution rules and the application of the 10 percent early withdrawal penalty are discussed in Chapter 7.

Hardship Distributions

(handwritten: Must use employee deferrals Only after using available liquid assets.)

Distributions on account of hardship must be limited to the maximum distributable amount. The maximum distributable amount is equal to the employee's total elective deferral contributions as of the date of distribution, reduced by the amount of previous distributions of elective contributions. Thus, the maximum distributable amount does not include earnings, Qualified Non-Elective Contributions (QNECs) or Qualified Matching Contributions (QMCs), unless certain grandfather rules apply. These grandfather rules relate to amounts that were credited to an employee's account prior to December 31, 1988.[22]

---

22. Treas. Reg. 1.401(k)-1(d)(3).

Case Study 1

In Sternberg v. IRS,[1] the plaintiff, Irwin Sternberg ("Sternberg") brought an action against the Internal Revenue Service ("IRS") seeking a refund of taxes he paid for the 1997 tax year and a release from taxes still owed for that year.

In 1990, Sternberg retired from the Harris Company. In July 1990, Sternberg received a lump-sum distribution of $147,512 from his employer's section 401(k) plan and timely rolled over this distribution into an IRA.

In 1997, Sternberg withdrew $211,007 from his IRA, representing the original roll-over of $147,512 plus deferred earnings from 1990 to 1997. On his 1997 tax return, Sternberg showed a tax liability of $40,956, primarily the result of a withdrawal of $211,007 from his IRA. Thereafter, Sternberg re-read the printed instructions accompanying IRS Form 1040 and "became aware of IRS Publication 590 and Form 8606 which were to be used in the determination of taxable distributions" from IRAs. On Form 8606 for "Nondeductible IRAs," Sternberg treated the original roll-over of $147,512 as a nondeductible contribution to his IRA. After following the remaining instructions on Form 8606, Sternberg calculated his taxable IRA distribution for 1997 as being $83,347, not $211,007. Based on this new number, Sternberg then filed an amended Form 1040 tax return in June 2000 that reported a total tax assessment of only $1,819 for the 1997 tax year. Accordingly, Sternberg claimed that the IRS owed him $36,741 in overpaid taxes. By letter, the IRS disallowed Sternberg's amended tax return on the grounds that, under I.R.C. Section 408(d), the IRA distribution taken in 1997 was fully taxable.

Both parties agreed that Sternerg rolled over $147,512 from his employer's 401(k) into an IRA in 1990 without having to pay tax on the 401(k) distribution. Both parties also agreed that Sternberg received a distribution of $211,007 in 1997 (the original rollover plus earnings from 1990 to 1997) from the IRA, and reported the distribution as taxable on his 1997 tax return. The court found that Sternberg erroneously characterized his $147,512 rollover in 1990 as a nondeductible contribution to his IRA, when the relevant statutes, regulations, and publications establish that the rollover only deferred the taxes that he would have owed had he elected to keep the 401(k) distribution. Under the Internal Revenue Code, if "any amount ... distributed from an individual retirement or individual retirement annuity" is paid to the owner of the annuity, and the entire amount is then rolled over into an individual retirement account within 60 days, the amount distributed is not subject to income tax at that time.[2]

---

1. Sternberg v. Internal Revenue Service, 2004 WL 790219 (E.D.N.Y.), 93 A.F.T.R.2d 2004-1388 (Feb. 9, 2004).
2. 26 U.S.C. 402(c); 26 C.F.R. Section 1.408 4(b).

The court continued its discussion by noting that IRS Publication 575 clearly provided that an individual who withdraws cash from a qualified retirement plan can defer tax on the distribution by rolling it over to another qualified retirement plan or a traditional IRA.[1] Ultimately, however, "any amount actually paid or distributed ... from an individual retirement account ... shall be included in the gross income of the payee or distributee for the taxable year in which the payment or distribution is received."[2] Furthermore, IRS Form 8606 and the accompanying instructions in IRS Publication 590 are not statutory exceptions to this rule, as these pertain to "nondeductible contributions" to an IRA - i.e., annual contributions to an IRA which are ineligible for a deduction on that year's tax return.[3]

1. See IRS Publication 575, at 25 (2003).
2. 26 C.F.R. Section 1.408-4(a)(1).
3. See IRS Publication 590 at 16 (2003).

| EXHIBIT 5.6 | MAXIMUM HARDSHIP DISTRIBUTIONS |

Employee Deferral Contribution at Date of Distribution

less: (Previous Distributions)

equals: Maximum Distributable Amount

EXAMPLE 5.19

Hardy defers $5,000 of his annual compensation into the company 401(k) plan every year. He has been doing so for the last ten years. Therefore, his maximum distributable amount is equal to his total elective deferrals, or $50,000. If he had previously received a hardship distribution then the amount of that distribution would reduce the $50,000 maximum distributable amount.

Hardship distributions can only be provided if there is an immediate and heavy financial need and the withdrawal is necessary to satisfy such need. Whether an employee has an immediate and heavy financial need is to be determined based on all the relevant facts and circumstances. Generally, for example, the need to pay funeral expenses of a family member would constitute an immediate and heavy financial need. A distribution made to an employee for the purchase of a boat or television would generally not constitute a distribution made on account of an immediate and heavy financial need. A financial need may be immediate and heavy even if it was reasonably foreseeable or voluntarily incurred by the employee.[23]

23. Treas. Reg. 1.401(k)-1(d)(3).

A distribution is deemed to be on account of an immediate and heavy financial need of the employee if the distribution is for any of the following:

- Expenses for medical care described in section 213(d) previously incurred by the employee, the employee's spouse, or any dependents of the employee (as defined in section 152) or necessary for these persons to obtain medical care described in section 213(d);

- Costs directly related to the purchase of a principal residence for the employee (excluding mortgage payments);

- Payment of tuition, related educational fees, and room and board expenses for up to the next 12 months of post-secondary education for the employee or the employee's spouse, children, or dependents (as defined in section 152); or

- Payments necessary to prevent the eviction of the employee from the employee's principal residence or foreclosure on the mortgage on that residence.

A distribution is treated as necessary to satisfy an immediate and heavy financial need of an employee only to the extent the amount of the distribution is not in excess of the amount required to satisfy the financial need. For this purpose, the amount required to satisfy the financial need may include any amounts necessary to pay any federal, state, or local income taxes or penalties reasonably anticipated to result from the distribution.

A distribution is not treated as necessary to satisfy an immediate and heavy financial need of an employee to the extent the need may be relieved from other resources that are reasonably available to the employee. This determination generally is to be made on the basis of all the relevant facts and circumstances. For these purposes, the employee's resources are deemed to include those assets of the employee's spouse and minor children that are reasonably available to the employee. Thus, for example, a vacation home owned by the employee and the employee's spouse, whether as community property, joint tenants, tenants by the entirety, or tenants in common, generally will be deemed a resource of the employee. However, property held for the employee's child under an irrevocable trust or under the Uniform Gifts to Minors Act (or comparable State law) is not treated as a resource of the employee.

Quick Quiz

Highlight the answer to these questions:

1. A distribution from a 401(k) plan is not available until the plan participant either retires or dies.
   a. True
   b. False

2. A hardship distribution can be taken from a 401(k) plan for an amount equal to the employee's total elective contribution less the value of any previous hardship distributions.
   a. True
   b. False

3. Hardship withdrawals are available if there is an immediate and heavy financial burden even if the participant has other assets available to satisfy the need.
   a. True
   b. False

False, True, False.

An immediate and heavy financial need generally may be treated as one not capable of being relieved from other resources that are reasonably available to the employee. An employer can rely upon the employee's written representation, unless the employer has actual knowledge to the contrary, that the need cannot reasonably be relieved from any of the following:

- Through reimbursement or compensation by insurance or otherwise;
- By liquidation of the employee's assets;
- By cessation of elective contributions or employee contributions under the plan;
- By other distributions or nontaxable loans (at the time of the loan) from plans maintained by the employer or by any other employer; or
- By borrowing from commercial sources on reasonable commercial terms in an amount sufficient to satisfy the need.

Hardship distributions are taxed as ordinary income and may be subject to the 10 percent early withdrawal penalty. Distributions are not subject to the 20 percent statutory withholding requirements since hardship distributions are not eligible for rollover treatment. Those taking a hardship distribution are suspended from making future contributions to the plan for six months.

EXAMPLE 5.20

Dalmart Co. maintains Plan Y, a profit sharing plan that includes a CODA but does not provide for participant loans. However, Plan Y provides that elective contributions under the arrangement may be distributed to an eligible employee on account of hardship using the deemed immediate and heavy financial need provisions. Amanda is an eligible employee in Plan Y with an account balance of $50,000. The total amount of elective deferral contributions made by Amanda, who has not previously received a distribution from Plan Y, is $20,000. Amanda requests a $15,000 hardship distribution of her elective deferral contributions to pay six months of college tuition and room and board expenses for her dependent child. At the time of the distribution request, Amanda's sole asset (that is reasonably available to Amanda within the meaning of the code) is a savings account with an available balance of $10,000.

A distribution is made on account of hardship only if the distribution is made both on account of Amanda's immediate and heavy financial need. A distribution for payment of up to the next 12 months of post-secondary education and room and board expenses for Amanda's dependent child is deemed to be on account of an immediate and heavy financial need of Amanda.

However, the distribution is only treated as necessary to satisfy Amanda's immediate and heavy financial need to the extent the need may not be relieved from other resources reasonably available to Amanda. Since Amanda has a $10,000 savings account as a reasonably available resource, it must be taken into account in determining the amount necessary to satisfy Amanda's immediate and heavy financial need. Thus, Amanda may only receive a distribution of $5,000 ($15,000 - $10,000) of her elective deferral contributions on account of this hardship plus an amount necessary to pay any federal, state, or local income taxes or penalties reasonably anticipated to result from the hardship distribution.

EXAMPLE 5.21

The facts are the same as in Example 5.20. Doug, another employee of Dalmart Co. has a vested account balance of $25,000. The total amount of elective deferral contributions made by Doug, who has not previously received a distribution from Plan Y, is $15,000. Doug requests a $10,000 distribution of his elective deferral contributions to pay six months of college tuition and room and board expenses for his dependent child. Doug makes a written representation (with respect to which Dalmart Co. has no actual knowledge to the contrary) that the need cannot reasonably be relieved:

- through reimbursement or compensation by insurance or otherwise;
- by liquidation of the employee's assets;
- by cessation of elective contributions or employee contributions under the plan;
- by other distributions or nontaxable (at the time of the loan) loans from plans maintained by the employer or by any other employer; or
- by borrowing from commercial sources on reasonable commercial terms in an amount sufficient to satisfy the need.

A distribution for payment of up to the next 12 months of post-secondary education and room and board expenses for Doug's dependent child is deemed to be on account of Doug's immediate and heavy financial need. In addition, because Dalmart Co. can rely on Doug's written representation, the distribution is considered necessary to satisfy Doug's immediate and heavy financial need. Therefore, Doug may receive a $10,000 distribution of his elective contributions on account of hardship plus an amount necessary to pay any federal, state, or local income taxes or penalties reasonably anticipated to result from the distribution.

Key Terms

Actual Contribution Percentage Test (ACP) - A nondiscrimination test that limits the sum of employee after-tax contributions and employer matching contributions for the HC based on the sum of employee after-tax contributions and employer matching contributions for the NHC.

Actual Deferral Percentage Test (ADP) - A nondiscrimination test that limits employee elective deferrals for the highly compensated employees (HC) based on the elective deferrals of non-highly compensated employees (NHC).

Age-Based Profit Sharing Plan - A qualified profit sharing plan that uses a combination of age and compensation as the basis for allocating the contribution to a participant's account.

Cash or Deferred Arrangement (CODA) - Permits an employee to defer a portion of their salary on a pretax basis to a qualified plan or receive the salary as current taxable income.

Catch-Up Contribution - A contribution that allows those nearing retirement to increase their deferral contributions to improve their financial situation for retirement. An elective contribution for employees 50 and over that allows them to increase their elective deferral limit by up to $4,000 for 2005.

Corrective Distribution - A distribution to satisfy the ADP or ACP test that reduces the elective deferrals or contributions of the HC employees by distributing or returning the funds to the HC employees.

Covered Compensation - The maximum compensation ($210,000 for 2005) that may be considered for purposes of making contributions to qualified retirement plans.

Employee Deferral Contributions - Pretax employee contributions to a qualified retirement plan with a CODA. The employee must chose to defer the compensation before earning the compensation.

Employer Matching Contributions - Employer provided contributions to a qualified retirement plan, usually a 401(k) plan that are based on the employee contributions.

Forfeitures - The percentage of a participant's accrued benefit that was not vested in the employee at the employee's termination from the plan sponsor. The forfeited amount stays with the plan and may be allocated to the other plan participants or reduce future plan costs.

Hardship Distributions - A distribution from a 401(k) plan because the employee has an immediate and heavy financial need and the withdrawal is necessary to satisfy the need. The distribution is taxable and subject to penalties to the extent the participant has other resources to have satisfied the financial need.

New Comparability Plan - A qualified profit sharing plan in which contributions are made to employees' accounts based on their respective classification in the company as defined by the plan sponsor.

Key Terms

Nondiscriminatory - A requirement of all qualified plans. The eligibility rules, coverage requirements, and contributions allocations of a qualified plan cannot discriminate against the rank-and-file employees for the benefit of shareholder, officers, and highly compensated employees.

One Year of Service - 1,000 hours of service with an employer within a 12 month period.

Permitted Disparity (Social Security Integration) - A technique or method of allocating qualified plan contributions to an employee account that provides a higher contribution to those employees whose compensation is in excess of the Social Security wage base ($90,000 for 2005) or selected integration level for the plan year.

Profit Sharing Plan - A qualified retirement plan established and maintained by an employer where the employer makes deductible contributions on behalf of the employees, the assets grow tax-deferred, and if there is a CODA feature, the employee also makes pretax contributions.

Qualified Matching Contribution (QMC) - Additional matching contributions made by the employer to satisfy the ADP or ACP test that increases the ACP or ADP of the NHC employees by who had deferred compensation during the plan year.

Qualified Nonelective Contribution (QNEC) - A contribution made by the employer to satisfy the ADP or ACP test that increases the ADP or ACP of the NHC employees by making additional contributions to all NHC eligible employees without regard to any elective deferral election made by the employees.

Recharacterization of Deferrals - To change the nature of any excess employee deferrals from pretax employee contributions to after-tax employee contributions.

Safe Harbor 401(k) Plans - A 401(k) plan that satisfies a minimum contribution or matching test and allows the plan sponsor to bypass the ADP test, the ACP test, and the top-heavy tests.

Social Security Integration (Permitted Disparity) - A technique or method of allocating qualified plan contributions to an employee account that provides a higher contribution to those employees whose compensation is in excess of the Social Security wage base ($90,000 for 2005) or selected integration level for the plan year ($90,000 for 2005).

Standard Eligibility - The general eligibility requirement that requires an employer to consider an employee eligible when he attains 21 years of age and has completed one-year of service (defined as 1,000 hours of service with an employer within a 12-month period).

Thrift Plan - A qualified retirement plan that permits employees to make after-tax contributions to the plan. Although the contributions are taxable before being contributed to the plan, the account still benefits from tax-deferred growth on earnings.

1. Describe the key elements of a profit sharing plan as discussed in Treasury Regulation 1.401-1(b).

2. List the differences between pension plans and profit sharing plans.

CHARACTERISTIC	PENSION PLAN	PROFIT-SHARING PLAN
Legal Promise of the Plan		
Are in-service withdrawals permitted?		
Is the plan subject to mandatory funding standards?		
Percent of plan assets available to be invested in employer securities.		
Employer annual contribution limit of covered compensation		

3. When is the last date during the year that a profit sharing plan may be established and by when must contributions be made to the profit sharing plan?

4. Explain the differences between the standard allocation formula, permitted disparity, age-based profit sharing plans, and new comparability plans.

5. How can forfeitures be used within a profit sharing plan?

6. What are the eligibility requirements for profit sharing plans?

7. What are the applicable vesting rules for profit sharing plans?

8. When may distributions be taken from a profit sharing plan and how will they be taxed?

9. Describe the characteristics of a cash or deferred arrangement.

10. List the advantages of 401(k) plans to both employees and employers.

11. Which entities may establish a 401(k) plan?

12. Describe the eligibility rules for 401(k) plans.

13. What are the entrance dates rules for 401(k) plans?

14. Define "participation" and "negative elections" with regards to 401(k) plans.

15. How can employees make contributions to a 401(k) plan and what are the applicable limits?

YEAR	ANNUAL DEFERRAL LIMIT	CATCH-UP CONTRIBUTIONS FOR THOSE OVER 50
2005		
2006		
2007 and beyond		

16. What is the income tax impact of employee deferrals?

17. When must the employer deposit employee deferrals?

18. Describe the catch-up contribution available for some employees.

19. How are employee after-tax contributions taxed?

20. Describe matching contributions and their associated vesting schedules.

21. How can a profit sharing contribution be used with a 401(k) plan?

22. What is the purpose of the ADP test and how does it work?

23. How is the ADP test calculated?

24. What are the remedies available if a company fails the ADP test?

25. What are corrective distributions and how are they used to correct the ADP test?

26. What is recharacterization and how is it used to correct the ADP test?

27. What are qualified non-elective and matching contributions and how are they used to correct the ADP test?

28. Explain the safe harbor rules and how they affect 401(k) contributions.

29. When may distributions be taken from a 401(k) plan?

30. Describe the hardship distribution rules.

1. Which of the following is not true regarding profit sharing plans?

   a. The plan is established and maintained by the individual employee.

   b. Allows employees to derive benefit from profits of the company.

   c. Profit sharing plans cannot discriminate in favor of officers and shareholders.

   d. Profit sharing plans provide a definite predetermined formula for allocating the contributions made to the plan among the participants and for distributing the funds accumulated under the plan.

2. Which of the following statements is true?

   a. Profit sharing plans may not offer in-service withdrawals.

   b. Pension and profit sharing plans are both subject to mandatory funding requirements.

   c. Profit sharing plans allow annual employer contributions up to 25 percent of the employer's covered compensation.

   d. The legal promise of a profit sharing plan is to pay a pension at retirement.

3. Andi, the 100 percent owner of Andi's Day Care, would like to establish a profit sharing plan. Andi's Day Care's tax year ends July 31 to coincide with the school year. What is the latest day Andi can establish and contribute to the plan?

   a. Andi must establish and contribute to the plan by December 31 of the year in which she would like to establish the plan.

   b. Andi must establish the plan by July 31 of the year in which she would like to have the plan and contribute by May 15 of the following year assuming she filed the appropriate extensions.

   c. Andi must establish the plan by July 31 of the year in which she would like to establish the plan and contribute by December 31.

   d. Andi must establish the plan by December 31 of the year in which she would like to establish the plan and contribute to the plan by April 15 of the following year.

4. Mikael opened a fabulous restaurant ten years ago. The food is so exceptional that the restaurant has become one of the top spots in the city. Mikael, age 55, is the sole owner with compensation of $250,000. Mikael's son Jamel, age 28, is the master chef with compensation of $100,000. Jamel has been with the restaurant full time since he turned 18. Mikael also employs 15 other individuals whose ages range between 25 and 35 and have compensation on average of $40,000 per year. Mikael wants to establish a profit sharing plan. Which of the following statements is true?

    a. If Mikael selected the standard allocation method and the plan contributes 10 percent per individual, the plan will contribute $25,000 to Mikael's account.

    b. If Mikael selected the permitted disparity method and the plan contributes 10 percent per individual, he will be able to increase the contribution the company makes for Mikael.

    c. Considering the needs and wants of Mikael and Jamel, an age-based profit sharing plan is the best plan for both of them.

    d. A new comparability plan is the least expensive, simplest way to meet both Mikael and Jamel's retirement needs.

5. Kathi's Cheerleading Uniforms has 4 employees. The company has a profit sharing plan that has made contributions every year. The plan is designed to maximize the contribution to Kathi and has reached Kathi's 415(c) limit each year. The company made a 20 percent contribution yesterday on behalf of all employees. The employee census and account balances are as follows:

EMPLOYEE	OWNERSHIP	COVERED COMPENSATION	CURRENT BALANCE	NONVESTED PLAN BALANCE	VESTED PLAN BALANCE
Kathi	100%	$210,000	$201,000	$0	$201,000
Darrin	0%	$30,000	$15,600	$10,800	$4,800
Carroll	0%	$20,000	$8,000	$6,400	$1,600
Lee	0%	$20,000	$8,000	$6,400	$1,600
Total	100%	$280,000	$232,600	$23,600	$209,000

Today, after a huge blow up, Kathi fired Carroll. Which of the following statements regarding forfeitures is correct (assume the plan meets all necessary testing requirements)?

    a. If the plan document permitted allocation of forfeitures based on compensation, then Kathi would receive $4,770.91 of Carroll's unvested plan balance.

    b. If the plan document permitted reduction of plan contributions for forfeitures, Carroll's $8,000 balance could be used to offset future plan contributions.

    c. Since Kathi fired Carroll, Carroll becomes 100 percent vested in her plan assets and there is no forfeiture of plan assets.

    d. Given the company census and plan information, the appropriate plan choice for forfeitures is to use them to reduce plan contributions.

6. Skatium, the city's most popular roller skating rink, has a profit sharing plan for their employees. Skatium has the following employee information:

EMPLOYEE	AGE	LENGTH OF SERVICE
Brett	62	14 years
Greer	57	14 years
Jennifer	32	6 months
Dan	22	3 years
Karen	19	3 years
Mike	17	6 months
Craig	16	1 year

The plan requires the standard eligibility and the least generous graduated vesting schedule available. The plan is not top-heavy. All of the following statements are correct except:

  false

a. Dan and Karen are 20 percent vested in their benefits.

b. Brett and Karen became 100 percent vested when they had been employed for five years.

c. Three of the seven people are eligible to participate in the plan.

d. Craig is eligible for the plan but is not yet vested in any benefits.

7. Which of the following statements is true regarding CODAs?

a. A 401(k) can only be established as a stand alone plan.

b. A CODA is allowed with a profit-sharing plan, stock bonus plan, and a cash balance pension plan.

c. Contributions can only be made after-tax.

d. CODAs are employee self-reliance plans.

8. All of the following are advantages of a 401(k) plan except:

a. Employees are permitted to shelter current income from taxation in a 401(k) plan.

b. Employers can sponsor 401(k) safe harbor plans without committing to annual contributions and without creating a deferred liability.

c. Earnings grow tax-deferred until distributed.

d. Employers can establish 401(k) plans with minimal expense.

9. Which of the following entities is unable to establish a 401(k) plan?

a. Government entity.

b. LLC.

c. Partnership.

d. Tax-exempt entity.

10. Ansley's Art Gallery has a profit sharing plan. The plan requires employees to be employed two years before they can enter the plan. The plan has two entrance dates per year, January and July 1st. Assume today is December 1, 2007 and the Gallery has the following employee information.

EMPLOYEE	AGE	START DATE
Ansley	42	1/1/2005
Ginny	37	5/1/2005
Max	31	8/12/2005
Alex	29	6/4/2006

Which of the following statements is true?

    a.   As of today, three individuals have entered the plan.

    b.   Ginny entered the plan on 5/1/2006.

    c.   Alex will enter the plan on 1/1/2008.

    d.   As of today, three individuals are eligible for the plan.

11. Which of the following is true regarding negative elections?

    1.   A negative election is a device where the employee is deemed to have elected a specific deferral unless the employee specifically elects out of such election in writing.

    2.   Negative elections are no longer approved by the IRS.

    3.   Negative elections are only available for employee's who enter the plan when it is first established and are not available for new employees.

    a.   1 only.

    b.   1 and 2.

    c.   2 and 3.

    d.   1, 2, and 3.

12. Rex, age 47, an employee at Water Waste, is considering contributing to a 401(k) plan during 2005. Which of the following statements are true?

    a.   Rex can potentially make a $18,000 contribution to a 401(k) plan for 2005.

    b.   If Rex does make a contribution, the amount is not subject to income or payroll taxes.

    c.   Rex can also contribute to a 401(k) Roth account in the current year.

    d.   Water Waste must deposit Rex's contribution to the plan as soon as reasonably possible.

13. Tyler's Bike Shop has a 401(k) plan that offers an employer match of dollar-for-dollar up to four percent of employee deferral contributions. Although the plan provides for the least generous graduated vesting schedule available, it does allow employees to enter the plan on their hire date. The employee census is as follows:

EMPLOYEE	AGE	COVERED COMP	EMPLOYEE DEFERRAL	YEARS IN PLAN
Tyler	57	$150,000	8.67%	10
Tanya	23	$100,000	Not yet participating	
Timmy	37	$80,000	16.25%	10
Tom	31	$76,000	4.00%	5

Tyler established the plan ten years ago to benefit him and his only employee, his son Timmy. Since then Tyler hired his other son, Tom, and his new wife Tanya. Tyler wanted to establish the 401(k) plan to encourage his children to save for their future. He also wanted a vesting schedule to ensure that they would learn the responsibility of sticking to their employment commitments. The family has come to you for recommendations to help them maximize their plan contributions. Since both of his sons have shown commitment over the past years, Tyler is willing to make some alterations to the plan in order to increase the retirement savings for all of them. Which of the following would not be one of your recommendations?

a. Tyler and Tom should increase their contributions in order to reach the total maximum deferral limit.

b. Tanya should enter the plan and contribute 16 percent.

c. Tom is not 100 percent vested in the employer match, thus he should stay employed at least one more year.

d. Tyler should consider adding a profit sharing contribution to the plan in order to increase the contributions.

14. Sew What, the best seamstress shop in town, sponsors a 401(k) plan. The plan provides a dollar-for-dollar match for employee contributions up to six percent and has immediate vesting for all contributions. For ADP purposes, the company has made the top 20 percent election for the determination of who is highly compensated. The company has the following employee information:

Employee	Ownership	Compensation	Elective Deferral	Deferral Percentage
Lois	93%	$201,000	$14,000	6.97%
Frank	5%	$150,000	$14,000	9.33%
Karen	2%	$100,000	$9,000	9.00%
Jeanette	-	$40,000	$4,000	10.00%
Joyce	-	$30,000	-	0.00%
Ronnie	-	$30,000	$1,800	6.00%
Kali	-	$30,000	-	0.00%

Which of the following statements is correct?

   a. Lois, Frank, and Karen are all highly compensated.
   b. The plan passes the ADP test.
   c. Joyce and Kali are not considered when calculating the ADP test because they do not contribute.
   d. Assuming Sew What has made the necessary safe harbor elections, the ADP is irrelevant.

15. Pandora's Box, a shop that specializes in custom trinket and storage boxes, has a 401(k) plan. The plan allows plan loans up to the legal limit allowed by law and they may be repaid under the most generous repayment schedule available by law. The plan has the following employee information:

EMPLOYEE	401(K) BALANCE	OUTSTANDING LOAN
Karen	$400,000	$0
Teddy	$250,000	$30,000
Josh	$75,000	$0
Justin	$15,000	$0

Which of the following statements is correct?

   a. If Teddy quit today, state law requires that he repay the loan within five days.
   b. The maximum Karen can borrow from her account is $200,000.
   c. The maximum Justin can borrow from his account is $10,000.
   d. If Josh wanted to borrow money from his plan for the purchase of a personal residence, he would have to pay the loan back within five years.

16. BigCorp, LLC has a 401(k) plan that allows for hardship distributions. Sandra would like to return to school to get a Masters degree. She has $3,000 in her savings account to use, but would like to take a hardship distribution from her 401(k) plan for the maximum amount available. Sandra's program will take two years and cost $7,000 per year. Sandra's 401(k) account balance is $20,000. Sandra has never made any hardship distributions and her elective contributions to the plan total $10,000. How much can Sandra withdraw as a hardship distribution?

   a. $4,000.

   b. $7,000.

   c. $10,000.

   d. $20,000.

17. ABS Company has three employees: Ann, Brenda, and Curtis. There compensations are $50,000, $150,000, and $200,000 respectively. ABC is considering establishing a straight 10% profit sharing plan or an Integrated profit sharing plan using a 10% contribution for base compensation and 15.7% for excess compensation. Which of the following statements are correct?

   a. If the integrated plan is selected, then the total contribution for all employees is $49,690.

   b. The effect of the integrated plan results in an increase in Brenda's contribution of $6,270.

   c. If the integrated plan is selected, the base contribution for all employees is $40,000.

   d. If the integrated plan is selected, Curtis's total contribution is $37,270.

Stock Bonus Plans and Employee Stock Ownership Plans

INTRODUCTION

As discussed in the previous chapter, profit sharing plans allow employers to make contributions to a qualified plan on behalf of employees of the organizations or companies. In some instances, an organization or company may wish to establish a qualified plan, in particular, a profit sharing plan, but are unable to contribute large amounts of cash due to internal growth needs. In this instance, both stock bonus plans and employee stock ownership plans (ESOPs) are available.

A **stock bonus plan** is a plan established and maintained by an employer to provide benefits similar to those of a profit sharing plan.[1] While the contributions by the employer are similar in deductibility to a profit sharing plan, a stock bonus plan is not necessarily dependent upon profits. Both contributions to and distributions paid from a stock bonus plan are generally in the form of the employer corporation's stock. Thus, a stock bonus plan does not require the corporation to use currently needed cash flow. For purposes of allocating and distributing the stock of the employer, which is to be shared among the employees or their beneficiaries, such a plan is subject to the same basic qualified plan requirements as a profit sharing plan.

An **Employee Stock Ownership Plan (ESOP)** is a qualified plan that invests primarily in "qualifying employer securities," typically shares of stock in the corporation creating the plan.[2] ESOPs were first enacted into federal legislation in 1974 under ERISA. At the time, Congress wanted to give employers an incentive to provide rank-and-file employees an ownership stake in the corporation for which they worked. Consequently, Congress established laws creating the stock bonus plan and ESOP to give qualified plans an incentive to invest primarily in employer securities. This chapter discusses both the stock bonus plan and the ESOP in detail.

1.   The term "stock bonus plan" is defined in the Treasury Regulations at Section 1.401-1(b)(1)(iii).
2.   29 U.S.C. Section 1107 (d)(6)(A).

	2005	2006	2007	2008
ESOP Account Balance	$850,000	$870,000[†]	$890,000[†]	$910,000[†]
Covered Compensation	$210,000	$215,000[†]	$220,000[†]	$225,000[†]

STOCK BONUS PLANS

Stock bonus plans are defined contribution profit sharing plans that allow employers to make contributions of stock to a qualified plan on behalf of their employees. As with all qualified plans, earnings within a stock bonus plan are not taxed until the stock, its value in cash, or other securities are distributed from the plan. Because stock bonus plans are not subject to mandatory funding, contributions can and generally are made on a discretionary basis. However, when contributions are made, they must be made to participant's accounts on a nondiscriminatory basis. The contributions cannot discriminate against the **rank-and-file employees** for the benefit of shareholders, officers, and highly compensated employees. Thus, a stock bonus plan is a variation of a profit sharing plan yet has some distinct differences from other profit sharing plans.

Generally, stock bonus plans must satisfy the following requirements:[1]

- Participants must have pass through voting rights on employer stock that is held by the plan.[2]
- Participants must have the right to demand employer securities on plan distributions.
- Participants must have the right to demand that the employer repurchase the employer's securities if they are not publicly traded (the put option).[3]
- Distributions must begin within one year of normal retirement age, death, or disability, or within five years for other modes of employment termination.
- Distributions must be fully paid within five years of commencement of distributions.[4]

ADVANTAGES AND DISADVANTAGES OF STOCK BONUS PLANS

Stock bonus plans are profit sharing plans for which an employer makes contributions of employer stock on behalf of a participant to a qualified plan as part of the employee's overall compensation package. Similar to profit sharing plans, stock bonus plans are designed to provide benefits to both employers and to employees. The fair market value of the contributions of the employer stock are tax deductible to the employer, which can result in decreased income tax costs for the corporation. The contributions are not required to be fixed in amount as there is no annual mandatory contribution requirement for stock bonus plans, which allows the corporation flexibility in funding. Stock bonus plans also promote productivity within the corporation

---

1. IRC Sections 401(a)(22) and 401(a)(23).
2. IRC Section 409(e).
3. IRC Section 409(h).
4. IRC Section 409(o).

because participants, as shareholders, have a vested financial interest in the growth and success of the corporation (although this does not always lead to an increase in stock prices).

While the advantages of stock bonus plans are attractive, stock bonus plans do have drawbacks. To the employee, there is the risk associated with the non-diversified investment portfolio. The employee earns income from the employer and also has an investment in the stock of the employer. In other words, if the corporation were to fail, the entire value in the employee retirement accounts may be lost as well as the employee's job and source of income (wages). Additionally, the ownership and control of the corporation is diminished or "**diluted**" as shares are granted to the employees. This has a greater impact on smaller, closely-held corporations.

With stock bonus plans, the required "**repurchase option**" (**put option**) could deplete the cash of the corporation. A repurchase option allows a terminating employee the choice to receive the cash equivalent of the employer's stock if the stock is not readily tradeable on an established market. If the repurchase occurs at an unexpected time (i.e. death of participant), the forced sale of stock back to the corporation may drain the corporations cash flow as well as result in a costly appraisal of the stock to determine the value to pay the employee-participant's heirs. In such a situation, the strain on the cash flow of the employer may have a negative impact on the corporation as a whole.

Key Concepts

Underline/highlight the answers to these questions as you read:

1. List the requirements of a stock bonus plan.

2. What are the advantages and disadvantages of a stock bonus plan?

3. What are the main differences between a stock bonus plan and a profit sharing plan?

4. Why are valuations performed for stock bonus plans?

FEATURES OF STOCK BONUS PLANS AS COMPARED TO PROFIT SHARING PLANS

As discussed above, stock bonus plans are a particular type of profit sharing plans and share many characteristics. Thus, the features of stock bonus plans will be discussed in relation to profit sharing plans in order to identify the similarities and differences between the two types of plans.

Contributions and Deductions

As with all qualified plans, stock bonus plans and profit sharing plans must be established by December 31st of the year for which the employer will be contributing to the plan. Meanwhile, contributions can be made to the plan as late as the due date of the tax return, including permitted extensions.

Contributions to stock bonus plans and profit sharing plans are **discretionary** but must meet the general profit sharing plan requirement of "**substantial and recurring**". While most contributions to stock bonus plans are tied to the corporation's profitability, there is no requirement that a corporation must contribute to the plan in a year in which it has earnings nor is there a prohibition against contributions to the plan in years in which the corporation has losses.

Quick Quiz

Highlight the answer to these questions:

1. A stock bonus plan is a particular type of profit sharing plan, so they share many characteristics.
   a. True
   b. False

2. A valuation of an employer's securities is performed only at the creation of the stock bonus plan.
   a. True
   b. False

3. A stock bonus plan may require an employee to attain six years of service before considering the employee eligible.
   a. True
   b. False

True, False, False.

Like profit sharing plans, stock bonus plans have a deductible contribution limit of 25 percent of covered compensation (limited to $210,000 for 2005, $215,000[†] for 2006).[1] When stock is contributed, the fair market value of the stock, as determined by a qualified appraiser, is deductible. In some instances, an employer may contribute more than the permitted 25 percent, in which case the employer would deduct the 25 percent and could carry forward the amount which exceeds the 25 percent limit and deduct the excess in a future year. However, the amount carried forward when added to the contribution made for the future year cannot exceed 25 percent, and the employer must pay a 10 percent excise tax on the portion of the contribution that exceeds 25 percent of covered compensation for the current year.

Valuation of Employer Stock in Stock Bonus Plans

An important area of plan administration for a stock bonus plan is the valuation or appraisal of the employer's securities. Valuations are performed to determine the value of the contribution for the corporation's tax deduction purposes and the corporation's financial statements. Valuations are also completed to periodically inform the participants of the stock's value. The employer will track the value of the contributions and therefore the amount of ordinary income that the employee will have to recognize upon distribution. A valuation also allows the employee to determine the sales price of the stock if he is exercising the repurchase option (put option).

For private or closely-held corporations, determining the value of securities is often very difficult. The law requires valuations of employers' securities and if those securities are not readily tradable on an established securities market, then these valuations must be undertaken by independent appraisers.[2] The appraiser must be an uninterested, independent party. The valuation must be done in good faith and must be based on all factors relevant to determining the securities' fair market value.[3] The valuation therefore involves an assessment of what a willing buyer would pay to a willing seller for the securities or business. These valuations are used on an annual basis for determining the value of the securities, that, for example, were contributed by the employer for tax deduction purposes or that were subjected to a repurchase option of a departing employee.

---

1. IRC Section 404(a)(3).
2. IRC Section 401 (a)(28)(C).
3. Regulations Section 54.4975-11(d)(5). See also *Donovan v. Cunningham* 541 ESOPs 246 (S.D. Texas 1982).

Eligibility

Stock bonus plans are subject to the standard eligibility rules as discussed in Chapter 3, the same as other qualified plans, including profit sharing plans. The standard eligibility of age 21 and one-year of service generally applies to stock bonus plans. As discussed before, plan sponsors could relax the eligibility requirements.

Like other qualified plans, stock bonus plans may require a two year waiting period before the employee is eligible. However, if the employer requires a two year waiting period, then all contributions must be 100 percent vested after the two year waiting period.

Key Concepts

Underline/highlight the answers to these questions as you read:

1. Define net unrealized appreciation.

2. What is the advantage to an employee of receiving a stock distribution from a stock bonus plan rather than receive the distribution in cash?

Allocation Methods

The allocation methods for contributions to participants' accounts in stock bonus plans are the same as those for profit sharing plans. The difference is that normally employer stock is contributed to the stock bonus plan rather than cash.

The standard allocation method for a stock bonus plan is to allocate contributions based on a percentage of each employee's compensation. Whenever stock is contributed, the stock must be valued by a qualified appraiser as discussed previously. Cash is generally only contributed when the plan expects cash distribution elections or the plan needs cash to meet its obligation to provide a market for the stock.

The percentage of compensation method is not the only acceptable allocation method for stock bonus plans. The formulas discussed for profit sharing plans based on age and past service also apply to stock bonus plans, as does the new comparability plan based on the employee's respective classification in the corporation. These methods apply as long as they do not discriminate in favor of highly compensated employees. As discussed in Chapter 5, stock bonus plans are also permitted to use the technique or method of permitted disparity, also known as Social Security Integration, which allocates plan contributions to employees' accounts and provides greater contributions to those employees whose earnings exceed the Social Security wage base.

Vesting

Similar to profit sharing plans, the vesting rules for stock bonus plans are the same as for other qualified plans as discussed in Chapter 3. The standard five-year cliff vesting schedules and the graduated 3 to 7 year vesting schedules apply unless the plan is top-heavy or if the employer selects a two year eligibility rule. If the plan is top heavy, the vesting period is reduced to a three-year cliff or a 2 to 6 year graduated vesting schedule. The plan sponsor may not exceed these vesting requirements yet is always permitted to be more generous if desired.

Portfolio Diversification

Profit sharing plans are generally designed to invest in **diversified investment portfolios**. Consequently, they are not normally invested exclusively in employer stock. Unlike profit sharing plans, stock bonus plans are usually funded with one hundred percent of the employer's stock. Profit sharing plans assist the employee in preparing for retirement through the growth of the individual participant's account with deferred compensation and tax deferral on earnings. As such, these plans are generally well diversified investment portfolios. In contrast, stock bonus plans are initially "cash free" to the employer as they are predominately funded with the employer's stock in order to provide benefits to employees without the need to use the corporation's cash. The exclusive use of employer stock as contributions results in an undiversified portfolio for the participant.

Voting Rights

If a profit sharing plan consists of employer stock, the plan participant generally does not have voting rights in the stock held by the plan. However, participants in a stock bonus plan must have pass through voting rights on employer stock that is held by the plan on their behalf. **"Pass through" voting rights** mean that the voting rights of the stock pass through from the plan all the way down to the participant. In this case, the participant could vote the shares of stock allocated to his stock bonus plan account. There are exceptions for closely-held corporations to limit voting to only those matters that are material. Also, unallocated shares are usually voted by the trustee. Unallocated shares are those shares in the trust that have not yet been allocated to individual participants.

Distributions

Stock bonus plan distributions are generally made in the form of employer stock. The distribution of stock provides additional income tax benefits because there is a deferral of income tax on the stock's appreciated value until the stock is later sold. Although the stock in the stock bonus plan is usually distributed to the employee, the plan may provide the employee with the choice of receiving the cash equivalent of the shares of stock at the time of distribution. However, if a cash equivalent is received, the deferral of income tax on the stock's appreciated value until the stock is sold is lost.

Generally, stock bonus plans do not permit employees to receive in-service withdrawal distributions from the plan except upon termination, hardship, disability, or retirement. However, stock bonus plans may permit, but are not required to allow, in-service withdrawals after a participant attains two years of participation in the plan. Similar to profit sharing plans, employee/participant loans are available from a stock bonus plan if the plan permits and the loans are available in a nondiscriminatory manner. Generally, employers choose not to permit loans from stock bonus plans.

Distributions of employer stock or securities from stock bonus plans are taxed depending on whether the distribution is a lump-sum distribution or an installment distribution. The employee is subject to ordinary income tax in the year of the distribution based on the securities' fair market value at the time of the contribution if there is a lump-sum distribution. The net unrealized appreciation (NUA) of the stock (i.e., the appreciation of the stock while being held in the plan) is not taxed at the time of the distribution but rather is taxed as a long-term capital gain when the stock is ultimately sold (discussed below).

On the other hand, if the distribution of the employer stock or securities is made in installments, the employee may only defer recognition of the appreciation on the stock purchased with after-tax employee contributions. Therefore, the fair market value of all employer securities distributed in the installment distribution attributable to employer contributions will be taxable as ordinary income; whereas, only the cost of the employer securities attributable to any after-tax employee contributions will be subjected to ordinary income tax and any appreciation will be taxed as capital gain at the ultimate date of disposition.[1]

Distributions may be subject to the 10 percent early withdrawal penalty if the participant is under the age of 59½. Distributions of stock may also be rolled into an IRA account or to another qualified plan that accepts stock and is willing to accept the rollover. Note that if the employer securities are rolled over to another tax-advantaged account, the ability to benefit from the NUA treatment is lost.

Net Unrealized Appreciation (NUA)

One of the principal benefits of stock bonus plans is net unrealized appreciation (NUA) treatment. **Net unrealized appreciation** is the appreciation in the value of employer stock from the time of contribution to the plan until the time that the stock is distributed to the plan participant. The NUA of the stock (i.e., the gain while being held in the plan) is not taxed as ordinary income at the time of the distribution, but rather is taxed as a capital gain when the stock is sold. The value of the stock at the date of contribution is taxable as ordinary income at the date of distribution.

---

1. IRC Section 402(e)(4)(A).

EXAMPLE 6.1	John is 65 years old. Over his career while working at ABC Corporation (a privately held corporation), he received stock contributions of ABC Corporation to his stock bonus plan. ABC's tax deduction was $20,000, or the combined value of contributions of stock valued at the time of contribution. John decides that he will retire, and he no longer wants to assume the risk that ABC Corporation will remain as an ongoing solvent entity; thus, he decides to take a full distribution from the plan and then sells all of his stock for cash. At distribution, John's ABC stock is valued by an independent appraiser at $100,000. Upon distribution of the stock, John would have $20,000 of ordinary income representing the total value of the employer's contribution. The remaining $80,000 ($100,000 - $20,000) of NUA will be taxed at the time of the sale as a long-term capital gain.

40k

If John sells the stock two years after distribution for $165,000, he will have a basis of $20,000 (the ordinary income recognized at distribution), $80,000 of NUA (long-term capital gain), and $65,000 of long-term capital gain representing the appreciation of the stock since the date of distribution. If the sale occurs before one year and a day, any post distribution appreciation would be taxed as short-term capital gain, but the long-term capital gain on the NUA would not be affected unless the sale was for less than $100,000.

This example not only stresses the tax implications involved, but it also points out that with an investment in ABC Corporation, John assumes the risk that ABC Corporation will continue as a viable entity. If ABC Corporation goes bankrupt or becomes insolvent, John's stock investment could be completely lost or seriously devalued. This investment risk is an important consideration for a participant in a stock bonus plan.

As illustrated, the benefit of NUA treatment is the deferral of taxation on the stock as a capital gain. The employee is taxed at ordinary income rates in the year of distribution only on the value of the securities deducted by the employer at the time of contribution to the plan. The net unrealized appreciation (i.e., the gain of the value of the stock while being held in the plan) is not taxed at the time of distribution but is taxed as a long-term capital gain when the stock is later sold by the participant.[1] In order to receive NUA treatment, there must be a 100 percent lump sum distribution. NUA is discussed in more detail in Chapter 7.

---

1. IRC Section 402(e)(4)(B); see also *Villarroel v. Commissioner*, 1998-247 T.C. Memo (1988), aff'd, 202 F.3d 271 (6th Cir. 2000).

	Stock Bonus Plans	Profit Sharing Plans
Plan Establishment	December 31	December 31
Date of Contribution	Due date of tax return plus extensions	Due date of tax return plus extensions
Type of Contributions	*Generally stock*	*Generally cash*
Deductible Contribution Limit	25% of covered compensation	25% of covered compensation
Valuation	*Generally needed annually*	*Generally unnecessary*
Eligibility	Same as other Qualified Plans (age 21 and 1 year of service or 2 years with 100% vesting)	Same as other Qualified Plans (age 21 and 1 year of service or 2 years with 100% vesting)
Allocation Method	% of compensation or formula based on age, service of classification	% of compensation or formula based on age, service of classification
Vesting	Same as other Qualified Plans (5-year cliff or 3 to 7 year graduated vesting unless top heavy)	Same as other Qualified Plans (5-year cliff or 3 to 7 year graduated vesting unless top heavy)
Portfolio Diversification	*No*	*Generally yes*
Voting Rights	*Generally yes*	*Generally no*
Type of Distributions	*Generally in stock*	*Generally in cash*
In-Service Withdrawals	May be allowed after two years	May be allowed after two years
Loans	May be allowed (but not usually)	May be allowed (but not usually)
Taxation of Distributions	*Ordinary income to the extent of employer deduction and NUA treatment available for lump sum distributions*	*Generally full distribution is ordinary income*

* Differences are highlighted in blue.

EMPLOYEE STOCK OWNERSHIP PLANS

Employee Stock Ownership Plans, referred to as ESOPs, are stock bonus plans for corporations that reward employees with both ownership in the corporation and substantial tax advantages. An ESOP is controlled through a trust. The sponsor company receives tax deductions for contributions of stock from the corporation. The ESOP then allocates the stock to separate accounts for the benefit of individual employee-participants.

Employee ownership in the context of ESOPs refers to ownership in the stock of the corporation through an employee benefit plan by most or all of the corporation's employees. ESOPs provide corporate owners with a way to transfer significant ownership interests to their employees while benefiting from favorable tax advantages. One underlying rationale for promoting employee ownership is that the long term health of the free economy is best served through providing employees with ownership of corporate securities beyond normal salaries and wages. Congress envisioned that ESOPs would function both as "an employee retirement benefit plan and a 'technique of corporate finance' that would encourage employee ownership."[1] Because of these dual purposes, ESOPs are not necessarily designed to guarantee retirement benefits because they place employee retirement assets at greater risk than the usual diversified ERISA qualified plans.[2]

Key Concepts

Underline/highlight the answers to these questions as you read:

1. What are ESOPs and why are they used?

2. List the parties of a typical leveraged ESOP.

3. List the requirements necessary for the owners of a closely-held corporation to qualify for nonrecognition of capital gain at the creation of an ESOP.

4. Discuss three advantages and disadvantages of an ESOP.

A key characteristic of the ESOP is that the trust may borrow money from a bank or other lender to purchase the employer stock. The corporation generally repays the loan through tax deductible contributions to the ESOP. Both the interest and the principal repayments for the loan are income tax deductible. The ESOP can thus be "leveraged." ESOPs with borrowings are referenced as LESOPs, which stands for "Leveraged" Employee Stock Ownership Plans (discussed below). When used in conjunction with financial and estate planning techniques and tax savings strategies, there can be substantial tax and investment benefits gained from utilization of an ESOP. ESOPs are, as one court wrote, "employee benefit plan[s] designed to invest primarily or when certain safeguards are present, solely in securities issued by the sponsoring corporation."

To become eligible for these tax advantages, the ESOP must satisfy various rules of the IRC and of ERISA. Similar to other qualified plans, the ESOP must satisfy applicable rules of employee vesting, participation, eligibility, and coverage. The ESOP must also have a trustee who is charged with a fiduciary duty to handle and maintain the plan in the best interest of plan participants and their beneficiaries.

1. *Martin v. Feilen*, 965 F.2d 660, 664 (8th Cir. 1992), *cert. denied*, 506 U.S. 1054, 113 S.Ct. 979, 122 L.Ed.2d 133 (1993).
2. *Moench v. Robinson,* 62 F.3d 553, 568 (3rd Cir. 1995) (quoting *Martin v. Feilen*, 965 F.2d 660, 664).

EXHIBIT 6.2

According to the National Center for Employee Ownership for 2003:[1]

- There were roughly 11,000 ESOPs in the United States covering more than 8.8 million participants.
- ESOPs controlled about $400 billion in assets.
- Of these ESOPs, roughly 95 percent were for closely-held corporations while about five-percent were for publicly traded corporations.
- The median percentage ownership for ESOPs in public corporations is about 10 percent to 15 percent.
- The median percentage ownership for private corporations is roughly 30 percent to 40 percent, and about 3,000 corporations are now majority employee-owned.
- About one-half of the ESOPs that are used for private firms are used to buy out an owner.
- The other 50 percent use ESOPs primarily as an employee benefit plan and sometimes in conjunction with borrowing money for capital acquisition.

The ESOP Association, which represents approximately 1,300 ESOP corporations, touts the following information concerning ESOPs:[2]

- Approximately 95 percent of the members of the ESOP Association are private, closely-held corporations.
- More than half of the members of the ESOP Association have less than 250 employees, although there are ESOPs in large businesses as well.
- While ESOPs exist in a broad range of industries, roughly 38 percent of the members of the ESOP Association are in manufacturing, followed by 13 percent in distribution.
- The ESOP Association's members had, on average, annual sales revenue ranging from 5 million to 50 million in the year 2000.
- On average, the members of the ESOP Association report that their ESOPs have been in place for at least 10 years.
- Roughly 65 percent of the members of the ESOP Association have corporations that are more than 50 percent owned by the ESOPs.
- Roughly 80 percent of the members of the ESOP Association provide a supplemental benefit plan as well as the ESOP, including 401(k) plans, pension plans, and profit sharing plans.
- Research shows that the implementation of an ESOP results in more information sharing, communications, and involvement in decision making for the employee-owners.
- Roughly 75 percent of the members of the ESOP Association report that motivation and productivity increased as a result of the ESOPs.
- ESOP Association members have, on average, an account balance of $173,224.00.

---

1. For other facts concerning ESOPs, see the informative website of www.nceo.org.
2. See www.esopassociation.org and its resource library for more information. The ESOP Association, founded in 1978, is a national association of corporations with employee stock ownership plans and service providers with a professional commitment to employee ownership through ESOPs. The ESOP Association has a library that is informative and provides much information concerning ESOPs. According to its website, the ESOP Association is the leading voice in America for employee ownership through ESOPs, and devotes considerable time to creating and maintaining favorable ESOPs legislation. Further, the ESOP Association is a prime source for educational materials necessary for successful implementation and administration of an ESOP.

THE ESOP TRANSACTION

The corporation, the principal shareholder of the corporation, the ESOP trust, the trustee or trustees, a lender, and employees are all part of the process of establishing an ESOP. Most ESOPs are leveraged because money must be borrowed to purchase the stock from the principal shareholder. In a **leveraged ESOP**, the corporation makes tax deductible contributions to the trust in the form of both principal and interest for the loan. The trust receives these funds, and the trust, through a trustee, then repays the acquisition loan from a bank or other lender. The trust purchases shares of the corporate stock from the principal shareholder, and these shares are normally pledged as security for the bank loan. The corporation and generally the principal shareholder (seller) guarantee the loan, and the corporation's assets are pledged as collateral for the loan. Prior to the allocation of the actual shares to the participant's account within the trust, the pledged shares are held in a separate holding account and referred to as unallocated.

As the trust repays the bank loan, an appropriate allocation of shares are withdrawn from the holding account and allocated to the account of the individual participant. Once a share of stock has been withdrawn from the holding account, that share may no longer act as pledged collateral for the debt. However, a proportionate amount of the loan was repaid; therefore, there is no need for additional cash or funds from the corporation to maintain the loan. There may, however, be a need for cash if the trust needs or wants to redeem distributed shares.

The following diagram illustrates the various relationships and transactions regarding a leveraged ESOP.

EXHIBIT 6.3	VARIOUS RELATIONSHIPS AND TRANSACTIONS IN A LEVERAGED ESOP

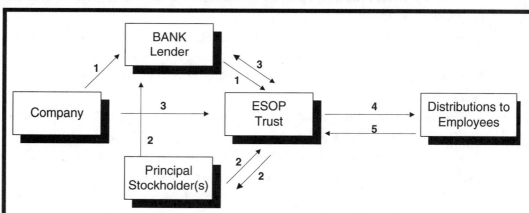

1. Bank loans to ESOP Trust with corporation's guarantee to purchase shares from the stockholders.
2. ESOP Trust buys stock from existing stockholder(s) who generally also guarantee the loan.
3. Corporation contributes annually (tax deductible) to the ESOP Trust, and ESOP Trust repays the bank both principal and interest.
4. Employees obtain stock when they retire or leave corporation (distributions).
5. The trust may have to purchase back "put option" shares from employees who exercise their buy back rights.

Practical Uses of ESOPs and Nonrecognition of Gain Treatment

Most commonly, an ESOP is used to buy the stock of the retiring or departing owner or owners of a closely-held corporation in order to achieve deferral of federal income taxes. The establishment of ESOPs allow owners of closely-held businesses to sell all or part of their interest in the corporation and defer recognition of the capital gain. This is known as **nonrecognition of gain treatment**. This attractive and substantial benefit is created by Section 1042 of the Internal Revenue Code.[1] In order to qualify for nonrecognition of gain treatment, the following requirements apply:[2]

1. The ESOP must own at least 30 percent of the corporation's stock immediately after the sale (notice that the controlling interest may remain owned elsewhere, but if this occurs the ESOP share should have been valued using a minority share discount).
2. The seller or sellers must reinvest the proceeds from the sale into qualified replacement securities (defined below) within 12 months after the sale and hold such securities three years.
3. The corporation that establishes the ESOP must have no class of stock outstanding that is tradable on an established securities market.
4. The seller or sellers, relatives of the seller or sellers, and 25 percent shareholders in the corporation are precluded from receiving allocations of stock acquired by the ESOP through the rollover.
5. The ESOP may not sell the stock acquired through the rollover transaction for three years. The requirement, however, will not apply if the corporation is sold. The three-year period is called a "holding" period, which prevents unnecessary, duplicative roll-overs by the corporation.
6. The stock sold to the ESOP must be common or convertible preferred stock and must have been owned by the seller for at least three years prior to the sale.

If all of these requirements are satisfied, the sellers (usually former principals of the corporation) may reinvest the proceeds from the sale within 12 months of the sale into qualified replacement securities (securities of domestic corporations as defined below), and carry over their former adjusted taxable basis from the corporation into the qualified replacement securities. As long as the seller retains these replacement securities, there will be no taxable event. If the seller later sells some or all of these replacement securities, the seller will have capital gains or losses determined by the carry over basis. If the seller dies, then the seller's heirs (or estate) are entitled to a new adjusted taxable basis equal to the date of death fair market value, thus avoiding capital gains taxation altogether. The nonrecognition of gain treatment is not available to the seller of an S Corporation that establishes an ESOP because IRC Section 1042 only allows owners of closely-held C Corporations to do so.

For the deferral of capital gain recognition to occur, the reinvestment must be made into qualified replacement securities. **Qualified replacement securities** are securities in a domestic corporation, including stocks, bonds, debentures, or warrants, which receive no more than 25 percent of their income from passive investments. The qualified replacement securities can be in the form of stock in an S corporation. However, stock of the corporation that issued the

---

1. IRC Section 1042.
2. *See* IRC Section 1042(c)(3); *see also* Temp. Regulations Section 1.1042-IT, Q and A-3(c).

employer securities (or a corporation that is part of a control group with that corporation) cannot serve as a qualified replacement security.

Advantages and Disadvantages of ESOPs

There are many reasons why the ESOP is the most common type of stock bonus plan. ESOPs benefit the employer-corporation and its participants in various ways. From the corporation's perspective, the ESOP creates a market for the stock of privately held corporations. It is crucial for shareholders to have a market for their stock for financial planning and estate planning issues. The shareholders, often owners who will soon retire, may sell shares to the plan which is a ready and available buyer. Hence, ESOPs are frequently used as estate planning vehicles for closely-held corporations and their owners. Without the ESOP, there may not be a market for the privately held corporate stock. Also, the corporation or trust is allowed to borrow money in order to provide contributions resulting in funds being provided immediately to the ESOP, while the employer repays the loan to the ESOP with tax deductible contributions. Not only do these tax deductions save the corporation cash, the cash flow of the corporation is further strengthened because in the ESOP exchange, the trust allocates shares to the employees' accounts while the corporation is paying cash to the bank (in a leveraged ESOP) and deducting such payments for both principal and interest. By providing employees with a stake in the corporation, employers give economic incentives to employees, which increases motivation and improves employee retention.

Quick Quiz

Highlight the answer to these questions:

1. In a leveraged ESOP, the corporation makes after-tax contributions to a trust on behalf of its employees.
   a. True
   b. False

2. Foreign securities may qualify as qualified replacement securities.
   a. True
   b. False

3. The creation of an ESOP may dilute ownership in the corporation.
   a. True
   b. False

False, False, True.

From the employees' perspective, the ESOP provides them with a type of retirement vehicle. The ESOP provides them with ownership in the corporation where they work, which tends to improve a worker's attitude, motivation, sense of loyalty, and belonging to the corporation. The employee-participant may also benefit from net unrealized appreciation (NUA) at the time of stock distributions because of favorable capital gains rates and deferred recognition.

There are disadvantages to ESOPs as well. First, there is an inherent lack of diversification of the individual "investment" portfolio because ESOPs must invest primarily in the stock of the corporation. As a result, an employee-participant's account is susceptible to fluctuations or drastic drops in the value because of the corporation's stock. This means that a long-time employee who has received large allocations of the stock has significant nondiversified portfolio risk. This risk can be mitigated somewhat for ESOP participants that are at least 55 years of age and who have completed at least 10 years of participation in the plan. This special diversification treatment is discussed later in this chapter.

From the shareholder's perspective, ESOPs "dilute" ownership in the corporation by reducing the concentration of shares from the sellers to broaden the employees holdings. Moreover, the repurchase option for stock that is not readily tradable can create cash flow problems and administrative concerns.[1] With the repurchase option, an employee can force the corporation to repurchase the stock originally issued and distributed to the employee-participant. In addition, the corporation creating the ESOP has substantial costs in setting up the plan, drafting plan documents, and staffing the plan.

Plan administration can also be costly, and the annual appraisals create significant and recurring expenses for closely-held corporations. These appraisals are necessary to determine the value of the tax deduction for the employer and to determine the price that an employer or trust would pay for the repurchase of ESOP distributed shares.

Employer-corporations must also be ready to purchase the shares of departing employees, which can further diminish or stretch the cash flow of a corporation. The lender involved with a leveraged ESOP may also place more scrutiny or requirements upon the employer, especially for annual valuations, which add to administrative costs of the plan.

ADVANTAGES AND DISADVANTAGES OF ESOPS

EXHIBIT 6.4

	Advantages	Disadvantages
Employer	• Creates a market for stock in a private/closely-held corporation • Helps retain employees • Improves employee loyalty • Employer-owners may create a diversified portfolio without recognition of capital gain • Corporation can borrow against stock • Corporation can improve the current cash flow of the corporation by taking a tax deduction on stock contributions	• Dilutes ownership • Administrative costs • May strain employer cash flow to meet pay-out requirements to departing employees at uncertain times • Periodic appraisal costs are expensive • Personal liability concerns for officers or management who also serve as trustees of ESOPs • Creates cash flow uncertainty in the future
Employee	• Acquires ownership in employer corporation • Employees have better perception of or attitude towards employer corporation • Favorable tax treatment on stock distributions (NUA) • Can force employer to repurchase stock at end of employment (put option) • Receives stock as form of compensation	• Employee bears risk of employer's insolvency (nondiversification) • Value of stock subject to appraiser • Stock value subject to fluctuation • Stock not liquid

---

1. See previous Section on Repurchase Option.

VOTING

Generally, ESOP participants have the same rights with their allocated shares as other shareholders, including the right to vote the shares and the right to earn dividends. For public ESOP corporations registered with the Securities and Exchange Commission, participants have full voting rights. However, ESOPs for privately held corporations are not required to provide full voting rights for these shares. The law merely requires that participants possess voting rights on major corporate decisions. Such major corporate decisions are considered to be mergers, acquisitions, consolidation, reclassification, liquidation, dissolution, recapitalization, or sale.

Key Concepts

Underline/highlight the answers to these questions as you read:

1. Explain the voting rights of ESOP participants of public corporations.

2. Discuss the scenario in which the employer's deduction related to an ESOP may exceed 25% of the total covered compensation.

3. If securities are not readily tradable, how is the value of the security determined for purposes of the ESOP contribution?

The trustee of the ESOP votes the shares on behalf of these participants on regular corporate matters beyond those listed above. For stock in a privately held corporation under these circumstances, the IRC allows the plan to authorize the ESOP trustee to vote the stock as one vote for each participant.[1]

ESOP trustees must discharge their duties by evaluating the best interests of the beneficiaries in the abstract as beneficiaries, not as directors who may lose control of the corporation nor should they discharge their duties as employees, some of whom may lose their jobs if control of the corporation changes hands.[2] Courts have commented that it is appropriate for trustees to put aside personal judgment in favor of carrying out the wishes of the trust participants.[3] The trust documents concerning an ESOP must be construed in light of ERISA's policies, and trust documents cannot excuse trustees from their fiduciary duties under ERISA.[4]

CONTRIBUTIONS TO ESOPS

ESOPs can provide generous tax benefits. These tax benefits were created to provide an incentive for employers and corporations to implement ESOPs and build work forces comprised of many employee-owners. Contributions to ESOPs are undertaken by the corporation and are made to the trust though the trustee. The corporation contributes cash or stock to the trust so that the trust can buy new or existing shares. The trust also has the option to borrow funds to buy shares while the corporation makes cash contributions to the plan so that the loan can be repaid. While there are significant tax benefits with ESOPs, there are limitations to contributions to an ESOP.[5] Contributions to ESOPs may be in cash or in the form of employer securities. The employer

---

1. IRC Section 409(e)(3). *See also Schoenholtz v. Doniger*, 657 F.Supp. 899 (S.D.N.Y. 1987).
2. *Danaher Corp. v. Chicago Pneumatic Tool Co.*, 635 F. Supp. 246, 249-250 (S.D.N.Y. 1986).
3. *Id.*
4. *Central States, Southeast and Southwest Areas Pension Fund v. Central Transport*, 472 U.S. 559, 568 (1985).

may deduct the value of the stock contributed and in the process, increase the corporation's cash profits by the taxes avoided.

Employer contributions to ESOPs are deductible by the employer just like any contribution to a qualified profit sharing plan or stock bonus plan, but contributions are subject to the 25 percent limit of covered compensation.[1] However, if the employer's stock is obtained by virtue of a loan (leveraged ESOP), then the permissible deductions for the employer are increased for the interest on the loan. In other words, the employer is allowed to deduct all interest paid on the loan over and above the 25 percent deduction of total eligible payroll of the plan participants.[2] The interest deduction is unlimited.

> If XYZ Corporation contributes 33% of covered compensation to the ESOP for principal and interest on the loan to the ESOP, this entire amount is deductible if 25% was applied to pay principal and 8% was applied to pay for interest payments.

Employers are further allowed tax deductions for dividends paid on stock held by an ESOP under various circumstances. Dividends that are paid in cash for stock purchases with an ESOP securities purchase loan are tax deductible.[3] Dividends, regardless of whether received outright or reinvested, are taxable as current ordinary income to the employee. These cash dividends on stock purchased with an ESOP securities acquisition loan are included in the 25 percent contribution limit for leveraged ESOPs. Also, employers may take a deduction on dividends applied to loan payments to a leveraged ESOP. Finally, if employees voluntarily reinvest dividends in the corporation's stock held by an ESOP, then these dividends are deductible by the employer.

DISTRIBUTIONS

Distributions from ESOPs, much like general stock bonus plans, are largely subject to the same restrictions applicable to distributions from any qualified plan. Therefore, the distribution rules for stock bonus plans discussed earlier in this chapter generally apply to ESOPs as well. The exceptions are discussed below. Aside from the general exceptions, distributions before age 59½, death, disability, or retirement are subject to the 10 percent penalty. There is no requirement for an ESOP or stock bonus plan to provide a joint and survivor annuity or a spousal death benefit.

An ESOP is subject to the minimum distribution requirements of IRC Section 401(a)(9) (as discussed in Chapter 7). However, plan participants can elect to receive substantial equal periodic payments of their account balance not less once per year after the participant separates from service. The substantially equal periodic payments must be for a period no longer than five years, unless the participant's account balance is valued at more than $850,000 for 2005 ($870,000[†] for 2006, $890,000[†] for 2007, and $910,000[†] for 2008), in which case the distribution period

---

5.   Effective January 1, 2002, the Economic Growth And Tax Relief Reconciliation Act of 2001 (EGTRRA 2001), IRC Section 616(c), expanded some tax benefits regarding contributions. Conversely, other areas were limited, including certain allocations to S Corporations.

1.   IRC Section 404 (a)(3).

2.   IRC Section 404(a)(9)(B).

3.   IRC Section 404.

may be extended one year for each additional $170,000 for 2005 ($175,000[†] for 2006, $180,000[†] for 2007, and $185,000[†] for 2008) of account value up to a total of ten years. If the participant's separation from service is due to the participant's attainment of the plan's normal retirement age, death, or disability, these substantially equal periodic payments must begin within one year after the participant's separation from service. If the participant's separation is for any other reason, these substantially equal periodic payments must begin within one year after the fifth year after the participant's separation.[1]

These rules simply provide the plan participant with a level of protection from the plan sponsor spreading out distributions over an extended period of time.

Any distribution from an ESOP that is not a lump distribution of the employer securities will not be eligible to receive NUA treatment and will be taxed as ordinary income. These distributions may also be subjected to the 10 percent early withdrawal penalty unless the distribution complies with one of the exceptions detailed in Chapter 7.

EXAMPLE 6.3

Fred retires, at normal retirement age, from his career with Risky Business in 2005. At his retirement, the value of Fred's ESOP is $400,000. Fred may have several options:

1. The plan may allow Fred to take distributions from the plan at his discretion.
2. The plan may allow Fred to roll over the account balance into an IRA rollover account.
3. Fred may leave the assets in his ESOP until he attains the age of 70 ½, at which time he will be required to begin taking his required minimum distributions.
4. The plan must allow Fred, if he elects, to begin taking annual substantially equal periodic payments in 2006.

In any case, if Fred's distribution is not a lump sum distribution of his employer's securities, the distribution will be taxed as ordinary income.

Valuation of Employer Stock in ESOPs

Valuation of the employer's securities is an important area of ESOP administration. Valuations are necessary for various reasons, which include:

- When contributions are made to an employee's account, the employer must know the value of the contribution for the corporation's tax deduction purposes.
- When contributions are made to an employee's account, the employee must know the value of the contribution for future NUA calculation.
- If a lender lends money to leverage the ESOP, the lender must know the value of the stock to determine if and how much money to lend to the corporation.
- If an employee exercises the put or repurchase option, the value of the stock must be determined.
- Valuations are needed for financial statements and reports.

---

1. IRC Section 409(o)(1).

Valuations for ESOP transactions should be guided by current appraisals by outside, independent valuation experts. Publicly traded stock is readily valued by looking to the stock's market price, whereas determining the value of a closely-held corporation's securities is much more involved and costly. If securities are not readily tradable on an established securities market, then valuations must be undertaken by independent appraisers, who must be uninterested, independent parties.[1] The corporation's lender may also place further requirements on the corporation regarding the valuation of the stock. The valuation must be done in good faith and must be based on all factors relevant to determining the securities' fair market value, resulting in an assessment of what a willing buyer would pay to a willing seller for the securities.[2]

If a valuation is overstated the corporation may be penalized. Any tax deduction based on these valuations can be lost if the value used is later determined to be overstated. Also, if the securities are purchased by the ESOP for an amount higher than their fair market value, then the corporation may be subject to exercise tax.[3] In some extreme cases, the ESOP may be disqualified altogether, losing its status as an ESOP and as a qualified plan. If the trustee is found to have caused the ESOP to buy stock at a price greater than its fair market value, the trustee may be deemed to have violated his fiduciary obligations and can be personally liable to the ESOP participants for the amount of the overpayment.

ERISA requires the ESOP to purchase the stock using an "**adequate consideration**" standard. Adequate consideration has been defined as fair market value determined in good faith.[4] **Fair market value** in the context of fiduciary breaches in ERISA cases has been defined as "the price that a willing buyer would pay a willing seller, both having reasonable knowledge of the pertinent facts."

Quick Quiz

Highlight the answer to these questions:

1. The majority of ESOPs are established by publicly traded corporations.
   a. True
   b. False

2. ESOPs for privately held corporations are not required to provide full voting rights for shares held in the plan.
   a. True
   b. False

3. Employer contributions to an ESOP are tax deductible.
   a. True
   b. False

4. An ESOP is not subject to the minimum distribution rules.
   a. True
   b. False

False, True, True, False.

---

1.   IRC Section 401 (a)(28)(C).
2.   Regulations Section 54.4975-11(d)(5). See also *Donovan v. Cunningham* 541 ESOPs 246 (S.D. Texas 1982).
3.   Revenue Ruling, 69-494, 1969-2 C.B. 88.
4.   29 U.S.C. Section 1002 (18)(B).

EXAMPLE 6.4

Matthew has owned a toy train business for 30 years. He wants to retire early. The business is worth approximately $10 million. Matthew cannot find a third-party buyer for his business, thus he has been advised to consider the establishment of an ESOP. Matthew hires an appraiser, who values the stock at $10 million. A banker agrees that the corporation is worth approximately $10 million, and the bank lends money to Matthew's train business to establish an ESOP. Matthew can, in effect, sell his stock to the ESOP and receive non-recognition of gain treatment if the ESOP holds the stock for more than three years, the ESOPs owns more than thirty percent (30%) of the stock, and Matthew purchases qualified replacement property within twelve months of the sale.

In the scenario above, Matthew was able to eliminate his concentrated portfolio and was also able to reduce his business risk in the train corporation by diversifying his portfolio without incurring taxation and related costs. Matthew was also able to align the economic incentives of the employees to that of the business by making employees part owners in the train business. Unfortunately, both Matthew and the corporation will probably be required by the bank to be guarantors of the loan to the trust; thus, Matthew will retain some risk until the loan is repaid.

EXAMPLE 6.5

Assume the same facts as above except that Matthew has an adjusted taxable basis of $300,000 in the corporation, and he sells seventy percent (70%) of his stock in the corporation to the ESOP and uses those funds to obtain a diversified portfolio of common stock by purchasing $1 million of stock in corporations A, B, C, D, E, F, and G ($1 million for each), for a total of $7 million. The basis of the $7 million is $210,000 (70% of $300,000). The qualified replacement property is all stock in domestic corporations. Assume that after the transactions and within applicable time periods, Matthew sells stock A for $1.5 million and sells stock B for $850,000. What is the tax treatment for the sale of A and B?

Matthew will be taxed once Matthew sells the stock. His adjusted taxable basis is his "carry over basis" in the original shares of stock. The basis in stock A is $30,000, 1/7th of 70% of $300,000. With an adjusted taxable basis of $30,000, the first $30,000 is a return of basis. The remaining $1,470,000 is taxed as a long-term capital gain. As for stock B, his adjusted taxable basis again is $30,000, 1/7th of 70% of $300,000. The first $30,000 is a return of basis, while the remaining $820,000 ($850,000 - $30,000) is taxed as a long-term capital gain.

EXAMPLE 6.6

Assume that Matthew bequeaths stock in corporations C, D, and E to Michael, his brother. At the time of Matthew's death, the stock in C, D, and E were worth $2 million each. If Michael inherits and then sells these stocks, what would his basis be?

With capital assets, there is a "step to fair market value" or an adjustment to fair market value of the adjusted taxable basis at the time of death. The "step up" in this case occurs at death, and Matthew's original adjusted taxable basis $300,000 is not taken into account. Therefore, Michael's (the heir of the stock) basis would be $2 million dollars for each stock C, D, and E.

DIVERSIFICATION ISSUES

ESOPs are permitted to hold 100 percent of the corporate stock in the trust. Most, if not all, of the stock in the ESOP trust is stock in the corporation where the employee-participant works. If the corporation files for bankruptcy or becomes insolvent, then the employee-participant will likely lose his entire investment. Employees with corporate stock in ESOPs are prohibited from selling their shares to diversify their holdings while employed unless they meet certain requirements. Under the IRC, qualified participants may force diversification of their holdings if they are at least 55 years old and have completed at least 10 years of participation in the ESOP.[1]

If the participant meets these qualification requirements, the ESOP must provide the participant with either the opportunity to receive a distribution from the ESOP or alternative investment options for a percentage of his account. The qualified participant must be offered a diversification election within 90 days

Key Concepts

Underline/highlight the answers to these questions as you read:

1. Under what circumstances can an ESOP participant require the employer to diversify his holdings?

2. When must a closely-held corporation provide a put option to the participants of an ESOP?

3. Explain the inherent conflict of interest within an ESOP.

4. Discuss the impact of an S Corporation ESOP participant demanding a stock distribution.

after the close of each plan year beginning with the year after the employee becomes qualified. The participant may elect to diversify up to 25 percent of the account balance into non-employer stock at this time. The election to diversify is cumulative; therefore, if an election is made to diversify 10 percent of the assets in the first eligible year, an election could be made to diversify

---

1.   IRC Section 401(a)(28).

an additional 15 percent of the account balance the following year. The final election year is the year before normal retirement age as determined by the plan document. In the final election year, the cumulative diversifiable percentage is increased to 50 percent.[1] The plan documents may satisfy the requirements of diversification of investments if the plan documents offer at least three investment options (consistent with regulations prescribed under the Internal Revenue Code, e.g., a cash fund, a bond fund, and a stock fund) to each participant making a diversification election. Within 90 days after the period during which the election was chosen, the plan must invest the portion of the participant's account covered by the election.[2]

<table>
<tr><td>EXAMPLE 6.7</td><td>Kerstin is a participant in Smith Corporation's ESOP. Kerstin has been with the company for 20 years. Kerstin turns 55 this year. The ESOP must allow Kerstin to diversify up to 25% of her account balance for the current year. Assume she has the plan diversify 15% for the current year, next year she could diversify the remaining 10% allowed for a total of 25%.

Assume the plan defines the normal retirement age as 60 years old. In the year that Kerstin turns 59, she will be able to diversify an additional 25%, bringing her total diversified portion to 50%. This allows her to minimize her exposure to the business risk resulting from her concentrated position.</td></tr>
</table>

PUT OPTIONS

Once a plan meets the distribution requirements and a participant is entitled to a distribution from the plan, the participant has the right to demand that the benefits be distributed in the form of employer securities. If the employer securities are not readily tradable on an established market, the participant has the right to require that the employer repurchase the employer securities under a fair market valuation formula. This is referred to as a "**put option**" or "**repurchase option**" under ESOPs.

The put or repurchase option is a substantial benefit to an employee-participant of an ESOP. A closely-held or private corporation that sponsors an ESOP must provide for a "put option" on corporate stock that is distributed to employee-participants.[3] The rank-and-file employees are protected with the put option because the employee may force the corporation to "buy back" the stock at the fair market value when there otherwise would be no market for the stock. If no put option is provided, then the corporation could choose not to purchase the departing employee's stock, leaving the employee with stock that he cannot sell or liquidate. Indeed, this rule applies to closely-held or private corporations because the inherent nature of closely-held or private corporations is that there is no readily established securities market for the stock. ESOPs may offer the right of first refusal to the corporation to buy back the stock from participants to prevent the stock from being owned and controlled by outside entities. At a minimum, the put

---

1.   IRC Section 401(a)(28).
2.   IRC Section 401(a)(28)(B)(ii).
3.   IRC Section 409(h).

option must be available during two time periods, one for no less than sixty (60) days immediately following the distribution and second, if the put option is not exercised within such 60-day period, for an additional period of at least 60 days in the following plan year.[1]

If a corporation is forced to repurchase the stock that was distributed to the employee as part of a total distribution,[2] then the corporation's repurchasing of that stock under a fair valuation formula[3] is satisfied if the corporation pays the participant in substantial equal periodic payments over a period beginning no later than 30 days after the exercise of the put option. However, this periodic payment must not be paid less frequently than annually and must be completed within five years.[4] For periodic repayments, reasonable interests and adequate security must be given.[5] If a put option is exercised after an installment distribution of the employer stock, then the employer must repurchase the stock within 30 days to fulfill the put option.[6]

<table>
<tr><td>

Michael, an employee of KAC corporation, receives a stock distribution of ten shares of stock in KAC corporation on October 10, 2003 as a participant of an ESOP. KAC is a closely-held corporation. If Michael exercises his put option ninety days after distribution, is KAC corporation required to honor his put option?

The answer is initially no, but ultimately yes. Michael must exercise his put option within 60 days following the distribution according to IRC Section 409(h)(4); however, IRC Section 409(h)(4) also provides an additional 60 day period in the following plan year, which would start on January 1, 2004 and continue through February 29, 2004, and thus Michael's exercise of his put option would be timely under IRC Section 409(h)(4) with respect to the additional 60 days within the following taxable year of the plan.

</td><td>

EXAMPLE 6.8

</td></tr>
</table>

---

1. IRC Section 409(h)(4).
2. Total distribution is defined as the distribution within one tax year of the balance of the recipient's account. IRC Section 409 (h) (5).
3. IRC Section 409(h)(1)(B).
4. IRC Section 409(h)(5), 409(h)(5)(A) and 409(h)(5)(B).

Case Study 1

The case of *Roth v. Sawyer-Cleaton Lumber Co.*,[1] dealt with the ESOP trustees' decisions concerning put options. Roth was a former employee of Sawyer-Cleaton, a closely-held corporation engaged in lumber sales. Under the corporation's ESOP plan documents, each participant had one account consisting of corporation stock and another consisting of other investments, and participants could exercise a put option on stock issued. At the time of Roth's retirement in 1988, Roth chose to exercise his put option. The stock sale was accomplished through a promissory note and stock pledge agreement. The Plan obligated itself to make payments to Roth over ten years with Roth retaining a security interest in his stock under the stock pledge agreement. Roth received partial payment of the sums due under the promissory note, but the corporation began to experience financial troubles. In 1990, the corporation terminated its business operations, and the Plan defaulted on payments due under the promissory note.

By 1991, the corporation was forced into Chapter 7 bankruptcy and Roth's stock and security became worthless.[2] Roth sued the ESOP and its trustees, claiming breach of fiduciary duty because of the failure to adequately secure notes given from the Plan and the assumption of the notes by the Plan. The court ultimately concluded that Roth's loss was caused by the trustees' decision to secure the plaintiff's promissory note with corporation stock and to make the ESOP the obligated party on the plaintiff's notes. Therefore, the trustees in that case could be liable for breach of fiduciary duty.[3]

---

1.   *Roth v. Sawyer-Cleaton Lumber Co.*, 61 F.3d 599 (8th Cir. 1995).
2.   *Roth*, 61 F.3d 599, 601.
3.   *Id*. at 605.

THE ESOP TRUSTEE AND "INHERENT" CONFLICTS

The ESOP is created by written plan documents, which are responsible for the establishment of the trust. The plan sponsor establishes the plan and the trust, and in some cases the trust borrows from a bank or other type of lender. The tax deductible contributions are paid to the trust, and in some cases the trust repays funds to the bank or lender. Under this complicated set of transactions, the trust must use the loan proceeds to acquire the employer stock. The trust is administered by the trustee, who, depending on the specific plan and the documents creating it, is an individual, a group of individuals, committee, or entity.[1] The trustee holds funds "in trust" for the benefit of employees, participants, and their beneficiaries. The trustee purchases employer

---

5.   IRC Section 409(h)(5)(B).
6.   IRC Section 409(h)(6).
1.   Interestingly, the corporation may have its own ESOP committee that is part of the corporation and not the ESOP, and the ESOP committee could have been charged with establishing and drafting the documents that formed the ESOP and its trustee.

securities, deals with the corporation, interacts with the bank or lender, and keeps the employee-participants apprised of the status and value of their accounts. In addition to all of these duties, the ESOP trustee must strive to preserve the ESOP's fundamental goal of investing plan assets into employer securities. The trustee is held to the standard of a fiduciary.

There are times where the interests of the employees, the interests of the corporation, and the interests of the management of the corporation are different or even at odds. Often times, the trustee is forced to navigate these complicated and perplexing issues and bear the brunt of criticism or claims. There has been much litigation over these issues in the case law.[1] Occasionally, individuals serve in a dual capacity concerning the ESOP, both as trustees of the ESOP and as officers, directors, or employees of the corporation. The corporation is the plan sponsor. A potential conflict of interest exists. Here, as detailed in *Shoen v. Americo, 885 F.Supp. 1332*, the ideal course of action for the trustee could be that "trustees of an [ESOP] must discharge their duties by evaluating the best interest of the beneficiaries in the abstract as beneficiaries, not as directors who may lose control of the corporation nor as employees, some of whom may lose their jobs if control of the corporation changes hands."[2] The courts have generally concluded that if the conflict of interest is so great that it is virtually impossible for the fiduciary to discharge the duties with "an eye to the beneficiaries' interests," then the preferred course of action for a fiduciary of a plan holding or acquiring the stock of a target, who is also an officer, director, or employee of a party in interest seeking to acquire or retain control of the target, is to resign and clear the way for the appointment of a genuinely neutral trustee to manage the assets involved in the control contest.[3]

There are cases in which the conflict of interest, although substantial, is not so great as to require the trustee's resignation. The question in these cases becomes whether the fiduciary engaged in an intensive and independent investigation of options to insure that the action taken was in the shareholders' best interests. One element of this inquiry is the extent to which the use of the trust's assets track the best interest of another party. The bottom line is, considering the duty imposed on the fiduciary under these circumstances, trustees must avoid placing themselves in a position where their acts as officers or directors of the corporation will prevent their functioning with the complete loyalty to participants demanded of them as trustees of the pension plan.[4] For instance, ESOP trustees will probably be found to have breached their fiduciary duties if they form a separate corporation designed to compete with the corporation where they are an ESOP trustee.[5]

The court in the *Shoen* decision also noted a second problem that is common in litigation concerning control of the corporation as it relates to the trustee's duty to monitor communications to participants. ESOPs, the court acknowledged in *Shoen*, typically contain provisions for "pass through" voting by the participants to qualify for favorable tax treatment under IRC Section 409. Basically each participant can direct the ESOP trustees on how to vote

---

1. *See*, for example, *Shoen v. Americo*, 885 F.Supp. 1332, 1348 (D. Nev. 1994); *Chas v. Archer*, 827 F.Supp. 159, 169 (W.D.N.Y. 1993).
2. *Central Trust corporation, N.A. v. American Avents Corp.*, 771 F.Supp. 871, 874-875 (S.D. Ohio 1989).
3. *Danaher Corp. v. Chicago Pneumatic Tool Co.*, 635 F. Supp. 246, 250 (S.D.N.Y. 1986) (*quoting Leigh v. Engle*, 727 F.2d 113, 122 (7th Cir. 1984).
4. *Shoen*, 885 F.Supp. at 1348; *Donovan v. Bierwirth*, 680 F.2d 263, 271 (2nd Cir. 1982).
5. *See Neyer, Tisco & Hindo, Ltd. v. Russell*, 1993 WL 52552 (E.D. Pa. 1993).

the shares allocated to his individual account in the ESOP if it is a closely-held corporation not concerning major corporate decisions. The court in *Shoen* explained that the contesting parties desired to communicate quickly and frequently with the participants, and in such a situation, according to the Department of Labor, the trustee's fiduciary duty mandates that the trustee insure that necessary information is given to participants, that misleading or false information is not provided to participants, and that participants render an independent decision free from duress or pressure from their employer as to how to vote.[1] The court also indicated that ESOPs have been known to be established to serve as anti-takeover devices, with the theory being that the ESOP will own a significant amount of the corporation's stock and will, because the voting of that stock is directed by the corporation's employees through the "pass through" framework, be friendlier in a contest of control to the incumbent management than to an outside, hostile force or entity.[2]

For an investment advisor to be deemed a "fiduciary" under ERISA's "renders investment advice" definition, the investment advisor must render advice pursuant to an agreement, be paid for such advice, and have influence approaching control over benefit plan's investment decisions.[3] The trustee must also be prudent. ERISA's "prudence" requirement commands a fiduciary to act "with the care, skill, prudence, and diligence under circumstances then prevailing that a prudent man acting in a like capacity and familiar with such matters would use in the conduct of an enterprise of a like character and with like aims."[4]

Case Study 2

In *Kuper v. Iovenko*,[1] the plaintiffs filed claims under ERISA for breach of fiduciary duty against the ESOP trustees and administrators. The plaintiffs were employees of the Emery Division of Quantum Chemical Corp. These employees were participants in the corporation's ESOP. Quantum entered into an agreement to sell its Emery Division to Henkel Corporation. Henkel Corporation, in the meantime, agreed to employ existing employees of Emery Division under comparable terms and to accept the trust-to-trust transfer of the ESOP assets of those employees who continued employment with Henkel Corporation following the sale. Although the sale was effective on April 17, 1989, the trust-to-trust transfer of ESOP assets was not completed until roughly a year and a half later. During this 18-month period, Quantum's stock declined in value from more than $50 per share to approximately $10 per share. Plaintiffs contended that Quantum's acknowledged failure to consider diversifying or liquidating the ESOP constituted a breach of fiduciary duty owed to the plan and its participants.

In defending the case, the defendants in *Kuper* asserted that the terms of the ESOP did not give them discretion to diversify or to liquidate the ESOP funds. The United States Sixth Circuit Court of Appeals discussed the duties of ERISA fiduciaries in general and the exemptions from those duties for ESOP fiduciaries.[2] Fiduciary duties under ERISA, the court explained, have three components:

- the duty of loyalty, which requires the fiduciary to make all decisions regarding an ERISA plan "with an eye single to the interests of the participants and beneficiaries;"[3]
- the "prudent man" obligation, which requires the fiduciary to act as a prudent person would act in a similar situation or under similar circumstances; and
- the exclusive purpose obligation, which requires the fiduciary to act for the exclusive purpose of providing benefits to plan beneficiaries.[4]

---

1. *Kuper v. Iovenko*, 66 F.3d 1447 (6th Cir.1995).
2. *Kuper v. Iovenko*, 66 F.3d 1447, 1458 (6th Cir.1995).
3. *Kuper*, 66 F.3d at 1458.
4. *Id.*

---

1. *Shoen,* 885 F.Supp. at 1349.
2. *Id.* at 1355 n.35.
3. ERISA, 29 U.S.C.A. Section 1002(21)(A)(ii).
4. 29 U.S.C. Section 1104(a)(1)(B).

Case Study 2 Continued

The United States Sixth Circuit reasoned that an ESOP fiduciary is exempt from the duty to diversify investments and cannot be held liable for failing to diversify investments even if diversification would be prudent under the terms of a non-ESOP plan. These statutory exemptions, however, do not relieve a fiduciary from the general fiduciary responsibilities enumerated above.[1] "Thus, ESOP fiduciaries must, then, wear two hats and are expected to administer ESOP investments consistent with the provisions of both a specific employee benefits plan and ERISA... These competing concerns make it more difficult to delineate the responsibilities of ESOP trustees."[2]

Finally, the United States Sixth Circuit conducted a balancing act of the competing concerns. After this delicate balancing of varying interests, the Court held that an ESOP fiduciary's decision to continue investing in employer securities is reviewed for abuse of discretion. This balancing act is done with the purpose of ERISA on the one hand and the nature of ESOPs on the other. In this scenario, the courts may presume that a fiduciary's decision to remain invested in employer securities was reasonable. A plaintiff may rebut this presumption of reasonableness by showing that a prudent ESOP fiduciary acting under similar circumstances would have made a different investment decision.[3]

---

1. *Id.* (*citing Martin v. Feilen*, 965 F.2d 660, 665 (8th Cir.1992)).
2. *Id.*
3. See also *Keach v. United States Trust Co., N.A.*, 222 F.Supp.2d 1224 (C.D.Ill. Dec. 30, 2002), 2002 WL 31887909.

Case Study 3

In *Wright v. Oregon Metallurgical Corp.*,[1] an Oregon District Court was asked to evaluate an ESOP trustee's fiduciary obligations. The fiduciary duties in that case arose with the creation of an ESOP designed to finance the leveraged buyout of the owner's shares. The Court explained that under ERISA, a fiduciary is required to discharge his duties:

- "Solely in the interest of the participants and beneficiaries;" and
- with the exclusive purpose of providing benefits to participants and their beneficiaries and defraying reasonable expenses of administering the plan [the exclusive purpose requirement];
- with the care, skill, prudence, and diligence under circumstances then prevailing that a prudent man acting in a like capacity and familiar with such matters would use in the conduct of an enterprise of a like character and with like aims [the prudence requirement];
- by diversifying the investments of the plan in order to minimize the risk of large losses, unless under the circumstances it is clearly prudent not to do so [the diversification requirement]; and
- in accordance with the documents and instruments governing the plan insofar as such documents and instruments are consistent with the provisions of ERISA.

---

1. *Wright v. Oregon Metallurgical Corp.*, 222 F. Supp. 2d 1224, 28 Employee Benefits Cas. 2006 (D. Oregon, Aug. 6, 2002).

Case Study 4

In some situations, an ESOP trustee may be deemed to have been required to obtain advice from a separate independent party. In *Leigh v. Eagle*,[1] plan administrators played a role in having the plan they directed to invest, along with corporations they controlled, into the stock of corporations that the plan administrators, i.e. fiduciaries, were attempting to acquire. The plan administrators did not perform an independent, diligent investigation into the investment options available to the trust. Nor did these fiduciaries seek out independent advice from separate third parties concerning investment options. Even though the trust did not lose money and the trust did not decrease in value based on the actions of these fiduciaries, the court found that the fiduciaries nonetheless breached their duty for failing to seek out independent advice or embark on an independent, diligent investigation into investment options available to the trust.

---

1. *Leigh v. Eagle*, 727 F.2d 113, 129 (7th Cir. 1984).

The law and jurisprudence relating to trustees shows that the ESOP trustee must strive to preserve the ESOP's fundamental goal of investing plan assets into employer securities, all the while being held to the standard of a fiduciary while purchasing employer securities, dealing with the corporation, interacting with the bank or lender, and keeping employee-participants updated as to the value of their accounts and status of the ESOP as a whole.

S Corporations' Role as an Owner of ESOPs

IRC Section 1361 was amended in 1996 by the Small Business Job Protection Act, which allowed qualified plan trusts and Section 501(c)(3) organizations to be shareholders of S Corporations. Therefore, S corporations may establish ESOPs, and ESOPs are permitted to own the stock of an S corporation.[1] **S Corporations** are generally small corporations that:

- have no more than 100 shareholders;

- have shareholders that are individuals; and[2]

- have only one class of stock.

A significant change in the law occurred when an ESOP maintained by an S Corporation was treated as not violating the Code's qualification requirements nor as engaging in a prohibited transaction. In accordance with plan documentation, distributions of S Corporation stock that constitute qualifying employer securities held by the ESOP may be used to make interest and principal payments on loans utilized to acquire securities.

At first, it would appear that the 100 shareholder limitation would create an issue with respect to the number of participants in the ESOP. Nonetheless, the participants in the ESOP are not counted towards the 100 shareholder limit for an S Corporation. Instead, the ESOP is deemed to be only one shareholder.

EXAMPLE 6.9	Matthew, Patrick, Michael, and American ESOP all hold shares in the same S Corporation. American ESOP has seven employee-participants in its ESOP. Matthew, Patrick and Michael are not employee-participants of American ESOP. Based on this factual scenario, how many shareholders are there of the S Corporation?
	The answer is four. Matthew, Patrick, and Michael count as three shareholders and American ESOP is considered to be one shareholder. American ESOP is not deemed to be seven shareholders because the employee-participants are not counted towards the aggregate number of shareholders in the S Corporation.

The Taxpayer Relief Act of 1997 also added several beneficial changes to the way ESOPs and S Corporations are treated, including an amendment to Section 409(h)(2) of the IRC. This amendment allowed ESOPs the power to prevent participants from demanding stock distributions. Otherwise, a participant could terminate a corporation's S Corporation status by

---

1. IRC Section 1361.
2. The shareholders can be individuals, an estate, some trusts, a qualified retirement plan, or other qualified entities, but generally must be an individual. Also, a non-resident alien cannot serve as a shareholder of an S Corporation.

demanding a stock distribution and then placing that stock in an IRA, which is not permitted to hold stock in an S Corporation.[1] This law was somewhat modified concerning banks that are S Corporations. Section 1361 of the Internal Revenue Code now provides that an IRA or Roth IRA may be a shareholder of a bank that is an S Corporation, but only to the extent of bank stock held by the IRA as of the date of enactment of the provision, which is October 22, 2004.[2] With respect to dividends, the IRC prohibits S Corporations from deducting dividends paid from employer securities that are held by ESOPs.[3]

The income of an S Corporation passes through to the ESOP, and because an ESOP is tax exempt, no tax is paid on the income until it is distributed to the ESOP participant. ESOPs are advantageous in S Corporations to the extent that, among the S Corporation owners, the ESOP is not required to pay federal income taxes on its profits. In sum, it is important to note in the financial planning and estate planning process that ESOPs used in conjunction with S Corporations can provide significant financial benefits to owners and employees. The same is likewise true for stock bonus plans.

SUMMARY

Stock bonus plans provide benefits similar to those of profit sharing plans, except that benefits are normally distributed in the form of employer securities. ESOPs are the most common type of stock bonus plans. An ESOP can be a very powerful tool for closely-held businesses. ESOPs provide tax benefits and satisfy the employer's goals of having motivated, loyal, and long-term employees. Meanwhile, the employees are provided with value for services rendered and are able to accumulate assets that are provided over time towards retirement. Employees also become part owners of a corporation in which they work, which should increase their productivity, efficiency, and motivations. A key ingredient of the ESOP is that the corporation has the ability to borrow (leverage) to purchase the employer stock.

Quick Quiz

Highlight the answer to these questions:

1. The put option protects the rank-and-file employees.
   a. True
   b. False

2. The trustee of an ESOP must act in the best interest of the plan participants.
   a. True
   b. False

3. An S Corporation cannot establish an ESOP.
   a. True
   b. False

True, True, False.

The leveraging aspect of ESOPs, along with the tax deductibility of the payments, make ESOPs a very attractive tool in the financial planning and estate planning areas. On the other hand, because the investments of ESOPs are primarily in employer securities, it is a highly non-diversified and risky investment depending on the strength, standing, and goodwill of the corporation as an on going entity. If the corporation were to fail, the ESOP and the accounts of

---

1. IRC Section 409(h)(2).
2. IRC Section 1361(c)(2)(A)(vi).
3. IRC Section 404(k)(1).

the individual employee-participants may be rendered worthless. Nonetheless, depending on each individual situation, financial planning advice and estate planning advice must be given with these advantages and disadvantages in mind. The ESOP trustees may be the ones named in subsequent lawsuits if ESOPs fail, or the businesses with which they are affiliated fail.

Stock bonus plans and ESOPs are primarily used to avoid putting cash into a qualified plan while a corporation is growing and needs the cash for growth. The problem with these plans is that eventually cash must be contributed to diversify the 55-year olds, those terminating participants, and in the case of a closely-held corporation to provide a market for those retirees or plan participants who wish to sell their shares. It is also important to remember that stock bonus plans and ESOPs are "pay me now or pay me later" qualified plans and as the employer stock becomes more valuable, the plan will need more and more cash to redeem any outstanding shares. Sponsors considering adopting a stock bonus or ESOP plan should carefully consider not only the initial tax deduction and cash flow impact but the ultimate necessity to fund the plan with sufficient cash to redeem shares under the put option and diversify the investment portfolios for those participants age 55 or older.

	Stock Bonus Plans	ESOPs
Plan Establishment	December 31	December 31
Date of Contribution	Due date of tax return plus extensions	Due date of tax return plus extensions
Type of Contributions	Generally stock	Generally stock
Deductible Contribution Limit	*25% of covered compensation*	*25% of covered compensation plus interest paid on loan*
Valuation	Generally needed	Generally needed plus dividends (in certain circumstances)
Eligibility	Same as other Qualified Plans (21 and 1 year of service or 2 years with 100% vesting)	Same as other Qualified Plans (21 and 1 year of service or 2 years with 100% vesting)
Allocation Method	% of compensation or formula based on age, service of classification	% of compensation or formula based on age, service of classification
Integration with Social Security	*Yes*	*No*
Vesting	Same as other Qualified Plans (5-year cliff or 3 to 7 year graduated vesting unless top heavy)	Same as other Qualified Plans (5-year cliff or 3 to 7 year graduated vesting unless top heavy)
Portfolio Diversification	No	No
Voting Rights	Generally yes	Generally yes
Distributions	Generally stock	Generally stock
In-Service Withdrawals	May be allowed after two years of participation	May be allowed after two years of participation
Loans	May be allowed (but not usually)	May be allowed (but not usually)
Taxation of Distributions	Ordinary income with NUA treatment available	Ordinary income with NUA treatment available

Note: The differences between Stock Bonus Plans and ESOPs are highlighted in blue.

Key Terms

Adequate Consideration Standard - Fair market value determined in good faith.

Dilution - The reduction in the monetary value or voting power of an owner's stock as a result of contributions to stock bonus plans and ESOPs.

Discretionary - The choice for a plan sponsor of a profit sharing plan as to the amount and frequency of a contribution.

Diversified Investment Portfolios - An investment portfolio invested in a broad range of investment classes to reduce investment risk.

Employee Stock Ownership Plan (ESOP) - A qualified profit sharing plan that utilizes employer contributions to the plan to purchase the stock of the employer's company and allocates the ownership to the plan participants.

Fair Market Value - The price that a willing buyer would pay a willing seller, both having reasonable knowledge of the pertinent facts and neither under duress.

Leveraged ESOP - An ESOP that borrows the funds necessary to purchase the employer's stock. The interest and principal repayments on the loan are tax deductible for the employer.

Net Unrealized Appreciation (NUA) - The appreciation in the value of employer stock after the date of contribution to the plan until the date of distribution.

Nonrecognition of Gain Treatment - A delay in the recognition of gain available to owners of a company that sell company stock to an ESOP. The transaction must meet the stated requirements of the IRC and the owner must reinvest the proceeds from the sale within 12 months of the sale into qualified domestic replacement securities.

Pass Through Voting - The voting rights of the stock pass through from the ESOP or the stock bonus plan to the participant.

Qualified Replacement Securities - Securities in a domestic corporation, including stocks, bonds, debentures, or warrants, which receive no more than 25% of their income from passive investments.

Rank-and-File Employees - The non-key, non-highly compensated employees.

Repurchase Option (Put Option) - An option that allows a terminating employee to receive in cash the fair market value of the employer's stock within a stock bonus plan or ESOP if the employer stock is not readily tradeable on an established market. An option to sell to the employer.

S Corporations - Small corporations taxed as pass-through entities that cannot have more than 100 individual shareholders and have only one class of stock.

Key Terms

Stock Bonus Plan - A qualified profit sharing plan funded solely with employer stock.

Substantial and Recurring - IRC standard defining the frequency requirement of contributions by employers to profit sharing plans.

1. List the required characteristics of a stock bonus plan.

2. List advantages and disadvantages of stock bonus plans.

3. List at least three distinctions between profit sharing plans and stock bonus plans.

4. Why are valuations of the employer's securities completed each year for the plan sponsor of a stock bonus plan?

5. What are the eligibility requirements for stock bonus plans?

6. Describe the standard method of allocating contributions to a stock bonus plan.

7. Explain the stock voting rights of stock bonus plan participants.

8. Define net unrealized appreciation and discuss the tax advantages related to it.

9. Define ESOPs and discuss when they are used.

10. Discuss how the leveraged ESOP works.

11. For the owner of a closely-held business to qualify for the nonrecognition of capital gain treatment certain requirements must be met. List these requirements.

12. Define qualified replacement securities.

13. List several advantages of an ESOP.

14. List several disadvantages of an ESOP.

15. Describe the voting rights of ESOP participants.

16. Discuss the limitations on contributions to ESOPs.

17. What are the requirements necessary for an employee to force diversification of his holdings in the ESOP?

18. Describe the requirements of the "put option" for an ESOP.

19. Discuss how the changes created by the Taxpayer Relief Act of 1997 with regard to ESOPs impact S Corporations.

1. Which of the following are requirements for a qualified stock bonus plan?

    1. Participants must have pass through voting rights for stock held by the plan.
    2. Participants must have the right to demand employer securities at a distribution, even if the plan sponsor is a closely-held corporation.

    a. 1 only.
    b. 2 only.
    c. 1 and 2.
    d. Neither 1 nor 2.

2. Mike, age 60, is a participant in the stock bonus plan of Tantalus, Inc., a closely-held corporation. Mike received contributions in shares to the stock bonus plan, and Tantalus, Inc. took income tax deductions as follows:

Year	# of Shares	Value per Share (At Time of Contribution)
2002	100	$10
2003	125	$12
2004	150	$13
2005	200	$15
2006	400	$18

    Mike terminates employment and takes a distribution from the plan of 975 shares of Tantalus, Inc., having a fair value of $19,500. What are Mike's tax consequences?

    a. There are no immediate tax consequences because he has not sold the stock.
    b. Mike has ordinary income of $14,650 at distribution.
    c. Mike has net unrealized appreciation of $19,500 at distribution.
    d. Mike has ordinary income of $19,500 at distribution.

3. Cavin sells stock several years after he received it as a distribution from a qualified stock bonus plan. When the stock was distributed, he had a net unrealized appreciation of $7,500. Cavin also had ordinary income from the distribution of $29,000. The fair market value of the stock and the sales price at the time of sale was $81,000. How much of the sale price will be subject to long-term capital gain treatment?

    a. $7,500.
    b. $44,500.
    c. $52,000.
    d. $73,500.

4. Davin sells stock six months after he received it as a distribution from a qualified stock bonus plan. When the stock was distributed, he had a net unrealized appreciation of $7,500. He also had ordinary income from the distribution of $29,000. The fair value of the stock at the time of sale was $81,000. How much of the sale price will be subject to long-term capital gain treatment?

    a. $7,500.

    b. $44,500.

    c. $52,000.

    d. $73,500.

5. Which of the following are costs of a stock bonus plan?

    1. Periodic appraisal costs.

    2. Periodic actuarial costs.

    a. 1 only.

    b. 2 only.

    c. 1 and 2.

    d. Neither 1 nor 2.

6. Patrick and Kevin own Irisha Corporation and plan to retire. They would like to leave their assets to their children; therefore, they transfer 70 percent of the stock to a trust for the benefit of their 10 children pro rata. Patrick and Kevin then plan to sell the remaining Irisha shares to a qualified ESOP plan. Which of the following is correct?

    1. The stock transfer to the ESOP is not a 50 percent transfer and therefore will not qualify for nonrecognition of capital gains.

    2. Any transfer to an ESOP of less than 50 percent ownership may be subject to a minority discount on valuation.

    a. 1 only.

    b. 2 only.

    c. 1 and 2.

    d. Neither 1 nor 2.

7. BJ owns NOCTM, Inc. and sells 100 percent of the corporate stock (all outstanding stock) on January 1, 2005 to an ESOP for $5,000,000. His adjusted taxable basis in the stock was $2,400,000. Which of the following is correct?

    1. If BJ reinvests the $5,000,000 in qualified domestic securities within 18 months, he has a carryover basis of $2,400,000 in the qualified domestic security portfolio and no current capital gain.

    2. BJ has a long-term capital gain of $2,600,000 reduced by the 20 percent small business credit; therefore, his gain is $2,080,000 if he does not reinvest in qualified domestic securities within 18 months.

       a. 1 only.

       b. 2 only.

       c. 1 and 2.

       d. Neither 1 nor 2.

8. One of the disadvantages of an ESOP is that the stock is an undiversified investment portfolio. Which of the following is correct?

    1. An employee, age 55 or older, who has completed 10 years of participation in an ESOP may require that 100 percent of the account balance be diversified.

    2. An employee who receives corporate stock as a distribution from an ESOP may enjoy net unrealized appreciation treatment at the time of distribution.

       a. 1 only.

       b. 2 only.

       c. 1 and 2.

       d. Neither 1 nor 2.

9. Taylor, age 65, retires from Tickle Tile corporation and receives 25,000 shares of Tickle Tile stock with a fair market value of $500,000 in 1998. Taylor recognized $48,000 of ordinary income upon the distribution. What is Taylor's NUA immediately after the distribution?

       a. $48,000.

       b. $348,000.

       c. $452,000.

       d. $500,000.

10. Meb, the owner of Meb's Hardware, is considering establishing a stock bonus plan. She recently talked with her financial planner, Don T. Know. Don T. Know never studied when he took his certificate program, therefore he gave Meb incorrect information about stock bonus plans. Which of the following statements given to Meb was correct?

   a. Meb can establish a stock bonus plan for the previous year anytime before the due date (plus extensions) of Meb's Hardware's tax return.

   b. When the employee's of Meb's Hardware receive distributions of stock from the stock bonus plan, they will receive capital gain treatment on the distribution equal to the value of the stock as contributed by Meb's Hardware.

   c. A valuation of the stock of Meb's Hardware is required when the stock bonus plan is established, but subsequent valuations are unnecessary.

   d. Meb can require the employees to be age 21 and employed for two years before becoming eligible for the stock bonus plan.

11. Sam is a participant in RFK, Inc.'s ESOP. Sam has been a participant in the plan for eight years and her account balance in the plan is $1,000,000 and is completely funded with employer securities. The plan defines the normal retirement age as 65 years old. Sam is 64 years old this year and would like to retire. Her financial planner mentioned that she should have a more diversified portfolio. What, if anything, can she do to diversify her portfolio?

   a. The only way Sam can diversify her portfolio is to take a distribution of the employer stock from the ESOP and reinvest the value in a diversified portfolio.

   b. Sam can require the ESOP to diversify her up to 25 percent of her portfolio.

   c. Since Sam is in the final election year she can require the ESOP to diversify 50 percent of her portfolio.

   d. Sam can diversify 10 percent each year until the portfolio is completely diversified.

12. Rustin recently retired from Fox, Inc., a national plastics supplier. When Rustin retired his stock bonus plan had 10,000 shares of Fox, Inc. stock. Fox, Inc. took deductions equal to $20 per share for the contributions made on Rustin's behalf. At retirement, Rustin took a lump-sum distribution of the employer stock. The fair market value of the stock at distribution was $35 per share. Six months after distribution, Rustin sold the stock for $40 per share. What amount was subject to ordinary income tax on Rustin's tax return at the date Fox, Inc. contributed the stock to the plan?

   a. $0.

   b. $200,000.

   c. $350,000.

   d. $400,000.

13. Assume the same facts presented in question 12. What amount was subject to ordinary income on Rustin's tax return at the date the stock was distributed?

    a. $0.

    b. $200,000.

    c. $350,000.

    d. $400,000.

14. Assume the same facts presented in question 12. Which of the following gain was Rustin subject to at the date the stock was distributed?

    a. $0.

    b. $50,000 short-term capital gain.

    c. $200,000 long-term capital gain.

    d. $150,000 long-term capital gain and $5,000 short-term capital gain.

    e. $400,000 long-term capital gain.

15. Assume the same facts presented in question 12. Which of the following gain was Rustin subject to at the date the stock was sold?

    a. $0.

    b. $50,000 short-term capital gain.

    c. $200,000 long-term capital gain.

    d. $150,000 long-term capital gain and $50,000 short-term capital gain.

    e. $400,000 long-term capital gain.

Distributions from Qualified Plans

INTRODUCTION

This chapter focuses on distributions from qualified plans and, as discussed in previous chapters, the relationship between the government, the participant, and the plan sponsor (employer). The government allows the participant and/or the plan sponsor to deposit pretax funds into an account that will grow tax-free until distribution to the participant (or the participant's beneficiaries), at which time the funds will be subject to income tax.

To receive the tax-free growth of the assets within the plan, the plan participant must follow precise rules and requirements regarding distributions from the plan. This chapter covers the requirements, benefits, stipulations, and consequences of taking distributions for retirement, as well as the impact of taking distributions prior to retirement or not using the funds during retirement.

While this chapter focuses on distributions from qualified plans, distributions from other tax-advantaged accounts, such as IRAs, SIMPLEs, 403(b) plans, and 457 plans will be discussed in Chapters 9 and 10.

DISTRIBUTION OPTIONS

Distributions are disbursements of assets from a qualified plan with no intention by the participant of returning the assets to the plan. Distributions include in-service withdrawals, payments made upon termination or retirement, and may also include certain distributions related to qualified domestic relations orders. Loans taken from a qualified plan are not distributions unless the loan is not repaid and the transaction is deemed a distribution (discussed below).

A qualified plan may, by law, offer a wide range of distribution options, but each plan document establishes the options actually available to the participants of a particular plan. Generally, qualified plans offer a variety of distribution options including a lump-sum distribution, a rollover distribution, a single life annuity, or a joint life annuity option. The plan may also offer in-service distributions and hardship withdrawals before retirement (discussed below).

DISTRIBUTION OPTIONS

- Annuities
- Lump-sum distributions
- Rollovers
- In-service withdrawals
- Non-repaid loans

PENSION PLANS

Pension plans are generally not permitted to offer in-service withdrawals to participants. (Note that in-service withdrawals could be made once the participant reaches retirement age, but because of the continued accrual of benefits, plans do not normally permit such withdrawals). Thus, distributions from pension plans are normally made because of the participant's termination of employment, early retirement, normal retirement, disability, or death.

Key Concepts

Underline/highlight the answers to these questions as you read:

1. What are the distribution options for pension plans?

2. What are the distribution options for profit sharing plans?

Early Termination

A participant who terminates employment before normal retirement age can have up to three options: receive a lump-sum distribution of the qualified plan assets, roll the assets over to an IRA or other qualified plan, or leave the funds in the pension plan. However, these options depend on the plan document. Many pension plans do not have lump sum options.

If the participant's vested account balance is less than $5,000, then the law allows, but does not require, the plan to disperse the balance to the participant if the participant does not make a timely election. This is called a forced payout. Before March 28, 2005, the plan could simply disperse the account balance and still meet its fiduciary duty. However, the Department of Labor issued final regulations that changed the responsibilities of plan administrators with regards to forced payouts. Section 2550.404a-2 of the Department of Labor now requires that forced payouts between $1,000 and $5,000 be directly rolled to an IRA if the participant has not made a timely election and the plan requires a forced payout. A forced payout for amounts less than $1,000 are not affected by this change.

Normal Retirement

At the participant's normal retirement age, the pension plan will typically distribute retirement benefits through an annuity payable for the remainder of the participant's life. The plan may also provide for a lump-sum distribution option that pays the participant an amount equal to the present value of the annuity. While the plan document dictates the distribution options available to the participant, a single life annuity is generally the automatic form of benefit for a single participant. However, married individuals must be offered a qualified joint and survivor annuity (QJSA). Regardless of the form, distributions from qualified pension plans are subjected to ordinary income tax.

Qualified Joint and Survivor Annuity (QJSA)

A **Qualified Joint and Survivor Annuity (QJSA)** must be provided to married participants of a pension plan and must also be provided to married participant's of profit sharing plans unless the plan meets the following criteria:

1. The plan provides that the participant's nonforfeitable accrued benefit is payable in full, upon the participant's death, to the participant's surviving spouse (unless the participant elects, with spousal consent, that such benefit be provided instead to a designated beneficiary).
2. The participant does not elect the payment of benefits in the form of a life annuity.

In order to meet the first requirement, two additional requirements must be met. First, the benefit must be available to the surviving spouse within a reasonable time after the participant's death. A "reasonable time" is defined by the IRC to mean within the 90-day period following the date of death. Longer periods may be deemed a reasonable time based on the particular facts and circumstances. Second, the benefit payable to the surviving spouse must be adjusted for gains or losses occurring after the participant's death in accordance with plan rules governing the adjustment of account balances for other plan distributions.[1]

The QJSA pays a benefit to the participant and spouse as long as either lives; although, at the death of the first spouse, the annuity may be reduced. Because the annuity is paid as long as either spouse is living, the QJSA is actuarially reduced; therefore, the annuity payment is less than it would have been using the participants' single life expectancy. The reduction is to actuarially compensate for the continuing payments to the surviving spouse after the first spouse's death. The nonparticipant spouse beneficiary may choose to waive her right to a QJSA by executing a notarized or otherwise official waiver of benefits. The waiver may be made during the 90-day period beginning 90 days before the annuity start date.

Quick Quiz

Highlight the answer to these questions:

1. Pension plans generally provide a lump-sum distribution.
    a. True
    b. False

2. A qualified joint and survivor annuity and qualified preretirement survivor annuity are required for pension plans.
    a. True
    b. False

3. Profit sharing plans may allow for inservice withdrawals.
    a. True
    b. False

False, True, True.

---

1. Treasury Regulation 1.401(a)-20 Q-A #3.

Qualified Preretirement Survivor Annuity (QPSA)

A **qualified preretirement survivor annuity (QPSA)** must also be provided to married participants of a pension plan or a profit sharing plan utilizing the same criteria as discussed above. A QPSA provides a benefit to the surviving spouse if the participant dies before attaining normal retirement age. A QPSA is essentially a term insurance policy paid for by a reduction in the ultimate pension plan retirement benefit that the participant would have received from the plan at normal retirement age.

The nonparticipant spouse is offered the QPSA and may choose whether to accept or waive the option. The QPSA may be waived by the nonparticipant spouse via a written notarized waiver. (In some cases, the signature can be witnessed by a plan official instead of being notarized.) The waiver may be made beginning the first day of the plan year in which the participant attains age 35 until the day the participant dies. In addition, the waiver can be revoked at any time during this period as well. Since any waiver is generally executed when the participant is age 35, this waiver or acceptance decision is critical, as it may impact the family's overall future financial plan. Financial planners should carefully review the couple's life insurance situation before making a determination as to whether they should waive the QPSA. Assuming the QPSA was elected and the surviving spouse receives the benefit, there is no adjusted taxable basis in the benefit. Thus, the full value of distribution under the QPSA is subject to ordinary income tax.

EXHIBIT 7.2	QPSA BENEFIT COMPARISON

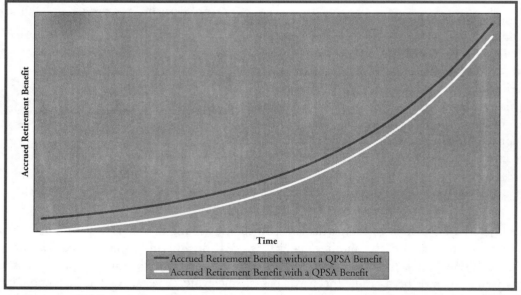

The difference between the two lines is the premium cost of life insurance associated with the QPSA.

PENSION PLAN NORMAL RETIREMENT AGE DISTRIBUTION OPTIONS

EXHIBIT 7.3

- Qualified Joint and Survivor Annuity (QJSA)
- Single Life Annuity if QJSA is waived or no spouse
- Lump Sum

AN EFFECTIVE WAIVER QPSA OR QJSA BENEFITS

EXHIBIT 7.4

- In writing;
- Clearly indicates that the QPSA or QJSA will be waived and the consequences of the waiver;
- Signed by the nonparticipant spouse; and
- Notarized or witnessed by a plan official

Rollover

A distribution from a pension plan may be rolled over into another qualified plan or an IRA provided the participant is not required to begin taking the required minimum distributions. If the assets are rolled over, the participant defers recognition of ordinary income until the assets are distributed from the rollover account. However, in certain situations when a distribution is taken as a lump-sum distribution, the recipient may receive favorable tax treatment on the distribution (Net Unrealized Appreciation (NUA), 10-year forward averaging, Pre-74 capital gain treatment) as discussed below. These favorable taxation treatments will be lost if the distribution is rolled over to an IRA or to a plan that is not a qualified plan.

PROFIT SHARING PLANS

Profit sharing plans generally provide participants with a distribution of the plan's assets at the participant's termination. At termination, the participant may be able to take the money as ordinary taxable income, annuitize the value, or roll the assets over into a rollover qualified plan or IRA to continue the deferral of the income tax depending on the options available. In contrast to pension plans, profit sharing plans are not required to offer survivor benefits if the plan does not pay the participant in the form of a life annuity benefit and the participant's nonforfeitable accrued benefit is payable to the surviving spouse upon the participant's death. (See discussion in QJSA above.) Profit sharing plans also differ from pension plans because profit sharing plans may allow for inservice withdrawals (plan dependent) and most 401(k) plans generally allow plan loans to participants in the plan document.

TAXATION OF DISTRIBUTIONS

Distributions from qualified retirement plans are generally subject to ordinary income tax because the plans usually contain both contributions and earnings that have never been subjected to income tax. The contributions to the plan were effectively wages that would have been taxed at ordinary income tax rates had they been paid directly to the participant. These contributions have not yet been subjected to income tax because the benefits were held in a qualified plan. Therefore, when the plan assets are distributed, the value of the distribution is included in the participant's income and is taxed as ordinary income.

Just as the government requires an employer to withhold a specific amount of tax from an employee's wages to ensure that the government receives the income tax, a distribution from a qualified retirement plan is also subject to withholding requirements. Generally, the plan custodian is required to withhold a mandatory 20 percent from most non-periodic distribution (any payment that is not part of an annuity) made to the participant (the 20% withholding requirement does not apply to hardship distributions or loans). If income tax is not withheld or insufficient income tax is withheld, the recipient may be required to pay estimated tax payments or otherwise be subject to penalties for insufficient withholdings or estimated tax payments. This withholding requirement only pertains to qualified plans and not from distributions of IRAs.

Key Concepts

Underline/highlight the answers to these questions as you read:

1. What are rollovers and when and how are they used?

2. Under what circumstances will a participant have an adjusted taxable basis in their qualified plan?

3. What special options are available for lump-sum distributions?

ROLLOVERS

Even when the participant has the option of taking a lump-sum distribution, the participant is not required to withdraw the account balance. Instead the participant may elect to **rollover** or transfer the balance of the account into another tax-advantaged qualified plan or an IRA account to continue to defer the recognition of income taxes until the ultimate distribution of the assets from the new plan. Generally, a participant will elect to rollover an account balance when the participant has terminated employment but would like to continue to benefit from the tax-deferred growth of the assets and plan for his retirement. A participant may also elect a rollover to increase his investment choices or to have more control over the plan assets. It is important to note that the rules regarding rollovers have been significantly broadened over the years, the expanded rules for 403(b) and 457 plans as discussed in Chapter 10.

The decision to rollover qualified plan assets into an IRA should be considered carefully. Once the assets are deposited into the IRA, the assets will continue to benefit from the tax-deferred growth until a distribution is taken from the IRA account. However, any assets deposited into the IRA lose the ERISA alienation protection, the benefit of **10-year forward averaging**, the benefit of **pre-1974 capital gain treatment**, and the benefit of **net unrealized appreciation** (NUA). The opportunity to benefit from 10-year forward averaging, pre-1974 capital gain treatment, and net unrealized appreciation does not exist for distributions from IRAs. All of these topics are discussed in detail below.

THE COST OF A ROLLOVER FROM A QUALIFIED PLAN TO AN IRA

EXHIBIT 7.5

> - Lose ERISA protection
> - Lose potential 10-year forward averaging
> - Lose potential Net Unrealized Appreciation (NUA)
> - Lose potential Pre-1974 capital gain treatment

Rollovers may be accomplished in one of the two following ways:
1. Direct rollover
2. Indirect rollover

Direct Rollover

A **direct rollover** occurs when the plan trustee distributes the account balance directly to the trustee of the recipient account. A direct rollover is usually completed with a wire transfer from the old custodian to the new custodian or a check from the old custodian negotiable only by the custodian of the new account. All qualified plans must provide for the availability of direct rollovers of certain distributions. If the participant elects a direct rollover, then the original plan custodian will not be required to withhold 20 percent of the distribution for federal income tax.

Indirect Rollover

The second method of completing a rollover is indirectly through a distribution to the participant with a subsequent transfer to another account. In this instance the original custodian issues a check to the participant in the amount of the full account balance reduced by the 20 percent subject to mandatory withholding allowance. In order to complete the rollover, the participant must then reinvest the full original account balance of the qualified plan (including the 20 percent subject to mandatory withholding) within 60 days of the original distribution into the new qualified plan or IRA. The 60-day clock starts with their constructive receipt of the distribution (usually when they receive the check).

One of the problems with the **indirect rollover** method is that the distribution is subject to the mandatory withholding of 20 percent, but 100 percent of the account balance must be deposited in the new qualified plan or IRA at the date of the distribution. Thus, the participant must utilize funds from other sources in the amount of the 20 percent withheld and deposit 100 percent of the distribution amount into the rollover account.

EXAMPLE 7.1

> Kristi, age 28, took a distribution from her 401(k) plan of her entire account balance of $85,000. She intended to roll-over the $85,000 to an IRA at a brokerage company, but decided to receive the check herself rather than have the custodian do a direct trustee to trustee rollover. The custodian of the 401(k) plan withheld 20% of the account balance ($17,000) (as required by law) and sent Kristi a check in the amount of $68,000. In order to avoid having to recognize any taxable income, Kristi must open the IRA and deposit $85,000 (not $68,000) within 60 days of receiving the $68,000 check. Kristi will then receive a tax refund of the

$17,000 withheld when she files her federal income tax return. To avoid the 20% withholding requirement, Kristi could have initiated a direct rollover from the 401(k) to her new IRA.

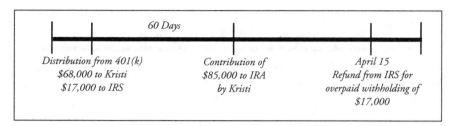

Indirect rollovers usually occur due to poor planning or because the account owner wants to use the funds during the 60-day period. To prevent potential abuse, the IRS only permits an individual to have one indirect rollover from one IRA to another IRA per year. The one year waiting period does not apply to indirect rollovers from qualified plans to IRAs. There can also be an unlimited number of direct rollovers during the year.

Planning for a Rollover

As mentioned above, plan sponsors are required to offer the participant the choice of a direct rollover at the time of the distribution, but qualified plans are not required to accept rollovers from other qualified plans or IRAs. Thus, without proper planning, an individual who takes a distribution from a qualified plan with the intention of completing an indirect rollover into another qualified plan may fail to meet the 60 day requirement if their new qualified plan does not accept rollovers from other plans. Qualified plans are required to provide participants with a written explanation of the distribution options, the mandatory withholding rules, and any other rules relating to the taxation of distributions. Additionally, any necessary spousal waivers must be secured in advance of any distribution.

Neither a direct or indirect rollover may consist of any distribution from a qualified plan that is one of a series of substantially equal periodic payments (not less frequently than annually) made for the life of the participant, the joint lives of the participant and the participant's designated beneficiary, or for a period of 10 years or more. In addition, any distribution on account of a required minimum distribution (discussed below) and hardship withdrawals may not be rolled over into another qualified plan or IRA.

After-Tax Contributions

If a qualified plan consists of employee after-tax contributions, these contributions may be rolled over into another qualified plan that accepts after-tax dollars or into a traditional IRA. In the case of a rollover of after-tax contributions from one qualified plan to another qualified plan, the rollover can only be accomplished through a direct rollover. A qualified plan is not permitted to accept rollovers of after-tax contributions unless the plan provides separate accounting for such contributions and the applicable earnings on those contributions. Conversely, after-tax contributions are not permitted to be rolled over from an IRA into a qualified plan.[2]

---

2. IRC Section 408(d)(3)(C).

ADJUSTED TAXABLE BASIS

A participant will have an **adjusted taxable basis** in distributions received from a qualified plan if either of the following have occurred:

- The participant made after-tax contributions to a contributory qualified plan, or
- The participant was taxed on the premiums for life insurance held in the qualified plan.

When an employer or plan participant contributes after-tax funds to a qualified plan, the participant will have an adjusted taxable basis in the qualified plan equal to the amount of after-tax funds contributed to the plan during participation. Distributions from qualified plans that have an adjusted taxable basis will be partially treated as a nontaxable return of basis while the remaining portion of the distribution will be taxed as ordinary income. The calculation will vary depending upon whether a distribution is taken as an annuity or lump sum. Lump-sum distributions are discussed in a later section.

Annuity Payments

Amounts distributed as an annuity are taxable to the participant of a qualified plan in the year in which the annuity payments are received. Each annuity payment is considered a partially tax-free return of adjusted taxable basis and partially ordinary income using an inclusion/exclusion ratio. The numerator for the exclusion ratio is the cost basis in the annuity, and the denominator of the exclusion ratio is the total of the expected benefit that will be payable from the annuity.

$$\frac{\text{Cost Basis in the Annuity}}{\text{Total Expected Benefit}} = \text{Exclusion Ratio}$$

Kim is a participant in a qualified plan from which she is to receive annuity payments of $3,000 per month for an expected period of 20 years. Kim has an adjusted taxable basis in the qualified plan in the amount of $180,000. How much of each annuity distribution to Kim is subject to ordinary income?

EXAMPLE 7.2

$$\frac{\text{Cost Basis in the Annuity}}{\text{Total Expected Benefit}} = \text{Exclusion Ratio}$$

$$\frac{\$180,000}{\$3,000 \times 20 \text{ years} \times 12 \text{ months}} = \text{Exclusion Ratio}$$

$$\frac{\$180,000}{\$720,000} = 25\% \text{ Exclusion Ratio}$$

$3,000 x 25% = $750 of each monthly payment is return of adjusted taxable basis

$3,000 - $750 = $2,250 of each monthly payment is subject to ordinary income tax.

Once the participant has recovered the entire cost basis of the annuity, all future monthly payments will be fully taxed.[3] In the event that the participant dies before recovering all of the

---

3. IRC Section 72(b)(2).

cost basis, a deduction (miscellaneous itemized deduction not subject to two percent) will be available on the participant's final income tax return for the unrecovered investment.[4] Distributions that are not lump-sum and are not in an annuity are taxed pro rata to the account balance in comparison to the pre-taxed portion.

Lump-Sum Distributions

Participants may take a full distribution, often called a lump-sum distribution, from a plan upon termination of employment. Any after-tax contributions will simply offset the taxable distribution. Lump-sum distributions are discussed in detail below.

LUMP-SUM DISTRIBUTIONS

Lump-sum distributions from a qualified pension or profit sharing plan may receive special income tax treatment. A lump-sum distribution must meet the following four requirements:

1. The distribution must represent the employee's entire accrued benefit in the case of a pension plan or the full account balance in the case of a defined contribution plan.
2. A distribution of the balance of a participant's entire accrued benefit or account balance must be made within one taxable year.
3. The distribution must be on account of either the participant's death, attainment of age 59½, separation from service (does not apply to self-employed individuals in the plan), or disability.
4. The employee must have participated in the plan for at least five taxable years prior to the tax year of distribution (waived if the distribution is on account of death).

The taxpayer must elect lump-sum distribution treatment by attaching Form 4972 to the taxpayer's federal income tax return. This must be filed by the participant, or (in the case of the participant's death) by his estate within one year of receipt of the distribution.

All of the four requirements must be met in order for the distribution to qualify as a lump-sum distribution and therefore qualify for any of the special tax treatments described below.

Distributions from qualified plans are generally taxed as ordinary income, but when a distribution is considered a lump-sum distribution, the distribution may qualify for one of the following special tax treatments:

- 10-year forward averaging.
- Pre-1974 capital gain treatment.
- Net Unrealized Appreciation (NUA).

However, simply because a distribution may qualify for one of the following special tax treatments does not mean that it is the best choice for the individual receiving the distribution. In many cases, the best choice may be to rollover the distribution into an IRA. However, it is always important to evaluate the options that are available.

EXHIBIT 7.6	SPECIAL TAX TREATMENT

> - 10-year forward averaging
> - Pre-1974 capital gains treatment
> - NUA treatment

---

4. IRC Section 72(b)(3).

EXHIBIT 7.7

Form **4972**

Department of the Treasury
Internal Revenue Service (99)

Tax on Lump-Sum Distributions
(From Qualified Plans of Participants Born Before January 2, 1936)

▶ **Attach to Form 1040 or Form 1041.**

OMB No. 1545-0193

20**04**

Attachment
Sequence No. **28**

Name of recipient of distribution

Identifying number

		Yes	No
Part I	**Complete this part to see if you can use Form 4972**		
1	Was this a distribution of a plan participant's entire balance (excluding deductible voluntary employee contributions and certain forfeited amounts) from all of an employer's qualified plans of one kind (pension, profit-sharing, or stock bonus)? If "No," **do not** use this form **1**		
2	Did you roll over any part of the distribution? If "Yes," **do not** use this form **2**		
3	Was this distribution paid to you as a beneficiary of a plan participant who was born before January 2, 1936? **3**		
4	Were you **(a)** a plan participant who received this distribution, **(b)** born before January 2, 1936, **and (c)** a participant in the plan for at least 5 years before the year of the distribution?. **4**		
	If you answered "No" to both questions 3 **and** 4, **do not** use this form.		
5a	Did you use Form 4972 after 1986 for a previous distribution from your own plan? If "Yes," **do not** use this form for a 2004 distribution from your own plan **5a**		
b	If you are receiving this distribution as a beneficiary of a plan participant who died, did you use Form 4972 for a previous distribution received for that participant after 1986? If "Yes," **do not** use the form for this distribution **5b**		

Part II	**Complete this part to choose the 20% capital gain election** (see instructions)		
6	Capital gain part from Form 1099-R, box 3	**6**	
7	Multiply line 6 by 20% (.20) . . . . ▶	**7**	
	If you also choose to use Part III, go to line 8. Otherwise, include the amount from line 7 in the total on Form 1040, line 43, or Form 1041, Schedule G, line 1b, whichever applies.		

Part III	**Complete this part to choose the 10-year tax option** (see instructions)		
8	Ordinary income from Form 1099-R, box 2a minus box 3. If you did not complete Part II, enter the taxable amount from Form 1099-R, box 2a.	**8**	
9	Death benefit exclusion for a beneficiary of a plan participant who died before August 21, 1996	**9**	
10	Total taxable amount. Subtract line 9 from line 8	**10**	
11	Current actuarial value of annuity from Form 1099-R, box 8. If none, enter -0-	**11**	
12	Adjusted total taxable amount. Add lines 10 and 11. If this amount is $70,000 or more, **skip** lines 13 through 16, enter this amount on line 17, and go to line 18	**12**	
13	Multiply line 12 by 50% (.50), but **do not** enter more than $10,000 .	**13**		
14	Subtract $20,000 from line 12. If line 12 is $20,000 or less, enter -0-	**14**		
15	Multiply line 14 by 20% (.20)	**15**		
16	Minimum distribution allowance. Subtract line 15 from line 13	**16**	
17	Subtract line 16 from line 12	**17**	
18	Federal estate tax attributable to lump-sum distribution	**18**	
19	Subtract line 18 from line 17. If line 11 is zero, **skip** lines 20 through 22 and go to line 23 . .	**19**	
20	Divide line 11 by line 12 and enter the result as a decimal (rounded to at least three places).	**20** .		
21	Multiply line 16 by the decimal on line 20	**21**		
22	Subtract line 21 from line 11	**22**		
23	Multiply line 19 by 10% (.10)	**23**	
24	Tax on amount on line 23. Use the Tax Rate Schedule in the instructions	**24**	
25	Multiply line 24 by ten (10). If line 11 is zero, **skip** lines 26 through 28, enter this amount on line 29, and go to line 30	**25**	
26	Multiply line 22 by 10% (.10)	**26**		
27	Tax on amount on line 26. Use the Tax Rate Schedule in the instructions	**27**		
28	Multiply line 27 by ten (10)	**28**	
29	Subtract line 28 from line 25. Multiple recipients, see instructions . . . . . ▶	**29**	
30	**Tax on lump-sum distribution.** Add lines 7 and 29. Also include this amount in the total on Form 1040, line 43, or Form 1041, Schedule G, line 1b, whichever applies . . . . . . ▶	**30**	

For Paperwork Reduction Act Notice, see instructions.

Cat. No. 13187U

Form **4972** (2004)

10-Year Forward Averaging

A participant born prior to January 1, 1936 may be eligible for **10-year forward averaging** when taking a lump-sum distribution from a qualified plan. Contrary to its title, 10-year forward averaging does not allow the taxpayer to pay the income tax attributable to the lump-sum distribution over a 10-year period, but it still may lower the current income tax attributable to the lump-sum distribution. Because the income tax system incorporates graduated tax rate schedules, any large or relatively large distribution will cause the taxpayer to pay tax at higher rates because the entire distribution is included as ordinary income. If the distribution were large enough, it could cause a taxpayer to move from the lowest tax bracket through all of the rates up to the top tax bracket. This result is often referred to as "bracket creep" since this type of distribution will cause the taxpayer to pay various rates of tax on different parts of the distribution. 10-year forward averaging is designed to mitigate the negative impact attributable to a move to a higher income tax bracket because of a lump-sum distribution.

Under 10-year forward averaging, the income tax due on a lump-sum distribution is calculated by dividing the taxable portion of the lump-sum distribution by 10 and then applying the 1986 individual income tax rates (see Exhibit 7.8) to the result (one-tenth of the total taxable distribution). This result is then multiplied by 10 to determine the total income tax due on the distribution.

The benefit of 10-year forward averaging is that the taxpayer avoids the distribution being taxed in the higher current income tax brackets. The averaging (calculating the taxable amounts as one tenth) mitigates against income tax bracket creep due to the lump-sum distribution. Because the 1986 individual income tax rates are used in the calculation and not the tax rates for the year of distribution, consideration must be given to both current rates and the 1986 rates. There has been a declining trend in income tax rates over the last 20 years, which has reduced the benefits of 10-year forward averaging. 10-year averaging does not allow the tax to be paid over various years; rather, the tax is paid in the year of the lump-sum distribution. The following exhibit illustrates the 10-year forward averaging calculation:

EXHIBIT 7.8

Step		Notes
1	**Lump-Sum distribution**	
2	Less employee's contributions that were previously taxed and the cost of insurance	This includes participant's after-tax contributions to a qualified plan, PS-58 costs (resulting from life insurance within a qualified plan), and certain loans from qualified plans that are treated as taxable distributions.
3	Less minimum distribution allowance (only applicable to small lump-sum distributions less than $70,000)	The minimum distribution allowance is the lesser of: 1. $10,000 or 2. one-half of the adjusted total taxable amount of the lump-sum distribution for the taxable year, reduced (but not below zero) by 20 percent of the excess (if any) of the adjusted total taxable amount over $20,000.
4	**Equals taxable amount of distribution**	
5	Divide the taxable amount by 10	
6	Determine the tax on the result determined in Step 5	Tax is calculated by using 1986 income tax rates.
7	Multiply the result of Step 6 by 10	Result is tax attributable to distribution.
8	Pay the tax from Step 7	The tax is paid in one payment.

EXHIBIT 7.9 **1986 INCOME TAX RATE TABLE FOR TEN-YEAR AVERAGING CALCULATION**

Over -	But Not Over --	The Tax Is	Amount Over --
$ -0-	$1,190	11%	$ -0-
1,190	2,270	$ 130.90 + 12%	1,190
2,270	4,530	260.50 + 14%	2,270
4,530	6,690	576.90 + 15%	4,530
6,690	9,170	900.90 + 16%	6,690
9,170	11,440	1,297.70 + 18%	9,170
11,440	13,710	1,706.30 + 20%	11,440
13,710	17,160	2,160.30 + 23%	13,710
17,160	22,880	2,953.80 + 26%	17,160
22,880	28,600	4,441.00 + 30%	22,880
28,600	34,320	6,157.00 + 34%	28,600
34,320	42,300	8,101.80 + 38%	34,320
42,300	57,190	11,134.20 + 42%	42,300
57,190	85,790	17,388.00 + 48%	57,190
85,790	....	31,116.00 + 50%	85,790

EXAMPLE 7.3

Kerstin is covered under a noncontributory qualified plan. She has never made any contributions to the plan; all contributions were pretax employer contributions. She was born before 1936 and takes a lump-sum distribution that qualifies for 10-year forward averaging. How much income tax will she pay utilizing 10-year forward averaging if her account balance is $100,000 at the time of the distribution?

Lump-sum distribution	$100,000.00	
Less minimum distribution allowance	0.00	*
Taxable portion of distribution	$100,000.00	
One tenth of taxable portion	$10,000.00	
Tax on one tenth of distribution	$1,447.10	10-year forward averaging rate table
Tax due on distribution ($1,447.10 x 10)	$14,471.00	Ten times the amount previously calculated

* The lesser of $10,000 or $50,000 (50,000 = 0.5 x $100,000)is $10,000.
The $10,000 is reduced by $16,000 (16,000 = 20% x ($100,000 - $20,000)), but not below zero.
Therefore, the minimum distribution allowance is zero.

Before electing 10-year averaging, a lump sum distribution recipient should evaluate the tax that would be paid under the current ordinary income tax rates versus the 10-year forward averaging rates. In addition, prior to electing a lump sum distribution, the participant might want to consider the long-run strategy of rolling the account balance into an IRA and taking a 72(t) distribution, which is explained later in this chapter.

2005 SINGLE INCOME TAX RATES

EXHIBIT 7.10

Over -	But Not Over --	The Tax Is	Amount Over --
$ -0-	$7,300	10%	$ -0-
$7,300	$29,700	$730.00 + 15%	$7,300
$29,700	$71,950	$4,090.00 + 25%	$29,700
$71,950	$150,150	$14,652.50 + 28%	$71,950
$150,150	$326,450	$36,548.50 + 33%	$150,150
$326,450	....	$94,727.50 + 35%	$326,450

2005 MARRIED FILING JOINTLY INCOME TAX RATES

EXHIBIT 7.11

Over -	But Not Over --	The Tax Is	Amount Over --
$ -0-	$14,600	10%	$ -0-
$14,600	$59,400	$1,460.00 + 15%	$14,600
$59,400	$119,950	$8,180.00 + 25%	$59,400
$119,950	$182,800	$23,317.50 + 28%	$119,950
$182,800	$326,450	$40,915.50 + 33%	$182,800
$326,450	....	$88,320.00 + 35%	$326,450

EXAMPLE 7.4

Joe Bob, a single taxpayer, takes a $600,000 lump-sum distribution from CR Inc. qualified plan. Joe Bob did not make any contributions and the plan did not contain any insurance. How much is Joe Bob's tax if he elects 10-year forward averaging?

Line 1	Lump Sum Distribution	$600,000	
Line 2	Less: Employee Contributions	0	
Line 3	Less: MD Allowance	0	
Line 4	Equals taxable amount of distribution	$600,000	
Line 5	Divide the taxable amount by 10	$60,000	
Line 6	Tax on Line 5	$18,736.80	
Line 7	Multiply the result of Step 6 by 10	$187,368.00	
Line 8	Pay the tax from Step 7	$187,368.00	(31.228%)

EXAMPLE 7.5

Assume the same facts as above except Joe Bob does not elect 10-year averaging? The tax is now $190,470.

Line 1	Lump Sum Distribution	$600,000	
Line 2	Tax on Line 1	$190,470	
Line 3	Pay the tax from Line 2	$190,470	(31.75%)

Notice that in this instance it is in Joe Bob's best interest to elect 10-year averaging because he will pay $3,102 less tax ($190,470 - $187,368).

If Joe Bob was married then the tax would be:

Line 1	Lump Sum Distribution	$600,000	
Line 2	Tax on Line 1	$184,063	
Line 3	Pay the Tax from Line 2	$184,063	(30.68%)

If Joe Bob was married, then not electing the 10-year averaging would be best because he would pay $3,305 less tax ($187,368 - $184,063).

Pre-1974 Capital Gain Treatment

Participants born prior to January 1, 1936 are also eligible to treat the portion of a lump-sum distribution attributable to pre-1974 participation in a qualified plan as long-term capital gain (taxable at 20 percent, not eligible for special 15 percent capital gains rate).[5] To calculate the portion that will be considered long-term capital gain, the total lump-sum distribution is multiplied by the ratio of the participant's number of months of pre-1974 participation in the qualified plan to the total number of months of the participant's plan participation. The portion remaining of the lump-sum distribution is eligible for ten-year forward averaging, or is otherwise taxed as ordinary income.

$$\text{Long-term capital gain portion} = \frac{\text{Months of pre-1974 participation}}{\text{Total months of participation}} \times \text{Taxable distribution}$$

EXAMPLE 7.6

Josh is covered under a noncontributory qualified plan. He has never made any contributions to the plan; all contributions have been pretax employer contributions. He was born before 1936 and qualifies for pre-1974 capital gain treatment. He has been in the plan since 1964 and is taking a lump-sum distribution of $1,000,000 in 2004. What portion of the distribution from the qualified plan qualifies for capital gain treatment?

---

5. Section 1122(h)(3) of the Tax Reform Act of 1986, PL 99-514 as amended by PL 100-647(1988).

$$\text{Long-term capital gain portion} = \frac{\text{10 years (1974-1964) x 12 months}}{\text{40 years (2004-1964) x 12 months}} \text{ x } \$1,000,000$$

$$\text{Long-term capital gain portion} = \frac{\text{120 months}}{\text{480 months}} \text{ x } \$1,000,000$$

$$\text{Long-term capital gain portion} = \$250,000$$

The remaining $750,000 ($1,000,000 - $250,000) is taxed at ordinary income tax rates or may be eligible for 10-year forward averaging.

Net Unrealized Appreciation (NUA)

Taxpayers that receive a lump-sum distribution of employer securities (such as stock) may receive special tax treatment on the distribution. This tax treatment consists of favorable capital gain treatment instead of ordinary income tax treatment on the NUA portion of the distribution as well as deferral of recognition of the gain on the NUA portion until the distributed employer securities are sold. Although this treatment certainly applies to lump-sum distributions of employer securities from any qualified plan, it is most likely to occur from a stock bonus plan or ESOP.

Employer securities generally include stocks, bonds, and debentures of the employer corporation as well as securities of a parent company or subsidiary. However, distributions generally consist of employer stock.

Net unrealized appreciation (NUA) is defined as the excess of the fair market value of the employer securities at the date of the lump-sum distribution over the cost of the employer securities at the date the securities were contributed to the qualified plan.

$$\text{Fair Market Value at Date of Distribution} - \text{Value of Securities Used at the Date of the Employer Contribution} = \text{Net Unrealized Appreciation}$$

The portion of the lump-sum distribution attributable to the cost of the employer securities (the value of the employer's tax deduction) will be taxable as ordinary income (eligible for 10-year forward averaging if the participant was born before January 1, 1936) to the participant in the year of the distribution and this value is considered the participant's adjusted taxable basis in the employer securities. At the date of the subsequent sale of the employer securities, the participant will be required to recognize the long-term capital gain deferred since the date of the distribution. Any subsequent gain after the distribution date will be treated as either short-term capital gain or long-term capital gain based on the holding period beginning at the date of the distribution. If at the date of the subsequent sale the value of the employer securities has decreased since the date of the initial distribution, the participant will decrease the recognition of the deferred long-term capital gain to an amount equal to the differences between the fair market value of the stock at the date of the subsequent sale and the adjusted taxable basis of the securities.

EXHIBIT 7.12 ILLUSTRATION OF NET UNREALIZED APPRECIATION

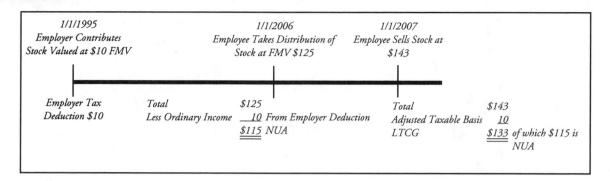

| **EXAMPLE 7.7** | Cody received a lump-sum distribution of his employer's stock from his qualified plan. The lump-sum distribution was 1,000 shares of the employer's stock valued at $2,000,000 as of the date of the distribution. The value of the stock at the date the employer contributed the stock to the plan was $500,000. When Cody receives the $2,000,000 lump-sum distribution of the employer stock, $500,000 of the distribution will be taxed as ordinary income in the year of the lump-sum distribution. The remaining gain of $1,500,000 will not be recognized until the employer stock is sold. At the date the employer stock is sold, Cody's adjusted taxable basis in the stock will be $500,000, the amount taxed as ordinary income in the year of distribution. If he subsequently sells the stock for any amount greater than $500 per share, then Cody will have a capital gain. The first $1,500,000 of gain will be taxable as long-term capital gain and any gain in excess will be short or long-term capital gain depending on the holding period after the distribution date. Thus, if he sold it at the date of distribution for $2,000,000 then he would have a long-term capital gain of $1,500,000, the NUA. |

Assume, utilizing the facts above, that Cody sells the stock two years after the distribution date for $2,120 per share. What would be the tax consequences?

$2,120,000	Sales Price ($2,120 x 1,000 shares)
$500,000	Adjusted taxable basis (taxed as ordinary income in the year of distribution)
$1,620,000	Long-term capital gain (NUA and subsequent long-term capital gain)

If Cody had held the stock for less than one year and one day (the long-term holding period requirement), the tax consequences would be as follows:

$2,120,000	Sales price ($2,120 x 1,000 shares)
$500,000	Adjusted taxable basis (taxed as ordinary income in the year of distribution)
$1,620,000	Total capital gain
$1,500,000	Long-term capital gain (NUA)
$120,000	Short-term capital gain since distribution

There are several issues involved in this type of transaction. First, the participant must qualify for lump-sum distribution treatment. Second, the NUA portion must be relatively high in comparison to the cost basis portion; otherwise, the recipient may be paying too much immediate ordinary income tax for the benefit of future long-term capital gain treatment. The next issue concerns whether the stock is to be held by the recipient. If so, then the investment risks of holding a large concentration of a single security must be considered. Finally, cash flow considerations must be evaluated to determine the impact of holding the securities versus selling the securities. Note: The amount subject to ordinary income tax is subject to a penalty if there is no exception in the Code.

In the event that this type of transaction does not make economic sense for a participant, the assets in the qualified plan can be rolled over into an IRA. However, if these assets are rolled into an IRA, the benefits of NUA are lost because distributions from IRAs are always characterized as ordinary income. The loss of the special tax treatment may not be that important if the NUA portion is relatively small compared to the ordinary income element, and the rollover allows for the continued deferral of income tax.

Inherited Securities with NUA resulting from a Qualified Plan Distribution

Stock that was part of a distribution from a qualified plan may be transferred upon the death of the participant to a beneficiary or heir. The question arises, "How should this stock be treated by the beneficiary for tax purposes?" There are two competing concepts in the IRC that must be considered. First is the concept of adjustment to FMV at the date of death. If this rule is applied, the stock, which is a capital asset, would simply have the same adjusted taxable basis to the heir as the fair market value reported for estate tax purposes. The second concept is that of income in respect to a decedent, which is income earned at death yet not recognized prior to death. Such income will not receive an adjustment to FMV at date of death. For example, the adjusted taxable basis of assets in a qualified plan or IRA are not adjusted to fair market value as a result of the death of the owner.

The appropriate tax treatment is a fair application of the competing concepts. The inherited stock will receive an adjustment of basis to FMV at date of death less any unrecognized NUA. The tax will be paid when the assets are disposed of by the heirs.

EXAMPLE 7.8	Assume the same facts from Example 7.7 above, except that Cody dies shortly after the lump-sum distribution. At his death, the total value of the stock is $2,750,000. There is still $1,500,00 of NUA that has not been taxed. Cody's heirs will generally receive the stock with a new adjusted taxable basis equal to the fair market value at the date of death (a step to the fair market value). However, when received as part of a lump-sum distribution of employer securities, the heirs' adjusted taxable basis in the stock is equal to the fair market value of the stock at the date of death less the NUA. Therefore in this example, Cody's heirs will have an adjusted taxable basis in the stock of $1,250,000 ($2,750,000 - $1,500,000).

QUALIFIED DOMESTIC RELATIONS ORDER

ERISA generally prevents a participant's qualified plan assets from being assigned or alienated in favor of a third party. However, a spouse or former spouse may be entitled to a portion of a participant's qualified plan benefits. An exception to the ERISA anti-alienation rules has been made if the assignment or alienation is at the direction of a **Qualified Domestic Relations Order (QDRO)**.

A QDRO is an order, judgment, or decree pursuant to a state domestic relations law that creates or recognizes the right of a third party alternate payee (nonparticipant) to receive benefits from a qualified plan. QDROs can be used for the provision of child support, alimony, or marital property rights to a spouse, former spouse, child, or other dependent of a participant. A QDRO can be issued by a judge or state agency that has the authority to issue orders, judgements, or decrees.

Although there is not a particular form that must be followed, a QDRO must specify the name and last known mailing address of the participant and the name and mailing address of each third party alternate payee covered by the order. It must also specify the amount or percentage of the participant's benefits to be paid by the plan to each third party alternate payee or the manner in which the amount or percentage is to be determined, the number of payments or period to which such order applies, and each plan to which the QDRO applies. A QDRO can give the 3rd party payee all or part of the retirement benefits. The QDRO cannot, however, provide for any distribution mechanism or benefit not allowed by the retirement plan itself.

The administrator of the qualified plan is responsible for determining whether a domestic relations order is qualified. Therefore, the plan document must establish reasonable procedures to determine the qualified status. Administrators are required to notify participants and alternate payees when they receive a domestic relations order and to furnish a copy of the plan's procedures for determining the qualified status of such orders. Once the administrator determines the plan is qualified, the administrator must follow the plan's procedures for making QDRO distributions.

QDROs are often used either to provide support payments to the alternate payee or to divide marital property pursuant to divorce. There are two basic approaches that may be used to divide the benefit depending on the reason the QDRO is being used. One approach, often called the "shared payment approach," splits the actual benefit payments made between the participant and the alternate payee. Thus, each payment that would be made to the participant under the plan is split such that the alternate payee receives part of the payment and the participant receives the remaining portion of the payment. Under this approach, the alternate payee will not receive any payments unless the participant receives a payment or is already in pay status. This approach is often used when a participant has already begun to receive a stream of payments from the plan, usually at retirement, such as a life annuity.

EXAMPLE 7.9

After many years of marriage, Paul and Lucy filed for divorce. Paul has a qualified retirement plan from his previous employer. He currently receives $800 per month in retirement benefits. Assume the qualified plan allows for a shared payment approach for QDRO distributions. If Paul and Lucy's QDRO allocated 50% of the benefit to be paid to each, then each month Paul will receive $400 and Lucy will receive $400.

The second approach, often called the "separate interest" approach, divides the participant's retirement benefit into two separate portions. Depending on the plan document, this may give the alternate payee the right to receive a lump-sum distribution equal to the present value of the account balance or a separate right to receive their portion of the retirement benefit payable at a later time similar to that of the participant. This approach is often used when the retirement plan is being divided pursuant to divorce but before the participant retires.

EXAMPLE 7.10

After several years of marriage, Steven and Jeanette have filed for divorce. Steven has a qualified retirement plan through his current employer with an account balance of $100,000. Assume the qualified plan allows for a separate interest approach for QDRO distributions. The plan states that if a QDRO is issued, then the QDRO must provide for a lump-sum distribution of a percentage of the account balance to the nonparticipant as ordered by the court. If Steven and Jeanette's QDRO states that Jeanette is to receive 40% of the account balance, then a lump distribution will be made by the plan to Jeanette in the amount of $40,000.

It should be noted that the plan document, and not the court, determines how the retirement plan will satisfy QDROs (i.e., split account, payout the present value). As long as the QDRO complies with the plan document, the participant and the alternate payee can agree to the approach utilized.

After several years of marriage, Chris and Jenn filed for divorce. Jenn has a qualified retirement plan through her current employer. Assume the qualified plan allows for a separate interest approach for QDRO distributions. The qualified plan documents provide that if a QDRO is issued, then the QDRO can provide for any one of the following:

- A lump-sum distribution to the alternate payee of the present value of the estimated future benefit.
- A lump-sum distribution of a percentage of the account balance.
- A separation of the account balance where a percentage of the account is allocated to each party and is maintained by the plan provider for each party payable when the participant reaches retirement age regardless of whether the participant actually retires.

Chris and Jenn's QDRO can utilize any one of these three methods to separate the plan interest.

A distribution pursuant to a QDRO will not be considered a taxable distribution to the third party alternate payee as long as the assets are deposited into the recipient's IRA or qualified plan. If a distribution pursuant to a QDRO is not deposited in an IRA or other qualified plan, the third party alternate payee will be subjected to tax at ordinary income tax rates on the value of the distribution. The distribution is also subject to the 10 percent early withdrawal penalty if it is not deposited into the recipient's IRA or qualified plan.

QUALIFIED DOMESTIC RELATIONS ORDER
PAUL AND LUCY SMITH

Parties

The Participant is Paul Smith. The Participant's address is 123 Blueberry Lane, Any City, All States, 12345. The Participant's Social Security number is 123-45-6789.

The Alternate Payee is Lucy Smith. The Alternate Payee's address is 987 Strawberry Lane, Any City, All States, 12345. The Alternate Payee's Social Security number is 987-65-4321. The Alternate Payee is the former spouse of the Participant.

Plan

This order applies to benefits under the ABC Retirement Plan, herein called the Plan.

Amount of Benefits to be Paid to Alternate Payee

The Alternate Payee shall receive 50% of each benefit payment made from the Plan.

Form and Commencement of Payment to Alternate Payee

The Alternate Payee shall receive payments from the Plan of the benefits assigned to the Alternate Payee under this Order (including payments attributable to the period in which the issue of whether this Order is a qualified domestic relations order is being determined) commencing as soon as practicable after this Order has been determined to be a qualified domestic relations order or, if later, on the date the Participant commences receiving benefit payments from the Plan. Payment to the Alternate Payee shall cease on the earlier of: Alternate Payee's remarriage, or the date that payments from the Plan with respect to the Participant cease.

PLAN LOANS

Although distributions of qualified plan assets to participants are generally not permitted until retirement or termination, qualified plans are permitted, but not required, to provide loans from the plan to participants. The **plan loans** must be made available to all participants and beneficiaries on an effectively equal basis, must be limited in amount, must be repaid within a certain time period, must bear a reasonable rate of interest, must be adequately secured, and the administrator must maintain proper accounting for the loans. Although any qualified plan could establish a loan provision, loan provisions are common only in cash or deferred arrangement (**CODA**) type plans such as 401(k) and 403(b) plans. Loans are prohibited on other tax-sheltered retirement savings vehicles, such as IRAs, SEPs, and SIMPLEs (discussed later).

Key Concepts

Underline/highlight the answers to these questions as you read:

1. What is the maximum amount a participant can borrow from a 401(k) plan?

2. When must loans from a 401(k) plan be repaid?

3. Discuss the impact of plan termination on plan loans.

Amount of Loan

Loans from qualified plans may not exceed the lesser of $50,000 or one-half of the fair market value of the participant's vested accrued benefit under the plan. However, where a participant's vested accrued benefit is less than $20,000, the available plan loan is limited to the lesser of the vested accrued benefit or $10,000. Consider the examples (A - F) in the following table:

	Vested Accrued Benefit	Maximum Permissible
A	$1,000,000	$50,000
B	$120,000	$50,000
C	$80,000	$40,000
D	$24,000	$12,000
E	$18,000	$10,000
F	$9,000	$9,000

Additionally, if the participant had an outstanding loan balance within the previous twelve months, the otherwise maximum permissible loan is reduced by the highest outstanding loan balance during the twelve month period ending the day prior to when the current loan is made.

EXAMPLE 7.12

Pat has $125,000 in vested plan benefits. He borrowed $40,000 on January 1, 2003 from his 401(k) plan and repaid $25,000 on August 14, 2003. On December 31, 2003, Pat's maximum permissible loan from the plan would be $10,000. Pat is subjected to this limitation because his highest outstanding balance within twelve months of December 30, 2003 (the day before the date of the calculation) is $40,000. The otherwise maximum permissible loan amount of $50,000 must be reduced by $40,000 to determine the ultimate maximum loan amount available of $10,000.

If instead, Pat calculated his maximum permissible loan on August 16, 2004, he could borrow $35,000 because of the previous repayment. This is calculated by reducing the maximum loan of $50,000 by the highest outstanding loan balance within the prior twelve months of $15,000 ($40,000 - $25,000).

For purposes of the loan calculation, all plans under the same employer are treated as one for the employer.

EXHIBIT 7.14

- Qualified plans may permit loans up to the lesser of one-half of the vested plan accrued benefit up to $50,000.
- Except, if the vested accrued benefit is less than or equal to $20,000, then a loan is permitted up to the lesser of $10,000 or the vested accrued benefit.
- Reduce available loan by maximum outstanding loan within the past year.
- Loans are usually associated with 401(k) and 403(b) plans.
- Loans must generally be repaid within five years with an exception for loans associated with the purchase of personal residences, which can be repaid over 30 years.

Repayment of Loans

Loans from qualified plans must generally be repaid within five years from the date the loan commences; otherwise, the loan is treated as a distribution as of the date of the original loan distribution. Loans treated as a distribution will be treated in the same manner as any other distribution from a qualified plan and will be subject to ordinary income tax and potentially the early withdrawal penalty of 10 percent if the participant fails to meet one of the exceptions (discussed below).

The five-year repayment rule does not apply to loans that are used for the purchase of a principal residence. In such a case, the IRC provides that the loan must be repaid over "a reasonable time" determined at the time of the loan. Presumably, the repayment of loans for purposes of a purchase of a personal residence could be over 30 years, the life of the mortgage, etc. As each plan may have different loan provisions, it is important to determine the provisions that are provided in the plan document and determine the policies from the loan administrator.

Quick Quiz

Highlight the answer to these questions:

1. Loans from qualified plans can never exceed 50% of the participant's vested account balance.
   a. True
   b. False

2. Loans from qualified plans must always be repaid within five years.
   a. True
   b. False

3. The law requires loans from qualified plans to be repaid upon the participant's termination of employment from the plan sponsor.
   a. True
   b. False

False, False, False.

Loans are not only required to be repaid within a specific period of time, but are also required to be repaid in a specific manner over the repayment period. Substantially level amortization of the loan is required over the term of the loan.[6] Loan repayments must be level over the repayment

6. IRC Section 72(p)(2)(C).

period and must be made at least quarterly. In other words, the loan cannot be repaid in full at the end of the five-year period. Generally employers require that loans be repaid only through payroll and if not repaid before termination, the loan may be treated as a distribution.

EXAMPLE 7.13

Kim has a vested accrued benefit of $200,000 and receives $70,000 to be repaid in level quarterly installments over five years. Kim has a deemed distribution of $20,000 (the excess of $70,000 over $50,000) at the time of the loan because the loan exceeds the $50,000 maximum permissible loan limit. The remaining $50,000 loan is not a deemed distribution.

EXAMPLE 7.14

Ginger has a vested accrued benefit of $30,000 and borrows $20,000 from her plan as a loan repayable in level monthly installments over five years. Ginger's maximum permissible loan is $15,000 (50% of $30,000), so her loan is $5,000 more than permissible. In this case, Ginger has a deemed distribution of $5,000 at the date of the loan. The remaining $15,000 is a permissible loan and would not be a deemed distribution. The $5,000 will be taxed as ordinary income and potentially subject to a 10% early withdrawal penalty unless George meets one of the exceptions.

EXAMPLE 7.15

Cindy has a vested accrued benefit of $100,000, and she takes a $50,000 loan. The loan is repayable in level quarterly installments over seven years, and Cindy is using the proceeds to buy a new car. Because the repayment period of the loan exceeds the maximum term of five years, Cindy has a deemed distribution of $50,000 at the date the loan is made. The $50,000 will be taxed as ordinary income and potentially subject to a 10% early withdrawal penalty unless Cindy meets one of the exceptions.

Impact of Loans When an Employee is Terminated

Most plan documents require that loans be repaid upon termination of employment; however, this is not a requirement under the law. Loan repayments are generally accommodated through payroll deduction, which, of course, is unavailable after termination occurs. If a participant fails to repay a loan from a qualified plan before termination, the employer will generally declare the unpaid portion a deemed distribution subject to ordinary income tax and possibly the 10 percent early withdrawal penalty.

However, plans may provide that the outstanding loan balance reduce the amount of a direct rollover distribution. The examples below illustrate this available option.

EXAMPLE 7.16

In 2006, Alina has a vested account balance of $10,000 in Plan Y, of which $3,000 is invested in a plan loan to Alina that is secured by the remainder of her vested account balance. Upon termination of employment in 2006, Alina, who is under the age of 70½, elects a direct rollover distribution of her entire account balance of Plan Y, and the outstanding plan loan is offset against the distributable account balance.

Plan Y must pay $7,000 ($10,000 - $3,000) directly to the eligible retirement plan chosen by Alina in the direct roll-over. When Alina's account balance was offset by the amount of the $3,000 unpaid loan balance, Alina received a plan loan offset amount (equivalent to $3,000), an eligible roll-over distribution. Alina must roll over $3,000 to an eligible retirement plan within a 60-day period, or else the $3,000 distribution will be treated as any other distribution from a qualified plan, subject to ordinary income tax and possibly early withdrawal penalty. [7]

EXAMPLE 7.17

Assume the same facts as in the previous example except that the terms governing the plan loan to Alina provide that upon termination of employment, Alina's account balance is automatically offset by the amount of any unpaid loan balance to repay the loan. Alina terminates employment but does not request a distribution from Plan Y. Nevertheless, pursuant to the terms governing the plan loan, Alina's account balance is automatically offset by the amount of the $3,000 unpaid loan balance.

The $3,000 plan loan offset amount attributable to the plan loan in this example is treated in the same manner as the $3,000 plan loan offset amount in the prior example. Alina will have ordinary income and possible early withdrawal penalty.

EXAMPLE 7.18

Assume the same facts as in the previous example except that instead of providing for an automatic offset upon termination of employment to repay the plan loan, the terms governing the plan loan require full repayment of the loan by Alina within 30 days of termination of employment. Alina terminates employment, does not elect a distribution from Plan Y and also fails to repay the plan loan within 30 days. The administrator of Plan Y declares the plan loan to Alina in default and executes on the loan by offsetting Alina's account balance by the amount of the $3,000 unpaid loan balance.

The $3,000 plan loan offset amount attributable to the plan loan in this example is treated in the same manner as the $3,000 plan loan offset amount in the previous two examples. The result in this example is the same even though the

---

7.   IRC Section 402(c)(3).

plan administrator treats the loan as in default before offsetting Alina's accrued benefit by the amount of the unpaid loan.

EXAMPLE 7.19

Again assume the same facts as the previous example except that Alina elects to receive the distribution of the account balance that remains after the $3,000 offset to repay the plan loan instead of electing a direct rollover of the remaining account balance.

In this case, the taxable amount of the distribution to Alina is $10,000, not $3,000. Because the amount of the $3,000 offset attributable to the loan is included in determining the amount that equals 20 percent of the eligible rollover distribution received by Alina, withholding in the amount of $2,000 (20 percent of $10,000) is required. The $2,000 is required to be withheld from the $7,000 to be distributed to Alina in cash so that Alina actually receives a check for $5,000.

Alina would still be entitled to roll over the entire $10,000 within the 60-day period and to avoid applicable income tax and penalties.

Alina's Vested Account Balance = $10,000			
Loan = $3,000			
Terminates and Rolls Over	**Terminates and Does Not Rollover**	**Terminates and Required Repayment within 30 Days**	**Terminates Takes Distribution of Vested Account Balance**
Alina must rollover $3,000 to an eligible retirement plan within a 60-day period (30-day period in the third example) of the termination, or the $3,000 will be subjected to ordinary income tax and possibly the 10 percent early withdrawal penalty.			Alina receives a distribution in the amount of $5,000, $10,000 less withholding and less the outstanding loan. To avoid taxation on the full $10,000, Alina must contribute $10,000 to a new retirement plan or IRA within a 60-day period.

EXAMPLE 7.20

Fred, age 40, has an account balance in Plan Z, a qualified profit sharing plan that includes a CODA. Plan Z does not permit after-tax employee contributions. In 2005, Fred receives a loan from Plan Z. In 2007, Fred stops repayment and is therefore taxed on a deemed distribution equal to the amount of the unpaid loan balance. The deemed distribution is not an eligible rollover distribution because Fred has not separated from service or experienced any other event that permits the distribution of the elective contributions that secure the loan. Plan Z is prohibited from executing on the loan. Accordingly, Fred's account balance is not offset by the amount of the unpaid loan balance at the time Fred stops repayment on the loan. Thus, there is no distribution of an offset amount that is an eligible rollover distribution in 2007. The deemed distribution is also subject to the 10% early withdrawal penalty.

| LOAN SUMMARY FOR FAILURE TO REPAY LOAN OR TERMINATION OF EMPLOYMENT | EXHIBIT 7.15 |

- Many qualified plans treat an outstanding loan as a distribution from the plan and issue the participant a Form 1099R (distributions from a retirement plan). The participant will then report this distribution as ordinary income, and it may be subject to the 10% early withdrawal penalty if the participant does not meet one of the exceptions.

- A qualified plan may provide that the employee has a certain period of time to repay the loan after termination, or it will otherwise treat the loan as a distribution.

- Finally, qualified plans may provide that the loan is simply an offset of the distribution, and this offset can either be treated as a taxable distribution or may be rolled over by the participant to another qualified plan.

DISTRIBUTIONS PRIOR TO 59½

In some cases, individuals may want or need to take distributions from a qualified plan before their retirement. To discourage taxpayers from using the funds before retirement, taxable distributions before the age of 59½ will generally be subject to a 10 percent early withdrawal penalty. Most plans also limit the ability of participants to take early distributions from a qualified plan except in the case of the participant's termination, death, or retirement. However, some plans may permit rollovers and substantially equal periodic payments as distributions before the age of 59½. Although not common, profit sharing plans may permit in-service distributions from the plan after the participant has participated in the plan for at least two years. This provision may be included in a plan to encourage plan participation within a company by alleviating the employees' fear of not being able to access the funds.

EARLY WITHDRAWAL PENALTY

In any case, a distribution prior to the participant attaining the age of 59½ may be subjected to a 10 percent **early withdrawal penalty** unless the distribution is on account of one of several exceptions. All of the exceptions coincide with the government's intention that participants use the plan assets for their retirement, but in circumstances like death and disability, it makes sense to allow the participant (or the participant's beneficiaries) to withdraw the assets prior to their scheduled retirement.

Exceptions to the 10 Percent Early Withdrawal Penalty

The 10 percent early withdrawal penalty will not apply if the distribution is made on account of the plan participant attaining the age of 59½, the participant's death, or the participant's disability. A participant is considered disabled if he is "unable to engage in any substantial gainful activity by reason of any medically determinable physical or mental impairment which can be expected to result in death or to be of long-continued and indefinite duration."[8] A participant must also provide proof substantiating his disability claim. Each case is evaluated on a case by case basis to determine if the participant meets the disability definition. Generally, although not always, suffering from one of the following will be considered disabled: loss of two limbs; certain progressive diseases that result in a loss of a limb; certain diseases of the heart, lungs or blood vessels that produce breathlessness, pain, or fatigue from slight exertion; cancer that is inoperable and progressive; damage to the brain that has resulted in severe loss of judgment, intellect, orientation, or memory; mental diseases requiring continued institutionalization or constant supervision of the individual; loss of vision such that the best correction leaves 20/200 eyesight; permanent and total loss of speech; and total deafness uncorrectible by a hearing aid.

Key Concepts

Underline/highlight the answers to these questions as you read:

1. What is the penalty for taking distributions from a qualified plan before the participant attains the age of 59½?

2. List the exceptions to the early withdrawal penalty.

| EXHIBIT 7.16 | SUMMARY OF 10 PERCENT PENALTY EXCEPTIONS |

Exceptions to 10% Early Withdrawal Penalty
• Death
• Attainment of age 59½
• Disability
• Substantially equal periodic payments (Section 72(t))
• Medical expenses that exceed 7.5 percent of AGI
• Qualified Domestic Relations Order (QDRO)
• Attainment of age 55 and separation from service

Additionally, if the distribution is part of a series of substantially equal periodic payments, also called Section 72(t) distributions, made at least annually for the life or life expectancy of the participant or the joint lives or joint life expectancies of the participant and his designated beneficiary, the payments will not be subjected to the 10 percent early withdrawal penalty. The payments must begin after the participant has separated from service, and to be considered substantially equal periodic payments, the payments must be made in any one of the following three ways: [9]

---

8. IRC Section 72(m).

1. **Required Minimum Distribution** Method.

   The payments are calculated in the same manner as required under minimum distribution rules (discussed below).

2. **Fixed Amortization** Method.

   The payment is calculated over the participant's life expectancy if single, or the joint life expectancy if married, and the interest rate is reasonable (not to exceed 120% of the federal midterm rate).

3. **Fixed Annuitization** Method.

   The participant takes distributions of the account over a number of years determined by dividing the account balance by an annuity factor using a reasonable interest rate and mortality table.

Jack, age 45, wanted to explore his distribution options under IRC Section 72(t) rules. His account balance is $1,000,000.

Option 1 - Required Minimum Distribution Method

Assume the required minimum distribution factor was 38.8 years.[10]

$$\frac{\$1,000,000}{38.8} = \$25,773.20 \text{ per year (1st year)}$$

Option 2 - Fixed Amortization Method

Assume the interest rate is 6.5%,[11] and the joint life expectancy is 38.8 years.

N = 38.8

i = 6.5

PV = $1,000,000

FV = 0

PMT $_{OA}$ = $75,254.61 per year

Option 3 - Fixed Annuitization Method

Assume a $1,000,000 annuity factor for 6.5% and 38.8 years which results in a factor of 15.19.[12]

$$\frac{\$1,000,000}{15.19} = \$65,832.78$$

---

9. These three methods are set forth in Notice 89-25 as modified by Rev. Ruling 2002-62. An alternate method may be used, but must be approved through the use of a private letter ruling.
10. The factor is determined by the "Single Life Table" in Reg. Section 1.401(a)(9) - 9.
11. The interest rate is 120% of the applicable midterm rate. The interest rate in this example is provided for illustration purposes.
12. The factor is calculated based on the mortality table in Appendix B of Rev. Ruling 2002-62. This calculation would normally be made by an actuary.

Notice that Options 2 and 3 provide a larger payment than Option 1. For example, a person may want the larger payment to help finance a new business venture. The participant can choose any of the methods.

In the case above, Jack may choose Option 1 if he needs some current income but does not want to significantly deplete his account balance. Recall that he must continue to withdraw until he is 59½. Jack could choose Option 2 or 3, which provide larger payments, if, for example, he were starting a new business and needed the extra cash flow, or expected that business losses from a flow-through entity would shelter part of the distributions.

The payment calculated under one of the methods determined above must continue exactly as calculated for the later of five years from the date of the first payment or the participant attaining the age of 59½.[13] If the payments change in any way, the participant will be considered to have made a distribution equal to the full account balance of the qualified plan in the first year of the substantially equal periodic payments. The addition of this amount to the participant's taxable income will also subject the participant to an early withdrawal penalty as well as penalties and interest for the years passed since the first year of the distribution.

Revenue Ruling 2002-62 allows a taxpayer to make a one-time irrevocable switch from the fixed amortization or fixed annuitization methods to the required minimum distribution method. If the switch is made then the required minimum distribution method must be used for all subsequent years. The change would be useful in cases where the value of the account had declined substantially and the taxpayer wanted to reduce the required annual payments for future years.

Quick Quiz

Highlight the answer to these questions:

1. Distributions before a participant attains the age of 59½ will generally be subject to a 10 percent penalty.
   a. True
   b. False

2. If the participants are already separated from service due to retirement and they wait until they attain age 55 to begin distributions, then they will not be subject to the 10 percent penalty.
   a. True
   b. False

True, False.

Once the distribution under 72(t) has been elected, the rules must be followed precisely to avoid being subject to the 10 percent penalty. If a mistake is made, the results are often irreversible and costly including unnecessary tax and penalties. Revenue Ruling 2002-62 states that additional contributions cannot be made to the account (other than investment gains) nor can amounts

---

13. Rev. Ruling 2002-62: Permits a participant a one-time election to change from the 2nd or 3rd method to the 1st (RMD) method.

from the plan be rolled over tax free into another account without subjecting the account to the 10 percent penalty.

If a distribution is made from a qualified plan on account of the participant's separation from service after attaining age 55, the distribution will not be subjected to the 10 percent early withdrawal penalty. This exception may be extremely helpful to those employees that take an early retirement package and need funds from their retirement plan prior to receiving Social Security benefits. It is important to note that this exception is only applicable to distributions from qualified plans and not available to distributions from IRAs.

The government also provides an exception to the 10 percent early withdrawal penalty if the distributions are dividends paid within 90 days of the plan year from an ESOP; if the distribution is made to pay certain unpaid income taxes because of a tax levy on the plan; if the distribution is made to the participant for certain medical expenses paid during the year greater than 7.5 percent of the participant's adjusted gross income (whether the person itemizes or not); and if the distribution is pursuant to a Qualified Domestic Relations Order (discussed above).

SUMMARY OF 10 PERCENT PENALTY EXCEPTIONS FOR QUALIFIED PLANS

EXHIBIT 7.17

- Distribution is made after the participant is age 59½.
- Distribution is made on account of death of the participant.
- Distribution is made on account of disability of the participant.
- Distribution is part of a series of substantially equal periodic payments made at least annually for the life or life expectancy of the participant or the joint lives or joint life expectancies of the participant and his designated beneficiary. (Section 72(t))
- Distribution is made after separation from service after the participant attains age 55.
- Distributions are dividends paid within 90 days of the plan year from an ESOP.
- Distribution is made to pay certain unpaid income taxes because of a tax levy on the plan.
- Distributions made to the participant for certain medical expenses paid during the year greater than 7.5 percent of adjusted gross income.
- Distributions pursuant to a Qualified Domestic Relations Order (QDRO).

Other exceptions to the 10 percent early withdrawal penalty are plan rollovers and plan loans. As discussed previously, these withdrawals receive preferential treatment. In addition, other exceptions discussed in Chapter 9 apply specifically to IRAs.

MINIMUM DISTRIBUTIONS

Assets in qualified plans and other tax-advantaged plans enjoy tax-deferred growth. However, this favorable tax treatment is for the purpose of encouraging individuals to save for retirement. The IRC has established age 70½ as the maximum deferral age before distributions must begin. Once a taxpayer attains the age of 70½, the minimum distribution rules must be complied with by the taxpayer. The minimum distribution rules require individuals to begin taking minimum distributions when the participant attains the age of 70½. If the funds are not distributed by the required date, a 50 percent excise tax will be levied on the participant for failure to take the

required minimum distribution (RMD). The penalty is on an amount equal to the RMD less any distribution that was taken, but the result cannot be less than zero.

The first distribution must be taken by April 1 of the year following the year the participant attains the age of 70½. However, for each year thereafter, the RMD must be taken before December 31 of the tax year. The special first year option allows a participant to delay the first payment until April 1 following the year in which the participant turns 70½. However, such a delay only applies to the first distribution and could cause a bunching of income in the year after the participant attains the age of 70½. If the participant delays taking the first RMD until April 1 of the year following the attainment of age 70½, the second RMD must still be taken by December 31 of that same year.

EXAMPLE 7.22	Paul turned 70½ in March of this year. He was a participant in a qualified plan with his previous employer but has not received any distributions since retirement. Since Paul turned 70½ this year, he will have to take the RMD from his retirement plan for this year. The last date he can take his distribution for this year without incurring a minimum distribution penalty is April 1 of next year. The last date he can withdraw his distribution for next year is December 31 of next year.

Case Study 1

In the case of Lee v. California Butchers' Pension Trust Fund,[1] Lee (the pensioner) who retired at age 73 brought action against pension trust fund ("Fund"), claiming that the Fund violated, among other things, ERISA by underpaying his pension. The United States Ninth Circuit Court of Appeals concluded that the Fund improperly denied increased benefits to the pensioner.

Lee worked at Safeway as a butcher for 30 years. He retired in 1992 at age 73. The dispute in this case dealt with the amount of money that Mr. Lee was entitled to be paid every month in his pension. He wanted to be paid as though he had worked 30 years and retired in 1992. The Fund insisted on paying him as though he had retired in 1990 instead of 1992, and then started working again. The effect of the Fund decision was to pay Mr. Lee $815.50 per month instead of $1,498.20. The Internal Revenue Code requires pension plans to begin paying people their pensions after they attain age 70½ whether they keep working or not. Thus, the plan started paying Lee his pension in 1990 because he had reached age 70½.

---

1. Lee v. California Butchers' Pension Trust Fund, 154 F.3d 1075 (9th Cir. 1998).

Case Study 1 Continued

A collective bargaining agreement increased pensions for people who retired beginning in 1992. When the 1992 increases came into effect, Lee obviously wanted them calculated on all his years of service. However, the Fund did not pay him on the basis that he had worked almost 30 years. Instead, it just applied the higher amounts to his two years of service following the 1990 beginning date of his distributions, as though he had only worked as a butcher covered by the plan for two years, resulting in his obtaining the pre-1992 calculation applied to almost all his years of work, and the post-1992 calculation only on his post-age-70½ work. Lee's lawyer initiated correspondence with the Fund about the calculation in December of 1991. After repeated inquiry, Lee's lawyer was told that the plan deemed him to have retired April 1, 1990.

Lee filed suit, claiming that the Fund discriminated against him based on his age (i.e., that he had turned 70½ before the 1992 increase) and violated the plan provisions because the tax provision just meant that Lee had to start drawing his pension so he would start paying income tax on the money, not that he had to retire at age 70½. Because Lee was not required to retire at age 70½ and had not in fact retired, he could not be "deemed" to have retired. The Fund argued that it correctly denied Lee's claim because the Internal Revenue Code required them to distribute his entire interest at age 70½. Congress amended the Internal Revenue Code in 1986 to require pension plans to begin distributing benefits when the pensioner reaches age 70½.[1] The Fund read this to mean that a person must be treated as having retired at age 70½ and referred to such an employee's status as "legally retired" and distinguished it from "physically retired."

The Court disagreed with the Fund and ruled in Lee's favor, explaining that there were no words in the statute or plan to support what the trustees did. Lee was not "legally" or "physically" retired in 1990; rather, he was indeed working at Safeway as a butcher. 26 U.S.C. Section 401(a)(9) limited use of pension funds as tax shelters beyond age 70½, but did not say a word about requiring people to quit working or authorizing plans to deprive them of increases and accruals following age 70½ when they are still working. The Court concluded that the law did not require the employee to be retired, just that his money be "distributed," beginning by the specified date. As no possible reading of the plan language could "deem" Lee to have retired in 1990, under the plan, Lee was to be "deemed retired" after he quit working in 1992, at which time he was entitled to the increased benefits available to all employees who stopped working after January 1, 1992. The Fund's denial of the increase to Lee was therefore considered to be an abuse of discretion.

---

1. See 26 U.S.C. Section 401(a)(9)(A)(ii) (1990).

An exception to the general RMD for qualified plans exists if a participant is still employed by the plan sponsor of a qualified plan upon attainment of age 70½. A participant that is still employed by the plan sponsor of the qualified plan does not have to begin taking RMD until April 1 of the year after the participant terminates employment with the plan sponsor. The exception is not available for any participant that owns more than five percent of the ownership of the plan sponsor in the year he reaches the age of 70½. In addition, if the participant is a more than 5 percent owner and begins taking the RMD, he cannot discontinue taking the distributions should he no longer own greater than five percent of the company at some future date. However, while the law permits the delay, a qualified plan may require all individuals, even those participants that have continued employment past the age of 70½, to take RMD at 70½; the discretion is given to the plan's sponsor.

EXHIBIT 7.18	REQUIRED MINIMUM DISTRIBUTIONS

- Must begin by April 1 of the year after the participant attains the age of 70½.
- Unless the participant is still employed by the plan sponsor, then the RMD must be taken by April 1 of the year after the participant terminates service with the plan sponsor. Exception: Does not apply for a more than 5 percent owner of the plan sponsor.

EXAMPLE 7.23	Mary, age 74, works at the local grocery store. She is a participant in the grocer's profit sharing plan but has not begun taking RMD. If Mary terminates employment in August 1 of this year, she must take her first RMD by April 1 of next year.

CALCULATING THE REQUIRED MINIMUM DISTRIBUTION

The required minimum distribution (RMD) is determined each year by dividing the account balance as of the close of business on December 31 of the year preceding the distribution year by the distribution period determined by participant's age as of December 31 of the distribution year in the uniform lifetime table (See Exhibit 7.19).[14] There is one exception where the beneficiary's age is ignored when determining the distribution period and is discussed below.

In the past, the above calculation permitted an exception. An alternate calculation was used for the second year of RMD when the first RMD was not taken until the subsequent tax year. In this case, to calculate the RMD for the second year, the plan account balance at the end of the preceding year was reduced by the first year's RMD that had not been taken at that time. This

---

14. Reg. Section 1.401(a)(9)-9.

adjustment only applied to the second distribution, and it was to the taxpayer's benefit. When the revised regulations were promulgated (Treasury Reg 1.401(a)(9)-5, A-3(c)) this exception was not part of the revised regulations, thus requiring all distributions to be calculated the same regardless of whether the first distribution was delayed until the second year.

Assume Paul's account balance at December 31, 2005 was $400,000, and he is 71 by December 31, 2006. He, therefore, uses a distribution period from the uniform lifetime table of 26.5 and will need to take a distribution for 2005 of $15,094.34 by April 1, 2006. If he delays until April 1, 2006, he must also take a distribution for 2006 by December 31, 2006.

EXAMPLE 7.24

$$\frac{\$400,000}{26.5} = \$15,094.34$$

Assume Paul's account balance at December 31, 2005 was $480,000, and he took his 2005 distribution in April of 2006. He will need to take $18,750 by December 31, 2006 for 2006, in addition to his April 1, 2006 distribution. Note that when two distributions are combined in one year, it can cause the recipient to move up in the progressive tax brackets due to the stacking of two payments.

$$\frac{\$480,000}{25.6} = \$18,750$$

Kendal attained the age of 70½ in October 2006. He retired several years ago but has not taken any distributions yet. His account balance on December 31, 2005 was $100,000, and his balance on December 31, 2006 was $110,000. The first year for which Kendal must take a minimum distribution is 2006 (although he may wait until April 1, 2007 to actually take the first distribution). To calculate the 2006 distribution, determine the factor from the uniform lifetime table based on his age at December 31, 2006 (70). The distribution period is 27.4. Utilizing the end of the prior year's account balance of $100,000, Kendal's required minimum distribution for 2006 is $3,649.64.

EXAMPLE 7.25

$$\frac{\$100,000}{27.4} = \$3,649.64$$

For 2007, the distribution will be $4,150.94. Each year after that, the end of the prior year account balance and the age related distribution period at current year end will be used to determine the RMD.

$$\frac{\$110,000}{26.5} = \$4,150.94$$

EXAMPLE 7.26

John is 70½ on October 15, 2006. John's year-end account balance for 2005, 2006, 2007, and 2008 are $300,000, $360,000, $420,000, and $502,000 respectively. Calculate John's minimum distribution for years 2005, 2006, 2007, 2008, and 2009 (See the Uniform Lifetime Table, Exhibit 7.19).

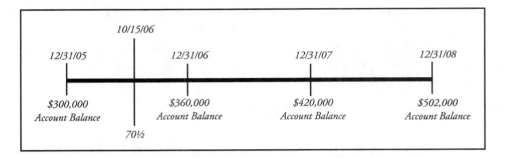

Minimum distribution calculation for 2005:

There is no minimum distribution required for 2005 because John is not yet 70½.

Minimum distribution calculation for 2006:

$$\frac{\$300,000}{27.4} = \$10,948.91$$

Minimum distribution calculation for 2007:

$$\frac{\$360,000}{26.5} = \$13,584.91$$

Minimum distribution calculation for 2008:

$$\frac{\$420,000}{25.6} = \$16,406.25$$

Minimum distribution calculation for 2009:

$$\frac{\$502,000}{24.7} = \$20,323.89$$

UNIFORM LIFETIME TABLE USED BY PARTICIPANTS

EXHIBIT 7.19

Age of Employee	Distribution Period	Age of Employee	Distribution Period
70	27.4	93	9.6
71	26.5	94	9.1
72	25.6	95	8.6
73	24.7	96	8.1
74	23.8	97	7.6
75	22.9	98	7.1
76	22.0	99	6.7
77	21.2	100	6.3
78	20.3	101	5.9
79	19.5	102	5.5
80	18.7	103	5.2
81	17.9	104	4.9
82	17.1	105	4.5
83	16.3	106	4.2
84	15.5	107	3.9
85	14.8	108	3.7
86	14.1	109	3.4
87	13.4	110	3.1
88	12.7	111	2.9
89	12.0	112	2.6
90	11.4	113	2.4
91	10.8	114	2.1

When calculating the RMD for the plan participant, always use the **uniform lifetime table** unless the participant's sole designated beneficiary is the participant's spouse and that spouse is more than 10 years younger than the participant. In that case, use the **joint life expectancy table** to calculate the RMD. Utilizing the joint life expectancy tables will result in a longer life expectancy and decrease the RMD. An excerpt of the joint life expectancy chart is provided below. The complete chart can be found at Treas. Reg. 1.401(a)(9)-9, and in IRS Publication 590.

EXAMPLE 7.27

Assume the same facts as Example 7.25 except that Kendal is married, and his wife Julie, age 69 at December 31, 2004, is the sole beneficiary. The minimum distribution will be calculated exactly as it was previously because Julie is not more than 10 years younger than Kendal.

EXAMPLE 7.28

Now, assume the same facts as the above example except that Kendal is married, and his wife Julie, age 39 at December 31, 2006, is the sole beneficiary. Now the joint and survivor tables are used to determine the life expectancy because Julie is more than 10 years younger than Kendal. Their joint life expectancy is 44.9. Under this scenario, Kendal's RMD will be $2,227.17 ($100,000/44.9).

EXAMPLE 7.29

Assume the same facts as the above example except that Kendal's daughter Jaime, age 22 on December 31, 2006, is the sole beneficiary. In this case, the single life table based on Kendal's life is used to determine the distribution period. Therefore, the RMD is the same as the first example ($100,000/27.4 = $3,649.64).

EXCERPT FROM THE JOINT AND LAST SURVIVOR TABLE (USED BY PARTICIPANTS WITH SPOUSES MORE THAN 10 YEARS YOUNGER THAN THE PARTICIPANT)

EXHIBIT 7.20

Ages	30	31	32	33	34	35	36	37	38	39
30	60.2	59.7	59.2	58.8	58.4	58.0	57.6	57.3	57.0	56.7
31	59.7	59.2	58.7	58.2	57.8	57.4	57.0	56.6	56.3	56.0
32	59.2	58.7	58.2	57.7	57.2	56.8	56.4	56.0	55.6	55.3
33	58.8	58.2	57.7	57.2	56.7	56.2	55.8	55.4	55.0	54.7
34	58.4	57.8	57.2	56.7	56.2	55.7	55.3	54.8	54.4	54.0
35	58.0	57.4	56.8	56.2	55.7	55.2	54.7	54.3	53.8	53.4
36	57.6	57.0	56.4	55.8	55.3	54.7	54.2	53.7	53.3	52.8
37	57.3	56.6	56.0	55.4	54.8	54.3	53.7	53.2	52.7	52.3
38	57.0	56.3	55.6	55.0	54.4	53.8	53.3	52.7	52.2	51.7
39	56.7	56.0	55.3	54.7	54.0	53.4	52.8	52.3	51.7	51.2
40	56.4	55.7	55.0	54.3	53.7	53.0	52.4	51.8	51.3	50.8
41	56.1	55.4	54.7	54.0	53.3	52.7	52.0	51.4	50.9	50.3
42	55.9	55.2	54.4	53.7	53.0	52.3	51.7	51.1	50.4	49.9
43	55.7	54.9	54.2	53.4	52.7	52.0	51.3	50.7	50.1	49.5
44	55.5	54.7	53.9	53.2	52.4	51.7	51.0	50.4	49.7	49.1
45	55.3	54.5	53.7	52.9	52.2	51.5	50.7	50.0	49.4	48.7
46	55.1	54.3	53.5	52.7	52.0	51.2	50.5	49.8	49.1	48.4
47	55.0	54.1	53.3	52.5	51.7	51.0	50.2	49.5	48.8	48.1
48	54.8	54.0	53.2	52.3	51.5	50.8	50.0	49.2	48.5	47.8
49	54.7	53.8	53.0	52.2	51.4	50.6	49.8	49.0	48.2	47.5
50	54.6	53.7	52.9	52.0	51.2	50.4	49.6	48.8	48.0	47.3
51	54.5	53.6	52.7	51.9	51.0	50.2	49.4	48.6	47.8	47.0
52	54.4	53.5	52.6	51.7	50.9	50.0	49.2	48.4	47.6	46.8
53	54.3	53.4	52.5	51.6	50.8	49.9	49.1	48.2	47.4	46.6
54	54.2	53.3	52.4	51.5	50.6	49.8	48.9	48.1	47.2	46.4
55	54.1	53.2	52.3	51.4	50.5	49.7	48.8	47.9	47.1	46.3
56	54.0	53.1	52.2	51.3	50.4	49.5	48.7	47.8	47.0	46.1
57	54.0	53.0	52.1	51.2	50.3	49.4	48.6	47.7	46.8	46.0
58	53.9	53.0	52.1	51.2	50.3	49.4	48.5	47.6	46.7	45.8
59	53.8	52.9	52.0	51.1	50.2	49.3	48.4	47.5	46.6	45.7
60	53.8	52.9	51.9	51.0	50.1	49.2	48.3	47.4	46.5	45.6
61	53.8	52.8	51.9	51.0	50.0	49.1	48.2	47.3	46.4	45.5
62	53.7	52.8	51.8	50.9	50.0	49.1	48.1	47.2	46.3	45.4
63	53.7	52.7	51.8	50.9	49.9	49.0	48.1	47.2	46.3	45.3
64	53.6	52.7	51.8	50.8	49.9	48.9	48.0	47.1	46.2	45.3
65	53.6	52.7	51.7	50.8	49.8	48.9	48.0	47.0	46.1	45.2
66	53.6	52.6	51.7	50.7	49.8	48.9	47.9	47.0	46.1	45.1
67	53.6	52.6	51.7	50.7	49.8	48.8	47.9	46.9	46.0	45.1
68	53.5	52.6	51.6	50.7	49.7	48.8	47.8	46.9	46.0	45.0
69	53.5	52.6	51.6	50.6	49.7	48.7	47.8	46.9	45.9	45.0
70	53.5	52.5	51.6	50.6	49.7	48.7	47.8	46.8	45.9	44.9
71	53.5	52.5	51.6	50.6	49.6	48.7	47.7	46.8	45.9	44.9
72	53.5	52.5	51.5	50.6	49.6	48.7	47.7	46.8	45.8	44.9
73	53.4	52.5	51.5	50.6	49.6	48.6	47.7	46.7	45.8	44.8
74	53.4	52.5	51.5	50.5	49.6	48.6	47.7	46.7	45.8	44.8
75	53.4	52.5	51.5	50.5	49.6	48.6	47.7	46.7	45.7	44.8
76	53.4	52.4	51.5	50.5	49.6	48.6	47.6	46.7	45.7	44.8
77	53.4	52.4	51.5	50.5	49.5	48.6	47.6	46.7	45.7	44.8
78	53.4	52.4	51.5	50.5	49.5	48.6	47.6	46.6	45.7	44.7
79	53.4	52.4	51.5	50.5	49.5	48.6	47.6	46.6	45.7	44.7

Ages	40	41	42	43	44	45	46	47	48	49
40	50.2	49.8	49.3	48.9	48.5	48.1	47.7	47.4	47.1	46.8
41	49.8	49.3	48.8	48.3	47.9	47.5	47.1	46.7	46.4	46.1
42	49.3	48.8	48.3	47.8	47.3	46.9	46.5	46.1	45.8	45.4
43	48.9	48.3	47.8	47.3	46.8	46.3	45.9	45.5	45.1	44.8
44	48.5	47.9	47.3	46.8	46.3	45.8	45.4	44.9	44.5	44.2
45	48.1	47.5	46.9	46.3	45.8	45.3	44.8	44.4	44.0	43.6
46	47.7	47.1	46.5	45.9	45.4	44.8	44.3	43.9	43.4	43.0
47	47.4	46.7	46.1	45.5	44.9	44.4	43.9	43.4	42.9	42.4
48	47.1	46.4	45.8	45.1	44.5	44.0	43.4	42.9	42.4	41.9
49	46.8	46.1	45.4	44.8	44.2	43.6	43.0	42.4	41.9	41.4
50	46.5	45.8	45.1	44.4	43.8	43.2	42.6	42.0	41.5	40.9
51	46.3	45.5	44.8	44.1	43.5	42.8	42.2	41.6	41.0	40.5
52	46.0	45.3	44.6	43.8	43.2	42.5	41.8	41.2	40.6	40.1
53	45.8	45.1	44.3	43.6	42.9	42.2	41.5	40.9	40.3	39.7
54	45.6	44.8	44.1	43.3	42.6	41.9	41.2	40.5	39.9	39.3
55	45.5	44.7	43.9	43.1	42.4	41.6	40.9	40.2	39.6	38.9
56	45.3	44.5	43.7	42.9	42.1	41.4	40.7	40.0	39.3	38.6
57	45.1	44.3	43.5	42.7	41.9	41.2	40.4	39.7	39.0	38.3
58	45.0	44.2	43.3	42.5	41.7	40.9	40.2	39.4	38.7	38.0
59	44.9	44.0	43.2	42.4	41.5	40.7	40.0	39.2	38.5	37.8
60	44.7	43.9	43.0	42.2	41.4	40.6	39.8	39.0	38.2	37.5
61	44.6	43.8	42.9	42.1	41.2	40.4	39.6	38.8	38.0	37.3
62	44.5	43.7	42.8	41.9	41.1	40.3	39.4	38.6	37.8	37.1
63	44.5	43.6	42.7	41.8	41.0	40.1	39.3	38.5	37.7	36.9
64	44.4	43.5	42.6	41.7	40.8	40.0	39.2	38.3	37.5	36.7
65	44.3	43.4	42.5	41.6	40.7	39.9	39.0	38.2	37.4	36.6
66	44.2	43.3	42.4	41.5	40.6	39.8	38.9	38.1	37.2	36.4
67	44.2	43.3	42.3	41.4	40.6	39.7	38.8	38.0	37.1	36.3
68	44.1	43.2	42.3	41.4	40.5	39.6	38.7	37.9	37.0	36.2
69	44.1	43.1	42.2	41.3	40.4	39.5	38.6	37.8	36.9	36.0
70	44.0	43.1	42.2	41.3	40.3	39.4	38.6	37.7	36.8	35.9
71	44.0	43.0	42.1	41.2	40.3	39.4	38.5	37.6	36.7	35.9
72	43.9	43.0	42.1	41.1	40.2	39.3	38.4	37.5	36.6	35.8
73	43.9	43.0	42.0	41.1	40.2	39.3	38.4	37.5	36.6	35.7
74	43.9	42.9	42.0	41.1	40.1	39.2	38.3	37.4	36.5	35.6
75	43.8	42.9	42.0	41.0	40.1	39.2	38.3	37.4	36.5	35.6
76	43.8	42.9	41.9	41.0	40.1	39.1	38.2	37.3	36.4	35.5
77	43.8	42.9	41.9	41.0	40.0	39.1	38.2	37.3	36.4	35.5
78	43.8	42.8	41.9	40.9	40.0	39.1	38.2	37.2	36.3	35.4
79	43.8	42.8	41.9	40.9	40.0	39.1	38.1	37.2	36.3	35.4
80	43.7	42.8	41.8	40.9	40.0	39.0	38.1	37.2	36.3	35.4
81	43.7	42.8	41.8	40.9	39.9	39.0	38.1	37.2	36.2	35.3
82	43.7	42.8	41.8	40.9	39.9	39.0	38.1	37.1	36.2	35.3
83	43.7	42.8	41.8	40.9	39.9	39.0	38.0	37.1	36.2	35.3
84	43.7	42.7	41.8	40.8	39.9	39.0	38.0	37.1	36.2	35.3
85	43.7	42.7	41.8	40.8	39.9	38.9	38.0	37.1	36.2	35.2
86	43.7	42.7	41.8	40.8	39.9	38.9	38.0	37.1	36.1	35.2
87	43.7	42.7	41.8	40.8	39.9	38.9	38.0	37.0	36.1	35.2
88	43.7	42.7	41.8	40.8	39.9	38.9	38.0	37.0	36.1	35.2
89	43.7	42.7	41.7	40.8	39.8	38.9	38.0	37.0	36.1	35.2

Effect of Multiple Qualified Plans or IRAs

As discussed, upon reaching age 70½, taxpayers are required to begin taking minimum distributions. However, it is important to understand that a minimum distribution must be taken from each qualified plan in which the taxpayer has an account balance. Therefore, if the taxpayer had three qualified plans resulting from previous jobs, then 3 minimum distributions would have to be taken.

Many taxpayers have multiple IRAs; however, taxpayers are permitted to combine the value of all of their IRAs in the determination of the required minimum distribution. In addition, the amount distributed for purposes of complying with the minimum distribution rules can be taken from one IRA or multiple IRAs depending on the wishes of the taxpayer.

EFFECT OF PARTICIPANT'S DEATH ON MINIMUM DISTRIBUTIONS

Minimum distributions are still required to be taken even after a participant dies. An important distinction is made depending on whether the participant died before or after beginning minimum distributions. In either case, in the year of the participant's death, the RMD is calculated as if the participant has not died.

Note that the beneficiary of a qualified plan may withdraw all of the assets of the qualified plan after the death of the participant with no penalty. Recall that the 10 percent early withdrawal penalty does not apply to distributions taken after death. The RMD rules only apply when the beneficiary wants to delay withdrawing the assets of the qualified plan.

Death after Beginning of Minimum Distributions

If the participant dies after beginning to take minimum distributions, then the calculation of subsequent minimum distributions depends on the designated beneficiary as determined on the last day of the year following the year of the participant's death.

Qualified plans may disregard any beneficiary eliminated by an effective disclaimer or distribution of the benefit during the period between the participant's death and December 31 of the following year. If there is more than one designated beneficiary, the beneficiary with the shortest life expectancy (usually the oldest beneficiary) is used as the measuring life, but the plan may also be divided into a separate account for each beneficiary to utilize the life expectancy of each beneficiary for the calculation of the required minimum distribution.

If a trust is named as the beneficiary, the beneficiaries of the trust will be treated as the designated beneficiaries provided:
- The trust is valid under state law;
- The trust is irrevocable or will become so upon the participant's death (e.g., inter vivos trust);
- The trust beneficiaries are identifiable from the trust instrument; and
- Appropriate documentation has been provided to the plan administrator.

Spouse Beneficiary

If the surviving spouse is a beneficiary of the plan, then the surviving spouse can receive distributions over his remaining single-life expectancy (see Exhibit 7.21), recalculated each year based on the single life expectancy table. Distributions must begin, however, in the year following the year of the participant's death. Alternatively, if the surviving spouse is the sole beneficiary, the surviving spouse may rollover the plan balance to his own account and wait until he attains age 70½ to begin taking minimum distributions utilizing the uniform life table for his own life expectancy at that point.

There are a number of reasons why a surviving spouse would choose to either leave the deceased spouse owner's account intact or, alternatively, roll the account over to the surviving spouse's name. If the account remains in the decedent's name, it will be retitled after death "Mr. John Doe Plan for the Benefit of Mrs. Jane Doe." If rolled over and put into spouse's name, the title of the account will be Mrs. Jane Doe, IRA. If placed in the surviving spouse's own name, then the surviving spouse can name the beneficiary. If left intact as a qualified plan, the ERISA protection remains. If rolled over to an IRA, ERISA protection is lost, but state law may provide creditor protection.

In the case of a spouse much younger than the decedent owner, leaving the account intact if distributions have begun will assure continuing cash flow. If a surviving spouse needs the money, this would provide penalty-free funds because the surviving spouse would generally have to wait until retirement to collect the funds if the assets are rolled over into the surviving spouse's name. In fact, the spouse would not be limited to taking just the minimum distributions. Alternatively, if the surviving spouse is older than the owner, leaving the account intact will allow the surviving spouse to stretch out the distributions. In the case of a surviving spouse who is younger than the decedent and does not need the cash flow, rolling the account over to the surviving spouse's name allows for continual deferral and the designation of a new beneficiary; thus, creating the opportunity to stretch out the minimum distributions far into the future.

EXAMPLE 7.30	Louise, age 72, had been taking minimum distributions from her qualified plan for the past two years. Louise died in 2006, the sole beneficiary of her qualified plan was her husband, Harry, age 68. The RMD for 2006 will be calculated based on the uniform life table and Louise's age at the end of 2006. After that RMD is taken, Henry can choose to either roll Louise's qualified plan balance into an IRA for himself and wait until he is 70½ to begin taking the required minimum distributions, or Harry may begin taking minimum distributions based on his life expectancy as calculated by the single life expectancy table in the year after Louise's death.

Assuming the following account balances and information:

Date	Account Balance	Louise's Age	Harry's Age
12/31/2005	$400,000	72	68
12/31/2006	$425,000	-	69
12/31/2007	$490,000	-	70

The RMD for 2006, the year Louise died, would be based on Louise's life expectancy utilizing the uniform life table and the account balance at 12/31/2005 as follows:

$$\frac{\$400,000}{24.7 \text{ (at age 73)}} = \$16,194.33$$

For 2006, Harry could roll the remaining plan balance to an IRA for himself, take a full taxable distribution of the account balance, or, alternatively, he may begin taking RMD over his life expectancy as determined by the single life expectancy table as follows:

$$\frac{\$425,000}{17.0 \text{ (at age 70)}} = \$25,000.00$$

For 2007, Harry's RMD would be calculated using the recalculated single life expectancy as follows:

$$\frac{\$490,000}{16.3 \text{ (at age 71)}} = \$30,061.35$$

Nonspouse Beneficiary

If the beneficiary is someone other than the participant's surviving spouse, then the distribution period is the remaining single, non-recalculated life expectancy of the designated beneficiary. If more than one nonspouse beneficiary exists the shortest life expectancy of the beneficiaries is used. As always in the year of the participant's death, the RMD is calculated based on the participant's life expectancy (Uniform Lifetime table). Subsequently, however, the life expectancy for the nonspouse beneficiary is calculated using the age of the designated beneficiary in the year following the year of the participant's death (Single Life Expectancy for Beneficiaries table, Exhibit 7.21), reduced by one for each subsequent year.

Cheryl dies in August 2006 at the age of 73. The beneficiary for her qualified plan is her daughter, Elizabeth, who was 42 when Cheryl died. Assuming the facts below, calculate the RMD for 2006, 2007, and 2008.

EXAMPLE 7.31

Date	Account Balance	Cheryl's Age	Elizabeth's Age
12/31/2005	$100,000	73	42
12/31/2006	$95,000	-	43
12/31/2007	$87,000	-	44

For 2006, the RMD is calculated utilizing the uniform life table life expectancy based on the age Cheryl would have been at 12/31/2006 and the account balance at 12/31/2005.

$$\frac{\$100,000}{23.8 \text{ (at age 74)}} = \$4,201.68$$

For 2007, the RMD is calculated based on Elizabeth's life expectancy utilizing the single life expectancy table for Elizabeth's age at 12/31/2007 and the plan account balance at 12/31/2006.

$$\frac{\$95,000}{39.8 \text{ (at age 44)}} = \$2,386.93$$

For 2008, the RMD is calculated utilizing the account balance at 12/31/2007 and Elizabeth's life expectancy as calculated in the prior year reduced by one.

$$\frac{\$87,000}{39.8 - 1} = \$2,242.27$$

The RMD calculations for all subsequent years would continue to reduce Elizabeth's life expectancy calculated in 2007 by one. The life expectancy would not be recalculated. In this example, Elizabeth can withdraw all of the account balance after Cheryl's death as a lump sum or in payments larger than the RMD, but in no case would Elizabeth be able to withdraw less than the RMD in any year.

EXHIBIT 7.21

Age	Life Expectancy	Age	Life Expectancy	Age	Life Expectancy	Age	Life Expectancy
0	82.4	28	55.3	56	28.7	84	8.1
1	81.6	29	54.3	57	27.9	85	7.6
2	80.6	30	53.3	58	27.0	86	7.1
3	79.7	31	52.4	59	26.1	87	6.7
4	78.7	32	51.4	60	25.2	88	6.3
5	77.7	33	50.4	61	24.4	89	5.9
6	76.7	34	49.4	62	23.5	90	5.5
7	75.8	35	48.5	63	22.7	91	5.2
8	74.8	36	47.5	64	21.8	92	4.9
9	73.8	37	46.5	65	21.0	93	4.6
10	72.8	38	45.6	66	20.2	94	4.3
11	71.8	39	44.6	67	19.4	95	4.1
12	70.8	40	43.6	68	18.6	96	3.8
13	69.9	41	42.7	69	17.8	97	3.6
14	68.9	42	41.7	70	17.0	98	3.4
15	67.9	43	40.7	71	16.3	99	3.1
16	66.9	44	39.8	72	15.5	100	2.9
17	66.0	45	38.8	73	14.8	101	2.7
18	65.0	46	37.9	74	14.1	102	2.5
19	64.0	47	37.0	75	13.4	103	2.3
20	63.0	48	36.0	76	12.7	104	2.1
21	62.1	49	35.1	77	12.1	105	1.9
22	61.1	50	34.2	78	11.4	106	1.7
23	60.1	51	33.3	79	10.8	107	1.5
24	59.1	52	32.3	80	10.2	108	1.4
25	58.2	53	31.4	81	9.7	109	1.2
26	57.2	54	30.5	82	9.1	110	1.1
27	56.2	55	29.6	83	8.6	111+	1.0

No Beneficiary

If no beneficiary has been named by December 31 of the year following the owner's death (or the beneficiary is the decedent's estate or a charity), then distributions must continue over the remaining distribution period of the deceased owner. The remaining distribution period is reduced by one each year.

EXAMPLE 7.32	Robin began taking the RMD from her profit sharing plan in 2005. In 2007, Robin died after suffering a heart attack. She had not named a beneficiary of her profit sharing plan at the time of her death. Robin's estate may choose to take a full distribution of Robin's profit sharing plan account balance or, alternatively, may choose to defer distributions from the plan to the RMD. In the year of Robin's death, the RMD would be calculated as if Robin had not died. In the year after Robin's death, the RMD would be calculated based on the account balance at the end of the prior year, and Robin's life expectancy is calculated in the year of her death from the uniform life table reduced by one.

Death Before Required Beginning Date

If the participant dies before the required beginning date (before minimum distributions have begun), then the minimum distribution rules will depend on the designated beneficiary.

Spouse Beneficiary

If the surviving spouse is the beneficiary of the plan, the surviving spouse can receive distributions over his remaining single-life expectancy, recalculated each year under the **single life expectancy table**.[15] Distributions must begin in the year in which the owner would have attained age 70½. Alternatively, if the surviving spouse is the sole beneficiary, the surviving spouse can roll the plan balance over and wait until he attains age 70½ to begin taking minimum distributions. The surviving spouse can also elect to distribute the entire account balance within five years after the year of the owner's death.

EXAMPLE 7.33	Matthew died at the age of 37 in 2005. His wife, Sara, was the sole beneficiary of his profit sharing plan. Since Matthew had not begun taking RMD before his death, Sara has four options in relation to Matthew's profit sharing plan.

1. Sara may withdraw Matthew's entire account balance immediately.
2. Sara may choose to leave the assets in the plan, but she must take a distribution of the account balance before the end of the fifth year after Matthew's death.
3. Sara may choose to roll the account balance to an IRA for her benefit. In this case, the RMD would begin when Sara attained the age of 70½ and would be based on Sara's life expectancy as determined by the uniform life expect-

---

15. IRC Section 401(a)(9)(B)(iv)(II) and Treas. Reg. Section 1.401(a)(9)-5 Q&A-5(c)(1) and (2).

ancy table. In addition, she could not take a distribution until age 59½ without having the 10 percent early withdrawal penalty apply.

4. Sara may elect to take distributions from the plan based on her recalculated life expectancy (single life expectancy table) each year. Sara may choose to begin the distribution immediately or wait until Matthew would have been 70½.

Nonspouse Beneficiary

If the beneficiary is someone other than the surviving spouse, then the distribution period is the remaining single, non-recalculated life expectancy of the designated beneficiary. Life expectancy is calculated using the age of the designated beneficiary in the year following the year of the employee's death, reduced by one for each subsequent year. Alternatively, the beneficiary can elect to distribute the entire account balance within five years after the year of the owner's death.

In this case, the RMD is calculated in the same manner as discussed above (distributions after RMD had begun), except that the beneficiary may choose to leave assets in the account and not take distributions from the plan until the fifth year after the participant's death. In the fifth year, however, the beneficiary must take a distribution of the entire account balance. The beneficiary cannot start taking distributions over their life expectancies at that time. The 5-year rule allows the beneficiary to forego taking distributions for the four years after the death of the participants; whereas, in all other cases, the beneficiary must take at least the annual minimum distributions calculated based on his non-recalculated single life expectancy.

No Beneficiary

If no beneficiary has been named by December 31 of the year following the owner's death (or the beneficiary is the decedent's estate or charity), the account must be fully distributed before the end of the fifth year following the year of death. The account balance may be distributed anytime before the end of the fifth year but may never extend beyond.

Quick Quiz

Highlight the answer to these questions:

1. The first minimum distribution must be made by April 15 of the year following the year the participant attains the age of 70½.
   a. True
   b. False

2. Designated beneficiaries for minimum distributions are determined on the last day of the year following the year of the participant's death.
   a. True
   b. False

3. With regard to minimum distributions, a surviving spouse receives more favorable options than any other type of beneficiary in the event of the owner's death.
   a. True
   b. False

False, True, True.

EXHIBIT 7.22   **DEATH OF PARTICIPANT SUMMARY**

	OPTIONS AFTER MINIMUM DISTRIBUTIONS BEGIN*
Spouse Beneficiary	1. Spouse can receive distributions over the surviving spouse's remaining single life expectancy as recalculated using the single life table. 2. Rollover plan balance to an IRA in surviving spouse's name and delay distributions until spouse is 70½.
Nonspouse Beneficiary	1. Distribution period is the longer of the remaining single life expectancy (not recalculated) of the designated beneficiary (reduced by one year) or the remaining life expectancy of the participant.
No Beneficiary	1. Distributions must continue over the remaining distribution period of the deceased owner (uniform life table). The decedent's remaining distribution period is reduced by one each year.
	OPTIONS BEFORE MINIMUM DISTRIBUTIONS BEGIN*
Spouse Beneficiary	1. Distribution over participant's remaining life expectancy as recalculated using single life expectancy table beginning when the participant would have turned 70½. 2. Distribute participant's account within 5 years. 3. Roll plan assets to an IRA in surviving spouse's name and wait until surviving spouse is 70½ to begin RMD.
Nonspouse Beneficiary	1. Distribute participant's account within 5 years. 2. Remaining single life expectancy (not recalculated) of designated beneficiary (reduced by one year).
No Beneficiary	1. Distribute participant's account within 5 years.

* In all cases, the beneficiary can take more than the minimum distribution.

Key Terms

Adjusted Taxable Basis - The portion of a distribution that is not subject to income tax. Usually, the return of after-tax contributions or nondeductible contributions.

CODA (Cash or Deferred Arrangement) - Permits an employee to defer a portion of their salary on a pretax basis to a qualified plan or receive the salary as current taxable income.

Direct Rollover - Occurs when the plan trustee distributes the account balance directly to the trustee of the recipient account.

Early Withdrawal Penalty - A 10 percent penalty on distributions made before the participant attains the age of 59½ (exceptions apply).

Fixed Amortization - The payment is calculated over the participant's life expectancy if single, or the joint life expectancy if married, and the interest rate is reasonable.

Fixed Annuitization - The participant takes distributions of the account over a number of years determined by dividing the account balance by an annuity factor using a reasonable interest rate and mortality table.

Indirect Rollover - A distribution to the participant with a subsequent transfer to another qualified account.

Joint Life Expectancy Table - The life expectancy table used to determine a participant's RMD when the participant's sole designated beneficiary is the participant's spouse and that spouse is more than 10 years younger than the participant.

Lump-Sum Distributions - A complete distribution of a participant's account balance within one taxable year on account of death, disability, attainment of age 59½, or separation from service. Some lump-sum distributions from qualified plans are eligible for special taxation options.

Net Unrealized Appreciation - A special taxation treatment for a lump-sum distribution from a qualified plan that treats part of the distribution as capital gain.

Plan Loans - Loans from a qualified plan made available to all participants on an effectively equal basis that are limited in amount, are repaid within a certain time period, bear a reasonable rate of interest, are adequately secured, and require the administrator to maintain a proper accounting.

Pre-1974 Capital Gain Treatment - A special taxation treatment for lump-sum distributions from qualified plans that treats the distribution attributable to pre-1974 participation in the plan as long-term capital gain.

Qualified Domestic Relations Order (QDRO) - A court order related to divorce, property settlement, or child support that can divide a participant's interest in a qualified plan.

Qualified Joint and Survivor Annuity (QJSA) - The QJSA pays a benefit to the participant and spouse as long as either lives; although, at the death of the first spouse, the annuity may be reduced.

Key Terms

Qualified Preretirement Survivor Annuity (QPSA) - Provides a benefit to the surviving spouse if the participant dies before attaining normal retirement age.

Required Minimum Distribution - A minimum amount that must be withdrawn from a qualified plan each year after the participant attains the age of 70½. The amount is calculated using either the uniform distribution table, the single life expectancy table, or the joint life expectancy tables.

Rollover - To elect to transfer funds from one tax-advantaged account to another tax-advantaged account to continue to defer the recognition of income taxes until the ultimate distribution of the assets.

Single Life Expectancy Table - Tables used to calculate the required minimum distribution for beneficiaries.

10-Year Forward Averaging - A method of income tax calculation for certain lump-sum distribution from qualified plans that divides the taxable portion of the lump-sum distribution by 10 and applies the result to the 1986 individual income tax rates. The resulting calculation is then multiplied by 10 to determine the total income tax due on the distribution.

Uniform Distribution Table - A table used to calculate the RMD for the plan participant unless the participant's sole designated beneficiary is the participant's spouse and that spouse is more than 10 years younger than the participant.

DISCUSSION QUESTIONS

1. Describe the distribution options for pension plans.

2. Describe the distribution options for profit sharing plans.

3. Describe rollovers and when and how they are used.

4. Discuss the circumstances that will result in a qualified retirement plan participant having adjusted taxable basis in plan assets.

5. List the three special options available for lump-sum distributions from a qualified plan.

6. Describe qualified plan loans and their limitations.

7. How are Qualified Domestic Relations Orders (QDRO) treated with regards to qualified retirement plans?

8. Discuss the penalty for distributions from a qualified plan before 59½.

9. Explain when minimum distributions must begin.

1. Which of the following distributions from a qualified plan would not be subject to the 10 percent early withdrawal penalty, assuming the participant has not attained age 59½?

    1. A distribution made to a spouse under a Qualified Domestic Relations Order (QDRO).

    2. A distribution from a qualified plan used to pay the private health insurance premiums of a current employee of Clinical Trials Company.

    3. A distribution to pay for costs of higher education.

    4. A distribution made immediately after separation from service at age 57.

        a. 1 and 2.

        b. 1 and 3.

        c. 1 and 4.

        d. 2 and 3.

2. Gerry is 70½ on April 1 of the current year and must receive a minimum distribution from his qualified plan. The account balance had a value of $423,598 at the end of last year. The distribution period for a 70 year old is 27.4, and for a 71 year old it is 26.5. If Gerry takes a $15,000 distribution next April 1st, what is the amount of the minimum distribution tax penalty?

    a. $0.

    b. $230.

    c. $492.

    d. $985.

3. Josh recently died at the age of 63, leaving a qualified plan account with a balance of $1,000,000. Josh was married to Kay, age 53, who is the designated beneficiary of the qualified plan. Which of the following is correct?

    a. Kay must distribute the entire account balance within five years of Josh's death.

    b. Kay must begin taking distributions over Josh's remaining single-life expectancy.

    c. Any distribution from the plan to Kay will be subject to a 10 percent early withdrawal penalty until she is 59½.

    d. Kay can receive annual distributions over her remaining single-life expectancy, recalculated each year.

4. Andrea recently died at age 77, leaving behind a qualified plan worth $200,000. Andrea began taking minimum distributions from the account after attaining age 70½ and correctly reported the minimum distributions on her federal income tax returns. Before her death, Andrea named her granddaughter, Reese age 22, as the designated beneficiary of the account. Now that Andrea has died, Reese has come to you for advice with respect to the account. Which of the following is correct?

    a. Reese must distribute the entire account balance within five years of Andrea's death.

    b. In the year following Andrea's death, Reese may begin taking distributions from the account based on Reese's remaining life expectancy.

    c. In the year following Andrea's death, Reese must begin taking distributions over Andrea's remaining single-life expectancy.

    d. Reese can roll the account over to her own name and name a new beneficiary.

5. The early distribution penalty of 10 percent does not apply to qualified plan distributions:

    1. Made after attainment of the age of 55 and separation from service.
    2. Made for the purpose of paying qualified higher education costs.
    3. Paid to a designated beneficiary after the death of the account owner who had not begun receiving minimum distributions.

    a. 1 only.
    b. 1 and 3.
    c. 2 and 3.
    d. 1, 2, and 3.

6. Which of the following statements is/are correct regarding the early distribution 10 percent penalty tax from a qualified plan?

    1. Retirement at age 55 or older exempts the distributions from the early withdrawal penalty tax.
    2. Distributions used to pay medical expenses in excess of the 7.5% of AGI for a tax filer who itemizes are exempt from the early withdrawal penalty.
    3. Distributions that are part of a series of equal periodic payments paid over the life or life expectancy of the participant are exempt from the early withdrawal penalty.

    a. 3 only.
    b. 1 and 3.
    c. 2 and 3.
    d. 1, 2, and 3.

7. Steve, age 69, is an employee of X2, Inc. He plans to work until age 75. He currently contributes 6% of his pay to his 401(k) plan, and his employer matches with 3%. Which one of the following statements is true?

   a. Steve is required to take minimum distributions from his 401(k) plan beginning April 1 of the year after he attains age 70½.

   b. Steve is required to take minimum distributions from his 401(k) plan beginning April 1 of the year after he retires.

   c. Steve is required to take minimum distributions from his Traditional IRA beginning April 1 of the year after he retires.

   d. Steve cannot contribute to his 401(k) plan after age 70½ in any case.

8. Jose Sequential, age 70½ in October of this year, worked for several companies over his lifetime. He has worked for the following companies (A-E) and still has the following qualified plan account balances at those companies.

Company	Jose's Account Balance
A	$250,000
B	$350,000
C	$150,000
D	$350,000
E	$200,000

Jose is currently employed with Company E. What, if any, is his required minimum distribution for the current year from all plans? Life expectancy tables are 27.4 for age 70 and 26.5 for age 71.

   a. $0.

   b. $40,146.

   c. $41,509.

   d. $47,445.

9. Tom, age 39, is an employee of Star, Inc., which has a profit sharing plan with a CODA feature. His total account balance is $412,000, $82,000 of which represents employee elective deferrals and earnings on those deferrals. The balance is profit sharing contributions made by the employer and earnings on those contributions. Tom is 100% vested. Which of the following statements is/are correct?

    1. Tom may take a loan from the plan, but the maximum loan is $41,000 and the normal repayment period will be 5 years.

    2. If Tom takes a distribution (plan permitting) to pay health care premiums (no coverage by employer) he will be subject to income tax, but not the 10% penalty.

      a. 1 only.

      b. 2 only.

      c. 1 and 2.

      d. Neither 1 nor 2.

10. On January 5, Cindy, age 39, withdrew $42,000 from her qualified plan. Cindy had an account balance of $180,000 and an adjusted taxable basis in the account of $30,000. Calculate any early withdrawal penalty.

      a. $0.

      b. $1,200.

      c. $3,500.

      d. $4,200.

11. Brenda, age 53 and a recent widow, is deciding between taking a lump-sum distribution from her husband's pension plan of $263,500 now or selecting a life annuity starting when she is age 65 (life expectancy at 65 is 21 years) of $2,479 per month. Current 30-year treasuries are yielding 6% annually. Which of the statements below are true?

    1. If she takes the lump-sum distribution, she will receive $263,500 in cash now and be able to reinvest for 34 years, creating an annuity of $4,570 per month.

    2. If she takes the lump-sum distribution she will be subject to the 10% early withdrawal penalty.

      a. 1 only.

      b. 2 only.

      c. 1 and 2.

      d. Neither 1 nor 2.

12. Nancy, age 70 on February 2, 2004, had the following account balances in a qualified retirement plan.

12/31/01	$300,000
12/31/02	$350,000
12/31/03	$500,000
12/31/04	$478,000
12/31/05	$519,000
12/31/06	$600,000

Assuming that Nancy is retired and has never taken a distribution prior to 2005, what is the total amount of minimum distribution required in 2005? Life expectancy factors according to the uniform life table are 27.4 for a 70 year old and 26.5 for a 71 year old.

    a. $18,037.

    b. $18,248.

    c. $35,597.

    d. $36,286.

13. Which of the following is/are elements of an effective waiver for a preretirement survivor annuity?

    1. Both spouses must sign the waiver.

    2. The waiver must be notarized or signed by a plan official.

    3. The waiver must indicate that the person(s) waiving understand the consequences of the waiver.

        a. 2 only.

        b. 1 and 3.

        c. 2 and 3.

        d. 1, 2, and 3.

14. Which of the following is true regarding QDROs?

    a. The court determines how the retirement plan will satisfy the QDRO. (i.e. split accounts, separate interest).

    b. In order for a QDRO to be valid, the order must be filed on Form 2932-QDRO provided by ERISA.

    c. All QDRO distributions are charged a 10% early withdrawal penalty.

    d. A QDRO distribution is not considered a taxable distribution if the distribution is deposited into the recipient's IRA or qualified plan.

Installation, Administration and Termination of Qualified Plans

8

INTRODUCTION

In today's economic environment, retirement plans are an essential component of the overall compensation package of an employer and are designed to recruit and retain talented employees. The selection of an appropriate qualified plan can be both time-consuming and expensive. Depending on the plan selected, numerous initial and continuing requirements must be met to ensure that the plan retains its qualified, and thus tax-advantaged, status. Once a plan is established, annual testing, yearly contributions, and yearly filings may also be required. Special rules also apply to plan amendments and terminations of qualified plans when needed. This chapter will discuss plan selection, installation, administration, and amending and terminating a qualified plan.

QUALIFIED PLAN SELECTION

Selecting a qualified plan begins with the consideration of a number of relevant issues including business, financial, and sometimes personal goals. Other issues that impact plan selection are the employee census, employee turnover, funding requirements, philosophy about employee savings, and the cost to adopt, implement, and maintain the plan. The retirement plan decision makers in a small company are usually the owners, while executive management and human resources management usually make the decisions for a large company. Decision makers are often assisted in plan selection by qualified plan experts who help the decision makers consider the many factors at issue when selecting a plan. For large companies, the decisions are usually based on the business objectives of the company, but for small or closely-held businesses, plan choice is often based on both the owner's business and personal objectives.

Key Concepts

Underline/highlight the answers to these questions as you read:

1. What business and personal issues should be considered when making a qualified plan selection?

2. What is an employee census and why is it important?

3. What are the general characteristics of qualified plans?

BUSINESS OBJECTIVES

The first step in plan selection is to determine the business objectives for establishing a qualified plan. Although they can vary, the typical objectives of a large company include being competitive in the labor market by offering a qualified plan that fits within an overall compensation package. For a smaller company, the ability to assist the small business owner with tax-deferred savings is frequently a primary personal objective. Other common reasons companies establish qualified plans are to attract, reward, and retain employees, assist employees in saving for retirement, or simply to benefit the employees through the adoption of a tax-advantaged plan.

EXHIBIT 8.1   **STEPS IN QUALIFIED RETIREMENT PLAN SELECTION**

Concept Summary

1. Establish the objectives for the plan (Sample Objectives)
     • To benefit owners of small businesses.
     • To benefit all employees.
     • To benefit select employees.
     • To attract, retain, or reward employees.
     • To encourage early retirement.
     • To provide a tax-advantaged benefit.
 2. Prepare an employee census to identify the beneficiaries of various plans and the financial impact of alternative plans on the employer sponsor.
 3. Identify the types of plans that can meet both the qualitative and quantitative objectives.
 4. Assess each plan's financial characteristics:
     • Contribution costs.
     • Costs of administration.
     • Flexibility of contributions.
     • Burden of investment risks.
     • Necessity of mandatory funding.
 5. Select plan.

EMPLOYEE CENSUS

An important first step to consider when selecting a qualified plan is to prepare an employee census. If the primary goal of having a plan is to simply provide a savings vehicle such as a 401(k) plan, the **employee census** may not be as important. However, if the purpose of the plan is to benefit the small business owner, the employee census is essential. The census will identify each employee, their age, compensation, number of years of employment, and any ownership interest. Each element of the census is important to consider because plans can be structured to benefit highly compensated employees, nonhighly compensated employees, older or younger employees, employees who have a certain length of service, a group of employees, or some mix of these employees. The census helps to identify which employees will benefit (and to what extent) from using various possible types of plans. In addition to a current census, a review of employee turnover is essential to plan selection because such a review can help determine the appropriate vesting schedules and how to deal with forfeitures resulting from employee termination.

EXAMPLE 8.1

SAMPLE EMPLOYEE CENSUS				
Employee	**Age**	**Compensation**	**Ownership Interest**	**Length of Service**
Alex	30	$200,000	100%	10 Years
Becky	35	$35,000	0	5 Years
Cameron	30	$30,000	0	2 Years
Derrick	30	$30,000	0	2 Years
Total		**$295,000**	**100%**	
Expected Turnover 0 for Alex and Becky and by year 4 for Cameron and Derrick				

Consider Example 8.1, suppose Alex wanted to establish a plan to benefit all employees who would save for their own retirement. He should consider a 401(k) plan with an employer match of up to 3% of covered compensation. Alex could simply reduce future compensation raises by 3% and thus have a net zero cost of funding the plan. The 401(k) employer match is also discretionary not mandatory, leaving the sponsor with cash flow flexibility.

Suppose an additional objective was to benefit only those who are employed by the company for at least five years. Because the plan utilizes an employer match, the longest cliff vesting schedules Alex could use is a 3-year cliff vesting schedule. This would still only require Alex to provide a match to those employees employed for three years.

If Alex was much older than Becky, Cameron, and Derrick, he might consider using an age-weighted profit sharing plan, so that most of the contributions and benefits would be contributed to the plan on his behalf.

An employee census is an essential tool in determining which employees will benefit and how much they will benefit using various plans. The employee census is then used to help select the best plan to accomplish the goals of the company and its owners.

CASH FLOW CONSIDERATIONS

The decision maker should always consider the company's financial stability and the predictability of its cash flows prior to plan selection. The company's cash flows dictate how committed the company can be with regard to mandatory contributions, such as those required for all pension plans. For example, if cash flows fluctuate widely from year to year, it is probably not prudent to install any pension plan because of the **mandatory funding requirement**. In the case of fluctuating cash flows, it is more prudent to select some type of qualified profit sharing plan because profit sharing plans have **discretionary contributions** each year. However, if cash flows are stable and predictable, then the company may want to consider either pension or profit sharing plans.

ADMINISTRATION COSTS

When a company implements a qualified plan, there are numerous costs associated with adopting and administering the plan. Establishing a plan generally requires a financial planner or retirement plan expert to assist the company in selecting and adopting the plan. In addition, once the plan has been adopted, the company must pay for the actual funding of the plan if the plan includes employer contributions. If the plan is large and has many participants, the sponsor may need to hire employees to administer the plan during the year and file the necessary compliance forms or outsource this to an outside vendor such as a **third party administrator** (TPA).

A company's ability to afford such costs impacts the type of plan chosen. For example, profit sharing plans are often very easy to set up with many prototype plans available, have discretionary contributions and minimal annual testing; therefore, they are relatively inexpensive to establish and maintain. Adding a 401(k) feature (**CODA**) to a profit sharing plan increases the cost slightly because of the annual **ADP** and **ACP** testing (as discussed in Chapter 5) and the matching contributions. The testing and its associated cost could be avoided by adopting a safe harbor 401(k) plan, which does not require certain nondiscrimination tests (such as ADP and ACP testing). Stock bonus plans and ESOPs often require annual valuations of the stock of the business by a valuation expert, making the administration of this type of plan more expensive than a simple profit sharing plan. Defined benefit plans require PBGC insurance premiums, and actuaries are needed annually to determine plan contributions, making the defined benefit plan potentially the most expensive plan to adopt. Large companies may be able to absorb the substantial costs associated with a defined benefit plan, while small companies may be more sensitive to controlling plan costs. However, today there is a trend for large companies to convert defined benefit plans to cash balance pension plans in an attempt to reduce certain costs and for newer companies to avoid defined benefit plans altogether. This illustrates the need for consideration to be given to plan costs for adoption and administration during plan selection.

OWNER'S BUSINESS AND PERSONAL OBJECTIVES

If the company is a small or closely-held company, then the owner's personal and business objectives are critical in plan selection. Small business owners typically want to reduce their current taxes and save for their own financial future. For example, key owners of small companies generally want a majority of plan benefits for themselves and less for the rank-and-file employees, especially those who do not stay with the employer for a long period. The owners may select a plan that will meet this need or use various techniques to modify the plan to primarily benefit owners and/or key employees. Since these are the decision-makers that financial planners will be working with, it is important to understand and try to achieve their goals.

PLAN SELECTION APPLICATION

After evaluating each of the above issues, a financial advisor/pension expert can assist the owner or key decision maker in determining which plan suits the owner and the company's needs. The following exhibit summarizes some of the important issues to consider in plan selection.

Quick Quiz

Highlight the answer to these questions:

1. Plan selection should only focus on the needs of the company and should never focus on the needs of the small business owner as this would be a conflict of interest.
   a. True
   b. False

2. While an employee census is generally essential, it may not be critical if the only objective is to provide a savings vehicle.
   a. True
   b. False

3. An employer with fluctuating cash flows will generally choose a pension plan.
   a. True
   b. False

False, True, False.

EXHIBIT 8.2 QUALIFIED PLAN SUMMARY OF CHARACTERISTICS

Qualified Plan	Who Generally Contributes	Mandatory Funding	Investment Risk	Company Stock %	Permits Soc. Sec. Integration	Required Expert	Who is Generally Favored?[1]	QJSA / QPSA
PENSION PLANS								
Defined Benefit Pension Plan	ER	Yes	ER	≤10%	Yes	Actuary and Pension Expert	Older Age Entrants	Yes
Cash Balance Pension Plan	ER	Yes	ER	≤10%	Yes	Actuary and Pension Expert	Younger Persons	Yes
Target Benefit Pension Plan	ER	Yes	EE	≤10%	Yes	Actuary once and Pension Expert	Older Age Entrants	No
Money Purchase Pension Plan	ER	Yes	EE	≤10%	Yes	None[2]	Younger Persons	No
PROFIT SHARING PLANS								
Profit Sharing Plan	ER	No	EE	≤100%	Yes	None[2]	Highly Compensated and younger persons	No
Stock Bonus Plan	ER	No	EE	≤100%	Yes	Valuation Specialist and Pension Expert	Highly Compensated and long length of service	No
ESOP	ER	No	EE	≤100%	No	Valuation Specialist and Pension Expert	Highly Compensated and long length of service	No
401(k) Plan	EE and ER	No[3]	EE	≤100%	No[4]	Pension Expert	Savers and Younger Persons	No
Thrift Plan	EE	No	EE	≤100%	Yes	Pension Expert	Savers and Younger Persons	No
Age-Based Profit Sharing Plan	ER	No	EE	≤100%	Yes	Pension Expert	Older Highly Compensated	No
New Comparability Plan	ER	No	EE	≤100%	Yes	Pension Expert	Owners	No

1. Where younger persons are favored, it is because they benefit from a greater number of compounding periods.
2. Many prototype plans are available.
3. 401(k) Plans may have mandatory funding if there is a matching contribution for a safe harbor plan.
4. If a CODA feature is a part of the profit sharing plan then, the profit sharing plan can be integrated, but not the CODA portion.

EE = Employee, ER = Employer.

The following examples demonstrate the plan selection process.

Assume Alex owns a small company with the following employee information:

EXAMPLE 8.2

EMPLOYEE CENSUS				
Employee	Age	Compensation	Ownership	Length of Service
Alex	30	$200,000	100%	10 Years
Becky	35	$35,000	0	5 Years
Cameron	30	$30,000	0	2 Years
Derrick	30	$30,000	0	2 Years
Total		**$295,000**	**100%**	

Assuming the company has sufficient cash flow to fund a plan, the most obvious plan recommendation would be a profit sharing plan. The plan could be integrated with Social Security, therefore providing Alex an even greater share of the contributions than a nonintegrated plan. A profit sharing plan would allow a contribution of up to 25% of covered compensation and would help maximize contributions to Alex.

The profit sharing plan could also include a CODA (401(k)) feature if Alex wanted the employees to contribute to the plan. The CODA feature would allow employees to make elective deferrals into the plan. The company could match employee contributions to encourage employee participation.

Assume instead that Alex is 51 years old and wants to maximize contributions for his own benefit. Since, in this case, Alex is significantly older than the other employees, a defined benefit plan or age-weighted profit sharing plan may be more appropriate than a straight profit sharing plan or an integrated profit sharing plan. Either of these plans would allow for higher contributions on behalf of Alex because of his age. In choosing between a defined benefit and an age-weighted profit sharing plan, Alex is choosing between mandatory funding for the defined benefit plan and discretionary funding for the age-based plan. Also, the costs of maintaining the plans will be quite different because a defined benefit plan requires annual actuarial determinations and a profit sharing plan does not utilize actuaries. Alex will have to compare the advantages and disadvantages of each of the plans in making his decision.

EXAMPLE 8.3

Edward and Fran each own 50% of a small company with the following employee census.

EMPLOYEE CENSUS				
Employee	Age	Compensation	Ownership	Length of Service
Edward	55	$300,000	50%	10 years
Fran	30	$300,000	50%	10 years
Gerry	35	$30,000	0	2 Years
Harriet	30	$30,000	0	2 Years
Total		$660,000	100%	

The age difference between Edward and Fran (owners) makes the plan selection more challenging. An age-weighted plan would be beneficial for Edward. However, because Fran is much younger than Edward, such a plan would not equally benefit Fran. Assuming they both wanted to benefit equally, a profit sharing plan would be most appropriate because it would allow them to each receive the maximum contribution of the annual additions limit ($42,000 for 2005, $43,000[†] for 2006, $44,000[†] for 2007, and $45,000[†] for 2008). In addition, the plan could be integrated with Social Security to provide higher benefits for the highly compensated employees, Edward and Fran. As an alternative, a new comparability plan would permit them to create classes of employees. The first class would be owners, and a new comparability plan would allow them to receive a larger portion of the contribution (remember this plan is highly scrutinized by the IRS).

EXAMPLE 8.4

Irene has been the owner of Irene's Pet Shop for 10 years. She decided to establish a retirement plan for her corporation. She has come to you and indicated that she wants to make all initial contributions to the plan using company stock. She may also want to integrate the plan with Social Security.

Either a qualified profit sharing or stock bonus plan would be an appropriate plan for Irene since she wants to use 100% company stock for the initial and subsequent contributions. Both plans also allow integration with Social Security.

1. Assume that the sponsor company wants a qualified plan. The sponsor must be willing to abide by the qualified plan requirements, including:
    - Nondiscrimination and broad coverage
    - Eligibility rules
    - Coverage rules
    - Reporting rules
    - Testing rules
    - Disclosure rules
    - Vesting rules

2. Prepare an employee census.

3. Determine if (A) mandatory or (B) discretionary funding is appropriate.
    A. Mandatory funding:
        - Determine whether the investment risk will be on the employer or employee:
            - Employer: Either defined benefit pension plan or cash balance pension plan
                - If the plan favors older age entrants - Defined benefit pension plan
                - If the plan favors younger age entrants - Cash balance pension plan
            - Employee: Either target benefit pension plan or money purchase pension plan
                - If the employer is willing to endure larger establishment costs - Target benefit pension plan
                - If the employer wants low establishment costs - Money purchase pension plan

    B. Discretionary funding:
        - If employee contributions to the qualified plan are desired (self reliance - contributory):
            - Pretax: 401(k) Plan
            - After-tax: Thrift Plan
        - If only the employer contributes to the qualified plan (noncontributory):
            - Contributions of company stock: Profit sharing plan, Stock bonus plan, ESOP
            - Test benefits for discrimination rather than contributions (cross-test): Age-based profit sharing plan, new comparability plan
        - If the employer wants low initial costs - Profit sharing plan
        - If the employer is willing to pay additional costs - Stock bonus plan, ESOP, age-based profit sharing plan, or new comparability plan
        - If the employer wants integration - Profit sharing plan or Stock bonus plan

EXHIBIT 8.4 **PLAN SELECTION FLOW CHART**

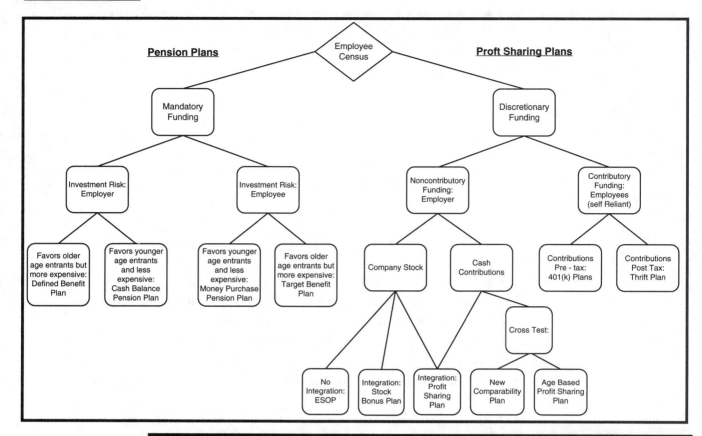

ESTABLISHING A QUALIFIED PLAN

The employer-sponsor is responsible for setting up and maintaining the qualified plan. There are several steps involved in establishing a qualified plan. First, the employer must select and adopt the appropriate plan. Next, the employer must communicate the plan to employees and establish a procedure for funding and administering the plan. Remember that the employer (owner) does not necessarily need to have employees other than himself to establish a qualified plan. A self-employed person who has no other employees can establish a qualified plan.

ADOPTING A WRITTEN PLAN

A qualified plan must be detailed in a written plan that is adopted by the company. To take an income tax deduction for contributions for a particular tax year, the plan must be adopted by

Key Concepts

Underline/highlight the answers to these questions as you read:

1. What are the requirements for establishing a qualified plan?

2. How and when should employees be notified when a qualified plan is established?

3. Who may manage the qualified plan assets?

the last day of that particular tax year. In some cases, the company may elect for the plan to have a different tax year than the company.

EXAMPLE 8.5

> If a company is on a calendar year basis, then the plan must be adopted by December 31 of the year in which the deduction is desired. If, instead, the company is on a fiscal year ending August 31, then the plan should be adopted by August 31.

The company can individually design the plan using an **ERISA attorney** (expensive), or the company can use an IRS-approved master or prototype plan (very inexpensive). Once adopted, information about the plan must be communicated in writing to the employees as detailed below.

Master or Prototype Plans

The majority of qualified plans follow standard forms called master or prototype plans. These plans have been pre-approved by the IRS and are available for employers to simply adopt. **Master plans** provide a single trust or custodial account that is jointly used by all adopting employers. **Prototype plans** allow each employer to establish their own separate trust or custodial account. IRS approved master or prototype plans can often be obtained from banks, trade or professional organizations, insurance companies, investment houses, or mutual funds. These organizations will assist the employer by offering them a basic plan and trust document. They will also use an adoption agreement, so that the employer can elect, by checking the box, various options such as participation requirements and vesting schedules.

Individually Designed Plans

If the company has specific needs that are not addressed in a master or prototype plan, or if they so choose, the company can have their own individually drafted plan. However, in order to be considered a qualified plan, the plan must be permanent and for the exclusive benefit of the employees and their beneficiaries. The adopted plan should detail the procedure for amending and identify who can amend the plan should it be necessary.

Individually designed plans are less common because of the cost to design and draft and because of the wide availability of prototype plans. While advance IRS approval is not required to adopt an individually drafted plan, approval can and usually is sought from the IRS. This is done by requesting a determination letter and paying the required fee. Creating an individually designed plan usually requires the services of an ERISA attorney, making the plan much more expensive than prototype plans.

Determination Letters

Determination letters may be used when a retirement plan is adopted, amended, or terminated. They may be filed in advance of the plan being adopted or immediately thereafter, usually by filing Form 5300. While they are not required in any of these circumstances, they are useful to the plan sponsor because they allow the plan sponsor to rely on the response from the IRS. If the IRS has any issues with the plan design, the plan can be amended immediately to ensure compliance.

Determination letters are usually accompanied by the appropriate fee. The fee is based on the type of transaction involved. Some small employers may be exempt from paying the fee if they meet certain criteria. The fee is determined on IRS Form 8717.

EXHIBIT 8.5 FORM 8717: USER FEE FOR EMPLOYEE PLAN DETERMINATION LETTER REQUESTED

Form **8717** (Rev. September 2004) Department of the Treasury Internal Revenue Service	**User Fee for Employee Plan Determination Letter Request** ▶ **Attach to determination letter application.**	**For IRS Use Only**	OMB No. 1545–1772 Control number _____ Amount paid _____ User fee screener

1 Name of plan sponsor (employer if single-employer plan)	2 Sponsor's employer identification number

3 Plan name	4 Plan number

Caution: *If you qualify for the exemption from user fees for small business employers, complete only the certification below (see the instructions on page 2 for details). For all other applications, leave the certification blank and check the appropriate box in column A or B of line 5.*

Certification

I certify that the application for a determination letter on the qualified status of _____ (name of the plan) meets the conditions for exemption from user fees described in section 620 of the Economic Growth and Tax Relief Reconciliation Act of 2001.

Signature ▶ _____ Title ▶ _____ Date ▶ _____

Form Submitted	Fee Schedule	
	A	**B**
5a Form 5300:	with Demo 5 and/or Demo 6: ☐ $1,250	no Demo 5 and no Demo 6 ☐ $700
b Form 5307:	with Demo 5 and/or Demo 6: ☐ $1,000	no Demo 5 and no Demo 6 ☐ $125
c Form 5310:	with Demo 5 and/or Demo 6: ☐ $375	no Demo 5 and no Demo 6 ☐ $225
d Form 6406:	Not applicable	☐ $125
e Multiple employer plans (Form 5300):	with Demo 5 and/or Demo 6:	no Demo 5 and no Demo 6
(1) 2 to 10 Forms 5300 submitted	☐ (1) $ 1,250	☐ (1) $ 700
(2) 11 to 99 Forms 5300 submitted	☐ (2) $ 2,000	☐ (2) $ 1,400
(3) 100 to 499 Forms 5300 submitted	☐ (3) $ 3,500	☐ (3) $ 2,800
(4) Over 499 Forms 5300 submitted	☐ (4) $ 6,500	☐ (4) $ 5,600
f Multiple employer plans (Form 5310):	with Demo 5 and/or Demo 6:	no Demo 5 and no Demo 6
(1) 2 to 10 employers maintaining the plan	☐ (1) $ 375	☐ (1) $ 225
(2) 11 to 99 employers maintaining the plan	☐ (2) $ 600	☐ (2) $ 450
(3) 100 to 499 employers maintaining the plan	☐ (3) $ 1,000	☐ (3) $ 900
(4) Over 499 employers maintaining the plan	☐ (4) $ 2,000	☐ (4) $ 1,800
g Volume submitter:		
(1) Specimen plan		☐ (1) $ 1,500
(2) Lead specimen plan (see Rev. Proc. 2000-20)		☐ (2) $ 3,000
(3) Specimen plan identical to lead specimen plan (see Rev. Proc. 2000-20)		☐ (3) $ 100
h Group trust		☐ $ 750

Attach Check or Money Order Here

Cat. No. 64727O   Form **8717** (Rev. 9-2004)

Determination letters are generally narrow in scope and address particular issues. For example, a favorable determination letter may be received that indicates that the plan meets the qualified plan rules, but the determination letter may or may not verify that certain types of contributions to the plan are income tax deductible. Just because a plan receives a favorable determination letter does not mean that it cannot lose its qualified status if it does not continue to comply with provisions of the plan document as well as with the IRC and ERISA. It is critical to understand that the sponsor must follow the provisions established in the plan document.

SAMPLE PLAN ADOPTION AGREEMENT

EXHIBIT 8.6

Sample Plan Adoption Agreement
401(k) Plan

Employer Information

Name: _____   Telephone: _____

Address: _____   EIN: _____

_____   Plan Administrator: _____

Plan Information

Name of Plan: _____

Plan Number: _____   Plan Year: ☐ Calendar year   ☐ Fiscal year ending

Effective Date: ☐ January 1, _____; or ☐ _____ (For initial plan year enter a date between January 1 and October 1.)
☐ This is a restatement of a prior plan known as:
The restated effective date of the plan is:

Coverage Information

The eligibility requirements for participation in the Plan will be:

1. Eligibility Service Requirement (check one)
☐ No eligibility service requirement.
☐ Six months of employment. (If this option is selected, an Employee will not be required to complete any specified number of Hours of Service in the six-month period.)
☐ One year of service.

2. Age Requirement
☐ No minimum age requirement
☐ _____ Years (cannot be more than 21).

The requirements listed above are (check one):
☐ Applicable to all Employees.
☐ Applicable to all Employees except those Employees employed on the Effective Date. Such Employees will participate immediately. All other Employees will need to satisfy the requirements listed above.

Employer Contribution Information

The Employer shall contribute on behalf of each Participant for each Plan Year in accordance with one of the following as indicated in the Summary Plan Description:
☐ Matching Contributions in the amount of the Participant's Elective Deferral up to 4%.
☐ Nonelective Contribution of 2% of each Participant's Compensation.

Vesting Information

A participant's vested interest in his or her Employer Contribution Account will be:
☐ 100% immediately vested at all times.
☐ 100% vested after _____ Years of Service (not to exceed 3 years). A Participant will be 0% vested prior to completing this period.
☐

Years of Service	Vested Percentage
1	0%
2	20%
3	40%
4	60%
5	80%
6	100%

Signatures

Employer: _____   Trustee (optional): _____
By (Authorized Signature): _____   By (Authorized Signature): _____
Date: _____   Date: _____

NOTIFYING ELIGIBLE EMPLOYEES

Information regarding the qualified plan must be distributed to employees who might be eligible for the plan. In addition, the information must be furnished to the eligible employees working at the same facility. This information helps to inform the employee of his rights under ERISA and the qualified retirement plan.

Before the IRS can issue a determination letter on the qualified status of a retirement plan, the employer must provide the IRS with satisfactory evidence that it has notified the persons who qualify as interested parties. **Interested parties** with regard to notification are present employees who are eligible to participate in the plan and present employees who are not eligible for the plan but whose principal place of employment is the same as the principal place of employment of any employee who is eligible to participate.

EXAMPLE 8.6	Loupili company wants to establish a qualified retirement plan that requires one year of service to participate. Loupili has two offices, one on the north side of town called the North office and one on the south side of town called the South office. The North office has 32 employees, and the South office has 10 employees. The North office has been operational for several years, and half of its employees are eligible to participate in the qualified retirement plan. The South office was recently opened, and none of the employees have met the service requirement to be eligible. Loupili must notify all of the employees in the North office because some of them are eligible and the others work in the same office as eligible individuals. The employees in the South office do not need to be notified at this time because none of them are eligible for the plan.

Notification can be made in person, via e-mail or mail, or by posting a notice in a location generally used for posting notices to employees. If notification is made to the eligible employees in person or by posting, then the notice must be given between seven and 21 days before the determination application is mailed to the IRS. If the notice is mailed to the eligible employees, then it must be mailed at least ten days before, but not more than 24 days before, the determination application is mailed to the IRS[1]. Below is a sample form taken from Revenue Procedure 2001-6 that can be used to notify employees.

---

1. Rev Proc 2001-6.

1. Notice To:_____[describe class or classes of interested parties]

An application is to be made to the Internal Revenue Service for an advance determination on the qualification of the following employee pension benefit plan:

2. _____
   (name of plan)

3. _____
   (plan number)

4. _____
   (name and address of applicant)

5. _____
   (applicant EIN)

6. _____
   (name and address of plan administrator)

7. The application will be filed on _____ for an advance determination as to whether the plan meets the qualification requirements of § 401 or 403(a) of the Internal Revenue Code of 1986, with respect to the plan's _____ [initial qualification, amendment, termination, or partial termination]. The application will be filed with:

   EP Determinations
   Internal Revenue Service
   P.O. Box 192
   Covington, KY 41012-0192

8. The employees eligible to participate under the plan are: _____

9. The Internal Revenue Service _____[has/has not] previously issued a determination letter with respect to the qualification of this plan.

RIGHTS OF INTERESTED PARTIES

10. You have the right to submit to EP Determinations, at the above address, either individually or jointly with other interested parties, your comments as to whether this plan meets the qualification requirements of the Internal Revenue Code.

    You may instead, individually or jointly with other interested parties, request the Department of Labor to submit, on your behalf, comments to EP Determinations regarding qualification of the plan. If the Department declines to comment on all or some of the matters you raise, you may, individually, or jointly if your request was made to the Department jointly, submit your comments on these matters directly to EP Determinations.

REQUESTS FOR COMMENTS BY THE DEPARTMENT OF LABOR

11. The Department of Labor may not comment on behalf of interested parties unless requested to do so by the lessor of 10 employees or 10 percent of the employees who qualify as interested parties. The number of persons needed for the Department to comment with respect to this plan is _____. If you request the Department to comment, your request must be in writing and must specify the matters upon which comments are requested, and must also include:

    (1) the information contained in items 2 through 5 of this Notice; and

    (2) the number of persons needed for the Department to comment.

A request to the Department to comment should be addressed as follows:

Deputy Assistant Secretary
Pension and Welfare Benefits Administration
ATTN: 3001 Comment Request
U.S. Department of Labor,
200 Constitution Avenue, N.W.
Washington, D.C. 20210

COMMENTS TO THE INTERNAL REVENUE SERVICE

12. Comments submitted by you to EP Determinations must be in writing and received by them by _____. However, if there are matters that you request the Department of Labor to comment upon on your behalf, and the Department declines, you may submit comments on these matters to EP Determinations to be received by them within 15 days from the time the Department notifies you that it will not comment on a particular matter, or by _____, whichever is later, but not after _____. A request to the Department to comment on your behalf must be received by it by_____if you wish to preserve your right to comment on a matter upon which the Department declines to comment, or by _____ if you wish to waive that right.

ADDITIONAL INFORMATION

13. Detailed instructions regarding the requirements for notification of interested parties may be found in sections 17 and 18 of Rev. Proc. 2001–6. Additional information concerning this application (including, where applicable, an updated copy of the plan and related trust; the application for determination; any additional documents dealing with the application that have submitted to the Service; and copies of section 17 of Rev. Proc. 2001–6 are available at _____ during the hours of _____ for inspection and copying. (There is a nominal charge for copying and/or mailing.)

The employer is required to provide, free of charge, a summary of the details of the qualified retirement plan, called a **Summary Plan Description**, to employees, participants, and beneficiaries under pay status (receiving benefits). The summary must be furnished within 90 days after the person becomes a participant, first receives benefits as a beneficiary, or within 120 days after the plan is established under ERISA. The Summary Plan Description explains in plain language what the plan provides and how it operates. It provides information on when an employee can begin to participate in the plan, how service and benefits are calculated, when benefits becomes vested, when and in what form benefits are paid, and how to file a claim for benefits. The Summary Plan Description is needed because the plan document is lengthy and has substantial legal jargon that many employees may not understand.

The employer should ensure that the Summary Plan Description accurately reflects what is included in the actual plan to avoid potential liability. Many employers use disclaimers in the Summary Plan Description that state that in the event that the Summary Plan Description is different than the plan document, the plan document controls the provisions of the qualified plan. This strategy has been effective for some companies in the past; although, it has and will continue to be a source of litigation until it is legislatively decided.

The employer is also required to provide the plan participants notices of any plan amendments or changes. This can be done either through a revised Summary Plan Description or in a separate document, called a **Summary of Material Modifications**. This document must be given to participants free of charge within 210 days after the end of the plan year in which a change is adopted.

In addition to the Summary Plan Description, the employer must automatically provide the participants, free of charge, a copy of the plan's Summary Annual Report each year. The Summary Annual Report is a summary of the annual financial report that the plan files with the

Department of Labor each year (Form 5500 discussed later in this chapter). Participants may also ask the plan administrator for a copy of the plan's annual report in its entirety if they wish to learn more about the plan.

SAMPLE SUMMARY ANNUAL REPORT

EXHIBIT 8.8

Summary Annual Report
ABC Company Defined Contribution Retirement Plan

This is a summary of the annual report for the **ABC Company Defined Contribution Retirement Plan** EIN XX-XXXXXXX, for the period January 1, 2006 through December 31, 2006. The annual report has been filed with the Pension and Welfare Benefits Administration, U.S. Department of Labor, as required under the Employee Retirement Income Security Act of 1974 (ERISA).

Basic Financial Statement

Benefits under the plan are provided by trust and insurance. Plan expenses were $XX,XXX,XXX. These expenses included $XX,XXX,XXX in administrative expenses and $XX,XXX,XXX in benefits paid to participants and beneficiaries. A total of XX,XXX persons were participants in or beneficiaries of the plan at the end of the plan year, although not all of these persons had yet earned the right to receive benefits.

The value of the plan assets, after subtracting liabilities of the plan was $XXX,XXX,XXX as of December 31, 2006, compared to $XXX,XXX,XXX as of January 1, 2006. During the plan year, the plan experienced a decrease in its net assets of $XX,XXX,XXX.

This decrease included unrealized depreciation in the value of plan assets; that is, the difference between the value of the plan's assets at the end of the year and the value of those assets at the beginning of the year. The plan had a total negative income of $X,XXX,XXX, including employer contributions of $X,XXX,XXX, realized losses of $X,XXX,XXX from the sale of assets, and negative net earnings from investments of $X,XXX,XXX (which includes unrealized losses on assets).

Minimum Funding Standards

Enough money was contributed to the plan to keep it funded in accordance with the minimum funding standards of ERISA.

Your Rights To Additional Information

You have the right to receive a copy of the full annual report, or any part thereof, on request. The following items are included in the report:
1. an accountant's report;
2. assets held for investment;
3. financial information; and
4. insurance information.

To obtain a copy of the full annual report, or any part thereof, write or call ABC Company, 123 Lovers Lane, Anytown, USA, telephone number (555) 555-2004. The charge to cover copying will be 25 cents per page or any part thereof.

You also have the right to receive from the plan administrator, on request and at no charge, a statement of the assets and liabilities of the plan and accompanying notes, or a statement of income and expenses of the plan and accompanying notes, or both. If you request a copy of the full annual report from the plan administrator, these two statements and accompanying notes will be included as part of that report. The charge to cover copying costs given above does not include a charge for the copying of these portions of the report because these portions are furnished without charge.

You also have the legally protected right to examine the annual report at ABC Company, 123 Lovers Lane, Anytown, USA, telephone number (555) 555-2004 and at the U.S. Department of Labor in Washington, D.C., or to obtain a copy from the U.S. Department of Labor upon payment of copying costs. Requests to the Department should be addressed to: Public Disclosure Room, Pension and Welfare Benefit Administration, Department of Labor, 200 Constitution Avenue, N.W., Washington, D.C. 20210.

EXHIBIT 8.9 **SOURCES OF PLAN INFORMATION**

Type of Document	Who You Can Get It From	When You Can Get It	Your Cost
Summary Plan Description (SPD): This summary of your retirement plan tells you what the plan provides and how it operates.	Plan Administrator	Upon written request	Reasonable Charge
		Automatically within 90 days after you become covered under the plan	Free
		Automatically every 5 years if your plan is amended	Free
		Automatically every 10 years if your plan has not been amended	Free
	Department of Labor	Upon Request	Copying Charge
Summary of Material Modifications (SMM): This summarizes material changes to your plan.	Plan Administrator	Automatically within 210 days after the end of the plan year for which the plan has been amended or modified (distribution of a revised SPD satisfies this requirement)	Free
	Department of Labor	Upon Request	Copying Charge
Summary Annual Report: This summarizes the annual financial reports that most retirement plans file with the Department of Labor.	Plan Administrator	Automatically within 9 months after the end of the plan year, or 2 months after the due date for filing the annual report	Free
Annual Report (Form 5500 Series): Annual financial reports that most retirement plans file with the Department of Labor.	Plan Administrator	Latest annual report upon written request	Reasonable Charge
	Department of Labor	Upon Request	Copying Charge
Individual Benefit Statement: A statement describing your total accrued and vested benefits is required to be provided by most retirement plans.	Plan Administrator	Upon written request once every 12 months	Free

Documents and Instructions under which the plan is established or operated: This includes, for example, the plan document, collective bargaining agreement, trust agreement, SPD, SMM, and latest annual report.	Plan Administrator	Upon written request	Reasonable Charge
		Available for Inspection upon request	Free
Notice to Participants in Underfunded Plans. Generally, single-employer pension plans that are less than 90% funded must give you notice reporting the funding level of the plan describing the and limits on PBGC's guarantees.	Plan Administrator	Within 2 months after the due date for filing the annual report	Free

http://www.dol.gov/ebsa/publications/wyskapr.html

*Documents filed with the Labor Department can be obtained by contacting the U.S. Department of Labor, EBSA, Public Disclosure Facility, Room N-1513, 200 Constitution Avenue, NW, Washington, D.C. 20210, telephone: 202.693.8673.

QUALIFIED TRUST

The assets of the qualified plan must be placed in a qualified trust or a custodial account.[2] IRC section 401(a) describes the specific requirements for a qualified trust. Generally, a **qualified trust** is a trust established or organized in the United States that is maintained by an employer for the exclusive benefit of the employer's employees. The trust must distribute assets to employees and not discriminate against certain employees. **Custodial Accounts** are generally maintained by a bank or other financial institutions.

---

2. IRC 401(a).

EXHIBIT 8.10   401(a) SUMMARY OF QUALIFIED TRUST[3]

- The trust must be established or organized in the United States and maintained at all times as a domestic trust in the United States.
- The trust must be part of a pension, profit-sharing, or stock bonus plan established by an employer for the exclusive benefit of his employees or their beneficiaries.
- The trust must be formed for the purpose of distributing to the employees or their beneficiaries the corpus and income of the fund accumulated by the trust in accordance with the plan.
- It must be impossible under the trust instrument at any time before the satisfaction of all liabilities with respect to employees and their beneficiaries under the trust, for any part of the corpus or income to be used for, or diverted to, purposes other than for the exclusive benefit of the employees or their beneficiaries.
- The trust must be part of a plan that benefits prescribed percentages of the employees or which benefits such employees as qualify under a classification set up by the employer and found by the Commissioner of the IRS not to be discriminatory in favor of certain specified classes of employees.
- The trust must be part of a plan under which contributions or benefits do not discriminate in favor of certain specified classes of employees.
- The trust must be part of a plan that provides certain nonforfeitable rights.
- If the trust forms part of a pension plan, the plan must provide that forfeitures must not be applied to increase the benefits any employee would receive under such plan.
- The trust must, if the plan benefits any self-employed individual who is an owner-employee, satisfy the additional requirements for qualification.

INVESTING PLAN ASSETS

Plan assets will either be managed by the plan sponsor (or an asset management firm hired by the plan sponsor) or individually by the plan participants. In many cases, the type of plan and who retains the investment risk will dictate whether the plan assets are managed by the plan sponsor or self-directed by the plan participants. Defined benefit plan sponsors are responsible for funding a determined retirement benefit for plan participants based upon a specific formula and therefore retain the investment risk. As a result, the sponsor will generally hire an outside asset management firm to invest the plan assets in such a way as to fund the pension liabilities over time. Cash balance pension plans function in a similar manner to defined benefit plans, and the assets are generally managed in a similar function.

---

3.   IRC 401(a) summarized.

Defined contribution plan participants bear the investment risk for the assets in their accounts. Despite this, plan sponsors may choose to manage the plan assets or hire an outside asset management firm to manage the assets for the plan participants.

Plan sponsors are generally considered a fiduciary of qualified plans. Being classified as a fiduciary requires a certain level of responsibility and prudence. Employers and plan sponsors have attempted to shift some or all of the fiduciary responsibility from the sponsor to the employees following the guidelines under ERISA Section 404(c).

Even when plan sponsors choose to shift the management responsibility of the investment assets to the plan participants, the plan sponsor still retains certain responsibilities over the choices and alternative investments available to the participants.

Retirement plan sponsors must provide a broad range of investment choices for participants to manage their retirement assets. A plan must offer a broad range of investment alternatives (at least three) that are sufficient to provide participants or beneficiaries with a reasonable opportunity to

Quick Quiz

Highlight the answer to these questions:

1. To take a deduction for contributions for a particular year, the qualified plan must be adopted by the due date of the tax return for the plan year.
   a. True
   b. False

2. Notification of the adoption of a qualified plan may be made in person, via e-mail, or by posting notice at the place of business.
   a. True
   b. False

3. If the plan sponsor shifts the management responsibility to the plan participants, then the sponsor no longer has any fiduciary responsibility.
   a. True
   b. False

False, True, False.

materially affect the potential return on amounts in his individual account. Generally, a plan will provide at least one stock investment option, one bond investment option, and one cash or money market type investment option. This combination of security options allows an investor to create relatively efficient portfolios by allocating different amounts to the three funds.

The plan must therefore provide the participants with at least three alternatives to invest in within the retirement plan. These alternatives must meet the following criteria:
- Be diversified;
- Have materially different risk and return characteristics, which in the aggregate enable the participant or beneficiary to achieve a portfolio with aggregate risk and return characteristics at any point within the range normally appropriate (efficient frontier) for the participant or beneficiary; and
- Each alternative, when combined with investments in the other alternatives tends to minimize through diversification the overall risk of a participant's or beneficiary's portfolio.

IRS regulations, directing the types of investments that should be included in a retirement plan, are consistent with concepts and notions that competent financial planners use in advising clients regarding investing, diversification, and the balance between increasing returns and reducing risk within a portfolio.

ADMINISTRATION

Qualified retirement plans require ongoing administration and maintenance. Informational compliance tax returns, such as IRS Form 5500, must be filed annually. The allocation of contributions to employees' accounts or determination of accrued benefits must also be completed at least annually. Other administrative duties include annual testing to comply with IRS regulations and amending the plan document for tax law changes. Besides performing the administrative duties, the plan sponsor frequently retains and is responsible for an investment adviser to assure that plan assets are managed for the sole benefit of participants and their beneficiaries. The plan sponsor may outsource each of these tasks to a third party administrator or other provider.

Key Concepts

Underline/highlight the answers to these questions as you read:

1. What are the minimum funding requirements for qualified plans, and when may contributions be deducted by the employer?

2. How are forfeitures treated in qualified plans?

3. What transactions are prohibited for a qualified plan?

4. What regulatory bodies and filing requirements are involved with the operation of a qualified plan?

OPERATING THE PLAN

Covering Eligible Employees
Recall from Chapter 3 that a qualified retirement plan must benefit a broad range of rank-and-file employees, not just the highly compensated or key employees. The company can establish age and service requirements (within the guidelines prescribed by the IRC) in order to control the number of individuals eligible to be in the plan. In addition, qualified plans require annual coverage testing to ensure that the rank-and-file employees (non-highly compensated and non-key) are sufficiently covered. Refer to Chapter 3 for more specific information on the coverage rules and Chapters 3 through 6 for detailed information on each plan's specific annual testing requirements.

Making Appropriate Contributions
Minimum Funding Requirement
In general, sponsors of money purchase pension plans, cash balance pension plans, defined benefit pension plans, and target benefit pension plans must contribute enough money into the plan to satisfy the minimum funding requirements as determined by an actuary for each year.

Loopili Corporation has a money purchase pension plan for which they contribute two percent of covered compensation each year. Loopili has four employees that each make $20,000. By the required contribution date (tax return due date plus extensions) Loopili must contribute $1,600 to the plan ($20,000 x 4 employees x 2%).

Determining the amount needed to satisfy the minimum funding standard for a defined benefit plan is complicated. The amount is based on what should be contributed under the plan formula using actuarial assumptions and formulas. Actuaries work with the plan sponsor to determine the minimum funding for a defined benefit plan. The actuarial assumptions will take into account factors such as life expectancy, likelihood of early retirement, mortality rates, inflation rates, investment return rates, and the expected rate of forfeitures.

Defined benefit plans must make quarterly installment payments of the required contributions. If installment payments are not made on time, then the company must pay interest on any underpayment for the period of the underpayment. The installment payment due dates are 15 days after the end of each quarter. For a calendar-year plan, the installment payments are due April 15, July 15, October 15, and January 15 (of the following year). Each quarterly installment payment must be 25 percent of the required annual payment.

Contributions in General

A qualified plan is generally funded by employer contributions (often called a noncontributory plan because employees do not contribute to the plan), but employees participating in the plan may also be permitted to make contributions (a contributory plan). As explained earlier, one of the benefits of qualified plans is that the employer is allowed to take a deduction in the year of contribution, but the employee does not have to include the income as taxable income in that year. The deductibility of these contributions in effect reduces the overall cost to the employer of the qualified plan.

A company can make deductible contributions for a tax year up to the due date of their tax return (plus extensions) for the year of contribution. A promissory note made out to the plan for contributions is a prohibited transaction and is not a payment that qualifies for an income tax deduction.

While the employer generally applies contributions in the year in which they are paid, the employer may apply the payment to the previous year if all the following requirements are met:
1. The contributions are made by the due date of the tax return for the previous year (plus extensions).
2. The plan was established by the end of the previous year (the plan year).
3. The plan treats the contributions as though it had received them on the last day of the previous year.
4. The company specifies in writing to the plan administrator or trustee that the contributions apply to the previous year, or the company takes a deduction for the amount of the contributions on the tax return for the previous year.

Self employed individuals can make contributions on behalf of themselves only if they have positive net earnings (compensation) from self-employment in the trade or business for which the plan was established. The net earnings must be from the self-employed individual's personal services and not from investments. A self-employed individual cannot make a contribution for himself in a year in which he has a loss, but he can still make contributions for other employees based on the employees' compensation.

There are certain limits on the contributions and other annual additions a company can make each year on behalf of plan participants (discussed in Chapter 3). There are also limits on the deductible amount of plan contributions. The limits differ depending on whether the plan is a defined contribution plan or a defined benefit plan.

For 2005, the annual benefit for a defined benefit plan participant cannot exceed the lesser of 100 percent of the participant's average compensation for his highest three consecutive calendar years or $170,000 ($175,000[†] for 2006, $180,000[†] for 2007, and $185,000[†] for 2008). For 2005, a defined contribution plan's annual contributions and other additions (excluding the earnings of the plan assets) to a participant account cannot exceed the lesser of 100% of the participant's compensation or $42,000 ($43,000[†] for 2006, $44,000[†] for 2007, and $45,000[†] for 2008). Catch-up contributions for those participants age 50 and over are not subject to the annual defined contribution limit and thus can be in addition to these limits.

In the event that more money is contributed to a defined contribution plan than is allowed under the limits above, the excess amount is called the excess annual addition. A plan can correct excess annual additions if the excess was caused by a reasonable error in estimating a participant's compensation, determining the elective deferrals permitted, or because of forfeitures allocated to participants' accounts. To do so, the plan can allocate the excess to other participants in the plan to the extent of their unused limits for the year. If these limits are exceeded, they can hold the excess in a separate account and allocate it to participants' accounts in later years before making any contributions for that year, or they can return employee after-tax contributions or elective deferrals. Returning employee after-tax contributions or distributing of elective deferrals to correct excess annual additions is considered a corrective distribution rather than a distribution of accrued benefits. The penalties for early distributions and excess distributions do not apply.

| EXHIBIT 8.11 | CORRECTING EXCESS ANNUAL ADDITIONS |

- Allocate the excess annual additions to other plan participants.
- Hold excess annual additions in a separate account and allocate in future years.
- Corrective distributions.

Participants may be permitted to make nondeductible contributions to a plan in addition to the employer's contributions. Even though these employee contributions are not deductible, the earnings will accrue tax free until distributed in later years. These contributions must satisfy certain nondiscrimination tests.

Taking Deductions

Employer Deduction

The employer can usually deduct, subject to certain limitations, contributions made to a qualified plan, including those made for their own retirement. The contributions (and the attributable earnings and gains) are generally not taxed to the employee until distributed by the plan. The deduction limit for contributions to a qualified plan depends on the type of plan.

The deduction for contributions to a defined contribution plan cannot exceed 25 percent of the compensation paid or accrued during the year to eligible employees participating in the plan. If the individual is self-employed, he must reduce this limit in figuring the deduction for contributions made to his own account. Recall that the maximum compensation that can be taken into account when calculating plan funding for each employee is the covered compensation limit, $210,000 for 2005 ($215,000[†] for 2006, $220,000[†] for 2007, and $225,000[†] for 2008).

The deduction for contributions to a defined benefit plan is based on actuarial assumptions and computations. Consequently, an actuary must calculate the appropriate amount of mandatory funding.

In the case of an employer who maintains both a defined benefit plan and a defined contribution plan, the funding limit set forth is combined. The maximum deductible amount is the greater of:
- 25 percent of the aggregate covered compensation of employees, or
- The required minimum funding standard of the defined benefit plan (as discussed in Chapter 4).

This limit does not apply if the contributions to the defined contribution plan consist entirely of employee elective deferrals. In other words, employee elective deferrals do not count against the plan limit.

Deduction Limit for Self-Employed Individuals (Keogh Plans)

Sole proprietors who file a Schedule C, partners of a partnership, and members of an LLC are generally treated as self-employed individuals for tax purposes. In contrast, owners of C-corporations and S-corporations may also be employees of those entities. While self-employed individuals may adopt basically any qualified plan (generally not a stock bonus plan or an ESOP since there is no stock involved with sole proprietorships, partnerships, or LLCs), the plan they choose to adopt will be referred to as a **Keogh plan**. A Keogh plan is simply a qualified plan for a self-employed person. An important distinction of Keogh plans is the reduced contribution that can be made on behalf of the self-employed individual. The employees of a firm that maintains a Keogh plan will generally be treated in the same manner as if the plan was not a Keogh plan. Employees will generally receive a benefit based on their W-2 income. The reason for the distinction is that self-employed individuals do not receive a form W-2 and will instead file a Schedule C or receive a form K-1 which details the owner's earnings.

There is a special computation needed to calculate the maximum contribution and tax deduction for a Keogh plan on behalf of self-employed individuals. Since self-employed individuals do not have W-2s, the IRC uses the term earned income to denote the amount of compensation that is earned and can be considered by the self-employed individual.

Earned income is defined as net earnings from self-employment less one-half of self-employment tax less the deduction for contributions to the qualified plan on behalf of the self employed person. Through this process, the IRC attempts to treat self-employed individuals as if they were corporations instead of self-employed. Both employers and employees each pay 1/2 of self-employment taxes; however, in the case of self-employed individuals, they are required to pay both halves. If the company was a corporation, then it would deduct one half of the self employment taxes paid on behalf of the individual in arriving at net income. Therefore, earned income for self employed individuals is the self-employment income reduced by one-half of self-employment tax. Similarly, a corporation would deduct the contribution made to a qualified retirement plan in arriving at net income. Therefore, calculating earned income for a self employed individual also requires a reduction for the amount of the contribution to the Keogh plan.

Recall from Chapter 4 that the two primary parts of the Social Security system are OASDI (Old Age Survivor Disability Insurance) and Medicare. Both employers and employees contribute to the system through FICA payments that consist of 6.2 percent for OASDI and 1.45 percent for Medicare. The OASDI portion of 6.2 percent applies to income up to the Social Security wage base ($90,000 for 2005) while the Medicare portion applies to all income with no limit.

The deduction for the self employed person's contributions and net earnings is interrelated and depends on each other. For this reason, the self-employed person must determine the deduction for their own contributions by using simultaneous equations or a circular calculation or by using the simpler method described below that adjusts the plan contribution rate for the self-employed person.

To calculate the self-employed individual's 2005 contribution to the Keogh plan, utilize the following formulas:

1. Calculate the self employed individual's contribution rate:

$$\text{Self-Employed Contribution Rate} = \left(\frac{\text{Contribution Rate to Other Participants}}{1 + \text{Contribution Rate to Other Participants}}\right)$$

2. Calculate Self Employment Tax:

   Net Self-Employment Income

   Times: 92.35%

   Net Earnings subject to Self Employment Tax

   Times: 15.3% up to $90,000 + 2.9% over $90,000

   Equals: Self Employment Tax

3. Calculate the self employed individual's contribution:

   Net Self-Employment Income

   Less: 1/2 of Self-Employment Taxes

   Equals: Adjusted Net Self-Employment Income (Earned Income)

   Times: Self-Employed Contribution Rate

   Equals: Self-Employed Individual's Qualified Plan Contribution

EXAMPLE 8.8

Jack has Schedule C net income of $200,000 and wants to know the maximum amount he can contribute to a Keogh profit sharing plan. In this instance Jack can contribute $38,374 to the plan. The contribution is calculated as follows:

1. Calculate the self employed individual's contribution rate:

$$\text{Self-Employed Contribution Rate} = \left(\frac{25\%}{1 + 25\%}\right)$$

   Self-Employed Contribution Rate = 20%

2. Calculate Self Employment Tax:

$200,000	Net Self-Employment Income
x 0.9235	Times: 92.35%
$184,700	**Net Earnings subject to Self Employment Tax**
x 15.3%/2.9%	Times: 15.3% up to $90,000 + 2.9% over $90,000
$16,516	**Equals: Self Employment Tax ($13,770 + $2,746)**

3. Calculate the self employed individual's contribution:

$200,000	Net Self-Employment Income
$8,258	Less: 1/2 of Self-Employment Taxes (50% x 16,516)
$191,742	**Equals: Adjusted Net Self-Employment Income**
x 0.20	Times: Self-Employed Contribution Rate
$38,348	**Equals: Self-Employed Individual's Qualified Plan Contribution**

Check figure:

$$\frac{\$38,348}{\$191,742 - \$38,348} = 25\%$$

When solving the Keogh contribution calculation, it is important to understand that while 25 percent is the limit for employee compensation, the self-employed individual maximum is 25 percent of the self employed individual's earned income. The 25 percent of earned income effectively translates to 20 percent of net self-employed income less ½ of self employment tax. The reason is because the self-employed individual is responsible for the employer's share of self-employment taxes, and the self-employed individual's ultimate compensation is relative to the retirement contribution made on his behalf.

EXAMPLE 8.9

Thus, in the example above, Jack's earned income is calculated as follows:

$200,000	Schedule C net income
- $8,258	Less: ½ self-employment taxes
- $38,348	Less: Keogh contribution
$153,394	Earned income
X 0.25	Times: 25% to determine Keogh contribution
$38,348	**Total Keogh contribution**

Notice that the total Keogh contribution is truly 25% of the earned income.

SCHEDULE SE (Form 1040) Department of the Treasury Internal Revenue Service	**Self-Employment Tax** ▶ Attach to Form 1040. ▶ See Instructions for Schedule SE (Form 1040).	OMB No. 1545-0074 20**04** Attachment Sequence No. **17**
Name of person with **self-employment** income (as shown on Form 1040)	Social security number of person with **self-employment** income ▶	

Who Must File Schedule SE

You must file Schedule SE if:

- You had net earnings from self-employment from **other than** church employee income (line 4 of Short Schedule SE or line 4c of Long Schedule SE) of $400 or more **or**
- You had church employee income of $108.28 or more. Income from services you performed as a minister or a member of a religious order **is not** church employee income (see page SE-1).

Note. Even if you had a loss or a small amount of income from self-employment, it may be to your benefit to file Schedule SE and use either "optional method" in Part II of Long Schedule SE (see page SE-3).

Exception. If your only self-employment income was from earnings as a minister, member of a religious order, or Christian Science practitioner **and** you filed Form 4361 and received IRS approval not to be taxed on those earnings, **do not** file Schedule SE. Instead, write "Exempt–Form 4361" on Form 1040, line 57.

May I Use Short Schedule SE or Must I Use Long Schedule SE?

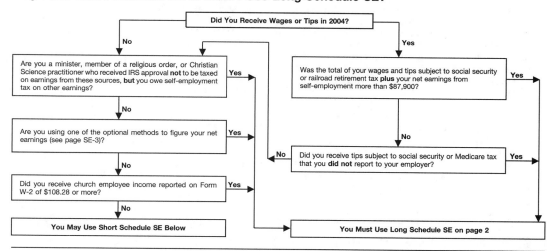

Section A—Short Schedule SE. Caution. Read above to see if you can use Short Schedule SE.

1	Net farm profit or (loss) from Schedule F, line 36, and farm partnerships, Schedule K-1 (Form 1065), box 14, code A	**1**	
2	Net profit or (loss) from Schedule C, line 31; Schedule C-EZ, line 3; Schedule K-1 (Form 1065), box 14, code A (other than farming); and Schedule K-1 (Form 1065-B), box 9. Ministers and members of religious orders, see page SE-1 for amounts to report on this line. See page SE-2 for other income to report	**2**	
3	Combine lines 1 and 2	**3**	
4	**Net earnings from self-employment.** Multiply line 3 by 92.35% (.9235). If less than $400, **do not** file this schedule; you do not owe self-employment tax . . . . ▶	**4**	
5	**Self-employment tax.** If the amount on line 4 is: • $87,900 or less, multiply line 4 by 15.3% (.153). Enter the result here and on **Form 1040, line 57.** • More than $87,900, multiply line 4 by 2.9% (.029). Then, add $10,899.60 to the result. Enter the total here and on **Form 1040, line 57.**	**5**	
6	**Deduction for one-half of self-employment tax.** Multiply line 5 by 50% (.5). Enter the result here and on **Form 1040, line 30**	**6**	

For Paperwork Reduction Act Notice, see Form 1040 instructions.   Cat. No. 11358Z   **Schedule SE (Form 1040) 2004**

Schedule SE (Form 1040) 2004   Attachment Sequence No. **17**   Page **2**

Name of person with **self-employment** income (as shown on Form 1040)	Social security number of person with **self-employment** income ▶	⋮ ⋮

Section B—Long Schedule SE

Part I   Self-Employment Tax

Note. If your only income subject to self-employment tax is **church employee income,** skip lines 1 through 4b. Enter -0- on line 4c and go to line 5a. Income from services you performed as a minister or a member of a religious order **is not** church employee income. See page SE-1.

A   If you are a minister, member of a religious order, or Christian Science practitioner **and** you filed Form 4361, but you had $400 or more of **other** net earnings from self-employment, check here and continue with Part I . . . . ▶ ☐

1   Net farm profit or (loss) from Schedule F, line 36, and farm partnerships, Schedule K-1 (Form 1065), box 14, code A. **Note.** Skip this line if you use the farm optional method (see page SE-4)   **1**

2   Net profit or (loss) from Schedule C, line 31; Schedule C-EZ, line 3; Schedule K-1 (Form 1065), box 14, code A (other than farming); and Schedule K-1 (Form 1065-B), box 9. Ministers and members of religious orders, see page SE-1 for amounts to report on this line. See page SE-2 for other income to report. **Note.** Skip this line if you use the nonfarm optional method (see page SE-4)   **2**

3   Combine lines 1 and 2 . . . .   **3**

4a   If line 3 is more than zero, multiply line 3 by 92.35% (.9235). Otherwise, enter amount from line 3   **4a**

   b   If you elect one or both of the optional methods, enter the total of lines 15 and 17 here .   **4b**

   c   Combine lines 4a and 4b. If less than $400, **stop;** you do not owe self-employment tax. **Exception.** If less than $400 and you had **church employee income,** enter -0- and continue. . . . . ▶   **4c**

5a   Enter your **church employee income** from Form W-2. See page SE-1 for definition of church employee income **5a**

   b   Multiply line 5a by 92.35% (.9235). If less than $100, enter -0- **5b**

6   **Net earnings from self-employment.** Add lines 4c and 5b **6**

7   Maximum amount of combined wages and self-employment earnings subject to social security tax or the 6.2% portion of the 7.65% railroad retirement (tier 1) tax for 2004 . . . .   **7**   87,900 | 00

8a   Total social security wages and tips (total of boxes 3 and 7 on Form(s) W-2) and railroad retirement (tier 1) compensation. If $87,900 or more, skip lines 8b through 10, and go to line 11 . . . .   **8a**

   b   Unreported tips subject to social security tax (from Form 4137, line 9)   **8b**

   c   Add lines 8a and 8b **8c**

9   Subtract line 8c from line 7. If zero or less, enter -0- here and on line 10 and go to line 11 . ▶   **9**

10   Multiply the **smaller** of line 6 or line 9 by 12.4% (.124) **10**

11   Multiply line 6 by 2.9% (.029) **11**

12   **Self-employment tax.** Add lines 10 and 11. Enter here and on **Form 1040, line 57** . .   **12**

13   **Deduction for one-half of self-employment tax.** Multiply line 12 by 50% (.5). Enter the result here and on **Form 1040, line 30** **13**

Part II   Optional Methods To Figure Net Earnings (see page SE-3)

Farm Optional Method. You may use this method **only** if **(a)** your gross farm income[1] was not more than $2,400 **or (b)** your net farm profits[2] were less than $1,733.

14   Maximum income for optional methods . . . .   **14**   1,600 | 00

15   Enter the **smaller** of: two-thirds (⅔) of gross farm income[1] (not less than zero) or $1,600. Also include this amount on line 4b above **15**

Nonfarm Optional Method. You may use this method **only** if **(a)** your net nonfarm profits[3] were less than $1,733 and also less than 72.189% of your gross nonfarm income[4] **and (b)** you had net earnings from self-employment of at least $400 in 2 of the prior 3 years.

Caution. You may use this method no more than five times.

16   Subtract line 15 from line 14 . . . .   **16**

17   Enter the **smaller** of: two-thirds (⅔) of gross nonfarm income[4] (not less than zero) **or** the amount on line 16. Also include this amount on line 4b above **17**

[1] From Sch. F, line 11, and Sch. K-1 (Form 1065), box 14, code B.

[2] From Sch. F, line 36, and Sch. K-1 (Form 1065), box 14, code A.

[3] From Sch. C, line 31; Sch. C-EZ, line 3; Sch. K-1 (Form 1065), box 14, code A; and Sch. K-1 (Form 1065-B), box 9.

[4] From Sch. C, line 7; Sch. C-EZ, line 1; Sch. K-1 (Form 1065), box 14, code C; and Sch. K-1 (Form 1065-B), box 9.

Schedule SE (Form 1040) 2004

Robbins Co., a sole proprietorship, employs B, C, D, and E as well as the sole proprietor, A, who files a Schedule C for his business.

EXAMPLE 8.10

	Compensation	Contributions
A*	150,000	See note below
B	100,000	15,000
C	80,000	12,000
D	50,000	7,500
E	20,000	3,000
	*A's compensation is Schedule C net income	

Robbins maintains a Keogh profit plan with a 15% contribution to each employee (not the owner). In spite of the fact that each employee receives exactly 15%, A is limited to receiving 13.04% (0.15/1.15) of $150,000 less one-half of the self-employment taxes due on his earnings.

$150,000	Schedule C net income
$6,000	Less: ½ self-employment taxes (12,000 assumed)
$144,000	Self-employment income
X 0.1304	Contribution rate (0.15/1.15)
$18,782.61	**Contribution on behalf of A ***

* Rounding was not utilized when applying the contribution rate.

The special calculation is required because Schedule C net income is presumed to include the qualified plan contribution and because one-half of the self-employment taxes are deductible for self-employed persons after the calculation of the Schedule C net income. For all of the other employees, their contribution is calculated based upon 15% of their compensation.

Where To Deduct Contributions

Deductions for contributions to qualified plans made for employee-participants are taken on the employer's tax return. For example, sole proprietors deduct contributions on Form 1040, either Schedule C (Profit or Loss From Business) or Schedule F (Profit or Loss From Farming). Partnerships, and most LLCs deduct contributions on Form 1065 (U.S. Return of Partnership Income Tax Return), Form 1120-A (U.S. Corporation Short-Form Income Tax Return), or Form 1120S (U.S. Income Tax Return for an S Corporation). Sole proprietors and partners deduct contributions for themselves on Form 1040, line 30. If the self employed person is a partner, then contributions for that partner from the partnership are shown on Form 1065, Schedule K-1 (Partner's Share of Income, Credits, Deductions, etc.).

Carryover of Excess Contributions

If the employer contributes more to the qualified plan than the permitted deduction for the year, the excess contribution can be carried over and deducted in future years, combined with, or in lieu of, contributions for those years. The combined deduction in a later year is limited to 25 percent of the participating employees' compensation for that year. This percentage limit must be reduced to figure the maximum deduction for contributions made for the self-employed individual.

The amount that can be carried over and deducted may be subject to an excise tax. If the employer contributes more than the deductible amount to a retirement plan, he has made a nondeductible contribution and may be liable for an excise tax. In general, a 10 percent excise tax applies to nondeductible excess contributions made to qualified pension and profit sharing plans.

The 10 percent excise tax does not apply to any contribution made for a self employed individual to meet the minimum funding requirements in a defined benefit plan. Even if that contribution is more than the earned income from the trade or business for which the plan is set up, the difference is not subject to this excise tax.

If the employer maintains a defined benefit plan, the following exceptions may enable them to avoid the 10 percent penalty on certain nondeductible contributions. If contributions to one or more defined contribution plans are not deductible only because they are more than the combined plan deduction limit, the 10 percent excise tax does not apply to the extent the difference is not more than the greater of six percent of the participants' compensation (including elective deferrals) for the year or the sum of employer matching contributions and the elective deferrals to a 401(k) plan.

In figuring the 10 percent excise tax, the employer can choose not to take into account as nondeductible contributions for any year contributions to a defined benefit plan that are not more than the full funding limit figured without considering the current liability limit. The employer applies the overall limits on deductible contributions first to contributions to defined contribution plans and then to contributions to defined benefit plans. If the employer uses this exception, the employer cannot also use the exception discussed above regarding contributions to one or more defined contribution plans.

Forfeitures

Generally, **forfeitures** occur when employees terminate employment. In the event that there are forfeitures from a defined contribution plan (profit sharing, stock bonus, etc.), the forfeited amounts can be used to either reduce the employer's contributions under the plan or can be reallocated to the remaining plan participants. Employers often anticipate the effect of forfeitures on remaining plan participants in determining the costs of a qualified plan.

EXAMPLE 8.11

Loopili Corporation recently established a profit sharing plan that requires five years of service before obtaining a vested right to benefits under the plan. Lucy, one of the company's employees, resigned from her position after two years of service and has an unvested account balance of $8,000. Loopili Corporation may reduce its next contribution to the plan by $8,000 or reallocate the $8,000 to the remaining participants.

Defined benefit plans are required to use forfeitures to reduce plan costs. Forfeitures cannot be allocated to the participant's accounts because participants of defined benefit plans do not have individual accounts. Contributions to defined benefit plans are made yearly to keep the plan actuarially on target to pay the expected required benefits. If the plan is over funded one year, then the company pays less in the subsequent year. The over funded amount is not returned to the employer until all claims from the plan have been paid, and the plan document allows the plan to distribute the assets to the employer.

EXAMPLE 8.12

Assume for this example Loopili Corporation established a defined benefit plan in favor of its employees based on years of service. Last year the plan assets were $1,000,000, and the actuary estimated that the plan needed to be at $1,200,000 to fund the required benefits. The company contributed the necessary $200,000 bringing the account balance to $1,200,000 for the current year. During the year, Andy, a long time employee, died prematurely. At the end of the year the actuary estimated that now the plan only needed $1,180,000 to fund the needed benefits. The company does not get back the excess $20,000. That amount will stay in the plan and reduce contributions in future years.

TREATMENT OF FORFEITURES FROM TERMINATIONS

EXHIBIT 8.13

Defined Benefit Plans	Defined Contribution Plans
• Forfeitures may reduce plan costs	• Forfeitures may reduce plan costs or • Allocate forfeitures to remaining participants

PROHIBITED TRANSACTIONS

Prohibited transactions are transactions between the plan and a disqualified person that are prohibited by law. If a disqualified person takes part in a prohibited transaction, that disqualified person will be subject to a tax as discussed below.

EXHIBIT 8.14 **DEFINITION OF DISQUALIFIED PERSON**

A disqualified person is any of the following:
1. A fiduciary of the plan.
2. A person providing services to the plan.
3. An employer, any of whose employees are covered by the plan.
4. An employee organization, any of whose members are covered by the plan.
5. Any direct or indirect owner of 50% or more of any of the following:
   - The combined voting power of all classes of stock entitled to vote, or the total value of shares of all classes of stock of a corporation that is an employer or employee organization described in (3) or (4).
   - The capital interest or profits interest of a partnership that is an employer or employee organization described in (3) or (4).
   - The beneficial interest of a trust or unincorporated enterprise that is an employer or an employee organization described in (3) or (4).
6. A member of the family of any individual described in (1), (2), (3), or (5). (A member of a family is the spouse, ancestor, lineal descendant, or any spouse of a lineal descendant.)
7. A corporation, partnership, trust, or estate of which (or in which) any direct or indirect owner described in (1) through (5) holds 50% or more of any of the following:
   - The combined voting power of all classes of stock entitled to vote or the total value of shares of all classes of stock of a corporation.
   - The capital interest or profits interest of a partnership.
   - The beneficial interest of a trust or estate.
8. An officer, director (or an individual having powers or responsibilities similar to those of officers or directors), a 10% or more shareholder, or highly compensated employee (earning 10% or more of the yearly wages of an employer) of a person described in (3), (4), (5), or (7).
9. A 10% or more (in capital or profits) partner or joint venture of a person described in (3), (4), (5), or (7).
10. Any disqualified person, as described in (1) through (9) above, who is a disqualified person with respect to any plan to which a section 501(c)(22) trust is permitted to make payments under section 4223 of ERISA.

Prohibited transactions generally include actions by a disqualified person that potentially could have adverse consequences to the plan or participants. A transfer of plan income or assets to, use of them by, or for the benefit of a disqualified person is a prohibited transaction. A prohibited transaction is also any act of a fiduciary that uses plan income or assets in his own interest. The receipt of consideration by a fiduciary for his own account from any party dealing with the plan in a transaction that involves plan income or assets is prohibited. Selling, exchanging with, or leasing property, as well as lending money or extending credit to a disqualified person by the plan is prohibited.

PROHIBITED TRANSACTIONS

EXHIBIT 8.15

- Transfer of plan income or assets to, use of them by, or for the benefit of a disqualified person.
- Self dealing by a fiduciary.
- Receipt of consideration by a fiduciary for his own account when dealing with a party in interest.
- Selling, exchanging, leasing, buying as well as lending or borrowing between a disqualified person and the plan.

Certain transactions are exempt from being treated as prohibited transactions. For example, a prohibited transaction does not take place if a disqualified person receives any benefit that they are entitled as a plan participant or beneficiary. However, the benefit must be figured and paid under the same terms as for all other participants and beneficiaries.

The initial penalty on a prohibited transaction is 15 percent of the amount involved for each year (or part of a year) in the taxable period (defined below). If the transaction is not corrected within the taxable period, an additional tax of 100 percent of the amount involved is imposed. Both taxes are payable by any disqualified person who participated in the transaction (other than a fiduciary acting only as such). If more than one person takes part in the transaction, each person can be jointly and severally liable for the entire tax. The amount involved in a prohibited transaction is the fair market value of any property given or received. If services are performed, the amount involved is any excess compensation given or received.

The taxable period starts on the transaction date and ends on the earliest of the following days:
- The day the IRS mails a notice of deficiency for the tax.
- The day the IRS assesses the tax.
- The day the correction of the transaction is completed.
- Payment of the 15 percent tax with Form 5330.

If a disqualified person participates in a prohibited transaction, he can avoid the 100 percent tax by correcting the transaction as soon as possible. Correcting the transaction means rectifying it to the fullest extent without putting the plan in a worse financial position than if the fiduciary had originally acted under the highest fiduciary standards.

Ortez, Inc. sponsors a 401(k) plan that allows participant contributions. The company pays its employees and withholds the contributions on a bi-weekly basis. The plan does not allow participants to direct their investments. The plan fiduciary invests the plan assets in a diversified portfolio of investments. Assume employee contributions were not deposited into the plan for the first pay period of the year. Therefore, the participant contributions that normally would have been deposited remained in Ortez, Inc's general assets. Since the employer was able to use the money that belonged to the participants, they engaged in a prohibited transaction (the use of assets for the benefit of a qualified person - the employer). Ortez Inc. realized the error a month later. To avoid the 100% penalty, Ortez Inc. must not only deposit the employee contributions into the participant's account, but they must also deposit additional funds to compensate for the earnings on the contribution the participants did not receive (the amount required is determined using the IRC Section 6621 rate compared to the plan's earning rate).[4]

If the prohibited transaction is not corrected during the taxable period, the disqualified person usually has an additional 90 days after the day the IRS mails a notice of deficiency for the 100 percent tax to correct the transaction. This correction period (the taxable period plus the 90 days) can be extended if the IRS grants reasonable time needed to correct the transaction or the disqualified person petitions the Tax Court. If he corrects the transaction within this period, the IRS will abate, credit, or refund the 100 percent tax.

ERISA AND FILING REQUIREMENTS

ERISA

The **Employee Retirement Income Security Act of 1974** (ERISA) places several burdens on retirement plan administration. One of the key obligations ERISA imposes is that of fiduciary responsibility. While several people may be imposed with the fiduciary duty, the duty is generally imposed on those individuals that have authority over the plan's management, administration, or disposition of the plan's assets. The duty is also imposed on individuals that render investment advice on the plan's assets for a fee. Plan fiduciaries may include plan administrators, plan trustees, and members of the plan's investment committee.

The **fiduciary** must exercise the care, skill, and diligence of a prudent person acting solely in the interest of plan participants and their beneficiaries. The fiduciary also has an obligation to diversify the plan's assets to reduce the risk of loss. The fiduciary must also act in accordance with the plan's provisions and must refrain from acts forbidden under the law.

---

4. http://www.dol.gov/ebsa/faqs/faq_vfcp.html

Fiduciaries are prohibited from engaging in certain activities. First, they may not be paid for their services if they are already receiving full-time pay from an employer or union whose employees or members are participants. Second, they cannot act in any transaction involving the plan on behalf of a party whose interests are adverse to those of the plan, its participants, or beneficiaries. They may not receive any consideration for their own personal account from any party dealing with the plan in connection with a transaction involving the assets of the plan. They may not cause a plan to engage in certain transactions with parties in interest. Also, they may not permit more than 10 percent of a pension plan's assets to be invested in employer securities.

If a plan fiduciary does not exercise the necessary care, skill, and diligence of a prudent person or engages in prohibited transactions, the fiduciary may be held personally liable for any losses the plan suffers. The plan fiduciary may also be required to remit to the plan any profits he earned through improper use of the assets. In some instances, a court may relieve a fiduciary of his services to the plan due to fiduciary misconduct.

Department of Labor

The **Department of Labor** administers and enforces more than 180 federal laws covering many workplace activities for about 10 million employers and 125 million workers. The Employee Benefits Security Administration (EBSA), an agency of the Department of Labor, oversees plan administration, primarily focusing on being an advocate for the employee. Applicable to this text, the Department of Labor is charged with enforcing the rules governing the conduct of plan managers, investment of plan assets, reporting and disclosure of plan information, enforcement of the fiduciary provisions of the law, and workers' benefit rights as regulated by ERISA.

Pension Benefit Guaranty Corporation

Recall from Chapter 4 that the **Pension Benefit Guaranty Corporation** was established in 1974 when President Gerald R. Ford signed ERISA into law. The PBGC, just as its name implies, acts to guarantee pension benefits. It is a federal corporation that acts as an insurance provider to maintain the benefits promised to employees by their defined benefit pension plans. The plan sponsors of defined benefit and cash balance pensions plans pay premiums for the insurance coverage, but the PBGC only provides plan participants with a limited benefit in the case of the plan completely or partially terminating with an unfunded or underfunded liability.

The PBGC does not cover defined contribution plans, nor does it cover defined benefit pension plans of professional services corporations with 25 or fewer participants. The PBGC does cover all other defined benefit plans at a cost to the plan sponsor of $19 per plan participant per year and $9 per $1,000 of plan underfunding for the year.

Quick Quiz

Highlight the answer to these questions:

1. Defined benefit plans must make quarterly installment payments of the required contributions.
   a. True
   b. False

2. Defined benefit plans may use forfeitures to reduce plan costs or reallocate them to plan participants.
   a. True
   b. False

3. If a prohibited transaction occurs in a qualified plan, a 100% penalty may be assessed if not timely corrected.
   a. True
   b. False

True, False, True.

Reporting Requirements

The employer generally must file an annual report with the Department of Labor. Generally this is accomplished by filing Form 5500, which is basically an informational return. Some employers are allowed to file an abbreviated form called Form 5500-EZ, and other organizations are exempt from filing altogether. If a report is due, then it must be filed with the Department of Labor by the last day of the 7th month after the plan year end. The Department of Labor will then provide the necessary information to the IRS and PBGC. Below is a discussion of the Form 5500.

Form 5500–EZ

Form 5500–EZ is used if the plan only provides benefits for the employer, the employer and their spouse, or one or more partners and their spouses. A plan that covers a business that is a member of an affiliated service group, a controlled group of corporations, or a group of businesses under common control, or a plan that covers a business that leases employees cannot file a Form 5500-EZ.

Form 5500

All other employers, unless exempt from filing, must file a Form 5500. Form 5500 contains the basic identifying information of the plan. As detailed in Exhibit 8.16, there are several schedules that may also have to be completed depending on the type and nature of the plan.

Exemption from Filing Form 5500

Form 5500–EZ and Form 5500 are not required if the employer has only a one-participant plan that had total plan assets of $100,000 or less at the end of every plan year beginning after December 31, 1993. The employer is also exempt if he has two or more one-participant plans with combined total plan assets of $100,000 or less at the end of every plan year beginning after December 31, 1993.

	LARGE PENSION PLAN[1]	SMALL PENSION PLAN[1]
Form 5500	Must complete	Must complete
Schedule A (Insurance Information)	Must complete if plan has insurance contracts for benefits or investments.	Must complete if plan has insurance contracts for benefits or investments.
Schedule B (Actuarial Information)	Must complete if defined benefit plan and subject to minimum funding standards.[2]	Must complete if defined benefit plan and subject to minimum funding standards.[2]
Schedule C (Service Provider Information)	Must complete if service provider was paid $5,000 or more and/or an accountant or actuary was terminated.	Not required.
Schedule D (DFE/Participating Plan Info.)	Must complete Part I if plan participated in a CCT, PSA, MTIA, or 103-12 IE.	Must complete Part I if plan participated in a CCT, PSA, MTIA, or 103-12 IE.
Schedule E (ESOP Annual Information)	Must complete if ESOP.	Must complete if ESOP.
Schedule G (Financial Transaction Schedules)	Must complete if Schedule H, line 4b, 4c, or 4d is "Yes."[3]	Not required.
Schedule H (Financial Information)	Must complete.[3]	Not required.
Schedule I (Financial Information - Small Plan)	Not required.	Must complete.
Schedule P (Annual Return of Fiduciary of Employee Benefit Trust)	Must file to start running of statute of limitations under Code Section 6501(a).	Must file to start running of statute of limitations under Code Section 6501(a).
Schedule R (Retirement Plan Information)	Must complete.[4]	Must complete.[4]
Schedule SSA (Annual Registration Statement Identifying Separated Participants with Deferred Vested Benefits)	Must complete if plan had separated participants with deferred vested benefits to report.	Must complete if plan had separated participants with deferred vested benefits to report.
Schedule T (Qualified Pension Plan Coverage Information)	Must complete if qualified plan unless permitted to rely on coverage testing information for prior year.	Must complete if qualified plan unless permitted to rely on coverage testing information for prior year.
Accountant's Report	Must attach.	Not required unless Schedule I, line 4k, is checked "No."

1. This chart provides only general guidance. Not all rules and requirements are reflected. A large plan is defined as a plan that covered 100 or more participants as of the beginning of the plan year. A small plan is a plan that covered fewer than 100 participants as of the beginning of the plan year.
2. Certain money purchase defined contribution plans are required to complete Schedule B, lines 3, 9, and 10 in accordance with the instructions for Schedule R, line 5.
3. Schedules of assets and reportable (5%) transactions also must be filed with the Form 5500 if Schedule H, line 4i or 4j is "Yes," but use of printed form not required.
4. A pension plan is exempt from filing Schedule R if all of the following four conditions are met:
   • The plan is not a defined benefit plan or otherwise subject to the minimum funding standards of Code section 412 or ERISA section 302.
   • No in-kind distributions reportable on line 1 of Schedule R were distributed during the plan year.
   • No benefits were distributed during the plan year that are reportable on Form 1099-R using an EIN other than that of the plan sponsor or plan administrator.
   • In the case of a plan that is not a profit sharing, ESOP, or stock bonus plan, no plan benefits were distributed during the plan year in the form of a single sum distribution.

EXHIBIT 8.17 **FORM 5500**

Form 5500

Department of the Treasury
Internal Revenue Service
Department of Labor
Employee Benefits Security
Administration
Pension Benefit
Guaranty Corporation

Annual Return/Report of Employee Benefit Plan

This form is required to be filed under sections 104 and 4065 of the Employee Retirement Income Security Act of 1974 (ERISA) and sections 6047(e), 6057(b), and 6058(a) of the Internal Revenue Code (the Code).

► **Complete all entries in accordance with the instructions to the Form 5500.**

Official Use Only

OMB Nos. 1210-0110 / 1210-0089

2004

This Form is Open to Public Inspection.

Part I Annual Report Identification Information

For the calendar plan year 2004
or fiscal plan year beginning   MM / DD / YYYY   and ending   MM / DD / YYYY

A This return/report is for:
(1) ☐ a multiemployer plan;
(2) ☐ a single-employer plan (other than a multiple-employer plan);
(3) ☐ a multiple-employer plan; or
(4) ☐ a DFE (specify) .... ☐

B This return/report is:
(1) ☐ the first return/report filed for the plan;
(2) ☐ an amended return/report;
(3) ☐ the final return/report filed for the plan;
(4) ☐ a short plan year return/report (less than 12 months).

C If the plan is a collectively-bargained plan, check here .... ► ☐

D If filing under an extension of time or the DFVC program, check box and attach required information. (see instructions) .... ► ☐

Part II Basic Plan Information — enter all requested information.

1a Name of plan

1b Three-digit plan number (PN) ►

1c Effective date of plan   MM / DD / YYYY

Caution: *A penalty for the late or incomplete filing of this return/report will be assessed unless reasonable cause is established.*

Under penalties of perjury and other penalties set forth in the instructions, I declare that I have examined this return/report, including accompanying schedules, statements and attachments, as well as the electronic version of this return/report if it is being filed electronically, and to the best of my knowledge and belief, it is true, correct and complete.

Signature of plan administrator

SIGN HERE ►   Date

Type or print name of individual signing as plan administrator

a

Signature of employer/plan sponsor/DFE

SIGN HERE ►   Date

Type or print name of individual signing as employer, plan sponsor or DFE

b

For Paperwork Reduction Act Notice and OMB Control Numbers, see the instructions for Form 5500.   Cat. No. 13500F   Form **5500** (2004)

0 1 0 4 0 0 0 1 0 6

v7.1

Form 5500 (2004)   Page **2**

2a Plan sponsor's name and address (employer, if for single-employer plan) (Address should include room or suite no.)

1) Name

   Name Continued

2) C / O

3) Street

4) City   **2b** Employer Identification Number (EIN)

5) State   Zip Code

6) Foreign Routing Code   **2c** Sponsor's telephone number

7) Foreign Country   **2d** Business code (see instructions)

8) DBA/

9) Location Address, if different than Street

   Location Address, City, State/Zip if different than 4) city

3a Plan administrator's name and address (If same as plan sponsor, enter "Same")

1) Name

   Name Continued

2) C / O

3) Street

4) City   **3b** Administrator's EIN

5) State   Zip Code

6) Foreign Routing Code   **3c** Administrator's telephone number

7) Foreign Country

4 If the name and/or EIN of the plan sponsor has changed since the last return/report filed for this plan, enter the name, EIN and the plan number from the last return/report below:

a Sponsor's name

b EIN   -   **c** PN

0 1 0 4 0 0 0 2 0 7

FORM 5500 CONTINUED

Form 5500 (2004)   Page **3**

5 Preparer information (optional)

a Name (including firm name, if applicable) and address

1) Name

Name Continued

2) Street

3) City

b EIN

4) State   Zip Code

5) Foreign Routing Code

c Telephone number

6) Foreign Country

6 Total number of participants at the beginning of the plan year ....

7 Number of participants as of the end of the plan year (welfare plans complete only lines **7a**, **7b**, **7c**, and **7d**)

a Active participants ....

b Retired or separated participants receiving benefits ....

c Other retired or separated participants entitled to future benefits ....

d Subtotal. Add lines **7a**, **7b**, and **7c** ....

e Deceased participants whose beneficiaries are receiving or are entitled to receive benefits ....

f Total. Add lines **7d** and **7e** ....

g Number of participants with account balances as of the end of the plan year (only defined contribution plans complete this item) ....

h Number of participants that terminated employment during the plan year with accrued benefits that were less than 100% vested ....

i If any participant(s) separated from service with a deferred vested benefit, enter the number of separated participants required to be reported on a Schedule SSA (Form 5500) ....

0 1 0 4 0 0 0 3 0 8

Form 5500 (2004)   Page **4**

8 Benefits provided under the plan (complete **8a** and **8b**, as applicable)

a ☐ Pension benefits (check this box if the plan provides pension benefits and enter below the applicable pension feature codes from the List of Plan Characteristics Codes printed in the instructions):

☐ ☐ ☐ ☐ ☐ ☐ ☐ ☐ ☐ ☐ ☐

b ☐ Welfare benefits (check this box if the plan provides welfare benefits and enter below the applicable welfare feature codes from the List of Plan Characteristics Codes printed in the instructions):

☐ ☐ ☐ ☐ ☐ ☐ ☐

9a Plan funding arrangement (check all that apply)

(1) ☐ Insurance

(2) ☐ Code section 412(i) insurance contracts

(3) ☐ Trust

(4) ☐ General assets of the sponsor

9b Plan benefit arrangement (check all that apply)

(1) ☐ Insurance

(2) ☐ Code section 412(i) insurance contracts

(3) ☐ Trust

(4) ☐ General assets of the sponsor

10 Schedules attached (Check all applicable boxes and, where indicated, enter the number attached. See instructions.)

a Pension Benefit Schedules

1) ☐ **R** (Retirement Plan Information)

2) ☐ ☐☐☐ **T** (Qualified Pension Plan Coverage Information)

If a Schedule T is not attached because the plan is relying on coverage testing information for a prior year, enter the year ▶ ☐☐☐☐

3) ☐ **B** (Actuarial Information)

4) ☐ **E** (ESOP Annual Information)

5) ☐ **SSA** (Separated Vested Participant Information)

b Financial Schedules

1) ☐ **H** (Financial Information)

2) ☐ **I** (Financial Information--Small Plan)

3) ☐ ☐☐☐ **A** (Insurance Information)

4) ☐ **C** (Service Provider Information)

5) ☐ **D** (DFE/Participating Plan Information)

6) ☐ **G** (Financial Transaction Schedules)

7) ☐ ☐☐☐ **P** (Trust Fiduciary Information)

0 1 0 4 0 0 0 4 0 9

AMENDING AND TERMINATING A QUALIFIED PLAN

Just as creating a qualified plan often makes good business sense, terminating or changing a qualified plan may also make good business sense. Employers may (and should) reserve the right to change or terminate the plan and to discontinue contributions within the plan document. There are many reasons for changing provisions of a qualified plan. Changes (amendments) are often used to solve original defects in the plan document, maximize benefits to key employees, or comply with a new tax law requirement. In addition, there are reasons for terminating a qualified plan. Terminations often occur when a law change occurs that makes one type of plan less advantageous than it was previously, the company can no longer financially maintain the plan, or the company realizes the plan no longer meets the needs of the employees or the company.

Key Concepts

Underline/highlight the answers to these questions as you read:

1. Why would a qualified plan be amended or terminated?

2. How is a qualified plan amended?

3. How is a qualified plan terminated?

REASONS TO AMEND OR TERMINATE A PLAN

Qualified plans, especially for small employers, are often changed to maximize the provision of benefits to key employees. Some plans allow forfeitures to be reallocated to other plan participant's or may be used to reduce plan costs. Small business owners frequently change this election based on the benefits they are able to receive from the plan. For example, consider an owner who has compensation of $100,000 when the plan is first established. Due to the amount of his compensation, he is unable to receive the maximum contribution allowed for the year (e.g. $42,000 for 2005, $43,000[†] for 2006, $44,000[†] for 2007, and $45,000[†] for 2008); therefore, the logical choice for him would be to allow forfeitures to be reallocated to remaining participants, so that his contributions can be increased by the other's forfeitures. In later years, when his compensation is $400,000 and he is able to receive the maximum contribution, it no longer makes sense from his perspective to allow reallocation. Since he has already reached his annual additions limit, the reallocated forfeitures could not increase his account. In such an instance, he may amend the plan to require that forfeitures only reduce future plan costs.

Another reason a plan may be changed or terminated is that a law change may make an entire plan or plan provision obsolete. For example, before the Economic Growth and Tax Relief and Reconciliation Act of 2001 (EGTRRA 2001) was enacted, the contribution limit for a profit sharing plan was 15 percent of employer compensation. An extra 10 percent was available for employers to increase their total contribution through the adoption of pension plans (namely money purchase pension plans). To do this, many employers selected what is referred to as a Tandem Plan (typically combined a 10 percent money purchase pension plan with a 15 percent profit sharing plan so that owners would be able to receive the maximum contribution each year into their qualified plan), while only exposing themselves to a 10 percent mandatory contribution. When EGTRRA 2001 passed, it increased the contribution limit for the profit sharing plan to 25 percent, which virtually made these Tandem Plans obsolete. The reason is simple. Recall the money purchase pension plan requires a mandatory fixed contribution each year, while the profit sharing plan allows the employer the discretion to determine the contribution percentage each year. With the profit sharing plan able to reach the maximum limit of 25 percent, it becomes unnecessary for the employer to take the risk involved with the fixed contribution of the money purchase pension plan. Therefore, many plans were amended so that the money purchase pension plan was terminated and the plan remaining consisted solely of a profit sharing plan.

A qualified plan may also be terminated when the employer finds that they can no longer financially support the plan they have in place. Sometimes the decision is made by the employer, while other times the decision is made by the PBGC. The employer will frequently reach out for debt relief when he has filed for bankruptcy, Chapter 7, or reorganization, Chapter 11. The PBGC also has the right to step in to terminate a plan if the plan is under-funded and the PBGC feels that it needs to protect its risk that the plan will go under.

A plan may also be terminated simply because the employer finds that the plan is not meeting the needs of the employees or the company. Sometimes the plan benefits are so small that the cost of administering the plan is prohibitive. The employer may realize that a simple increase in compensation for the employees will satisfy the same goodwill as a qualified plan and at a lower cost.

AMENDING OR TERMINATING A QUALIFIED PLAN

EXHIBIT 8.18

- To maximize benefits for key employees
- Law changes
- Employer is unable to support
- Benefits were not sufficient

AMENDING A QUALIFIED PLAN

Plan changes are very common due to tax law changes, business changes, or to solve a defect in the plan. Changes are often easily implemented by amending the plan document. When the plan document is amended, the administrator must also revise the Summary Plan Description. The employer is also required to provide the plan participants notices of any plan amendments or changes. Notice can be made either through a revised Summary Plan Description or in a separate document called a Summary of Material Modifications. This document must also be provided to participants free of charge within 210 days after the end of the plan year in which a change is adopted.

TERMINATING A QUALIFIED PLAN

When a qualified plan is terminated, and presuming that sufficient funds are available, all of the participants in the plan become fully vested in their benefits as of the date of termination. Sponsors that terminate a qualified plan must discontinue all contributions and benefit accruals and must distribute all plan assets within a reasonable period of time after the termination of the plan. The method of obtaining a termination and the requirements that need to be met are different for defined-benefit plans and defined-contribution plans.

Permanency Requirement

Although qualified plans are required to be permanent, permanency does not necessarily require that the plan never terminate or continue in existence forever. Permanency in this context just means that the plan must not be established as a temporary program. The goal behind the "permanency" requirement is to dissuade owners from creating plans that will only benefit the owners and key employees and then having the plan vanish before benefits can be accrued by rank-and-file employees. Unfortunately, the abandonment of the plan for any reason other than business necessity within the first few years after it is established will be evidence that the plan was not a bona fide program for the exclusive benefit of employees. This is especially true when a pension plan is abandoned soon after pensions have been fully funded for officers or shareholders. The permanency of the plan is indicated by all of the surrounding facts and circumstances, including the likelihood of the employer's ability to continue contributions as provided under the plan.

Defined-Benefit Plan Terminations

Because the PBGC is responsible for under-funded defined benefit plans, there are more requirements for terminating a defined benefit plan than for a defined contribution plan. Title IV of ERISA requires that a defined benefit plan terminate under a standard, distress, or involuntary termination. See Example 8.14.

Standard Termination

A **standard termination** is one in which the employer has sufficient assets to pay all benefits (liabilities) at the time of final distribution. To terminate a defined benefit plan this way, the administrator must first notify all affected parties between 60 and 90 days before the proposed termination date. The termination date can be any date selected by the administrator, including a weekend or holiday. The administrator must then notify the PBGC. The PBGC must approve the termination because it will be liable should the organization not be able to pay the intended debts. Assuming the plan has met the PBGC requirements, then the date of termination will generally be the date proposed by the administrator in the notice of intent to terminate.

Distress Termination

A **distress termination** occurs when the employer is in financial difficulty and is unable to continue with the plan financially. Generally a distress termination occurs when the company is in liquidation, in bankruptcy (Chapter 7), or has filed for reorganization (Chapter 11). It can also occur when the company can no longer pay debts or the pension costs are simply unreasonable. The administrator must also notify the affected parties and the PBGC as discussed above.

EXAMPLE 8.14

US Airways is an example of a company that decided it could no longer fund the plan it had in place. In 2003, US Airways filed for Chapter 11 bankruptcy and requested that the bankruptcy court allow them to terminate the pension plan they had in place for the pilots. At the time, the plan was underfunded by approximately $2.5 billion dollars, and the company claimed that fulfilling this obligation would prevent them from successfully reorganizing and emerging from bankruptcy. The court allowed the termination and left the company free to establish a more conservative defined contribution plan. The impact was that the PBGC took over the plan and only protected benefits up to the 2003 PBGC limit, approximately $43,000 (2004 benefits were approximately $44,000). Many pilots saw their benefits reduced from as much as $144,000 annually to approximately $19,000 annually for those age 55, due to the PBGC limit and the actuarial reduction from normal retirement age of 65 to 55.

Involuntary Termination

An **involuntary termination** may be initiated by the PBGC for a plan that is unable to pay benefits from the plan in order to limit the amount of exposure to the PBGC. The PBGC <u>may</u> terminate a pension plan, even if a company has not filed to terminate a plan on its own initiative, if:

- the plan has not met the minimum funding requirements;
- the plan cannot pay current benefits when due;
- a lump-sum payment has been made to a participant who is a substantial owner of the sponsoring company; or
- the loss to PBGC is expected to increase unreasonably if the plan is not terminated.[5]

The PBGC <u>must</u> terminate a plan if assets are unavailable to pay benefits currently due.

Defined Contribution Plan Terminations

Compared to defined benefit plans, terminating a defined contribution plan is relatively easy. Defined contribution plans are already funded and not subject to PBGC. Essentially, all the employer must do to terminate the plan is pass a corporate resolution to do so. At that point, any final promised contributions must be completed and the assets must be distributed from the plan.

Partial Terminations

In some instances, a plan, by operation of law, will experience a partial termination. This can occur when the employer changes the plan so that it is very adverse to the employees, or there is a significant severance of employees covered by the plan (i.e. a layoff). A partial termination is decided on a facts and circumstances test; therefore, companies who plan to make decisions that will affect a large number of employees should consider how their actions will affect their

---

5. www.pbgc.gov.

qualified plans. Similar to a full termination, the benefits of the plan participants will be 100 percent vested in the event there is a partial termination.

Case Study 1

A request for a distress termination was made in the Chapter 11 bankruptcy reorganization in In re Diversified Industries, Inc.[1] The Chapter 11 debtor-employer filed a motion with the Bankruptcy Court for authorization to file a notice of intent with Pension Benefit Guaranty Corporation ("PBGC") to terminate five defined benefit plans. The facts showed that the plans were underfunded. The total unpaid minimum contributions for all of these plans as of December 31, 1992 was $2,841,000. The Debtor gave notice of its intent to seek termination of all pension plans. Since there were no objections to the termination of four of these plans, the Court granted authorization and the Debtor initiated the process with PBGC to terminate those four. The benefits for all the participants in those four plans were fully guaranteed by PBGC. The Debtor elected to seek authorization from the PBGC to terminate the remaining plan ("the Plan") pursuant to ERISA's distress termination procedure.

The Plan provided substantial pension benefits for Mr. Ben Fixman and certain other present and former members of the Debtor's senior management team, but a large portion of these benefits were not guaranteed by the PBGC. It was uncontested that if the senior management pension plans were terminated, Mr. Fixman would lose a greater sum than any other employee. Mr. Fixman's pension plan provided him with an annual payment of approximately $136,000. If the Plan were to be terminated, his annual pension would drop to approximately $27,000, the maximum payment that PBGC insured. Mr. Fixman filed an objection to the Debtor's motion, claiming in part that the Debtor was required under ERISA to have the Bankruptcy Court determine whether the Plan could be terminated.

The Bankruptcy Court concluded that due to the Plan's insolvency, the only method of termination was by means of distress termination, which required the plan administrator to provide 60 days' advance notice of intent to terminate to the affected parties, to submit to the PBGC various information as required by ERISA, and to submit information for the PBGC to determine whether the distress criteria had been met.[2] Before submitting the request to terminate the Plan to the PBGC, the Bankruptcy Court explained, the Debtor must satisfy a "business judgment" test and show that the decision is a reasonable exercise of its business judgment. At a hearing, the Debtor proved that it was in its best interest to seek termination of the Plan because, unless the Plan was terminated, the Debtor and its subsidiaries would be unable to pay their debts when due, resulting in the Debtor being unable to continue in business outside the Chapter 11 reorganization process. Accordingly, the court ordered that the Debtor submit the appropriate notices under ERISA to the PBGC to institute the proceedings at that agency to terminate the Plan.

---

1. In re Diversified Industries, Inc., 166 B.R. 141 (Bkrtcy. E.D. Mo. 1993).
2. See Employee Retirement Income Security Act of 1974, Section 4041(c); 29 U.S.C.A. Section 1341(c).

PLAN FREEZE

In some cases, an employer may find that they no longer want to contribute to a plan but do not want to fully terminate the plan. This can be accomplished by freezing the plan. For defined contribution plans, a freeze simply means that the employer will no longer make any contributions. For a defined benefit plan, participants will no longer accrue additional benefits but the plan sponsor must maintain the previously accrued benefits. The plan will continue to benefit from the tax deferral on the plan's earnings until the plan distributes its assets according to the plan document.

Quick
Quiz

Highlight the answer to these questions:

1. Qualified plans are often amended to maximize benefits to key employees.
   a. True
   b. False

2. Qualified plan amendments are difficult and require approval by ERISA.
   a. True
   b. False

3. Qualified plans may never terminate without losing their qualified status retroactively to inception.
   a. True
   b. False

True, False, False.

Key Terms

Actual Contribution Percentage Test (ACP) - A nondiscrimination test that limits the sum of employee after-tax contributions and employer matching contributions for the HC based on the sum of employee after-tax contributions and employer matching contributions of the NHC.

Actual Deferral Percentage Test (ADP) - A nondiscrimination test that limits employee elective deferrals for the HC based on the elective deferrals of the NHC.

Cash or Deferred Arrangement (CODA) - Permits an employee to defer a portion of their salary on a pretax basis to a qualified plan or receive the salary as current taxable income.

Custodial Accounts - Accounts generally maintained by a bank or other financial institution for the benefit of participants.

Department of Labor - Governmental department charged with enforcing the rules governing the conduct of plan managers, investment of plan assets, reporting and disclosure of plan information, enforcement of the fiduciary provisions of the law, and workers' benefit rights as regulated by ERISA.

Determination Letter - A request filed with the IRS requesting a determination on a particular topic. In the case of a retirement plan, they are used when a plan is adopted, amended, or terminated to assure the plan sponsor that the qualified plan complies with applicable provisions.

Distress Termination - Termination that occurs when the employer is in financial difficulty and is unable to continue with a defined benefit plan.

Employee Census - A matrix of information that is used in plan selection and identifies each employee, their age, compensation, number of years of employment, and any ownership interest in the plan sponsor.

Employee Retirement Income and Security Act (ERISA) - Enacted by Congress in 1974 because of various abuses by plan sponsors to provide protection for an employee's retirement assets, both from creditors and from plan sponsors.

ERISA Attorney - An attorney who specializes in ERISA law.

Fiduciary - An individual that has a special relationship of trust, confidence, and responsibility in certain financial obligations.

Forfeitures - The percentage or amount of a participant's accrued benefit that was not vested to the employee at the employee's termination from the plan sponsor. The forfeited amount stays in the plan and may be allocated to the other plan participants (defined contribution plan) or reduce future plan costs (defined contribution plan or defined benefit plan).

Key Terms

Interested Parties - Present employees who are eligible to participate in the plan and present employees who are not eligible for the plan but whose principal place of employment is the same as the principal place of employment of any employee who is eligible to participate.

Involuntary Termination - Termination initiated by the PBGC for a defined benefit plan that is unable to pay benefits from the plan.

Keogh Plan - A qualified plan for a self-employed individual.

Mandatory Funding - An amount or percentage that must be contributed to a qualified pension plan by the employer each plan year.

Master Plan - Provides a single trust or custodial account that is jointly used by all adopting employers.

Pension Benefit Guaranty Corporation (PBGC) - Established in 1974 when President Gerald R. Ford signed the Employee Retirement Income Security Act (ERISA) into law. The PBGC guarantees qualified pension benefits. It is a federal corporation that acts as an insurance provider to maintain the benefits promised to employees by their defined benefit pension plans.

Plan Freeze - Employer will no longer make any contributions to the plan, but does not want to fully terminate the plan.

Prohibited Transactions - Transactions between the plan and a disqualified person that are prohibited by law.

Prototype Plan - A prepackaged plan that allows the sponsor to use a check the box approach to plan choices.

Qualified Trust - A trust established or organized in the U.S. that is maintained by the employer for the exclusive benefit of employees.

Standard Termination - Termination in which the employer has sufficient assets to pay all benefits (liabilities) at the time of final distribution.

Summary of Material Modifications - Document that provides in plain language the modifications made to a qualified plan.

Summary Plan Description - Document that explains in plain language the details of a retirement plan and how it operates. It provides information on when an employee can begin to participate in the plan, how service and benefits are calculated, when benefits become vested, when and in what form benefits are paid, and how to file a claim for benefits.

Third Party Administrator - An organization unrelated to the plan sponsor who is paid to administer the plan sponsor's qualified or other retirement plan.

1. Describe the business and personal issues that should be considered when making a qualified plan selection.

2. What is an employee census and why is it important?

3. Explain the steps involved in adopting a qualified plan.

4. How and when should employees be notified when a qualified plan is established?

5. What are the minimum funding requirements for qualified plans?

6. When may contributions to a qualified plan be deducted by the employer?

7. Explain how forfeitures are treated in qualified plans.

8. List the transactions that are prohibited in a qualified plan and the exceptions.

9. Describe the regulatory bodies, other than the IRS, and filing requirements involved with the operation of a qualified plan.

10. Under what circumstances would a qualified plan be amended or terminated?

11. Describe how a qualified plan is amended.

12. Describe how a qualified plan is terminated.

1. Generally, which of the following are contributory plans?

    a. 401(k) and money purchase pension plans.

    b. 401(k) and thrift plans.

    c. Thrift plans and ESOPs.

    d. Money purchase pension plans and profit sharing plans.

2. Which of the following generally contribute to defined benefit plans, profit sharing plans and money purchase pension plans?

    a. Employees only.

    b. Employer only.

    c. Both employer and employees.

    d. Employer, employees, and government.

3. Who generally makes elective deferrals to a 401(k) plan?

    a. Employees only.

    b. Employer only.

    c. Employees and employer.

    d. Employees, employers, and forfeitures.

4. Plans which require mandatory funding are generally funded by?

    a. The employee.

    b. The employer.

    c. The employee and the employer.

    d. For PBGC insured plans, the employee and the employer.

5. Employees generally contribute either pre- or post-tax to which of the following plans?

    1. 401(k) plans.

    2. Thrift plans.

    3. Cash balance pension plans.

    4. Defined benefit pension plans.

    a. 1 and 2.

    b. 1 and 4.

    c. 2 and 3.

    d. 3 and 4.

6. Which of the following qualified plans require mandatory funding?

    1. Defined benefit pension plans.

    2. 401(k) plans with an employer match organized as a profit sharing plan.

    3. Cash balance pension plans.

    4. Money purchase pension plans.

        a. 1 and 3.

        b. 1, 2, and 3.

        c. 1, 3, and 4.

        d. 1, 2, 3, and 4.

7. Company A has been capitalized by MJBJ Vulture Capital, a venture capital company. Company A's cash flows are expected to fluctuate significantly from year to year, due to phenomenal growth. They expect to go public within three years. Which of the following would be the best qualified plan for them to consider adopting?

        a. Profit sharing plan.

        b. New comparability plan.

        c. 401(k) plan with a match.

        d. Stock bonus plan.

8. Investment portfolio risk is generally borne by the participant/employee in all of the listed qualified plans, except:

    1. Defined benefit pension plan.

    2. Cash balance pension plan.

    3. 401(k) plan.

    4. Profit sharing plan.

        a. 1 and 2.

        b. 2 and 3.

        c. 3 and 4.

        d. 1, 3, and 4.

9. The target benefit pension plan and the money purchase pension plan provide some employee/participant investment diversification protections by limiting the investment amount in employer stock to less than or equal to:

        a. 0%.

        b. 5%.

        c. 10%.

        d. 20%.

10. Qualified retirement plans that permit the employer unlimited investment in sponsor company stock are:

1. 401(k) plans.
2. Stock bonus plans.
3. Profit sharing plans.
4. ESOPs.
    a. 3 only.
    b. 4 only.
    c. 3 and 4.
    d. 1, 2, 3, and 4.

11. Generally, older age entrants are favored in which of the following plans?

1. Defined benefit pension plans.
2. Cash balance pension plans.
3. Target benefit pension plans.
4. Money purchase pension plans.
    a. 1 and 2.
    b. 2 and 3.
    c. 1 and 3.
    d. 4 only.

12. A distress termination of a qualified retirement plan occurs when:

1. The PBGC initiates a termination because the plan was determined to be unable to pay benefits from the plan.
2. An employer is in financial difficulty and is unable to continue with the plan financially. Generally, this occurs when the company has filed for bankruptcy, either Chapter 7 liquidation or Chapter 11 reorganization.
3. The employer has sufficient assets to pay all benefits vested at the time, but is distressed about it.
4. When the PBGC notifies the employer that it wishes to change the plan due to the increasing unfunded risk.
    a. 2 only.
    b. 1 and 2.
    c. 1, 2, and 3.
    d. 1, 2, and 4.

13. Marie, the sole shareholder in Marie's Pastries, is contemplating establishing a qualified plan. The corporation's employee census is as follows:

MARIE'S PASTRIES EMPLOYEE CENSUS				
Employee	**Age**	**Compensation**	**Ownership**	**Length of Service**
Marie	55	$200,000	100%	30 Years
Cheryl	38	$45,000	0	20 Years
Jeff	42	$28,000	0	14 Years
Ruby	34	$24,000	0	11 Years
Total		**$297,000**	**100%**	
The company experiences very low turnover.				

Marie, a long-time widow, has always treated the employees like her family and the company has experienced very low turnover. She would like to use the retirement plan to assist her in transferring ownership interest to the employees as she is ready to retire. She has a strong preference for avoiding and deferring taxes. She is opposed to mandatory funding and indifferent to integration. Which plan would be appropriate for Marie?

    a. Stock bonus plan.

    b. Money purchase pension plan.

    c. Defined benefit plan.

    d. Employee stock ownership plan.

14. Westgate Inc., recently adopted a profit sharing plan. Westgate has two offices, the North Westgate office and the South Westgate office. There are 10 employees in the North Westgate office, 5 of which are eligible for the plan, and 15 employees in the South Westgate office that are all eligible for the plan. Which of the following statements is true?

    a. If Westgate decides to notify the employees about the plan via mail, the letters must be mailed at least 30 days before mailing the determination letter to the IRS.

    b. A Summary Plan Description must be furnished to each participant within 120 days of plan establishment.

    c. If Westgate adopted a prototype plan, then it would use a single trust or custodial account that has been adopted by all employers using that prototype plan.

    d. Westgate only needs to notify the employees that are eligible for the plan that the company has adopted a qualified plan.

15. Tracy, age 46, is a self-employed financial planner and has Schedule C income from self-employment of $56,000. He has failed to save for retirement until now. Therefore, he would like to make the maximum contribution to his profit sharing plan. How much can he contribute to his profit sharing plan account?

    a. $9,552.

    b. $11,200.

    c. $12,929.

    d. $14,000.

IRAs and SEPs

9

INTRODUCTION

The Individual Retirement Arrangement (IRA) has been available since 1974. The amount that once could be contributed on a tax-deferred basis per person per year was limited to $2,000, but that has now been changed to $4,000 for 2005 ($4,000 for 2006, $4,000 for 2007, and $5,000 for 2008) with an additional deferral of $500 for 2005 ($1,000 for 2006, $1,000 for 2007, and $1,000 for 2008) for persons age 50 or older. The rules regarding deductibility have also changed as will be explained in this chapter. The IRA has great potential as an accumulation device for retirement when started early and funded annually. Consider an individual making annual year-end deposits of $4,000 in a mutual fund earning 10.4 percent returns for 40 years (age 25-65).[1] The future accumulated balance of the account at age 65 is $1,974,287 even though the individual only deposited a total of $160,000. The compound growth potential of such accounts often makes the tax deductibility of the contribution a less significant issue than the accumulation as illustrated in the graph below.

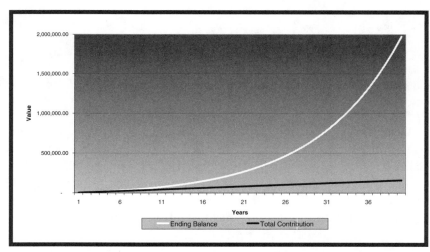

---

1.   10.4 percent is the average return of large capitalization stock over the last 60 years.

Although the Roth IRA does not permit income tax deductible contributions, distributions are generally tax free. Additionally, a new 401(k) with a Roth feature will be available beginning in 2006 and could be one of the best retirement tools available for small businesses, their principals, and employees.

Know The Numbers

	Traditional IRA	Roth IRA	SEP	SARSEP
Contribution Limit	$4,000 for 2005 $4,000 for 2006 $4,000 for 2007 $5,000 for 2008	$4,000 for 2005 $4,000 for 2006 $4,000 for 2007 $5,000 for 2008	25 % or $42,000 for 2005 $43,000† for 2006 $44,000† for 2007 $45,000† for 2008	$14,000 for 2005 $15,000 for 2006 $15,000† for 2007 $15,500† for 2008
Catch Up (Over age 50)	$500 for 2005 $1,000 for 2006 $1,000 for 2007 $1,000 for 2008	$500 for 2005 $1,000 for 2006 $1,000 for 2007 $1,000 for 2008	Not Applicable	$4,000 for 2005 $5,000 for 2006 $5,000† for 2007 $5,000† for 2008
Contribution Phaseout	Not Applicable	Single: 95k - 110k MFJ: 150k - 160k MFS: 0k - 10k	Not Applicable	Not Applicable
Conversion Limit	Not Applicable	Single: $100,000 MFJ: $100,000 MFS: Not Applicable	Not Applicable	Not Applicable

Deduction Phaseouts	No QP: No Limit
	Single with QP: 50k - 60k
	MFJ both with QP:
	   70k - 80k for 2005
	   75k - 85k for 2006
	80k - 100k for 2007 and after
	MFJ one with QP:150k-160k
		Not Applicable	Not Applicable	Not Applicable

Provide to Employee With	Not Applicable	Not Applicable	Compensation > $450	Not Applicable

IRAs, SEPs, SARSEPs, SIMPLEs, and tax sheltered annuities (403(b) plans) are not qualified plans, do not meet the requirements under IRC Section 401(a), and are not entitled to the same benefits as qualified plans. They are referred to as "other tax-advantaged plans" to indicate that, while not qualified plans, they have many of the same benefits and features as qualified plans. While all of these plans have many of the benefits of qualified plans, they also have certain advantages over qualified plans. Similar to qualified plans, tax-advantaged plans are all tax deferred, meaning that earnings within the trust or plan are not taxed until a distribution occurs. In addition, all of these tax-advantaged plans provide for sheltering of current income from taxation. Finally, IRAs, SEPs, and SIMPLEs are not subject to the same federal reporting requirements as qualified plans.

IRAs, SEPs, SIMPLEs, and 403(b) plans do not permit 10-year averaging, do not have the same non-alienation of benefits protection found under ERISA, and do not receive special capital gains treatment for distributions of employer securities. In addition, these plans, with the exception of the 403(b) plan, are not permitted to allow loans. Qualified plans typically have specific vesting schedules for contributions made by the employer on behalf of the employee. Other tax-advantaged plans always provide for 100 percent vesting.

CHARACTERISTICS OF QUALIFIED PLANS AND OTHER TAX-EXEMPT PLANS

EXHIBIT 9.1

Characteristic	Qualified Plans	IRAs	SEP IRAs	SIMPLE IRAs**	403(b) Plans
Provides for tax deferral for deposits and savings	✓	✓	✓	✓	✓
Provides shelter for current income	✓	✓	✓	✓	✓
Annual reporting – Form 5500	✓	✗	✗	✗	Maybe***
Vesting required	✓	✗	✗	✗	✗
Loans are permitted	✓	✗	✗	✗	✓
Protection under ERISA	✓	✗****	✗****	✗****	Maybe*
10-year averaging permitted	✓	✗	✗	✗	✗
Pre-74 capital gain treatment	✓	✗	✗	✗	✗
Distributions eligible for NUA	✓	✗	✗	✗	✗

*Many 403(b) plans provide for ERISA protection; however, some do not.   ** There are very few, if any, SIMPLE 401(k)s.

Employer maintained 403(b) plans must file Form 5500.   * Although state law and bankruptcy protection may be available.

✓ YES ✗ NO

This chapter discusses the rules surrounding Traditional IRAs, IRA annuities, Roth IRAs, SEPs, and SARSEPs. SIMPLE plans, 403(b) plans, and 457 plans are discussed in the following chapter.

INDIVIDUAL RETIREMENT ARRANGEMENT

There are two general types of **individual retirement arrangements** (IRAs) under present law: traditional IRAs, to which both deductible and nondeductible contributions may be made, and Roth IRAs, to which only nondeductible contributions may be made.[2] Many of the rules relating to traditional IRAs and Roth IRAs are the same and will be discussed together under traditional IRAs. The differences in the types of IRAs are discussed later in this chapter.

TRADITIONAL IRAS

Traditional IRAs have been available for many years and although the limits on both contributions and deductions have changed, these retirement vehicles remain an important part of retirement planning for individuals. IRAs take one of two forms, an IRA account or an **IRA annuity**. An IRA account can hold a wide variety of investments and can be held by a wide variety of **custodians** (e.g., brokerage, bank, mutual fund, etc.). An IRA annuity is usually held by an insurance company as custodian. As a result of the EGTRRA 2001, IRAs have become a more significant part of planning for retirement. There are important distinctions with traditional IRAs that must be considered, including contribution limits and deductibility limits.

Contribution Limits

Individuals have historically been able to contribute each year the lesser of $2,000 or their earned income to traditional IRAs. However, this limit was increased as a result of the EGTRRA 2001 for years beginning after 2001. In addition, individuals who have attained the age of 50 before the end of the current taxable year are also eligible to make catch-up contributions, thereby further increasing the annual IRA contribution limits. These new limits, which are combined limits between traditional and Roth IRAs, are summarized in the following chart.

Key Concepts

Underline/highlight the answers to these questions as you read:

1. What is the limit on contributions to an IRA for 2005?

2. What is considered earned income for purposes of IRA contributions?

EXHIBIT 9.2   **CONTRIBUTION LIMIT FOR IRAS (TRADITIONAL & ROTH)**

Year	Annual Limit	Catch-Up Limit (for those over age 50)	Maximum Contribution
2005	$4,000	$500	$4,500
2006	$4,000	$1,000	$5,000
2007	$4,000	$1,000	$5,000
2008	$5,000	$1,000	$6,000
After 2008	Limit is adjusted upward in $500 increments	$1,000	

---

2.   This chapter does not consider Coverdell IRAs (formerly known as Education IRAs).

With the increases in the contribution limit, IRAs have become a more significant part of an individual's retirement planning and a better savings and investment tool for use by financial planners.

The following graphs depict the accumulation over time in an IRA assuming a $4,000 contribution was made to the account at the beginning of each year and without considering the availability of the catch-up contribution and the increase in the limits. Notice that after ten years, $70,125 has accumulated assuming a 10 percent rate of return. After thirty years, over $723,774 has accumulated assuming a 10 percent rate of return.

EXAMPLE 9.1

Years	Amount Deposited	8% Return	10% Return	12% Return
1-5	$20,000	$25,344	$26,862	$28,461
1-10	$40,000	$62,582	$70,125	$78,618
1-15	$60,000	$117,297	$139,799	$167,013
1-20	$80,000	$197,692	$252,010	$322,795
1-25	$100,000	$315,818	$432,727	$597,336
1-30	$120,000	$489,383	$723,774	$1,081,170

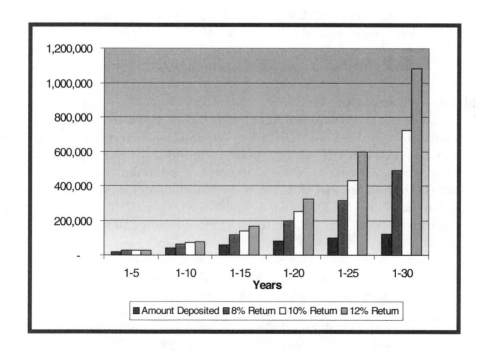

EXAMPLE 9.2

A straight deposit equal to the 2005 IRA limit of $4,000 per year assuming contributions are made at the end of each year at various earning rates for 30 and 40 years are:

Years (N)	Rate (i)	PMT	Amount Deposited	FV
30	8%	$4,000	$120,000	$453,133
30	10%	$4,000	$120,000	$657,976
30	12%	$4,000	$120,000	$965,331
40	8%	$4,000	$160,000	$1,036,226
40	10%	$4,000	$160,000	$1,770,370
40	12%	$4,000	$160,000	$3,068,366

Earned Income - Individual IRA

The annual contributions to an IRA are limited to the lesser of an individual's earned income or the annual limit in effect. Earned income includes any type of compensation where the individual has performed some level of services for an employer or is considered self-employed. Compensation includes earnings for W-2 employees or those individuals who are self-employed, whether they operate a sole proprietorship, partnership, or an LLC taxed as a sole proprietorship or partnership. Earned income also includes alimony received by the taxpayer. For federal income tax purposes, **alimony** is deductible by the payor and is includible as earned income by the recipient. Exhibit 9.3 provides a list of earned income and a separate list of what is not earned income.

EXAMPLE 9.3

In Letter Ruling 9202003, the IRS ruled that hogs transferred from a husband to his wife (a bona fide employee) did in fact constitute compensation (earned income) and could be used as the basis for contributions to an IRA.

Earned Income - Spousal IRA

Individuals who do not have any earned income may still be eligible to establish an IRA if their spouse has sufficient earned income. An IRA for a spouse who has no earned income is generally referred to as a spousal IRA and can be established provided the other spouse has sufficient earned income. The necessary level of earned income is equal to the total amount that is to be contributed to both IRAs. **Spousal IRAs** can be established up to the contribution limit for the year in question (i.e. $4,000 for 2005, $4,000 for 2006, $4,000 for 2007, and $5,000 for 2008). The catch-up contribution is also available for those individuals age 50 and over.

EXAMPLE 9.4

Jack, age 48, and Sydney, age 43, have been married for twenty years and are currently retired. Although Jack is currently unemployed, Sydney earns $8,000 from her part-time work at the local market during 2005. Because Sydney has income of $8,000, both Jack and Sydney can contribute up to $4,000 to each of their IRAs in the year 2005.

EXAMPLE 9.5

Jeff, age 54, and Brit, age 52, have been married for twenty years and are planning to retire in six years. Although Jeff is currently unemployed, Brit earns $38,000 from her work at the local school. Brit's income of $38,000 would allow each of them to contribute up to $4,000 to each of their IRAs during 2005. In addition, each of them can contribute an extra $500 for 2005 as a catch-up contribution because they are both over age 50.   Their total deductible IRA contribution could be as much as $9,000 in 2005 ($10,000 in 2006 and 2007).

EXAMPLES OF EARNED INCOME AND WHAT IS NOT EARNED INCOME

EXHIBIT 9.3

Earned Income:
• W-2 income • Schedule C net income • K-1 income from an LLC • K-1 income from a partnership where the partner is a material participant • Alimony
Not Earned Income:
• Earnings and profits from property, such as rental income, interest income, and dividend income • Capital gains • Pension and annuity income • Deferred compensation received (compensation payments postponed from a past year) • Income from a partnership for which you do not provide services that are a material income producing factor • Any amounts excluded from income, such as foreign income and housing costs • Unemployment benefits • Investment returns as a limited partner in a partnership • Income flowing from an S-corporation via Schedule K-1 • Social Security benefits • Worker's compensation

Earned Income - Attainment of 70½

Contributions to a traditional IRA are not permitted in the year or any years after the year in which an individual attains age 70½.[3] This limitation for traditional IRAs does not apply to Roth IRAs. Individuals who have sufficient earned income may continue to contribute to a Roth IRA after the attainment of age 70½.

---

3.   IRC Section 219(d)(1).

EXAMPLE 9.6

Billy and Alice have been married for many years. Although Billy is currently retired, he has a part-time position at the local superstore earning $13,000 each year. Billy turned 70 on March 8th of 2005. Alice is 40 and is a stay-home mom. Because Billy will attain the age of 70½ during the current year, he is not permitted to contribute to a traditional IRA. However, Alice may contribute $4,000 for 2005 to a spousal IRA (either traditional or Roth), and Billy can contribute $4,000 to a Roth IRA (with the availability of a $500 catch-up contribution).

Excess Contributions

Contributions that exceed the limits discussed above (i.e. $4,000 for 2005, $4,000 for 2006, $4,000 for 2007, and $5,000 for 2008) are subject to an excise tax of six percent. This penalty is charged each year that the excess contribution remains in the IRA.[4] The taxpayer can avoid the excise penalty on excess contributions by withdrawing the excess contribution and the earnings attributable to the excess contributions by the due date (excluding extensions) of the federal income tax return (April 15th for calendar year taxpayers). These excess contributions rules and the penalty apply to both traditional and Roth IRAs.

EXAMPLE 9.7

In 2005, Sara, age 32, contributed $4,900 to her IRA. She made an excess contribution of $900 that will be subject to a six percent penalty if she does not withdraw the excess contribution and any related earnings by April 15th of 2006.

EXAMPLE 9.8

In 2005, Sara, age 32, contributed $3,500 to her traditional IRA and $1,500 to her Roth IRA. She has made an excess contribution of $1,000. She can avoid the six percent penalty by withdrawing the excess contribution and any related earnings from either the IRA or the Roth IRA account (or both) by the following April 15th.

The calculation of earnings attributable to the excess IRA contribution is based on a prorated portion of the earnings accrued by the IRA while the excess contribution remained in the IRA.

Timing of Contributions to IRAs

As discussed in Chapter 8, contributions to qualified plans can be made as late as the due date of the tax return including extensions. For corporations with a calendar year end, the final date a contribution can be made to a qualified plan is September 15th. For partnerships and self-employed individuals, the final date a contribution can be made to a qualified plan is October 15th. However, for IRAs, contributions must be made to both traditional and Roth IRA accounts by the due date of the individual federal income tax return without considering extensions. For most taxpayers, this due date is April 15th of the year following the tax year end.

---

4.   IRC Section 4973.

Finally, the contribution to a traditional IRA or Roth IRA must be made in cash with an exception for rollover contributions.[5] No other type of asset may be contributed to an IRA.

Deductibility of IRA Contributions

Provided an individual has sufficient earned income, he may contribute the maximum amount to a traditional IRA on an annual basis. However, the deductibility of the traditional IRA contribution on an individual's federal income tax return is dependent on several factors, including coverage or participation in a qualified plan or other retirement plan and the amount of the individual's **adjusted gross income** (AGI). If the individual and spouse (if any) are not active participants in a qualified plan or retirement plan (defined later), they may contribute to a deductible IRA to the lesser of the IRA contribution limit or earned income. Even if the individual or their spouse is an active participant, they still may be able to contribute to a deductible IRA if the AGI of the taxpayer (and spouse, if any) is below certain threshold limits as discussed below.

No Qualified Plan

An individual who is not an active participant does not have any income limitation for purposes of deducting his IRA contributions. Therefore, if an individual earns a substantial amount of income (e.g., $1,000,000) and is not an active participant in a qualified plan, then the individual may fully deduct a contribution (within the contribution limit) to his traditional IRA account.

Quick Quiz

Highlight the answer to these questions:

1. A 55-year old individual can contribute a maximum of $4,000 to an IRA in 2005.
   a. True
   b. False

2. Annual contributions to an IRA are limited to the lesser of a single individual's earned income or the annual limit in effect.
   a. True
   b. False

3. Persons who do not have any earned income may not contribute to an IRA.
   a. True
   b. False

False, True, False.

---

5.   IRC Section 408(a)(1).

EXHIBIT 9.4 **WHO CAN DEDUCT CONTRIBUTIONS TO A TRADITIONAL IRA**

Taxpayer does not have a qualified plan	Taxpayer(s) has/have a qualified plan(s)		One spouse has a qualified plan, one does not
No AGI Limit	Single	**AGI Phaseout** $50k - $60k (2005, 2006, 2007, and 2008)	The spouse without the qualified plan may have a deductible traditional IRA contribution as long as their joint AGI does not exceed $160,000. The deductible IRA contribution is phased out between $150,000 and $160,000.
	MFJ	**AGI Phaseout** $70k - $80k (2005) $75k - $85k (2006) $80k - $100k (2007 and after)	

Active Participants of Qualified Plans

For individuals or married couples filing jointly who are considered active participants (defined below) of a qualified plan or other retirement plan (see discussion below), there is an income test to determine the deductibility of IRA contributions. If the taxpayer's AGI is greater than the upper limit of the phaseout, no deduction is permitted. If the taxpayer's AGI is less than the lower limit of the phaseout, then a full deduction is permitted. If the taxpayer's AGI is between the limits, then the deduction is ratably phased out. The AGI phaseout limits for unmarried (single) taxpayers and married couples filing jointly are depicted in the following table:[6]

EXHIBIT 9.5 **SCHEDULE OF AGI PHASEOUT RANGES**

Tax Year	AGI Phaseout Range Single	AGI Phaseout Range Married Filing Jointly
2005	$50,000 – $60,000	$70,000 – $80,000
2006	$50,000 – $60,000	$75,000 – $85,000
2007 and after	$50,000 – $60,000	$80,000 – $100,000

Married couples filing separately are effectively phased out between an AGI of $0 and $10,000. Individuals falling within these phaseout ranges must calculate the deductible amount of the contribution utilizing the calculation discussed below.

As illustrated in Exhibit 9.4, simply because one spouse is covered by a qualified plan does not prohibit the other spouse from deducting a contribution to a traditional IRA. However, this ability to deduct the contribution is phased out for married individuals with AGI beginning at $150,000 and is completely phased out for AGI at or above $160,000.

---

6. IRC Section 219(g)(3)(A).

Calculation of IRA Deduction – Subject to Phaseout

An individual who is an active participant in a retirement plan and has an AGI within the **phaseout** range will have a reduced maximum deductible IRA contribution. The deduction limit ($4,000 for 2005, $4,000 for 2006, $4,000 for 2007, and $5,000 for 2008) will be reduced based on a proportion equal to the amount by which the individual's AGI exceeds the lower limit of the phaseout range divided by $10,000 (or $20,000 in the case of a joint return for a taxable year beginning after December 31, 2006). The calculation of this reduction in the IRA deductibility limit is as follows:

$$\text{Reduction} = \text{Contribution Limit} \times \frac{\text{AGI} - \text{Lower Limit}}{\$10,000}$$

Consider the following examples:

Fred is single, age 38, and an active participant in his employer's qualified retirement plan. His AGI for 2006 is $51,000, and he makes the maximum contribution ($4,000) to his traditional IRA.

EXAMPLE 9.9

$$\text{Reduction} = \$4,000 \times \frac{\$51,000 - \$50,000}{\$10,000} = \$400$$

Thus, Fred's traditional IRA deduction for 2006 is reduced by $400 to $3,600 ($4,000 - $400).

Assume the same facts as above except that Fred is over the age of 50 and is eligible for the catch-up contribution of $1,000. In this case, the traditional IRA deduction is reduced by $500.

EXAMPLE 9.10

$$\text{Reduction} = \$5,000 \times \frac{\$51,000 - \$50,000}{\$10,000} = \$500$$

Thus, Fred's traditional IRA deduction for 2006 is reduced to $4,500 ($5,000 - $500). Notice that the portion that is phased out represents 10 percent of the contribution. Therefore, with the additional $1,000 contribution, only 90 percent or $900 will be deductible ($3,600 + $900 = $4,500).

Rob, age 32, and Sara, age 31, are married and are active participants in qualified plans. They file a joint return and have AGI of $79,000. Both Rob and Sara make the maximum contribution to their respective traditional IRAs in 2006.

EXAMPLE 9.11

$$\text{Reduction} = \$4,000 \times \frac{\$79,000 - \$75,000}{10,000} = \$1,600$$

Thus, Rob and Sara can each deduct $2,400 ($4,000 - $1,600).

EXAMPLE 9.12

Nick and Kim are married and file jointly. Kim is an attorney who earns $130,000 per year and is an active participant in the firm's qualified plan. She also has portfolio income of $15,000 per year. Nick is unemployed and goes to the bar every day and plays Gin Rummy. Can Nick make a contribution to a traditional IRA and is it deductible? Yes. Nick can contribute because together Kim and Nick have sufficient earned income and the contribution is deductible because their joint AGI is less than $150,000. Therefore, Nick can make the maximum contribution (subject to his age) to the IRA for the current year and fully deduct it.

Where is the Traditional IRA Deduction Taken

The deduction for contributions to traditional IRAs is a deduction for AGI. The deduction is listed on line 25 of the individual's 2004 Form 1040 (The 2005 form was not available at the time of printing).

EXHIBIT 9.6 **ADJUSTED GROSS INCOME SECTION OF FORM 1040**

Adjusted Gross Income	23	Educator expenses (see page 26)	23			
	24	Certain business expenses of reservists, performing artists, and fee-basis government officials. Attach Form 2106 or 2106-EZ	24			
	25	IRA deduction (see page 26)	25			
	26	Student loan interest deduction (see page 28)	26			
	27	Tuition and fees deduction (see page 29)	27			
	28	Health savings account deduction. Attach Form 8889	28			
	29	Moving expenses. Attach Form 3903	29			
	30	One-half of self-employment tax. Attach Schedule SE	30			
	31	Self-employed health insurance deduction (see page 30)	31			
	32	Self-employed SEP, SIMPLE, and qualified plans	32			
	33	Penalty on early withdrawal of savings	33			
	34a	Alimony paid b Recipient's SSN ▶	34a			
	35	Add lines 23 through 34a			35	
	36	Subtract line 35 from line 22. This is your **adjusted gross income** ▶			36	

Active Participant Status

As discussed above, the deductibility of traditional IRA contributions may be reduced if the taxpayer is an active participant in a retirement plan for the year of contribution to the traditional IRA. An active participant is an employee who has benefitted under one of the following plans through a contribution or an accrued benefit:[7]

- qualified plan
- annuity plan
- tax sheltered annuity (403(b) plan)
- certain government plans[8]
- simplified employee pension plans (SEPs)
- simple retirement accounts (SIMPLEs)

---

7.   IRC Section 219(g)(5).
8.   Does not include 457 plans – IRC Section 219(g)(5). In addition, certain armed forces reserve members and volunteer firefighters may not be considered active participants.

Contributions made to a plan include contributions made by the employer, the employee, or any plan forfeiture allocations. In addition, the accrual of benefits under a defined benefit plan also counts for purposes of determining active participant status. An accrual of benefits occurs when a plan has mandatory funding and an employee is eligible to receive benefits even though the account balance may not be funded. For example, when a participant completes an additional year of service in a defined benefit plan that calculates the benefit based on years of service, then, the participant has accrued additional benefits in that year. An employee is considered an active participant even if the contributions to the account are completely forfeitable. In other words, even if the employee is zero percent vested in the benefit, he will still be considered an active participant if he receives a contribution to his account for the current year.

Key Concepts

Underline/highlight the answers to these questions as you read:

1. What is the penalty for excess contributions to an IRA?

2. List the factors that affect the deductibility of IRA contributions on an individual's federal tax return.

3. What are the required minimum distribution rules for IRAs?

Active participant status for an employee depends on the type of retirement plan. For a defined benefit plan, an employee is an active participant if the individual participates or meets the eligibility requirements of the plan. When an individual is eligible for a defined benefit plan, the individual is an active participant regardless of whether he participates or the employer makes the required contribution for the employee to receive the accrued benefit. However, an individual may elect out of participating, and in the subsequent year(s), the individual will not be considered as an active participant. In most cases, employees who meet the eligibility requirements will be active participants since it is rare for an individual to elect out of receiving benefits.

An individual is an active participant in a money purchase pension plan or target benefit pension plan if the employer is required to make a contribution on behalf of that employee. Since these plans must comply with mandatory funding requirements, most employees who are eligible for such plans and are covered will be active participants.

Because contributions to profit sharing plans (and stock bonus plans) are discretionary from the employer, the determination of active participant status is dependent on whether the individual receives a contribution for the year. Remember the contribution may come from the employer, employee, or from a plan forfeiture allocation. Also, qualified nonelective contributions, as well as qualified matching contributions, will qualify as a contribution to the plan for the year. Any of these contributions will cause an individual to be classified as an active participant for the year for which the contribution was made.

As previously discussed, contributions to traditional IRAs are required to be made by April 15th for the previous year, while contributions to qualified plans can be made as late as the due date of the company's income tax return including extensions. With a profit-sharing plan, an individual may not know whether or not he will be an active participant for a particular year until after he is required to make the contribution to the IRA account. Because of the timing difference, certain provisions permit such qualified plan contributions to be considered for the following year for purposes of traditional IRA deductibility.

<table>
<tr><td>EXAMPLE 9.13</td><td>George is employed by Hone Company, which sponsors a profit-sharing plan. The plan was established in 2001. Hone decides in August of 2006 to make a contribution to the plan for the year 2005. Since Hone made the contribution in 2006, George would be considered an active participant for the year 2006, not 2005. However, if a contribution was made for George in 2005, then George would be an active participant for 2005.</td></tr>
</table>

As discussed, an employee who makes an employee elective deferral contribution to a plan, such as a 401(k) plan, is considered an active participant for the current year. However, just because an employee is eligible to defer a portion of his salary into a 401(k) plan does not automatically make him an active participant for the current year (e.g., the employee does not defer).[9]

For spouses filing jointly, the active participation status of one spouse does not constitute active participant status of the other spouse.[10] If only one spouse is an active participant, then the spouse that is not an active participant may make a deductible IRA contribution as long as the couple's joint income (adjusted gross income) does not exceed $160,000 (the ability to take a deduction phases out from $150,000 to $160,000).

<table>
<tr><td>EXAMPLE 9.14</td><td>Bob's employer sponsors a money purchase pension plan with a contribution level of seven percent of compensation. Bob meets the eligibility requirements. Therefore, Bob is an active participant for purposes of IRA deductibility.</td></tr>
</table>

<table>
<tr><td>EXAMPLE 9.15</td><td>Joe is a participant of his company's profit sharing plan. However, the company had a bad year and did not make a contribution to the profit sharing plan, and no employees terminated employment with non-vested benefits during the current year. Joe is not an active participant in the plan because he did not receive any employer contribution or any forfeiture allocation.</td></tr>
</table>

<table>
<tr><td>EXAMPLE 9.16</td><td>Deanna is employed with Kensington Company where she is eligible to defer up to 80 percent of her salary into the 401(k) plan. Deanna does not defer anything in her 401(k) plan, nor does she receive a contribution by the employer or a forfeiture allocation. Deanna is not an active participant for purposes of IRA deductibility for that year.[11]</td></tr>
</table>

---

9.   Treas. Reg. 1.219-2(e).
10.   IRC Section 219(g)(7).

Deanna, who is a non-highly compensated employee, is employed with Kensington Company where she is eligible to defer up to 80 percent of her salary into the 401(k) plan. Deanna does not defer anything in her 401(k) plan, nor does she receive a forfeiture allocation. However, Deanna does receive a small contribution from the employer in the form of a qualified non-elective contribution.[12] Deanna is considered an active participant for purposes of IRA deductibility.

EXAMPLE 9.17

Aaron and Stacey are married and file a joint income tax return. Their joint AGI is $125,000. Stacey is a dentist who earns a salary of $80,000 per year, and she defers the maximum to her 401(k) plan. Aaron is a personal trainer earning $45,000 in fees per year. He files a Schedule C with his federal income tax return. Stacey is an active participant in a qualified plan, but Aaron is not. Although he should likely establish a Keogh plan for his self-employment income, he is not currently an active participant. Because their joint AGI is less than $150,000 and he is not an active participant in a qualified plan, Aaron can make a fully deductible traditional IRA contribution. Stacey could make a non-deductible IRA contribution or a contribution to a Roth IRA.

EXAMPLE 9.18

Non-Deductible IRA Contributions

Although one of the advantages of an IRA contribution is that they are often income tax deductible for AGI, contributions to an IRA can be non-deductible.[13] Generally, taxpayers make non-deductible contributions to traditional IRAs if they are active participants in a qualified plan and their income exceeds the phaseout limits. However, any taxpayer can make a non-deductible contribution as long as they have earned income. These non-deductible contributions receive the benefit of the deferral of income tax on the current earnings within the IRA.

When an individual makes a non-deductible contribution to an IRA, the individual has an adjusted taxable basis in the IRA. Withdrawals from the IRA will consist partially of account earnings that have not been subject to income tax and partially of return of adjusted taxable basis for which the individual has already paid income tax.

Individuals who have non-deductible IRA contributions should file Form 8606 with their federal income tax return. This form should be filed each year to track the adjusted taxable basis of an individual's IRA account (see lines 1 and 2 on Form 8606).

---

11. However, Deanna is considered covered for purposes of the coverage rules.
12. Qualified non-elective contributions (QNECs) are contributions made to non-highly compensated employees so that the plan sponsor meets the ADP requirements.
13. 408(o)(2)(B)(ii).

EXHIBIT 9.7 **FORM 8606**

Form **8606**	**Nondeductible IRAs**	OMB No. 1545-1007
Department of the Treasury Internal Revenue Service (99)	▶ See separate instructions. ▶ Attach to Form 1040, Form 1040A, or Form 1040NR.	20**04** Attachment Sequence No. **48**

Name. If married, file a separate form for each spouse required to file Form 8606. See page 5 of the instructions. | Your social security number

Fill in Your Address Only if You Are Filing This Form by Itself and Not With Your Tax Return ▷

Home address (number and street, or P.O. box if mail is not delivered to your home) | Apt. no.

City, town or post office, state, and ZIP code

Part I   Nondeductible Contributions to Traditional IRAs and Distributions From Traditional, SEP, and SIMPLE IRAs

Complete this part only if:
- You made nondeductible contributions to a traditional IRA for 2004,
- You took distributions from a traditional, SEP, or SIMPLE IRA in 2004 (other than a rollover, conversion, recharacterization, or return of certain contributions) **and** you made nondeductible contributions to a traditional IRA in 2004 or an earlier year, **or**
- You converted part, but not all, of your traditional, SEP, and SIMPLE IRAs to Roth IRAs in 2004 (excluding any portion you recharacterized) **and** you made nondeductible contributions to a traditional IRA in 2004 or an earlier year.

1	Enter your nondeductible contributions to traditional IRAs for 2004, including those made for 2004 from January 1, 2005, through April 15, 2005 (see page 5 of the instructions)	**1**	
2	Enter your total basis in traditional IRAs (see page 5 of the instructions)	**2**	
3	Add lines 1 and 2	**3**	

In 2004, did you take a distribution from traditional, SEP, or SIMPLE IRAs or make a Roth IRA conversion?
— **No** ⟶ Enter the amount from line 3 on line 14. Do not complete the rest of Part I.
— **Yes** ⟶ Go to line 4.

4	Enter those contributions included on line 1 that were made from January 1, 2005, through April 15, 2005	**4**	
5	Subtract line 4 from line 3	**5**	
6	Enter the value of **all** your traditional, SEP, and SIMPLE IRAs as of December 31, 2004, plus any outstanding rollovers (see page 6 of the instructions)	**6**	
7	Enter your distributions from traditional, SEP, and SIMPLE IRAs in 2004. **Do not** include rollovers, conversions to a Roth IRA, certain returned contributions, or recharacterizations of traditional IRA contributions (see page 6 of the instructions)	**7**	
8	Enter the net amount you converted from traditional, SEP, and SIMPLE IRAs to Roth IRAs in 2004. **Do not** include amounts converted that you later recharacterized (see page 6 of the instructions). Also enter this amount on line 16	**8**	
9	Add lines 6, 7, and 8	**9**	
10	Divide line 5 by line 9. Enter the result as a decimal rounded to at least 3 places. If the result is 1.000 or more, enter "1.000" . . .	**10**	× .
11	Multiply line 8 by line 10. This is the nontaxable portion of the amount you converted to Roth IRAs. Also enter this amount on line 17	**11**	
12	Multiply line 7 by line 10. This is the nontaxable portion of your distributions that you did not convert to a Roth IRA	**12**	
13	Add lines 11 and 12. This is the nontaxable portion of all your distributions	**13**	
14	Subtract line 13 from line 3. This is **your total basis in traditional IRAs for 2004 and earlier years**	**14**	
15	**Taxable amount.** Subtract line 12 from line 7. Also include this amount on Form 1040, line 15b; Form 1040A, line 11b; or Form 1040NR, line 16b	**15**	

Note: *You may be subject to an additional 10% tax on the amount on line 15 if you were under age 59½ at the time of the distribution (see page 7 of the instructions).*

For Paperwork Reduction Act Notice, see page 8 of the instructions.   Cat. No. 63966F   Form **8606** (2004)

FORM 8606

Part II 2004 Conversions From Traditional, SEP, or SIMPLE IRAs to Roth IRAs

Complete this part if you converted part or all of your traditional, SEP, and SIMPLE IRAs to a Roth IRA in 2004 (excluding any portion you recharacterized).

Caution: *If your modified adjusted gross income is over $100,000 **or** you are married filing separately and you lived with your spouse at any time in 2004, you **cannot** convert any amount from traditional, SEP, or SIMPLE IRAs to Roth IRAs for 2004. If you erroneously made a conversion, you must recharacterize (correct) it (see page 7 of the instructions).*

16	If you completed Part I, enter the amount from line 8. Otherwise, enter the net amount you converted from traditional, SEP, and SIMPLE IRAs to Roth IRAs in 2004. **Do not** include amounts you later recharacterized back to traditional, SEP, or SIMPLE IRAs in 2004 or 2005 (see page 7 of the instructions)	16
17	If you completed Part I, enter the amount from line 11. Otherwise, enter your basis in the amount on line 16 (see page 7 of the instructions)	17
18	**Taxable amount.** Subtract line 17 from line 16. Also include this amount on Form 1040, line 15b; Form 1040A, line 11b; or Form 1040NR, line 16b	18

Part III Distributions From Roth IRAs

Complete this part only if you took a distribution from a Roth IRA in 2004 (other than a rollover, recharacterization, or return of certain contributions—see page 7 of the instructions).

19	Enter your total nonqualified distributions from Roth IRAs in 2004 including any qualified first-time homebuyer distributions (see page 7 of the instructions)	19
20	Qualified first-time homebuyer expenses (see page 7 of the instructions). **Do not** enter more than $10,000	20
21	Subtract line 20 from line 19. If zero or less, enter -0- and skip lines 22 through 25	21
22	Enter your basis in Roth IRA contributions (see page 7 of the instructions)	22
23	Subtract line 22 from line 21. If zero or less, enter -0- and skip lines 24 and 25. If more than zero, you may be subject to an additional tax (see page 8 of the instructions)	23
24	Enter your basis in Roth IRA conversions (see page 8 of the instructions)	24
25	**Taxable amount.** Subtract line 24 from line 23. If zero or less, enter -0-. Also include this amount on Form 1040, line 15b; Form 1040A, line 11b; or Form 1040NR, line 16b	25

Sign Here Only if You Are Filing This Form by Itself and Not With Your Tax Return	Under penalties of perjury, I declare that I have examined this form, including accompanying attachments, and to the best of my knowledge and belief, it is true, correct, and complete.

▶ Your signature   ▶ Date

Form **8606** (2004)

Printed on recycled paper

Distributions from Traditional IRAs

Generally, distributions from traditional IRAs are taxed as ordinary income. The one exception is for distributions consisting of a combination of tax-deferred earnings and the return of adjusted taxable basis that results from either non-deductible IRA contributions or rollovers of contributions from qualified plan balances that included after-tax contributions (such as thrift plans). In such cases, each distribution will consist of a combination of return of **adjusted taxable basis** (ATB) and ordinary income. The ratio of return of ATB is equal to the ratio of the total ATB of the account before the withdrawal to the fair market value of the total account balance. The calculation will be made each year on Form 8606 (see lines 1-12).

$$\text{Ratio of ATB} = \frac{\text{ATB before withdrawal}}{\text{FMV of account at withdrawal}}$$

EXAMPLE 9.19

Andy has a traditional IRA with an account balance of $100,000. Over the years, he made after-tax contributions of $25,000, and the remaining $75,000 is attributable to pretax contributions and earnings. Therefore, Andy has an adjustable taxable basis of $25,000 because that is the amount contributed after tax. When Andy begins receiving distributions, the assets distributed will be partially a return of basis and partially ordinary income. The ratio is calculated by dividing the ATB over the fair market value ($25,000/$100,000 = ¼). Thus, if Andy took a $10,000 distribution then ¼ ($2,500) would be a return of basis and ¾ ($7,500) would be ordinary income.

Required Minimum Distributions

Traditional IRA distributions can be taken at anytime, but the **required minimum distribution** (RMD) rules state that the distributions must (except Roth IRAs) begin by April 1st of the year following the year in which the owner attains the age of 70½.[14] The minimum distribution rules require that traditional IRA owners begin receiving distributions from their accounts based on the same factors as discussed in Chapter 8 for qualified plans. These rules prohibit a taxpayer from continuing to indefinitely accrue tax-deferred earnings within their traditional IRA. Distributions that are not taken are subject to a 50 percent excise tax.

---

14. The minimum distribution rules do not apply to Roth IRAs.

The 10 Percent Penalty and its Exceptions for Early Withdrawals

By allowing deductions for traditional IRA contributions and by allowing balances in IRAs (both traditional and Roth) to grow on a tax-deferred basis, the government forfeits current income (tax revenue) to encourage taxpayers to save for retirement in their IRAs. The government also encourages taxpayers to leave funds in their traditional and Roth IRAs until retirement by imposing a 10 percent premature withdrawal penalty for distributions prior to age 59½. Therefore, traditional and Roth IRA distributions before the age of 59½ will be subject to the 10 percent penalty unless a specific exception applies. Exhibit 9.8 summarizes the exceptions to the 10 percent withdrawal penalty for distributions from IRAs and qualified plans. Exhibit 9.9 provides a comparison of the early withdrawal penalty for qualified plans and IRAs.

SUMMARY OF 10 PERCENT PENALTY EXCEPTIONS

EXHIBIT 9.8

Applies to Distributions from:	Exception to 10% Early Withdrawal Penalty
Both Qualified Plans & IRAs	Death
Both Qualified Plans & IRAs	Attainment of age 59½
Both Qualified Plans & IRAs	Disability
Both Qualified Plans & IRAs	Substantially equal periodic payments (Section 72(t))
Both Qualified Plans & IRAs	Medical expenses that exceed 7.5% of AGI
Both Qualified Plans & IRAs	Qualified Domestic Relations Order (QDRO)
Only Qualified Plans	Attainment of age 55 and separation from service
Only IRAs	Higher education expenses
Only IRAs	First time home purchase (up to $10,000)
Only IRAs	Payment of health insurance premiums by unemployed

COMPARISON OF QUALIFIED PLANS AND IRAS (10% PENALTY)

EXHIBIT 9.9

Exception to 10% Early Withdrawal Penalty ✗ = Not Permitted	Qualified Plans	Traditional IRAs	Roth IRAs
Death	✓	✓	✓
Attainment of age 59½	✓	✓	✓
Disability	✓	✓	✓
Substantially equal payments	✓	✓	✓
Medical expenses that exceed 7.5% AGI	✓	✓	✓
Qualified Domestic Relations Order (QDRO)	✓	✓	✓
Attainment of age 55 and separated from service	✓	✗	✗
Education expenses	✗	✓	✓
First time home purchase (up to $10,000)	✗	✓	✓
Payment of health insurance premiums by unemployed	✗	✓	✓

The 10 percent penalty does not apply if a distribution is received after the owner attains the age of 59½, by a beneficiary after the account owner's death, because of the account owner's disability, for medical expenses in excess of 7.5 percent of the participant's AGI, or if the distribution is part of a series of substantially equal periodic payments. The final exceptions from the 10 percent penalty apply only for withdrawals from IRAs (not qualified plans) for higher education expenses, for acquisition costs of a first home (up to $10,000), and for health insurance premiums for the unemployed.

Higher Education Expenses

The education expense exception is for higher education expenses (post secondary educational institutions) for the benefit of the taxpayer, taxpayer's spouse, child, or grandchild at an eligible educational institution. Qualified expenses include tuition, fees, books, supplies. Room and board will also be included if the student is at least half time.[15]

First Time Home Purchase

The first time home purchase exception applies up to a lifetime maximum of $10,000 for the acquisition of a home for the taxpayer, taxpayer's spouse, child, grandchild, or ancestor of such taxpayer or taxpayer's spouse. A first time home buyer is defined as an individual (and if married, such individual's spouse) that had no present ownership interest in a principal residence during the 2-year period ending on the date of acquisition of the principal residence to which the exception applies.[16]

Health Insurance Premiums

The payment of health insurance premiums by an unemployed individual is not subject to the 10 percent penalty. The individual must have received unemployment compensation for 12 consecutive weeks under any Federal or State unemployment compensation law.[17] The exception no longer applies when the individual has regained employment and has been employed for 60 days.

IRA ANNUITY V. IRA ACCOUNTS

An individual retirement annuity is different than a traditional IRA account because it is an annuity contract or endowment contract issued by an insurance company. However, an IRA annuity must meet certain similar requirements regarding transferability, nonforfeitability, premiums, and distributions.

Transferability and Nonforfeitability

An IRA annuity is not transferable by the owner and the benefits must not be forfeitable. The proceeds from an IRA annuity must be received by the owner or by a beneficiary of the contract. Similar to traditional IRAs, these IRA annuities cannot be pledged as collateral nor can loans be taken from the contract.

---

15. IRC Section 529(e)(3).
16. IRC Section 72(t)(8)(D)(i)(I).
17. IRC Section 72(t)(2)(D)(i).

Premiums

The annual premiums for an IRA annuity may not exceed $4,000 for 2005. The premiums for the IRA annuity cannot be fixed. In the event that premium payments cease, the owner must be given the right to receive a paid up annuity and the owner of the annuity must also be allowed to forego payment of the annuity premium.

Distributions

The distribution rules for IRA annuities are the same as for traditional IRAs. This includes the required minimum distribution beginning April 1st of the year following the year the owner attains the age of 70½ and the 10 percent penalty for distributions before age 59½.

ROTH IRAS

Roth IRAs were created by the Taxpayer Relief Act of 1997. Roth IRAs are very attractive because, although the contributions to a Roth IRA are not deductible, qualified distributions (defined below) from Roth IRA accounts consist solely of non-taxable income. In other words, the tax-deferred earnings may be distributed without ever being subjected to income tax. Additionally, Roth IRAs may be funded after the owner attains the age of 70½ and are not subject to the required minimum distribution rules during the owner's life.

Roth IRAs and traditional IRAs share many of the same features and characteristics. The same contribution limitations that apply to traditional IRAs also apply to Roth IRAs, and this limit is an aggregate limit that includes contributions to both types of IRAs. Roth IRAs and traditional IRAs also share the prohibited transaction rules (as discussed below), the permitted investment rules, and the definition of earned income.

Key Concepts

Underline/highlight the answers to these questions as you read:

1. What is the difference between a traditional IRA and an individual retirement annuity?

2. How does a Roth IRA differ from a traditional IRA?

3. What are the income limits for Roth IRA contributions?

4. How can qualified plan assets be converted to a Roth IRA?

5. What are the requirements for a distribution from a Roth IRA to be classified as a qualified distribution?

EXHIBIT 9.10 **SIMILARITIES AND DIFFERENCES OF TRADITIONAL V. ROTH IRAS**

	Traditional IRA	**Roth IRA**
Earned Income	✓	✓
Contributions	✓	✓
Deductions	✓	N/A
Investment Choices	✓	✓
Minimum Distribution Rules	During life and after death	Only after death
Prohibited Transactions	✓	✓

✓ = *same*

Taxpayers can fund Roth IRAs by either making cash contributions or by converting traditional IRAs into Roth IRAs. Note that qualified plans cannot be converted to Roth IRAs. If converting to a Roth IRA is desired, it is necessary to first convert the qualified plan to a traditional IRA and then convert the traditional IRA to the Roth IRA. When funding a Roth IRA, dollar limitations prevent contributions and conversions beyond certain income levels. As a result, high net worth taxpayers generally cannot establish or fund Roth IRAs. However, Roth IRAs are a proven powerful planning tool for taxpayers within the appropriate income limits.

EXAMPLE 9.20

Assume Laura contributes $4,000 per year for 30 years to a Roth IRA earning 10 percent. After 30 years she will have contributed $120,000 but have an account balance of $657,976. The account balance is over five times the amount of the contribution, and all distributions will be tax free (if the distributions are qualified).

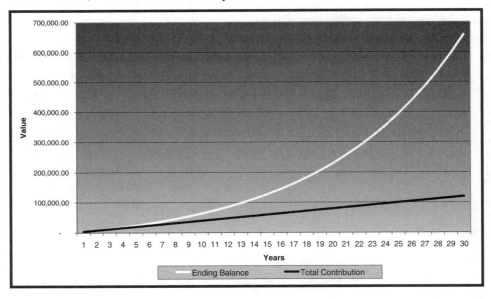

Contributions

Both Roth IRAs and traditional IRAs share an annual single contribution limit and use the same definition for earned income. However, taxpayers may only contribute to a Roth IRA if they fall within the prescribed income limits. For single individuals, the limit, based on AGI, ranges from $95,000 to $110,000. If a single taxpayer's adjusted gross income is below $95,000, then a full contribution can be made to a Roth IRA. If the taxpayer's AGI exceeds $110,000, then the taxpayer may not contribute to a Roth IRA. If the taxpayer's AGI falls between the limits, then the contribution limited is based on a phaseout calculation. For married taxpayers filing jointly, the AGI limit ranges from $150,000 to $160,000, so a couple (both below the age of 50) filing jointly could contribute $8,000 to their Roth IRAs for the year 2006 if their income is below $150,000.

FUNDING ROTH IRAs (AGI LIMITS)

EXHIBIT 9.11

Contribution AGI Phaseout Limit ($)		Conversion AGI Limit ($)	
Single	$95,000 – $110,000	Single	$100,000
Married Filing Jointly	$150,000 – $160,000	Married Filing Jointly	$100,000
Married Filing Separate	$0 – $10,000	Married Filing Separate	Not Available

Roth 401(k)

For years beginning after 2005, a 401(k) plan may include a Roth contribution program in which employees will be able to make after-tax contributions. Similar to how the Roth feature is beneficial for IRAs, it is expected to be beneficial for 401(k) plans.

Conversions

Taxpayers are permitted to convert traditional IRAs to Roth IRAs if their AGI is less than or equal to $100,000. This same dollar limitation applies to single taxpayers and married taxpayers filing jointly and does not include the conversion amount in the calculation of AGI. Married taxpayers filing separate returns are not eligible to convert a traditional IRA to a Roth IRA.

By converting a traditional IRA to a Roth IRA, a taxpayer hopes to receive distributions that are completely tax free. However, at the time of the conversion, the taxpayer must include the value of the **conversion** amount in their taxable income. Therefore, the taxpayer is making the choice to forego funds (those used to pay the tax) by paying tax today to save tax in the future. Generally, this is an effective strategy when the person converting to the Roth has lower current income tax rates than their future expected tax.

Recharacterized Contributions

IRA owners may **recharacterize** certain **contributions**[18] made to one type of IRA as made to a different type of IRA for a taxable year. For example, this may occur if a contribution is made to a traditional IRA, and the owner subsequently decides that it is better to contribute the funds to a Roth IRA. The individual can transfer the contribution (or a portion of the contribution) and

---

18.   Treas. Reg. 1.408A.

its attributable earnings in a trustee-to-trustee transfer from the trustee of the FIRST IRA to the trustee of the Roth IRA (the SECOND IRA), and the individual can elect to treat the contribution as having been made to the SECOND IRA, instead of to the FIRST IRA, for federal income tax purposes.

These types of recharacterizations must be made by the due date of the individual's tax return (including extensions). However, the IRS has made exceptions in certain cases.

EXAMPLE 9.21

Andrea contributes $4,000 to her traditional IRA. Prior to the due date (plus extensions) for filing her federal income tax return, she decides that she would prefer to contribute to a Roth IRA instead. Andrea instructs the trustee of the traditional IRA to transfer in a trustee-to-trustee transfer the amount of the contribution, plus attributable earnings, to the trustee of a Roth IRA. She notifies the trustee of the traditional IRA and the trustee of the Roth IRA that she is recharacterizing the $4,000 contribution. On her federal income tax return, Andrea treats the $4,000 as having been contributed to the Roth IRA and not the traditional IRA.

Contributions to Roth IRAs can also be recharacterized as traditional IRA contributions. This type of recharacterization might apply in the event that a taxpayer made a contribution to a Roth IRA because he anticipated meeting the income limitations and later realized that his income exceeded the income limits.

EXAMPLE 9.22

Kristi, who is single, contributes $4,000 to her Roth IRA for 2006. However, she receives a significantly larger bonus because of her hard work and dedication to the firm. This unusually large bonus causes her income to exceed $110,000 (the income limit for contributions to Roth IRAs). As a result, she recharacterizes the contribution to the Roth IRA as a contribution to her traditional IRA. If Kristi is not covered by a qualified plan, she can deduct this contribution on her federal tax return. However, if she is covered by a qualified plan, then she would effectively be making an after-tax contribution to her traditional IRA and would be required to file Form 8606.

Distributions

A distribution from a Roth IRA is not included in the owner's gross income if it is a "**qualified distribution**." In addition, qualified distributions from Roths are not subject to the 10 percent early withdrawal penalty.

Qualified Distributions

A qualified distribution is a distribution from a Roth IRA that satisfies both of the following tests:

1. The distribution must be made after a five-taxable-year period (which begins January 1st of the taxable year for which the first regular contribution is made to any Roth IRA of the individual or, if earlier, January 1st of the taxable year in which the first conversion contribution is made to any Roth IRA of the individual), **AND**
2. The distribution satisfies one of the following four requirements:
   - Made on or after the date on which the owner attains the age 59½;
   - Made to a beneficiary or estate of the owner on or after the date of the owner's death;
   - Is attributable to the owner being disabled; or
   - For first time home purchase (lifetime cap of $10,000 for first time homebuyers includes taxpayer, spouse, child, or grandchild who has not owned a house for at least 2 years).

On July 5th, 2006, Tom Hall established a Roth IRA for year 2006 with a $1,200 contribution. Since this was his first contribution to a Roth IRA, his five-year period begins on January 1st, 2006.	**EXAMPLE 9.23**

On February 16th, 2006, Mary made an initial contribution of $900 to a Roth IRA. She made the contribution for the 2005 tax year (recall that a taxpayer can make contributions until April 15th of the following year to a traditional or Roth IRA for the prior tax year). Mary's five-year period begins on January 1st, 2005 even though she made her initial contribution in 2006 because the contribution was for 2005.	**EXAMPLE 9.24**

The five-taxable-year period is not re-determined when the owner of a Roth IRA dies. Thus, the beneficiary of the Roth IRA would only have to wait until the end of the original five-taxable-year period for the distribution to be a qualified distribution. Prior to the end of the five-year period, minimum distribution could be taken from the contribution and conversion layers without tax or penalty.

Nonqualified Distributions

Any amount distributed from an individual's Roth IRA that is not a qualified distribution is treated as made in the following order (determined as of the end of a taxable year and exhausting each category before moving to the following category):

- from regular contributions (i.e. the $4,000 for 2005 annual contributions),
- from conversion contributions on a first-in-first-out basis, and then
- from earnings.

In the event a distribution is not a qualified distribution, the first layer will be return of adjusted taxable basis (from after-tax contributions), followed by post-tax conversion contributions. Since these contributions have already been taxed there will be no income tax consequences, the final layer consists of the tax-deferred earnings on contributions and conversions within the Roth IRA. Such earnings will be subject to tax and penalty if the distribution is not a qualified distribution.

EXHIBIT 9.12   **ROTH DISTRIBUTIONS**

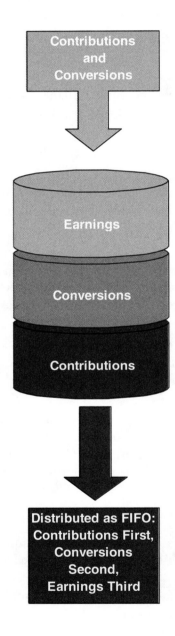

Distributions will generally not be taxable to the extent that total distributions do not exceed total contributions and conversions. However, if an individual takes a distribution that is not a qualified distributions and the amount of the distribution is neither contributed to another Roth IRA in a qualified rollover contribution nor constitutes a corrective distribution, part of the distributions may be includible in the individual's gross income. The amount included in the owner's gross income is the amount by which the total of all distributions (qualified or not) taken through the years exceeds the amount of all contributions and conversions to all of the individual's Roth IRAs.

ROTH DISTRIBUTION ORDER FLOW DIAGRAM

EXHIBIT 9.13

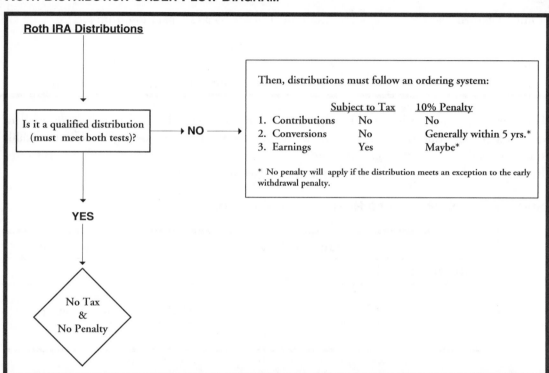

10 Percent Early Withdrawal Penalty

The 10 percent early withdrawal penalty will generally apply to any portion of a distribution from a Roth IRA that is includible in gross income (such as distributions that consist of earnings within the Roth IRA). The penalty also applies to a nonqualified distribution, even if it is not includible in gross income, to the extent it is allocable to a conversion contribution if the distribution is made within the five-taxable-year period beginning with the first day of the individual's taxable year in which the conversion contribution was made.

It is important to note that although a nonqualified distribution may be subject to the 10 percent penalty based on the Roth IRA rules, the penalty may be avoided if the distribution falls within one of the exceptions.

Recall that the exceptions to the 10 percent early withdrawal penalty include the following:

Applies to Distributions from:	Exception to 10% Early Withdrawal Penalty
Both Qualified Plans & IRAs	Death
Both Qualified Plans & IRAs	Attainment of age 59½
Both Qualified Plans & IRAs	Disability
Both Qualified Plans & IRAs	Substantially equal payments periodic payments
Both Qualified Plans & IRAs	Medical expenses that exceed 7.5% of AGI
Both Qualified Plans & IRAs	Qualified Domestic Relations Order (QDRO)
Only Qualified Plans	Attainment of age 55 and separation from service
Only IRAs	Higher education expenses
Only IRAs	First time home purchase (up to $10,000)
Only IRAs	Payment of health insurance premiums by unemployed

For example, a distribution could avoid the 10 percent penalty if the proceeds were used for qualified higher education expenses or to pay for certain medical costs. The following table summarizes the treatment from the standpoint of taxation and penalties of distributions from a Roth IRA to the extent the distribution is not a qualified distribution.

EXHIBIT 9.14 **SUMMARY OF NONQUALIFIED ROTH IRA DISTRIBUTIONS**

	Subject to Taxation?	Subject to 10% Penalty?
Contributions	No	No
Conversions	No	Yes Within five years of conversion*
Earnings	Yes	Yes*

Penalty will not apply if the distribution falls within the exceptions listed above.

EXAMPLE 9.25

Joyce, age 45, contributed a total of $10,000 to her Roth IRA beginning six years ago. She also converted a traditional IRA with a balance of $25,000 to a Roth IRA two years ago. Her current account balance in both Roth IRAs is $43,000. If she receives a complete distribution from both of these Roth IRAs and uses the proceeds to pay for her son's college tuition, then the distribution will have the following tax treatment:

The distribution does not meet both of the requirements of a qualified distribution. Therefore, the earnings portion of the distribution ($8,000) is subject to ordinary income tax, but none of the distribution will be subject to the 10 percent early withdrawal penalty. The penalty does not apply because the proceeds are being used for qualified higher education expenses, one of the exceptions to the 10 percent early withdrawal penalty.

EXAMPLE 9.26

Assume the same facts as above, except that Joyce took the distribution from her Roth IRAs to be used as a down payment on her son's new Porsche sports car. The distribution will have the following tax treatment:

The distribution does not meet both of the requirements of a qualified distribution. Therefore, the earnings portion of the distribution ($8,000) is subject to ordinary income tax. In addition, the 10% early withdrawal penalty applies to the conversion portion of the distribution because she has converted from a traditional IRA to a Roth IRA within the last five years. Therefore, the $8,000 of earnings that is considered taxable income is also subject to the 10 percent early withdrawal penalty and the $25,000 conversion is subject to the 10 percent penalty but is not taxable.

If Joyce was over the age of 59½, then the distribution would have been a qualified distribution and none of the distribution would be subject to ordinary income tax or penalty. The year of the conversion is only a factor when the distribution is not a qualified distribution. In this case, the Roth IRA was established six years ago, and Joyce was over 59½, thus the distribution was a qualified distribution.

<table>
<tr><td>

EXAMPLE 9.27

</td><td>

Brad is 61 years old and first contributed to a Roth IRA three years ago. His contributions to the Roth IRA total $6,000. In addition, Brad converted his traditional IRA to a Roth IRA last year. The conversion was in the amount of $20,000. If Brad takes a $35,000 distribution from the Roth IRA, it will have the following tax treatment:

The distribution has not met the five-year requirement to be a qualified distribution. Therefore, the portion of the distribution that consists of earnings ($9,000) is subject to ordinary income tax, but none of the distribution will be subject to the 10 percent early withdrawal penalty. The penalty does not apply because Brad is over the age of 59½, one of the exceptions to the 10 percent early withdrawal penalty.

</td></tr>
</table>

COMPARING ROTH IRAs TO TRADITIONAL IRAs

Two important distinctions when comparing Roth IRAs to traditional IRAs are:

1. Unlike traditional IRAs, an individual can make a contribution to a Roth IRA after the age of 70½, and
2. The required minimum distribution rules do not apply to Roth IRAs during life.

Key Concepts

Underline/highlight the answers to these questions as you read:

1. What are the limitations on the types of investments that can be held in an IRA?

2. What are the rollover rules for transferring balances from a qualified plan to an IRA?

3. What are the distribution rules for an IRA?

4. What transactions are considered prohibited for an IRA?

OTHER IRA ISSUES

Investments

Individuals have a plethora of options regarding the investment choices for assets purchased or held in an IRA. Investments in cash, stocks, bonds, and even options are permitted. However, custodians often limit IRA owners from investing in certain option contracts, especially naked options, within an IRA.

Although there is great freedom of investment choices, certain types of investments are prohibited and are not allowed to be held within an IRA, mainly life insurance and collectibles.[19] If either life insurance or collectibles are purchased within an IRA, the value of the purchase is treated as a distribution from the IRA account and is subject to tax and/or penalty.

---

19. IRC Section 408(a)(3).

Collectibles include all of the following:[20]

- any work of art;
- any rug or antique;
- any metal or gem;
- any stamp or coin; and
- any alcoholic beverage.

An exception to the collectibles rule exists for certain coins and bullion. U.S. gold, silver, and platinum minted coins, such as American Gold, Silver, and Platinum Eagle coins, are permitted to be held in an IRA account. However, coins of most foreign countries, such as South African Krugerrands, are considered collectibles and are therefore not permissible investments for an IRA. In addition, investments in gold, silver, platinum, or palladium bullion are permitted.

IRA Rollovers

There are a variety of rollover rules that facilitate taxpayers transferring their retirement balances from one type of plan or account to another. These rules address transfers from qualified plans and from IRAs. EGTRRA 2001 greatly enhanced the portability and flexibility of transferring retirement funds.

Distributions from Qualified Plans

When an individual terminates employment with the plan sponsor of a qualified plan, the individual may roll the qualified plan balance over into an IRA. Typically, an IRA that holds funds that have been transferred from a qualified plan is referred to as a "conduit" IRA or an IRA rollover account. The funds in such a conduit IRA are allowed to be rolled back into another qualified plan, assuming the new plan permits such rollovers.

> Craig leaves his employer, Planet Source, where he was a participant in a qualified plan. Craig can rollover his balance in his qualified plan into an IRA, which is generally referred to as a conduit IRA. Once Craig finds a new employer, he can rollover the funds in the conduit IRA into the new qualified plan (assuming that the plan permits such a rollover contribution). Alternatively, Craig could maintain the conduit IRA until he was 70½, at which point he would be required to begin taking minimum distributions.

EXAMPLE 9.28

It is important to consider the assets that are being transferred from the qualified plan to the IRA. If assets that are not permitted to be held in an IRA, although allowed in a qualified plan, are rolled into an IRA, then there may be a deemed distribution that will be subject to taxable income and possibly the 10 percent premature withdrawal penalty. For example, life insurance can be held in a qualified plan but not in an IRA.

---

20.   IRC Section 408(m).

If a participant in a qualified plan wishes to convert to a Roth IRA through a rollover, the participant must first roll the qualified plan proceeds into a traditional IRA and then to the Roth IRA.

Many taxpayers and advisors often leave funds in a conduit IRA and never roll the funds over to another qualified plan because there are few real benefits to having funds in a qualified plan versus having funds in an IRA. The following exhibit identifies some of the benefits of a qualified plan versus an IRA.

EXHIBIT 9.15 COMPARISON OF BENEFITS FOR QUALIFIED PLANS V. IRAS

Benefits	Qualified Plan	IRA
Ten-year forward averaging and Pre-1974 capital gain treatment permitted?	Yes, if participant is born prior to 1/1/36	No
Loans may be permitted?	Yes, if plan permits loans	No
Assets are protected from creditors (ERISA or state law)?	Yes, ERISA	Yes, if resident state law provides or in selected situations under the bankruptcy laws.
Assets can be invested in life insurance?	Yes	No
Participants/owners have complete discretion of investment decisions?	Generally No	Yes
60 day rollover?	No	Yes

As discussed in Chapter 7, although 10-year forward averaging and capital gain treatment for pre-1974 participation is available for lump-sum distributions from a qualified plan, it is only available for those taxpayers born prior to January 1, 1936. Thus, the number of taxpayers who would qualify for **10-year forward averaging** or **pre-1974 capital gain treatment** is minimal. One advantage of a qualified plan is that participants may be able to withdraw a portion of the plan balance as a loan. However, the plan must provide for this feature and many plans do not permit loans. Although IRAs do not allow for loans, they do permit a rollover of 60 days that can, in effect, be a short-term loan (see discussion below). One of the most advantageous features of a qualified plan is the creditor protection that is provided by ERISA. This type of protection is not available to IRAs although many states do provide some level of creditor protection for the assets held in IRAs and the Supreme Court has provided some protection under the bankruptcy laws as discussed below.

Employee after-tax contributions from a qualified plan may be rolled over into another qualified plan or a traditional IRA for years after December 31, 2001. In the case of a rollover from a qualified plan to another qualified plan, the rollover is permitted only through a direct transfer. In addition, a qualified plan is not permitted to accept rollovers of after-tax contributions unless the plan provides separate accounting for such contributions and earnings. After-tax contributions, including nondeductible contributions to an IRA, are not permitted to be rolled over from an IRA into a qualified plan or 403(b) plan.

60-day Period

Taxpayers have the ability to take a distribution from an IRA at any time. However, distributions from IRAs will generally be taxed as ordinary income and may be subject to the 10 percent early withdrawal penalty (as discussed above). If an individual takes a distribution from an IRA, the distribution must generally be rolled back into another IRA within 60 days from the original distribution. (Although, the IRS may waive the 60-day requirement in the event the delay is caused by casualty, disaster, or other events beyond the taxpayers control.) This rule permits taxpayers to receive a distribution, make use of the funds for a period of 60 days, and then redeposit the funds into an IRA without any tax consequences.

Generally, if the taxpayer makes a tax-free rollover of any part of a distribution from a traditional IRA they cannot make another tax-free rollover from that same IRA or the same funds within a 1-year period. (Certain exceptions apply for failed institutions.) The 1-year period begins on the date the taxpayer received the IRA distribution, not on the date they rolled it back into an IRA.

> Kole has two traditional IRAs, IRA-1 and IRA-2. Kole makes a tax-free rollover of a distribution from IRA-1 into a new traditional IRA (IRA-3). Kole cannot within 1 year of the distribution from IRA-1, make a tax-free rollover of any distribution from either IRA-1 or IRA-3 into another traditional IRA. However, the rollover from IRA-1 into IRA-3 does not prevent Kole from making a tax-free rollover from IRA-2 into any other traditional IRA. This is because Kole has not, within the last year, rolled over tax-free any distribution from IRA-2 or made a tax-free rollover into IRA-2.

EXAMPLE 9.29

Rollover to Qualified Plans

In the past, only funds held in a conduit IRA could be rolled back into a qualified plan. However, distributions after December 31, 2001 from an IRA are now permitted to be rolled over into a qualified plan, section 403(b) annuity, or governmental section 457 plan. Although it is now permissible to roll an IRA balance into a qualified plan, 403(b), or 457 plan, these plans are not required to accept such rollovers.

Lump-sum distributions from qualified plans may receive special tax treatment, including pre-74 capital gains treatment and 10-year forward averaging. However, a distribution from a qualified plan is not eligible for capital gains or averaging treatment if there was a rollover to the plan that would not have been permitted under present law.   Thus, in order to preserve capital gains and averaging treatment for a qualified plan distribution that is rolled over, the rollover would have to be made to a conduit IRA and then rolled back into a qualified plan. In effect, the IRS does not permit taxpayers to receive special tax treatment on funds held in an IRA that would never have qualified for special tax treatment.

ERISA Protection v. State Law Protection

As discussed in Chapter 3, qualified plans are protected by ERISA, which provides that a participant's accounts and benefits under the plan may not be alienated or assigned.[21] However, IRAs are not afforded this same protection because as IRAs are not exempt from creditor's claims by ERISA.

The Supreme Court ruled on April 4, 2005 that IRAs can be exempt property in a bankruptcy proceeding. Although providing some protection where there was none previously, the ruling does not provide a blanket protection for IRAs. IRAs are only exempt to the extent they are reasonably necessary for the support of the debtor or his dependents.[22] In addition, a debtor's state law may determine whether this case is applicable to the debtor. Consideration should be given to the facts and circumstances surrounding a rollover since IRAs are still not provided the same creditor protection as other qualified plans under ERISA.

Case Study 1

Rousey Et Ux v. Jacoway: Several years after petitioners deposited distributions from their pension plans into Individual Retirement Accounts (IRAs), the Rouseys filed a joint petition under Chapter 7 of the Bankruptcy Code. They sought to shield portions of their IRAs from their creditors by claiming them as exempt from the bankruptcy estate under 11 U. S. C. Section 522(d)(10)(E), which provides, inter alia, that a debtor may withdraw from the estate his "right to receive . . . a payment under a stock bonus, pension, profit sharing, annuity, or similar plan or contract on account of . . . age." Respondent Jacoway, the Bankruptcy Trustee, objected to the Rouseys' exemption and moved for turnover of the IRAs to her. The Bankruptcy Court sustained her objection and granted her motion, and the Bankruptcy Appellate Panel (BAP) agreed. The Eighth Circuit affirmed, concluding that, even if the Rouseys' IRAs were "similar plans or contracts" to the plans specified in Section 522(d)(10)(E), their IRAs gave them no right to receive payment "on account of age," but were instead savings accounts readily accessible at any time for any purpose.

However, the Supreme Court held that the Rouseys can exempt IRA assets from the bankruptcy estate because the IRAs fulfill both of the Section 522(d)(10)(E) requirements at issue here—they confer a right to receive payment on account of age and they are similar plans or contracts to those enumerated in Section 522(d)(10)(E).

---

21. ERISA Section 206(d).
22. Rousey v. Jacoway.

Prohibited Transactions

There are certain transactions that an owner or beneficiary is not permitted to engage in with an IRA. An IRA loses its tax exemption when the account ceases to be an IRA by reason of a **prohibited transaction**. If an individual or beneficiary of an IRA engages in any of the following transactions, then the account will cease to be an IRA as of the first day of the current taxable year[23]:

- Selling, exchanging, or leasing of any property to an IRA;
- Lending money to an IRA;
- Receiving unreasonable compensation for managing an IRA;
- Pledging an IRA as security for a loan;
- Borrowing money from an IRA; or
- Buying property for personal use (present or future) with IRA funds.

In the event that a prohibited transaction has occurred, the account ceases to be an IRA as of the beginning of the year and the entire balance in the IRA is treated as having been distributed.[24] In this case, the taxpayer will be subject to ordinary income tax on the entire balance and will also be subject to the 10 percent early withdrawal penalty if not otherwise exempted, as discussed above.

---

23. IRC Section 408(e)(2).
24. IRC Section 408(e)(2)(B).

A similar rule applies to an IRA annuity. If an individual borrows money against an IRA annuity contract, the individual must include the fair market value of the annuity contract as of the first day of the tax year in his gross income. The distribution may also be subject to the 10 percent early withdrawal penalty.

Transfers Incident to Divorce

If an interest in an IRA is transferred from a spouse or former spouse (transferor) to an individual (transferee) by reason of divorce, **qualified domestic relations order (QDRO)**, separate maintenance decree, or a written document related to such a decree, starting from the date of the transfer, the interest in the IRA is treated as the individual's (transferee's) IRA.[25]

However, if an owner receives a distribution from an IRA and subsequently transfers the distributed funds to the other spouse pursuant to a divorce decree, the distribution is subject to ordinary income tax and, potentially, a 10 percent premature withdrawal penalty.

If an individual is required to transfer some or all of the assets of his traditional IRA to a spouse or former spouse, there are two commonly used methods to make the transfer. The individual can instruct the custodian to simply change the name on the account to the name of the spouse or former spouse, or one spouse can direct the trustee of his IRA to transfer the funds directly to the trustee of the other spouse's IRA.

Quick Quiz

Highlight the answer to these questions:

1. Cash, stock, bonds, life insurance, and collectibles are permitted investments for IRAs.
   a. True
   b. False

2. Funds in an IRA may be transferred to a qualified plan.
   a. True
   b. False

3. IRAs are exempt from creditor's claims by ERISA.
   a. True
   b. False

4. Loans from an IRA are considered prohibited transactions.
   a. True
   b. False

False, True, False, True.

SIMPLIFIED EMPLOYEE PENSION (SEPS)

A **simplified employee pension (SEP)** is a practical retirement plan alternative to a qualified plan that can be used by small businesses and sole proprietors. SEPs are easier to establish than qualified plans and have practically no filing requirements. Because SEPs use IRAs as the receptacle for contributions, there is no trust accounting for the plan sponsor. In addition, SEPs have similar characteristics to profit sharing plans.

Because a SEP is not a qualified plan, it has some unique rules that are different than qualified plans. For example, SEPs have more liberal participation requirements than qualified plans, have a later establishment date, and have different contribution, distribution, and vesting rules.

---

25. IRC Section 408(d)(6).

PARTICIPATION

Employers that sponsor SEPs must provide benefits to almost all employees. The requirements for coverage include the following:

- Attainment of age 21 or older;
- Performance of services for three of the last five years; and
- Received compensation of at least $450 during the year.

The participation rules for SEPs mean that an employer must cover all employees that are 21 years of age, have worked for the company for a period of three years or more, and have earned more than $450 during the year. Based on this definition, even part-time employees must be covered. However, the three-year requirement allows the employer to exclude anyone who has not worked for at least three years. Therefore, if a company has high employee turnover, a SEP may be used to exclude the employees who do not remain employed for a period of at least three years.

It is important to note that contributions must be made on behalf of all employees who meet the participation rules during the calendar year whether or not they are still employed as of the end of the year and whether or not they are still alive. For example, an employee who resigned in March and earned more than $450 would be entitled to a contribution based on his earnings through his termination date.

In addition, those employees over the age of 70½ who meet the eligibility rules must also receive an employer contribution to their SEP.

As with qualified plans, the employer may impose less restrictive participation requirement for its employees than those discussed above but not more restrictive requirements.

Employees can also be excluded from participation in a SEP if they are members of any of the following groups:

- Employees covered by a union agreement if their retirement benefits were bargained for in good faith by their union and their employer.
- Nonresident alien employees who have no U.S. source earned income from their employer.

ESTABLISHMENT OF A SEP

SEPs can be established, as well as funded, for a plan year as late as the due date of the federal income tax return including extensions. Therefore, SEPs can be established for the following entities as late as the date indicated below:

Entity	Due date of return	Final extension
Sole proprietorship (Schedule C)	April 15th	October 15th
Partnership (Form 1065)	April 15th	October 15th
Corporation (Form 1120)	March 15th	September 15th
S-Corporation (Form 1120S)	March 15th	September 15th

The ability to establish a SEP as late as ten months after the tax-year end is a significant advantage over qualified plans. Recall from Chapter 8 that qualified plans must be established by December 31st of the plan year. This establishment feature allows a planner to recommend establishing a retirement plan and implementing it for the previous year.

To establish a SEP, the employer must complete three basic steps:
- A formal written agreement to provide benefits to all eligible employees must be executed.
- All eligible employees must be given notice about the SEP.
- A SEP-IRA (the receptacle account) must be set up for each eligible employee.

The standard method of complying with the first requirement is to adopt the IRS model SEP using Form 5305-SEP (See Exhibit 9.16). Using Form 5305-SEP allows the plan to be established without IRS approval or a determination letter, and the form does not have to be filed with the IRS or the Department of Labor. The plan sponsor should keep the original form. Most financial service companies, including banks, mutual funds, brokerage houses, and insurance companies, have prototype SEP documents that can be used by employers.

EXHIBIT 9.16

Form **5305-SEP** (Rev. December 2004) Department of the Treasury Internal Revenue Service	**Simplified Employee Pension—Individual Retirement Accounts Contribution Agreement** (Under section 408(k) of the Internal Revenue Code)	OMB No. 1545-0499 **Do not** file with the Internal Revenue Service

_____ makes the following agreement under section 408(k) of the
(Name of employer) Internal Revenue Code and the instructions to this form.

Article I—Eligibility Requirements (check applicable boxes—see instructions)

The employer agrees to provide discretionary contributions in each calendar year to the individual retirement account or individual retirement annuity (IRA) of all employees who are at least _____ years old (not to exceed 21 years old) and have performed services for the employer in at least _____ years (not to exceed 3 years) of the immediately preceding 5 years. This simplified employee pension (SEP) ☐ includes ☐ **does not** include employees covered under a collective bargaining agreement, ☐ includes ☐ **does not** include certain nonresident aliens, and ☐ includes ☐ **does not** include employees whose total compensation during the year is less than $450*.

Article II—SEP Requirements (see instructions)

The employer agrees that contributions made on behalf of each eligible employee will be:

A. Based only on the first $205,000* of compensation.

B. The same percentage of compensation for every employee.

C. Limited annually to the smaller of $41,000* or 25% of compensation.

D. Paid to the employee's IRA trustee, custodian, or insurance company (for an annuity contract).

_____   _____
Employer's signature and date   Name and title

According to the IRS, Form 5305-SEP cannot be used in the following situations:

- The employer currently maintains another qualified retirement plan. However, this does not prevent the employer from sponsoring a SEP.
- If IRAs have not been established for any eligible employees.
- If the employer is a member of any of the following groups (unless all eligible employees of all the members of these groups, trades, or businesses participate in the SEP):
  - An affiliated group described in section 414(m);
  - A controlled group of corporations described in section 414(b);
  - Trades or businesses under common control described in section 414(c); or
  - The employer does not pay the cost of the SEP contributions.

The employer must provide eligible employees with a copy of Form 5305-SEP, its instructions, and other information. This notification is a key element in establishing a SEP and is consistent with the establishment of qualified plans. Employees must be given notice of their rights relating to the employer's retirement plan.

CONTRIBUTIONS

Similar to profit sharing plans, employer contributions to SEPs are discretionary from year to year. Because of the discretionary nature of the contributions, SEPs are often used by small businesses that can not or do not wish to commit to a mandatory contribution every year. However, in years that a contribution is made to a SEP, a contribution must be made to all employees eligible during the year, whether or not they are employed or alive as of the end of the year.

Contributions to SEPs are made by the employer and must be made to employees' IRA accounts based on a written formula that does not discriminate in favor of highly compensated employees. However, contributions to SEPs may be integrated with Social Security (permitted disparity). The contribution, subject to the limits discussed below, made for the employee is excluded from the employee's gross income and not subject to FICA or FUTA.

The limit for contributions to a SEP is the lesser of 25 percent of an employee's compensation or $42,000[26] for 2005 ($43,000[†] for 2006, $44,000[†] for 2007, and $45,000[†] for 2008). As with qualified plans, no more than $210,000 for 2005 of compensation can be considered for purposes of contributions to a SEP. Therefore, the maximum contribution for any employee in year 2005 is $42,000. It is important to understand that an employee might receive more than 25 percent of his compensation in a qualified plan through integration or cross-testing, but an employee cannot receive more than 25 percent of his compensation in a SEP.

For self-employed individuals, the 25 percent limit converts to 20 percent ($0.25 \div 1.25$) of net self-employment income. Recall that the 25 percent limit for self-employed individuals is based on earned income, not total income.

Contributions to a SEP are included under IRC Section 415(c) for purposes of determining the annual contributions limit under IRC Section 415(c). Therefore, if the employer maintains a defined contribution qualified plan in addition to a SEP, both the SEP contribution and the qualified plan contribution are added together to determine whether or not the annual

Quick Quiz

Highlight the answer to these questions:

1. Requirements for coverage in a SEP include an employee's performance of service for three of the last five years.
   a. True
   b. False

2. Part-time employees are exempt from being included in a SEP.
   a. True
   b. False

3. Employer contributions to SEPs are discretionary and do not have to be made each year.
   a. True
   b. False

4. Employer contributions to a SEP are 100% vested.
   a. True
   b. False

True, False, True, True.

---

26. IRC Section 402(h)(2) and Section 408(j).

contributions limit ($42,000 for 2005, $43,000[†] for 2006, $44,000[†] for 2007, and $45,000[†] for 2008) has been violated.

If the employer maintains a profit sharing plan in addition to a SEP, then contributions to the SEP reduce the 25 percent limit of the profit-sharing plan. In other words, the maximum that could be contributed to a SEP and a profit-sharing plan in total cannot exceed 25 percent of total covered compensation.

Excess contributions are contributions in excess of the 25 percent or $42,000 limit for 2005 ($43,000[†] for 2006, $44,000[†] for 2007, and $45,000[†] for 2008). These excess contributions cannot be deducted in the current year but may be carried forward and deducted in a future year. However, excess contributions are generally subject to a 10 percent excise tax. This treatment is the same as with qualified plans.

DEDUCTIONS

Contributions to a SEP are deductible for the employer and excludable for the employees up to the limits discussed above. The employer's deduction for contributions to a SEP is generally claimed on the following forms:

Entity	Where to Deduct Contribution
Unincorporated business	Schedule C or Schedule F of Form 1040
Partnership	Form 1065
Corporation	Form 1120
S-Corporation	Form 1120S

The employer's deduction for contributions to a SEP is claimed on line 32 of Form 1040 if self-employed. This includes both sole proprietors and partners. Partnerships must distribute Schedule K-1 to all of its partners and passes its deduction for contributions to a SEP to the partner by way of Schedule K-1. The partner deducts this pass-through deduction on line 32 of Form 1040.

ADJUSTED GROSS INCOME SECTION OF FORM 1040

EXHIBIT 9.17

Adjusted Gross Income

23	Educator expenses (see page 26)	23
24	Certain business expenses of reservists, performing artists, and fee-basis government officials. Attach Form 2106 or 2106-EZ	24
25	IRA deduction (see page 26)	25
26	Student loan interest deduction (see page 28)	26
27	Tuition and fees deduction (see page 29)	27
28	Health savings account deduction. Attach Form 8889	28
29	Moving expenses. Attach Form 3903	29
30	One-half of self-employment tax. Attach Schedule SE	30
31	Self-employed health insurance deduction (see page 30)	31
32	Self-employed SEP, SIMPLE, and qualified plans	32
33	Penalty on early withdrawal of savings	33
34a	Alimony paid b Recipient's SSN ▶	34a
35	Add lines 23 through 34a	35
36	Subtract line 35 from line 22. This is your **adjusted gross income** ▶	36

The deduction for contributions made to a SEP on behalf of the employer will be deducted on the tax return for corporations and S-corporations as with the deduction for contributions made on behalf of the employees.

VESTING AND WITHDRAWALS

Contributions for a SEP are made to IRA accounts on behalf of employees. As a result, there is no vesting for employer contributions. Once the contribution is made to an employee's SEP-IRA, the funds within that account immediately belong to the employee.

Further, employees are able to withdraw funds in any amount from their SEP-IRA because of the nature of the account – that is because it is an IRA. This ability to withdraw funds is available at all times, including while the employee is still employed. However, if the employee does receive a distribution from the SEP-IRA, the distribution will be subject to ordinary income tax and may be subject to the early withdrawal penalty unless the distribution qualifies for any of the exceptions to the 10 percent early withdrawal penalty as discussed earlier for IRAs and Roth IRAs.

Note that contributions to SEPs are made to traditional IRA accounts and cannot be made to Roth IRA accounts.

SALARY REDUCTION SIMPLIFIED EMPLOYEE PENSION (SARSEPS)

Although SIMPLE plans were introduced to replace **SARSEPs**, which are not permitted to be established for years after 1996, many of the SARSEPs in existence prior to 1997 are still in operation. SARSEPs allow employees to elect to defer a portion of their current salary into a SEP-IRA in a similar fashion to 401(k) plans. In fact, the SARSEP deferral limit is the same as 401(k) plans. However, the SARSEP was very easy to establish and had minimal reporting and testing requirements.

To establish a SARSEP, an employer had to meet the following provisions:

- At least 50 percent of the employees eligible to participate must choose to defer a portion of their salary.
- The employer had to have no more than 25 eligible employees.
- The elective deferrals of the highly compensated employees had to meet the SARSEP ADP test (discussed below).

Key Concepts

Underline/highlight the answers to these questions as you read:

1. What provisions were required in order for an employer to establish a SARSEP?

2. How do elective deferrals into a SARSEP work with other salary deferral type plans?

SARSEP ADP Test

Under this test, the amount deferred each year by each eligible highly compensated employee as a percentage of pay (the deferral percentage) cannot be more than 125 percent of the average deferral percentage (ADP) of all nonhighly compensated employees eligible to participate.[27]

The deferral percentage equals:

ADP = Elective employee deferral ÷ Employee's compensation

Consider the following example for Affable Company:

EXAMPLE 9.30

Employee	Ownership	Compensation	Elective Deferral	ADP
A	60%	$200,000	$11,000	5.50%
B	30%	$140,000	$9,800	7.00%
C	5%	$85,000	$3,400	4.00%
D	3%	$80,000	$5,000	6.25%
E	2%	$50,000	$2,500	5.00%
F	-	$40,000	$2,000	5.00%

Employees A and B are the only highly compensated employees. Their actual deferral percentage equals 6.25 percent [(5.50 + 7.00)/2]. The other four employees are non-highly compensated and have an actual deferral percentage of 5.06 percent [(4.00 + 6.25 + 5.00 + 5.00)/4]. The plan meets the ADP test because the ADP of the HCs is less than 1.25 times the ADP of the NHCs. The ADP of the NHCs times 1.25 equals 6.33; whereas, the ADP for the HCs equals 6.25 percent.

Elective Deferral Limit

An employee cannot defer more than $14,000 for 2005 of their compensation into a SARSEP. However, those taxpayers who have attained the age of 50 by the end of the tax year may make additional catch-up contributions as detailed in the chart that follows.

---

27.   The ADP test for 401(k) plans consists of three separate tests, one of which is the 125 percent test.

EXHIBIT 9.18 | SUMMARY OF ELECTIVE DEFERRAL LIMITS

SARSEPs, 401(k) Plans, 403(b) Plans, 457 Plans			ROTH 401(k) Plans		SIMPLE Plans	
Year	Annual Deferral Limit	Catch-Up Contributions	Annual Deferral Limit	Catch-Up Contributions	Annual Deferral Limit	Catch-Up Contributions
2005	$14,000	$4,000	N/A	N/A	$10,000	$2,000
2006	$15,000	$5,000	$15,000	$5,000	Indexed in $500 increments thereafter	$2,500
2007 and beyond	Indexed in $500 increments thereafter	Indexed in $500 increments thereafter	Indexed in $500 increments thereafter	Indexed in $500 increments thereafter		Indexed in $500 increments thereafter

It is important to note that the $14,000 deferral limit for 2005 applies to the aggregate elective deferrals the employee makes for the year to a SARSEP and any of the following plans:

- Cash or deferred arrangement (401(k) plan)
- Salary reduction arrangement under a tax-sheltered annuity plan (403(b) plan)
- SIMPLE IRA plan

Quick Quiz

Highlight the answer to these questions:

1. To establish a SARSEP, an employer had to have a minimum of 25 employees.
   a. True
   b. False

2. An employee, age 40, cannot defer more than $14,000 for 2005 of their compensation into a SARSEP in a single year.
   a. True
   b. False

False, True.

This rule prevents an employee of a company who defers the maximum into his employer's 401(k) plan from also deferring salary from another source into one of the above plans. However, other income sources may be eligible to be considered for some other type of qualified plan arrangement or simplified employee pension.

If the employer makes nonelective contributions to the SARSEP, the combined employee and employer contributions cannot exceed the lesser of 25 percent of the employee's compensation or $42,000 for 2005.

EXCESS DEFERRALS

Excess deferrals in a SARSEP are elective contributions made by highly compensated employees that violate the SARSEP ADP test. The highly compensated employees must be given notice within 2½ months after the end of the plan year of their excess contributions. These deferral contributions must then be removed from the SARSEP. If the employer does not inform the highly compensated employees, then the employer must pay a 10 percent excise tax on the excess portion.

Key Terms

Adjusted Gross Income (AGI) - A tax return amount that includes an individual's income less certain deductions, known as "above-the-line" deductions. AGI is calculated before subtracting the standard or itemized deductions and the personal and dependency exemptions. The calculated AGI affects the deductibility of traditional IRA contributions and the ability to make Roth IRA contributions.

Adjusted Taxable Basis (ATB) - The portion of a distribution that is not subject to income tax. Usually, the return of after-tax contributions or nondeductible contributions.

Alimony - Support payments from one ex-spouse to the other. Alimony received is considered earned income for purposes of making IRA contributions.

Contributions - Payments to an IRA.

Conversion - When a traditional IRA is converted to a Roth IRA. At the date of conversion, an individual includes the fair market value of the traditional IRA into their adjusted gross income.

Custodians - Brokerage company, bank, or mutual fund company that holds an individual's IRA.

Earned Income - Any type of compensation where the individual has performed some level of service for an employer or is considered self-employed.

Individual Retirement Arrangement (IRA) - Two general types under present law: traditional IRAs, to which both deductible and nondeductible contributions may be made, and Roth IRAs, to which only nondeductible contributions may be made.

IRA Annuity - An annuity contract or endowment contract issued by an insurance company that follows many of the same rules for deductibility of premium payments and the limits for premium payments as a traditional IRA.

Phaseout - The AGI range that will affect the deductibility of IRA contributions and an individual's ability to make contributions to a Roth IRA.

Prohibited Transaction - Transactions that an owner or beneficiary is not permitted to engage in with an IRA.

Qualified Distribution - A distribution from a Roth IRA that is made after a five-taxable-year period and on account of the account owner's death, disability, attainment of age 59½, or first-time home purchase.

Qualified Domestic Relations Order (QDRO) - A court order related to divorce, property settlement, or child support.

Key Terms

Recharacterize - Transferring a contribution and its attributable earnings from a traditional IRA to a Roth IRA or vice versa. The recharacterization must occur by the tax return filing date including extensions for the year of the recharacterization.

Required Minimum Distribution - Requires individuals to begin taking minimum distributions when the participant attains the age of 70½.

Roth IRA - An IRA created by the Taxpayer Relief Act of 1997. Contributions to a Roth IRA are nondeductible and qualified distributions are excluded from an individual's taxable income.

SARSEP - Salary Reduction Simplified Employee Pension. A plan that can no longer be established but allowed employees to elect to defer a portion of their current salary into a SEP-IRA in a similar fashion to a 401(k) plan.

Simplified Employee Pension (SEP) - A practical retirement plan alternative to a qualified plan that can be used by small businesses and sole proprietors. It follows many of the same limits as qualified plans but may require the employer to cover more employees.

Spousal IRA - An IRA created on behalf of a spouse who does not have the necessary earned income to make a contribution to an IRA of their own but can borrow earned income from their spouse.

Traditional IRA - An IRA that may accept deductible and nondeductible contributions and whose assets grow tax-deferred until distribution.

DISCUSSION QUESTIONS

1. What is the limit on contributions to an IRA for 2005 and 2006?

2. List items of income considered earned income for purposes of IRA contributions.

3. What is a spousal IRA?

4. Why is age 70½ significant to traditional IRA contributions?

5. How are excess contributions to an IRA penalized?

6. Discuss the ability to deduct a contribution made to a traditional IRA given a person that is not covered by a qualified retirement plan.

7. Discuss the ability to deduct a contribution made to a traditional IRA when an employee is covered by a qualified retirement plan.

8. Discuss the ability to deduct a contribution made to a traditional IRA given an employee covered by a qualified retirement plan who has a spouse who is not covered by a qualified retirement plan.

9. Define active participant status for purposes of deducting IRA contributions.

10. What are the minimum distribution rules for traditional IRAs?

11. When is the early withdrawal penalty applicable to traditional IRAs?

12. How do individual retirement annuities differ from a traditional IRA account?

13. Compare and contrast a traditional IRA to a Roth IRA.

14. How does the definition of earned income for a Roth IRA compare with the definition of earned income for a traditional IRA?

15. Identify the 2005 AGI income limits for contributions to a Roth IRA.

16. What are the income limits for converting a traditional IRA to a Roth IRA?

17. How can the assets of a qualified plan be converted into a Roth IRA?

18. What is a "qualified distribution" from a Roth IRA?

19. How is a nonqualified distribution from a Roth IRA taxed?

20. What are the minimum distribution rules relating to Roth IRAs?

21. What types of investments may be held in an IRA and what investments are specifically prohibited from being held in an IRA?

22. What types of coins are permitted IRA investments?

23. Discuss the impact of violating the prohibited transaction rules of an IRA.

24. What are the SEP coverage requirements?

25. What employees may be excluded from participation in a SEP?

26. What is the 2005 contribution limit for a SEP?

27. How and when is a SEP established?

28. What vesting options are available for a SEP?

29. Compare and contrast a SEP and a profit sharing plan.

30. How are the elective deferrals into a SARSEP considered in relation to other salary deferral type plans?

MULTIPLE CHOICE PROBLEMS

1. Which statements are correct regarding penalties associated with IRA accounts?

    1. Generally, distributions made prior to 59½ are subject to the 10% premature distribution penalty.

    2. There is a 50% excise tax on a required minimum distribution not made by <u>April 1</u> of the year following the year in which age 70½ is attained.

    a. 1 only.

    b. 2 only.

    c. 1 and 2.

    d. Neither 1 nor 2.

2. David took a lump-sum distribution from his employer's qualified plan at age 56 when he terminated his service. He rolled over his distribution using a direct rollover to an IRA. Assuming David has met 10-year forward averaging requirements, which of the following is/are correct regarding tax treatment of the transaction?

    1. If at age 59 he distributes the IRA, he benefits from 10-year forward averaging.

    2. If he rolls the entire IRA to a new employer's qualified plan, he may be eligible for forward averaging treatment in the future.

    3. If he rolls over a portion of the IRA to a new employer's qualified plan, he may preserve any eligibility for forward averaging on that portion that was rolled over.

    4. If David immediately withdraws the entire amount from his IRA, he may benefit from 10-year forward averaging.

    a. 2 only.

    b. 2 and 3.

    c. 2, 3, and 4.

    d. 1, 2, 3, and 4.

3. Robin and Robbie, both age 35, are married and filed a joint return for 2005. Robbie earned a salary of $90,000 in 2005 and is covered by his employer's 401(k) plan. Robbie and Robin earned interest of $15,000 in 2005 from a joint savings account. Robin is not employed, and the couple had no other income. On April 15, 2006, Robbie contributed $4,000 to an IRA for himself and $4,000 to an IRA for Robin. The maximum allowable IRA deduction on the 2005 joint return is:

    a. $1,500.

    b. $4,000.

    c. $4,500.

    d. $8,000.

4. Amy, divorced and age 55, received taxable alimony of $50,000 in 2005. In addition, she received $1,800 in earnings from a part-time job. Amy is not covered by a qualified plan. What was the maximum deductible IRA contribution that Amy could have made for 2005?

    a. $1,800.

    b. $2,000.

    c. $4,000.

    d. $4,500.

5. For the year 2005, Katy (age 35) and Stefen (age 38) reported the following items of income:

	Katy	Stefen	Total
Wages	$50,000	--	$50,000
Dividend income	$2,000	$1,200	$3,200
Cash won from lottery		$500	$500
	$52,000	$1,700	$53,700

Katy is covered by a qualified plan. Stefen does not work and makes wine all day. Assuming a joint return was filed for 2005, what is the maximum amount that they can contribute and deduct to their IRAs?

    a. $2,000.

    b. $4,000.

    c. $6,000.

    d. $8,000.

6. Which of the following cannot be held in an IRA account as an investment?

    a. A U.S. gold coin.

    b. Option contracts (calls).

    c. Variable life insurance.

    d. Municipal bonds.

7. Phillip, who is currently age 52, made his only contribution to his Roth IRA in 2005 in the amount of $4,000. If he were to receive a total distribution of $8,000 from his Roth IRA in the year 2010, how would he be taxed?

   a. Since Phillip waited five years, the distribution will be classified as a "qualified distribution" and will therefore not be taxable or subject to the 10% early distribution penalty.

   b. Since Phillip waited five years, the distribution will be classified as a "qualified distribution" and will therefore not be taxable but will be subject to the 10% early distribution penalty.

   c. Although Phillip waited five years, the distribution will not be classified as a "qualified distribution" and will therefore be taxable and will be subject to the 10% early distribution penalty.

   d. Although Phillip waited five years, the distribution will not be classified as a "qualified distribution" and will therefore be taxable to the extent of earnings and will be subject to the 10% early distribution penalty on the amount that is taxable.

8. Which of the following is <u>not</u> a permitted method of converting a Traditional IRA to a Roth IRA?

   a. An amount distributed from a Traditional IRA can be rolled over into a Roth IRA within 60 days after the initial distribution.

   b. An amount in a Traditional IRA can be transferred in a trustee-to-trustee transfer from the trustee of the Traditional IRA to the trustee of the Roth IRA.

   c. An amount in a Traditional IRA can be transferred to a Roth IRA maintained by the same trustee.

   d. An amount from a qualified plan can be transferred via a direct trustee-to-trustee transfer to a Roth IRA.

9. Jim, who is age 39, converts a $72,000 Traditional IRA to a Roth IRA in 2006. Jim's adjusted taxable basis in the Traditional IRA is $10,000. He also makes a contribution of $4,000 to a Roth IRA in 2006 for the tax year 2005. If Jim takes a $4,000 distribution from his Roth IRA in 2006, how much total federal income tax, including penalties, is due as a result of the distribution assuming his 2006 federal income tax rate is 28 percent?

   a. $0.

   b. $300.

   c. $840.

   d. $1,140.

10. Jack and Jill, both age 43, are married, made $20,000 each, and file a joint tax return. Jill has made a $4,000 contribution to her Traditional IRA account and has made a contribution of $2,000 to a Coverdell Education Savings Account for 2005. What is the most that can be contributed to a Roth IRA for Jack for 2005?

    a. $0.
    b. $2,000.
    c. $4,000.
    d. $8,000.

11. Ah and Ha, both age 33, are married, not covered by a qualified plan, and file a joint tax return. They have AGI of $155,000 and have each contributed $2,000 to a Roth IRA during 2005 for the year 2005. Ah's mother contributed $2,000 to a Coverdell Education Savings Account for each of their two children. What is the most that Ah and Ha can contribute in total together to a Traditional IRA for 2005?

    a. $0.
    b. $1,000.
    c. $4,000.
    d. $8,000.

12. What is the first year in which a single taxpayer, age 54 in 2005, could receive a qualified distribution from a Roth IRA if he made his first $3,500 contribution to the Roth IRA on April 1, 2006, for the tax year 2005?

    a. 2008.
    b. 2009.
    c. 2010.
    d. 2011.

13. Kathy (age 55) is single, recently divorced, and has received the following items of income this year:

Pension annuity income from QDRO	$21,000
Interest and dividends	$5,000
Alimony	$1,000
W-2 Income	$1,200

    What is the most that Kathy can contribute to a Roth IRA for 2005?

    a. $1,200.
    b. $2,200.
    c. $4,000.
    d. $4,500.

14. Which of the following statements is/are correct regarding SEP contributions made by an employer?

    1. Contributions are subject to FICA and FUTA.

    2. Contributions are currently excludable from employee-participant's gross income.

    3. Contributions are capped at $14,000 for 2005.

      a. 1 only.

      b. 2 only.

      c. 1 and 2.

      d. 1, 2, and 3.

15. For 2005, what is the maximum amount that can be contributed to a SEP?

      a. $10,000.

      b. $14,000.

      c. $18,000.

      d. $42,000.

16. A SEP is not a qualified plan and is not subject to all of the rules as qualified plans. However, it is subject to many of the same rules. Which of the following are true statements?

    1. SEPs and qualified plans have the same funding deadlines.

    2. The contribution limit for SEPs and qualified plans (defined contribution) is $42,000 for the year 2005.

    3. SEPs and qualified plans have the same ERISA protection from creditors.

    4. SEPs and qualified plans have different nondiscriminatory and top-heavy rules.

      a. 1 only.

      b. 1 and 2.

      c. 2 and 4.

      d. 1, 2, 3, and 4.

17. Mary, age 50, has an IRA with an account balance of $165,000. Mary has recently been diagnosed with an unusual disease that will require treatment costing $50,000, which she will have to pay personally. Mary's AGI will be $100,000 this year. Which of the following statements are true?

    1. Mary can immediately borrow up to $50,000 from her account and repay within five years.

    2. Mary can distribute $50,000 subject to income tax but not subject to the 10% penalty because it will be used to pay medical expenses.

      a. 1 only.

      b. 2 only.

      c. 1 and 2.

      d. Neither 1 nor 2.

18. Delores, age 62, single, and retired, receives a defined benefit pension annuity of $1,200 per month from Bertancinni Corporation. She is currently working part time for Deanna's Interior Design and will be paid $18,000 this year (2005). Deanna's Interior has a 401(k) plan, but Delores has made no contribution to the plan and neither will Deanna this year. Can Delores contribute to a traditional IRA or a Roth IRA for the year and what is the maximum contribution?

      a. $4,000 to a traditional IRA/$4,000 to a Roth IRA.

      b. $0 to a traditional IRA/$4,000 to a Roth IRA.

      c. $4,500 to a traditional IRA/$0 to a Roth IRA.

      d. $4,500 to a traditional IRA/$4,500 to a Roth IRA.

19. Which of the following people can contribute to a traditional IRA for 2005?

	Person	AGI	Covered by Qualified Plan	Marital Status
1.	Dianne	$70,000	Yes	Married
2.	Joy	$50,000	Yes	Single
3.	Kim	$280,000	No	Married
4.	Loretta	$60,000	Yes	Single

      a. None.

      b. 1, 2, and 3.

      c. 1, 2, and 4.

      d. 1, 2, 3, and 4.

20. The early distribution penalty of 10 percent does not apply to IRA distributions:

1. Made after attainment of the age of 55 and separated from service.
2. Made for the purpose of paying qualified higher education costs.
3. Paid to a designated beneficiary after the death of the account owner who had not begun receiving minimum distributions.

    a. 1 only.

    b. 1 and 3.

    c. 2 and 3.

    d. 1, 2, and 3.

SIMPLE, 403(b), and 457 Plans

10

INTRODUCTION

A company may wish to establish a retirement plan but may be unable or unwilling to incur the costs associated with a qualified plan. The IRC provides for "other tax-advantaged plans" that provide favorable tax treatment but are not qualified plans. These plans are often easier and less costly to administer. This chapter discusses in detail three of these "other tax-advantaged plans," SIMPLEs, 403(b)s, and 457 plans.

SIMPLEs (Savings Incentive Match Plans for Employees) provide incentives to "small employers" (less than 100 employees)[1] to adopt retirement plans for employees with less administrative costs and fewer set-up procedures than qualified plans and no annual filing requirements.

Section 403(b) plans, also called "Tax Sheltered Annuities" (TSAs) or "Tax-Deferred Annuities" (TDAs), are plans available to certain non-profit organizations and to employees of public educational systems. Recently, the limits for employee elective deferral contributions to 403(b) plans were increased as were added catch-up provisions for those persons over 50 years old, allowing for employee elective deferrals equal to that of 401(k) plans.

Section 457 plans re deferred compensation plans that allow certain employees of state and local governments and of nongovernmental tax-exempt entities the ability to defer compensation free from current income taxation. These employee deferral contributions to 457 plans are separate and not combined with other deferral contributions to retirement plans such as SARSEPs, 401(k)s, SIMPLEs, or 403(b)s for purposes of overall contribution limits.

---

1. IRC Section 408(p).

Know The Numbers

SIMPLEs	Total Elective Contribution	Catch Up > 50	
2005	$10,000	$2,000	
2006	$10,000†	$2,500	
2007	$10,500†	$2,500†	
2008	$10,500†	$2,500†	
403(b) Plans	**Annual Deferral Limit**	**Catch Up > 50**	
2005	$14,000	$4,000	
2006	$15,000	$5,000	
2007	$15,000†	$5,000†	
2008	$15,500†	$5,000†	
457 Plans	**Annual Deferral Limit**	**Catch Up > 50**	**Final 3-Year Catch Up**
2005	$14,000	$4,000	$14,000
2006	$15,000	$5,000	$15,000
2007	$15,000†	$5,000†	$15,000†
2008	$15,500†	$5,000†	$15,500†

Sep - non contributory
S. MPLE - contributory

SIMPLES

Savings Incentive Match Plans for Employees, referred to as "SIMPLEs", are retirement plans for small employers. Many smaller employers are reluctant to set up qualified retirement plans because of the complicated rules and administrative costs that accompany qualified plans. SIMPLEs, however, are both easy to establish and maintain and provide an incentive to small employers to adopt retirement plans because they posses the similar tax advantages of qualified plans. In addition, SIMPLE plans are attractive to employers because they are not required to meet all of the nondiscrimination rules applicable to qualified retirement plans and they do not have the burdensome annual filing requirements.

A SIMPLE allows employees to make elective deferral contributions similar to a 401(k) plan. The employer sponsor is required to match employee elective deferral contributions made by employees or, alternatively, to make non-elective contributions for all employees who are eligible. The employer and employee enter into a written agreement that directs the employer to make employee elective deferral contributions to the accounts of eligible employees in exchange for a salary reduction.

EXAMPLE 10.1

Karli makes an election to reduce her salary from $50,000 to $45,000 and have her employer deposit the $5,000 into a SIMPLE IRA. The employer will also match the employee's contribution up to 3% of salary ($50,000 x 0.03 = $1,500) into the SIMPLE IRA.

A SUMMARY OF THE CHARACTERISTICS OF SIMPLEs

EXHIBIT 10.1

- Employer establishes SIMPLE plan
- Employer contracts with employee to have salary reduction
- Employer withholds employee deferral over the course of a year
- Employee elective deferrals are not subject to income tax but are subject to payroll tax
- Employer deposits match on a regular basis tax deferred without payroll tax
- Earnings grow tax deferred on all contributions

TYPES OF SIMPLEs

When establishing a SIMPLE, the sponsor company has two choices in determining the vehicle used to hold the assets of the plan. A company may choose either an IRA or 401(k) for the plan. Therefore, a sponsor company may establish the SIMPLE as either a SIMPLE IRA plan or a SIMPLE 401(k) plan. In most instances, the company will establish a SIMPLE IRA because there are less administrative burdens than for SIMPLE 401(k) plans. SIMPLE 401(k) plans are very rare in practice.

The SIMPLE IRA

A **SIMPLE IRA** is a SIMPLE plan that utilizes an IRA account as the funding vehicle of the plan. The SIMPLE IRA is established utilizing an individual retirement account (or an individual retirement annuity). The plan is established by the employer via a written plan that allows each employee to choose between directing the employer to make contributions to the SIMPLE IRA plan or allowing the employee to receive such payments directly in cash (a CODA feature) as compensation. SIMPLE IRAs require the employer to either match the employee contributions of those that participate or provide nonelective contributions to all employees who are eligible. All contributions made under a SIMPLE IRA must be paid to a SIMPLE IRA, not to any other type of IRA. SIMPLE IRA plans can be established by for-profit entities, tax-exempt employers, and governmental entities.

Key Concepts

Underline/highlight the answers to these questions as you read:

1. What are SIMPLE plans?

2. What types of SIMPLE plans are available?

3. List the requirements to establish a SIMPLE plan.

The SIMPLE 401(k)

A **SIMPLE 401(k)** is a SIMPLE plan that utilizes a 401(k) plan as the funding vehicle of the plan. SIMPLE 401(k) plans must be maintained by an eligible employer and satisfy contribution requirements, eligibility requirements, and vesting requirements. A SIMPLE 401(k) plan must be maintained on a calendar year basis and not a fiscal year basis. An employer may adopt a SIMPLE 401(k) plan if it meets the less than or equal to 100 employee limit. A SIMPLE 401(k) is not subject to nondiscrimination requirements or top heavy restrictions if it meets certain contribution and other requirements that are discussed in this chapter.

ESTABLISHING A SIMPLE

A SIMPLE IRA plan can be maintained only on a calendar year basis. As such, plan contributions to the SIMPLE IRA, as well as the eligibility of employers who establish the SIMPLE IRA, are determined on a calendar year basis.[2]

SIMPLEs are designed for the small employer. A SIMPLE is very easy to establish and maintain as it has minor administrative costs and does not have any annual filing requirements. There are definite advantages for SIMPLEs compared to qualified plans. As discussed throughout this book, qualified plans have significant administrative costs and burdensome rules and requirements.

Who Can Establish A SIMPLE?

SIMPLE plans can only be established for companies who employ 100 or fewer employees who earned at least $5,000 of compensation from the employer for the preceding calendar year. The employer can be a C corporation, partnership, S corporation, limited liability company, sole proprietorship, a tax-exempt entity, or a governmental entity. Whether the employees are eligible to participate in the SIMPLE or not, all employees who earned $5,000 or more in the previous year that are employed at any time during the calendar year are taken into consideration for purposes of counting the 100 employee limitation. Accordingly, even employees that can be excluded, such as nonresident aliens or those employees who do not meet the plan's minimum eligibility requirements, must all be considered in the 100 employee limitation to avoid a company that truly has more than 100 employees being eligible to establish a SIMPLE. Leased employees or self-employed individuals who received earned income from the employer in the preceding calendar year are also included in the calculation for the 100 employee limitation rule.[3]

EXAMPLE 10.2	Z-Mart Corporation employed 150 employees in 2005, 115 of whom were nonresident aliens. For calendar year 2006, the company would only have 35 employees eligible to participate in the year 2006, but Z-Mart Corporation may not establish a SIMPLE IRA plan in calendar year 2005 because the company employed 150 employees (though 115 of them were nonresident aliens). The company had under 100 eligible participants, but for purposes of the 100 employee limitation, nonresident aliens must be considered for the preceding calendar year in the calculation of the eligibility of the company as a whole.

---

2. IRC Section 408(p)(6)(C).
3. IRC Section 408(p)(2)(C)(i)(I).

ENTITIES THAT CAN ESTABLISH SIMPLE PLANS

EXHIBIT 10.2

C Corporations
S Corporations
Limited Liability Companies (LLC)
Partnerships
Proprietorships
Government Entities

Two-Year Grace Period for Employers Who Cease to Comply with 100 Employee Limit

If an employer meets the 100 employee limitation in a given year, then the employer will have a two year "**grace period**" where the employer can exceed the limitation without losing eligibility to maintain the SIMPLE. In other words, if an employer in a calendar year satisfies the 100 employee limitation, that employer is treated as if it satisfied the 100 employee limitation for two calendar years immediately after the calendar year for which it last satisfied the 100 employee limitation.

However, if the employer undergoes an acquisition, disposition, or other similar transaction, the employer will retain eligibility (i.e., not deemed as exceeding the 100 employee limitation) for the year of the transaction plus the two subsequent years, only if both of the following two rules are met:

1. The plan coverage has not significantly changed during the grace period and
2. The SIMPLE plan would have continued to qualify after the transaction if the employer had remained as a separate employer.[4]

If at anytime within the two years the employer does not meet the requirements listed above, neither the employer nor the employee will be permitted to make contributions to the plan.

---

4. IRC Section 408(p)(4), Section 408(p)(10).

Other Plans Not Allowed

An employer may not establish a SIMPLE if the employer contributes to a defined contribution plan for its employees during the year, if its employees accrue a benefit from a defined benefit plan during the year, or if the employer contributes to a SEP or 403(b) during the year.

If an employer maintains another qualified plan solely to benefit union employees whose retirement benefits were the subject of good faith bargaining, the employer can make contributions to a SIMPLE plan. All the eligibility and contribution rules will apply and the SIMPLE must exclude those union employees.

How Is a SIMPLE Established

SIMPLEs are easy to establish and maintain in comparison to other types of qualified retirement plans. There are few administrative costs associated with the SIMPLE plan because there are no annual filing requirements. At the inception, an employer files **Form 5304-SIMPLE** or **Form 5305-SIMPLE** to establish a SIMPLE IRA plan. These are model SIMPLE plan documents. Form 5304 applies to employers who allow plan participants to select the financial institution that will receive their contributions while Form 5305 applies to those SIMPLEs that require initial contributions to be deposited at a designated financial institution. As a further illustration of the relaxed administrative rules and required paperwork, Forms 5304-SIMPLE and 5305-SIMPLE by themselves (i) satisfy employer notification requirements for SIMPLEs, (ii) maintain the SIMPLE plan records, and (iii) establish proof that the employer set up a SIMPLE plan for its employees.

EXHIBIT 10.3

Form **5304-SIMPLE** (Rev. March 2002) Department of the Treasury Internal Revenue Service	Savings Incentive Match Plan for Employees of Small Employers (SIMPLE)—Not for Use With a Designated Financial Institution	OMB No. 1545-1502 Do not file with the Internal Revenue Service

_____ establishes the following SIMPLE

Name of Employer

IRA plan under section 408(p) of the Internal Revenue Code and pursuant to the instructions contained in this form.

Article I—Employee Eligibility Requirements   (complete applicable box(es) and blanks—see instructions)

1   General Eligibility Requirements.   The Employer agrees to permit salary reduction contributions to be made in each calendar year to the SIMPLE IRA established by each employee who meets the following requirements (select either 1a or 1b):

a   ☐ Full Eligibility. All employees are eligible.

b   ☐ Limited Eligibility.   Eligibility is limited to employees who are described in both (i) and (ii) below:

　　(i) Current compensation.   Employees who are reasonably expected to receive at least $ _____ in compensation (not to exceed $5,000) for the calendar year.

　　(ii) Prior compensation.   Employees who have received at least $ _____ in compensation (not to exceed $5,000) during any _____ calendar year(s) (insert 0, 1, or 2) preceding the calendar year.

2   Excludable Employees.

　　☐ The Employer elects to exclude employees covered under a collective bargaining agreement for which retirement benefits were the subject of good faith bargaining. Note: This box is deemed checked if the Employer maintains a qualified plan covering only such employees.

Article II—Salary Reduction Agreements   (complete the box and blank, if applicable—see instructions)

1   Salary Reduction Election.   An eligible employee may make an election to have his or her compensation for each pay period reduced. The total amount of the reduction in the employee's compensation for a calendar year cannot exceed the applicable amount for that y ear.

2   Timing of Salary Reduction Elections

a   For a calendar year, an eligible employee may make or modify a salary reduction election during the 60-day period immediately p receding January 1 of that year. However, for the year in which the employee becomes eligible to make salary reduction contributions, th e period during which the employee may make or modify the election is a 60-day period that includes either the date the employee becomes eligible or the day before.

b   In addition to the election periods in 2a, eligible employees may make salary reduction elections or modify prior elections _____
_____. If the Employer chooses this option, insert a period or periods (e.g. semi-annually, quarterly, monthly, or daily) that will apply uniformly to all eli gible employees.

c   No salary reduction election may apply to compensation that an employee received, or had a right to immediately receive, before execution of the salary reduction election.

d   An employee may terminate a salary reduction election at any time during the calendar year. ☐ If this box is checked, an employee who terminates a salary reduction election not in accordance with 2b may not resume salary reduction contributions during the calen dar year.

Article III—Contributions   (complete the blank, if applicable—see instructions)

1   Salary Reduction Contributions.   The amount by which the employee agrees to reduce his or her compensation will be contributed by the Employer to the employee's SIMPLE IRA.

2a   Matching Contributions

　　(i) For each calendar year, the Employer will contribute a matching contribution to each eligible employee's SIMPLE IRA equal to th e employee's salary reduction contributions up to a limit of 3% of the employee's compensation for the calendar year.

　　(ii) The Employer may reduce the 3% limit for the calendar year in (i) only if:

　　　　(1) The limit is not reduced below 1%; (2) The limit is not reduced for more than 2 calendar years during the 5-year period ending with the calendar year the reduction is effective; and (3) Each employee is notified of the reduced limit within a reasonable period of time before the employees' 60-day election period for the calendar year (described in Article II, item 2a).

b   Nonelective Contributions

　　(i) For any calendar year, instead of making matching contributions, the Employer may make nonelective contributions equal to 2% of compensation for the calendar year to the SIMPLE IRA of each eligible employee who has at least $ _____ (not more than $5,000) in compensation for the calendar year. No more than $200,000* in compensation can be taken into account in determining the nonelective contribution for each eligible employee.

　　(ii) For any calendar year, the Employer may make 2% nonelective contributions instead of matching contributions only if:

　　　　(1) Each eligible employee is notified that a 2% nonelective contribution will be made instead of a matching contribution; and

　　　　(2) This notification is provided within a reasonable period of time before the employees' 60-day election period for the calendar   year (described in Article II, item 2a).

3   Time and Manner of Contributions

a   The Employer will make the salary reduction contributions (described in 1 above) for each eligible employee to the SIMPLE IRA e stablished at the financial institution selected by that employee no later than 30 days after the end of the month in which the money is withheld from the   employee's pay. See instructions.

b   The Employer will make the matching or nonelective contributions (described in 2a and 2b above) for each eligible employee to t he SIMPLE IRA established at the financial institution selected by that employee no later than the due date for filing the Employe r's tax return, including extensions, for the taxable year that includes the last day of the calendar year for which the contributions are made .

* For 2003 and later years, this amount is subject to annual cost-of-living adjustments. The IRS announces the increase, if any, in a news release, in the Internal Revenue Bulletin, and on the IRS's internet web site at www.irs.gov.

Form 5304-SIMPLE (Rev. 3-2002)   Page 2

Article IV —Other Requirements and Provisions

1   Contributions in General.   The Employer will make no contributions to the SIMPLE IRAs other than salary reduction contributions (described in Article III, item 1) and matching or nonelective contributions (described in Article III, items 2a and 2b).

2   Vesting Requirements.   All contributions made under this SIMPLE IRA plan are fully vested and nonforfeitable.

3   No Withdrawal Restrictions.   The Employer may not require the employee to retain any portion of the contributions in his or her SIMPLE IRA or otherwise impose any withdrawal restrictions.

4   Selection of IRA Trustee.   The employer must permit each eligible employee to select the financial institution that will serve as the trustee, custodian, or issuer of the SIMPLE IRA to which the employer will make all contributions on behalf of that employee.

5   Amendments To This SIMPLE IRA Plan.   This SIMPLE IRA plan may not be amended except to modify the entries inserted in the blanks or boxes provided in Articles I, II, III, VI, and VII.

6   Effects Of Withdrawals and Rollovers

a   An amount withdrawn from the SIMPLE IRA is generally includible in gross income. However, a SIMPLE IRA balance may be rolled over or transferred on a tax-free basis to another IRA designed solely to hold funds under a SIMPLE IRA plan. In addition, an individual may roll over or transfer his or her SIMPLE IRA balance to any IRA after a 2-year period has expired since the individual first participated in any SIMPLE IRA plan of the Employer. Any rollover or transfer must comply with the requirements under section 408.

b   If an individual withdraws an amount from a SIMPLE IRA during the 2-year period beginning when the individual first participated in any SIMPLE IRA plan of the Employer and the amount is subject to the additional tax on early distributions under section 72(t), this additional tax is increased from 10% to 25%.

Article V —Definitions

1   Compensation

a   General Definition of Compensation.   Compensation means the sum of the wages, tips, and other compensation from the Employer subject to federal income tax withholding (as described in section 6051(a)(3)) and the employee's salary reduction contributions made under this plan, and, if applicable, elective deferrals under a section 401(k) plan, a SARSEP, or a section 403(b) annuity contract and compensation deferred under a section 457 plan required to be reported by the Employer on Form W-2 (as described in section 6051(a)(8)).

b   Compensation for Self-Employed Individuals.   For self-employed individuals, compensation means the net earnings from self-employment determined under section 1402(a), without regard to section 1402(c)(6), prior to subtracting any contributions made pursuant to this plan on behalf of the individual.

2   Employee. Employee means a common-law employee of the Employer. The term employee also includes a self-employed individual and a leased employee described in section 414(n) but does not include a nonresident alien who received no earned income from the Employer that constitutes income from sources within the United States.

3   Eligible Employee.   An eligible employee means an employee who satisfies the conditions in Article I, item 1 and is not excluded under Article I, item 2.

4   SIMPLE IRA. A SIMPLE IRA is an individual retirement account described in section 408(a), or an individual retirement annuity described in section 408(b), to which the only contributions that can be made are contributions under a SIMPLE IRA plan and rollovers or transfers from another SIMPLE IRA.

Article VI —Procedures for Withdrawal   (The employer will provide each employee with the procedures for withdrawals of contributions received by the financial institution selected by that employee, and that financial institution's name and address (by attaching that information or inserting it in the space below) unless: (1) that financial institution's procedures are unavailable, or (2) that financial institution provides the procedures directly to the employee. See Employee Notification   on page 5.)

Article VII —Effective Date

This SIMPLE IRA plan is effective _____ . See instructions.

                                 *   *   *   *   *

_____   _____
Name of Employer   By: Signature   Date

_____   _____
Address of Employer   Name and title

FORM 5304-SIMPLE CONTINUED

Model Notification to Eligible Employees

I. Opportunity to Participate in the SIMPLE IRA Plan

You are eligible to make salary reduction contributions to the _____ SIMPLE IRA plan. This notice and the attached summary description provide you with information that you should consider before you decide whether to start, continue, or change your salary reduction agreement.

II. Employer Contribution Election

For the _____ calendar year, the employer elects to contribute to your SIMPLE IRA (employer must select either (1), (2), or (3)):

☐ (1) A matching contribution equal to your salary reduction contributions up to a limit of 3% of your compensation for the year;

☐ (2) A matching contribution equal to your salary reduction contributions up to a limit of _____% (employer must insert a number from 1 to 3 and is subject to certain restrictions) of your compensation for the year; or

☐ (3) A nonelective contribution equal to 2% of your compensation for the year (limited to $200,000*) if you are an employee who makes at least $ _____ (employer must insert an amount that is $5,000 or less) in compensation for the year.

III. Administrative Procedures

To start or change your salary reduction contributions, you must complete the salary reduction agreement and return it to _____ (employer should designate a place or individual) by _____ (employer should insert a date that is not less than 60 days after notice is given).

IV. Employee Selection of Financial Institution

You must select the financial institution that will serve as the trustee, custodian, or issuer of your SIMPLE IRA and notify your employer of your selection.

Model Salary Reduction Agreement

I. Salary Reduction Election

Subject to the requirements of the SIMPLE IRA plan of _____ (name of employer) I authorize _____ % or $ _____ (which equals _____ % of my current rate of pay) to be withheld from my pay for each pay period and contributed to my SIMPLE IRA as a salary reduction contribution.

II. Maximum Salary Reduction

I understand that the total amount of my salary reduction contributions in any calendar year cannot exceed the applicable amount for that year. See instructions.

III. Date Salary Reduction Begins

I understand that my salary reduction contributions will start as soon as permitted under the SIMPLE IRA plan and as soon as administratively feasible or, if later, _____. (Fill in the date you want the salary reduction contributions to begin. The date must be after you sign this agreement.)

IV. Employee Selection of Financial Institution

I select the following financial institution to serve as the trustee, custodian, or issuer of my SIMPLE IRA.

_____
Name of financial institution

_____
Address of financial institution

_____
SIMPLE IRA account name and number

I understand that I must establish a SIMPLE IRA to receive any contributions made on my behalf under this SIMPLE IRA plan. If the information regarding my SIMPLE IRA is incomplete when I first submit my salary reduction agreement, I realize that it must be completed by the date contributions must be made under the SIMPLE IRA plan. If I fail to update my agreement to provide this information by that date, I understand that my employer may select a financial institution for my SIMPLE IRA.

V. Duration of Election

This salary reduction agreement replaces any earlier agreement and will remain in effect as long as I remain an eligible employee under the SIMPLE IRA plan or until I provide my employer with a request to end my salary reduction contributions or provide a new salary reduction agreement as permitted under this SIMPLE IRA plan.

Signature of employee _____ Date _____

* For 2003 and later years, this amount is subject to cost-of-living adjustments. The IRS announces the increase, if any, in a news release, in the Internal Revenue Bulletin, and on the IRS Web Site at www.irs.gov.

EXHIBIT 10.4 FORM 5305-SIMPLE

| Form **5305-SIMPLE**
(Rev. March 2002)

Department of the Treasury
Internal Revenue Service | Savings Incentive Match Plan for
Employees of Small Employers (SIMPLE)—
for Use With a Designated Financial Institution | OMB No. 1545-1502

Do not file
with the Internal
Revenue Service |

_____ establishes the following SIMPLE
_____ Name of Employer

IRA plan under section 408(p) of the Internal Revenue Code and pursuant to the instructions contained in this form.

Article I—Employee Eligibility Requirements   (complete applicable box(es) and blanks—see instructions)

1   General Eligibility Requirements.   The Employer agrees to permit salary reduction contributions to be made in each calendar year to the SIMPLE individual retirement account or annuity established at the designated financial institution (SIMPLE IRA) for each employee who meets the following requirements (select either 1a or 1b):

a ☐ Full Eligibility. All employees are eligible.

b ☐ Limited Eligibility.   Eligibility is limited to employees who are described in both (i) and (ii) below:

   (i) Current compensation.   Employees who are reasonably expected to receive at least $ _____ in compensation (not to exceed $5,000) for the calendar year.

   (ii) Prior compensation.   Employees who have received at least $ _____ in compensation (not to exceed $5,000) during any _____ calendar year(s) (insert 0, 1, or 2) preceding the calendar year.

2   Excludable Employees

   ☐ The Employer elects to exclude employees covered under a collective bargaining agreement for which retirement benefits were the subject of good faith bargaining. Note: This box is deemed checked if the Employer maintains a qualified plan covering only such employees.

Article II—Salary Reduction Agreements   (complete the box and blank, if applicable—see instructions)

1   Salary Reduction Election.   An eligible employee may make an election to have his or her compensation for each pay period reduced. The total amount of the reduction in the employee's compensation for a calendar year cannot exceed the applicable amount for that year. S ee instructions.

2   Timing of Salary Reduction Elections

a For a calendar year, an eligible employee may make or modify a salary reduction election during the 60-day period immediately p receding January 1 of that year. However, for the year in which the employee becomes eligible to make salary reduction contributions, th e period during which the employee may make or modify the election is a 60-day period that includes either the date the employee becomes eligible or the day before.

b In addition to the election periods in 2a, eligible employees may make salary reduction elections or modify prior elections _____
_____ . If the Employer chooses this option, insert a period or periods (e.g. semi-annually, quarterly, monthly, or daily) that will apply uniformly to all eli gible employees.

c No salary reduction election may apply to compensation that an employee received, or had a right to immediately receive, before execution of the salary reduction election.

d An employee may terminate a salary reduction election at any time during the calendar year.   ☐ If this box is checked, an employee who terminates a salary reduction election not in accordance with 2b may not resume salary reduction contributions during the calen dar year.

Article III—Contributions   (complete the blank, if applicable—see instructions)

1   Salary Reduction Contributions.   The amount by which the employee agrees to reduce his or her compensation will be contributed by the Employer to the employee's SIMPLE IRA.

2 a   Matching Contributions

   (i) For each calendar year, the Employer will contribute a matching contribution to each eligible employee's SIMPLE IRA equal to th e employee's salary reduction contributions up to a limit of 3% of the employee's compensation for the calendar year.

   (ii) The Employer may reduce the 3% limit for the calendar year in (i) only if:

      (1) The limit is not reduced below 1%; (2) The limit is not reduced for more than 2 calendar years during the 5-year period ending with the calendar year the reduction is effective; and (3) Each employee is notified of the reduced limit within a reasonable period of time before the employees' 60-day election period for the calendar year (described in Article II, item 2a).

b   Nonelective Contributions

   (i) For any calendar year, instead of making matching contributions, the Employer may make nonelective contributions equal to 2% of compensation for the calendar year to the SIMPLE IRA of each eligible employee who has at least $ _____ (not more than $5,000) in compensation for the calendar year. No more than $200,000* in compensation can be taken into account in determining the nonelective contribution for each eligible employee.

   (ii) For any calendar year, the Employer may make 2% nonelective contributions instead of matching contributions only if:

      (1) Each eligible employee is notified that a 2% nonelective contribution will be made instead of a matching contribution; and

      (2) This notification is provided within a reasonable period of time before the employees' 60-day election period for the calendar   year (described in Article II, item 2a).

3   Time and Manner of Contributions

a The Employer will make the salary reduction contributions (described in 1 above) to the designated financial institution for th e IRAs established under this SIMPLE IRA plan no later than 30 days after the end of the month in which the money is withheld from the employee's pay. S ee instructions.

b The Employer will make the matching or nonelective contributions (described in 2a and 2b above) to the designated financial ins titution for the IRAs established under this SIMPLE IRA plan no later than the due date for filing the Employer's tax return, including exte nsions, for the taxable year that includes the last day of the calendar year for which the contributions are made.

* For 2003 and later years, this amount is subject to annual cost-of-living adjustments. The IRS announces the increase, if any, in a news release, in the Internal Revenue Bulletin, and on the IRS's internet web site at www.irs.gov .

FORM 5305-SIMPLE CONTINUED

Article IV —Other Requirements and Provisions

1 Contributions in General. The Employer will make no contributions to the SIMPLE IRAs other than salary reduction contributions (described in Article III, item 1) and matching or nonelective contributions (described in Article III, items 2a and 2b).

2 Vesting Requirements. All contributions made under this SIMPLE IRA plan are fully vested and nonforfeitable.

3 No Withdrawal Restrictions. The Employer may not require the employee to retain any portion of the contributions in his or her SIMPLE IRA or otherwise impose any withdrawal restrictions.

4 No Cost Or Penalty For Transfers. The Employer will not impose any cost or penalty on a participant for the transfer of the participant 's SIMPLE IRA balance to another IRA.

5 Amendments To This SIMPLE IRA Plan. This SIMPLE IRA plan may not be amended except to modify the entries inserted in the blanks or boxes provided in Articles I, II, III, VI, and VII.

6 Effects Of Withdrawals and Rollovers

a An amount withdrawn from the SIMPLE IRA is generally includible in gross income. However, a SIMPLE IRA balance may be rolled ov er or transferred on a tax-free basis to another IRA designed solely to hold funds under a SIMPLE IRA plan. In addition, an individua l may roll over or transfer his or her SIMPLE IRA balance to any IRA after a 2-year period has expired since the individual first particip ated in any SIMPLE IRA plan of the Employer. Any rollover or transfer must comply with the requirements of section 408.

b If an individual withdraws an amount from a SIMPLE IRA during the 2-year period beginning when the individual first participate d in any SIMPLE IRA plan of the Employer and the amount is subject to the additional tax on early distributions under section 72(t), thi s additional tax is increased from 10% to 25%.

Article V —Definitions

1 Compensation

a General Definition of Compensation. Compensation means the sum of wages, tips, and other compensation from the Employer subject to federal income tax withholding (as described in section 6051(a)(3)) and the employee's salary reduction contributions made under this plan, and, if applicable, elective deferrals under a section 401(k) plan, a SARSEP, or a section 403(b) annuity contract and co mpensation deferred under a section 457 plan required to be reported by the Employer on Form W-2 (as described in section 6058(a)(8)).

b Compensation for Self-Employed Individuals. For self-employed individuals, compensation means the net earnings from self-employment determined under section 1402(a), without regard to section 1402(c)(6), prior to subtracting any contributions made pursuant to this plan on behalf of the individual.

2 Employee. Employee means a common-law employee of the Employer. The term employee also includes a self-employed individual and a leased employee described in section 414(n) but does not include a nonresident alien who received no earned income from the Emp loyer that constitutes income from sources within the United States.

3 Eligible Employee. An eligible employee means an employee who satisfies the conditions in Article I, item 1 and is not excluded under Article I, item 2.

4 Designated Financial Institution. A designated financial institution is a trustee, custodian, or insurance company (that issues annuity contracts) for the SIMPLE IRA plan that receives all contributions made pursuant to the SIMPLE IRA plan and deposits those cont ributions to the SIMPLE IRA of each eligible employee.

Article VI —Procedures for Withdrawal (The designated financial institution will provide the instructions (to be attached or inserted in the space below) on the procedures for withdrawals of cont ributions by employees.)

Article VII —Effective Date

This SIMPLE IRA plan is effective _____ . See instructions.

              *   *   *   *   *

Name of Employer _____   By: Signature _____   Date _____

Address of Employer _____   Name and title _____

The undersigned agrees to serve as designated financial institution, receiving all contributions made pursuant to this SIMPLE I RA plan and depositing those contributions to the SIMPLE IRA of each eligible employee as soon as practicable. Upon the request of any part icipant, the undersigned also agrees to transfer the participant 's balance in a SIMPLE IRA established under this SIMPLE IRA plan to another IRA without cost or penalty to the participant.

Name of designated financial institution _____   By: Signature _____   Date _____

Address _____   Name and title _____

FORM 5305-SIMPLE CONTINUED

Model Notification to Eligible Employees

I. Opportunity to Participate in the SIMPLE IRA Plan

You are eligible to make salary reduction contributions to the _____
SIMPLE IRA plan. This notice and the attached summary description provide you with information that you should consider before you decide whether to start, continue, or change your salary reduction agreement.

II. Employer Contribution Election

For the _____ calendar year, the employer elects to contribute to your SIMPLE IRA (employer must select either (1), (2), or (3)):

☐ (1) A matching contribution equal to your salary reduction contributions up to a limit of 3% of your compensation for the year;

☐ (2) A matching contribution equal to your salary reduction contributions up to a limit of _____% (employer must insert a number from 1 to 3 and is subject to certain restrictions) of your compensation for the year; or

☐ (3) A nonelective contribution equal to 2% of your compensation for the year (limited to $200,000*) if you are an employee who makes at least $ _____ (employer must insert an amount that is $5,000 or less) in compensation for the year.

III. Administrative Procedures

To start or change your salary reduction contributions, you must complete the salary reduction agreement and return it to _____ (employer should designate a place or individual) by _____ (employer should insert a date that is not less than 60 days after notice is given).

Model Salary Reduction Agreement

I. Salary Reduction Election

Subject to the requirements of the SIMPLE IRA plan of _____ (name of employer) I authorize _____ % or
$ _____ (which equals _____ % of my current rate of pay)
to be withheld from my pay for each pay period and contributed to my SIMPLE IRA as a salary reduction contribution.

II. Maximum Salary Reduction

I understand that the total amount of my salary reduction contributions in any calendar year cannot exceed the applicable amount for that year. See instructions.

III. Date Salary Reduction Begins

I understand that my salary reduction contributions will start as soon as permitted under the SIMPLE IRA plan and as soon as administratively feasible or, if later, _____. (Fill in the date you want the salary reduction contributions to begin. The date must be after you sign this agreement.)

IV. Duration of Election

This salary reduction agreement replaces any earlier agreement and will remain in effect as long as I remain an eligible employee under the SIMPLE IRA plan or until I provide my employer with a request to end my salary reduction contributions or provide a new salary reduction agreement as permitted under this SIMPLE IRA plan.

Signature of employee _____   Date _____

* For 2003 and later years, this amount is subject to cost-of-living adjustments. The IRS announces the increase, if any, in a news release, in the Internal Revenue Bulletin, and on the IRS Web Site at www.irs.gov.

An employer can establish a SIMPLE IRA plan any time between January 1 and October 1 of the year in which it wants the plan to begin unless the employer or one of its predecessors previously maintained a SIMPLE IRA plan. If the employer previously maintained a SIMPLE IRA plan, then the employer must establish the SIMPLE IRA by January 1 of the year in which it wants the plan to begin. New employers who begin business after October 1 of the year may establish a SIMPLE IRA after October 1 if the SIMPLE is established as soon as it is administratively feasible.

In any case, the employer must provide the participants with a 60-day period of time during when they can make their deferral elections. This 60-day period must occur every plan year between November 2 and December 31. If a plan is established during the year, or an employee becomes eligible during the year, the participant's 60-day election period must include the date of eligibility.

Eligibility

To be eligible for a SIMPLE, an employer can not have more than 100 employees and all employees considered eligible must benefit from the SIMPLE. Eligible employees are those employees who earned at least $5,000 in compensation from the employer during any two preceding calendar years and who are reasonably expected to earn at least $5,000 in compensation during the current calendar year. Air pilots, nonresident aliens, and union employees whose retirement benefits were the subject of good faith bargaining may be excluded from the eligibility requirements of a SIMPLE IRA plan by the employer.

The employer and employee eligibility for a SIMPLE is determined based on the calendar year, January 1 to December 31. A SIMPLE plan cannot use any other fiscal years (other than those that mimic calendar years) to determine eligibility requirements.

ELIGIBILITY CHARACTERISTICS

EXHIBIT 10.5

- Employees who earned $5,000 during any two preceding calendar years
- Employees who are expected to earn $5,000 during the current calendar year

Vesting

All employer contributions to SIMPLE IRA accounts on behalf of employees and the related earnings are fully (100%) and immediately vested and cannot be forfeited by the employee.[5] All contributions under the SIMPLE 401(k) plan are likewise fully and immediately vested.

---

5. IRC Section 408(p)(3).

SIMPLE IRAs

Employee Elective Deferral Contributions

With the exception of certain rollover contributions, the only contributions that may be made under a SIMPLE IRA plan are the employee's elective deferral contributions and the required employer matching contributions or nonelective contributions.[6] Similar to other cash or deferred arrangement (CODA) type plans, rather than have funds paid directly in cash to the employee through payroll, an employee's elective deferral contribution or salary reduction contribution is made to the employee's SIMPLE IRA account.

The SIMPLE IRA permits the employee to defer a percentage or a dollar amount of his compensation for the year. Within 60 days prior to the beginning of the plan year, the employee elects the amount to defer under the plan. The employer is not allowed to place any restriction on the employee's elective deferral unless the annual limit on the salary reduction amount is reached, $10,000 for 2005 ($10,000[†] for 2006, $10,500[†] for 2007, $10,500[†] for 2008).[7]

| EXHIBIT 10.6 | SIMPLE CHARACTERISTICS |

- Employee elective deferral (optional)
- Employer match (or non-elective contribution)
- 100% vesting in all contributions and earnings
- Employer must have ≤ 100 employees

Annual Limit on Employee Elective Contributions for SIMPLE IRAs

Employees may make annual elective deferrals to a SIMPLE IRA plan for 2005 and thereafter, in the amount of $10,000 adjusted for inflation.

Year	Total Elective Contribution	Catch-Up
2005	$10,000	$2,000
2006	$10,000[†]	$2,500
2007	$10,500[†]	$2,500[†]
2008	$10,500[†]	$2,500[†]

---

6. IRC Section 408(p)(2)(A), Section 408(p)(2)(A)(iii).
7. IRC Section 408(p)(2)(A)(ii).

The $10,000 limitation is adjusted for inflation in increments of $500 (the inflation adjustment is rounded downward to the nearest $500). The base period for calculating the inflation adjustment is the calendar quarter beginning July 1, 2004.[8]

Salary Reduction Catch-up Contributions for SIMPLE IRAs

For employees who have attained the age of 50 by the end of the calendar year and if there are no other elective contributions that can be made for them during the calendar year, such employees are permitted to make additional elective contributions, also known as "catch-up contributions," to the plan for that calendar year. The maximum catch-up contribution for such an eligible employee for the calendar year is the lesser of:

- the catch-up contribution limit, of $2,000 for 2005, $2,500 for 2006, $2,500[†] for 2007, and $2,500[†] for 2008;[9] or
- the employee's compensation for the year reduced by all of the employee's other catch-up contributions for the year to other SIMPLEs, or 401(k)'s, SEPs, and 403(b)s.

EXAMPLE 10.3

> Joseph, age 54, worked for Wondering Industries between January 1 and May 31 of 2005. During that period, he made elective deferral contributions to his 401(k) of $14,000 and elected to defer an additional $600 under the available catch-up of the 401(k). In July of 2005, Joseph began working for Knowledger Contributions, which had a SIMPLE. Between July and December of 2005, Joseph can only defer an additional $1,400 ($2,000 - $600) to the SIMPLE under the catch-up provision because of catch-up deferrals under the 401(k) plan.

Employer Contributions

An employer who sponsors a SIMPLE IRA is required to make either matching contributions to those employees who make elective deferrals or, alternatively, to make nonelective contributions to all eligible employees.

Employer Matching Contributions

If the employer elects to make matching contributions, the employer is generally required to match the employee's elective deferral contributions on a dollar-for-dollar matching basis up to three percent of the compensation of the employee (without regard to the covered compensation limit) for the entire calendar year.[10]

---

8. IRC Section 408(p)(2)(A)(ii), as amended by EGTRRA 2001, Section 611(f)(1), Section 408(p)(2)(E), as amended by EGTRRA 2001, Section 611(f)(2); EGTRRA 2001, Section 611(i)(1).

9. After 2006 calendar year, the $2,500 limitation will be adjusted for inflation in increments of $500, and the base period for calculating the inflation adjustment will be the calendar quarter starting July 1, 2005. IRC Section 414(v), as amended by EGTRRA, 2001, Section 631(a).

10. IRC Section 408(p)(2)(A)(iii).

The employer may reduce the three percent matching contribution requirement for a calendar year, but only under all of the following circumstances:[11]

- the limit is reduced to no less than one percent;
- the limit is not reduced for more than two years out of the five year period that ends with (and includes) the year for which the election is effective; and
- employees are notified of the reduced limit within a reasonable period of time before the sixty day election period for a salary reduction agreement.

This only applies to SIMPLE IRAs (not available for SIMPLE 401(k)s).[12]

EXAMPLE 10.4

An employer normally must match each employee's elective deferral contribution dollar-for-dollar up to 3% of the employee's compensation. Michael is employed by Thomas in 2005. Michael earned $30,000 and elected to defer 10% of his salary. Thomas was self-employed and his net earnings were $300,000. Thomas chose to defer 3% of his earnings to his SIMPLE IRA. Thomas makes a 3% matching contribution. The total contribution to Michael's SIMPLE IRA for 2005 is $3,900 as calculated below. Notice that the match for Thomas is not limited to 3% of $210,000 (the covered compensation limit for qualified plans). The limit is $9,000 (3% of $300,000).

Michael's elective deferral contribution ($30,000 x 10%)	$3,000
Matching contribution by Thomas Co. ($30,000 x 3%)	$900
2005 Total SIMPLE IRA Contribution	**$3,900**

Using the same facts as above, the total contribution for 2005 to Thomas' SIMPLE IRA is $18,000 as calculated below:

Thomas' elective deferral contribution ($300,000 x 3%)	$9,000
Matching contribution by Thomas Co. ($300,000 x 3%)	$9,000
2005 Total SIMPLE IRA Contribution	**$18,000**

Nonelective Contributions by Employer

The alternative for the employer who chooses not to match employee elective deferrals is to make nonelective contributions for all eligible employees. If the employer chooses to make **nonelective contributions**, then the employer must contribute two percent of each eligible employee's compensation (up to the covered compensation limit of $210,000 for 2005, $215,000[†] for 2006, $220,000[†] for 2007, $225,000[†] for 2008) to the SIMPLE IRA. The contribution must be made for all eligible employees who earn at least $5,000 from the employer for the year, or less if elected by the employer. If the employer decides to make nonelective contributions, the

---

11. IRC Section 408(p)(2)(C)(ii).
12. IRC Section 401(k)(11)(B)(i).

employer is required to make those nonelective contributions whether or not the employee chooses to make any elective deferral contributions. The employees must be notified within a reasonable time period before the 60 day election period of the employer's choice of the two percent nonelective contribution method or the matching contribution.

EXAMPLE 10.5

Matthew, an employee of Kathleen's Company, earned $40,000 in 2005 and agreed to make elective deferral contributions of 9% of his salary to his SIMPLE IRA. Kathleen earned $60,000 net self-employment income and chose to make elective deferral contributions of 10% of her earnings. Kathleen's Company, as the employer, made a nonelective contribution of 2% to each eligible employee. The total contribution to Matthew's SIMPLE IRA for 2005 is $4,400 as calculated below.

Matthew's elective deferral contribution ($40,000 x 0.09)	$3,600
Non elective contribution by Kathleen Co. ($40,000 x 0.02)	$800
2005 Total Contribution for Matthew	**$4,400**

Using the same facts as above, the total contribution to Kathleen's SIMPLE IRA for 2005 is $7,200 as calculated below.

Kathleen's elective deferral contribution ($60,000 x 0.10)	$6,000
Non elective contribution by Kathleen Co. ($60,000 x 0.02)	$1,200
2005 Total Contribution for Kathleen	**$7,200**

Taxation of Contributions

SIMPLE IRA contributions are contemporaneously tax deductible for the small employer. The deductible amount includes the employee elective deferral contributions (as compensation) and any employer match or nonelective contribution. The contributions to a SIMPLE IRA are not subject to a limitation based on a percentage of compensation, but the employee's elective deferral is limited to $10,000 for 2005 ($10,000[†] for 2006, $10,500[†] for 2007, $10,500[†] for 2008).

Employer Contributions	Employee Elective Deferrals
• 3% match, or • 2% nonelective contribution for all eligible employees	• % or $ contribution up to $10,000 plus $2,000 for over 50 for 2005

Employers are allowed to deduct contributions for the taxable year only if the contributions are made on or before the date that the employer's tax return is due. The elective contributions of the employee that are being made into the SIMPLE IRA account must be contributed by the employer no later than 30 days following the last day of the month of the contributions. [13] The employer must also make any matching contributions or nonelective contributions by the date that its tax return is due for that tax year, including extensions.

Employee elective deferral contributions and employer contributions made to SIMPLE IRAs are excluded from an employee's taxable income and are not subject to federal income tax withholding. An employee's elective deferral contributions are, however, subject to payroll taxes (OASDI and Medicare), but the employer matching or nonelective contributions made to SIMPLE IRA accounts are not subject to payroll tax (OASDI and Medicare).

Withdrawals and Distributions

Distributions from a SIMPLE IRA plan are includible as ordinary income in the individual employee's taxable income in the year in which they are withdrawn. SIMPLE IRA plan distributions are taxed in the same manner as distributions from a traditional IRA. As a general rule, trustee-to-trustee transfers (direct), and rollovers of SIMPLE IRAs are not taxable distributions. SIMPLE distributions may be subjected to an early withdrawal penalty of 10 percent if received prior to age 59½. The exclusions from the 10 percent penalty for SIMPLE IRAs are the same as described in Chapter 9 for IRAs.

A distribution or transfer made from a SIMPLE IRA during the first two years of an employee's participation in the SIMPLE must be contributed to another SIMPLE IRA to avoid taxation and penalty. After the two year participation period, a SIMPLE IRA can be transferred or rolled over tax-free to:

- an IRA other than a SIMPLE IRA;
- a qualified plan;
- a 403(b) account or tax sheltered annuity; or
- a deferred compensation plan of a State or local government (457 plan).

If a distribution is taken from a SIMPLE IRA plan during the first two years of an employee's participation in the plan and if the distribution is subject to the early withdrawal penalty, the penalty tax increases from 10 percent to 25 percent. If the distribution is made on account of a penalty exclusion (as described in Chapter 9) then the 25 percent penalty tax will not apply.[14] After the employee's first two years of plan participation, the 10 percent penalty for early withdrawal will apply if the distribution is not because of a penalty excluded reason.

SIMPLE 401(k) PLANS

A SIMPLE 401(k) plan is a qualified plan and must generally satisfy the same requirements as 401(k) plans and SIMPLE IRA plans. The differences between SIMPLE 401(k)s and SIMPLE IRAs or between SIMPLE 401(k)s and 401(k)s are discussed below, along with other attributes of SIMPLE 401(k)s.

---

13. IRC Section 408(p)(5)(B).
14. IRC Section 72(t)(6).

Under a SIMPLE 401(k) plan, an employee may choose to reduce his salary in return for "salary reduction contributions" or deferrals to a SIMPLE 401(k) account. This salary reduction contribution is expressly stated as a percentage of the employee's compensation but may not exceed $10,000 for 2005. The employer may, but is not required to, permit certain employees to use the catch-up feature, under which employees age 50 and over may defer a contribution of up to $2,000 for 2005.

The rules concerning contributions for employers to regular 401(k) plans, discussed in Chapter 5, also apply to SIMPLE 401(k)s. The limitation of $10,000 for 2005 or employee elective deferral contributions to the SIMPLE IRA plans (discussed above) also apply to the SIMPLE 401(k)s.

A participant of a SIMPLE 401(k) may take a loan (plan permitting) from his SIMPLE 401(k), unlike a participant of a SIMPLE IRA. The amount of the loan is subject to the same restrictions, discussed in Chapter 7, as loans from qualified plans.

Employers who sponsor SIMPLE 401(k) plans must make either (1) a matching contribution or (2) a nonelective contribution to the plan. An employer is required to match the elective deferral contribution of the employee on a dollar-for-dollar basis up to three percent of the employee's compensation for the calendar year.[15] In contrast to a SIMPLE IRA plan, the employer does not have the available option of reducing matching contributions to less than three percent of the compensation of each employee.

As an alternative to matching elective deferral contributions, an employer that has established a SIMPLE 401(k) plan may elect to provide nonelective contributions of two percent of each eligible employee's compensation. The nonelective contributions of the employer are required to be made for each eligible employee, regardless of whether that employee elects to make any salary reduction deferral contributions. Under these circumstances, the employer is permitted, but is not required, to limit nonelective contributions to only those eligible employees (those employees who meet the eligibility rules).[16]

Quick Quiz

Highlight the answer to these questions:

1. Employers who sponsor a SIMPLE IRA must make either matching contributions or nonelective contributions.
   a. True
   b. False

2. Distributions from SIMPLE IRAs are generally taxed like traditional IRAs.
   a. True
   b. False

3. Employers that sponsor SIMPLE 401(k) plans must allow for catch up contributions for participants over 50.
   a. True
   b. False

True, True, False.

---

15. IRC Section 401(k)(11)(B)(i)(II).
16. IRC Section 401(k)(11)(B)(ii).

No other contribution may be made to the trust comprising the SIMPLE 401(k) account. No contributions can be made nor may benefits accrue for services during the year pursuant to any other qualified retirement plan of the employer for any employee participating in the SIMPLE 401(k) plan. The ADP test, ACP test, and top-heavy rules, explained in prior chapters, do not apply to SIMPLE 401(k)s because they are essentially safe harbor plans. Once again, though, there are few if any SIMPLE 401(k) plans that have been established.

CONCLUSION

SIMPLEs are retirement plans for small employers, and like their name implies, are very easy to establish and maintain, have less administrative costs than other retirement plans, and do not have any annual filing requirements. As discussed, SIMPLEs can take the form of a SIMPLE IRA or SIMPLE 401(k), both of which essentially share the same rules. In practice, most employers chose the SIMPLE IRA instead of the SIMPLE 401(k). Although the 401(k) version has loans as an available option, it also has greater administrative requirements.

EXHIBIT 10.7 CONCEPT SUMMARY - SIMPLE PLANS

SIMPLE	Savings Incentive Match Plan for Employees
Application	Small employers (limit of 100 employee's with compensation > $5,000)
Style	Self-reliant employee elective deferral contributions and employer match
Type	Could be SIMPLE 401(k), but almost all are SIMPLE IRAs
Established By What Date	Generally, October 1 of year the plan starts
Characteristics	No annual filing requirement, minor costs No other retirement plans are permitted
Employee Elective Deferral Contribution Limit	Lesser of $10,000 for 2005 salary reduction or 100% salary
Catch-Up Contribution for Age 50	Yes, $2,000 for 2005
Available Employer Contributions	Dollar-for-dollar match up to the lesser of 3% of compensation (without regard to covered compensation limit) or $10,000 or 2% of compensation (up to covered compensation limit of $210,000 for 2005) nonelective contribution for each eligible employee regardless of deferral
Penalties for Withdrawals	25% if within 2 years, unless penalty exception applies; 10% after 2 years unless penalty exception applies.
Loans Permitted	No - SIMPLE IRA; Yes - SIMPLE 401(k)
In-Service Withdrawals	Yes, subject to income and penalties

SIMPLE IRA, SIMPLE 401(k), AND 401(k) PLAN COMPARISON

EXHIBIT 10.8

	SIMPLE IRA	SIMPLE 401(k)	401(k) Plans
Application	Small employers (limit of 100 employee's with compensation > $5,000)	Same as SIMPLE IRA	Most employers
Style	Self-reliant employee elective deferral contributions and employer match		
Established By What Date	Generally, October 1 of the year the plan starts	Same as SIMPLE IRA	By 12/31 of year before
Ability to have Other Plans	Must not have another retirement plan	Same as SIMPLE IRA	There may be other plans
Filings and Costs	No annual filing requirement, minor costs	Same as 401(k)	Annual filing required and administrative costs
Annual Testing	None required if meet contribution requirements	None required if meet contribution requirements	Required.
Vesting	All contributions are fully vested	All contributions are fully vested	Vesting schedules allowed
Employee Elective Deferral Contribution Limit	$10,000 for 2005 $10,000[†] for 2006 $10,500[†] for 2007 $10,500[†] for 2008	Same as SIMPLE IRA	$14,000 for 2005 $15,000 for 2006 $15,000[†] for 2007 $15,500[†] for 2008
Catch-Up Contribution for Age 50	$2,000 for 2005 $2,500 for 2006 $2,500[†] for 2007 $2,500[†] for 2008	Same as SIMPLE IRA	$4,000 for 2005 $5,000 for 2006 $5,000[†] for 2007 $5,000[†] for 2008
Employer Contribution	The employer must generally make: • A dollar-for-dollar match up to 3% of pay or • A 2% nonelective contri-bution for each eligible employee.	Same as SIMPLE IRA except for the employer-match cannot be reduced to as low as 1% for no more than 2 out of 5 years, including the year of election.	Employer may contribute
Loans Permitted	No	Same as 401(k)	Yes
In-Service Withdrawals	Permitted, but possible 10% penalty if under age 59-1/2. If withdrawals are made within the first two years of participation, the 10% additional tax is increased to 25%.	Same as 401(k)	Permitted, but possible 10% penalty if under age 59-1/2

Under Section 403(b) of the IRC, plans called **tax sheltered or deferred annuities,** or "**403(b) plans,**" are available to certain qualified nonprofit organizations or to employees of public educational systems. Recently, the employee elective deferral contributions limits of 403(b) plans have been increased along with the addition of the catch-up provisions that allow for deferral of significant amounts for those employees who are age 50 or older.

WHAT IS A 403(b) PLAN

A 403(b) plan is a retirement plan for certain employees of public schools, certain ministers, and employees of various tax exempt organizations. It is a tax-sheltered retirement plan, but not a qualified plan. The 403(b) plan is established by the employer, and the employee has an individual account earmarked as his 403(b) plan account. Many consider 403(b) plans of nonprofit entities to be the counterpart to the 401(k) plans of for-profit entities. Sometimes, 403(b)s are termed "401(k)s for nonprofits." Many 403(b) plans offer similar attributes as qualified defined contribution plans.

Key Concepts

Underline/highlight the answers to these questions as you read:

1. What are 403(b) plans?

2. When does ERISA apply to 403(b) plans?

3. Who is eligible for a 403(b) plan?

4. What rules are applicable to employee contributions to 403(b) plans?

Which Entities Can Establish 403(b) Plans

Only employers can set up 403(b) accounts. Individuals cannot establish 403(b) accounts on their own. Interestingly, however, self-employed ministers (discussed briefly below) are considered both employees and employers, and thus; are able to contribute to a retirement 403(b) income account for their own benefit. Generally, employers that are eligible to establish 403(b) plans are nonprofit religious, charitable, scientific, educational, and other public interest organizations like private schools, colleges, universities, and teaching hospitals.

Technically, the two types of entities that can establish 403(b) plans are:
1. Tax exempt organizations under IRC Section 501(c)(3), or
2. Public schools or public educational organizations.

Section 501(c)(3) Organizations

Section 501(c)(3) organizations are nonprofit tax-exempt organizations that are established under IRC Section 501(c)(3) of the Internal Revenue Code. Section 501(c)(3) organizations are nonprofit entities such as corporations, community chests, funds, or foundations. They are organized exclusively (i) for religious, charitable, scientific, literary, or educational purposes, (ii) to foster amateur sports competition nationally or internationally, unless any of their activities involve providing athletic equipment or facilities, or (iii) to prevent cruelty to children or animals. Net earnings of the organization may not inure to the benefit of private shareholders. Further, no lobbying activities (other than by public charities) can comprise a substantial part of

[Handwritten margin notes:]
Annuities & M Funds
No individual stocks

$220k covered comp
$15K EE deferral
$5K ≥ 50 catch up contrib.
100% vesting

the organization's activities, nor can the organization participate in any political campaign for any candidate for public office.[17]

Public Schools or Public Educational Organizations

In general, public schools can establish 403(b)s, and most often the public educational system of a state or community will establish a 403(b) plan. A public educational system is an organization run by a state, political subdivision, or agency that maintains a faculty and curriculum and has regularly enrolled students in attendance where educational activities are conducted.[18]

ERISA APPLICABILITY

The issue of whether ERISA applies to a 403(b) plan is important. If ERISA applies, then the plan requirements change. ERISA applies if the 403(b) plan is considered to be an "employee benefit pension plan." An employee benefit pension plan is defined as any plan, fund, or program established or maintained by an employer that provides retirement income to employees or defers income of employees for periods until termination of employment or beyond. Governmental TSAs and church-related TSAs are not subject to ERISA, but plans of Section 501(c)(3) organizations may be subject to ERISA unless employer involvement is so minimal that it falls short of the requirement that a plan be sponsored by an employer (as discussed below).

It is very common for a 403(b) plan to be a part of an overall pension or retirement plan. The 403(b) portion may be referred to as the supplemental retirement plan. If this is the case then the plan is subject to ERISA requirements.

Generally 403(b) plans are not subject to ERISA rules if the following are true:
- employee participation is voluntary;
- there are no employer contributions;
- employee has solely enforceable rights under the plan;
- employer's involvement is limited in scope; and
- sponsored by a government or religious institution.

Suppose Loyola University had a retirement plan that required employees to contribute 3.5 percent of their salary to the plan and the university contributed eight percent to the plan. Loyola also maintained a 403(b) plan that allowed employees to choose elective deferrals up to the maximum provided by the law. In this case Loyola's 403(b) plan would be subject to ERISA requirements because it is maintained as an "employer benefit pension plan."	**EXAMPLE 10.6**

---

17. IRC Section 501(c)(3).
18. IRC Section 403(b)(1)(A)(ii).

If a 403(b) plan only provides for salary reduction agreements, then the plan is not considered to be established or maintained by the employer and ERISA is inapplicable. If ERISA applies, nonelective deferral contributions must satisfy nondiscrimination requirements, matching contributions must satisfy the ACP test, and the plan is subject to preretirement joint and survivor annuity elections and joint and survivor elections at retirement as distribution requirements.

To illustrate this point, consider the scenario of a 403(b) plan that only provides for elective deferrals (i.e., salary reduction contributions). In such a case, only one nondiscrimination requirement will apply: If one employee has the right to elect to have the employer make salary reduction contributions under a salary reduction agreement, then all employees must be permitted to elect to salary deferral contributions. If, however, the plan contains employer contributions beyond salary reduction contributions, then contributions to the 403(b) plan are subject to the general nondiscrimination rules applicable to qualified retirement plans and may not discriminate in favor of the HC.

ELIGIBILITY

Eligible employees can participate in a 403(b) plan sponsored through an employer. Similar to 401(k) plans, a 403(b) plan may require employees to attain age 21 and complete one year of service to become eligible to participate. The following are considered eligible employees (who must meet the age and service requirements) to participate in a 403(b) plan:

1. Employees of tax-exempt organizations as defined under IRC Section 501(c)(3).
2. Employees who are involved in the day-to-day operations of a public school or public school system.
3. Employees of cooperative hospital service organizations.[19]
4. Ministers who meet one of the following criteria:
   - Ministers that are employed by Section 501(c)(3) organizations (discussed above);
   - Ministers that are self-employed. A self-employed minister is deemed as employed by a tax-exempt organization that is a qualified employer.
   - Ministers who are employed by organizations that are not Section 501(c)(3) organizations and function as ministers in their day-to-day responsibilities with their employer.

   Self-employed ministers must report total contributions to 403(b) accounts as a tax deduction on their tax returns.

Notes on Employees

When the term "employee" is used in discussing these rules, an employer-employee relationship must exist to allow the employee to be eligible to participate. The individual must be an employee, not an independent contractor. There are many IRS guidelines for characterizing someone as an employee or independent contractor based on the relationship between the individual and the company. Some emphasis is placed on the amount of control, direction, and supervision that the employer has over the individual.

---

19. Cooperative hospital service organizations are codified in IRC Section 501(e). They are deemed to be Section 501(c)(3) organizations, and thus are allowed to form a 403(b) plan for employees.

In *Azad v U.S.*[20], a radiologist was on salary at a hospital. The radiologist's work at the hospital was not supervised nor was it directed by the hospital. The Court concluded that the radiologist was not an employee as defined by the IRC, and was not permitted to exclude from his gross income those amounts contributed to an annuity contract by the employer.

EXAMPLE 10.7

EMPLOYEE CONTRIBUTIONS

Employees' elective deferral contributions to 403(b) accounts are very similar to employee elective deferral contributions to 401(k)s, SARSEPs, and 457s. While a 403(b) plan is established by the employer, the employee has an individual 403(b) account for his own benefit. Only the employer is allowed to make contributions to the 403(b) account on behalf of the employee (usually through employee salary reduction), but some plans may also allow employees to make after-tax contributions similar to a thrift plan.

The following contributions are permissible contributions (but are not required) for 403(b) accounts:
- employee elective deferrals;
- nonelective contributions;
- after-tax contributions; and
- any combination of the above.

With employee "elective deferrals," contributions can be made under a salary reduction agreement where the employee agrees that the employer will withhold money from the employee's paycheck so that these funds can be contributed directly into the 403(b) account for the benefit of the employee. The employee is not subject to income tax on the contribution until the funds are withdrawn from the 403(b) account by the employee. However, the elective deferral amounts are subject to payroll taxes exactly as are 401(k) elective deferrals. For 2005, an employee can electively defer no more than $14,000, subject to catch-up provisions discussed later in this chapter.

Unlike employee elective deferrals, "nonelective contributions" are not made under a salary reduction agreement. Instead, nonelective contributions are matching contributions, mandatory contributions from the employer, or even discretionary contributions by the employer. Again, the employee does not pay taxes on these contributions until withdrawn by the employee from the account.

Finally, an employee may contribute after-tax or non-deductible funds to a 403(b) account. Unlike the elective deferral and non-elective contributions, however, the amount contributed in after-tax contributions are not excluded from the income of the employee and will therefore create an adjusted taxable basis in the 403(b) account. When the participant takes a withdrawal from such an account, some of the funds will be return of capital and, therefore, nontaxable.

---

20. *Azad v. U.S.*, 277 F. Supp. 258 (D.C. Minn. 1966), *aff'd*, 388 F.2d 74 (8th Cir. 1968).

Limits on Elective Deferrals

An elective deferral is basically an employee's contribution to an employee's account through a voluntary salary reduction agreement. While technically only employers can actually make contributions into the 403(b) accounts on behalf of the employees, an employee has voluntarily elected or decided to reduce his salary by a certain amount and that forgone amount is contributed by the employer for the benefit of the employer into the 403(b) account. Commonly, this is referred to as a cash or deferred arrangement (CODA) because the employee has the choice of receiving the funds in cash or deferring the income. Therefore, the employee is directing the employer to place these deferral amounts into this account on his behalf.

During a given year, an employee may enter into more than one salary reduction agreement. If elective deferrals are made to more than one 403(b) account for a given employee (irrespective of whether the contributions were made by the same employer) in the same year, then there must be a summary of all such elective deferrals to determine if the aggregate amount exceeds more than the employee's limit for that year, $14,000 for 2005. If elective deferrals are made to other retirement plans on behalf of the employee, then the limit on elective deferrals applies to the total, aggregate amount. Other accounts that are included in the aggregate total are 401(k) plans, Section 501(c)(18) plans, SIMPLEs, SARSEPs, and all 403(b) plans. If an amount contributed exceeds the limit, the employee must include the excess in gross income on his tax return for the year contributed.

EXHIBIT 10.9	**403(b) ANNUAL ELECTIVE DEFERRALS LIMITS***

Year	Annual Deferral Limit	Catch-Up Contributions **	Total Deferral
2005	$14,000	$4,000	$18,000
2006	$15,000	$5,000	$20,000
2007	$15,000[†]	$5,000[†]	$20,000[†]
2008	$15,500[†]	$5,000[†]	$20,500[†]

* The same limits apply to SARSEPs, 401(k) plans, and 457 plans.
** Age 50 or older

The limit on elective deferrals for 2005 that can be contributed to a 403(b) account through a salary reduction agreement is $14,000. There are certain exceptions to the general limit of $14,000 for 2005 for contributions to 403(b) plans. Those age 50 and over and those with at least 15 years of service to the employer can make additional, or catch-up, contributions.

Vesting

All contributions to 403(b) accounts and related earnings are 100 percent vested.

Catch-Up Contributions

Age 50 Catch-Up Provisions

There are "catch-up" provisions for certain employees participating in a 403(b). In addition to the contribution limits to a 403(b), employees age 50 and over at the end of the year may make additional contributions under the catch-up provisions of IRC Section 403(b). An employee is eligible to make catch up contributions if the employee has reached age 50 by the end of the year, and the maximum amount of elective deferrals that can be made to the employee's account have been satisfied for the year. If these two elements exist, then the total amount of "catch up contributions" for the employee age 50 and over would be the lesser of $4,000 for 2005, or includable compensation (explained below) subtracted by other elective deferrals for the year. When determining what catch up contributions are allowable under 403(b), all catch up contributions made by the employer on behalf of the employee must be combined, and these amounts include contributions made to qualified retirement plans, 401(k)s, 403(b) plans, SEPs, and SIMPLEs.

"15 Year Rule" Exception

There is a special catch-up rule, in addition to the $4,000 catch-up for participants age 50 and over, that applies only for 403(b) plans for employees that have worked for the same employer for 15 years (not required to be consecutive). If an employee has worked for 15 years with an organization that qualifies for eligibility under a 403(b) plan, then the limit of elective deferrals to the 403(b) account is increased by the lesser of the following:

- $3,000,
- $15,000, reduced by increases to the general limit that were allowed in previous years due to the **15-year rule**, or
- $5,000 times the number of years of service for the organization by the employee, subtracted by the total elective deferrals made by the employer on behalf of the employee for earlier years.

Quick Quiz

Highlight the answer to these questions:

1. Employers or individuals can establish a 403(b) plan.
   a. True
   b. False

2. 403(b) plans may be covered under ERISA.
   a. True
   b. False

3. Additional catch-up contributions to a 403(b) plan may be after-tax contributions from the employee.
   a. True
   b. False

False, True, False.

[handwritten margin notes: Can be nonconsecutive. allows EE to put away extra $15K in deferrals over at least 5 yrs. (max 3k/yr)]

If an employee qualifies for the 15-year rule, the maximum elective deferrals for the 403(b) plan for the plan year may be as high as $21,000 for 2005 ($14,000 maximum deferral plus $3,000 from the 15-year rule plus $4,000 for the 50 and over catch-up rule) .

Employee	Age	Years of Service	Maximum Deferral
A	25	2	$14,000
B	52	3	$18,000
C	52	16	$21,000

→ *Roth Contributions (Roth Accounts)*

Effective after December 31, 2005, 403(b) plans and 401(k) plans may allow employees to make Roth contributions to the 403(b) plan. These contributions are not excludable from the employee's gross income. Instead, these contributions will consist of after-tax dollars, just like contributions to Roth IRAs. Distributions attributable to these Roth contributions will be non-taxable and will not be subject to penalties if the distribution is a qualifying distribution. The qualifying distribution rules are the same as those for distributions from Roth IRAs as discussed in Chapter 9. Qualified plans that adopt availability of Roth contributions are required to adopt separate accounts and maintain separate records for these Roth contributions and earnings allocable to the contributions.

These Roth contributions will provide a great opportunity for employees to save for retirement. Although the contributions are not pretax, all qualifying distributions will be tax-free and penalty free. The contribution limit for Roth accounts increases in 2006 to $15,000, significantly higher than the limits for contributions to Roth IRAs outside a qualified plan. Contributions to Roth IRAs are also limited based on annual income, but Roth accounts within 403(b)s do not have such income limitations. However, some Roth IRAs are subject to the higher deferral limits for 403(b)s. Therefore, an HCE would be able to fund a Roth only through a Roth account, not a Roth IRA.

EMPLOYER CONTRIBUTIONS

Nonelective contributions are matching contributions, mandatory contributions, or even discretionary contributions from the employer. Employer matching contributions are based on the employee's deferral, and the employer may make other contributions without regard to the employee's elective deferral. Unlike employee elective deferrals, nonelective contributions are not made under a salary reduction agreement. As discussed earlier, the nonelective employer contributions (other than salary reduction contributions) to the 403(b) account subject the plan to ERISA.

The Limit on Annual Additions

There is a limit on "annual additions" or amounts added to an account over the course of a year for an employee in a 403(b) plan to comply with IRC Section 415(c). The limitation applies to an aggregate of all contributions. The total contributions are comprised of elective deferrals, nonelective contributions, and after-tax contributions. The maximum for 2005 is the lesser of $42,000, or 100 percent of the employee's covered compensation for the employee's most recent year of service. If an employee contributed to more than one 403(b) account, all employer contributions to the accounts must be combined when determining if they exceed acceptable limits.

Includable Compensation in the Most Recent Year of Service

The definition of **includable compensation** for the most recent year of service is that amount of taxable wages and benefits that are received by the employee from the employer. When figuring includable compensation for the most recent year of service, it could be that the most recent year of service is not the same as the employer's most recent annual work period. In such a case, the most recent year of service is determined by calculating the previous full year of service for the employee's position.

A full year of service is equal to full time employment for the annual work period of the employer. For instance, if an employee worked the last four months of 2005 and the next nine months of 2006, then the most recent year of service would have been the first nine months of 2006 and the last three months of 2005, totaling the most previous 12-month period of work.

Once the most recent year of service has been identified, the next step is to quantify the includable compensation earned during that full year of service. Includable compensation is the total of income and benefits received from an employer maintaining a 403(b) account and the amount included in the income of the employee. The following amounts are considered as includible compensation:

- Elective deferrals;
- Amounts contributed by an employer under a Cafeteria Plan;
- Amounts contributed under an eligible Section 457 Nonqualified Deferred Compensation plan;
- Wages, salaries, and fees for personal services earned with the employer maintaining the 403(b) account;
- Income excluded under the Foreign Earned Income exclusion; and
- Qualified transportation or fringe benefits.

Key Concepts

Underline/highlight the answers to these questions as you read:

1. What are the available investment choices for 403(b) plans?

2. How are loans and distributions from a 403(b) plan taxed?

3. What rollover, distribution, and minimum distribution rules apply to 403(b) plans?

Meanwhile, the following items are not considered includible compensation:
- The employer's contributions to the employee's 403(b) account;
- Compensation earned while the employee was not eligible;
- The employer's contributions to a qualified plan on behalf of the employee that are excluded from income; and
- The cost of incidental life insurance.

INVESTMENT CHOICES AND LIMITATIONS

Funds within a 403(b) account can only be invested in either insurance annuity contracts or mutual funds. Specifically, individual accounts in 403(b) plans must be one of the following forms:

- A contract provided through an insurance company called an annuity contract;
- An account invested in mutual funds only, which is referred to as a custodial account; or
- An account for church employees that is a retirement income account, which invests in either annuities or mutual funds.

Annuity Contracts

"**Annuity contracts**" are not specifically defined in the Internal Revenue Code. An annuity contract must be purchased for the employee from an insurance company and may give a fixed benefit or a variable benefit depending on the performance of the investment.[21] Any contract or certificate that is transferable to a person other than a trustee is not an annuity contract.

EXAMPLE 10.8

In *Corbin v. U.S.*,[22] the question before the Court was whether an annuity must be purchased from an insurance company in order to qualify for this special treatment. The United States Eighth Circuit Court of Appeals noted that the IRS had issued Revenue Ruling 82-102, 1982-1, C.B., revoking prior rulings that seemed to extend to non-insurance company-purchased annuities the special benefits of IRC Section 403(b)(1). The Court concluded that the wording of the statute using the word "premiums" indicated that the privilege is limited to annuities purchased from insurance companies.

LOANS

While in-service withdrawal distributions to employees are generally not permitted until retirement or termination, ERISA plans are permitted to make loans to plan participants. Loans to 403(b) employee-participants are allowed and are subject to the same limitations and requirements applicable to loans from qualified retirement plans (e.g., 401(k)). Although any qualified plan may establish a loan provision, they are generally found only in 401(k) plans and 403(b) plans. As discussed fully in Chapter 5 regarding loans from 401(k) plans, the plan loans must be made available to all participants and beneficiaries on an effectively equal basis, must be limited in amount, must be repaid within a certain time period, must bear a reasonable rate of interest, must be adequately secured, and the administrator must maintain proper accounting for the loans.

When an employee is terminated or if the TSA is terminated, then any outstanding loan will be affected. Loan repayments are generally accomplished through payroll deduction, which of course is unavailable after employee termination occurs. If an employee fails to repay a loan from a qualified plan upon termination, the employer will generally declare the unpaid portion a deemed distribution, which will be subject to ordinary income tax and possibly an early withdrawal penalty of 10 percent if under the age of 59½. However, plans may provide alternatives such as reducing the amount of a direct rollover distribution and providing the employee a certain period of time to repay the loan before it will be treated as a distribution.

---

21. Treasury Regulation Section 1.403(b)-1(c)(3).
22. *Corbin v. U.S.*, 760 F.2d 234, 6 Employee Benefits Cas. 1417 (8th Cir. 1985).

DISTRIBUTIONS

Because 403(b) plans fall within the ERISA plan area, they follow many of the same rules regarding distributions applicable to other qualified plans. Generally, distributions can be paid from a 403(b) account only after the following events:

- the employee turns age 59½;
- the employee is separated from service;
- the employee dies;
- the employee becomes disabled; or
- for salary reduction contributions, the employee endures a severe hardship.[23]

These restrictions apply only to contributions from salary reduction agreements. Nonelective deferral contributions have no such restrictions upon distribution. However, if distributions attributable to salary reduction contributions or nonelective deferrals occur before the employee turns 59½, then a 10 percent penalty for early withdrawal may apply.

Hardship distributions are permitted in 403(b)s. Therefore, the hardship rules discussed in Chapter 5 for CODAs can be used for guidance. Hardship distributions from TSAs cannot be rolled over to an IRA and are not subject to the 20 percent income tax withholding rules as discussed in Chapter 7.

ROLLOVERS TO/FROM 403(b)S

Employee-participants can generally roll over tax free all or any part of a distribution from a 403(b) plan to a qualified plan, a traditional IRA, or to another 403(b) retirement plan. Any rollover that is not a direct trustee-to-trustee rollover will be subject to mandatory 20 percent withholding and 100 percent of the distribution must be deposited into the new account by the 60th day following the day on which the employee receives the distribution.

Hardship Exception to Rollover Rules

The IRS may waive the 60-day rollover period if the participant's failure to waive such requirement would be against equity or good conscience, including cases of casualty, disaster, or other events beyond the reasonable control of the individual. To obtain a hardship exception, the participant must apply to the IRS for a waiver of the 60-day rollover requirement. In its determination as to the grant of a waiver, the IRS will consider all relevant facts and circumstances, including:

- Whether errors were made by the financial institution facilitating the roll over;
- Whether the participant was unable to complete the rollover due to death, disability, hospitalization, incarceration, restrictions imposed by a foreign country or postal error;
- Whether the participant used the amount distributed; and
- The time passed since the date of distribution.

---

23. IRC Section 403(b)(11).

MINIMUM DISTRIBUTION REQUIREMENTS

403(b)s are subject to the same minimum distribution requirements applicable to IRAs and qualified plans, which require that an individual begin taking withdrawals from the plan by April 1st of the year after the participant attains the age of 70½. These rules include the latest time that distributions from 403(b)s may begin and the minimum amount that may be distributed from the 403(b), which are similar to the rules for IRAs and for qualified retirement plans. For a more complete explanation of the minimum distribution requirements, see Chapter 7.

Excess Employer Contributions

If a distribution from a 403(b) plan consists of income that was previously included in income as an excess employer contribution, then that portion of the transfer is not eligible as a rollover distribution to an IRA. This transfer does not affect the rollover treatment of the eligible portion of the transferred amounts; however, the ineligible portion is subject to the traditional IRA contribution limits and may create an excess IRA contribution subject to a six percent excise tax. Chapter 9 discusses the traditional IRA contribution limits and the six percent excise tax.

TAXATION OF 403(b) DISTRIBUTIONS

The tax rules that apply to 403(b) distributions are basically the same tax rules that apply to distributions from other qualified retirement plans and IRAs. In most instances, the distributions from 403(b) accounts received by participants are taxable as ordinary income in the year received; however, the employee-participant's return of adjusted taxable basis is not subject to tax. This basis includes the employee's voluntary after-tax contributions, life insurance protection costs, employer contributions previously includible in the employee's income, and loans to the employee secured by the TSA that were deemed as taxable distributions.

QUALIFIED JOINT AND SURVIVOR ANNUITY

As discussed in Chapter 7, a **qualified joint and survivor annuity (QJSA)** is an immediate annuity for the life of the participant coupled with an annuity for the surviving spouse of the participant for the remainder of the spouse's life. The survivor annuity may not be less than 50 percent, nor more than 100 percent, of the payable amount of the annuity during the lifetime of the participant and spouse. While the IRC does not specifically provide that QJSA apply to 403(b)s, the QJSA requirements control whether ERISA is applicable to the 403(b) plan. Recall that ERISA will apply if the 403(b) plan is an employee benefit pension plan or provides employer contributions beyond salary deferrals. If ERISA does apply to the 403(b) plan, then the QJSA requirements will generally apply.

THE BENEFITS OF 403(b) PLANS AND CONTRIBUTING TO 403(b)S

There are some significant benefits to making employee elective deferral contributions to 403(b) plans. First, the employee does not pay income taxes on the contributions to the plan. This, of course, does not apply to any after-tax contribution but does apply to the elective deferral and the nonelective contributions from the employer. The employee only pays taxes on allowable contributions once withdrawals from the plan are taken. Secondly, earnings and gains on the amounts placed in a 403(b) account are not subjected to income tax until withdrawn by the employee. Thirdly, the benefits are similar to those in 401(k) plans (as discussed in Chapter 5) and other retirement vehicles because the employees have the tax-deferred benefits of growth over time, along with a vehicle where an employer may match benefits and may provide for other incidental contributions for an employee's benefit.

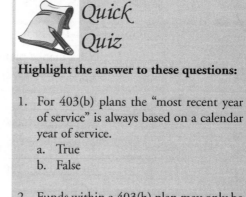

Quick Quiz

Highlight the answer to these questions:

1. For 403(b) plans the "most recent year of service" is always based on a calendar year of service.
   a. True
   b. False

2. Funds within a 403(b) plan may only be invested in either annuity contracts or mutual funds.
   a. True
   b. False

3. 403(b) plans generally provide for 100% immediate vesting of contributions.
   a. True
   b. False

False, True, True.

SIMILARITIES AND DIFFERENCES BETWEEN 401(k) PLANS AND 403(b) PLANS

403(b) plans for nonprofit organizations are similar to the 401(k) plans used by for-profit businesses. Like 401(k) plans, 403(b) plans allow employees to defer a portion of their salary. The funds accumulate and grow over time and are not subjected to income taxation by federal or state governments until distributed to the employee.

The tax advantages associated with 401(k) qualified defined-contribution plans are the same as those for 403(b) plans, namely that allowable contributions and the earnings of these contributions are not subject to federal income taxation until withdrawn. The amount of contributions to 401(k) plans and to 403(b) plans may consist of employee elective deferrals, employer contributions, and after-tax employee contributions. 403(b) plans may provide for employer matching contributions, much like 401(k)s. Participants in a 403(b) have the same contribution limits each year as 401(k) participants, and the early withdrawal rules are basically the same for both types of plans.

Obviously, there are differences between the two types of plans. An employer must establish, administer, and maintain 401(k)s; whereas, 403(b) plans do not require any employer involvement beyond payroll deductions for the employee elective deferral agreements. The 3-year cliff vesting periods on employer matching contributions are common for 401(k) plans, but 403(b)s provide 100 percent immediate vesting.

EXHIBIT 10.10   CONCEPT SUMMARY - 403(b) PLANS

Application	Not-For-Profit institution (large universities)
Style	Self reliance plans; employee only contributions
Subject to ERISA	Maybe (If organized as a qualified plan)
Established By What Date	End of year
Characteristics	Self-reliant savings plan
Elective Deferral Contribution Limit	$14,000 + $4,000 catch-up contribution (2005)
Available Contribution	$42,000 for 2005 or 100% of compensation including elective deferrals
Additional After-Tax Contributions Permitted	Permissible by plan document
Investment Risk	Employee has investment choices and risks
Investment Alternatives	Limited to Insurance Annuities and Mutual Funds
Penalties	10% early withdrawal (if applicable)
Loans Permitted	Yes (regular qualified plan rules on loans if plan permits)
Rollovers	Yes, to IRA, qualified plan, or other 403(b)
ERISA Protected	Yes, if ERISA plan. ERISA not applicable if governmental or church TDA.
In-Service Withdrawals	Generally no, except hardships, which are plan specific
Vesting	100% at all times for contributions and earnings

457 PLANS

No coordination w/ other plans

Under Section 457 of the Internal Revenue Code, employees of state and local governments and of nongovernmental tax-exempt entities may participate in tax-free deferred compensation plans to aid employees in saving for retirement. Employee elective deferrals into a **457 plan** do not count against deferrals into 401(k)s or 403(b)s.

WHAT IS A 457 PLAN

Section 457 of the Internal Revenue Code allows employees of state and local governments and employees of tax-exempt nongovernmental entities to save tax-deferred compensation for retirement. 457 plans work in many ways like 401(k)s and 403(b)s. Employees contribute a portion of their salary through a payroll reduction. The annual amount that an employee may contribute is limited (except for ineligible 457(f) plans explained below), and employee elective deferral contributions are not includible in an employee's gross income in the year earned but are deferred until paid out or made available to the employee. 457 plans are not "qualified plans" and, thus, are not subject to many of the eligibility standards of the Internal Revenue Code, including such requirements as nondiscrimination, minimum participation, and funding and vesting standards. A 457 plan is a "nonqualified" deferred compensation plan.[24]

There are three types of 457 plans: i) eligible governmental plans under IRC Section 457(b), ii) eligible tax-exempt plans under IRC Section 457(b), and iii) "ineligible plans" under IRC Section 457(f). The following exhibit illustrates how these three types of 457 plans are related.

RELATIONSHIP BETWEEN 457 PLANS

EXHIBIT 10.11

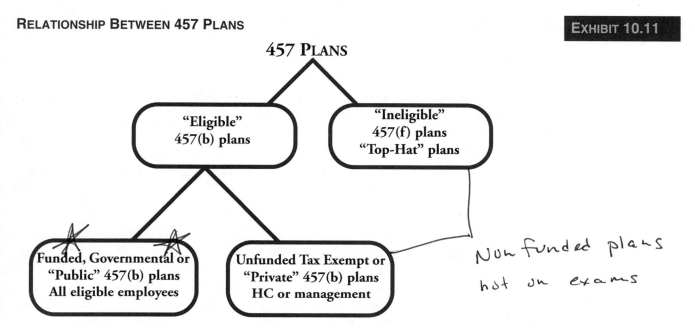

Plans that are **"eligible" under 457(b)** allow employees of sponsoring organizations to defer income taxation on savings for retirement into future years. Plans that are "**ineligible**", found under **Section 457(f)**, may trigger different tax treatment under Section 457(f). The main distinction between eligible plans (457(b) plans) and ineligible plans (457(f) plans) is that ineligible plans provide for greater deferral of funds. Most of this section on 457s will address rules applicable to 457(b)s. Ineligible plans and their differences compared to 457(b) plans will also be addressed.

WHICH ENTITIES CAN ESTABLISH 457(b) PLANS

457(b) plans may only be formed and maintained by employers that are "eligible" as defined under Section 457.[25] The term eligible employer is defined as a State, a political subdivision of a State, or any agency or instrumentality of a State or political subdivision of a State, and any other organization other than a governmental unit that is exempt from tax.[26] These tax-exempt organizations include trade associations, religious organizations, private hospitals, rural electric cooperatives, farmers' cooperatives, private schools and foundations, labor unions, and charitable organizations. Churches[27] and qualified church-controlled organizations[28] are not considered eligible employers under Section 457.

---

24. Rheal v. Commissioner, T.C. Memo 1989 - 525.
25. IRC Section 457(e)(1).
26. IRC Section 457(e)(1)(A)(B).
27. IRC Section 3121(w)(3)(A).
28. IRC Section 3121(w)(3)(B).

ERISA APPLICABILITY

457(b) plans sponsored by governmental employers are also called "public 457(b) plans." 457(b) plans for tax-exempt employers are called "private 457(b) plans." Public 457(b) plans are required to be funded through a trust holding all assets and income for the exclusive benefit of plan participants and their beneficiaries.[29] Under private 457(b) plans for tax-exempt employers, ERISA limits participation to a select group of highly compensated employees or management. Private 457(b) plans are offered only to HC employees or top management because funds in the plan are not placed in trust. The private 457(b) plan is "unfunded" and remains vulnerable to the employer's creditors. This poses a potential conflict between ERISA and Section 457. As a general matter, ERISA requires that private retirement plans be funded through a trust or annuity contract, yet private 457(b) plans must not be funded to receive tax benefits. Nonetheless, this conflict is avoided if the tax-exempt organization under a private 457(b) plan limits participation to HC employees or top management, as the tax-exempt employer would be exempt from ERISA under those circumstances.

Key Concepts

Underline/highlight the answers to these questions as you read:

1. What are 457 plans and which entities may establish them?

2. To what extent is ERISA applicable to 457 plans?

3. Who is eligible to establish a 457 plan?

4. What are the applicable rules for employee contributions to 457 plans?

Case Study 1

The case of In re Leadbetter[1] dealt with the requirement that funds in a 457 plan remain solely the property and rights of the employer until, of course, such funds made available to the participant or other beneficiary. While the funds are under the employer's control, they are subject to the claims of the employer's general creditors.

In this bankruptcy appeal, the state of Ohio refused to relinquish deferred compensation held on behalf of the debtor, Walter C. Leadbetter ("Leadbetter") in the Ohio Public Employees Deferred Compensation Program ("Ohio Program"), which was a 457 plan of deferred compensation for state employees. The state of Ohio administered the Ohio Program for state employees. The Ohio Program qualified for tax-deferred status under Section 457, allowing compensation to be placed in a deferred compensation plan, free from federal income tax until withdrawn from the plan by the employee. Leadbetter, a state employee, agreed to the terms of the program and began deferring compensation into the Ohio Program, and subsequently, Leadbetter filed a voluntary petition for bankruptcy.

---

1. In re Leadbetter, 992 F.2d 1216, 1993 WL 141068 (6th Cir. 1993).

---

29. IRC Section 457(g).

Case Study 1 Continued

During the bankruptcy proceeding, the trustee for the bankruptcy estate discovered over $3,500 in deferred compensation held by the Ohio Program. The trustee sought turnover of those funds to the bankruptcy estate. The Ohio Program objected, arguing that including the deferred compensation in the bankruptcy estate would violate Section 457(b)(6)'s requirement that the funds remain solely the property of the employer.

Section 457 specifically requires as a condition of tax-deferred status that the funds "remain (until made available to the participant or other beneficiary) solely the property and rights of the employer ... subject only to the claims of the employer's general creditors."[1] Accordingly, the key question before the Court was whether Section 457(b)(6)'s requirement that the funds remain "solely" the property of the employer prevented the funds from being placed into the bankruptcy estate. The Ohio Program argued that Section 457(b)(6)'s requirement that the deferred compensation remain "solely" the property of the employer allowed exclusion of the funds from the bankruptcy estate. The Court disagreed. Under the Ohio Program, an employee can readily surmise that any participant in the 457 plan has an expectancy of a return of investment at some future date as a result of the very purpose of the 457 plan. The Court also reasoned that under Section 457, a requirement for deferential tax status is that the plan not be a trust.[2] Furthermore, the plan document expressly stated that it did not create a trust and that participants are general creditors, not beneficiaries.

As a result, the Court ruled that the Ohio Program's status as a tax-exempt deferred compensation plan under Section 457 did not prevent inclusion of the deferred compensation as "property of the estate" under bankruptcy laws.[3] The Court then ordered that the state of Ohio turnover the over $3,500 of deferred compensation to the bankruptcy trustee.

---

1. 26 U.S.C. Section 457(b)(6).
2. See Foil v. Commissioner, 920 F.2d 1196, 1209 (5th Cir.1990) (funds placed in a retirement plan did not qualify for the deferred taxation of Section 457 because "the funds held in the [retirement] trust belong[ed] to the members as beneficiaries, and [were] not the sole property of the State").
3. The Court cited the following cases in support of this statement. See, e.g., Scott v. Council, 122 B.R. 64, 66-67 (Bankr.S.D.Ohio 1990); In re Petrey, 116 B.R. 95, 98-99 (Bankr.S.D.Ohio 1990).

An employer does not have to make public 457(b) plans available to all employees but can selectively choose which employees may participate in the plan.

ELIGIBILITY

Participants in 457(b) plans must enter into a salary reduction agreement prior to the first day of the month in which compensation will be deferred. New employees may be allowed to defer compensation during the calendar month that the employee starts if he completed a salary reduction agreement before his first day of work. A 457 plan may not accept after-tax contributions from the employee.

Any contributions made by the employer are not vested immediately. 457(b) plans follow the cliff vesting system explained in Chapter 3. However, for ineligible 457(f) plans, the employer agrees to pay the participant a certain amount of money after a specified period of employment, at which time the employee is no longer at "substantial risk of forfeiture" of the funds (discussed below).

EMPLOYEE CONTRIBUTIONS

Limits

457(b) plans generally operate with employees deferring compensation on a pretax basis through salary reduction agreements with their employer. The deferral amount, instead of being paid as income to the employee, is paid directly to the 457 plan. The annual amount deferred by an employee for an eligible 457(b) plan must not exceed the lesser of 100 percent of the employee's compensation or of the applicable dollar limit for the given calendar year. Stated differently, employees are able to contribute up to the lesser of the following amounts:

- The employee elective deferral of $14,000 for 2005, or
- Up to 100 percent of includible compensation, but this amount must be less than the employee elective deferral limit.

Age 50 Catch-Up Contributions for Governmental 457(b) Plans

Section 457(b) permits governmental entities to allow for catch-up contributions for employees age 50 and over. Employees age 50 or over may contribute an additional $4,000 above the elective deferral limit of $14,000 for 2005. This catch-up provision increases to $5,000 for 2006 and to $5,000[†] for 2007. Thereafter, the catch-up amount will be increased for cost-of-living adjustments in increments of $500. This catch-up benefit is available only for eligible governmental (public) 457(b) plans.[30] The age 50 catch up is not available to employees of eligible tax-exempt (private) 457(b) plans.

---

30. IRC Section 414(v).

EXHIBIT 10.12

Year	Employee Elective Deferral Limit	Catch-Up Amounts (Age 50 or Over)
2005	$14,000	$4,000
2006	$15,000	$5,000
2007	$15,000[†]	$5,000[†]
2008	$15,500[†]	$5,000[†]

Special "Final 3-Year" Additional Catch-Up Provision

457(b) plans may also have a special catch-up option that is termed the **"final 3-year" catch-up provision**. It applies to both public and private 457(b) plans. It is designed for employees approaching retirement that have not contributed the maximum amount to a 457 plan in previous years. It effectively doubles the employee deferral limit of IRC Section 402(g), but is limited to prior year employee deferrals not taken. It allows these employees to make up for previously missed contributions as follows: Three years prior to normal retirement age (as defined by the plan) an employee may contribute an additional amount equal to the elective deferral limit, which for 2005 is $14,000. Thus, an employee with adequate compensation could defer $14,000 under the regular deferral limitation and $14,000 as catch-up for a total of $28,000 in 2005. The limits are listed as follows:

MAXIMUM EMPLOYEE ELECTIVE DEFERRAL WITH THE "FINAL 3-YEAR" CATCH-UP

EXHIBIT 10.13

Year	Normal Deferral	Catch-up Deferral	Total Deferral in the Final 3-Years
2005	$14,000	$14,000	$28,000
2006	$15,000	$15,000	$30,000
2007	$15,000[†]	$15,000[†]	$30,000
2008	$15,500[†]	$15,500[†]	$31,000

This final 3-year catch-up option is further limited to prior unused maximum deferral amounts. The catch-up deferral is limited to any unused deferral in the plan.

EXAMPLE 10.9

Robby has worked for New York City for the last 20 years. He deferred $10,000 into his 457(b) plan for 2003. His normal retirement age, as defined under New York City's 457(b) plan, will be 2008. Robby has a prior unused maximum deferral amount of $33,000 as of December 31, 2004. How much can Robby contribute as his final three-year catch-up contributions and when?

MAX is 30k

Robby can contribute "final 3-year" catch-up contributions of up to $14,000 in 2005, up to $15,000 in 2006, and up to $4,000 in 2007. He is limited to $4,000 in 2007 because his prior unused maximum deferral amount of $33,000 has been exhausted ($33,000 - $14,000 - $15,000 - $4,000 = 0). Notice, during the three years prior to his normal retirement age (2008) of 2005, 2006, and 2007, Robby could also defer up to the regular elective deferral contribution limits.

Employers that sponsor 457 plans are not required to offer the "final 3-year" catch-up option. Furthermore, participants who utilize the "final 3-year" catch-up cannot simultaneously use the age 50 or older catch-up provisions.

EMPLOYER CONTRIBUTIONS

As with other retirement plans, an employer may make matching contributions or nonelective deferrals into the 457 plan. Interestingly, the 457(b) contribution limit of $14,000 for 2005 and $15,000 for 2006 includes both employee contributions and employer matching contributions. This is a significant difference between 457(b) plans and 401(k)s or 403(b)s. As a result, matching contributions by employers in 457 plans are very infrequent compared to those for 401(k) or 403(b) plans. Many 457 plans do not offer a matching contribution at all.

NO INTEGRATION WITH OTHER SALARY DEFERRAL PLANS

A vital and substantial benefit of contributing to a 457 plan is that the contributions to the 457 plan are not aggregated or combined with contributions to other tax-deferred retirement plans. An employee may contribute the maximum amount to a 401(k) plan, 403(b) plan, SARSEP, or SIMPLE IRA, in addition to the deferral limits for 457(b)s. This means that in 2004, an employee could contribute up to $14,000 for 2005 and $15,000 for 2006 to a 457(b) plan and up to $14,000 for 2005 and $15,000 for 2006 to another 403(b) or 401(k) plan if available. Beginning in 2002, the law separated the 457(b) deferral limit from the limit on other retirement plans, resulting in a boost in popularity of the 457 plan.

| EXHIBIT 10.14 | SUMMARY OF CONTRIBUTION LIMITS |

	457 Contribution	403(b)/401(k)/SARSEP Contribution	Aggregate Total for the Year
2005	$14,000	$14,000	$28,000
2006	$15,000	$15,000	$30,000
2007	$15,000[†]	$15,000[†]	$30,000
2008	$15,500[†]	$15,500[†]	$31,000

EXAMPLE 10.10

Mike, age 35, works for the State of California. The State of California offers a 403(b) and a 457 (b) plan to its employees. What is the maximum amount that Mike can defer into both plans in 2006? The answer is $30,000, $15,000 into the 457(b) and another $15,000 into the 403(b).

DISTRIBUTIONS

Public (governmental) 457(b) plans must maintain and keep all plan assets and income in trust or custodial accounts or annuity contracts for the exclusive benefit of their participants and beneficiaries. 457(b) distributions must be included as ordinary income in the calendar year in which the distributions are made. A distinct advantage of a public 457(b) plan is that the age 59½ withdrawal rule does not apply. Basically, there is no 10 percent penalty for early withdrawal at retirement or upon termination of employment for participants in public 457(b) plans.

However, private 457(b) plans are still subject to a 10 percent penalty for early withdrawal prior to age 59½, unless the employee has terminated employment or is faced with an unforeseeable emergency. When the participant is faced with an "unforeseeable emergency"[31] such as an unexpected injury or illness, accident, or severe financial hardship, the participant's rights to early withdrawal are subject to the rules specified in the actual plan of the employer.

In contrast to 403(b) plans, an employer creating and maintaining a 457(b) must establish a plan document that details the rules of the plan. As discussed, public 457(b)s are more flexible than private 457(b)s concerning distributions. Withdrawals from a 457(b) plan must begin by age 70½.

ROLLOVERS

The rules for rollovers from 457(b) plans are the same as those that apply to rollovers from qualified plans. The important distinction is whether the 457 plan is a public (governmental) 457(b) plan. Public 457(b) plans allow funds to be rolled over into a new employer's 403(b), 401(k), or 457(b) plan if that plan accepts such transfers. Otherwise, the assets can be rolled into an IRA. However, 457(b) plans for nongovernmental tax-exempt entities may allow funds only to be rolled over from the 457(b) plan into another tax-exempt organization's 457(b) if the plan accepts such transfers. However, these funds cannot be rolled into an IRA or any another type of employer-sponsored retirement plan.

BENEFITS AND DISADVANTAGES OF A SECTION 457 PLANS

457 plans reduce current taxable income. They allow the participant to save on a tax-deferred basis for retirement. The contributions and earnings are able to grow tax deferred. The participant has the ability to contribute to a 457(b) plan, in addition to a 403(b) or a 401(k) plan, depending on whether or not it is offered by the employer. The 457(b) plan also provides "portability" for the participant. Offering portability allows the employee-participant to rollover his savings to another public sector employer's 457 plan, if applicable. In other words, a public

---

31. IRC Section 457(d)(1)(A)(iii).

457(b) may rollover funds into a new employer's 457(b) plan, or even a 401(k) or 403(b), if the plan accepts such transfers. Such funds can also be rolled into an IRA.

Notably, EGTRRA 2001 allows 457 plan participants to be subject to the same, but separate, contribution limit as their 401(k) and 403(b) counterparts. 457 plan participants were formerly restricted to contributions totaling up to $8,500, this put them at a disadvantage in relation to other competing plans for private companies and private schools.

One significant drawback to a non-governmental tax-exempt organization offering a 457 plan is that there is a lack of creditor protection concerning the plan assets. A public 457(b) plan for governmental entities requires funds to be placed in a trust for the exclusive benefit of the participant and beneficiaries. However, there is no such requirement for private 457(b) plans for non-governmental, tax-exempt organizations, and therefore private 457(b) plan assets are available to the employer's creditors and the employee may lose access to the funds. This is one very important distinction that should be considered in the financial planning process.

SECTION 457(f) "INELIGIBLE" PLANS

Ineligible plans, under IRC Section 457(f), are nonqualified deferred compensation plans for state and local governmental employers and for tax-exempt employers. These ineligible plans are also called "top-hat" plans. Only HC employees or top management may participate in a 457(f) plan. Ineligible plans are those plans under Section 457 that fail to meet one or more requirements of the "eligible plan." 457(f) plans are frequently intentionally ineligible while some are unintentionally ineligible. With ineligible plans under 457(f), there is no limit on the amount of deferral.

However, the amounts contributed to the 457(f) are subject to a "substantial risk of forfeiture." This means that the participant is considered to be a general unsecured creditor of the plan sponsor or employer. The substantial risk of forfeiture is conditioned upon (i) the unsecured status of the employee and (ii) the employee's future performance of substantial services for the employer. The employer agrees to pay the participant a certain amount of money after a specified period of employment, at which time the employee is no longer at "substantial risk of forfeiture" of the funds.

Taxation of funds in an ineligible plan occurs when there is no risk of forfeiture. Amounts may therefore be taxable prior to the actual payment or distribution to the participant. The amounts that are taxable prior to actual payment are included in the gross income of the participant in the first year that the deferral amount is not subject to a substantial risk of forfeiture. The typical deferred compensation arrangement for ineligible 457(f) plans is for presidents, CEOs, and coaches.

Disadvantages to 457(f) Plans

If the participant terminates employment before the stated payment period, the participant may forfeit all of the 457(f) plan funds. Also, because the funds in the plan remain the employer's property until vested, the employee-participant may lose all the 457(f) account and the funds if the employer goes bankrupt. Also, even though a distribution may not occur, the participant may be taxed on the value of the plan once the funds vest in the participant or are no longer subject to substantial risk of forfeiture.

457 PLAN COMPARISON

EXHIBIT 10.15

	Public 457(b) Plans	Private 457(b) Plans	457(f) Plans
Eligible/Ineligible	Eligible	Eligible	Ineligible
Employer/Sponsors	Governmental Entities	Tax-Exempt Organizations under 501(c)	Governmental Entities (Rare) & Tax-Exempt Entities under 501(c)
Assets in Plan	Protected by Trust	Not Protected by Trust; Available to Employer's Creditors	Not Protected by Trust; Available to Employer's Creditors
Elective Deferral Contribution Limits	2005 - $14,000 2006 - $15,000 2007 - $15,000[†] 2008 - $15,500[†]	2005 - $14,000 2006 - $15,000 2007 - $15,000[†] 2008 - $15,500[†]	No Limit
Employees that Participate	Rank and File Employees and Key Management	Key Management and HCs for Tax Exempt Organizations; All Employees if Church-Related Organization	Key Management and HCs
Pretax Contribution	Yes	Yes	Yes
Funds Grow Tax Deferred	Yes	Yes	Yes
Age 50 and Over Catch-Up Provisions	Yes	No	No
3-Year Catch-Up Provisions	Yes 2005 - $14,000 2006 - $15,000 2007 - $15,000[†] 2008 - $15,500[†]	Yes 2005 - $14,000 2006 - $15,000 2007 - $15,000[†] 2008 - $15,500[†]	No
Rollovers	Permitted to 401(k), 403(b), 457(b), or IRA plans	Not Permitted Unless Rolled Into Another 457(b)	Not Permitted

In conclusion, 457 plans allow employees of tax-exempt organizations and of governments to defer compensation into retirement savings plans. Public 457(b) plans hold funds in trust and are available to all employees while private 457(b) plans are not funded and are available only to HC employees or upper management. Salary deferrals into 457(b) plans are not aggregated or combined with salary deferrals to other retirement plans such as 401(k)s and 403(b)s. 457(f) plans are ineligible but allow for an unlimited amount of contributions to the plan. Nonetheless, the participant's funds in a 457(b) are subject to a substantial risk of forfeiture.

EXHIBIT 10.16	CONCEPT SUMMARY - 457 PLANS

Type of Plan	Nonqualified Deferred Compensation Plan
Application	Employees of state and local government, tax-exempt governmental agencies, and 501 entities
Style	Self-reliant, employee elective tax-deferred savings
Qualified Plan	No
Established By What Date	End of year
Characteristics	Deferred compensation plan
Elective Deferral Contribution Limit	Lesser of $14,000 for 2005 ($15,000 for 2006) or 100% of compensation + $4,000 catch-up for 2005 ($5,000 catch-up for 2006) for age 50 or older (catch-up for public only)
Available Employer Contribution	Permitted, but very unusual
Additional After-Tax Contributions Permitted	No
Investment Risk	Employee selects investments and bears risk
Investment Alternatives	Broad
Penalties	10% for early withdrawal
Loans Permitted	No
Rollovers	Public 457(b) plans may be rolled over to 457, 403(b), 401(k), or IRA plans permitting. Private 457(b) plans can only be rolled to other 457(b) plans. 457(f) plans cannot be rolled over.
ERISA Protected	No
In-Service Withdrawals	Yes

Key Terms

Annuity Contracts - While the contracts are not specifically defined in the Internal Revenue Code, an annuity contract must be purchased for the employee from an insurance company and may give a fixed benefit or a variable benefit depending on the performance of the investment. Any contract or certificate that is transferable to a person other than a trustee is not an annuity contract.

Eligible 457 Plans - 457(b) plans for governmental and tax-exempt organizations under 501(c) that allow employees to defer income taxation on savings for retirement into future years. Eligible plans are available to most of an employers employees.

15-Year Rule - A special catch-up provision for 403(b) plan participants that have worked for the plan sponsor for 15 years. The catch-up allows them to defer up to an additional $15,000 during the plan year.

Final 3-Year Catch-Up Provision - A special catch-up provision for public and private 457(b) plans that allows an individual to defer an additional $14,000 for 2005 ($15,000 for 2006) to the plan in their final three years before the plan's normal retirement age.

Form 5304-SIMPLE - The IRS form used to establish a SIMPLE IRA plan when the employees choose the financial institution.

Form 5305-SIMPLE - The IRS form used to establish a SIMPLE IRA plan when the employer chooses the financial institution.

457 Plan - A nonqualified deferred compensation plan for employees of state and local government and tax-exempt entities.

Grace Period - If an employer meets the 100 employee limitation in a given year, then the employer will have a two year "grace period" when the employer can exceed the limitation without losing eligibility to maintain the SIMPLE.

Includible Compensation - An employee's taxable wages and benefits for the most recent year of service.

Ineligible 457 Plans - 457(f) plans for employees of governmental entities and tax-exempt entities under 501(c)(3). Ineligible plans are only available to highly compensated and management employees.

Nonelective Contributions - Contributions to a qualified plan on behalf of all eligible employees.

Qualified Joint and Survivor Annuity (QJSA) - The QJSA pays a benefit to the participant and spouse as long as either lives; although, at the death of the first spouse, the annuity may be reduced.

Savings Incentive Match Plans for Employees (SIMPLEs) - Retirement plans for small employers with 100 or fewer employees who earn more than $5,000 in a year. SIMPLEs may be established as SIMPLE 401(k)s or SIMPLE IRAs.

Key Terms

Section 501(c)(3) Organizations - Nonprofit tax-exempt organizations that are established under IRC Section 501(c)(3) of the Internal Revenue Code.

SIMPLE 401(k) - A SIMPLE plan that utilizes a 401(k) plan as the funding vehicle of the plan.

SIMPLE IRA - A SIMPLE plan that utilizes an IRA account as the funding vehicle of the plan

Tax Sheltered or Deferred Annuities (403(b) Plans) - Retirement plans for certain qualified non-profit organizations or employees of public educational systems – often called 401(k)s for non-profit organizations.

DISCUSSION QUESTIONS

1. Describe SIMPLE plans.

2. List and define the different types of SIMPLE plans.

3. What are the rules for establishing a SIMPLE plan?

4. Identify the characteristics of SIMPLE IRAs.

5. Identify the characteristics of SIMPLE 401(k) plans.

6. Describe 403(b) plans.

7. When does ERISA apply to a 403(b) plan?

8. Who is eligible to establish a 403(b) plan?

9. What are the applicable rules regarding employee contributions to 403(b) plans?

10. What are the applicable rules regarding employer contributions to 403(b) plans?

11. What investment options are available for 403(b) plans?

12. How are distributions from 403(b) plans taxed?

13. What are the rollover, distribution, and minimum distribution rules applicable to 403(b) plans?

14. What are 457 plans and what entities may establish them?

15. Who is eligible to establish a 457 plan?

16. What are the applicable rules regarding employee contributions to 457 plans?

17. What are the applicable rules regarding employer contributions to 457 plans?

18. How does a participant's salary deferral to a 457 plan affect his contributions to a qualified plan?

19. How are distributions from a 457 plan taxed?

20. What are the benefits and disadvantages of a 457 plan?

21. What are Section 457(f) plans and how are the distributions taxed?

1. Kim Cat, age 42, earns $210,000 annually as an employee for CTM, Inc. Her employer sponsors a SIMPLE retirement plan and matches all employee contributions made to the plan dollar-for-dollar up to 3% of covered compensation. What is the maximum contribution (employer and employee) that can be made to Kim's SIMPLE account in 2005?

    a. $10,000.

    b. $12,000.

    c. $16,300.

    d. $20,000.

2. Taylor, age 25, works for Swim America. Swim America adopted a SIMPLE plan 6 months ago. Taylor made an elective deferral contribution to the plan of $8,000, and Swim made a matching contribution of $2,400. Which of the following statements is/are correct?

    1. Taylor can withdraw his entire account balance without terminating employment.

    2. He can roll his SIMPLE IRA into his Traditional IRA.

    3. Taylor will be subject to ordinary income taxes on withdrawals from the SIMPLE.

    4. Taylor may be subject to a 25% early withdrawal penalty on amounts withdrawn from the SIMPLE.

    a. 1 and 2.

    b. 1 and 3.

    c. 2, 3, and 4.

    d. 1, 3, and 4.

3. Which of the following is/are correct regarding SIMPLE plans?

    1. A SIMPLE plan does not require annual testing.

    2. A SIMPLE IRA must follow a 3-year cliff vesting schedule if the plan is top heavy.

    3. A 25% early withdrawal penalty may apply to distributions taken within the first two years of participation in a SIMPLE plan.

    4. The maximum elective deferral contribution to a SIMPLE 401(k) plan is $14,000 for 2005 and $18,000 for 2005 for an employee who has attained the age of 50.

    a. 3 only.

    b. 1 and 3.

    c. 1, 2, and 3.

    d. 2, 3, and 4.

4. All of the following statements is/are incorrect regarding tax-sheltered annuities (403(b)s) except?

   1. A catch-up provision is available to all employees of 501(c)(3) organization employers that sponsor a TSA.
   2. Active employees who take withdrawals from TSAs prior to 59½ are subject to a 10% penalty tax.
   3. TSAs are available to all employees of 501(c)(3) organizations who adopt such a plan.
   4. If an employee has had at least 15 years of service with an eligible employer, an additional catch-up contribution may be allowed.
      a. 1 only.
      b. 1 and 2.
      c. 1, 2, and 3.
      d. 2, 3, and 4.

5. Which of the following statements is/are correct regarding TSAs and 457 deferred compensation plans?

   1. Both plans require contracts between an employer and an employee.
   2. Participation in either a TSA or a 457 plan will cause an individual to be considered an "active participant" for purposes of phasing out the deductibility of Traditional IRA contributions.
   3. Both plans allow 10-year forward averaging tax treatment for lump-sum distributions.
   4. Both plans must meet minimum distribution requirements that apply to qualified plans.
      a. 1 only.
      b. 1 and 4.
      c. 2, 3, and 4.
      d. 1, 2, and 4.

6. What is the maximum employee elective deferral contribution (salary reduction) for an employee who is 45 years old under a 403(b) plan in 2006?
      a. $9,000.
      b. $11,000.
      c. $15,000.
      d. $20,000.

7. Which of the following are permitted investments in a 403(b) TSA (TDA) plan?

    1. An annuity contract from an insurance company.

    2. An international gold stock mutual fund.

    3. A self-directed brokerage account consisting solely of U.S. stocks, bonds and mutual funds.

       a. 1 only.

       b. 2 only.

       c. 1 and 2.

       d. 1, 2, and 3.

8. Which of the following characteristics accurately describes a 403(b) plan?

    1. A self-reliant employee elective deferral plan.

    2. The retirement benefit is dependent on the investment results.

    3. The plan generally permits loans.

       a. 1 only.

       b. 2 only.

       c. 1 and 2.

       d. 1, 2, and 3.

9. Which of the following statements is/are correct regarding 403(b) plans?

    1. 403(b)s are eligible for rollover treatment to IRAs, qualified plans, and other 403(b)s.

    2. Investments in stocks, bonds, and money markets are available.

    3. Assets in a 403(b) plan are always 100% vested.

       a. 1 only.

       b. 2 only.

       c. 1 and 3.

       d. 1, 2, and 3.

10. Which of the following types of 457 plans permit employees to defer recognition of income without a risk of forfeiture?

    1. Public 457(b) plans.

    2. 457(f) plans.

    3. Private 457(b) plans.

       a. 1 only.

       b. 2 only.

       c. 1 and 3.

       d. 1, 2, and 3.

11. What is the maximum elective deferral contribution to a 457(b) plan for 2006 (including the catch-up)?

    a. $10,000.
    b. $14,000.
    c. $15,000.
    d. $20,000.

12. What is the maximum catch up for 2006 under the 457(b) plan "Final 3-Year" rule?

    a. $2,500.
    b. $5,000.
    c. $15,000.
    d. $30,000.

13. James, age 57, has compensation of $150,000 and wants to defer the maximum to his public 457(b) plan. The normal retirement age for his plan is age 60. How much can he defer in 2006 if he has unused deferral of $60,000 from age 40 to age 49?

    a. $15,000.
    b. $20,000.
    c. $30,000.
    d. $35,000.

14. Henry Hobbs age 58 has compensation of $72,000. The normal retirement age for his 457(b) plan is age 62. Henry has unused deferrals totaling $21,000 as of January 1, 2006. How much can Henry defer into his 457(b) public plan for the current year?

    a. $14,000.
    b. $20,000.
    c. $30,000.
    d. $35,000.

15. Ben Reynolds, age 62 in 2006, is planning for retirement at normal retirement age of 65 from the Salt Lake City coroner's office which has a 457(b) plan. Ben has an unused deferral amount of $9,000. Ben has compensation of $128,000 per year as a mortician/autopsy specialist. Ben wants to know the maximum amount he can defer in 2006 the 457(b) plan.

    a. $15,000.
    b. $20,000.
    c. $24,000.
    d. $30,000.

16. Which of the following plans permits employers to match employee elective deferral contributions or make nonelective contributions?

    1. 457(b).

    2. 401(k).

    3. 403(b).

        a. 2 only.

        b. 3 only.

        c. 2 and 3.

        d. 1, 2, and 3.

Social Security

INTRODUCTION

Social Security benefits were never intended to provide total preretirement wage replacement upon retirement. Social Security was created to supplement a covered worker's pension, savings, investments, and other earnings from assets to make up an appropriate wage replacement ratio (e.g., 70%). As illustrated in Chapter 2, individuals who retire typically need a minimum of 70 to 80 percent of their preretirement income during their retirement to maintain their same standard of living.

Low wage earners receive Social Security retirement benefits approximating 60 percent of preretirement income. Average wage earners receive only 42 percent of preretirement income from Social Security benefits and high wage earners may receive only 26 percent of preretirement income (see Exhibit 11.1).

From a financial planning standpoint it is important to understand Social Security law and the various benefits that are available from Social Security. This chapter provides a basic overview of the Social Security system and its benefits. There are six major categories of benefits administered by the Social Security Administration:
1. Retirement benefits;
2. Disability benefits;
3. Family benefits;
4. Survivors' benefits;
5. Medicare; and
6. Supplemental Security Income (SSI) benefits. SSI benefits are not funded by Social Security taxes but are funded by general funds from the Treasury.

The **retirement benefit** is the benefit that most people are aware of from Social Security. Full retirement benefits are payable at "full retirement age," reduced benefits as early as age 62, to anyone who has obtained at least a minimum amount (40 quarters) of Social Security credits. Based on a change in Social Security law in 1983, the age when full retirement benefits are paid begins to rise from age 65 in the year 2000 and increases to age 67 by the year 2027. Those workers who delay retirement beyond the full retirement age will receive a special scheduled increase (Exhibit 11.10) in their Social Security retirement benefits when they ultimately retire.

EXHIBIT 11.1 **SOCIAL SECURITY BENEFITS AS A PERCENTAGE OF PRERETIREMENT INCOME**

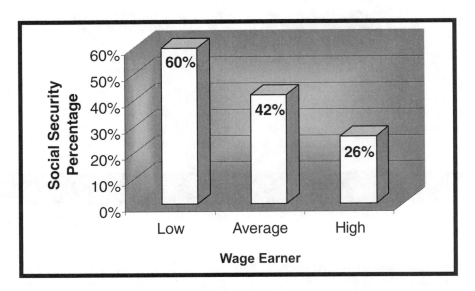

The **disability benefit** is payable at any age to workers who have sufficient credits under the Social Security system. Recipients must have a severe physical or mental impairment that is expected to prevent them from performing "substantial" work for at least a year or result in death. Monthly earnings of $830 for 2005 (if the individual is blind then the amount is increased to $1,380 per month for 2005) or more are considered substantial. The disability insurance program has built-in incentives to smooth the transition back to the workforce including continuation of benefits and health care coverage.

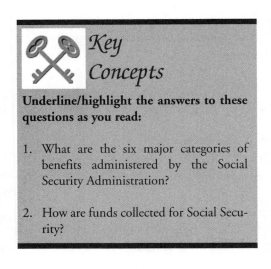

Key Concepts

Underline/highlight the answers to these questions as you read:

1. What are the six major categories of benefits administered by the Social Security Administration?

2. How are funds collected for Social Security?

The **family benefit** is provided to certain family members of workers eligible for retirement or disability benefits. Such family members include spouses age 62 or older, spouses under age 62 but caring for a child under age 16, unmarried children under 18, unmarried children under age 19 and full-time students, and unmarried children of any age who were disabled before age 22.

Survivors benefits apply to certain members of the deceased worker's family if the worker earned sufficient Social Security credits. Family members entitled to survivors benefits include those listed for family benefits and may also include the worker's parents if the worker was their primary means of support. A special one-time payment of $255 may be made to the spouse or minor children upon the death of a Social Security covered worker.

Medicare provides hospital and medical insurance. Those who have attained full retirement age or those who receive disability benefits for at least two years automatically qualify for Medicare. Others must file an application to become qualified.

Finally, **Supplemental Security Income (SSI)** (funded by general tax revenues and not by Social Security taxes) is another benefit that provides monthly payments to those disabled or at full retirement age who have a low income and few assets. Generally, those who receive SSI also qualify for **Medicaid**, food stamps, and other government assistance.

SOCIAL SECURITY TAXES AND CONTRIBUTIONS

Although the Social Security retirement benefits program is thought by many to be one of the most complicated and confusing programs created, the basic concept is quite simple. Employees, employers, and self-employed individuals pay Social Security taxes, known as FICA taxes, during their working years. These payments are pooled in special trust funds. Contributing workers become "covered" workers, meaning that they will fall under the Social Security umbrella of benefits after contributing for approximately 10 years (40 quarters) and will receive retirement benefits based on those contributions and the Social Security formula.

The **Federal Insurance Contributions Act (FICA)** is the law allowing Social Security taxes, including Medicare taxes, to be deducted from paychecks. A portion of these FICA taxes pays

Quick Quiz

Highlight the answer to these questions:

1. Social Security benefits cannot be withdrawn until an individual reaches full retirement age.
   a. True
   b. False

2. Social Security contributions are placed in the following trust funds: OASI, DI, and SMI.
   a. True
   b. False

False, False.

part of the Medicare coverage. Separate and apart from Social Security taxes, general tax revenues are used to finance Supplemental Security Income, commonly referred to as "SSI." SSI is a program administered by the Social Security Administration that pays benefits to persons who have limited income and assets.

Both employers and employees pay the taxes for Social Security and Medicare. For the year 2005, an employer and employee each pay 6.2 percent of the employee's gross salary up to a limit of $90,000 for **OASDI (Old Age and Survivor Disability Insurance)**. The salary limit rises annually based on annual increases in average wages. Self-employed workers pay 12.4 percent (6.2 percent x 2) of their taxable income up to the same salary limit. The Medicare portion of the Social Security tax is 1.45 percent for employers and employees each and is 2.9 percent for self-employed workers with no limit on the amount of compensation taxed.

EXAMPLE 11.1

If an employee earns a salary of $100,000 in 2005, the first $90,000 of the employee's salary will receive a tax of 7.65 (6.2 + 1.45) percent while the remaining $10,000 will be subject to a tax of only 1.45 percent. The employer pays the same amount as the employee.

	Taxable Amount	x	Tax Rate	Total Tax
Employee - Social Security	$90,000		6.20%	$5,580
Employee - Medicare	$100,000		1.45%	$1,450
Total				$7,030

Case Study 1

The case of Veterinary Surgical Consultants, P.C. v. C.I.R., involved an owner of an S corporation who attempted to avoid FICA and FUTA taxes by declaring his remuneration as K-1 distribution of corporate net income and not W-2 wages.[1] Dr. Sadanaga performed substantial services for the S corporation, Veterinary Surgical Consultants, P.C. ("VSC"). Dr. Sadanaga worked approximately 33 hours a week for VSC. He was the only individual working for VSC. Tellingly, all of VSC's income was generated from the consulting and surgical services provided by Dr. Sadanaga. As officer and sole shareholder, Dr. Sadanaga declared all remuneration he received on a K-1 form, not on a W-2 form, thus avoiding FICA and FUTA taxes.

VSC claimed that the amounts paid to Dr. Sadanaga were distributions of its corporate net income, rather than wages, and that as an S corporation it passed its net income to Dr. Sadanaga as its sole shareholder. Not surprisingly, the Court disagreed with VSC, i.e. Dr. Sadanaga, and concluded that an S corporation cannot avoid federal FICA and FUTA employment taxes by characterizing compensation paid to its sole director and shareholder as distributions of the S corporation's net income rather than wages. The Court's analysis focused on whether payments represented remuneration for services rendered. To characterize the payments to Dr. Sadanaga as distributions of VSC's net income was "but a subterfuge for reality." The payments constituted remuneration for services performed by Dr. Sadanaga on behalf of VSC. Regardless of how an employer may choose to characterize payments made to its employees, the true analysis is whether the payments represent remuneration for services rendered.[2] Dr. Sadanaga's reporting of the distributions as nonpassive income from an S corporation had no bearing on the Federal employment tax treatment of those wages. He was VSC's sole source of income, thereby requiring treatment as an employee.[3] In short, while an S corporation is permitted to passthrough items of income in calculating its income tax liability, it may not passthrough its tax liability for federal employment taxes.

1. Veterinary Surgical Consultants, P.C. v. C.I.R., 117 T.C. No. 14, 117 T.C. 141, 2001 WL 1242120 (U.S.Tax Ct.), Tax Ct. Rep. (CCH) 54,527, Tax Ct. Rep. Dec. (RIA) 117.14 (U.S.Tax Ct. 2001).
2. See also Spicer Accounting, Inc. v. United States, 918 F.2d 90 (9th Cir. 1990); Joseph Radtke, S.C. v. United States, 895 F.2d 1196 (7th Cir. 1990).
3. See also Spicer Accounting, Inc. v. United States, supra, at 94-95.

The United States Social Security system operates on a "pay-as-you-go" basis. Social Security taxes are collected and divided among several trust funds. The federal **Old Age and Survivors Insurance ("OASI")** Trust Fund pays retirement and survivors' benefits. The OASI Trust Fund receives 5.30 percent of the FICA tax. The federal **Disability Insurance ("DI") Trust Fund** pays benefits to workers with disabilities and their families. The DI Trust Fund receives 0.90 percent of the FICA tax. OASI and DI are the two trust funds used for payment of Social Security benefits (total 6.2 percent).

The two Medicare trust funds are the federal **Hospital Insurance ("HI") Trust Fund**, which pays for services covered under the hospital insurance provisions of Medicare (Part A), and the federal **Supplementary Medical Insurance ("SMI") Trust Fund**, which pays for services covered under the medical insurance provisions of Medicare, known as Part B and the new prescription drug provisions known as Part D.[1] The SMI Trust Fund is partially funded by the general fund of the Treasury with the remaining funding coming from monthly premiums paid by the individuals enrolled in Part B.

SOURCES OF FUNDING TO SOCIAL SECURITY TRUST FUNDS   **EXHIBIT 11.2**

OASI Trust Fund	5.30 percent (limited to the maximum taxable earnings)
DI Trust Fund	0.90 percent (limited to the maximum taxable earnings)
HI Trust Fund	1.45 percent (all earnings are taxed) (In 1993, the Omnibus Budget Reconciliation Act of 1993 abolished the ceiling on taxable earnings for Medicare)
SMI Trust Fund	-0- (no FICA taxes used; funded by general federal tax revenues and monthly premiums paid by enrollees)

---

1. Medicare Prescription Drug. Improvement and Modernization Act of 2003 (PL 108-173).

SOCIAL SECURITY BENEFITS – ELIGIBILITY AND CALCULATIONS

COVERED WORKERS AND INSURED STATUS

To qualify for retirement benefits, a worker must be **"fully insured,"** which means that a worker has earned a certain number of quarters of coverage under the Social Security system. Since 1978, quarters of coverage have been determined based on annual earnings. In other words, earning a designated amount of money, regardless of when it was earned during the year, will credit the worker with a quarter of coverage for that year. In 2005, the designated amount for a quarter of coverage is $920. Thus, workers who earn at least $3,680 are credited with four quarters of coverage for 2005. No worker may earn more than four quarters in one year, regardless of earnings. The following is a list of the designated amounts for a quarter of coverage dating back to 1980:

Key Concepts

Underline/highlight the answers to these questions as you read:

1. Who are covered workers with regards to Social Security?

2. Who are beneficiaries of Social Security benefits?

EXHIBIT 11.3 | **DESIGNATED AMOUNTS FOR A QUARTER OF SOCIAL SECURITY COVERAGE**

Year	Amount Needed to Receive a Credit for One Quarter	Year	Amount Needed to Receive a Credit for One Quarter
1980	$290	1993	$590
1981	$310	1994	$620
1982	$340	1995	$630
1983	$370	1996	$640
1984	$390	1997	$670
1985	$410	1998	$700
1986	$440	1999	$740
1987	$460	2000	$780
1988	$470	2001	$830
1989	$500	2002	$870
1990	$520	2003	$890
1991	$540	2004	$900
1992	$570	2005	$920

For most persons, 40 quarters of coverage (10 years of work in employment covered by Social Security) or one quarter per year from age 21 to age 62 will fully insure a worker for life. Fully insured workers are entitled to the benefits under the Social Security system. Some benefits, like survivor's benefits, are available to "currently" (although not necessarily fully) insured individuals. **"Currently" insured** workers are those individuals who have at least six quarters of coverage out of the previous 13 quarters.

In 2005, William earned $4,200 from employment subject to Social Security between January 1 and March 31. He was then unemployed for the remainder of the year. How many quarters of coverage did he earn for Social Security for 2005?

EXAMPLE 11.2

For 2005, a worker receives one quarter credit for each $920 in annual earnings on which Social Security taxes are withheld up to a maximum of four quarters. It is irrelevant that William earned the $4,200 all in the first quarter. William has earned four quarters.

How is a worker's insured status determined under Social Security?

EXAMPLE 11.3

By the number of quarters of coverage received. To achieve currently insured status under Social Security, a worker must have at least six quarters of coverage out of 13 calendar quarters prior to retirement, disability, or death. Any worker with 40 covered quarters is fully insured.

SOCIAL SECURITY BENEFICIARIES

Social Security benefits are paid upon retirement, disability, or death if the eligibility requirements are satisfied. The worker's spouse and children may also be eligible to receive benefits when the worker satisfies eligibility requirements. Generally, monthly Social Security benefits can be paid to:

- A disabled insured worker under age 65.
- A retired insured worker at age 62 or older.
- The spouse of a retired or disabled worker entitled to benefits who:
  - is at least 62 years old, or
  - is caring for a child who is under age 16 or disabled.
- The divorced spouse of a retired or disabled worker entitled to benefits if the divorced spouse is age 62 or older and was married to the worker for at least 10 years.
- The divorced spouse of a fully insured worker who has not yet filed a claim for benefits if both are at least age 62, were married for at least 10 years, and have been finally divorced for at least two continuous years.

Memorize

- The dependent, unmarried child of a retired or disabled worker entitled to benefits or of a deceased insured worker if the child is:
  - under age 18;
  - under age 19 and a full-time elementary or secondary school student; or
  - Age 18 or over but disabled (if the disability began before age 22).
- The surviving spouse (including a surviving divorced spouse) of a deceased insured worker if the widow(er) is age 60 or older.
- The disabled surviving spouse (including a surviving divorced spouse in some cases) of a deceased insured worker if the widow(er) is age 50 or older.
- The surviving spouse (including a surviving divorced spouse) of a deceased insured worker, regardless of age, if caring for an entitled child of the deceased who is either under age 16 or disabled before age 22.
- The dependent parents of a deceased insured worker at age 62 or older.

In addition to monthly survivors benefits, a lump-sum death payment of $255 is payable upon the death of an insured worker. Exhibit 11.4 provides a summary of those eligible for OASDI benefits and the percentages of the worker's primary insurance amount ("PIA") that each beneficiary will receive. The PIA is the retirement benefit that the worker would receive if he or she retires at full retirement age.

Quick Quiz

Highlight the answer to these questions:

1. Fully insured means that a worker has earned a certain number of quarters (generally 40) of coverage under the Social Security system.
   a. True
   b. False

2. Social Security benefits can be paid to the dependent parents of a deceased insured worker at age 62.
   a. True
   b. False

True, True.

EXAMPLE 11.4

Steve, age 38, has just died. He has been credited with the last 35 consecutive quarters of Social Security coverage since he left college. He did not work before leaving college. Which of the following persons are eligible to receive Social Security survivor benefits as a result of Steve's death?

1. Tim, Steve's 16-year-old son.
2. Grace, Steve's 18-year-old daughter.
3. Olivia, Steve's 38-year-old widow.
4. Arline, Steve's 60-year-old dependent mother.

Grace is too old; Olivia does not have a child under 16 and she is too young; and Arline is not eligible because she is too young. Thus, only Tim is eligible.

SUMMARY OF SOCIAL SECURITY OASDI BENEFITS (AS A % OF PIA)

EXHIBIT 11.4

| | Assuming Full Retirement Age of the Worker | | | |
| | Retirement | Survivorship | | Disability |
	Fully Insured (2)	Fully Insured (2)	Currently Insured (3)	(4)
Participant	100%	Deceased	Deceased	100%
Child Under 18 (6)	50%	75%	75%	50%
Spouse with child under 16 (7)	50%	75%	75%	50%
Spouse - Age 65 (1)	50%	100%	0%	50%
Spouse - Age 62 (1)	40%	83%	0%	40%
Spouse - Age 60 (1)	N/A	71.5%	0%	N/A
Dependent Parent (age 62)	0%	75/82.5% (5)	0%	0%

1. Includes divorced spouse if married at least 10 years (unless they have remarried). Survivorship benefits are also available to divorced spouse if remarried after age 60.
2. Fully insured is 40 quarters of coverage or one quarter for each year after age 21 but before age 62.
3. Currently insured is at least six quarters of coverage in the last 13 quarters.
4. Disability insured is based on age as follows:
   - Before age 24 - Must have 6 quarters of coverage in the last 12 quarters.
   - Age 24 through 30 - Must be covered for half of the available quarters after age 21.
   - Age 31 or older - Must be fully insured and have 20 quarters of coverage in the last 40 quarters.
5. Parent benefit is 82.5 percent for one parent and 75 percent for each parent if two parents.
6. Child under age 19 and a full-time student or of any age and disabled before age 22 also qualifies.
7. Spouse with child disabled before age 22 also qualifies.

Note: Notice that when the participant worker is alive (retirement and disability), beneficiaries who qualify for a benefit, qualify for 50% of PIA. When the participant dies, all qualified beneficiaries generally receive 75% of PIA with the exceptions being the spouse who replaces the participant at 100% and any qualified dependent parents. See note 5.

Under Social Security (OASDI), what benefits are available to the survivors of a deceased but only currently insured worker?

A $255 lump-sum death benefit, which is generally payable to the insured's spouse, and 75 percent of the worker's PIA is available to a child under 18 or to a surviving spouse with a dependent child under the age of 16.

EXAMPLE 11.5

SOCIAL SECURITY RETIREMENT BENEFITS – A CLOSER LOOK

The most well known Social Security benefit is the Retirement Benefit. Until 2000, normal age retirement, the age where full retirement benefits are available to the retiree, was 65 years. The age at which full benefits are paid began to rise in the year 2000. Exhibit 11.5 illustrates the new law, which eventually raises normal age retirement with full benefits to age 67.

| EXHIBIT 11.5 | AGE FULL RETIREMENT BENEFITS BEGIN (NORMAL AGE RETIREMENT) |

Full Retirement Age With Full Benefits	Year Born
65 years	Before 1938
65 years, 2 months	1938
65 years, 4 months	1939
65 years, 6 months	1940
65 years, 8 months	1941
65 years, 10 months	1942
66 years	1943-1954
66 years, 2 months	1955
66 years, 4 months	1956
66 years, 6 months	1957
66 years, 8 months	1958
66 years, 10 months	1959
67 years	1960-present

Key Concepts

Underline/highlight the answers to these questions as you read:

1. How is a person's Social Security retirement benefit calculated?

2. How does retiring early or retiring late affect Social Security retirement benefits?

People who delay receiving Social Security retirement benefits beyond full retirement age receive an increase in their benefit when they do retire. People who take early retirement, currently as early as age 62, receive an actuarially reduced monthly benefit. (Early and late retirement options are discussed later in this chapter.)

When planning for an individual, it may be appropriate to calculate the individual's expected Social Security retirement benefit or to ask the client to request a Social Security statement and consider the benefit in that individual's retirement plan. Some financial planners, however, choose not to consider the estimated retirement benefit in order to be conservative in developing a retirement plan. Others justify the exclusion of Social Security retirement benefits from retirement planning based on the belief that there will be drastic changes to the Social Security system through legislative action or through economically driven forces.

THE RETIREMENT BENEFIT CALCULATION

Determining a worker's Social Security retirement benefit requires specific, detailed information pertaining to the persons age, actual earnings history that was subject to Social Security taxes, and the worker's retirement date. Social Security benefits are based on earnings averaged over most of a worker's lifetime. Actual earnings, in historical dollars, are first adjusted or "indexed" to current dollars to account for changes in average wages and inflation since the year the earnings were received. Then, the Social Security Administration calculates **average indexed monthly earnings ("AIME")** during the 35 years in which the applicant earned the most. The Social Security Administration applies a formula to these earnings and arrives at a basic benefit, which is referred to as the **primary insurance amount (PIA)**. The Social Security retirement benefit is based on the worker's PIA. The PIA determines the amount the applicant will receive at his or her full retirement age, but the dollar amount of the benefit depends on the year in which the worker retires. The PIA is indexed to the consumer price index (CPI) annually.

Figuring the Worker's Average Indexed Monthly Earnings (AIME)

To determine a worker's AIME, the worker's actual annual earnings from age 22 to 62 must be converted into current dollars by multiplying the worker's total annual earnings for each year by an indexing factor. The indexing factor is the result of dividing the national average wage for the year in which the worker attains age 60 by the national average wage for the actual year being indexed. Exhibit 11.6 provides national average wages from 1953 to 2003.

NATIONAL AVERAGE WAGE INDEXING SERIES, 1953-2003

EXHIBIT 11.6

Year	Amount	Year	Amount	Year	Amount
1953	$3,139.44	1970	$6,186.24	1987	$18,426.51
1954	$3,155.64	1971	$6,497.08	1988	$19,334.04
1955	$3,301.44	1972	$7,133.80	1989	$20,099.55
1956	$3,532.36	1973	$7,580.16	1990	$21,027.98
1957	$3,641.72	1974	$8,030.76	1991	$21,811.60
1958	$3,673.80	1975	$8,630.92	1992	$22,935.42
1959	$3,855.80	1976	$9,226.48	1993	$23,132.67
1960	$4,007.12	1977	$9,779.44	1994	$23,753.53
1961	$4,086.76	1978	$10,556.03	1995	$24,705.66
1962	$4,291.40	1979	$11,479.46	1996	$25,913.90
1963	$4,396.64	1980	$12,513.46	1997	$27,426.00
1964	$4,576.32	1981	$13,773.10	1998	$28,861.44
1965	$4,658.72	1982	$14,531.34	1999	$30,469.84
1966	$4,938.36	1983	$15,239.24	2000	$32,154.82
1967	$5,213.44	1984	$16,135.07	2001	$32,921.92
1968	$5,571.76	1985	$16,822.51	2002	$33,252.09
1969	$5,893.76	1986	$17,321.82	2003	$34,064.95

Source: Social Security Administration (www.ssa.gov)

EXAMPLE 11.6

For a worker age 62 in 2005, the indexing factor for the year 1970 is determined by dividing the national average wage for 2003 (when the worker attained age 60), which was $34,065, by the national average wage for 1970 (the year being indexed), which was $6,186.23, yielding a factor of 5.5066.

Year	AWI	Age 62 in 2005		Age 65 in 2005	
		Age	Factor	Age	Factor
1951	2,799	8	12.1697	11	11.8793
1952	2,973	9	11.4569	12	11.1835
1953	3,139	10	10.8506	13	10.2422
1954	3,156	11	10.7949	14	10.1896
1955	3,301	12	10.3182	15	9.7396
1956	3,532	13	9.6437	16	9.1029
1957	3,642	14	9.3541	17	8.8296
1958	3,674	15	9.2724	18	8.7525
1959	3,856	16	8.8347	19	8.3393
1960	4,007	17	8.5011	20	8.0244
1961	4,087	18	8.3354	21	7.8680
1962	4,291	19	7.9380	22	7.4929
1963	4,397	20	7.7480	23	7.3135
1964	4,576	21	7.4437	24	7.0263
1965	4,659	22	7.3121	25	6.9021
1966	4,938	23	6.8980	26	6.5112
1967	5,213	24	6.5341	27	6.1677
1968	5,572	25	6.1139	28	5.7710
1969	5,893.76	26	5.7798	29	5.4557
1970	**6,186.24**	27	**5.5066**	30	5.1978
1971	6,497.08	28	5.2431	31	4.9491
1972	7,133.80	29	4.7751	32	4.5074
1973	7,580.16	30	4.4940	33	4.2420
1974	8,030.76	31	4.2418	34	4.0040
1975	8,630.92	32	3.9469	35	3.7255
1976	9,226.48	33	3.6921	36	3.4851
1977	9,779.44	34	3.4833	37	3.2880
1978	10,556.03	35	3.2271	38	3.0461
1979	11,479.46	36	2.9675	39	2.8011
1980	12,513.46	37	2.7223	40	2.5696
1981	13,773.10	38	2.4733	41	2.3346
1982	14,531.34	39	2.3442	42	2.2128
1983	15,239.24	40	2.2353	43	2.1100
1984	16,135.07	41	2.1112	44	1.9929
1985	16,822.51	42	2.0250	45	1.9114
1986	17,321.82	43	1.9666	46	1.8563
1987	18,426.51	44	1.8487	47	1.7450
1988	19,334.04	45	1.7619	48	1.6631
1989	20,099.55	46	1.6948	49	1.5998
1990	21,027.98	47	1.6200	50	1.5291
1991	21,811.60	48	1.5618	51	1.4742
1992	22,935.42	49	1.4853	52	1.4020
1993	23,132.67	50	1.4726	53	1.3900
1994	23,753.53	51	1.4341	54	1.3537
1995	24,705.66	52	1.3788	55	1.3015
1996	25,913.90	53	1.3145	56	1.2408
1997	27,426.00	54	1.2421	57	1.1724
1998	28,861.44	55	1.1803	58	1.1141
1999	30,469.84	56	1.1180	59	1.0553
2000	32,154.82	57	1.0594	60	1.0000
2001	32,921.92	58	1.0347	61	1.0000
2002	33,252.09	59	1.0244	62	1.0000
2003	**34,064.95**	60	1.0000	63	1.0000
2004	-	61	1.0000	64	1.0000
2005	-	62	1.0000	65	1.0000

Next, each year's annual earnings must be multiplied by its indexing factor to arrive at the indexed earnings for the years from age 22 to 60. Note that the indexing factor will always equal one for the years in which the worker is 60 or older. After all annual earnings are indexed, or converted to current dollar amounts, the highest 35 years of indexed earnings are added together for a total. The sum of the highest 35 years is then divided by 420 (which represents 35 years multiplied by 12 months per year). This calculation yields the average amount of monthly earnings for all indexed years, hence the name Average Indexed Monthly Earnings (AIME). Once the worker's AIME is determined, the next step in determining the worker's retirement benefit is to calculate the primary insurance amount (PIA) for the worker.

EXAMPLE 11.7

Assume you have two clients, Ronnie and Karen. Both clients retire in 2005. Ronnie, born in 1943, retires at age 62. Karen, born in 1940, retires at her normal (or full) retirement age. In each case, we assume the worker has covered earnings from 1965 through 2004, as shown in columns labeled "nominal earnings."

Indexing brings nominal earnings up to near-current wage levels. For each case, the table shows columns of earnings before and after indexing. Between these columns is a column showing the indexing factors. A factor will always equal one for the year in which the person attains age 60 and all later years. The indexing factor for a prior year Y is the result of dividing the average wage index for the year in which the person attains age 60 by the average wage index for year Y. For example, Ronnie's indexing factor for 1965 is the average wage for 2003 ($34,064.95) divided by the average wage for 1965 ($4,658.72).

The highest 35 years of indexed earnings are used in the benefit computation. The selected indexed amounts are bold. Below the indexed earnings are the sums for the highest 35 years of indexed earnings and the corresponding average monthly amounts of such earnings. (The average is the result of dividing the sum of the 35 highest amounts by the number of months in 35 years.) Such an average is called the "Average Indexed Monthly Earnings" (AIME).

As you can see from the following chart, Ronnie's AIME is $2,844 and Karen's AIME is $3,727.

Year	Ronnie, born in 1943			Karen, born in 1940		
	Nominal earnings	Indexing factor	Indexed earnings	Nominal earnings	Indexing factor	Indexed earnings
1965	$4,612	7.3121	$33,723	$4,193	6.9021	$28,940
1966	$4,892	6.8980	$33,745	$4,713	6.5112	$30,687
1967	$5,167	6.5341	$33,762	$5,194	6.1677	$32,035
1968	$5,525	6.1139	$33,779	$5,747	5.7710	$33,166
1969	$5,847	5.7798	$33,795	$6,262	5.4557	$34,164
1970	$6,140	5.5066	**$33,810**	$6,746	5.1978	**$35,064**
1971	$6,452	5.2431	**$33,829**	$7,253	4.9491	**$35,896**
1972	$7,088	4.7751	**$33,846**	$8,135	4.5074	**$36,668**
1973	$7,535	4.4940	**$33,862**	$8,815	4.2420	**$37,393**
1974	$7,988	4.2418	**$33,884**	$9,511	4.0040	**$38,082**
1975	$8,589	3.9469	**$33,900**	$10,396	3.7255	**$38,731**
1976	$9,186	3.6921	**$33,915**	$11,293	3.4851	**$39,357**
1977	$9,742	3.4833	**$33,935**	$12,151	3.2880	**$39,953**
1978	$10,521	3.2271	**$33,952**	$13,305	3.0461	**$40,528**
1979	$11,447	2.9675	**$33,969**	$14,667	2.8011	**$41,083**
1980	$12,485	2.7223	**$33,987**	$16,197	2.5696	**$41,620**
1981	$13,748	2.4733	**$34,003**	$18,051	2.3346	**$42,142**
1982	$14,513	2.3442	**$34,022**	$19,273	2.2128	**$42,647**
1983	$15,228	2.2353	**$34,040**	$20,445	2.1100	**$43,139**
1984	$16,131	2.1112	**$34,056**	$21,887	1.9929	**$43,618**
1985	$16,827	2.0250	**$34,074**	$23,063	1.9114	**$44,083**
1986	$17,335	1.9666	**$34,091**	$23,994	1.8563	**$44,541**
1987	$18,450	1.8487	**$34,108**	$25,779	1.7450	**$44,985**
1988	$19,369	1.7619	**$34,127**	$27,311	1.6631	**$45,421**
1989	$20,146	1.6948	**$34,144**	$28,659	1.5998	**$45,848**
1990	$21,087	1.6200	**$34,161**	$30,257	1.5291	**$46,267**
1991	$21,884	1.5618	**$34,178**	$31,663	1.4742	**$46,678**
1992	$23,024	1.4853	**$34,197**	$33,582	1.4020	**$47,081**
1993	$23,234	1.4726	**$34,214**	$34,155	1.3900	**$47,476**
1994	$23,869	1.4341	**$34,231**	$35,360	1.3537	**$47,866**
1995	$24,839	1.3788	**$34,249**	$37,071	1.3015	**$48,249**
1996	$26,067	1.3145	**$34,266**	$39,188	1.2408	**$48,626**
1997	$27,602	1.2421	**$34,284**	$41,790	1.1724	**$48,995**
1998	$29,061	1.1803	**$34,300**	$44,305	1.1141	**$49,361**
1999	$30,696	1.1180	**$34,318**	$47,115	1.0553	**$49,720**
2000	$32,410	1.0594	**$34,335**	$50,076	1.0000	**$50,076**
2001	$33,200	1.0347	**$34,353**	$51,629	1.0000	**$51,629**
2002	$33,551	1.0244	**$34,371**	$52,503	1.0000	**$52,503**
2003	$34,388	1.0000	**$34,388**	$54,148	1.0000	**$54,148**
2004	$35,408	1.0000	**$35,408**	$56,092	1.0000	**$56,092**
Highest-35 total			$1,194,805	Highest-35 total		$1,565,566
AIME			$2,844	AIME		$3,727

Calculating the Worker's Primary Insurance Amount (PIA)

Generally, the PIA is the actual Social Security retirement benefit for the single retiree who retires at full retirement age. For those who retire early or late and for family or surviving beneficiaries, the PIA is not the actual amount of the benefit but the PIA is used to determine their actual benefit.

The PIA is a result of applying the AIME to the PIA formula. This benefit formula changes the dollar amounts (by CPI) but not the percentages from year to year and depends on the worker's first year of eligibility, that is, when the worker turns 62, becomes disabled, or dies.

The PIA is the sum of three separate percentages of portions of the AIME. These portions are also known as "bend points." For the year 2005, these portions are the first $627 of AIME, the amount of AIME between $627 and $3,779, and the AIME over $3,779. The bend points for 2005 are thus $627 and $3,779. For individuals who first become eligible for retirement benefits or disability insurance benefits in 2005 or who die in 2005 before becoming eligible for benefits, their PIA will be the sum of:

> 90 percent of the first $627 of their AIME, *plus*
> 32 percent of their AIME over $627 up to $3,779, *plus*
> 15 percent of their AIME that exceeds $3,779.
> (Maximum PIA for 2005 is $1,926, or an AIME of $6,137)

The sum of these three calculations is rounded down to the next lower multiple of $0.10 (if it is not already a multiple of $0.10). For calculations in subsequent years, it is useful to know how to determine a given year's bend points. Exhibit 11.7 shows the established bend points from 1979 through 2005.

BEND POINT TABLE

EXHIBIT 11.7

Dollar Amounts (bend points) in PIA Formula		
Year	First	Second
1979	$180	$1,085
1980	$194	$1,171
1981	$211	$1,274
1982	$230	$1,388
1983	$254	$1,528
1984	$267	$1,612
1985	$280	$1,691
1986	$297	$1,790
1987	$310	$1,866
1988	$319	$1,922
1989	$339	$2,044
1990	$356	$2,145
1991	$370	$2,230
1992	$387	$2,333
1993	$401	$2,420
1994	$422	$2,545
1995	$426	$2,567
1996	$437	$2,635
1997	$455	$2,741
1998	$477	$2,875
1999	$505	$3,043
2000	$531	$3,202
2001	$561	$3,381
2002	$592	$3,567
2003	$606	$3,653
2004	$612	$3,689
2005	$627	$3,779

Source: Social Security Administration (www.ssa.gov)

In order to determine future years' bend points, the 1979 bend points are converted into dollars for that year. The bend points for 2005 were determined by multiplying the 1979 bend points ($180 and $1,085) by the ratio between the national average wage for 2003, which was $34,064.95, and the national average wage for 1977, which was $9,779.44, rounded to the nearest dollar. $34,064.95 divided by $9,779.44 is 3.4833. When multiplying the 1979 bend points of $180 and $1,085 by 3.4833, the rounded results are $627 and $3,779, the bend points for 2005. For subsequent years, the 1979 bend points should be indexed by multiplying them by the ratio for the national average wage for the year the worker attains age 60 over the national average wage for 1977.

These figures for the PIA rise each year based on a cost of living adjustment (COLA) that is applied to reflect changes in the cost of living. Recent COLAs, which are based on inflation, are shown in Exhibit 11.8.

EXHIBIT 11.8   **COST OF LIVING ADJUSTMENT (COLA) PER YEAR**

Year	COLA	Year	COLA	Year	COLA
1990	5.4%	1995	2.6%	2000	3.5%
1991	3.7%	1996	2.9%	2001	2.6%
1992	3.0%	1997	2.1%	2002	1.4%
1993	2.6%	1998	1.3%	2003	2.1%
1994	2.8%	1999	2.5%	2004	2.7%

Annual COLA increases are determined by October of each year and go into effect in time so that they first appear on monthly benefit checks received in the following January. In 2005, the maximum monthly retirement benefit for retirees at full retirement age is $1,926, compared to $1,825 in 2004.

EXAMPLE 11.8

Recall from the previous example Ronnie retired in 2005, 2005 is the year in which he is first eligible for benefits and his AIME is $2,844. Ronnie's PIA is $1,273.74 (rounded down to $1,273.70) which is calculated below.

90% x $627	$564.30
32% x ($2,844 - $627)	$709.44
15% x $0	$0.00
PIA	**$1,273.74**

Recall that Karen's AIME is $3,727. Since she was first eligible for benefits in 2002 (the year Karen reached age 62), the bend points for 2002 must be used. In addition her PIA must be increased by cost-of-living adjustments, or COLAs, for 2002 through 2004. These COLAs are 1.4 percent, 2.1 percent, and 2.7 percent respectively. The resulting PIA is $1,604.23 (rounded down to $1,604.20).

90% x $592	$532.80
32% x ($3,567 - $592)	$952.00
15% x ($3,727 - $3,567)	$24.00
PIA	$1,508.80
2002 adjustment	X 1.014
2003 adjustment .	X 1.021
2004 adjustment	X 1.027
Resulting PIA	**$1,604.23**

Early and Late Retirement Options

Workers entitled to retirement benefits can currently take early retirement benefits as early as age 62. The worker will receive a reduced benefit because he or she will receive more monthly benefit payments than if the worker had waited and retired at full retirement age. The reduction to one's monthly benefit for early retirement is permanent. Conversely, a delayed or postponed retirement will permanently increase the monthly retirement benefit for a worker.

For each month of early retirement, a worker will receive a reduction in his or her monthly retirement benefit of 5/9 of one percent for up to the first 36 months. For subsequent months of early retirement, the permanent reduction percentage is 5/12 of one percent per month.

Assume Ronnie begins receiving benefits at the earliest possible age, which is age 62. Then the benefit amount for Ronnie is reduced for 48 months of retirement before Ronnie's normal retirement age, which is 66 years. The $1,273.70 PIA is thus reduced to a monthly benefit of $955.28.

EXAMPLE 11.9

PIA	$1,273.70
5/9 x 1% x 36 months	Less 20% reduction
5/12 x 1% x 12 months	Less 5% reduction
Monthly Benefit	$955.28

The benefit amount for Karen, assuming that benefits begin exactly at her normal retirement age of 65 years and 6 months, is not reduced except for rounding down to the next lower tenth of a dollar. The $1,604.23 PIA is thus reduced to a monthly benefit of $1,604.20.

Although the full retirement age will increase to age 67, workers will still have the option of taking early retirement at age 62. However, the reduction percentage that is applied to the monthly retirement benefit will increase until 2027. Before 2000, those who retired at age 62 received 80 percent of their retirement benefit, but the increase in full retirement age has increased the number of months from 62 until full retirement age. For instance, in the year 2009, covered workers who retire at age 62 will receive 75 percent of their monthly retirement benefit, or 25 percent less than his or her full retirement benefit. By 2027, a covered worker retiring at age 62 (full retirement age would be 67) will receive only 70 percent of his or her monthly retirement benefit. Exhibit 11.9, which was compiled by the Social Security Administration, shows the phase-in of the Social Security full retirement age and accompanying reductions for early retirement at age 62.

| EXHIBIT 11.9 | SOCIAL SECURITY FULL RETIREMENT AND REDUCTIONS* BY AGE |

Year of Birth	Full Retirement Age	Age 62 Reduction Months	Monthly Percent Reduction	Total Percent Reduction
1937 or earlier	65	36	0.555	20.00
1938	65 & 2 months	38	0.548	20.83
1939	65 & 4 months	40	0.541	21.67
1940	65 & 6 months	42	0.535	22.50
1941	65 & 8 months	44	0.530	23.33
1942	65 & 10 months	46	0.525	24.17
1943-1954	66	48	0.520	25.00
1955	66 & 2 months	50	0.516	25.84
1956	66 & 4 months	52	0.512	26.66
1957	66 & 6 months	54	0.509	27.50
1958	66 & 8 months	56	0.505	28.33
1959	66 & 10 months	58	0.502	29.17
1960 and later	67	60	0.500	30.00

*Percentage monthly and total reductions are approximate due to rounding. The actual reductions are .555 or 5/9 of 1 percent per month for the first 36 months and .416 or 5/12 of 1 percent for subsequent months.
Source: Social Security Administration (www.ssa.gov)

No matter what the full retirement age is, a worker may start receiving benefits as early as age 62 and can also retire at any time between age 62 and full retirement age. However, if a worker starts benefits at one of these early ages, the benefits are reduced a fraction of a percent for each month before the full retirement age.

| EXAMPLE 11.10 |

Assume that Josephine, a worker born in 1939, decided to retire on her 62nd birthday. Assume that her full retirement benefit would have been $1,429.20 at age 65 and four months, her full retirement age. If she retires at age 62, what will her monthly retirement benefit be?

The answer is $1,119. Josephine is retiring 40 months early. The monthly retirement benefit reduction percentage is 1/180 for the first 36 months (1/180 x 36 = 20 percent) and 1/240 for the 4 subsequent months of early retirement (1/240 x 4 = 1.6668 percent), yielding a total permanent reduction to Josephine's monthly retirement benefit of 21.6667 percent. 21.6667 percent x $1,429.20 = $309.66. $1,429.20 - $309.66 = $1,119.50 (rounded off).

What if Josephine retires at age 64 and six months? What will her permanent monthly retirement benefit be (subject to COLA increases)? Note she is retiring 10 months early from normal retirement age.

EXAMPLE 11.11

The answer is $1,349. 1/180 x 10 = 5.5556 percent. 5.5556 percent x $1,429.20 = $79.40. $1,429.20 - $79.40 = $1,349.80 (rounded off).

For those covered individuals who take late retirement, or when benefits are lost due to the earnings limitation, the monthly retirement benefit and the benefit paid to the surviving spouse will increase each year (until age 70) as follows:

PERCENTAGE INCREASES FOR DELAYED RETIREMENT

EXHIBIT 11.10

Increase For Year Born	Annual Percentage Each Year Of Late Retirement	After Age
1917-1924	3.0%	65
1925-1926	3.5%	65
1927-1928	4.0%	65
1929-1930	4.5%	65
1931-1932	5.0%	65
1933-1934	5.5%	65
1935-1936	6.0%	65
1937	6.5%	65
1938	6.5%	65 and 2 months
1939	7.0%	65 and 4 months
1940	7.0%	65 and 6 months
1941	7.5%	65 and 8 months
1942	7.5%	65 and 10 months
1943	8.0%	66

EXAMPLE 11.12

Jeanette will turn 66 in 2009 (thus she was born in 1943). She is considering taking her Social Security benefits at age 62, 66, or 70. Assume her monthly benefit is expected to be $1,000 at full retirement age, inflation is expected to be 4% and she is expected to live to age 90. The calculations below compare her choices (A,B, or C).

Choice A – Begin Benefits at age 62.

PMT	$750	($1,000 less 25% reduction)
N	336	(90-62) x 12
i	0.3333	4/12
FV	0	
PV$_{@62}$	**$151,450.19**	

Choice B – Begin Benefits at age 66.

PMT	$1,000	Full benefit at full retirement age
N	288	(90-66) x 12
i	0.3333	4/12
FV	0	
PV$_{@66}$	$184,948.61	

PMT	$0	
N	4	(66-62)
i	4	
FV	$184,948.61	
PV$_{@62}$	**$158,094.84**	

Choice C – Begin Benefits at age 70.

PMT	$1,320	($1,000 plus 8% x 4 years increase)
N	240	(90-70) x 12
i	0.3333	4/12
FV	0	
PV$_{@70}$	$217,828.85	

PMT	$0	
N	8	(70-62)
i	4	
FV	$217,828.85	
PV$_{@62}$	**$159,165.41**	

As you can see, even though the benefit is reduced if Jeanette begins her benefit early, the PV of the total benefit at age 62 is not much less than if she took the benefit at age 66. Similarly, if she begins her payments later, her yearly payments will be higher but the PV of the benefit at age 62 is not much more than if she had taken benefits at age 66. The significance here is that all things being equal, the acceleration or delay of benefit generally has little impact on the PV of the benefit at age 62. However, the choice of retirement age is significant when considering the annual income need required to maintain one's standard of living.

Although the calculations explained above can provide estimates of the Social Security benefits a retiring worker may receive, a financial planner should have the client obtain his entire Social Security earnings history up to the moment of retirement from the Social Security Administration to get the most accurate benefit estimate.

Reduction of Social Security Benefits

Besides early retirement, there are two other situations in which beneficiaries can have benefits reduced. The first instance is a reduction of benefits based on earnings, referred to as the **retirement earnings limitations test**. The other instance is through taxation of Social Security benefits. Both of these measures reduce one's net benefits.

A person can continue to work even though he is considered "retired" under Social Security. For a retiree who receives Social Security retirement benefits before his normal retirement age, the earnings received by the beneficiary cannot exceed certain limitations without triggering a reduction in Social Security benefits. Beneficiaries can earn up to the limitation amount and receive all of their benefits, but if their earnings exceed the designated limit for the calendar year, then benefits will be reduced or eliminated. The law provides for earnings limitations of $12,000 for those under the full retirement age for 2005. The Social Security Administration reduces $1 in benefits for each $2 earned by those beneficiaries above $12,000. In the year that the retiree reaches full retirement age, $1 in benefits will be deducted for each $3 earned above the given year's limit but only for earnings before the month the retiree reaches full retirement age. For 2005, the limit for earnings in the year the retiree reaches full retirement age was $31,800. The earnings limitation increases every year as median earnings nationwide increase. Once the retiree reaches his normal retirement age, benefits will not be reduced regardless of the earnings limitations.

In the event that a beneficiary, who is younger than normal retirement age, has earnings exceed the limitation, that beneficiary's benefits will be reduced depending on his or her age. The beneficiary must file an annual report of his or her earnings to the Social Security Administration by April 15 of the year following the year worked and must provide the exact earnings for that year and an estimate for the current year. The filing of a federal tax return with the IRS does not satisfy the filing requirement with the Social Security Administration. Also, the wages count toward the earnings limitation when they are earned, not when paid, whereas income for the self-employed normally counts when paid, not earned. If other family members receive benefits based on the beneficiary's Social Security record, then the total family benefits may be affected by the beneficiary's earnings that exceed the earnings limitation. In such a case, the Social Security Administration will withhold not only the worker's benefits but will withhold those benefits payable to family members as well.

EXAMPLE 11.13

Matthew is 64 years old and despite being retired from his occupation as an attorney, earned $20,000 in 2005 while working as a golf instructor at a local golf course. Matthew's monthly retirement benefit from Social Security is normally $1,200, which totals $14,400 for the entire year. Because Matthew exceeded the retirement earnings limitation, how much money will be reduced from Matthew's Social Security retirement benefit for 2005?

Matthew's total earnings in 2005	$20,000
Earnings limitation	($12,000)
Remainder excess	$8,000
One-half deduction	÷ 2
Benefits reduced by:	**$ 4,000**

The Social Security Administration will reduce Matthew's benefits for the year by $4,000. Matthew will receive $10,400 in retirement benefits ($14,400 annual retirement benefit less $4,000 reduction). Matthew's total income for 2005 will be $30,400, instead of $34,400.

EXAMPLE 11.14

Mike is 66 years old. He has a full-time job working as a masseur. This year (2005) he anticipates earning $22,000 from his job. How much, in dollars, will Mike's Social Security benefits be reduced for the earnings test?

None, because Mike is over normal retirement age.

Generally, only wages and net self-employment income count towards the retirement earnings limitation, whereas income from savings, investments, and insurance does not. The following is a nonexclusive list of sources of income that DO NOT count toward the earnings limitation:

- Pension or retirement income.
- 401(k) and IRA withdrawals.
- Dividends and interest from investments.
- Capital gains.
- Rental income.
- Workers' compensation benefits (generally not payable after a worker has retired).
- Unemployment benefits.
- Court-awarded judgments, less components of award that include lost wages.
- Contest winnings.

TAXATION OF SOCIAL SECURITY BENEFITS

Apart from the earnings limitation, some beneficiaries may be required to pay income tax on their Social Security benefits. For persons with substantial income in addition to Social Security benefits, up to 85 percent of their annual Social Security benefits may be subject to federal income tax. The Social Security Administration is concerned with beneficiaries' **modified adjusted gross income** (MAGI). For purposes of Social Security, MAGI is equal to the taxpayer's adjusted gross income plus tax exempt interest, including:

- interest earned on savings bonds used for higher education;
- amounts excluded from the tax payer's income for employer provided adoption assistance;
- amounts deducted for interest paid for educational loans;
- amounts deducted as qualified tuition expense; and
- income earned in a foreign country, a U.S. possession, or Puerto Rico, that is excluded from income.

Key Concepts

Underline/highlight the answers to these questions as you read:

1. How are Social Security benefits taxed?

2. What benefits are available from Social Security other than retirement benefits?

3. What is the maximum family benefit?

EXAMPLE 11.15

Last year Charlie and Eva had adjusted gross income of $40,000. They also had the following items:

- Eva spent 3 months during the year in Mexico visiting her mother. While she was there she earned $5,000 that has been excluded from their AGI.

- While in Mexico, Eva fell in love with a little orphan girl. Luckily, Charlie's company has an Adoption Assistance Program. The program paid $8,000 towards the adoption and the amount was excluded from Charlie's AGI.

- Charlie has been attending night school for several years and has several student loans. Last year he paid and deducted $200 in student loan interest. He also took a qualified tuition expense deduction for $600 he paid to the school.

- Charlie and Eva had $900 in interest. $400 was from Tax Exempt bonds and the remaining $500 was from corporate bonds.

Charlie and Eva's MAGI for last year is:

Adjusted Gross Income (AGI)	$40,000
+ Foreign Income Excluded	$5,000
+ Adoption Assistance Excluded	$8,000
+ Student Loan Interest Deduction	$200
+ Qualified Tuition Expense Deduction	$600
+ Tax Exempt Bonds Interest	$400
= Modified Adjusted Gross Income (MAGI)	**$54,200**

Generally, 50 percent of Social Security benefits may be subject to federal income taxes for beneficiaries who file a federal tax return as an "individual" and have a modified adjusted gross income between $25,000 and $34,000. For those with a modified adjusted gross income plus one-half of Social Security greater than $34,000, up to 85 percent of their Social Security benefits may be subject to federal income taxation. For those beneficiaries that file a joint federal tax return and have a modified adjusted gross income with their spouse between $32,000 and $44,000, 50 percent of their Social Security benefits will be subject to federal income taxes. Finally, if beneficiaries filing a joint tax return have a modified adjusted-gross income plus one-half Social Security benefits that exceeds $44,000, 85 percent of their Social Security benefits may be subject to federal income taxation.

In sum, for persons with substantial income in addition to their Social Security benefits, up to 85 percent of their annual benefits may be subject to federal income tax.

SOCIAL SECURITY HURDLE AMOUNTS

EXHIBIT 11.11

	Married Filing Jointly	All Others Except MFS = 0
1st Hurdle	$32,000	$25,000
2nd Hurdle	$44,000	$34,000

If MAGI plus one half of Social Security benefits exceeds the first hurdle but not the second, the taxable amount of Social Security benefits is the lesser of:
- 50% Social Security Benefits or
- 50% [MAGI + 0.50 (Social Security Benefits) - Hurdle 1].

EXAMPLE 11.16

A married couple has interest income of $18,000 and Social Security income of $20,000. What amount of their Social Security benefits must be included in their taxable income?

Lesser of:

- 0.50($20,000) = $10,000, or

- 0.50 [$18,000 + 0.50 (20,000) - 32,000] = Negative

They would have $0 inclusion due to a negative result.

EXAMPLE 11.17

A married couple has income of $30,000 and Social Security benefits of $20,000. What amount of their Social Security benefits must be included in their taxable income?

Lesser of:

- 0.50($20,000) = $10,000, or

- 0.50 [30,000 + 0.50 (20,000) - 32,000] = $4,000

They would have $4,000 of Social Security benefits included in taxable income.

If MAGI plus one-half the Social Security benefits exceeds the second hurdle, the taxable amount of Social Security benefits is the lesser of:
- 85% Social Security Benefits, or
- 85% [MAGI + 0.50 (Social Security Benefits) - Hurdle 2], plus the lesser of:
  - $6,000 for MFJ or $4,500 for all other taxpayers, or
  - The taxable amount calculated under the 50% formula and only considering Hurdle 1.

EXAMPLE 11.18

A married couple has income of $60,000 and Social Security income of $20,000. What amount of their Social Security benefits must be included in their taxable income?

0.85 ($20,000) = **$17,000**

0.85 [$60,000 + 0.50 ($20,000) - $44,000] = $22,100
   Plus the lesser of:
   • $6,000, or
   • 0.50($20,000) = $10,000, or
   • 0.50[$60,000+0.50($20,000)-$32,000] = $19,000

                                                                                          $6,000
                                                                                        $28,100

Therefore, **$17,000** must be included in their taxable income.

EXAMPLE 11.19

A married couple has income of $45,000 and Social Security benefits of $20,000. What amount of their Social Security benefits must be included in their taxable income?

0.85 ($20,000) = **$17,000**

0.85 [$45,000 + 0.50 ($20,000) - $44,000] = $9,350
   Plus the lesser of:
   • $6,000, or
   • 0.50($20,000) = $10,000, or
   • 0.50[$45,000+0.50($20,000)-$32,000] = $11,500

                                                                                          $6,000
                                                                                        $15,350

Therefore, **$15,350** must be included in their taxable income.

Last year Michelle, a single taxpayer, received $10,400 in Social Security benefits. For the entire year, she had an adjusted gross income of $28,000. How much, if any, of her Social Security benefit is taxable?

EXAMPLE 11.20

First, determine Michelle's modified adjusted gross income. Modified adjusted gross income is the sum of adjusted gross income, nontaxable interest, foreign-earned income, plus one-half of Social Security benefits. For Michelle, the equation is as follows: $28,000 + [$10,400 x 0.50] = $33,200 in modified adjusted gross income. Since Michelle's modified adjusted gross income is between the two base amounts for a single individual of $25,000 and $34,000, we can use the following formula to determine her taxable amount. The income tax base will be the lesser of 50% of her Social Security Benefits _OR_ 50% of the difference between Michelle's modified adjusted gross income less the base amount of $25,000. Based on this formula, Michelle will be subject to income tax on $4,100 of her Social Security Benefit.

- 0.50($10,400) = $5,200

- 0.50($33,200 - $25,000) = $4,100 (the LESSER amount)

A married couple files jointly and has an adjusted gross income of $38,000, no tax-exempt interest, and $11,000 of Social Security benefits. How much, if any, of their Social Security benefits is included in gross income?

EXAMPLE 11.21

The lesser of the following:

- 0.50 ($11,000) = $5,500 or

- 0.50[$38,000+0.50($11,000)-$32,000]=0.50($11,500) = $5,750

They will include $5,500 in gross income. If the couple's adjusted gross income was $15,000 and their Social Security benefits totaled $5,000, none of the benefits would be taxable since 0.50 [$15,000 + 0.50 ($5,000) - $32,000] is negative.

<table>
<tr><td></td><td></td></tr>
</table>

EXAMPLE 11.22							

Frank and Lois, married filing jointly, have tax-free municipal bond interest of $2,000. Assuming that Frank and Lois have differing AGI amounts ranging from $20,000 to $50,000 the social security amount includable in taxable income is shown below. Thus, if Frank and Lois have $20,000 in AGI then only $1,000 of the social security benefit is included (4% of the benefit is included), but if they have AGI of $50,000 then $20,400 is includable (85% of the benefit is included). Notice that once an individual is substantially over the second hurdle they can expect to include 85% of the Social Security benefit.

Preliminary AGI	$20,000	$25,000	$30,000	$35,000	$40,000	$45,000	$50,000
Tax free bond interest	$2,000	$2,000	$2,000	$2,000	$2,000	$2,000	$2,000
MAGI	$22,000	$27,000	$32,000	$37,000	$42,000	$47,000	$52,000
50% of Social Security	$12,000	$12,000	$12,000	$12,000	$12,000	$12,000	$12,000
MAGI plus 1/2 Social Security	$34,000	$39,000	$44,000	$49,000	$54,000	$59,000	$64,000
First hurdle	$32,000	$32,000	$32,000	$32,000	$32,000	$32,000	$32,000
Second hurdle	$44,000	$44,000	$44,000	$44,000	$44,000	$44,000	$44,000
Excess of income over first hurdle	$2,000	$7,000	$12,000	$17,000	$22,000	$27,000	$32,000
Excess of income over second hurdle	$0	$0	$0	$5,000	$10,000	$15,000	$20,000
1. 50% of SSB	$12,000	$12,000	$12,000				
2. 50% [MAGI + 0.50 (SSB) - Hurdle 1]	$1,000	$3,500	$6,000				
3. 85% of SSB				$20,400	$20,400	$20,400	**$20,400**
4. [85% [MAGI + 0.5 (SSB)- Hurdle 2]] + 6000				$10,250	$14,500	$18,750	$23,000
5. [85% [MAGI + 0.5 (SSB)- Hurdle 2]] + 50% [MAGI + 0.50 (SSB) - Hurdle 1]				$14,450	$18,700	$22,950	$27,200
5. [85% [MAGI + 0.5 (SSB)- Hurdle 2]] + 50% of SSB				$16,250	$20,500	$24,750	$29,000
Includable portion of Social Security	$1,000	$3,500	$6,000	$10,250	$14,500	$18,750	$20,400
Percent of SS Taxed	4%	15%	25%	43%	60%	78%	85%

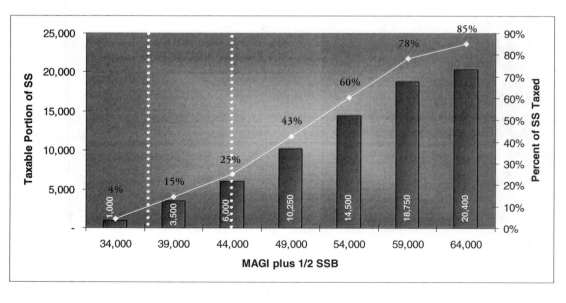

DISABILITY BENEFITS AND DISABILITY INSURED

Benefits are payable at any age to workers who have enough Social Security credits and who have a severe physical or mental impairment that is expected to prevent them from doing "substantial" work for a year or more or who have a condition that is expected to result in death. Workers are insured for disability if they are fully insured and, except for persons who are blind or disabled before age 31, have a total of at least 20 quarters of coverage during the 40-quarter period ending with the quarter in which the worker became disabled. Workers who are disabled before age 31 must have total quarters of coverage equal to one-half the calendar quarters that have elapsed since the worker reached age 21 ending in the quarter in which the worker became disabled. However, a minimum of six quarters is required.

WORK CREDITS FOR DISABILITY BENEFITS

EXHIBIT 11.12

Born After 1929, Become Disabled at Age:	Number of Credits You Need:
31 through 42	20
44	22
46	24
48	26
50	28
52	30
54	32
56	34
58	36
60	38
62 or older	40

- Before age 24 - The disabled individual may qualify if they have 6 credits earned in the 3-year period ending when the disability starts.

- Age 24 to 31 - The disabled individual may qualify if they have credit for working half the time between age 21 and the time they become disabled. For example, if they become disabled at age 27, they would need credit for 3 years of work (12 credits) out of the past 6 years (between ages 21 and 27).

- Age 31 or older - In general, the disabled individual needs to have the number of work credits shown in the chart. Unless they are blind, they must have earned at least 20 of the credits in the 10 years immediately before they became disabled.

In 2005, earnings of $830 or more per month are considered substantial; therefore, a worker earning more than $830 per month would not be eligible for Social Security disability benefits. (If the individual is blind, then the amount is increased to $1,380.) The disability program includes incentives to smooth the disabled individual's transition back into the workforce, including continuation of benefits and health care coverage. Disability under the Social Security system is defined as an inability to engage in substantial gainful activity by reason of a physical or mental impairment expected to last at least 12 months or result in death. The impairment must be of such severity that the applicant is not only unable to do his or her previous work but cannot, considering age, education, and work experience, engage in any other kind of substantial gainful work that exists in the national economy.

FAMILY BENEFITS

If an individual is eligible for retirement or disability benefits, other members of the individual's family might receive benefits as well. Family members who may receive retirement or disability benefits include the following:

- A spouse, if the spouse is 62 years old, caring for a child under age 16, or caring for a child who was disabled before age 22.
- A child, if the child is unmarried and under age 18, under age 19 but still in school, or age 18 or older but disabled.

For those workers who are entitled to retirement or disability benefits, an ex-spouse who was married to the worker for more than 10 years could also be eligible for retirement benefits based on the worker's record.

A child's benefit stops the month before the child reaches 18, unless the child is unmarried and is either disabled or is a full-time elementary or secondary school student. Approximately five months before the child's 18th birthday, the person receiving the child's benefits will get a form explaining how benefits can continue. A child whose benefits stop at 18 can have them started again if the child becomes disabled before reaching 22 or becomes a full-time elementary or secondary school student before reaching 19. If the child continues to receive benefits after age 18 due to a disability, the child also may qualify for SSI disability benefits. When a student's 19th birthday occurs during a school term, benefits can be continued up to two months to allow completion of the school term.

SURVIVORS BENEFITS

If a worker earned enough Social Security credits during his or her lifetime, certain members of the worker's family may be eligible for benefits when the worker dies. The family members of the deceased worker who may be entitled to survivors' benefits include:

- A widow or widower age 60, age 50 if disabled, or any age if caring for a child under age 16 or a disabled child.
- A child of the deceased worker, if the child is unmarried and under age 18, under age 19 but still in school, or age 18 or older but disabled.
- Parents of the deceased worker, if the deceased worker was their primary means of support.

A special one-time payment of $255 may be made to a deceased worker's spouse or minor children upon death. If a spouse was living with the beneficiary at the time of death, the spouse will receive a one-time payment of $255. The payment may be made to a spouse who was not living with the beneficiary at the time of death or an ex-spouse if the spouse or ex-spouse was receiving Social Security benefits based on the deceased's earnings record. If there is no surviving spouse, a child (or children) who is eligible for benefits on the deceased's work record in the month of death may claim the payment.

THE MAXIMUM FAMILY BENEFIT

When a person dies, his survivors receive a percentage of the worker's Social Security benefits ranging from 75 percent to 100 percent each. There is a limit on the amount of monthly Social Security benefits that may be paid to a family. This limit is called the **maximum family benefit** and it is determined through a formula based on the worker's PIA. While the limit varies, it is equal to roughly 150 to 180 percent of the deceased worker's PIA. If the sum of the family members' benefits exceeds the limit, the family members' benefits are proportionately reduced. For old-age and survivor family benefits, the formula computes the sum of four separate percentages of portions of the worker's PIA. For 2005, these portions are the first $801 of PIA, the amount between $801 and $1,156, the amount between $1,156 and $1,508, and the amount over $1,508. These are the bend points for the maximum family benefit formula for the year 2005, with the following percentage calculations:

Quick Quiz

Highlight the answer to these questions:

1. Up to 85% of an individual's Social Security benefits may be included in their taxable income.
   a. True
   b. False

2. Once divorced, non-working ex-spouses will not receive Social Security benefits.
   a. True
   b. False

3. The maximum family benefit establishes a limit on the benefits that can be received by one family.
   a. True
   b. False

True, False, True.

> 150 percent of the first $801 of the worker's PIA, *plus*
>
> 272 percent of the worker's PIA over $801 through $1,156, *plus*
>
> 134 percent of the worker's PIA over $1,156 through $1,508, *plus*
>
> 175 percent of the worker's PIA over $1,508.
>
> This number is rounded to the next lower $0.10.

EXAMPLE 11.23

If an individual has the maximum PIA for 2005, $1,926 per month, this would provide a maximum family benefit of $3,370.20 per month as shown by the calculation below:

$801 x 1.50 =	$1,201.50
($1,156 - $801) x 2.72 =	965.60
($1,508 - $1,156) x 1.34 =	471.68
($1,926 - $1,508) x 1.75 =	731.50
	$3,370.28 rounded to $3,370.20

EXAMPLE 11.24

Natalie and Brian, both age 50, are married and have two children, Ashley (age 15) and Kayli (age 5). Brian is disabled and has a PIA amount equal to the maximum PIA ($1,926). As seen in the example above, the maximum family benefit is $3,370.20. Because Brian is disabled, Natalie, Ashley, and Kayli are each entitled to receive a benefit equal to 50% of Brian's PIA, subject to the maximum family benefit limit, because the two children are under 18 and Natalie is a spouse/caretaker of a child under 18. Without regard to the maximum family benefit, they would each receive:

Brian	$1,926	100% of PIA
Natalie	$963	50% of Brian's PIA
Ashley	$963	50% of Brian's PIA
Kayli	$963	50% of Brian's PIA
Total	$4,815	

Because the benefit exceeds the maximum family benefit, the amounts for Natalie, Ashley, and Kayli must be prorated. Therefore, they will each receive $481.40 [($3,370.20-$1,926)/3]

Brian	$1,926.00	100% of PIA
Natalie	$481.40	50% of Brian's PIA subject to maximum family benefit
Ashley	$481.40	50% of Brian's PIA subject to maximum family benefit
Kayli	$481.40	50% of Brian's PIA subject to maximum family benefit
Total	$3,370.20	

Assume instead that Ashley is 19 and no longer eligible to receive benefits under Brian. The maximum family benefit would be calculated as follows:

Brian	$1,926.00	100% of PIA
Natalie	$722.10	50% of Brian's PIA subject to maximum family benefit
Ashley	$0.00	Not eligible
Kayli	$722.10	50% of Brian's PIA subject to maximum family benefit
Total	$3,370.20	

Now assume Ashley is 19 and Kayli is 17. In this case, Natalie is no longer eligible because she is not caring for a child under 16. The family benefit would be calculated as follows:

Brian	$1,926.00	100% of PIA
Natalie	$0.00	Not eligible
Ashley	$0.00	Not eligible
Kayli	$963.00	50% of Brian's PIA
Total	$2,889.00	

Notice that Kayli is limited to 50% of Brian's PIA, thus they do not reach the maximum family benefit.

MEDICARE BENEFITS

Medicare is a federal health insurance plan for people who are 65 and older, whether retired or still working. People who are disabled or have permanent kidney failure can get Medicare at any age. The Health Care Financing Administration, now known as Centers for Medicare and Medicaid Services (or CMS), part of the United States Department of Health and Human Services, administers Medicare. Medicare is the nation's largest health insurance program, covering over 39 million individuals. There are two parts to Medicare: Hospital Insurance (sometimes called Part A) and Medical Insurance (sometimes called Part B).

Generally, individuals who are over age 65 and receive Social Security benefits automatically qualify for Medicare. Also, individuals who have received Social Security disability benefits for at

Key Concepts

Underline/highlight the answers to these questions as you read:

1. What benefits are provided by Medicare?

2. What benefits are provided by Supplemental Security Income?

3. How does marriage or divorce affect Social Security benefits?

least two years automatically qualify for Medicare. All other individuals must file an application for Medicare.

Part A, Hospital Insurance, is paid for by a portion of the Social Security tax. Part A helps pay for necessary medical care furnished by Medicare-certified providers, including inpatient hospital care, skilled nursing care, home health care, hospice care, and other care. The number of days that Medicare covers care in hospitals and skilled nursing facilities is measured in what is termed **benefit periods.** A benefit period begins on the first day a patient receives services in a hospital or skilled nursing facility and ends after 60 consecutive days without further skilled care. There is no limit to the number of benefit periods a beneficiary may have.

Benefit periods are identified because deductibles, coinsurance, and premiums relate to a benefit period instead of a calendar year. For instance, for coverage under Medicare under Part A, a deductible of $912 applies per benefit period. For the 61st through the 90th day of each benefit period, the insured individual must pay $228 a day in the form of coinsurance. Any days over 90 in a benefit period are considered lifetime reserve days. There are 60 lifetime reserve days available with coinsurance of $456 per day. Lifetime reserve days do not renew with each benefit period. It is important, therefore, to determine the number of days used in each benefit period.

| EXHIBIT 11.13 | MEDICARE TIME LINE |

Beneficiary enters hospital

	60 Days	61-90	91-150
Deductible: $912 per benefit period	$228 per day	$456 per day
Coinsurance: $0		lifetime reserve

| EXHIBIT 11.14 | SKILLED NURSING FACILITY TIME LINE |

Beneficiary enters nursing facility

| 20 Days | 21-100 |
| Coinsurance: $0 | $114 per day |

EXHIBIT 11.15

Hospital Insurance (Part A)
• **Deductible** - $912 per Benefit Period
• **Coinsurance**
• $228 a day for the 61st through the 90th day
• $456 a day for the 91st through the 150th day for each lifetime reserve day (total of 60 lifetime reserve days – nonrenewable)
• **Skilled Nursing Facility coinsurance** - $114 a day for the 21st through the 100th day per Benefit Period
• **Hospital Insurance Premium** - $375 per month (Note: This premium is paid only by individuals who are not otherwise eligible for premium-free hospital insurance and have less than 30 quarters of Medicare covered employment)
• **Reduced Hospital Insurance Premium** - $206 (Note: For individuals having 30 to 39 quarters of coverage) Note: The $912 is 4 x $228, 2 x $456, and 8 x $114.

Medical Insurance (Part B)
• **Deductible** - $110 per year
• **Monthly Premium** - $78.20

Source: Social Security Administration (www.ssa.gov)

Medicare Part A helps pay for up to 90 days of inpatient hospital care during each benefit period. Covered services for inpatient hospital care include: semiprivate room and meals, operating and recovery room costs, intensive care, drugs, laboratory tests, x-rays, general nursing services, and any other necessary medical services and supplies. Convenience items such as television and telephones provided by hospitals in private rooms (unless medically necessary) are generally not covered. Medicare does not pay for custodial services for daily living activities such as eating, bathing, and getting dressed. Medicare does, however, pay for skilled nursing facility care for rehabilitation, such as recovery time after a hospital discharge. Part A may help pay for up to 100 days in a participating skilled nursing facility in each benefit period. Medicare pays all approved charges for the first 20 days relating to skilled nursing facility care, and the patient pays a coinsurance amount for days 21 through 100. Medicare may also pay the full, approved cost of covered home health care services, which includes part-time or intermittent skilled nursing services prescribed by a physician for treatment or rehabilitation of home bound patients. Normally, the only cost to the insured for home health care is a 20 percent coinsurance charge for medical equipment, such as wheelchairs and walkers.

Medicare Part B, Medical Insurance, is optional and a premium is charged. Part B is financed by the monthly premiums paid by those who are enrolled and out of the general revenues from the U.S. Treasury. Medicare Part B is used to pay for doctor's services; ambulance transportation; diagnostic tests; outpatient therapy services; outpatient hospital services including emergency room visits; X-rays and laboratory services; some preventative care; home health care services not covered by Part A; durable medical equipment and supplies; and a variety of other health services.

Medicare Part B pays for 80 percent of approved charges for most covered services. Unless an individual declines Part B medical insurance protection, the premium will automatically be deducted from their Social Security benefits. The 2005 premium amount is $78.20 a month. The deductible for Part B is $110 per year. The insured is responsible for paying a $110 deductible per calendar year and the remaining 20 percent of the Medicare-approved charges. Medicare Part B usually does not cover charges for prescription drugs, routine physical examinations, or services unrelated to treatment of injury or illness. Dental care, dentures, cosmetic surgery, hearing aids, and eye examinations are not covered by Part B.

Various plans under Medicare are available to insureds. The original Medicare Plan is the way most individuals get their Medicare Part A and Part B benefits. This is the traditional payment-per-service arrangement where the individual insured may go to any doctor, specialist, or hospital that accepts Medicare and Medicare pays its share after services are rendered. Medicare carriers and fiscal intermediaries are private insurance organizations that handle claims under the original Medicare Plan. Carriers handle Part B claims while fiscal intermediaries handle Part A plans. The Social Security Administration does not handle claims for Medicare payments.

Many private insurance companies sell Medicare supplemental insurance policies, such as Medigap, and Medicare SELECT. These supplemental policies help bridge the coverage gaps in the original Medicare Plan. These supplemental policies also help pay Medicare's coinsurance amounts and deductibles, as well as other out-of-pocket expenses for health care.

When a worker is first enrolled in Part B at age 65, there is a six-month open enrollment period in Medigap. During the time of open enrollment, the health status of the applicant cannot be used as a reason to refuse a Medigap policy or to charge more than other open enrollment applicants. The insurer may require a six-month waiting period for coverage of pre-existing conditions. If, however, the open enrollment period has expired, the applicant may be denied a policy based on health status or may be charged higher rates.

MEDICARE PART D SUBSIDY

Beginning January 1, 2006, new Medicare prescription drug plans will be available to individuals with Medicare (called Medicare Part D Subsidy). Insurance companies and other private companies will work with Medicare to offer these drug plans. They will negotiate discounts on drug prices. These plans are different from the Medicare-approved drug discount cards, which will phaseout by the earlier of May 15, 2006 or when an individual's enrollment in a Medicare prescription drug plan takes effect.

Medicare prescription drug plans provide insurance coverage for prescription drugs. Like other insurance, if an individual joins they will pay a monthly premium (generally around $35 in 2006) and pay a share of the cost of their prescriptions. Costs will vary depending on the drug plan the individual chooses.

Drug plans may vary in what prescription drugs are covered, how much the individual has to pay, and which pharmacies they can use. All drug plans will have to provide at least a standard level of coverage, which Medicare will set. However, some plans might offer more coverage and additional drugs for a higher monthly premium. When an individual joins a drug plan, it is important for them to choose one that meets their prescription drug needs.

OTHER MEDICARE HEALTH PLAN CHOICES

Medicare offers alternative methods of obtaining Medicare benefits through other health plan choices. Choices that vary by area include coordinated-care or Medicare managed care plans such as Health Maintenance Organizations (HMOs), HMOs with a point of service option, Provider Sponsored Organizations (PSOs), and Preferred Provider Organizations (PPOs). These plans involve specific groups of doctors, hospitals, and other providers who provide care to the insured as a member of the plan, like many employer-sponsored plans throughout the country. Medicare managed care plans not only provide the same services that are covered by Part A and Part B, but most Medicare managed plans offer a variety of additional benefits like preventative care, prescription drugs, dental care, eyeglasses, and other items not covered by the original Medicare Plan. The cost of these extra benefits varies among the plans.

For those who receive Medicare and have low income and few resources, states may pay Medicare premiums and, in some cases, other out-of-pocket Medicare expenses, such as deductibles and coinsurance. The state decides if individuals qualify. For more general information about Medicare, the Social Security Administration's leaflet *Medicare Savings for Qualified Beneficiaries* (HCFA Publication No. 02184) is helpful, as are the websites *www.ssa.gov* and *www.medicare.gov.*

SUPPLEMENTAL SECURITY INCOME BENEFITS

Supplemental Security Income (SSI) makes monthly payments to individuals with low incomes and few assets. In order to obtain SSI benefits, an individual must be age 65, disabled, or blind. The definition of disability is satisfied when the individual is unable to engage in any substantial gainful activity due to a physical or mental problem expected to last at least a year or expected to result in death. Children as well as adults qualify for SSI disability payments. As its name implies, Supplemental Security Income supplements the beneficiary's income up to various levels depending on where the beneficiary lives. If an otherwise eligible SSI applicant lives in another's household and receives support from that person, the federal SSI benefit is reduced by one-third.

The federal government pays a basic rate. In 2005 the basic monthly SSI check was $579 per month for one person and $869 per month for married couples. Some states supply additional funds to qualified individuals. To ascertain the SSI benefit rates in a certain state, the financial planner or client can contact a local Social Security office in that state or visit the Social Security Administration's website. Generally, individuals who receive SSI benefits also qualify for Medicaid, food stamps, and other government assistance.

To be eligible for the monthly SSI benefit, the beneficiary must not have assets that exceed $2,000 for one person or $3,000 for married couples. This asset determination does not include the value of the home and some personal belongings, such as one car. If the potential beneficiary does not work, he or she may be eligible for SSI benefits if monthly income is less than $599 for one person and $889 for a couple. If the potential beneficiary works, more monthly income is allowed -- $1,243 for one person and $1,823 for a couple. SSI benefits are not paid from Social Security trust funds and are not based on past earnings of the beneficiary. Rather, SSI benefits are financed by general tax revenues and assure a minimum monthly income for needy elderly, disabled, or blind persons.

FILING FOR SOCIAL SECURITY CLAIMS

The Social Security Administration reports that many people fail to file claims with the Social Security Administration or fail to do so in a timely fashion. Individuals should file for Social Security or SSI disability benefits as soon they become too disabled to work or for survivors benefits, when a family breadwinner dies. Social Security benefits do not start automatically. Social Security will not begin payment of benefits until the beneficiary files an application. When filling for benefits, applicants must submit documents that show eligibility, such as a birth certificate for each family member applying for benefits, a marriage certificate if a spouse is applying, and the most recent W-2 forms or tax returns.

To file for benefits, obtain information, or to speak to a Social Security representative, individuals must call the Social Security Administration's toll-free number, 800-772-1213, or visit the Social Security Administration's website. The toll-free number can be used to schedule an appointment at a local Social Security office. The Social Security Administration treats all calls confidentially. Periodically, a second Social Security representative will monitor incoming and outgoing telephone calls to ensure accurate and courteous service.

OTHER ISSUES

EFFECT OF MARRIAGE OR DIVORCE ON BENEFITS

Marriage or divorce may affect one's Social Security benefits, depending on the kind of benefits received. If a worker receives retirement benefits based on his or her own earnings record, the worker's retirement benefits will continue whether married or divorced. If an individual receives benefits based on his or her spouse's record, the individual's benefits will cease upon divorce unless the individual is age 62 or older and was married longer than 10 years. Widows and widowers, whether divorced or not, will continue to receive survivors' benefits upon remarriage if the widow or widower is age 60 or older. Disabled widows and widowers, whether divorced or not, will continue to receive survivors' benefits upon remarriage if the disabled widow or widower is age 50 or older.

Larry was married at the following ages and to the following wives. Larry is now 62 and married to Dawn.

EXAMPLE 11.25

	Wife	Current Age	Larry's Age at Marriage	Current Marital Status	Length of Marriage
1	Alice	62	20	Single	10 years, 1 month
2	Betty	63	31	Single	10 years, 1 month
3	Claire	64	42	Single	9 years
4	Dawn	65	53	Married	9 years

Who, among the wives, may be eligible to receive Social Security retirement benefits based upon Larry's earnings if Larry is retired or not retired?

Any divorced spouse, age 62 and married to Larry for 10 years or longer, and his current wife, Dawn, if he is retired. His current spouse cannot collect if he is not retired.

If Larry is retired: Alice, Betty, and Dawn

If Larry is not retired: Alice and Betty.

For all other forms of Social Security benefits, benefits will cease upon remarriage, except in special circumstances. When a person marries, it is presumed that at least one person in the marriage can provide adequate support. Likewise, Social Security benefits may recommence based on the previous spouse's benefits if the marriage ends.

CHANGE OF NAME

If an individual changes his or her name due to marriage, divorce, or a court order, that individual must notify the Social Security Administration of the name change so the Social Security Administration will be able to show the new name in their records and properly credit that individual for earnings. This will ensure that the individual's work history will be accurately recorded and maintained.

Quick Quiz

Highlight the answer to these questions:

1. Medicare Part A generally pays for "Places" while Part B pays for "Services."
   a. True
   b. False

2. In order to obtain Supplemental Social Security benefits, the individual must be 62, disabled, or blind.
   a. True
   b. False

3. Social Security beneficiaries who are United States citizens may live in most foreign countries without affecting their eligibility for Social Security benefits.
   a. True
   b. False

True, False, True.

LEAVING THE UNITED STATES

Beneficiaries who are United States citizens may travel or live in most foreign countries without affecting their eligibility for Social Security benefits. However, there are a few countries where Social Security checks cannot be sent. These countries currently include Cuba, Cambodia, North Korea, Vietnam, and the republics that were formerly in the U.S.S.R. (except Estonia, Latvia, and Lithuania).

Beneficiaries should inform the Social Security Administration of their plans to go outside the United States for a trip that lasts 30 days or more. By providing the name of the country or countries to be visited and the expected departure and return dates, the Social Security Administration will send special reporting instructions to the beneficiaries and arrange for delivery of checks while abroad.

EXHIBIT 11.16

Information for people who are working

Social Security and Medicare taxes

Social Security taxes	2004	2005
Employee/employer (each)	6.2% on earnings up to $87,900	6.2% on earnings up to $90,000
Self-employed *Can be offset by income tax provisions	12.4%* on earnings up to $87,900	12.4%* on earnings up to $90,000

Medicare taxes	2004	2005
Employee/employer (each)	1.45% on all earnings	1.45% on all earnings
Self-employed *Can be offset by income tax provisions	2.9%* on all earnings	2.9%* on all earnings

Work credits—When you work, you earn credits toward Social Security benefits. You need a certain number of credits to be eligible for Social Security benefits. The number you need depends on your age and the type of benefit for which you are applying. You can earn a maximum of four credits each year. Most people need 40 credits to qualify for retirement benefits.

	2004	2005
	$900 earns one credit	$920 earns one credit

Information for people who receive Social Security benefits

Earnings limits

Under federal law, people who are receiving Social Security benefits who have not reached full retirement age are entitled to receive all of their benefits as long as their earnings are under the limits indicated below. In 2005, the full retirement age is 65 and 6 months. The full retirement age will increase gradually each year until it reaches age 67 for people born in 1960 or later.

	2004	2005
At full retirement age or older	No limit on earnings	No limit on earnings
Under full retirement age	$11,640 For every $2 over the limit, $1 is withheld from benefits.	$12,000 For every $2 over the limit, $1 is withheld from benefits.
In the year you reach full retirement age	$31,080 For every $3 over the limit, $1 is withheld from benefits until the month you reach full retirement age.	$31,800 For every $3 over the limit, $1 is withheld from benefits until the month you reach full retirement age.

Disability beneficiaries' earnings limits: If you work while receiving disability benefits you must tell us about your earnings no matter how little you earn. You may have unlimited earnings during a trial work period of up to nine months (not necessarily in a row) and still receive full benefits. Once you have completed your nine-month trial work period, we will determine if you are still entitled to disability benefits. You also may be eligible for other work incentives to help you make the transition back to work.

Substantial Gainful Activity (Non-blind)	$810 per month	$830 per month
Substantial Gainful Activity (Blind)	$1,350 per month	$1,380 per month
Trial work period month	$580 per month	$590 per month

Information for people who receive Supplemental Security Income (SSI)

Monthly federal SSI payment (maximum)

	2004	2005
Individual	$564	$579
Couple	$846	$869
Monthly income limits		
Individual whose income is only from wages	$1,213	$1,243
Individual whose income is not from wages	$584	$599
Couple whose income is only from wages	$1,777	$1,823
Couple whose income is not from wages	$866	$889

NOTE: *If you have income, your monthly benefit generally will be lower than the maximum federal SSI payment. Remember, you must report all of your income to us. Some states add money to the federal SSI payment. If you live in one of these states, you may qualify for a higher payment. Your income can be greater than the limits indicated and you still may qualify.*

Information for people on Medicare

Most Medicare costs are increasing this year to keep up with the rise in health care costs.

	2004	2005
Hospital Insurance (Part A)		
For first 60 days in a hospital, patient pays	$876	$912
For 61st through 90th days in a hospital, patient pays	$219 per day	$228 per day
Beyond 90 days in a hospital, patient pays (for up to 60 more days)	$438 per day	$456 per day
For first 20 days in a skilled nursing facility, patient pays	$0	$0
For 21st through 100th days in a skilled nursing facility, patient pays	$109.50 per day	$114 per day
Part A Premium Buy-In: The amount of the premium you pay to buy Medicare Part A depends on the number of Social Security credits you have earned. If you have:		
40 credits	$0	$0
30-39 credits	$189 per month	$206 per month
less than 30 credits	$343 per month	$375 per month
Medical Insurance (Part B)		
Premium	$66.60 per month	$78.20 per month
Deductible	$100 per year	$110 per year
	After the patient has paid the deductible, Part B pays for 80 percent of covered services.	

NOTE: *If you get Medicare and your income is low, your state may pay your Medicare premiums and, in some cases, your deductibles and other out-of-pocket medical expenses. Contact your local medical assistance (Medicaid) agency, social services or welfare office for more information.*

http://www.ssa.gov/pubs/10003.html

Key Terms

AIME (Average Indexed Monthly Earnings) - The adjustment, or index, to a worker's historic earnings to create an equivalent current dollar value.

Benefit Periods - Begins on the first day an individual receives services as a patient in a hospital or skilled nursing facility and ends after 60 consecutive days without further skilled care.

COLA - The cost-of-living adjustments applied to Social Security benefits.

Currently Insured Workers - A worker who has earned at least six quarters of coverage out of the previous 13 quarters for Social Security.

Disability Benefit - A Social Security benefit available to recipients who have a severe physical or mental impairment that is expected to prevent them from performing "substantial" work for at least a year or result in death. To qualify for these benefits, the recipient must have the sufficient amount of Social Security credits.

Disability Insurance (DI) Trust Fund - The trust fund that pays benefits to workers with disabilities and their families. It is funded by 0.90 percent of an individual's taxable earnings up to $90,000.

Family Benefit - A Social Security benefit available to certain family members of workers eligible for retirement or disability benefits.

FICA (Federal Insurance Contributions Act) - A law allowing Social Security taxes, including Medicare taxes, to be deducted from employee's paychecks.

Fully Insured - A worker who has earned 40 quarters of coverage under the Social Security system.

Hospital Insurance (HI) Trust Fund - The trust fund that pays for services covered under the hospital insurance provisions of Medicare (Part A). It is funded by 1.45 percent of an individual's taxable earnings (no limitation).

Maximum Family Benefit - The limit on the amount of monthly Social Security benefits that may be paid to a family.

Medicaid - Provides medical assistance for persons with low incomes and resources.

Medicare - A federal health insurance plan for those who have attained full retirement age or have been disabled whether retired or still working.

Key Terms

Modified Adjusted Gross Income (when calculating taxable Social Security) - The sum of an individual's adjusted gross income plus tax exempt interest, including interest earned on savings bonds used for higher education; amounts excluded from the tax payer's income for employer provided adoption assistance; amounts deducted for interest paid for educational loans; amounts deducted as qualified tuition expense; and income earned in a foreign country, a U.S. possession, or Puerto Rico that is excluded from income.

Old Age and Survivor Disability Insurance (OASDI) - An inclusive title given to the Social Security benefit system.

Old Age and Survivors Insurance (OASI) - The trust fund that pays retirement and survivors' benefits funded by 5.30 percent of an individual's taxable earnings up to $90,000.

PIA (Primary Insurance Amount) - The amount on which a worker's retirement benefit is based; the PIA determines the amount the applicant will receive at his or her full retirement age based on the year in which the retiree turns 62. The PIA is indexed to the Consumer Price Index (CPI) annually.

Retirement Benefit - The most familiar Social Security benefit, full retirement benefits are payable at normal retirement age and reduced benefits as early as age 62 to anyone who has obtained at least a minimum (40 quarters) amount of Social Security credits.

Retirement Earnings Limitations Test - A test that may reduce the Social Security benefit paid to an individual based on their other income.

Social Security Statement, Form SSA-7005 - A written report mailed by the Social Security Administration to all workers age 25 and over who are not yet receiving Social Security benefits that provides an estimate of the worker's eventual Social Security benefits and instructions on how to qualify for those benefits.

SSI (Supplemental Security Income) - A program administered by the Social Security Administration and funded by the general Treasury that is available to those at full retirement age or the disabled who have a low income and few assets.

Supplementary Medical Insurance (SMI) Trust Fund - The trust fund that pays for services covered under the medical insurance provisions of Medicare, known as Part B. The coverage is funded by general federal tax revenues and monthly medicare premiums paid by enrollees.

Survivors Benefit - Social Security benefit available to surviving family members of a deceased, eligible worker.

DISCUSSION QUESTIONS

1. List and describe the six major categories of benefits administered by the Social Security Association.

2. How are Social Security funds collected?

3. Which individuals are covered workers under the Social Security system?

4. List the beneficiaries of Social Security benefits.

5. How is a person's Social Security retirement benefit calculated?

6. How does retiring early or retiring late affect the calculation of Social Security benefits?

7. How are Social Security benefits taxed?

8. What other benefits are available from Social Security other than retirement benefits?

9. Discuss the maximum family benefit.

10. What Social Security benefits does Medicare provide?

11. Describe Supplemental Security Income benefits and when they are available.

12. How does marriage or divorce affect Social Security benefits?

1. Social Security is funded through all of the following except:

    a. Employee payroll tax.

    b. Employer payroll tax.

    (c.) Sales tax.

    d. Self-employment tax.

2. Brisco, now deceased, was married for 12 years. He had two dependent children, ages 10 and 12, who are cared for by their mother age 48. His mother, age 75, was his dependent and survived him. At the time of his death, he was currently but not fully insured under Social Security. His dependents are entitled to all of the following benefits except:

    a. A lump-sum death benefit of $255.

    b. A children's benefit equal to 75% of Brisco's PIA.

    c. A caretaker's benefit for the children's mother.

    (d.) A parent's benefit.

3. Medicare Part A provides hospital coverage. Which of the following persons is not covered under Part A?

    (a.) A person 62 or older and receiving railroad retirement.

    b. Disabled beneficiaries regardless of age that have received Social Security for two years.

    c. Chronic kidney patients who require dialysis or a renal transplant.

    d. A person 65 or older entitled to a monthly Social Security check.

4. Part B of Medicare is considered to be supplemental insurance and provides additional coverage to participants. Which of the following is true regarding Part B coverage?

    a. The election to participate must be made at the time the insured is eligible for Part A Medicare and at no time after.

    (b.) The premiums for Part B are paid monthly through withholding from Social Security benefits.

    c. Once a participant elects Part B, he must maintain the coverage until death.

    d. Coverage under Part B does not include deductibles or coinsurance.

5.	A person receiving Social Security benefits under the age of 65 can receive earned income up to a maximum threshold without reducing Social Security benefits by the earnings test. Which of the following count against the earnings threshold?

    a.	Dividends from stocks.

    b.	Rental income.

    c.	Pensions and insurance annuities.

    d.	Gambling winnings.

6.	It is possible for a person receiving Social Security benefits to lose eligibility (be disqualified) for those benefits. Which of the following is not considered grounds for disqualification?

    a.	Marriage.

    b.	Divorce.

    c.	Conviction of fraud.

    d.	Engaging in illegal employment.

7.	Betty Sue, age 75, is a widow with no close relatives. She is very ill, unable to walk, and confined to a custodial nursing home. Which of the following programs is likely to pay benefits towards the cost of the nursing home?

    1.	Medicare may pay for up to 100 days of care after a 20-day deductible.

    2.	Medicaid may pay if the client has income and assets below state-mandated thresholds.

    a.	1 only.

    b.	2 only.

    c.	1 and 2.

    d.	Neither 1 nor 2.

8.	Which of the following concerning the Social Security system is correct?

    a.	SSI benefits are funded by the Treasury, not Social Security taxes, as are the other benefits.

    b.	The Social Security retirement benefit is payable at full retirement age with reduced benefits as early as age 59 to anyone who has obtained at least a minimum amount of Social Security benefits.

    c.	The two Medicare trust funds are the federal Medical Insurance Trust Fund for Part A and the Supplementary Hospital Insurance Trust Fund for Part B of Medicare benefits.

    d.	Benefits can be paid to the dependent parents of a deceased insured worker at age 59 or over.

9. Which of the following concerning the Social Security system is correct?

   a. Workers entitled to retirement benefits can currently take early retirement benefits as early as age 59.

   b. A worker who takes early retirement benefits will receive a reduced benefit because he or she will receive more monthly benefit payments as payments commence earlier than if the worker had waited and retired at full retirement age.

   c. Family members of an individual who are eligible for retirement or disability benefits include a spouse if the spouse is at least 59 years old or under 59 but caring for a child under age 16.

   d. Generally, individuals who are over the age of 59 and receive Social Security benefits automatically qualify for Medicare benefits.

10. All of the following statements concerning the Social Security system are correct except:

   a. If a worker receives retirement benefits based on his or her own earnings record, the worker's retirement benefits will continue whether married or divorced.

   b. Widows and widowers, whether divorced or not, will continue to receive survivors benefits upon remarriage if the widow or widower is age 60 or older.

   c. By providing the name of a country or countries to be visited and the expected departure and return dates, the Social Security Administration will send special reporting instructions to the beneficiaries and arrange for delivery of checks while abroad.

   d. A special one-time payment of $1,000 may be made to a deceased worker's spouse or minor children upon death.

11. All of the following statements concerning Social Security benefits are correct except:

   a. The maximum family benefit is determined through a formula based on the worker's PIA.

   b. If a worker applies for retirement or survivors benefits before his or her 65th birthday, he or she must also file a separate application for Medicare.

   c. People who are disabled or have permanent kidney failure can get Medicare at any age.

   d. The Social Security Administration is concerned with beneficiaries' combined income, which, on the 1040 federal tax return, includes adjusted gross income and nontaxable interest income.

12. All of the following statements concerning Social Security benefits are correct except:

    (a.) In order to obtain SSI benefits, an individual must be age 65 or older and must be disabled.

    b. The number of days that Medicare covers care in hospitals and skilled nursing facilities is measured in what is termed benefit periods.

    c. The definition of disability is that the individual is unable to engage in any substantial gainful activity due to a physical or mental problem expected to last at least a year or expected to result in death.

    d. Benefits are payable at any age to workers who have enough Social Security credits and who have a severe physical or mental impairment that is expected to prevent them from doing "substantial" work for a year or more or who have a condition that is expected to result in death.

13. Joyce and Melvin have been married for 30 years. In 2005, they received $22,000 of Social Security income and had $12,000 of interest income. What portion of the Social Security benefit is taxable?

    (a.) $0.

    b. $6,000.

    c. $10,200.

    d. $11,500.

$$12,000 + (.5 \times 22000)$$
$$= 23,000$$

14. Emile is single and received $28,000 of dividend income during the year. He also received $18,000 of Social Security benefits. What portion of his Social Security benefits are taxable?

    a. $0.

    (b.) $7,050.

    c. $9,000.

    d. $15,300.

12

Deferred Compensation and Nonqualified Plans

INTRODUCTION

Employers establish **deferred compensation arrangements** to provide benefits to a select group of employees without the limitations of a qualified plan. These types of arrangements, usually in the form of **nonqualified plans** or other executive compensation, often discriminate in favor of key employees and can exceed the dollar limits imposed on qualified plans. These arrangements may take many forms but ultimately the common objectives are recruiting and retaining key executives. While qualified plans and the other tax-advantaged plans are effective with respect to mid-paid and lower-paid employees, the limitations imposed by these plans, especially the dollar limits and testing requirements, do not provide sufficient retirement resources for key executives who earn in excess of $210,000, the covered compensation limit for qualified plans for 2005.

The general characteristics of the deferred compensation arrangements presented in this chapter are:
1. They do not have the tax advantages of qualified plans.
2. They usually involve some deferral of income to the executive.
3. The employer generally does not receive an income tax deduction until the key employee receives the payment and it becomes recognizable as taxable income, thus following the traditional income tax matching principle of deduction by one party only upon inclusion by another party.
4. There is generally a requirement that the employee/executive have a "substantial risk of forfeiture" or else the government will claim that the executive, while perhaps not having actual receipt of the money, has "constructive receipt" of the money and, therefore, current income subject to income tax.

Correspondingly, deferred compensation arrangements are most often used for one or all of the three following reasons:
1. To increase the executive's wage replacement ratio;
2. To defer the executive's compensation; or
3. In lieu of qualified plans.

Some different arrangements include:

1. Golden Handshakes - severance package, often designed to encourage early retirement;
2. Golden Parachutes - substantial payments made to executives being terminated due to changes in corporate ownership; and
3. Golden Handcuffs - designed to keep the employee with the company.

It is also important to understand that employers also use deferred compensation arrangements as a method of retaining key employees. This can be done either by vesting schedules or through increased benefits with additional years of service.

In 2004 Congress and President Bush passed into law the American Jobs Creations Act and IRC Section 409A impacting deferred compensation arrangements.

The American Jobs Creation Act of 2004 was signed into law on October 22, 2004 and created IRC Section 409A which deals with nonqualified deferred compensation plans. The purpose of this section is to provide clear structure and guidance for these types of plans. The new rules also enact harsh penalties for those plans that do not comply with Section 409A. Plans failing to meet the requirements of this section are subject to acceleration of prior deferrals, interest, penalties, and a 20 percent additional tax on the amount of the deferrals. These are serious ramifications for plans that fail to comply with the new rules.

The law attempts to define nonqualified deferred compensation plans as any plan that provides for "deferral of compensation." However, it excludes most qualified plans, incentive stock option plans, nonqualified stock option plans, employee stock purchase plans, stock appreciation rights plans, and standard type bonuses that are paid within 2½ months after the close of the taxable year. Eligible plans under IRC Section 457(b) are also excluded. However, the new rules do apply to plans under IRC Section 457(f) (Discussed in Chapter 10).

Compensation is subject to a substantial risk of forfeiture if entitlement to the amount is conditioned on the performance of substantial future services by any person or the occurrence of an event related to a purpose of the compensation, such as the attainment of certain earnings or equity value.

Although the new law does provide that a plan may permit a payment upon the occurrence of a change in ownership of the corporation, it greatly restricts the conditions under which a plan may permit the acceleration of the time or schedule of payments under the plan. The more that the timing of receipt of the payments can be controlled, the more likely that the payments will be deemed constructively received. The exceptions that the law provides are minimal but include domestic relations orders, distributions for paying income tax for 457(f) plans, and the payment of employment taxes.

WAGE REPLACEMENT RATIO

An individual may need approximately 70-80 percent of his preretirement income during his retirement years to maintain his preretirement lifestyle. Most low-income and middle-income employees are capable of accumulating the amounts necessary to attain their target **wage replacement ratio** utilizing the qualified plans offered by their employer in conjunction with Social Security and their own savings. However, executives who earn substantially more than the qualified plan covered compensation limit, $210,000 for 2005, cannot attain a significant wage component replacement ratio from qualified plans because qualified plans adhere to strict limits on either contributions (e.g., $42,000 per year in 2005 for defined contribution plans) or benefits (e.g., a defined benefit limit of $170,000 in 2005).

Key Concepts

Underline/highlight the answers to these questions as you read:

1. What are deferred compensation arrangements?

2. What are the three common reasons employers use deferred compensation arrangements?

Consider the following employer data from Meyer Group.

EXAMPLE 12.1

QUALIFIED SAVINGS AS A PERCENTAGE OF GROSS PAY FOR 2005

Person	Current Compensation	Covered Compensation	Contribution to Qualified Plan (Limit)	Savings Rate (As a% of Gross Compensation)
Al	$400,000	$210,000	$42,000	10.50%
John	$210,000	$210,000	$42,000	20.00%
Kelly	$40,000	$40,000	$20,000*	50.0%

* Kelly could have a larger contribution under IRC 415(c) under certain scenarios.

Each employee's final compensation can be projected using a 3.5 percent assumed wage rate increase and assuming that each employee is 20 years from retirement.

PROJECTED FUTURE COMPENSATION

Person	Current Compensation	Compensation 20 Years from Today (Assume 3.5% Raises)
Al	$400,000	$795,916
John	$210,000	$417,856
Kelly	$40,000	$79,592

Assuming that each employee saves the stated contribution amount each year at year end and the funds earn eight percent per year, determine the accumulated account balance and the dollar size of a 20-year annuity paid in arrears on an annual basis.

PROJECTED ACCUMULATION AT RETIREMENT AND A 20-YEAR ANNUITY

Person	Savings from Qualified Plan Today	Future Accumulated Balance at 8% in 20 Years	Accumulation 20-Year Annuity
Al	$42,000	$1,922,003	$195,760
John	$42,000	$1,922,003	$195,760
Kelly	$20,000	$915,239	$93,219

The wage replacement ratio that the annuity provides can then be calculated as a <u>fraction</u> of each employee's final pre retirement compensation.

WAGE REPLACEMENT RATIO

Person	Wage Replacement (Annuity/Future Compensation)	
Al	25%	($195,760 ÷ $795,916)
John	47%	($195,760 ÷ $417,856)
Kelly	117%	($93,219 ÷ $79,592)

As illustrated, Al saves 10.50 percent of his gross compensation in the qualified plan, resulting in a wage replacement ratio from that qualified plan at retirement of 25 percent. This amount is substantially less than the 70-80 percent recommended wage replacement ratio that he will need.

The qualified plan restricted Al to this wage replacement ratio of 25 percent because the maximum contribution to the plan each year was limited ($42,000 for 2005).

The establishment of a deferred compensation plan allows an employer to provide nonqualified benefits to an executive. The purpose is to increase the executive's wage replacement ratio to a level commensurate with the executive's actual compensation instead of a wage replacement ratio limited by the qualified covered compensation limit of $210,000 for 2005 and the other limits of qualified plans (contributions $42,000 for 2005). A common application of deferred compensation plans is to supplement qualified retirement plans.

DEFERRED EXECUTIVE COMPENSATION

Deferred compensations arrangements may also be established simply to defer an executive's compensation to a future year. When an executive agrees to defer his compensation, the executive is agreeing to defer receipt of current income for a promise from the employer to pay that compensation at some later date. It is important to note that an agreement to defer compensation into the future must be made prior to the compensation being earned. Deferred compensation arrangements usually create income tax benefits for both the executive and the employer.

Employee Tax Benefit

An executive who elects to defer compensation generally earns a significantly greater amount than the covered compensation limit, is usually in the highest marginal income tax bracket, and does not need the income to be deferred currently to sustain his current standard of living. If the executive chooses to defer the compensation, the executive generally defers the compensation to a time when he expects to be in a lower marginal income tax bracket and thus, at the date of receipt, expects to pay less income tax on the compensation than would have been paid currently.

Employer Tax Benefit

The IRC places a $1,000,000 limit on a public company's employer's deduction for compensation payable to any one of the top five executives of a publicly traded company. For example, when a CEO is paid $1,250,000 per year, the employer can only deduct $1,000,000 for income tax purposes. In this case, if the executive elects to defer any income over the $1,000,000 limit to a year in which the executive earns less than the limit, the employer would be able to deduct the total compensation over the period of deferral and subsequent payment.

Quick Quiz

Highlight the answer to these questions:

1. Deferred compensation plans allow the employer to take a current deduction for compensation expense while the employee can defer the income tax on the compensation.
   a. True
   b. False

2. Public companies are limited to a $1,000,000 compensation deduction for some executives.
   a. True
   b. False

False, True.

> Josephine, the CFO of Eighteen Corporation, a publicly traded company, earns $1,250,000 per year. Without an election to defer any of her compensation, Eighteen Corporation will only be able to deduct $1,000,000 in relation to Josephine's compensation.
>
> If, however, Josephine elected to defer $250,000 of her compensation until her retirement, Eighteen Corporation would be able to deduct $1,000,000 in the current year as Josephine's compensation and at Josephine's retirement, would be able to deduct the additional $250,000 payment to Josephine as deferred compensation.

EXAMPLE 12.2

Alternative to Qualified Plans

Deferred compensation plans are also used where the employer does not have a qualified plan because the employer does not desire to cover a broad group of employees with a qualified retirement plan. The employer may nonetheless be compelled to provide retirement benefits to certain key executives and can accomplish this goal by utilizing a deferred compensation plan. Nonqualified plans can discriminate in favor of key employees and are not subject to the limits imposed on qualified plans.

INCOME TAX ISSUES

Deferred compensation arrangements are typically used to benefit the highly compensated and key executives in an organization. One of the primary benefits to these types of plans is the deferral of income taxation for the key executive. For deferral of income tax to be realized, the deferred compensation plan must comply with certain income tax provisions.

CONSTRUCTIVE RECEIPT

Constructive receipt is an income tax concept that establishes when income is includible by a taxpayer and therefore subject to income tax. The rules on constructive receipt are found in Treasury Regulations 1.451-2.

Key Concepts

Underline/highlight the answers to these questions as you read:

1. What is constructive receipt, and how does it affect deferred compensation plans?

2. What is a substantial risk of forfeiture, and how does it affect deferred compensation plans?

3. What is the Economic Benefit Doctrine, and how does it affect deferred compensation plans?

Income, although not actually in a taxpayer's possession, is nonetheless constructively received by the taxpayer in the taxable year during which it is credited to his account, set apart for him, or otherwise made available so that he may draw upon it at any time, or so that he could have drawn upon it during the taxable year if notice of intention to withdraw had been given. Generally, an individual will be deemed to have constructive receipt of income if he can choose to receive the income today or in the future. However, income is not constructively received if the taxpayer's control of its receipt is subject to substantial limitations or restrictions. Thus, if a corporation credits its employees with stock as a bonus but the stock is not available to the employees until some future date, the mere crediting of the stock on the books of the corporation does not constitute constructive receipt of the stock.

Examples of Constructive Receipt

Amounts payable with respect to interest coupons that have matured and are payable but which have not been cashed are constructively received in the taxable year during which the coupons mature, unless it can be shown that there are no funds available for payment of the interest during such year. Dividends on corporate stock are constructively received when made subject to the demand of the shareholder without qualifications. However, if a dividend is declared payable on December 31 and the corporation followed its normal practice of paying the dividends by mailing checks so that the shareholders would not receive them until January of the following year, such dividends are not considered to have been constructively received in December. Generally, the amount of dividends or interest credited on savings bank deposits or to shareholders of organizations, such as building and loan associations or cooperative banks, is income to the depositors or shareholders for the taxable year when credited. However, if any portion of such dividends or interest is not subject to withdrawal at the time credited, that portion is not constructively received and does not constitute income to the depositor or shareholder until the taxable year in which the portion first may be withdrawn.

Deferred compensation plans are structured so that employees benefiting under the plan will avoid constructive receipt and will therefore be allowed the deferral of income taxation.

As mentioned, an employee that elects to defer compensation, such as bonuses, into the future under a deferred compensation arrangement must do so prior to the compensation being earned. Otherwise, the employee would effectively have the choice of receiving current income or deferring. This choice would result in the income being considered constructively received whether or not there was a subsequent substantial risk of forfeiture.

The following are some examples of what is not considered constructive receipt:
- an unsecured promise to pay;
- the benefits are subject to substantial limitations or restrictions; and
- the triggering event is beyond the recipient's control (i.e. company is acquired).

SUBSTANTIAL RISK OF FORFEITURE

Substantial risk of forfeiture is another income tax concept that relates to when income is subject to income tax. The rules for substantial risk of forfeiture are found in Treasury Regulations 1.83-3(c).

Payroll tax

A substantial risk of forfeiture exists when rights in property that are transferred are conditioned, directly or indirectly, upon the future performance (or refraining from performance) of substantial services by any person, or the occurrence of a condition related to a purpose of the transfer and the possibility of forfeiture is substantial if the condition is not satisfied. The issue of whether a risk of forfeiture is substantial remains a matter of facts and circumstances. When there is a substantial risk of forfeiture, the taxpayer is not required to include the income as taxable income. When there is not a substantial risk of forfeiture, the taxpayer is required to recognize the income currently as taxable income.

Often, deferred compensation agreements are structured as a simple contractual promises from the employer to a key employee. Generally, this puts the employee at risk that the employer might default or breach the contract and not pay. The obligation of a deferred compensation agreement is reflected on the balance sheet of the organization as a liability. However, in terms of the ranking of creditors in the case of liquidation, all secured and unsecured creditors would be paid in full prior to paying the deferred compensation obligation. A participant in a deferred compensation plan will be paid ahead of both preferred and common shareholders in liquidation. Thus, it can be said that for an unfunded deferred compensation arrangements based on a simple contractual promise to pay, the employee is at a "substantial risk of forfeiture." Most deferred compensation arrangements are unfunded and, therefore, subject to the risk of non-payment. Deferred compensation arrangements can, however, be funded.

EXAMPLE 12.3

On November 25, 2005, Carb Corporation gives Edward, an employee, a bonus of 100 shares of Carb Corporation stock. The terms of the bonus arrangement obligate Edward to return the stock to Carb Corporation if he terminates his employment for any reason. However, for each year occurring after November 25, 2005, during which Edward remains employed with Carb Corporation, Edward ceases to be obligated to return 10 shares of the Carb Corporation stock. Therefore, each year occurring after November 25, 2005 that Edward remains employed, his rights in 10 shares of stock cease to be subject to a substantial risk of forfeiture. Thus, the value of the 10 shares of stock will be included in Edward's income when the substantial risk of forfeiture expires.

Quick Quiz

Highlight the answer to these questions:

1. Deferred compensation plans are structured so that employees benefiting under the plan will avoid constructive receipt.
   a. True
   b. False

2. A substantial risk of forfeiture is the risk that the employee will leave the corporation prematurely and take the plan assets with them.
   a. True
   b. False

3. For contributions to a deferred compensation plan to be taxed because of the economic benefit doctrine, there must be no restrictions or risks that the funds would not be paid to the employee.
   a. True
   b. False

True, False, True.

Since one of the primary purposes of deferred compensation arrangements is to avoid taxation for the key executive, these plans will almost always include a substantial risk of forfeiture so that the executive can defer payment of income tax. Employers may simply promise to pay the employee or may use some form of vesting schedule in an attempt to meet the substantial risk of forfeiture standard.

ECONOMIC BENEFIT DOCTRINE

The **economic benefit doctrine** provides that an employee will be taxed on funds or property set aside for the employee if the funds or property are unrestricted and nonforfeitable, even if the employee was not given a choice to receive the income currently. In other words, if an employer sets aside funds for an employee and there is no risk that the employee will not receive the funds, then the funds are taxable under this doctrine at the point in time at which there are no longer any restrictions attached to the property.

Deferred compensation plans may provide for a trust to hold the funds for the employee prior to retirement or termination. Contributions to an employee's trust made by an employer will generally be included in the gross income of the employee in accordance with IRC Section 83 (discussed below, except that the value of the employee's interest in the trust shall be substituted for the fair market value of the property for purposes of applying such section). This means that contributions to a trust are taxable to the employee even if there is not a distribution from the trust. To be subject to income tax, the funds simply have to be unrestricted and nonforfeitable, which could occur once the employee becomes partially or fully vested.[1] An exception to this rule can be achieved through use of a rabbi trust, discussed later in this chapter.

Under no circumstances would a simple promise to pay be subject to current income tax since there are substantial risks as to whether the payments will be made. To be taxable under the economic benefit doctrine, there must be no restrictions or risks that the funds would not be paid to the employee.

IRC Section 83: Property Transferred in Connection with Performance of Service

When an employer transfers property to an employee in connection with performance of service, the employee will be taxed on the difference between the fair market value of the property and the amount paid for the property. For example, if an employer transferred stock worth $10 to an employee and the employee paid $3 for the stock, then the employee would be taxed on the difference of $7.

The fair market value of the property is determined at the time the rights of the person having the beneficial interest in the property are transferable or are not subject to a substantial risk of forfeiture, whichever occurs earlier. For example, if a company grants $50,000 worth of company stock to Randy, a key executive, and provides that he can only receive it if he is employed for five years, then there is clearly a substantial risk of forfeiture during that five year vesting period.

Generally, the gain or difference between the fair market value of the property and any amounts paid by the employee will be taxed as ordinary income to the employee. Usually, this amount is included in the employee's Form W-2 and is also subject to withholding and payroll taxes. Further appreciation from the point at which the income is included in taxable income will be capital gain (assuming that the property is of a capital nature).

Key Concepts

Underline/highlight the answers to these questions as you read:

1. What is the 83(b) election with regards to a deferred compensation plan?

2. When are payroll taxes due on compensation placed into a deferred compensation plan?

3. When does the employer receive an income tax deduction for assets contributed to a deferred compensation plan?

These rules are typically applicable to grants of stock, especially restricted stock, and employee stock options but can also be applied to other transfers of property to an employee. The 83(b) election allows an employee to include into income the net value of a transfer from an employer for the purpose of establishing a basis in a capital asset. This election is discussed in greater detail later in the chapter.

---

1. IRC Section 402(b).

PAYROLL TAX

Deferred compensation is considered to be earned income at the time a substantial risk of forfeiture expires and, therefore, is subject to payroll taxes at that time even though the employee will not receive payment until sometime in the future. The general rule is that payroll tax will apply at the later of when the deferred income is earned or the point at which the deferred income becomes nonforfeitable. Restricted stock or other benefits may be subject to vesting or other restrictions that would result in an employee forfeiting benefits if employment was terminated prior to a specific point in time. Once the restrictions are lifted, the benefits are deemed nonforfeitable and payroll taxes are due. Benefits from these plans are reported on Form W-2 since it is literally deferred compensation. The taxable event occurs when there is no longer a substantial risk of forfeiture.

If an employee defers a bonus of $50,000 in a deferred compensation plan, then the employee would be subject to payroll tax in the year in which the bonus was earned. If, however, the employee received $50,000 of restricted stock that did not vest for two years, then the value of the stock at the end of the two year period would be subject to payroll tax.

Quick Quiz

Highlight the answer to these questions:

1. An 83(b) election allows the employer to elect to include contributions to the deferred compensation plan into the employee's income.
   a. True
   b. False

2. Deferred compensation will never be subject to payroll taxes until the employee receives distributions from the plan.
   a. True
   b. False

3. An employer receives a current income tax deduction for contributions to a qualified plan.
   a. True
   b. False

False, False, True.

Executives and key employees who participate in deferred compensation plans generally have current earnings in excess of the Social Security wage base of $90,000 for 2005 and, therefore, only pay the 1.45 percent Medicare portion on income that is deferred in the deferred compensation plan. While the funds are subject to payroll tax in the year earned, the employee is better off since he does not have to pay the OASDI portion at 6.2 percent. Likewise, the employer will also avoid paying the 6.2 percent for OASDI.

When the income is later paid to the executive, it will be subject to income tax. However, the payments will not constitute "earned income" in the period received and, therefore, will not be subject to payroll taxes and will not qualify for the earned income test for IRAs and other qualified plans.

EMPLOYER INCOME TAX DEDUCTION

As discussed in the first chapters of the book, one of the greatest benefits of qualified plans is that the employer receives a current income tax deduction for contributions to a qualified plan and the employee is not taxed on those contributed amounts until they are received as a distribution from the plan. This tax benefit does not extend to deferred compensation arrangements. In deferred compensation plans, the employer is entitled to receive an income tax deduction for contributions to the plan only when the employee is required to include the payments as taxable income. This concept is referred to as the matching principle - the employer's deduction follows the employee's inclusion taxable income.

A **nonqualified deferred compensation plan (NQDC)** is a contractual arrangement between the employer and an executive whereby the employer promises to pay the executive a predetermined amount of money sometime in the future. In the future may mean at or during retirement or at or after termination of employment. These types of plans are neither required nor intended to meet the ERISA or IRC requirements to be a qualified plan. Therefore, the employer does not realize the tax advantages of a qualified plan.

There are certain benefits to employers and employees in setting up deferred compensation plans. The advantages of deferred compensation plans to the employer are: (1) cash outflows are often deferred until the future, (2) the employer will save on payroll taxes except for the 1.45 percent Medicare match (since the employee's income is probably over the Social Security wage base), and (3) the employer can discriminate and provide these benefits exclusively to a select group of key employees. The employee benefits from a deferred compensation plan by deferring the receipt of income, thus increasing the possibility of lower federal income taxes at the time of the actual payment and avoiding Social Security taxes (except the 1.45% for Medicare) at the time it was earned. In addition, both the employee and employer benefit in these types of plans because the total compensation, including deferred compensation, may exceed the $1 million annual limit on deductible compensation.

Key Concepts

Underline/highlight the answers to these questions as you read:

1. What funding arrangements are available for deferred compensation plans?

2. What impact does Title I of ERISA have on deferred compensation plans?

3. What types of deferred compensation plans are available?

4. What are 401(k) wraps?

Although the characteristics discussed above apply to most NQDC plans, there are a variety of funding arrangements and types of plans that need to be discussed. These include unfunded promises to pay, secular trusts, rabbi trusts, phantom stock plans, and other types of deferred compensation arrangements.

UNFUNDED PROMISE TO PAY

Deferred compensation may take any form due to the flexibility and lack of requirements under ERISA and the IRC. An unfunded promise to pay falls within the spectrum of deferred compensation. This type of arrangement will meet the standards of a substantial risk of forfeiture and will, therefore, meet the objective of tax deferral. However, the employee is at a some risk of not being paid. The employer may choose not to pay or claim that the employee did not meet the conditions of the contract or the employer may not have sufficient funds to pay the obligation. Obviously, the employee has the right to claim that the employer is in violation of the agreement, which may or may not yield any tangible benefit. To mitigate against such risk, employees would prefer that the employer set funds aside for the purpose of providing for the payment of the deferred obligation. However, as discussed, if there are no restrictions on the set aside funds or there is not a risk of forfeiture, then the funds become immediately taxable, thereby defeating the tax-deferral objective.

Secular Trust

Secular trusts are irrevocable trusts designed to hold funds and assets for the purpose of paying benefits under a nonqualified deferred compensation arrangement. This type of plan provides protection for the assets in the trust. The funds are set aside for the benefit of employees and are not available to the employer or subject to the claims of the employer's creditors. Since a secular trust does not create a substantial risk of forfeiture for the employee, assets set aside in a secular trust result in immediate taxation to the employee.[2] This tax consequence is the cost of eliminating the risk that the funds will not be paid in the future.

Secular trusts are generally subject to Title I of ERISA and, therefore, have to comply with certain reporting, disclosure, vesting, and other requirements. Secular trusts may use a graduated vesting schedule, and the vesting of benefits will trigger the recognition of income for purposes of income tax. Once the funds are vested, and the employee is required to include the value of the vested benefit in income and the employer will have an income tax deduction of an equal amount.

To compensate for the increased taxable income without necessarily having an increase in cash distributions, secular trusts may provide for distributions to the participants for the purpose of paying the income tax attributable to the taxability of the benefits in the trust.

The funds contributed to the trust will be invested and will generate income. The income will usually be taxable to the employee as it is earned if it is not subject to a substantial risk of forfeiture.

Rabbi Trust

Rabbi trusts strike a good balance between the risk of an unfunded promise to pay and the lack of substantial risk of forfeiture in a secular trust. Like a secular trust, a rabbi trust is an irrevocable trust that is designed to hold funds and assets for the purpose of paying benefits under a nonqualified deferred compensation arrangement. However, there are certain critical differences between rabbi trusts and secular trusts. Although the assets in a rabbi trust are for the sole purpose of providing benefits to employees and may not be accessed by the employer, they may be seized and used for the purpose of paying general creditors in the event of the liquidation of the company. In this regard, they do not protect the executive employee from bankruptcy of the employer. Because of this possibility, the IRS has ruled that rabbi trusts that are established and follow specific guidelines will create a substantial risk of forfeiture. When these guidelines are followed, any assets within a rabbi trust are not currently taxable to the employee yet provide significantly more protection to the employee than a simple unfunded promise to pay.

---

2. IRC Section 402(b) and the Economic Benefit Doctrine.

Even though assets are set aside in a trust, rabbi trusts are treated as unfunded (also can be informally funded) for purposes of Title I of ERISA due to the presence of a substantial risk of forfeiture. As a result, these plans do not have to comply with as many rules as secular trusts.

The income generated from the assets within the trust is taxed to the employer. However, the employer will receive an income tax deduction upon distribution from the trust. Many deferred compensation plans will use life insurance products to avoid taxation of income to the employer.

The American Jobs Creation Act of 2004 and the creation of 409A had an impact on Rabbi trusts. Section 409A(b) states that in most cases, assets set aside in a trust outside of the United States (i.e., an offshore trust account) are treated as property transferred in connection with the performance of service whether or not such assets are available to satisfy claims of general creditors. Thus, any such assets will be taxed to the executive as constructively received at the date of transfer.

Model Rabbi Trust

The IRS provided clear and specific rules defining a model rabbi trust in Revenue Procedure 92-64 that must be followed to make certain that the plan will result in the desired outcome. The Rev. Proc. provides for many rules, some of which are listed below:

- The model language must be adopted almost verbatim;
- The trust must be valid under state law;
- The trust must state that the assets are subject to the claims of creditors in the case of insolvency;
- The trustee must be an independent third party, such as a bank; and
- The trustee must be given some level of discretion over investment of plan assets.

	Unfunded Promise to Pay	Rabbi Trust	Secular Trust
Funded with assets	No	Yes	Yes
Funded (for purposes of ERISA)	No	No	Yes
Risk of forfeiture without employer financial instability	Yes	No	No
Risk of forfeiture if employer is insolvent	Yes Claim is below general creditors	Yes Claim is below general creditors	No
When is there taxable income to the executive?	When actual or "constructively received"	When actually or "constructively received"	Immediately upon funding by employer or vesting
When is the payment deductible to employer?	Deferred until payment is made to executive	Deferred until payment is made to executive	Immediately as funded and "constructively received"
Accomplishes the objective of deferral	Yes	Yes	If vesting is required

Case Study 1

Bank of America, N.A. v. Moglia addressed creditors' interests in a "rabbi trust" that a Chapter 7 debtor established before filing for bankruptcy to create a source of funding for its otherwise unfunded employee benefit plans.[1] The Chapter 7 debtor, Outboard Marine Corporation ("Outboard"), had approximately $14 million in assets in a "rabbi trust." Bank of America, the agent of Outboard's secured creditors, claimed rights in those assets, while the trustee in bankruptcy claimed them for the unsecured creditors. The security agreement on which Bank of America relied covers all Outboard's "general intangibles," a term of great breadth in commercial law and broadly defined in the agreement as well to include "all other intangible personal property of every kind and nature."

The Court defined a "rabbi trust" as a form of trust whose tax treatment was first addressed in an IRS letter ruling on a trust for the benefit of a rabbi.[2] Under a rabbi trust, a trust is created by a corporation or other institution for the benefit of one or more of its executives (the rabbi in the IRS's original ruling).[3]

1. Bank of America, N.A. v. Moglia, 330 F.3d 942 (7th Cir. 2003).
2. See Private Letter Ruling 8113107 (Dec. 31, 1980); see also IRS General Counsel Memorandum, 39230 (Jan. 20, 1984).
3. See, for example, Westport Bank & Trust Co. v. Geraghty, 90 F.3d 661, 663-64 (2nd Cir. 1996).

Case Study 1 Continued

According to the Court, the main reason for a rabbi trust is that should the control of the institution change, the trust could then be funded to cushion the fall of the old executives if the new management intends to reduce the compensation of, or even fire, the old executives. However, as the IRS explained in the letter ruling, unless an executive's right to receive money from the trust is "subject to substantial limitations or restrictions" rather than being his to draw on at any time (making it income to him in a practical sense), the executive must include any contribution to the trust and any interest or other earnings of the trust in his gross income in the year in which the contribution was made or the interest obtained.[1] Bank of America conceded that Outboard established a bona fide Rabbi Trust, so that its contributions to the trust and the income that those contributions generated were not includible in the executives' gross income.

The "substantial limitations or restrictions" condition was satisfied in the transaction on which the IRS ruled. The trust agreement provided that the rabbi would not receive the trust assets until he retired or otherwise ended his employment with the congregation. Until then, the corpus of the trust and any interest on it would be owned by the congregation, so the rabbi would have no right to the money.[2]

What was also key in the Moglia case, was that the trust document instrument provided that "the assets of the trust estate shall be subject to the claims of [the congregation's] creditors as if the assets were the general assets of [the congregation]," thus reserving those assets for the unsecured creditors and preventing Outboard from creating a security interest in favor not only of the executives but also of any creditor.

The United States Seventh Circuit Court of Appeals concluded that the creditor's security interest in general intangibles of the debtor did not extend to the corpus of the rabbi trust and that the clause in the trust agreement creating the rabbi trust that prohibited the settlor from granting any creditor a security interest in trust corpus was enforceable. The Court explained that the creditors' security interest in general intangibles of Outboard did not extend to the corpus of "rabbi trust" because the corpus was to remain available at all times for payment of the debtor's general creditors pursuant under the terms of trust agreement and because Outboard was barred from creating any security interest in the trust corpus in favor of beneficiaries or creditors.[3]

---

1. See McAllister v. Resolution Trust Corp., 201 F.3d 570, 572-73, 575 (5th Cir.2000).
2. See Maher v. Harris Trust & Savings Bank, 75 F.3d 1182, 1185 (7th Cir.1996); Goodman v. Resolution Trust Corp., 7 F.3d 1123, 1125 (4th Cir.1993).
3. 26 U.S.C.A. Section 457(f)(1)(A).

FUNDING WITH INSURANCE

For NQDC plans that have funds set aside to pay obligations under the plan, the employer will be responsible for paying income tax attributable to earnings on assets held in the plan. As assets accumulate for executives and remain "at risk", earnings will be subject to taxation by the employer. Ultimately the employer will receive an income tax deduction when the funds are distributed to the executives. However, employers will often use insurance products because the increase in cash surrender value is not taxed if payments are not made from the policy.

PHANTOM STOCK PLANS

A **phantom stock plan** is a nonqualified deferred compensation arrangement where the employer gives fictional shares of stock to a key employee that is initially valued at the time of the grant. The stock is later valued at some terminal point (usually at termination or retirement), and the executive is then paid in cash the differential value of the stock. Phantom stock provides the same benefit as stock ownership except the final payment is made in cash. The employer has a deductible compensation expense equal to the payment made to the employee. The goal of phantom stock plans is to align the economic incentives of the executive with those of the company. Actual stock is not issued, usually because the current stockholders do not want to dilute their equity position (e.g., no non-family shareholders). This is particularly important in family and closely-held business situations.

| EXAMPLE 12.4 | Mike became the president of Tantalus, a closely-held family business. At the time of employment, the value of the company is $2 million and there are 2,000,000 shares of stock outstanding. Mike is granted phantom stock at the end of the first year valued at $100,000 because the value of the company has increased to $3 million or $1.50 per share. When Mike terminates, the value of the company is $5 million and he has phantom stock representing 300,000 shares at $2.50 per share. Tantalus will pay Mike $750,000 at termination as a result of the phantom stock plan. However, at no time did Mike actually own any shares or their voting rights. |

TITLE I OF ERISA

Most NQDC plans do not have to meet the coverage, participation, funding, and discrimination requirements of ERISA imposed on qualified plans. Top-hat plans and unfunded excess benefit plans are statutorily exempted from **Title I of ERISA**. As such, these plans have minimal compliance requirements. There are, however, some reporting and disclosure requirements even for nonqualified plans (including SERP and Top-Hat Plans). These include an initial, one-time filing of a Form 5500 disclosing that the company has such a plan. This "Alternative Reporting and Disclosure Statement" must be filed within 120 days of plan inception date. Additionally, the employer must be fair to all those in that plan and has disclosure requirements to them. Most employers establishing these types of plans will attempt to have the plan be classified as a Top-Hat Plan so that the plan is exempt from Title I.

TYPES AND APPLICATIONS OF NQDC PLANS

There are several types of nonqualified deferred compensation plans that can be established to benefit key executives. Salary reduction plans allow employees to elect to reduce their current salary and defer it until future years, generally until retirement or termination. Salary continuation plans typically provide benefits after retirement on an ongoing basis or for a predetermined period of time.

Supplemental executive retirement plans (generally referred to as SERPs) are nonqualified deferred compensation arrangements designed to provide additional benefits to an executive during retirement. These plans are also referred to as **Top-Hat plans** since they are designed to benefit a select group of top management or key employees. **Excess-benefit plans** are a type of SERP that is designed solely to provide benefits in excess of the benefits available in qualified plans based on the limits under IRC Section 415. As mentioned, unfunded excess benefit plans are not subject to Title I of ERISA while funded excess benefit plans are generally subject to these provisions.

> People's Bank and Dorothy, the vice-president and a cash-basis employee, enter into an employment agreement providing an annual total salary of $300,000 to Dorothy. People's promises to pay Dorothy $100,000 of the $300,000 in ten equal annual installments beginning at Dorothy's retirement or to her heirs beginning at her death. The agreement is a non-funded, nonqualified deferred compensation agreement. The $100,000 is not constructively received by Dorothy and is not deductible to People's Bank until actually paid. The entire $300,000 is currently subject to the 1.45 percent Medicare tax. When ultimately received, the $100,000 will be subject to income tax but not subject to Social Security taxes. Likewise, the payment will then be deductible to People's Bank as compensation. This plan could be an excess benefit plan or a SERP/Top-Hat Plan depending on the purpose. If the only purpose is to provide excess benefits over qualified plan limits, it is an excess benefit plan. However, most plans have additional purposes and are, therefore, SERPs/Top-Hat Plans.

EXAMPLE 12.5

Salary-reduction plans are common with professional athletes. A large signing bonus, or a part thereof, is frequently transferred to an escrow agent to defer the receipt of taxable income until such time as the athlete is beyond his/her peak earning period, thereby helping to assure the athlete's future financial security.

401(k) WRAP PLAN

401(k) wrap plans are a form of salary reduction plans that enable executives who are subject to salary deferral limitations due to the nondiscrimination rules to contribute higher amounts than otherwise permitted under a 401(k) plan. From the executive's perspective, there is not a significant difference between funds being contributed in these plans and 401(k) plans. The contribution to both plans are subject to payroll tax and income tax is deferred. However, there is a risk that the funds within the wrap plan might not be paid. Otherwise, there would not be substantial risk of forfeiture and the funds would then be taxable.

The usual motivation for use of a nonqualified deferred compensation plan where a qualified plan is in existence is to increase the wage replacement ratio (WRR) for key employees. Recall that qualified plans have compensation limits ($210,000 for 2005). If a key executive makes exactly $210,000, the qualified plan may deliver a suitable wage replacement ratio at retirement. However, for a key employee whose compensation is $400,000, the qualified plan will deliver benefits as if that employee earned $210,000, not $400,000. Thus, the greater the current compensation in excess of the qualified plan limit, the smaller the wage replacement ratio delivered by the qualified plan. Nonqualified plans are used to make up for this inequity.

EXAMPLE 12.6

Rob, age 50 (president), and Joe, age 50 (vice-president), are the top two executives in AFA, Inc. Joe's compensation is $205,000 and Rob's is $400,000. Joe is expected to receive $120,000 per year in retirement from AFA's qualified plan, thus achieving a wage replacement ratio of 58.5% ($120,000/$205,000). Unfortunately for Rob, he will also receive the same $120,000 from the qualified plan, thus producing a WRR of 30% ($120,000/$400,000). To make their retirement WRRs equal, AFA might use a NQDC arrangement to pay Rob an additional $114,000 per year in retirement [($120,000 + 114,000) / 400,000 = 58.5%]. This is an example of an excess benefits plan.

NQDC plans may be established for a wide variety of key employees, shareholder employees, officers, highly compensated employees, or any particular person. Their disadvantage, when compared to qualified plans, is the lack of a current income tax deduction for the employer.

Despite this fact, there is widespread use of NQDCs due to their great flexibility, and they have none of the disadvantages of qualified plans.

NQDC CONCEPT SUMMARY

EXHIBIT 12.2

Employer Viewpoint	Employee Viewpoint
• Unfunded promise to pay • Not a qualified plan • Cash outflows are deferred • Employer saves on payroll taxes • Income tax deduction deferred until paid • Sometimes used if compensation exceeds $1 million and, therefore, non-deductible • May discriminate among employees	• Employee is at risk for nonpayment • Fund by using a rabbi trust; if unfunded, best with a financially secure company • No current taxable income • Employee saves on payroll taxes • May provide future cash flow at lower income tax rate

EMPLOYER STOCK OPTIONS AND STOCK PLANS

STOCK OPTIONS

An employee **stock option** gives the employee a right to buy stock at a specified price for a specified period of time. As part of an employer's overall compensation package, an employee's stock option program can be used to attract or retain talented management and to tie the financial compensation of selected key executives to the performance of the company, thus aligning the interest of management executives with outside shareholders.

Through the technology bubble and the accounting scandals of the recent past, stock options were extremely popular with publicly trading companies. However, with the recent requirement that options be expensed, the use of options is on a decline. Companies are choosing to reward executives in other ways that do not have the same negative impact on a firm's financial statements.

Stock options are usually granted to select employees for the purchase of stock of the employer or a subsidiary. The option agreement must be in writing, and the option holder has no obligation to exercise the option. The terms of the option agreement must be stated (e.g., 10 years) in the agreement.

Key Concepts

Underline/highlight the answers to these questions as you read:

1. What are stock options?

2. What are Incentive Stock Options, and what are the tax consequences associated with the grant, exercise, and sale of ISOs?

3. What are Nonqualified Stock Options and what are the tax consequences associated with the grant, exercise, and sale of NQSOs?

Option Price

Generally, the **option price (exercise price)** is equal to the fair market value at the **grant date** (the date of issuance). If the option does not have a readily ascertainable fair market value at the grant date, there is no taxable income to the option holder as of the grant date. Employee stock options usually have substantial restrictions and vesting requirements such that a readily ascertainable fair market value for the options is not available. If values were available and the value was ascertainable, it would be taxable income to the recipient. An option is a form of deferred compensation if the price of the stock increases. If the stock price declines, the option holder will simply allow the option to lapse.

Vesting

Generally, stock options vest over time, thus continuing to provide an incentive to the executive who is receiving the option to remain with the employer and to be productive. As the fortunes of the company improve, it is common for more options to be granted. A common vesting schedule is 20 percent per year of service after the grant. However, the vesting schedule could take any form, even immediate 100 percent vesting, although that is uncommon.

Types of Options

There are two standard types of stock options: **Incentive Stock Options** (ISOs) and **Nonqualified Stock Options** (NQSOs). The goal of utilizing either type of option is to motivate employees by providing them with employer stock at a price that is expected to appreciate. From a tax perspective, however, ISOs can have more favorable tax treatment than NQSOs. The cost of this tax benefit is that ISOs have more restrictions.

INCENTIVE STOCK OPTIONS (ISOs)

An incentive stock option (ISO) is a right given to an employee to purchase an employer's common stock at a stated exercise price. If the requirements of IRC Section 422 are met when the incentive stock option is granted (provided the exercise price is equal to the fair market value of the stock), the employee will not recognize any taxable income at the date of grant. Further, at the date of exercise, the employee will also not be subject to ordinary income tax on the difference between the fair market value of the stock and the exercise price. However, this difference is a positive adjustment for the alternative minimum tax calculation. When the employee sells the stock subsequent to the exercise, the difference between the sales price of the stock and the original exercise price is considered long-term capital gain and there is a negative adjustment for the alternative minimum tax calculation. For an employee in the 35 percent ordinary income tax bracket, the long-term capital gain rate of 15 percent is very attractive, but to attain this tax benefit, ISOs have strictly defined requirements.

1. ISOs can only be granted to an employee of the corporation issuing the ISOs.

2. The ISO plan must be approved by the stockholders of the issuing corporation.

3. The ISOs must be granted within 10 years of the ISO plan date.

4. The exercise of the ISO is limited to a 10-year period (5 years for 10%+ owners).

5. At the date of the ISO grant, the exercise price must be greater than or equal to the fair market value of the stock.

6. An ISO cannot be transferred except at death.

7. An owner of more than 10% of a corporation cannot be given ISOs unless the exercise price is 110% of the fair market value at the date of grant and the option term is less than 5 years.

8. The aggregate fair market value of ISO grants must be less than or equal to $100,000 per year per executive. Any excess grant over the $100,000 is treated as a NQSO.

9. To qualify as an ISO, the executive must not dispose of the stock within two years of the grant of the ISO or within one year of the exercise of the ISO.

10. The executive must be an employee of the corporation continuously from the date of the grant until at least three months prior to the exercise.

Taxation

Grant Date

At the date of the ISO grant there is no taxable income to the employee if the exercise price is greater than or equal to the fair market value of the employer stock. If the exercise price is less than the fair market value of the employer stock, the executive will have W-2 income equal to the difference and the employer will have compensation expense for the same amount.

Exercise of the ISO

Once the ISO is exercisable, the executive purchases the employer stock at the exercise price. At the date of exercise in a qualifying ISO transaction, the executive will purchase the stock with his funds with an intent to hold the stock for at least the holding period requirement (as discussed below). The exercise of the ISO in a qualifying transaction will not create any regular tax impact for either the employee or the employer but will create an alternative minimum tax (AMT) adjustment for the executive equal to the difference between the exercise price and the fair market value of the stock at the exercise date.

The exercise price of the ISO creates the executive's adjusted taxable basis in the employer stock for regular tax purposes since the executive used after-tax dollars to purchase the stock under the ISO. However, the executive's AMT adjusted taxable basis is the fair market value at the date of exercise.

Sale of the Stock from the ISO Exercise After Holding Period Requirement

An executive will receive favorable gain treatment on the appreciation of employer stock above the exercise price provided the executive does not sell the employer stock before two years from the date of grant and one year from the date of exercise, referred to as the holding period requirement. If the holding period requirement is met, the employer will never receive a tax deduction in relation to the ISO.

If the executive meets this holding period requirement and the value of the stock is greater than the exercise price of the ISO, the executive will have long-term capital gain treatment on the appreciation above the exercise price and a negative AMT adjustment equal to the AMT adjustment at the date of the exercise.

EXAMPLE 12.7

On January 5, 2005, Bob, vice president of XYZ Corporation, is granted 10,000 ISOs at an exercise price of $10. On February 6, 2006, he exercises all of the options when the price of XYZ stock is $42. Bob subsequently sells the stock at $60 on February 14, 2007. What are his tax consequences?

At the date of exercise, Bob has no W-2 income, or ordinary income, but does have an AMT adjustment of $320,000 ($420,000 - $100,000) which may cause Bob to pay AMT. For regular tax, he has an adjustable taxable basis of $100,000. When he subsequently sells the stock for $600,000, he has a long-term capital gain of $500,000 subject to a capital gains rate of 15% and a negative AMT adjustment equal to $320,000.

Case Study 2

SPELTZ (124 T.C. No. 9) Ronald and June Speltz incurred AMT liability as a result of their exercise of incentive stock options in 2000. The stock declined precipitously in value after the date of exercise. Mr. and Mrs. Speltz partially paid the tax liability and submitted an offer in compromise with respect to the unpaid balance. The IRS rejected the offer in compromise and filed a lien on their property. The tax court held it was not an abuse of the IRS's discretion to reject Mr. and Mrs. Speltz's offer in compromise and to continue the lien. Mr. and Mrs. Speltz reasoned that their offer in compromise should have been accepted because of the unfair application of the alternative minimum tax (AMT).

Ronald Speltz was employed by McLeodUSA as a senior manager earning wages over $75,000 in 2000 and over $90,000 in 2004. As part of his compensation package he received ISOs for acquisition of McLeod Stock. In 2000, Mr. Speltz exercised some of the ISOs. Mr. and Mrs. Speltz filed their 1040 and the ISOs resulted in "excess of AMT income over regular tax income" of $711,118.

Case Study 2 Continued

On their Form 1040, petitioners reported that their "regular" adjusted gross income was $142,070. Their taxable income was $105,461, and their "regular" tax was $18,678. They reported AMT of $206,191 for a total tax liability of $224,869. After application of Federal income tax withheld, the balance owed on Speltz's tax liability for 2000 was $210,065. The value of their McLeod stock dropped precipitously. On their tax return for 2000, the Speltzs reported that they sold 200 shares of McLeod stock on January 14 for a total of $14,011 and 500 shares of McLeod stock on March 10 for a total of $52,282. On their tax return for 2002, they reported that they sold 2,070 shares of McLeod stock on December 30 for a total of $1,647. The Speltzs partially paid the liability reported on their 2000 Form 1040 at the time that it was filed and paid an additional $75,000 in installments prior to November 2, 2001.

In November of 2001, they submitted to the Internal Revenue Service (IRS) a Form 656, Offer in Compromise. The Speltzs offered a cash payment of $4,457, the cash value of Mr. Speltz's life insurance policy, against the liability that then exceeded $125,000. On the Form 656, petitioners checked the box for "Doubt as to Collectibility" stating they had insufficient assets and income to pay the full amount. Petitioners also attached to Form 656 a statement in which they explained that an offer in compromise was necessary because of the impact the AMT in 2000 had on their finances and their lifestyle.

Specifically, petitioner's income in 2000 was at a comfortable level for a family of five including three young daughters; the McLeod stock they held was nearly worthless and declining and had been used to secure a $134,000 loan with a bank to pay part of the 2000 Federal and State taxes; and, in the event of a sale of the stock (forced or otherwise), petitioners would be unable to carry back the capital loss to offset their 2000 gain. They began building a new home in 2000 and sold their prior home in 2001, using the proceeds of sale to repay the bank. Lifestyle changes were necessary, including: Petitioner June M. Speltz had to get a job instead of staying home with the children; the oldest daughter had to switch schools; petitioners were unable to contribute to their retirement and to their children's education fund; and they had to reduce their charitable donations. Finally, they could not afford to have a fourth child, which they had wanted.

In the statement, petitioners expressed their mental anguish and frustration with the unfairness of their situation. The offer was ultimately rejected because the IRS believed the Speltzs did have the ability to pay.

The Speltzs did not actually dispute the AMT, instead they claimed that the IRS abused its discretion by not allowing them to pay less because of the decline in stock. While the Tax Court was sympathetic, it found that the IRS did not abuse its discretion.

EXHIBIT 12.4   ISO ILLUSTRATED

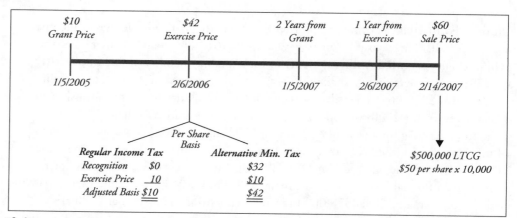

If the executive meets the holding period requirement but the value of the stock is less than exercise price, the executive will have a long-term capital loss equal to the difference between the exercise price and the sales price. The executive will also have a negative AMT adjustment equal to the AMT adjustment at the exercise date.

Disqualifying Disposition

If stock acquired after exercising an ISO is disposed before either two years from the date of the grant or one year from the date of exercise, the sale is known as a **disqualifying disposition** and some of the favorable tax treatment is lost. For such a sale, any gain on the sale of the stock attributable to the difference between the exercise price and the fair market value at the date of exercise will be considered ordinary income and per I.R.B. 2002-28, 97, reported on the executive's W-2, but it will not subject to payroll tax or federal income tax withholding. Any gain in excess of the amount reported on the W-2 will be short or long-term capital gain considering the executive's holding period. Any AMT adjustment created at the date of exercise will be reversed at the date of the disqualifying disposition. Also, at this time, the employer will have a tax deductible expense equal to the amount reported on the executive's W-2.

EXAMPLE 12.8

On October 12, 2005, Donald was granted 15,000 ISOs at an exercise price of $2 per share when the fair market value of the stock was also equal to $2. On November 14, 2006, Donald exercised the stock when the fair market value was $8 per share. Subsequently, on January 1, 2007, Donald sold all the stock for $6 per share.

At the date of grant there was no taxable income because the exercise price of the stock was equal to the fair market value of the stock. At the date of exercise, there was no regular income tax but there was AMT income equal to $6 per share ($8-$2). Because Donald did not hold the stock for at least two years from the date of the grant and one year from the date of exercise, Donald has a disqualifying disposition at the date of sale. The gain on the stock of $4 per share ($6-$2) is ordinary income, and Donald's employer will receive a tax deduction for the same amount ($60,000). Donald will also have a negative AMT adjustment equal to $6 per share at the date of sale to reverse the adjustment at the date of exercise.

EXAMPLE 12.9

Assume the same facts as above, except that the stock price at the time of sale is $11 instead of $6. There is still a disqualifying disposition since the holding period was not met. However, in this case, there will be ordinary income equal to $6 ($8 - $2) per share and a short-term capital gain of $3 per share. As before, Donald will have a negative AMT adjustment equal to $6 per share.

Cashless Exercise

A **cashless exercise** is an exercise of an option where the executive does not utilize any cash. Cashless exercises are quite common as many executives have little, if any, additional cash to exercise the option. At the time of a cashless exercise, a third-party lender lends the executive the cash needed to exercise the option and the lender is immediately repaid with the proceeds of the almost simultaneous sale of the stock. A cashless exercise of incentive stock options automatically triggers at least a partial disqualifying disposition since the holding period requirements will not be met.

Because the executive does not hold the stock for at least two years from grant and one year from exercise, the disposition of the stock is a disqualifying disposition and any gain recognized from the transaction will be treated as ordinary income (reportable on the W-2) not subject to payroll taxes. From the executive's perspective, the entire transaction is a form of cash bonus. Like a disqualifying disposition when the executive recognizes the ordinary income, the employer will have a tax deductible compensation expense.

EXAMPLE 12.10

Jason, an executive, has 10,000 ISOs with a $8 exercise price. When the value of the stock increases to $32, the stock has a total value of $320,000. If Jason exercised today, he would need $80,000 to exercise the option (ignoring any potential AMT consequence). Like many individuals, Jason does not have the $80,000 cash available to exercise the option. Therefore, Jason makes a cashless exercise of the option and receives $240,000 (the proceeds from the sale of the stock less the exercise price of $80,000).

Since the sale of the stock did not meet the holding period requirements of an ISO, $240,000 will be subjected to ordinary income tax.

NONQUALIFIED STOCK OPTIONS (NQSOS)

An NQSO is an option that does not meet the requirements of an incentive stock option or it is explicitly identified as nonqualified. As such, the exercise of an NQSO does not receive favorable capital gains treatment but also does not require the holding period associated with ISOs. A

NQSO is designed to tie a benefit given to an executive to the stock price of the company, but unlike an ISO, it does not provide the executive or the employer with substantial tax benefits.

From a risk perspective, the executive takes no risk in an NQSO. If the stock price falls below the exercise price, the executive simply does not exercise. If the stock appreciates, the executive may chose to exercise and may immediately sell the stock or hold it (there is investment risk to holding the stock).

Taxation
Grant Date

The grant of an NQSO will not create a taxable effect assuming that there is no readily ascertainable value for the NQSO. Generally an option will not have a readily ascertainable value if the exercise price of the option is greater than or equal to the fair market value of the underlying stock. If, however, the option does have a readily ascertainable value at the date of grant or at anytime after the grant, the executive will otherwise have W-2 income equal to the value and the employer will have an income tax deduction.

Exercise of the NQSO

At the exercise date of the NQSO, the executive will deliver to the employer both the option and the exercise price per share. The executive will recognize W-2 income for the appreciation of the fair market value of the stock over the exercise price (often referred to as the bargain element), income tax withholding will apply, and the employer will have an income tax deduction for the same amount.

The fair market value of the stock at the exercise date (which is equal to the sum of the exercise price plus the appreciation of the stock after the date of grant) is the executive's adjusted taxable basis in the employer stock. The executive's holding period for calculation of subsequent gains and losses also begins on the exercise date.

Sale of the Stock from the NQSO Exercise

Stock acquired through the exercise of an NQSO does not have a specified holding period requirement. When the stock is sold, the executive's gain or loss will be considered capital gain or loss and will receive short or long-term capital gain treatment according to the elapsed time between the date of the sale and the exercise date. The employer corporation does not have a tax effect at the sale date.

EXAMPLE 12.11

On January 2, 2005 (the grant date), Ned, an executive with ABC Corporation, is issued one nonqualified stock option from ABC Corporation with an exercise price of $10 (the current market price). On January 3, 2006, Ned exercises his option when the ABC stock price is $35. Ned brings the option and $10 to ABC. ABC issues the stock and Ned recognizes $25 in W-2 income from ABC. Ned's new basis in the stock is $35. He later sells the stock, on March 4, 2006 for $50, which creates a short-term capital gain of $15. If instead, Ned sold the stock on or after January 4, 2007, the gain would be long term.

EXAMPLE 12.12

On January 5, 2005, Gerry was issued 10,000 nonqualified stock options of L&O Corporation, his employer. At the date of the grant, the fair market value of the stock was $35 and the exercise price was $35. Due to the time, vesting, and transferability provisions, there was no readily ascertainable value for the options at the time of the grant. The options vest 20% per year and are exercisable as vested. On January 5, 2006, Gerry exercised 2,000 options when the fair market value of the stock was $48. Gerry will surrender 2,000 options and $70,000 to L&O Corporation. He will receive 2,000 shares of L&O having a current fair market value of $96,000. He will have W-2 income of $26,000 and will have an adjustable taxable basis in the stock of $96,000. If Gerry subsequently sells the stock, he will have a capital gain or loss, depending on the sale price of the stock. L&O Corporation will deduct $26,000 as compensation expense at the time of exercise.

Quick Quiz

Highlight the answer to these questions:

1. A stock option agreement must be in writing and must state an option term.
   a. True
   b. False

2. The exercise of an ISO triggers W-2 income for the employee.
   a. True
   b. False

3. At the exercise date of an NQSO, the employee will recognize W-2 income for the appreciation of the fair market value of the stock over the exercise price.
   a. True
   b. False

True, False, True.

Cashless Exercise

As discussed above, a cashless exercise is the exercise of an option when the executive does not utilize any cash. A NQSO can be exercised with a cashless exercise just as described above with the ISO, and the executive will receive the difference between the exercise price and the fair market value of the stock at the date of the cashless exercise as W-2 income.

Gifting of ISOs and NQSOs

Lifetime transfers of unexercised ISOs by the employee are not permitted. The requirement to obtain long-term capital gain treatment for the stock received upon exercise is that the stock must be transferred only after the holding period requirement. Any transfer of ISO stock before the completion of the holding period may cause the appreciation on the stock to be taxed as ordinary income rather than capital gain.

A NQSO can be gifted provided the NQSO plan permits transfer of ownership. There are no immediate income tax consequences on the transfer. Upon exercise of the NQSO by the donee, the employee will have W-2 income for the difference between the exercise price and the fair market value on the date of exercise. The donee's basis post the exercise will be equal to the fair market value on the date of exercise (exercise price plus employee's tax recognition). If the employee also pays the exercise price, it is an additional gift to the donee. Any gift of a NQSO that is neither vested nor exercisable is an incomplete gift. Valuation of options is determined using the **Black Scholes Method.** NQSOs are not good items to transfer to charities except after the option has been exercised and the stock held for more than a year and a day, which is when the stock can qualify as long-term capital gain property and is then available for a higher charitable deduction.

EXHIBIT 12.5 **NQSO AND ISO SUMMARY**

	NQSO	**ISO**
At Grant Date	No taxable income to holder if issued at the current or greater share price.	No taxable income to holder if issued at current or greater share price.
At Exercise	Executive gives options and exercise price to company. Company issues stock to executive to replace option.	Executive gives options and exercise price to company. Company issues stock to executive to replace option.
Taxation	At exercise, executive recognizes W-2 income to extent of difference between current stock price and exercise price.	At exercise, executive does not recognize any regular taxable income but will have an AMT adjustment for the appreciation over the exercise price.
Adjustable Taxable Basis	Executive's adjusted taxable basis in stock is equal to the fair market value of stock (exercise price in cash plus the recognition of W-2 income).	Executive's adjusted taxable basis in stock is equal to the exercise price.
When Stock is Sold	Capital gain or loss treatment.	Capital gain or loss treatment.

STOCK APPRECIATION RIGHTS

Stock Appreciation Rights (SARs) are rights that grant to the holder cash in an amount equal to the excess of the fair market value of the stock over the exercise price.

EXAMPLE 12.13

> Jamie is a key executive in NT Company. She is granted 1,000 SARs at $10, the current trading price of NT. If Jamie exercises the SAR two years from the grant when NT's stock price is $32, she will be entitled to receive $22,000 as W-2 income subject to both income and payroll taxes.

The SAR is essentially a way to achieve a "cashless exercise." Notice in the above example, Jamie did not have to come up with the exercise price of $10,000 (1,000 x $10). The rights cannot be exercised before one year, and if they are not exercised within five years, they are deemed exercised on the fifth anniversary of the grant. At that time, the employee will be paid the amount of the appreciation. Payments received for the stock appreciation rights are includable in gross income in the year the rights are exercised.

An employee who possesses stock appreciation rights is not in constructive receipt of income by virtue of the appreciation of the employer's stock. The cash payment to which the employee is entitled is includible in gross income in the year a stock appreciation right is exercised.

The grant of the SAR does not constitute constructive receipt, even if immediately exercisable, because of the future potential appreciation of the SAR. If, however, the SAR has a cap or limit, there is constructive receipt when the stock reaches that limit price, unless the SAR is issued in tandem with the option and the option is terminated if not exercised simultaneously with the SAR. In such case, there is no constructive receipt. (rev. rule 82-121).

Generally, SARs are granted with NQSOs or ISOs and may be used to provide cash to the executive, which is necessary to exercise the NQSO or ISO. Usually, the number of NQSOs or ISOs is reduced by any exercised SARs.

Key Concepts

Underline/highlight the answers to these questions as you read:

1. What are stock appreciation rights?

2. Explain the characteristics of restricted stock plans.

3. What are employee stock purchase plans?

RESTRICTED STOCK PLANS

A **restricted stock plan** is an employer-provided plan designed to increase retention and compensate employees with a non-cash outflow. The plan pays executives with shares of the employer's stock. The executive does not pay any amount towards the allocation of the stock and is restricted by the employer from selling or transferring the stock. The restriction most often gives the employer the ability to repurchase the stock during a set period of years or prohibits the executive from selling the stock during a set number of years or until a defined occurrence or event (i.e., the executive attains 10 years of service with the company).

At receipt of the restricted stock, the executive will generally not recognize any taxable income (see 83(b) discussion below) as the restrictions generally create a substantial risk of forfeiture. In addition the employer will not have a deductible expense. However, when this substantial risk of forfeiture is eliminated the executive recognizes W-2 income equal to the value of the stock at that date and the employer will have a tax deductible expense for an equal amount. The amount recognized by the executive becomes the executive's adjusted taxable basis in the stock for purposes of any subsequent gain or loss calculation. The executive's holding period of the stock also begins at the date the restrictions are lifted.

EXAMPLE 12.14

Dana was entitled to a $100,000 incentive bonus from Significant Corp. in 2005. However, Significant was short on cash due to poor planning and instead paid Dana $25,000 and gave her $75,000 worth of restricted stock (5,000 shares at $15 per share). In 2008, after all of the restrictions were lifted, Dana's shares are worth $30 per share. In 2008, Dana has W-2 income of $150,000 and Significant has a deduction of $150,000. Dana now has an adjusted taxable basis in the Significant stock of $150,000.

The 83(b) Election

If property is transferred in connection with the performance of services, the person performing such services may elect to include in gross income under **IRC section 83(b)** the excess (if any) of the fair market value of the property at the time of transfer over the amount (if any) paid for such property as compensation for services. The fact that the transferee has paid full value for the property transferred, realizing no bargain element in the transaction, does not preclude the use of the election as provided for in this section. If this election is made, any subsequent appreciation in the value of the property is not taxable as compensation to the person who performed the services but as capital gain at the date of sale. Thus, property with respect to which this election is made shall be includible in gross income as of the time of transfer even though such property is substantially nonvested at the time of transfer and no compensation will be includible in gross income when such property becomes substantially vested.

In computing the gain or loss from the subsequent sale or exchange of such property, its basis shall be the amount paid for the property increased by the amount included in gross income under section 83(b). Its holding period shall be determined based upon the date the value was included in gross income. If property for which a section 83(b) election is in effect is forfeited while substantially nonvested, such forfeiture shall be treated as a sale or exchange upon which there is realized a loss equal to the excess (if any) of the amount paid (if any) for such property over the amount realized (if any) upon such forfeiture. Therefore, the taxpayer would not receive any loss for the amount included in income, only a loss for the amount paid.

The economic benefit of this election is that the appreciation from the time of the grant through the vesting period will be treated as capital gain instead of W-2 income. However, the taxpayer must consider not only the tax issues of such an election but also the investment issues surrounding the value of the property (generally stock) in deciding whether or not to make the election.

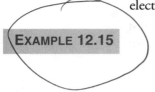

EXAMPLE 12.15

Assume SARs Inc. has a restricted stock plan. Stock granted to employees of SARs under this plan vest after a 5-year period. Kristi, a new executive, was granted restricted stock worth $10,000 on January 5, 2004. Kristi believes that the value of the stock will increase significantly over the next five years. Kristi can make an 83(b) election and include the $10,000 into her current income.

Assuming the stock is worth $25,000 at the end of five years, Kristi will not recognize any gain upon vesting of the stock. When the stock is sold, Kristi will have capital gain equal to the difference between the sale proceeds and the value of the stock at the time of the grant. Kristi has effectively converted ordinary income into capital gain income.

If Kristi had not filed the election, then she would include the $25,000 in taxable income for the year in which the vesting was complete. Any future appreciation above $25,000 would be treated as a capital gain.

Assume the same facts as above, including the fact that Kristi made the 83(b) election, except that Kristi quit two years after the grant. In this case, at the date of 83(b) election, Kristi would have ordinary income of $10,000 but at termination would not have a loss.

EXAMPLE 12.16

Making the Election

The 83(b) election must be filed no later than 30 days after the date the property was transferred and may be filed prior to the date of transfer. The election is made by filing one copy of a written statement with the internal revenue officer with whom the person who performed the services files his return. In addition, one copy of such statement shall be submitted with his income tax return for the taxable year in which such property was transferred.

The statement shall be signed by the person making the election, shall indicate that it is being made under section 83(b) of the Code, and shall contain the following information:

- The name, address, and taxpayer identification number of the taxpayer;
- A description of each property with respect to which the election is being made;
- The date or dates on which the property is transferred and the taxable year (for example, "calendar year 2005" or "fiscal year ending May 31, 2006") for which such election was made;
- The nature of the restriction or restrictions to which the property is subject;
- The fair market value at the time of each property with respect to which the election is being made;
- The amount (if any) paid for such property; and
- A statement to the effect that copies have been furnished to other persons as provided in the regulations.

EMPLOYEE STOCK PURCHASE PLANS (ESPP)

Intended to benefit all or a large portion of an employer's employees (the plan cannot be discriminatory), per IRC Section 423, an **employee stock purchase plan** (ESPP) gives employees an incentive to buy employer stock by allowing the employees to purchase the stock at a discounted price and receive favorable tax treatment for any gains if the stock meets certain holding period requirements. As discussed in other areas of the text, an employee who owns stock in his employer is connected to the productivity of the company and, in most cases, will work more efficiently and effectively towards the goals of the company.

Generally, an employee elects to defer after-tax compensation throughout the plan year through payroll deductions to the ESPP established by the employer. The employee is able to purchase the employer stock through the ESPP for a price equal to no less than 85 percent of a date determined stock price or an average stock price.[3] An example of a date determined price is the lesser of fair market value (1) at the beginning of the plan period, grant date or (2) the end of the plan period, exercise date. An example of an average price is the average price for the quarter. The grant date and exercise date generally coincide with the beginning and end of the calendar year, but either could follow quarters, months, or any other time period that the employer selects.

EXAMPLE 12.17

DTY Corporation's ESPP has a plan year of December 1, 2005 to November 30, 2006. DTY's employees are permitted to defer after-tax compensation into the plan from December 1, 2005 to November 30, 2006, and the ESPP will purchase the DTY stock for 85% of the lesser of the fair market value on December 1, 2005 or the fair market value on November 30, 2006. The fair market value of the stock at December 1, 2005 was $20, and the fair market value of the stock at November 30, 2006 was $28. The employee would be able to purchase the employer stock through the ESPP for $17 (85% of $20).

EXAMPLE 12.18

Tribro's ESPP operates four plan periods during the year following the normal quarters of the calendar year. Employees must elect to defer their after-tax compensation prior to the beginning of each period to participate in the ESPP. After the end of each quarter, the employee purchases the employer stock for 85% of the average price during the quarter.

At the date of purchase, the employee will not have any taxable consequences but will immediately have an unrealized gain at least equal to the price discount off the fair market value of the stock. Consider an employee who was able to purchase the stock of his employer through the ESPP for $11.05, 85% of the fair market value on the date of exercise ($13.00). This employee would have $1.95 ($13.00-$11.05) or a 17.6% ($1.95÷$11.05) immediate pre-tax gain. Even with a 30% marginal tax rate, the gain would be 12.32% (17.6% x (1 - 30%) without considering the benefits of future appreciation and lower tax rates (discussed below).

---

3. Most ESPPs utilize the 85% of the date determined price or average price; although, it may be any amount or percentage greater than 85%.

Employee Dollar Limit

An employee is statutorily limited to purchasing $25,000 of employer stock per year as determined based on the fair market value at the date of grant of the employer stock through the ESPP. For example, if at the grant date the fair market value of the stock was $31.25 and at the exercise date the stock had a fair market value of $28.00, the employee could only purchase 800 shares ($25,000 ÷ $31.25) for $23.80 (85% of $28.00) for a total of $19,040 (800 x $23.80). If the employee deferred more to the ESPP than necessary, the difference would be returned to him. The refund would not create any taxable consequences as the funds in the ESPP are post-tax. Some employers may place additional limitations on their employees by restricting the amount of stock they may purchase (i.e., 15% of compensation or 2,500 shares) through the ESPP. Such restrictions cannot be applied on a discriminatory basis.

Qualifying Disposition

If the employee holds the stock purchased through the ESPP for two years from the date of grant and one year from the date of exercise, any subsequent sale is a qualifying disposition of the stock. The employee's gain on the sale of the stock will be ordinary income to the extent the gain is attributable to the discount at the date of purchase. Any gain in excess of the ordinary income portion will be long-term capital gain. For example, if the employees were able to purchase the employer stock for $85.00 (85% of fair market value) and after meeting the required holding period requirements sold the stock for $90.00, then $5.00 ($90.00 - $85.00) would be considered as ordinary gain. This treatment occurs because the $5 represents part of the original discount. However, if after meeting the holding period requirement the employee sold the stock for $110.00, the total gain would be $25.00 ($110.00 - $85.00) and $15.00, the amount attributable to the discount, would be treated as ordinary income and the remaining $10.00 would be treated as long-term capital gain.

> Stanley, Inc. has an ESPP, and the stock traded on January 2, 2005 for $12.00 and on December 31, 2005 for $15.00. The plan permitted Cline, an employee, to buy at 85% of the lesser of the two prices ($12.00 x 0.85 = $10.20 per share). Cline, who contracted to purchase $25,000 worth of stock, will receive 2,083 shares of Stanley, Inc. stock ($25,000 ÷ $12.00). Note that since the stock price has risen to $15.00 per share, Cline has a portfolio worth $31,245 for which he paid $21,247. If he holds the stock 2 years from the date of the original purchase before selling at $20 per share, Cline will have an ordinary income of $3,749 ($12.00-$10.20 x 2,083) and long-term capital gain of $16,664 ($8.00 x 2,083).

EXAMPLE 12.19

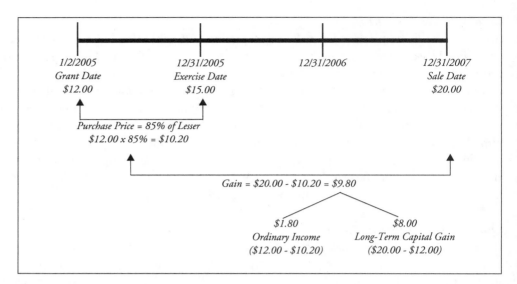

1/2/2005	12/31/2005	12/31/2006	12/31/2007
Grant Date	Exercise Date		Sale Date
$12.00	$15.00		$20.00

Purchase Price = 85% of Lesser
$12.00 x 85% = $10.20

Gain = $20.00 - $10.20 = $9.80

$1.80
Ordinary Income
($12.00 - $10.20)

$8.00
Long-Term Capital Gain
($20.00 - $12.00)

EXAMPLE 12.20

Assume the same facts as above, except that Cline sells the stock for $11.00. In this case, since the entire gain, $0.80 per share ($11.00 - $10.20), is less than Cline's purchase discount, ($1.80 per share), Cline will have ordinary income equal to $1,666 ($0.80 x 2,083).

Disqualifying Disposition

If an employee does not hold the stock purchased through the ESPP for at least two years from the date of grant and one year from the exercise date, any sale is a disqualifying disposition. The primary difference as compared to a qualifying disposition is that the gain attributable to the discount will be W-2 income rather than ordinary income. The employee's gain on the sale will be W-2 income to the extent the gain is attributable to the purchase discount. Any gain in excess of the ordinary income portion will be long or short-term capital gain dependent upon the holding period, which begins on the exercise date. For example, if an employee were able to purchase employer stock for $85.00 or 85 percent of fair market value, and BEFORE meeting the required holding period, sold the stock for $90.00, $5.00 ($90.00-$85.00) would be W-2 income. However, if the employee had sold the stock six months after the exercise date for $110.00, the

total gain would be $25.00 ($110.00 - $85.00) and $15.00, the amount attributable to the discount, would be W-2 income and the remaining $10.00 would be short-term capital gain.

EXAMPLE 12.21

Timer, Inc. has an ESPP and its stock traded on June 30, 2005 for $30.00 and July 31, 2005 for $25.00. Rhonda had elected to defer after-tax income to the ESPP and purchased 400 shares of the stock at 85% of the lower of the two values. Rhonda purchased 400 shares of the Timer, Inc. stock for $8,500 ($21.25 x 400 shares). Six months later, Rhonda sold the 400 shares at $27 per share. Since Rhonda did not hold the stock for the required holding period, Rhonda will have W-2 income at the date of sale of $1,500 [($25.00 - $21.25) x 400] and a short-term capital gain of $800 [($27.00 - $25.00) x 400].

Loss

If the employee sells the stock purchased through the ESPP at a price less than the exercise price, the employee will have a short or long-term capital loss as determined based upon the holding period beginning at the date of exercise and the difference between the exercise price and the sales price.

ESPP SUMMARY

EXHIBIT 12.6

- Employee usually buys employer stock at 85% of fair market value.
- When the stock is sold, the price discount of 15% is ordinary income.
- The excess of the sales price over the undiscounted purchase price is long-term capital gain if a qualifying disposition.
- The stock purchase has a built-in return of 17.5% pretax.
- There is a $25,000 limit for purchases.

Key Terms

Black Scholes Method - An option valuation model.

Cashless Exercise - An exercise of an option where the option holder does not utilize any cash.

Constructive Receipt - An income tax concept that establishes when income is includible by a taxpayer and therefore subject to income tax. Income is constructively received in the taxable year during which it is credited to the employee's account, set apart for him, or otherwise made available so that he may draw upon it at any time or so that he could have drawn upon it during the taxable year if notice of intention to withdraw had been given.

Deferred Compensation Arrangements - An arrangement to pay an executive compensation in a future year.

Disqualifying Disposition - If stock acquired after exercising an ISO is disposed before either two years from the date of the grant or one year from the date of exercise.

Economic Benefit Doctrine - An employee will be taxed on funds or property set aside for the employee if the funds or property are unrestricted and nonforfeitable even if the employee was not given a choice to receive the income currently.

Employee Stock Purchase Plan - A plan designed to benefit all or a large portion of an employer's employees that gives employees an incentive to buy employer stock by allowing the employees to purchase the stock at a discounted price and receive favorable tax treatment for any gains if the stock meets certain holding period requirements.

Excess Benefit Plans - A type of SERP that is designed solely to provide benefits in excess of the benefits available in qualified plans based on the limits under IRC Section 415.

401(k) Wrap Plans - A form of salary reduction plan that enable executives who are subject to salary deferral limitations due to the nondiscrimination rules to contribute higher amounts than otherwise permitted under a 401(k) plan.

Grant Date - The date of issuance of a stock or option.

Incentive Stock Options (ISOs) - A right given to an employee to purchase an employer's common stock at a stated exercise price. If the requirements of IRC Section 422 are met, the employee will not recognize any taxable income at the date of grant. Further, at the date of exercise, the employee will also not be subject to ordinary income tax on the difference between the fair market value of the stock and the exercise price. This difference is a positive adjustment for the alternative minimum tax calculation. When the employee sells the stock subsequent to the exercise, the difference between the sales price of the stock and the original exercise price is considered long-term capital gain and there is a negative adjustment for the alternative minimum tax calculation.

Key Terms

IRC Section 83(b) - Elect to include in gross income the difference between the fair market value of restricted stock and its purchase price.

Nonqualified Deferred Compensation Plan (NQDC) - A contractual arrangement between the employer and an executive whereby the employer promises to pay the executive a predetermined amount of money sometime in the future.

Nonqualified Plans - Plans that do not meet the requirements of the IRC Section 401(a) and therefore do not have the benefits of qualified plans.

Nonqualified Stock Options (NQSOs) - An option that does not meet the requirements of an incentive stock option. The exercise of an NQSO does not receive favorable long-term capital gains treatment but also does not require the holding period associated with ISOs.

Option Price (Exercise Price) - Usually the fair market value at the grant date.

Phantom Stock Plan - A nonqualified deferred compensation arrangement where the employer gives fictional shares of stock to a key employee that are initially valued at the time of the grant. The stock is later valued at some terminal point and the executive is then paid in cash the differential value of the stock as compensation.

Rabbi Trust - An irrevocable trust that is designed to hold funds and assets for the purpose of paying benefits under a nonqualified deferred compensation arrangement. The assets in a rabbi trust are for the sole purpose of providing benefits to employees and may not be accessed by the employer, but they may be seized and used for the purpose of paying general creditors in the event of a liquidation of the company. Assets within a rabbi trust are not currently taxable to the employee.

Restricted Stock Plan - An employer provided plan designed to increase retention and compensate employees with a non-cash outflow. The plan pays executives with shares of the employer's stock. The executive does not pay any amount towards the allocation of the stock and, in fact, is restricted by the employer from selling or transferring the stock.

Salary Reduction Plans - A nonqualified plan designed to receive deferral contributions from executives to reduce their current taxable income.

Secular Trusts - Irrevocable trusts designed to hold funds and assets for the purpose of paying benefits under a nonqualified deferred compensation arrangement. A secular trust does not create a substantial risk of forfeiture for the employee. Assets set aside in a secular trust results in immediate inclusion of income to the employee.

Stock Appreciation Rights (SARs) - Rights that grant to the holder cash in an amount equal to the excess of the fair market value of the stock over the exercise price.

Key Terms

Stock Option - A right to buy stock at a specified price for a specified period of time.

Substantial Risk of Forfeiture - An income tax concept that relates to when income is subject to income tax. A substantial risk of forfeiture exists when rights in property that are transferred are conditioned, directly or indirectly, upon the future performance (or refraining from performance) of substantial services by any person, or the occurrence of a condition related to a purpose of the transfer and the possibility of forfeiture is substantial if the condition is not satisfied.

Supplemental Executive Retirement Plans (SERP) - Nonqualified deferred compensation arrangements designed to provide additional benefits to an executive during retirement.

Title I of ERISA - Coverage, participation, funding, and discrimination requirements of ERISA imposed on qualified plans.

Wage Replacement Ratio - An estimate of the percent of income needed at retirement compared to income just prior to retirement.

DISCUSSION QUESTIONS

1. Why are deferred compensation arrangements established?

2. List three common reasons deferred compensation arrangements are used.

3. Define "constructive receipt" and how it affects deferred compensation plans.

4. What is a substantial risk of forfeiture and how does it affect deferred compensation plans?

5. Describe the Economic Benefit Doctrine and how it affects deferred compensation plans.

6. How is the 83(b) election used with regards to deferred compensation plans?

7. When are payroll taxes due on compensation contributed to a deferred compensation plan?

8. When will the employer receive an income tax deduction for assets contributed to a deferred compensation plan?

9. Discuss the funding arrangements available for deferred compensation plans.

10. What is the impact of Title I of ERISA on deferred compensation plans?

11. List and describe the types of deferred compensation plans available.

12. Describe 401(k) wraps.

13. What is an incentive stock option and what are the tax consequences associated with the grant, exercise and sale of ISOs?

14. What is a nonqualified stock option and what are the tax consequences associated with the grant, exercise, and sale of NQSOs?

15. What are stock appreciation rights?

16. What are restricted stock plans?

17. What is an employee stock purchase plan?

1. All of the following are reasons that an employer might favor a nonqualified plan over a qualified retirement plan except:

    a. There is more design flexibility with a nonqualified plan.

    b. A nonqualified plan typically has lower administrative costs.

    c. Nonqualified plans typically allow the employer an immediate income tax deduction.

    d. Employers can generally exclude rank-and-file employees from a nonqualified plan.

2. Rick has an 18% nonqualified deferred compensation plan that is funded annually by his employer. Payments are made to a separate trustee of a secular trust who was selected by Rick and his employer. The employer contributions are discontinued at Rick's death, disability, or employment termination. When Rick retires or terminates employment, he will receive the proceeds from the trust.

    Which of the following is/are correct regarding the deferred compensation plan?

    1. The contributions are not currently taxable to Rick because they are subject to a substantial risk of forfeiture.

    2. The contributions to the plan are currently subject to payroll taxes.

    3. The employer can deduct the contributions to the plan at the time of the contribution.

        a. 3 only.

        b. 1 and 3.

        c. 2 and 3.

        d. 1, 2, and 3.

3. Which of the following is false regarding a deferred compensation plan that is funded utilizing a Rabbi Trust?

    1. Participants have security against the employer's unwillingness to pay.

    2. Rabbi Trust provide the participant with security against employer bankruptcy.

    3. Rabbi Trusts provide tax deferral for participants.

    4. Rabbi Trusts provide the employer with a current tax deduction.

        a. None, they are all true.

        b. 2 and 4.

        c. 1, 2, and 4.

        d. 1, 2, 3, and 4.

4. Which of the following is true regarding employer contributions to secular trusts for employee-participants of a nonqualified deferred compensation agreement?

1. Participants have security against an employer's unwillingness to pay at termination.
2. Participants have security against an employer's bankruptcy.
3. Secular trusts provide tax deferral for employees until distribution.
4. Secular trusts provide employers with a current income tax deduction.

   a. 3 only.
   b. 1 and 2.
   c. 1, 2, and 4.
   d. 1, 2, 3, and 4.

5. Ricky receives stock options for 12,000 shares of XYZ Corporation with an exercise price of $10 when the stock is trading on the national exchange for $10 per share. The XYZ company plan is an Incentive Stock Option Plan. Which of the following statements are true regarding the options?

1. Ricky will be required to hold any ISOs for more than a year after exercise and more than two years from the grant date to have long-term capital gains.
2. 2,000 of the options are NQSOs.

   a. 1 only.
   b. 2 only.
   c. 1 and 2.
   d. Neither 1 nor 2.

6. Joe Bob receives stock options (ISOs) with an exercise price of $18 when the stock is trading at $18. Joe Bob exercises these options two years after the date of the grant when the stock price is $39 per share. Which of the following statements is correct?

   a. Upon exercise Joe Bob will have no regular income for tax purposes.
   b. Joe Bob will have W-2 income of $21 per share upon exercise.
   c. Joe Bob will have $18 of AMT income upon exercise.
   d. Joe Bob's adjusted taxable basis for regular income tax will be $39 at exercise.

7. Mary Jane received 1,000 NQSOs with an exercise price of $25 per share when the stock was $25 on the market. Two years from the date of grant Mary Jane exercises when the stock price is $102. Mary Jane:

   a. Has W-2 income of $25,000.
   b. Has an AMT adjustment of $77,000.
   c. Has W-2 income of $77,000.
   d. Has an AMT adjustment of $25,000.

8. Which of the following are characteristics of a phantom stock plan?

1. Benefits are paid in cash.
2. There is no equity dilution from additional shares being issued.

   a. 1 only.
   b. 2 only.
   c. 1 and 2.
   d. Neither 1 nor 2.

9. ABC has an Employee Stock Purchase Plan (ESPP). Which statements regarding an ESPP are correct?

1. The price may be as low as 85% of the stock value.
2. When an employee sells stock at a gain in a qualifying disposition, all of the gain will be capital gain.
3. There is an annual limit of $25,000 per employee.

   a. 1 only.
   b. 1 and 2.
   c. 1 and 3.
   d. 2 and 3.

10. Arnie, the CEO of The Producers Inc., was awarded the following stock options from The Producers Inc.

Option	Grant Date	Type	Exercise Price	FMV	Number of Shares
1	1/1/2002	NQSO	$15	$15	1,000
2	1/1/2004	NQSO	$25	$25	1,000

During 2004 Arnie had the following transactions regarding the above options.

Option	Date	Action	Number of Options (O)/ Shares (S)	Market Price on Date
1	2/1/2004	Exercised	1,000 (O)	$27
1	2/1/2004	Sold	1,000 (S)	$27
2	12/12/2004	Exercised	1,000 (O)	$36

Which of the following is correct?

    a. Arnie has $11,000 of W-2 income and a $12,000 capital gain.

    b. Arnie has $23,000 of W-2 income.

    c. Arnie has capital gain of $12,000.

    d. Arnie has $66,000 of W-2 income.

11. Mike was awarded 1,000 shares of restricted stock of B Corp at a time when the stock price was $14. Assume Mike properly makes an 83(b) election at the date of the award. The stock vests 2 years later at a price of $12 and Mike sells it then. What are Mike's tax consequences in the year of sale?

    a. Mike has W-2 income of $12,000.

    b. Mike has a long-term capital loss of $2,000.

    c. Mike has W-2 income of $14,000.

    d. Mike has a $12,000 long-term capital gain.

12. Cindy Sue has been with CS Designs, Inc. for 5 years. CS Designs has a deferred compensation plan to provide benefits to key executives only. CS Designs contributed $400,000 into a trust for Cindy Sue's benefit under the companies deferred compensation plan. The plan requires that executives must work for the company for 10 years before any benefits can be obtained from the plan. Cindy Sue has come to you to determine when she will be subject to income tax on the contribution by the employer. Which of the following is correct?

   a. Since the assets were placed into a trust, the economic benefit doctrine will require inclusion in income for the current year contributions made by the employer.

   b. Since Cindy Sue cannot receive the benefits until she has been with the employer for 10 years, the substantial risk of forfeiture doctrine will not require inclusion in income for the current year contributions made by the employer.

   c. Since the assets were placed into a trust, the constructive receipt doctrine will require inclusion in income for the current year contributions made by the employer.

   d. Cindy Sue is subject to income tax in the current year because the plan is discriminatory.

13. In 2004, Chip, an accomplished professional race car driver, is to receive a signing bonus for agreeing to drive for Hot-Lap International, a racing team. Hot-Lap agrees to establish a NQDC agreement with Chip to defer the bonus beyond Chip's peak income producing years. Hot-Lap transfers the bonuses to an escrow agent who invests the funds in securities acting as a hedge against inflation. The bonus is deferred until 2011 and is then paid to Chip in years 2011-2020. When is the income deductible by the employer and includible by Chip?

Option	Employer Deduction	Employee Inclusion
A	2004	2004
B	2011	2011
C	2011-2020	2011
D	2011-2020	2011-2020

14. On July 31, 2000, B Corp sold 1,000 shares of its stock to Mike, an employee, for $12 per share. At the time of the sale, B stock was trading for $30 per share. The stock was to vest in 4 years on July 31, 2004. This restriction was stamped on the certificates. On July 31, 2004, the B stock was trading for $125 per share. Mike sold the stock in 2005 for $125 per share. Assuming no special elections, how much must Mike include in income and in what year?

Option	Year	Amount
A	2000	$18,000
B	2000 - 2004	$18,000 ratably
C	2004	$113,000
D	2005	$113,000

15. Jennifer received 1,000 SARs at $22, the current trading price of Clippers, Inc., her employer. If Jennifer exercises the SARs three years after the grant and Clipper's stock is $34 per share, which of the following statements is true?

    a.   Jennifer will have an adjusted taxable basis of $22,000 in the Clippers, Inc. stock.

    b.   Jennifer will have W-2 income equal to $12,000.

    c.   Jennifer will have long-term capital gain of $12,000.

    d.   Jennifer will have ordinary income equal to $22,000.

Employee Benefits: Fringe Benefits

13

INTRODUCTION

When an employee provides services to an employer in return for compensation, the employee will often receive certain benefits, known as fringe benefits, that otherwise would be taxable income if the Internal Revenue Code (IRC) did not statutorily exclude the value of these benefits from the employee's gross income. Many employees do not even consider utilizing the office copier or fax machine for personal reasons as an employer provided fringe benefit, whereas other fringe benefits are more obvious, such as employer provided health insurance.

Generally, when a fringe benefit is provided as a requirement of employment or is for the convenience of the employer (i.e. meals, lodging), the value of the benefits will not be included in the employee's gross income. However, this general statement is not always complete as the value of some fringe benefits are excluded from an employee's gross income merely based on statutory provisions that focus on social goals, fitness, and education (i.e. health insurance, fitness center use, tuition). In order for the value of a fringe benefit to be excluded from the employee's gross income, the fringe benefit must be provided to the employees following a specific set of rules and qualifications as set forth in the IRC and as detailed below.

FRINGE BENEFITS DEFINED

A "**fringe benefit**" is a form of compensation where a benefit other than customary taxable wages is provided by the employer to the employee for the performance of services. These benefits are considered on the "fringe" because such benefits merely accompany, or are in addition to, an employee's salary, wages, or other compensation. Broadly, fringe benefits include paid vacation, sick leave, family leave, health insurance, life insurance, pension plans, profit sharing plans, the use of recreational facilities, personal use of employer's property, holidays, parking, prizes and awards, discounted products and services, and many others. When any of these fringe benefits is provided in return for the performance of services, the value of the fringe benefit is initially deemed compensation for those services. However, not all of the value of all fringe benefits will be included in the employee's gross pay even though the employer has a current income tax deduction. The presence of an employer's income tax deduction with no taxable income to the employee is similar to some benefits of qualified plans.

Know The Numbers	
Employee Benefits	**2005**
Achievement Awards: Nonqualified	$400
Achievement Awards: Qualified	$1,600
Adoption Assistance	$10,630
Adoption Assistance Beginning Phaseout	$159,450
Adoption Assistance Ending Phaseout	$199,450
Business Miles Expense	40.5 cents per mile
Dependent Care Assistance	$5,000
Educational Assistance Program	$5,250
Group Term Insurance	$50,000
Moving Expense	15 cents per mile
Public Transit Pass, Tokens, or Fare Cards	$21 per month
Qualified Parking	$200 per month

Key Concepts

Underline/highlight the answers to these questions as you read:

1. Define employee "Fringe Benefit."

2. In general, what are the tax consequences with regards to employee fringe benefits?

3. What are the nondiscrimination rules that apply to employee fringe benefits?

TAXATION OF FRINGE BENEFITS

Under IRS Treasury Regulations, all fringe benefits provided to an employee are taxable as wages unless a specific provision of the IRC excludes the requirement that the fringe benefit be taxed or unless the employee pays fair value for the fringe benefit. Although a fringe benefit may not be specifically excluded by the regulations, the value of the fringe benefit is not taxable if it is paid for by the employee. The IRC and the regulations, while providing no definition for the phrase "fringe benefit," list various examples of fringe benefits. Of paramount importance when dealing with fringe benefits is the issue of whether the fringe benefit is subject to income taxation and subject to withholding requirements by the employer and employee.

The value of a fringe benefit provided to the employee is deductible as compensation expense by the employer unless the fringe benefit is excludable from the employee's taxable income. Even if the expenditure by the employer is not deductible as compensation expense, it may very well be deductible under ordinary and necessary business expense. Employers should be aware that providing certain fringe benefits may trigger reporting requirements on W-2s for employees, on K-1s for partners, or 1099s for independent contractors. The employer may further be required to withhold monies for FICA, FUTA, SUTA, or federal and state income taxes. Other issues that arise with fringe benefits are whether the exclusions have a limit, the amount of any limit, who is eligible for the fringe benefit, and whether nondiscrimination requirements apply to the provision of the fringe benefit.

NONDISCRIMINATION OF FRINGE BENEFITS

A vital area of concern with some fringe benefits is the requirement that the employer not discriminate against different classes of employees. When these "nondiscrimination requirements" apply, and the fringe benefit is only provided to a "highly compensated employee," and is not available on substantially the same terms to all employees, then the fringe benefit is deemed discriminatory. If the provision of a fringe benefit is discriminatory, then the exclusion may be lost, resulting in the value of the fringe benefit being included or added to an employee's income. As discussed below, some fringe benefits have nondiscrimination requirements while others do not.

BENEFITING INDIVIDUALS

An employee performing services in return for a fringe benefit need not be the person who actually uses or enjoys the fringe benefit. For instance, a spouse or child of an employee may receive or use the fringe benefit of an employer-provided athletic facility. Other individuals beyond current employees who may be taxed on the value of the fringe benefit or who may be eligible to receive the fringe benefit without taxable income include retired employees, spouses of employees, dependent children, spouses of deceased employees, partners, directors, and independent contractors. The description of each fringe benefit includes a detail of those individuals who may receive or benefit from the fringe benefit.

SUMMARY OF AVAILABLE FRINGE BENEFITS

The fringe benefits that will be addressed in this chapter are those that are normally addressed in the regulations and are as follows:

1. Meals and lodging furnished for the convenience of the employer;[1]
2. Athletic facilities furnished by the employer;
3. Educational assistance programs;[2]
4. Dependent care programs;[3]
5. No additional cost services (airlines/ hotels/line of business);[4]
6. Qualified employee discounts (products versus services);
7. Working condition fringe benefits;[5]
8. *de minimus* fringe benefits;[6]
9. Qualified moving expense reimbursement (W-2) for AGI;
10. Qualified transportation and parking;
11. Adoption assistance programs;[7]
12. Prizes and awards;[8] and
13. Qualified tuition reduction plans.[9]

Quick Quiz

Highlight the answer to these questions:

1. An employee fringe benefit is not a form of compensation, instead a fringe benefit is merely an extra that is given to employees.
    a. True
    b. False

2. Employee fringe benefits are taxable as wages unless specifically excluded by the IRC.
    a. True
    b. False

3. If an employee fringe benefit is discriminatory then it will always cause inclusion in the employee's income.
    a. True
    b. False

False, True, False.

SPECIFIC FRINGE BENEFITS

MEALS AND LODGING PROVIDED BY THE EMPLOYER TO THE EMPLOYEE

Meals

In general, an employee may exclude from gross income the value of all meals provided in-kind (not as cash reimbursement) to him, his spouse, or any of his dependents as long as the meals meet the following two conditions:

*   The meals are furnished for the convenience of the employer, and
*   The meals are furnished on the employer's business premises.

---

1. IRC Section 119.
2. IRC Section 127.
3. IRC Section 129.
4. IRC Section 132.
5. IRC Section 132.
6. IRC Section 132.
7. IRC Section 137.
8. IRC Section 274.
9. IRC Section 117.

The Convenience of the Employer

Meals furnished by an employer without charge to the employee will be regarded as furnished for the convenience of the employer if the meals are furnished for a substantial business reason of the employer, not just as a means of providing additional compensation to the employee. The determination of "for the convenience of the employer" is made based on all of the surrounding facts and circumstances of each employer. The IRS provides some of the following examples as guidance when determining which meals provided by an employer would qualify, or be deemed, as furnished for the convenience of the employer.

Key Concepts

Underline/highlight the answers to these questions as you read:

1. What requirements are necessary for meals to be excluded from income?

2. What requirements are necessary for lodging to be excluded from income?

MEALS DEEMED FOR THE CONVENIENCE OF THE EMPLOYER

EXHIBIT 13.1

- Meals furnished to the employee during working hours so that the employee will be available for emergency calls. It must be shown that emergencies have actually occurred or can reasonably be expected to occur in the employer's business during mealtime. For example, when a hospital provides a meal to an on-call doctor.

- Meals furnished to the employee during working hours because the employer's business requires restricted short meal periods, 30 or 45 minutes, and the employee could not be expected to eat elsewhere in such a short meal period.

- Meals furnished to the employee during working hours because the employee could not otherwise secure proper meals within a reasonable meal period and when there may be insufficient eating facilities in the vicinity of the employer's premises.

- Meals furnished to restaurant employees for each meal period in which the employee works, despite whether the meal is furnished during, immediately before, or immediately after the employee's working hours.

- If the employer furnishes a meal to all employees, and the reason for furnishing the meal for more than 50% of the employees is deemed for the convenience of the employer, 100% of the meals are deemed to be for the convenience of the employer.

- If the employer would have furnished a meal to an employee for any reason deemed to be for the convenience of the employer during the employee's working hours, but the employee's duties prevented him from obtaining a meal during those working hours, a meal provided by the employer immediately after the employee's working hours is deemed for the convenience of the employer.

- If an employer charges the employee a fixed amount for the meal, the meal will be regarded as furnished for the convenience of the employer if the employee pays the fixed charge regardless of whether he accepts the meal or provides his own meal.

The IRS also provides specific examples as to what is not considered "for the convenience of the employer."

<table>
<tr><td></td><td>**MEALS DEEMED NOT FOR THE CONVENIENCE OF THE EMPLOYER**</td></tr>
</table>

- Any meal provided to promote the morale or goodwill of the employee or to attract prospective employees does not qualify for the exclusion.

- If the employer charges the employee for the meal, the meal will not be regarded as furnished for the convenience of the employer if the employee has a choice of accepting the meal and paying for it or of not paying for it and providing his own meals.

The Employer's Business Premises

The term "**business premises of the employer**" is defined as the place of employment of the employee. For example, meals provided in the employer's home to a domestic servant would constitute meals furnished on the business premises of the employer. Similarly, meals furnished to cowhands while herding their employer's cattle on leased land would be regarded as furnished on the business premises of the employer.

EXAMPLE 13.1

Barbara, a waitress at Circle Bar and Grill, works from 7 a.m. to 4 p.m. five days a week. Each workday she is furnished, without charge, two meals. The manager of Circle Bar and Grill encourages her to eat breakfast in the employee break room each day before 7 a.m. but does not expressly require her to do this. The manager does, however, require her to eat her lunch in the employee break room. Since Barbara is a food service employee and works during the normal breakfast and lunch periods, she can exclude the value of the breakfast and lunch from her gross income.

EXAMPLE 13.2

Mobile Processing and Manufacturing (MPM) built a cafeteria in its main building. Mark, a foreman at MPM, can purchase his lunch in the cafeteria or bring his lunch from home, but there are no other dining facilities nearby. Mark cannot exclude the value of any meals purchased in the cafeteria from his gross income because Mark has the choice to pay for and eat the cafeteria meal or to not pay for the cafeteria meal and bring his lunch from home.

EXAMPLE 13.3

In the above example, had MPM required Mark to pay $40 each month for food from the cafeteria whether he ate the food or not, the $40 would be excludable from Mark's gross income. This exclusion only applies because Mark is required to pay for the meal whether he eats it or not. The payment of $40 for the meal can be through payroll withholding or can be a cash payment by Mark. In either case, the payment will be excluded from the Mark's gross income.

Case Study 1

Dr. Walter Jacob was the executive director of the Training School Unit of the American Institute for Mental Studies. He was required, as a condition of his employment, to reside on the premises of Institute and be available 24 hours a day. Because of this burden, Institute provided his family housing and free groceries from the institute's commissary. The provision of groceries to Mr. Jacob's family is excluded from his gross income as in-kind because the groceries were prepared into meals and consumed by Mr. Jacobs and his family on the Institute's premises.[1] In addition, the court held that the value of non-food items such as napkins, toilet tissue, and soap were an integral part of either lodging or meals and was excluded from gross income.

---

1.   74-1 USTC 9316.

Lodging

The IRC also provides an exclusion from an employee's gross income for the value of lodging furnished by an employer to an employee if all three of the following qualifications are met:
1.   The lodging is furnished on the employer's business premises;
2.   The lodging is furnished for the convenience of the employer; and
3.   The employee is required to accept the lodging as a condition of employment.

If all three elements of this test are satisfied, the exclusion applies regardless of whether the employee is charged a fee for the lodging.

The Employer's Business Premises

The requirement that lodging be provided on the employer's premises is similar to the requirement that meals be provided on the employer's business premises. Generally, the business premises of the employer means the place of employment of the employee. Lodging furnished in the home of an employer to a domestic servant constitutes lodging furnished on the business premises of the employer.[10] Likewise, lodging for cowhands while herding their employer's cattle on leased land is deemed lodging furnished on the business premises of the employer.

The Convenience of the Employer

Similar to the rules concerning meals above, lodging furnished by an employer without charge to the employee will be regarded as furnished for the convenience of the employer if the lodging is furnished for a substantial business reason of the employer, not just as a means of providing additional compensation to the employee. The determination of "for the convenience of the employer" is made based on all of the surrounding facts and circumstances of each employer.

---

10.   IRC Section 119 (C).

Condition of Employment

The value of lodging is not includable in an employee's gross income if the employee is required to accept the lodging as a condition of employment. Requiring the employee to accept the lodging as a condition of employment is defined as the employee being required to accept the lodging to "enable him to perform the duties of his employment." In other words, the lodging is furnished because the employee is required to be available for duty at all times or because the employee could not perform the services required unless the employee is furnished such lodging.[11] If the employer provides lodging to the employee and the employee is charged a fixed amount whether or not the employee actually accepts the lodging, then the amount of the charge by the employer is not included in the employee's gross income.

Includable Lodging

If the lodging is not furnished on the business premises of the employer, or the lodging is not furnished for the convenience of the employer, or the employee is not required to accept the lodging as a condition of the employment, then the employee must include the value of the lodging in gross income irrespective of whether the value exceeds or is less than the amount charged. Unless evidence is shown to the contrary, the value of the lodging is considered to be equal to the amount charged.[12]

Case Study 2

Even if an employee is convenienced by the lodging, this has no effect on the exclusion. This was one of the issues raised in **Wilhelm v. United States.**[1] In **Wilhelm,** supervisory employees of a cattle ranch, who were required to be available for duty at all times, were allowed to exclude from gross income the lodging furnished by their employer. Although there was alternative housing available within a short distance, the **Wilhelm** court stated at the outset of its discussion that "there is no requirement... that the employee be deprived of his free choice in lodging and boarding or that he be inconvenienced. There is no statutory provision that the employee may not exclude from his gross income the value of the food and lodging furnished by his employer because the employee, too, is convenienced."

---

1. Wilhelm v. United States, 257 F.Supp. 16, 20-21 (D.Wyo.1966).

---

11. IRC Section 119 (B).
12. IRC Section 119 (B).

EXAMPLE 13.4

An employee of an institution is given the choice of residing at the institution free of charge or of residing elsewhere and receiving a cash allowance in addition to his regular salary. If he elects to reside at the institution, the value to the employee of the lodging furnished by the employer will be includible in the employee's gross income because his residence at the institution is not required in order for him to perform properly the duties of his employment.

EXAMPLE 13.5

A construction worker is employed at a construction project at a remote job site in Alaska. Due to the inaccessibility of facilities for the employees who are working at the job site to obtain food and lodging in the prevailing weather conditions, the employer is required to furnish meals and lodging to the employee at the camp site in order to carry on the construction project. The employee is required to pay $40 a week for the meals and lodging. The weekly charge of $40 is not part of the compensation includible in the gross income of the employee, and the value of the meals and lodging is excludable from his gross income.

There has been significant litigation concerning what constitutes the business premises of the employer. The courts have been somewhat flexible on this issue and consider all facts and circumstances.[13]

Case Study 3

In the case of **Erdelt v. United States,** 715 F.Supp. 278 (D.N.D. 1989), the school district purchased a house that was occupied by the district's superintendent. The house was located one block from the school facility. The fact that the house was not on the same contiguous piece of real estate as the school facility did not prevent the house from being considered on the district's business premises. The house was a "residence required as a condition of employment." The nature of the superintendent's position and uniqueness of the school district itself, the court reasoned, required that the superintendent be available to the community at all times through his presence and availability near the school. As such, the reasonable rental value of the house was not includible in his gross income for income tax purposes.

Nonetheless, some exclusions have been found to not apply under somewhat similar circumstances, like in **Wilson v. United States**, 412 F.2d 694 (1st Cir. 1969). There, a state trooper was reimbursed for "mid-shift" meals or lunches if he was more than 10 miles from his home. The court considered this to be includable in gross income of the state trooper.

ATHLETIC FACILITIES FURNISHED BY THE EMPLOYER

Under the regulations, the value of any "on premises athletic facility" provided by an employer to an employee is not included in the employee's gross income.[14] An "**on premises athletic facility**" is defined as a gym or other athletic facility such as a tennis court, pool, or golf course that meets all of the following requirements:
1. Operated by the employer;
2. Located on the employer's premises; and
3. "Substantially all" of the use of the facility is by employees of the employer, their spouses or, their dependent children.[15]

---

13. This flexible position was seen in the case of Saunders v. Commissioner, 215 F.2d 768, 771 (3rd Cir. 1954), where the court articulated: ". . . (T)he rationale of the rule should make it applicable to determine the extent of gross income either when quarters and meals are furnished in kind or cash is paid in lieu thereof . . . Admittedly, the payment of cash to an employee is normally compensatory and probably more obviously so than payment in kind. Nevertheless, just as an employee is often furnished tangible property which cannot be regarded as compensation, an employee may be furnished cash which is not compensation . . ."
14. Treasury Regulation Section 1.132-1(e)(1).

Operated by the Employer

The employer is deemed to operate an athletic facility when the employer operates the facility by hiring its own employees or hires an independent contractor to operate the athletic facility. If the athletic facility is operated by an unpaid separate unrelated entity, then the exclusion does not apply and the value of the athletic facility will be included in an employee's taxable income. Also, the facility may be operated by more than one employer, and as long as an employer pays rent either directly to the owner of the premises or to a sub-lessor of the premises, that employer is eligible for the exclusion.[16]

Key Concepts

Underline/highlight the answers to these questions as you read:

1. What requirements are necessary for athletic facilities provided to an employee as a fringe benefit to be excluded from income?

2. What requirements are necessary for education assistance programs provided to an employee as a fringe benefit to be excluded from income?

Located on the Employer's Premises

The requirement that the athletic facility be located on the employer's "premises" does not necessarily mean that the employer must own the facility or that the facility be located on the employer's *business* premises.[17] In other words, the premises could be leased or rented by the employer. As long as the employer pays reasonable rent for the premises, the facility may be considered the employer's premises. If the athletic facility is for "residential use" (like a tennis court, pool, or gym that are part of a resort), then this exclusion is lost.[18]

Use by Employees
General Public

The exclusion for on premises athletic facilities[19] is inapplicable to any athletic facilities made available to the general public through the sale or rental of memberships or similar arrangements.[20] For example, if the on-premises facility is a health club where others from the general public pay monthly membership dues, then the value of the use of the facility is included in an employee's gross income.

Discriminatory

Nondiscrimination requirements[21] do not apply to on-premises athletic facilities.[22] Thus, the employer has discretion to determine who may or may not have access to on-premises athletic facilities without jeopardizing the eligibility for the exclusion from the employee's gross income.

---

15. Treasury Regulation Section 1.132-1(e). See also Treasury Regulation Section 1.132-1(b)(5) for the deposition of dependent children. A dependent child or children of an employee under this section is a child or step-child who is a dependent of the employee or who is twenty-four years of age or younger whose parents are both deceased.
16. Treasury Regulation Section 1-132.1(e)(4).
17. Treasury Regulation Section 1.132-1(e)(2).
18. Treasury Regulation Section 1.132-1(e)(2).
19. Treasury Regulation Section 1.132-1(e).
20. Treasury Regulation Section 1.132-1(e)(1).
21. The nondiscrimination requirements of Section 132 and Section 1.132-A do not apply to the on-site athletic facility.
22. Treasury Regulation Section 1.132-1(e)(5).

Covered Employees

The following individuals are treated as employees for the purposes of the athletic facility exclusion:

- current employees;
- former retired or disabled employees;
- widow(er)s of those who died while employed;
- widow(er)s of former retired or disabled employees;
- partners; or
- leased employees providing services to an employer on a substantially full-time basis for at least a year where the services are performed under the employer's primary control.

EXAMPLE 13.6	Thomas works at ABC Insurance Company in a high rise building in downtown Austin, Texas. Adjacent to the main office, ABC rents out a gym from the building management. Under these circumstances, as long as the general public does not use the gym, the ABC employees may exclude the value of the use of the on-premises gym from their gross income. However, if the high rise building was a resort for residential use, then the value of the use of the athletic facility would need to be included in each employee's gross income.

EDUCATIONAL ASSISTANCE PROGRAMS

The value of an educational assistance program[23] provided by an employer for the benefit of an employee is excluded from the employee's gross income subject to certain limitations and requirements. Under the regulations, a **qualified educational assistance program** is a plan established and maintained by an employer that provides employees with educational assistance.[24] The program need not be funded, nor must the employer apply to the IRS for a determination of whether the plan is qualified.[25] The program must be a separate written plan of the employer set forth in a separate document and must only provide educational assistance.[26]

The gross income exclusion for educational assistance is limited to the value of $5,250. Nonetheless, as discussed below, an employer may exclude part or all of the excess of educational assistance over $5,250 from an employee's taxable income as a working condition benefit, assuming that the working condition benefit tests apply.

Educational Assistance

"Educational assistance" is defined as either:

1. the employer's payment of expenses incurred on behalf of an employee for education, or
2. the employer's provision of education to an employee.[27]

---

23. IRC Section 127.
24. Treasury Regulation Section 1.127-2.
25. Nonetheless, an employer may request that the IRS determine whether a plan is a qualified program.
26. Treasury Regulation Section 1.127-2(b).
27. Treasury Regulation Section 1.127-2(c)(1).

If the program provides the employee with a choice between the employer providing educational assistance or the employer providing other remuneration to the employee that is includible in the employee's gross income, the value of any benefit received from the plan is taxable to the employee.[28] More particularly, educational assistance does <u>not include:</u>

- the employer's payment for tools or supplies other than textbooks that the employee may retain after completion of the course;
- the employer's payment for meals, lodging or transportation; or
- the employer's payment for education involving sports, games, or hobbies, *unless* the education involves the employer's business or is a required part of a degree program.

The value of any of the above are included in the employee's gross income if provided by the employer.

Eligible Individuals

An educational assistance program must be an exclusive benefit for employees (defined below) of the employer. An educational assistance program must also be nondiscriminatory. Any educational assistance program for an employee's spouses or dependents does not apply to this exclusion.

Nondiscrimination

The IRC prohibits discrimination in the provision of the educational assistance program. If the program discriminates in favor of officers, shareholders, self-employed, or highly compensated employees, then the exclusion from gross income is lost. In other words, if the program is discriminatory, then the value of any benefit paid from the plan on behalf of an employee will be taxable to the employee. Specifically, the program meets the nondiscrimination requirements if the following conditions are met:

- the program benefits employees and does not favor highly compensated employees (as defined in Chapter 3);
- the program does not provide more than 5% of its benefits during the year to shareholders or owners (or their spouses or dependents) who own more than 5% of the stock, of the capital, or of the profit interest in the employer;
- the employees are not allowed to choose cash that must be included in gross income in lieu of educational assistance; and
- reasonable notice is given to the employees that the program is provided to eligible employees.

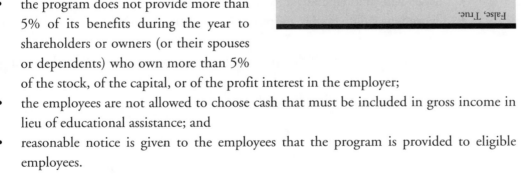

Highlight the answer to these questions:

1. Athletic facility dues provided to employees for an off-site gym are excludable from income.
   a. True
   b. False

2. Educational assistance programs lose their tax benefits if the plan is discriminatory.
   a. True
   b. False

False, True.

---

28. Treasury Regulation Section 1.127-2(c)(2).

Covered Employees

The following individuals are considered employees under this exclusion:

- current employees;
- former employees who are retired, disabled, or laid off;
- a leased employee who provided services on a substantially full-time basis for at least a year and the services were performed under the employer's primary control;
- sole proprietors; and
- partners performing services for the partnership.

EXAMPLE 13.7	Todd is a covered employee of Toys, Toys & More Toys. The company implemented a qualified educational assistance program and offered educational assistance to Todd and all other employees. Todd incurred $5,000 of educational expenses that was paid for by the company. Todd and other employees had a choice between the company providing educational assistance or the company providing other remuneration that would be includable in employees' gross income. In this case, any benefit paid from the plan is taxable to Todd because the plan offered a choice between the company providing educational assistance or the company providing other remuneration that would be includable in the employees' gross income. If Todd's only choice was to either receive educational assistance or nothing at all, then the full $5,000 would be excluded from Todd's gross income.

DEPENDENT CARE ASSISTANCE

The IRC allows an employee to exclude the value of dependent care assistance[29] (as defined below) provided by an employer from the employee's gross income. This exclusion for **dependent care assistance** applies to household and dependent care services paid for or provided by the employer to an employee under a dependent care assistance program. The services must be provided under the following conditions:

1. The services must be provided for one of the following qualifying persons:
   - dependent children under 13 years of age;
   - dependent children who are physically or mentally incapable of caring for themselves; or
   - an employee's spouse if the spouse is physically or mentally incapable of caring for himself.
2. The services must also allow an employee to work.

---

29. These are programs under IRC Section 129.

3. An employee may exclude up to the lesser of:
   - $5,000 annually ($2,500 for married couples filing separate returns) in benefits received through a dependent care assistance program from his gross income, or
   - the earned income of the employee or his spouse.
4. The plan must provide beneficiaries with advance notice of the program to permit them to make informed decisions about dependent care.[30]

Nondiscrimination

Nondiscrimination requirements apply to the dependent care assistance exclusion. In other words, highly compensated employees may not exclude any benefits paid as dependent care assistance from their taxable wages unless the benefits provided under the program do not favor highly compensated employees and are not discriminatory as to the other employees.

"NO-ADDITIONAL-COST SERVICES"

The exclusion for **no-additional-cost services** applies to any service provided by an employer to an employee that does not cause the employer to incur any substantial additional cost or lose revenue. The service provided as a fringe benefit must be offered to customers in the ordinary course of the line of business in which the employee performs substantial services. Examples of no-additional-cost services include providing free airline, bus, or train tickets, and hotel accommodations or telephone services either free or at reduced prices to employees working in those lines of business.[31] Also, an employee working as a parking lot attendant would have parking provided as a no-additional-cost service if the parking lot is not at capacity on a given day.[32]

Key Concepts

Underline/highlight the answers to these questions as you read:

1. What requirements are necessary for dependent care assistance programs provided to an employee as a fringe benefit to be excluded from income?

2. What are no additional cost services, and when are they excluded from income?

3. What are qualified employee discounts, and when are they excluded from income?

Lost or Forgone Revenue

One of the most important distinctions in determining if a no-additional-cost service is excludable from an employee's gross income involves whether the employer loses revenue or incurs an opportunity cost by providing the fringe benefit to the employee. Stated differently, any lost or **forgone revenue** is deemed to be a cost when determining whether the employer has incurred substantial additional costs when providing a service to an employee. The employer is considered to incur substantial additional cost if the employer or the employee spends a

---

30. This was the precise situation in *American Family Mut. Ins. Co. v. United States,* 815 F.Supp. 1206 (W.D.Wis.1992), where the Court found that the exclusion was unavailable because the plan did not provide the beneficiaries with advance notice.
31. Treasury Regulation Section 1.132-2(a)(2).
32. Note that other exclusions could apply to this as well, such as a working condition fringe or de minimus fringe benefit if applicable.

substantial amount of time providing the service even if the time spent would otherwise be inactive or idle or if the services are provided outside normal business hours.

Exception - Special Flight Rule

Airlines frequently provide personal flights at no charge for employees or family members of employees. Whether the no-additional-cost exclusion is available depends upon seat availability to other customers and if reserved seating is provided to the employee. The key distinction is that the airline must not forego revenue in order to provide the fringe benefit.

EXAMPLE 13.8

Commercial Airline permits its employees to take personal flights on the airline at no charge and receive reserved seating. Because Commercial Airline foregoes potential revenue by permitting the employees to reserve seats, employees receiving such free flights are not eligible for the no-additional-cost exclusion and must include the value of the flight in their gross income.[33] However, if the employees are not allowed to reserve seats and only board the flight if there is available capacity, then employees receiving those flights are eligible for the no-additional-costs exclusion and may exclude the value of the flight from their gross income.

Covered Employees

The following individuals are considered employees under the no-additional-cost service exclusion:

- current employees;
- former employees retired or on disability;
- widow(er)s of an individual who died while employed;
- widow(er)s of a former employee who retired or left on disability;
- a leased employee providing services to the employer on a substantially full-time basis for at least a year if the services were performed under the primary control of the employer; or
- a partner.

Providing this service to an employee's spouse or dependent child is viewed as being provided to the employee individually. Use of air transportation by an employee's parents is also considered use by the employee.

Case Study 5

In ***Charley v. Commissioner of Internal Revenue Service***,[1] Dr. Philip Charley, in his capacity as an employee of Truesdail Laboratories, traveled to various accident sites to inspect machinery. Truesdail had an "unwritten policy" that frequent flyer miles earned during employee travel became the sole property of the employee. If Dr. Charley chose to travel to an inspection by air, Truesdail would bill the client for round-trip, first class air travel. However, Dr. Charley would instruct the travel agent to arrange for coach service to and from the site but to charge Truesdail for first class travel. Dr. Charley would then use his frequent flyer miles (largely earned in connection with his business travel for Truesdail) to upgrade the coach ticket to first class and would instruct the travel agent to transfer funds equal to the difference in price between the first class ticket for which Truesdail was charged and the coach ticket to his personal travel account. Over the course of the taxable year, the travel agent maintained separate travel accounts for Dr. Charley and Truesdail. Dr. Charley took four business trips that year and using the procedures outlined above, received $3,149.93 in his personal travel account from his "sale" of the frequent flyer miles.

The IRS argued that Dr. Charley was wealthier after the transaction than before, showing that he received income. While the travel credits converted to cash can be characterized as additional compensation, Dr. Charley received property from his employer in the account upon which he could draw up to $3,149.93. Truesdail paid for first-class airfare and allowed the travel agent to credit Philip's account with the difference between the first-class price and the coach price. The funds constituting the difference therefore came from Truesdail, and the fact that travel credits were exchanged for frequent flyer miles was, according to the Court, irrelevant to their analysis. Dr. Charley asserted that the credits were "no-additional-cost services" that should be excluded under the IRC. However, the service in question must, among other things, be "offered for sale to customers in the ordinary course of the line of business of the employer in which the employee is performing services."[2] Truesdail did not offer frequent flyer miles to customers in the ordinary course of its business; thus, the travel credits at issue could not be deemed an excludable no-additional-cost service.

1. Charley v. Commissioner of Internal Revenue Service, 91 F.3d 72 (9th Cir. 1996).
2. IRC Section 132(b).

33. Treasury Regulation Section 1.132-2(c).

Unrelated Employers

A no-additional-cost service provided to an employee by an unrelated employer may qualify as an excludable benefit if:

- the service is the same type of service provided generally to customers in both the line of business of the employee and of the service provided;
- the employer of the employee and the employer providing the service have a written reciprocal agreement whereby a group of employees of each employer in the same line of business receive no additional cost services from the other employer; and
- the employer of the employee and the unrelated employer do not incur any substantial additional cost in providing this service or because of the written agreement.[34]

Nondiscrimination

Employers may not exclude the value of the services to highly compensated employees (as defined in Chapter 3) if the value of the no-additional-cost service is not available on the same terms to all employees or at least to a group of employees defined under a reasonable classification that does not favor highly compensated employees. If the provision of the no additional cost service is discriminatory, then no aspect or portion of the exclusion applies to highly compensated employees. Therefore, the entire value of the exclusion is disallowed with the amount of the benefit included in the highly compensated employees' gross income.[35]

QUALIFIED EMPLOYEE DISCOUNTS

Under the regulations, the value of "**qualified employee discounts**" on property or services offered to an employer's customers in the ordinary course of the employer's business may be excluded from an employee's income (subject to certain limits).[36] However, this exclusion does not apply to discounts on real property or on personal property commonly held for investment purposes.[37]

Limits

The exclusion for an employee discount is limited to the lesser of:

- twenty percent (20%) of the price at which the service is offered to nonemployee customers, or
- for merchandise or other property, the employer's gross profit percentage[38] multiplied by the price the employer charges nonemployee customers for the property.

---

34. Treasury Regulation Section 1.132-2(b). If one employer receives a substantial payment from the other employer with respect to the reciprocal agreement, the paying employer will be considered to have incurred a substantial additional cost pursuant to the agreement, and consequently services performed under the reciprocal agreement will not qualify for exclusion as no-additional-cost services.
35. Treasury Regulation Section 1.132-8(a)(2).
36. Treasury Regulation Section 1.132-3.
37. For instance, stocks and bonds are personal property commonly held for investment purposes.
38. An employer's gross profit percentage is determined based on all property offered to customers during the year preceding the year the discount is available, by subtracting the total cost of the property from the total sales price, and dividing the result by the total sales price of the property.

Covered Employees

The following individuals are treated as employees for the purposes of the qualified employee discount exclusion:

- current employees;
- former retired or disabled employees;
- widow(er)s of those who died while employed;
- widow(er)s of former retired or disabled employees;
- partners performing services for the partnership; or
- leased employees providing services to an employer on a substantially full-time basis for at least a year where the services are performed under the employer's primary control.

Nondiscrimination

Nondiscrimination rules apply to the exclusion for qualified employee discounts. The discount must be made available to all employees or to a group of employees defined under a reasonable classification designated by the employer that does not favor highly compensated employees.

EXAMPLE 13.9

Randy's Parts Depot sells radiators for $100 to its customers. The radiator cost Randy's $80. If Randy's allows its employees to purchase the radiator for $90, the employee can exclude the $10 discount from his gross income. If, however, Randy's sold the radiator to the employee at $75, then the employee would be required to include $5 in his gross income. The maximum excludable discount in this situation is $20 ($100 - $80).

WORKING CONDITION FRINGE BENEFITS

The value of "**working condition fringe benefits**"[39] provided by an employer are excluded from an employee's gross income. Working condition fringes are defined as any property or service provided to an employee that enables the employee to perform his work and, if paid for by the employee, would be deductible as a trade or business expense.[40]

---

39. IRC Section 132.
40. IRC Sections 162 or 167.

Covered Employees

Under the regulations, the following individuals are considered to be employees under the working conditions fringe exclusion:

- a current employee;
- a partner who performs services for a partnership;
- a director of the company; and
- an independent contractor performing services for the employer.[41]

Discriminatory

Working condition fringes are not subject to nondiscrimination requirements; therefore, the exclusion applies even if they favor highly compensated employees.

Key Concepts

Underline/highlight the answers to these questions as you read:

1. What are working condition employee fringe benefits, and when are they excluded from income?

2. What are "de minimus" employee fringe benefits, and when are they excluded from income?

Eligible Benefits

The working condition fringe exclusion applies to cash payments provided for an employee's expenses for a business activity as long as the employee may deduct the expenses had the employee paid for the expenses without reimbursement. It is imperative that the employee keep sufficient documentation to verify the payment is actually used for those expenses and any unused portion of the payment is returned to the employer.

The exclusion will not apply to:

- a service or property provided under a flexible spending account that provides the employee a certain level of unspecified non-cash benefits with a pre-determined cash value;
- a physical examination program provided by the employer; and
- any employee expense the employee may deduct as an expense for a trade or business other than the employer's trade or business.[42]

The property or service must be received by the employee and there must be a legitimate business expense that relates to the employee's work. Business related security devices, job related education, parking, and use of company cars are some examples of working condition fringes.[43]

Company Car as a Working Condition Fringe Benefit

As listed above, a common working condition fringe benefit is the provision of a company car. If the employee utilizes the car for both personal and business purposes, the portion used for business is considered the value of the working condition fringe benefit, whereas the personal use value of the car will be included in the employee's gross income. Also, use of a demonstration car

---

41. Treasury Regulation Section 1.132-1(b)(2).
42. Treasury Regulation Section 1.132-5(a)(1).
43. Treasury Regulation Section 1.132-5.

by full-time automobile salespersons qualifies as a working condition fringe benefit if the demonstration car is predominately used to facilitate the services the sales person provided to the employer and there are restrictions on personal use of the automobile.[44]

Qualified Vehicles for "Non-Personal Use"

A **qualified non-personal use vehicle** is a vehicle that the employee does not use more than a minimal amount for personal reasons due to the design of the vehicle. If an employee is provided a vehicle that is deemed to be a qualified non-personal use vehicle, the value of the provision will be excluded from his gross income. Qualified non-personal use vehicles may include:

- clearly marked police and fire vehicles;
- unmarked vehicles utilized by law enforcement individuals if the use is officially authorized;
- an ambulance or hearse;
- any vehicle designed to carry cargo with a loaded gross weight over 14,000 pounds;
- delivery trucks with seating for the driver only or the driver with a folding jump seat;
- a passenger bus with the capacity of at least 20 passengers;
- school buses; and
- tractors or other farm-type vehicles.

Meanwhile, a pickup truck with a loaded gross vehicle weight of 14,000 pounds or less may be a qualified non-personal use vehicle if it has been modified so that it will unlikely be used more than for minimal personal use. Such pickup trucks that are clearly marked with decals, special painting, or other advertising associated with the function of the business may qualify if the pickup truck is equipped with a hydraulic lift tank, permanent tank or drum, permanent side boards that materially raise the level of the sides of the truck or the bed, or other heavy equipment are part of the vehicle. Also, if the pickup truck is primarily used to transport a particular type of load in construction, manufacturing, farming, drilling, timbering, or other similar operation for which it was specially designed, it will be considered as a qualified non-personal use vehicle.

"DE MINIMUS" FRINGE BENEFITS

The term **"de minimus" fringe benefit** is defined in IRC Section 132(e) as any property or service provided by an employer to an employee that is so small in value that it makes accounting for it unreasonable or administratively impracticable when taking into account the frequency that similar fringes are provided by the employer to employees. "De minimus" is a term that means minimal, very trifling, or small.

---

44. Treasury Regulation Section 1.132-5(o).

Examples of De Minimus Fringe Benefits

The following is an illustrative but not exclusive list of de minimus fringe benefits as discussed in the regulations[45]:

- Occasional typing of personal letters by a secretary hired by an employer;
- Occasional personal use of an employer's copying machine, providing that the employer exercises sufficient control and imposes significant restrictions on the personal use of the machine so that at least 85% of the use of the machine is for business purposes;
- Occasional cocktail parties, group meals, or picnics for the employees and their guests;
- Traditional birthday or holiday gifts or property (not cash) with a low fair market value;
- Occasional theater or sporting event tickets;
- Coffee, donuts, or soft drinks;
- Local telephone calls; and
- Flowers, fruit, or books, or similar property provided to employees under special circumstances (i.e., on account of illness, outstanding performance or family crisis).[46]

Examples of Fringe Benefits that are not De Minimus

The regulations also discuss examples of benefits that are not excludable as de minimus benefits:

- Season tickets for sporting or theatrical events;
- The commuting use of an employer-provided automobile or other vehicle more than one day a month;
- Membership in a private country club or athletic facility, regardless of the frequency with which the employee uses the facility;
- employer-provided group term life insurance on the life of the spouse or child of an employee;
- use of employer-owned or leased facilities (such as an apartment, hunting lodge, boat, etc.) for a weekend.[47]

The Exclusion

The value of some or all of de minimus fringe benefits may be excluded from an employee's gross income under other statutory provisions or regulations such as the exclusion for meals furnished for the convenience of the employer discussed later in this section.[48]

The frequency of which similar fringes are furnished by the employer to the employee is generally calculated by reference to the frequency of which the employer furnishes the fringes to each individual employee.[49] An example of this employee-measured frequency is where an employer provides a free meal to one employee on a daily basis but not to any other employee, and the value of such meals is not de minimus concerning that one employee even though the meals are infrequently furnished to the employer's entire work force.[50]

---

45. Treasury Regulation Section 1.132-6.
46. Treasury Regulation Section 1.132-6(e)(1).
47. Treasury Regulation Section 1.132-6(e)(2).
48. Treasury Regulation Section 1.132-6(e)(2).
49. Treasury Regulation Section 1.132-6(b)(1).

EXAMPLE 13.10

Make You Well Hospital provides meals in the hospital cafeteria free of charge to nurses that work shifts greater than 24 hours. On average, each nurse receives one free meal every two weeks. The hospital also provides the director of the hospital a free meal in the hospital cafeteria every day. While the free meals to the nurses may be de minimus because they are infrequent, the meals to the director are not because they are provided everyday.

Irrespective of the "employee-measured frequency" rule above, the frequency with which the benefits are furnished in the aggregate to the entire work force is used where it would be administratively difficult to determine frequency considering individual employees. [51]

A cash fringe benefit is never excludable[52] unless the cash is for reasonable, occasional meal money or local transportation fare.[53] The "occasional" requirement depends on the frequency, availability, and regularity of the benefit. The furnishing of meals, money, or local transportation fare on a regular or routine basis is not considered to be "occasional".[54] Further, the meals, meal money, or local transportation fare must be provided due to overtime work necessitating an extension of the employee's normal work schedule.[55] The meals or meal money are excludable if they are provided to allow the employee to work overtime. For instance, meal money given to the employee for meals consumed during overtime work satisfies this test.[56]

De Minimus Meals

When meals or meal money furnished is so small in value that accounting for it is unreasonable or administratively impractical, the de minimus fringe benefits exclusion will apply. There is some overlap between de minimus meals and meals furnished for the "convenience of the employer" under IRC Section 119. In numerous lawsuits, employers attempt to argue that meals furnished satisfy both de minimus fringe benefit requirements and meals for the convenience of the employer.[57] Aside from coffee, donuts, soft drinks, occasional meals or meal money to enable the employee to work overtime, and occasional picnics and parties, this exclusion deals largely with employer-operated eating facilities.[58] Employer-operated eating facilities for employees qualify for this exclusion if:

- the facility is located on or near the business premises of the employer, and
- the annual revenue of the facility is equal to or greater than the direct operating costs of the facility.[59]

---

50. Treasury Regulation Section 1.132-6(b)(1).
51. Treasury Regulation Section 1.132-6(b)(2).
52. IRC Section 132(a).
53. Treasury Regulation Section 1.132-6(d)(2).
54. Treasury Regulation Section 1.132-6(d)(2)(A).
55. Treasury Regulation Section 1.132-6(d)(2)(B).
56. Treasury Regulation Section 1.132-6(d)(2)(C).
57. See *Boyd Gaming Corp. v. Commissioner of Internal Revenue Service,* 17 F. 3d. 1096 (9th Cir. 1999), discussed later in this Chapter. See also IRC Section 119.
58. The facility may be operated "directly or through a hired third party" by the employer and owned or leased by the employer as well.
59. IRC Section 132(e).

If access to the facility is available on substantially the same terms to all members of a group of employees defined under a reasonable classification set up by the employer that does not discriminate in favor of highly compensated employees, then this de minimus fringe benefit is excludable from the gross income of all employees including highly compensated employees.[60] The revenue from furnishing a meal is presumed to be equal to the facility's direct operating costs if its value can be excluded from an employee's gross income.[61] It is here where the de minimus meal overlaps with meals furnished for the convenience of the employer.[62] Under Section 119, an employee may exclude meals furnished on the business premises of the employer for the convenience of the employer.[63]

One attractive feature of de minimus meals is that they are fully deductible for income tax purposes by the employer without the 50 percent statutory limit on deductions for cost of meals yet excludable from the employee's gross income.

Case Study 6

The issues of de minimus meals for the convenience of the employer were presented to the United States 9th Circuit Court of Appeals in **Boyd Gaming Corp. v. Commissioner of Internal Revenue Service**.[1]

Although decided in 1999, the Boyd Gaming case dealt with facts occurring in the 1987 - 1988 taxable years when 26 U.S.C. Section 274(n) provided for an 80% cap on meal and entertainment expenses. Concerned with tax laws that purportedly "unfairly allowed high income taxpayers to structure their business affairs in a manner that generated deductions for personal living expenses," Congress imposed a cap on the amount of deductions for business meals and entertainment.[2] Boyd Gaming Corporation and California Hotel and Casino was a hotel and casino operator that required their employees to stay on the business premises throughout their work shift, resulting in the employees receiving free meals at onsite cafeterias. Boyd asserted that it was exempt from the then 80% cap on deductions because the meals provided were "de minimus fringe benefits".[3] The Tax Court rejected Boyd's argument and ruled that Boyd's deductions were limited to 80% under Section 274(n). The United States Ninth Circuit disagreed and reversed the Tax Court, finding that Boyd's stay-on-the-premises policy rendered the employee's meals furnished for the convenience of the employer and the meals constituted de minimus fringe benefits under 26 U.S.C. Section 132(e)(2).[4]

---

1.   *Boyd Gaming Corp. v. Commissioner of Internal of Revenue,* 177 F. 3d 1096 (9th Cir. 1999).
2.   177 F. 3d at 1097.
3.   *Id.* (*citing* 26 U.S.C. Section 274(n)(2)); 26 U.S.C. Section 132 (e)).

---

60.   IRC Section 132(e)(2).
61.   *Id.*
62.   See also Boyd Gaming Corporation, *Supra,* at page 1099.
63.   26 U.S.C. Section 119(a).

Case Study 6 Continued

More specifically, Boyd offered reasons for its stay-on-the-premises policy, including security and efficiency concerns,[1] maintaining work force control,[2] handling business emergencies and continuous customer demands, and the impracticability of obtaining meals within a reasonable proximity. The Court analyzed the statutes that dealt with the test of deductibility and indicated that Section 132(e)(2) defined de minimus fringe benefits as an employer's operation of an eating facility for employees if the facility was located on or near the business premises of the employer and the revenue derived from the facility met or exceeded the direct operating costs of the facility.

Because there was no evidence as to the revenue derived, Boyd had to rely on the statutory presumption in Section 132(e)(2) that treats revenue as equal to operating costs if employees are entitled to exclude the value of the meals under IRC Section 119. Thus, in order to determine the applicability of the 80% cap on deductions, the Court resorted to Section 132(e)(2), which in turn required an analysis of Section 119's "convenience of the employer" test.[3] Boyd asserted that the stay-on-the-premises requirement constituted a "substantial non-compensatory business reason" for furnishing meals. The Court reasoned that Boyd furnished meals as a consequence of its stay-on-the-premises policy, as employees could not leave the premises during their shifts. The Court articulated that common sense dictated that, once the policy was embraced, the employees had no choice but to eat on the premises and were "indispensable to the proper discharge of the employee's duties."[4] Because Boyd supported its "closed campus policy" with adequate evidence of legitimate business reasons, the Court found that non-compensatory business reasons existed, and thus the employees could exclude the meals under Section 119, which consequently meant that the presumption in Section 132(e)(2) applied. Once the presumption of Section 132(e)(2) applied, the cap on deductions was inapplicable and Boyd was allowed to deduct all meal expenses from its income.

---

1. The Court described the fact behind Boyd's stay on the premises policy. The casino environment is one in which vast amounts of cash flow in fast-moving transactions and special security precautions are imposed by state regulations, and many of Boyd's employees handle or have easy access to cash and gambling chips. Consequently, each property performs special check-out procedures for certain employees before they are permitted to leave the premises. The "stay-on-premises" policy minimizes the number of entries and departures during each work shift, thereby reducing security risks and the costs of security measures.
2. Boyd contends that the "stay-on-premises" requirement allows it to maintain tight control over its workforce, thereby reducing the chances of employees succumbing to the distractions and temptations of the "festive" Las Vegas atmosphere.
3. IRC Section 119 (B) (4) considers meals to be furnished for the convenience of the employer if they are provided to more than half of the employees for a "substantial non-compensatory business reason." *Boyd Gaming*, 177 F.3d at 1099-1100.
4. *Boyd Gaming*, 177 F.3d at 1100.

De Minimus Transportation

Transportation provided with minimal value may also qualify as a "de minimus" fringe benefit. If an employer furnishes an employee with taxi fare based on unusual circumstances and due to unsafe alternative transportation, the excess of the value of each one way trip over $1.50 is excluded from the employee's gross income.[64] Unusual circumstances are determined by consideration of all facts and circumstances relating to the situation, like a temporary change in employee's work schedule or being called to the work place at 1:00 a.m. when an employee usually works from 8:00 a.m. - 4:00 p.m.[65]

A public transit pass, tokens, or fare cards provided to the employee at a discount to defray commuting costs may be excluded from the employee's gross income as a de minimus fringe benefit <u>if</u> the discount or net value of the employee's costs does not exceed $21.00 per month.[66] Reimbursement of such expenses are excludable if the employee receives no more than $21.00 per month under a bona fide reimbursement arrangement.

Benefits Exceeding Value and Frequency Limits - All or Nothing

If a benefit is provided to an employee that is not deemed de minimus due to excess value or excess frequency, then no amount is considered a de minimus fringe.[67] If, for example, an employer reimburses an employee $40.00 per month for taxi fare, then the entire $40.00 per month will be included in the employee's gross income, not merely the $19.00 ($40 minus the $21 total cost threshold) per month excess value.

Quick Quiz

Highlight the answer to these questions:

1. Working condition fringes may be discriminatory and still maintain the favored tax treatment.
   a. True
   b. False

2. A de minimus employee fringe benefit is property or service provided to an employee that is so small in value that accounting for it is unreasonable.
   a. True
   b. False

True, True.

EXAMPLE 13.11

Jane works for ABC Company. ABC reimburses Jane $15 per month for a ferry pass. The ferry pass costs Jane $40 per month. In this situation, $15 is excluded from Jane's gross income.

If in the same example, ABC reimburses Jane $21 per month for the ferry pass, $21 is excluded from Jane's income.

If in the same example, ABC reimburses Jane $25 per month, then none of the $25 could be excluded from Jane's income.

---

64. Treasury Regulation Section 1.132-6(D)(2)(ii).
65. Treasury Regulation Section 1.132-6(D)(2)(iii)(B).
66. Treasury Regulation Section 1.132-6(D)(1).
67. Treasury Regulation Section 1.132-6(D)(4).

Nondiscrimination Rules

The nondiscrimination rules do not apply in determining the amount of a de minimus fringe benefit or working condition fringe benefit.[68] However, the nondiscrimination rules do apply to most other types of fringe benefits. Thus, the ability to classify a benefit that would ordinarily not allow discrimination as a de minimus fringe benefit may allow the employer to in effect discriminate.

RULES FOR SELECTED FRINGE BENEFITS

EXHIBIT 13.3

Type of Fringe Benefit	Treatment Under Employment Taxes		
	Income Tax Withholding	Social Security and Medicare	Federal Unemployment (FUTA)
Accident and health benefits	Exempt[1,2], except for certain long-term care benefits	Exempt, except for certain payments to S corporation employees who are 2% shareholders.	Exempt
Achievement awards	Exempt[1] up to $1,600 ($400 for nonqualified awards).		
Adoption assistance	Exempt[1]	Taxable	Taxable
Athletic facilities	Exempt if substantially all use during the calendar year is by employees, their spouses, and their dependent children.		
De minimis (minimal) benefits	Exempt	Exempt	Exempt
Dependent care assistance	Exempt[3] up to certain limits, $5,000 ($2,500 for married employee filing separate return).		
Educational assistance	Exempt up to $5,250 of benefits each year. (See *Educational Assistance* on page 7.)		
Employee discounts	Exempt[4] up to certain limits. (See *Employee Discounts* on page 8.)		
Employee stock options	See *Employee Stock Options* on page 8.		
Group-term life insurance coverage	Exempt	Exempt[1,5] up to cost of $50,000 of coverage. (Special rules apply to former employees.)	Exempt
Lodging on your business premises	Exempt[1] if furnished for your convenience as a condition of employment.		
Meals	Exempt if furnished on your business premises for your convenience.		
	Exempt if de minimis.		
Moving expense reimbursements	Exempt[1] if expenses would be deductible if the employee had paid them.		
No-additional cost services	Exempt[4]	Exempt[4]	Exempt[4]
Transportation (commuting) benefits	Exempt[1] up to certain limits if for rides in a commuter highway vehicle ($105), transit passes ($105), or qualified parking ($200). (See *Transportation (Commuting Benefits)* on page 14.)		
	Exempt if de minimis.		
Tuition reduction	Exempt[4] if for undergraduate education (or graduate education if the employee performs teaching or research activities).		
Working condition benefits	Exempt	Exempt	Exempt

[1] Exemption does not apply to S corporation employees who are 2% shareholders.
[2] Exemption does not apply to certain highly compensated employees under a self-insured plan that favors those employees.
[3] Exemption does not apply to certain highly compensated employees under a program that favors those employees.
[4] Exemption does not apply to certain highly compensated employees.
[5] Exemption does not apply to certain key employees under a plan that favors those employees.

Source: IRS Publication 15-b: Table 2-1 "Special Rules for Various Types of Fringe Benefits"

---

68. Section132(h)(1) and Treasury Regulations Section 132-(A).

QUALIFIED MOVING EXPENSE REIMBURSEMENT

A "**qualified moving expenses reimbursement**" may be excluded from an employee's gross income as a fringe benefit whether provided through services in kind, direct payment or reimbursement. Generally, employers may exclude qualified moving reimbursement expenses that are provided to an employee from the employee's wages. This exclusion applies to reimbursement of moving expenses that the employee could have deducted on his income tax return if the employee paid or incurred them without reimbursement, provided the employee did not deduct the moving expenses.[69]

Key Concepts

Underline/highlight the answers to these questions as you read:

1. What is a qualified moving expense reimbursement, and when is it excluded from income?

2. What is qualified transportation and parking, and when is it excluded from income?

3. What requirements are necessary for adoption assistance programs to be excluded from income?

Qualifying Move

The move must be to a new principal place of work at least fifty miles from the employee's former home. The employee needs to be either (i) full time in the new location for no less than 39 weeks during the 12 month period immediately after arrival or (ii) full time or self employed at least 78 weeks during the 24 month period immediately after arrival and at least 39 weeks during the 12 month period immediately after arrival. This exclusion for the qualified moving expense reimbursement applies to current employees and leased employees who provided services substantially full time for at least a year and perform under the employer's primary control. Those who own two percent or more of the corporation's stock are not considered employees under the rules for this exclusion.

Deductible Moving Expenses

Deductible moving expenses are confined to reasonable expenses for the following:
- moving household goods and personal effects from the former home to the new home (15 cents per mile for 2005), and
- traveling and associative lodging during the move from the former home to the new home.[70]

EXAMPLE 13.12

Thomas, an employee of MC Corp., works and maintains his principal residence in Pittsburgh, Pennsylvania. Upon receiving orders from his employer that he is to be transferred to the corporation's San Francisco, California office, Thomas drives to San Francisco with his family with stopovers at various cities between Pittsburgh and San Francisco to visit friends and relatives. In addition, Thomas detours

---

69. IRC Section 217.
70. IRC Section 217(b).

into Texas for sight-seeing. Because of the stopovers and tour into Texas, Thomas' travel time and distance are increased over what they would have been had he proceeded directly to San Francisco. To the extent that Thomas' route of travel between Pittsburgh and San Francisco is in a generally south-westerly direction, it may be said that he is traveling by the shortest and most direct route available by motor vehicle. Since Thomas' excursion into Texas is away from the usual Pittsburgh-San Francisco route, the portion of the expenses paid or incurred attributable to the Texas excursion is not deductible. Likewise, that portion of the expenses attributable to Thomas' delays en route not necessitated by reasons of rest or repair of his vehicle is not deductible.

Any portion or amount of deductible expenses that is not reimbursed by an employer may be deducted on the employer's individual tax return as an "above the line" (or "For AGI") deduction.

Nondeductible Moving Expenses

Examples of items non-deductible as moving expenses include, but are not limited to, the following:[71]

- storage charges (other than in-transit);
- costs incurred in the acquisition of property;
- costs incurred and losses sustained in the disposition of property;
- penalties for breaking leases;
- mortgage penalties;
- expenses of refitting rugs or draperies;
- expenses of connecting or disconnecting utilities;
- losses sustained on the disposal of memberships in clubs, tuition fees, and similar items;
- meals while in-route;
- pre-move house hunting expenses; and
- temporary living expenses.

If an employer reimburses an employee for any nondeductible expense, the employee must include that portion of the reimbursement in his gross income.

QUALIFIED TRANSPORTATION AND PARKING

The regulations provide for an exclusion of the value of qualified transportation benefits from an employee's gross income.[72] This exclusion for transportation benefits is subject to the following limitations:

- $100 per month for commuter highway transportation and transit passes combined, and
- $200 per month for 2005 ($205[†] per month for 2006) for qualified parking).

---

71. Treasury Regulations Section 1.217-1(b)(3).
72. Treasury Regulation Section 1.132-9.

For any given month, if the value of a benefit is more than the limit, then any excess amount above the limit, less any amount the employee paid, is included in the employee's income. The excess may not qualify as a de minimus benefit.

Covered Employees

The provision of the benefit may be discriminatory. Current employees and leased employees providing services substantially full time for at least a year under the employer's control are considered employees under this exclusion. Nonetheless, those who own two percent or more of the stock of an S corporation are not considered employees.

Excludable Transportation and Parking Benefits

The following examples are excludable transportation and parking benefits:

- a transit pass;
- a ride in a commuter highway vehicle between the home of the employee and the workplace; and
- qualified parking.[73]

The value of each one of these benefits are excludable from an employee's gross income without regard to whether one or all are provided by the employer to the employee. **Qualified parking** is parking provided by the employer on or near the employer's business premises. It also includes parking on or near the location where employees commute to work using mass transit, carpools, or commuter highway vehicles but not at the employee's home.

Quick Quiz

Highlight the answer to these questions:

1. Deductible moving expenses include moving household goods, lodging, and meals during the move.
   a. True
   b. False

2. Qualified transportation benefits may be given by the employer directly or through a bona fide reimbursement arrangement.
   a. True
   b. False

3. Adoption assistance benefits may be excluded from the employee's gross income and are not subject to Social Security and Medicare taxes.
   a. True
   b. False

False, True, False.

Qualified transportation benefits may be given by the employer directly or through a bona fide reimbursement arrangement. However, cash reimbursements for transit passes may qualify only when a voucher is not readily available for direct distribution by the employer.

---

73. Treasury Regulation Section 1.132-9.

ADOPTION ASSISTANCE PROGRAMS

Ordinarily, an employee may exclude from an employee's gross income amounts paid for, or expenses incurred, by the employer for qualified adoption expenses[74] concerning the adoption of a child by an employee if these amounts are furnished according to a written adoption assistance program.[75] An employer may establish a written **adoption assistance program** intended to promote adoption and that will pay expenses related to an adoption not exceeding $10,630 for 2005 to an employee.[76] The limitation of $10,630 for 2005 applies to an adoption for each child (there is no longer an increased amount for special needs adoptions). The amount paid is excluded from the employee's income, but there is a phaseout of this exclusion starting at $159,450 of adjusted gross income (AGI) for 2005 through $199,450. If the employee's AGI is greater than or equal to $199,450 for 2005, then the exclusion is eliminated.

The plan must comply with nondiscrimination requirements. The plan may pay for qualified adoption expenses consisting of adoption fees and related charges, court costs, attorney's fees, and other expenses directly tied to the adoption of a child under 18 or who is physically or mentally incapable of caring for themselves.[77] While the payments or reimbursements made under the program are excluded from an employee's gross income, such payments continue to be subject to Social Security, Medicare, and federal unemployment taxes.

AWARDS AND PRIZES

Certain prizes and awards (as defined below) given to employees by his employer may be excluded from the employee's gross income.[78] An employee achievement award is defined in the IRC as an item of tangible personal property that is:

- Transferred by an employer to an employee for length of service achievement or safety achievement,
- Awarded as part of a meaningful presentation, and
- Awarded under conditions and circumstances that do not create a significant likelihood of the payment of disguised compensation.[79]

Key Concepts

Underline/highlight the answers to these questions as you read:

1. What requirements are necessary for awards and prizes to be excluded from income?

2. What requirements are necessary for qualified tuition reduction plans to be excluded from income?

For purposes of this section, the term "tangible personal property" does <u>not</u> include cash. Other items that will not be considered tangible personal property include vacations, meals, lodging, tickets to theater and sporting events, and stocks, bonds, and other securities.

---

74. IRC Section 137.
75. IRC Section 137(a).
76. The employer may institute a program providing $6,000 for children with special needs. See IRC Section 137.
77. IRC Section 23(d)(2).
78. IRC Section 274.
79. IRC Section 274(j)(3)(A) and 74(c).

Limits on Value of Awards

An employee is allowed to exclude from his gross income the value of any employee achievement awards insofar as the cost of the award does not exceed the following limitations:[80]

- $400 for all nonqualified plan awards when added to the employer's cost for all other employee achievement awards made to such employee during the taxable year that are not qualified plan awards, and
- $1,600 for all qualified plan awards when added to the employer's cost for all other employee achievement awards made to such employee during the taxable year (including employee achievement awards that are not qualified plan awards).[81]

Only the excess amount over the $400 and $1,600 limitations is included in the employees income (but not deductible by the employer); the initial $400 or $1,600 limitations are not included in the employees income (and deductible by the employer). In other words, if an employee achievement award exceeds the $1,600 limit and constitutes a qualified plan award, then only the excess amount above $1,600 is included in the employee's gross income and no penalty occurs that would render the entire amount taxable.

If the cost of the award provided to an employee is more than the employer's allowable deduction, then the larger of the following amounts must be included in the employee's wages: (a) the portion of the cost that is more than the employer's allowable deduction (up to the value of the award), (b) the amount of the value of the award that exceeds the employer's allowable deduction.

Qualified Plan Award

A "**qualified plan award**" is defined as an employee achievement award bestowed as part of an established written plan of the taxpayer that does not discriminate in favor of highly compensated employees (within the meaning of Section 414(q)) for eligibility or benefits.[82]

However, there are limitations on this exclusion. If the "average cost"[83] of all employee achievement awards provided by the employer during the year exceeds $400, then such employee achievement award shall not be treated as a qualified plan award for any taxable year.

---

80. IRC Section 274 (j)(1) and (2).
81. IRC Section 274 (j)(2).
82. IRC Section 274(j)(3)(B)(i).
83. IRC Section 274(J)(3)(ii). For purposes of this provision, average cost shall be determined by including the entire cost of all qualified plan awards given by the employer without taking into account employee achievement awards of nominal value (less than $50).

Special Rules

In the event that an employee achievement award is granted by a partnership, the deduction limitations apply to the partnership as well as to each member.[84] For length of service awards, an award is not deemed as being provided for length of service achievement if it is accepted during the recipient's first five (5) years of employment, or within any other five year period.[85] Meanwhile, an item is not considered a safety achievement award if:

- such safety achievement awards have been granted to more than 10 percent of the employees of the employer during the taxable year, or
- such item is awarded to a manager, administrator, clerical employee, or other professional employee.[86]

Covered Employees

Under this exclusion, employees are considered (1) current employees or (2) leased employees providing services to an employer on a substantially full-time basis for at least a year if the services performed are under the employer's primary control. Two percent shareholders of S corporation are not considered employees of the corporation for this exclusion.

> Kathleen is a professor at the University of Georgia. She receives an employee achievement award for her work during the year. She is given a crystal trophy and matching serving dishes for a total value of $1,500. The award is a qualified plan award. Is this amount excluded from her income for that taxable year?
>
> Answer: Yes. In this scenario, Kathleen can exclude from her income $1,500 because it is a qualified plan award. If the plan was not qualified, then Kathleen could only exclude up to $400.

EXAMPLE 13.13

QUALIFIED TUITION REDUCTION PLANS

An employee may exclude from gross income any amount representing a qualified tuition reduction.[87] **Qualified tuition reduction** is defined in the IRC as the amount of any reduction in tuition provided to an employee of an educational organization for education below the graduate level of:[88]

- current employees;
- former employees who retired or left on disability;
- widow(er)s of a person who died while employed;
- widow(er)s of former employees who retired or left on disability; or
- dependent children or spouses of any of the above.

---

84. IRC Section 274(j)(4)(A).
85. IRC Section 274(j)(4)(B).
86. IRC Section 274(j)(4)(C).
87. IRC Section 117(d)(1).
88. IRC Section 117(d)(2).

Qualified Educational Organizations

Although this exclusion normally does not apply to the graduate level, if the individual is a graduate student teaching or performing research activities for an educational organization, then that individual may be eligible if he or she meets all other requirements of this exclusion.[89] To be qualified, an educational organization must normally maintain a regular faculty and curriculum and have a regularly enrolled body of students in attendance at the place where its educational activities are carried out in the normal course of business. This educational organization can be elementary, secondary, a college, or university.

Nondiscriminatory

For the exclusion to apply, the tuition reduction must not discriminate in favor of highly compensated employees, or stated differently, the reduction must be made available on substantially the same terms to each member of a group of employees defined under a reasonable classification set up by the employer that does not discriminate in favor of highly compensated employees.[90]

VALUATION RULES APPLYING TO FRINGE BENEFITS

In determining whether a fringe benefit is excludable from taxation, a common problem is the valuation of the fringe benefit in the event that the entire fringe benefit is taxable or a portion of the fringe benefit is taxable. Various taxation rules apply in determining the value of a fringe benefit. Ordinarily, the general valuation rules apply to the value of a fringe benefit. However, there are special valuation rules for certain benefits, which are discussed in this section. Aside from the general valuation rule, there are special valuation rules for employee transportation benefits, which include the cents-per-mile rule, the commuting rule, the lease value rule, and the unsafe conditions commuting rule.

THE GENERAL VALUATION RULE

Most fringe benefits are valued under the general valuation rule. Basically, the fair market value should be the value assigned to a fringe benefit. Under the regulations, the amount that an employee would be required to pay a third party in an arms-length transaction to purchase or lease the benefit, or what one would pay in the market place, is considered the fair market value of a fringe benefit. This figure is different than the cost an employer may incur in providing the benefit to an employee. Likewise, this figure is not what an employee considers to be the value or the amount the employer would be willing to pay for the fringe benefit. Instead, the amount that is determined to be fair market value depends on the facts and circumstances of the particular situation.

---

89. 26 U.S.C.A. Section 117(d)(5).
90. 26 U.S.C.A. Section 117(d)(3).

For instance, with employer-provided vacations, the fair market value of an employer-provided vacation is the amount the employer would have to pay a third party, travel agent, or directly to the service provider for the same or similar vacation on the same or comparable terms in the geographic area where the vacation is taking place. Additionally, when ascertaining the value of an employer-provided vehicle, the fair market value is the amount the employee would need to pay a third party or dealership to lease the same or similar vehicle in the same or similar terms in the geographic area where the employer uses the vehicle. The duration of the lease is also relevant in this determination, so the comparable lease term should be a similar period as the period provided by the employer-provided vehicle. In other words, if the employer is providing the vehicle to the employee for a two year period, then comparable lease terms of two years should be used in determining the fair market value.

Key Concepts

Underline/highlight the answers to these questions as you read:

1. How are employee fringe benefits valued under the general rule?

2. What is the cents per mile rule?

3. What is the commuting rule?

4. What is the lease value rule?

5. What is the unsafe conditions commuting rule?

THE CENTS PER MILE RULE

Valuation under the **cents per mile rule** requires multiplying the standard mileage rate by the total miles the employee drives the vehicle for personal purposes. Personal use is any use of the vehicle other than use in the employer's business or trade. The standard mileage rate for 2005 is 40.5 cents per mile. Of course, the vehicle must be provided by an employer to the employee for both business use and personal use. Under the regulations, a vehicle is considered to be any motorized wheeled vehicle, which would include those manufactured primarily for use on public roads, streets, and highways.[91] One important issue in using this valuation is whether the vehicle is used regularly in the employee's business.[92]

The test for determining whether the vehicle is used regularly in the employee's business requires that any of the following conditions are satisfied:

- 50% or more of the total annual mileage of the vehicle is for the employer's trade or business;

- the employer sponsors a commuting pool that uses the vehicle each work day to transport no less than three employees to and from work; or

- the vehicle is "regularly used", and not subject to infrequent business use such as occasional trips between multiple business premises, and this regular use is in the employer's business based on all the facts and circumstances.[93]

---

91. Treasury Regulation Section 1.61-21(f)(4).
92. Treasury Regulation Section 1.61-21(f).
93. Treasury Regulation Section 1.61-21(e)(1)(iv).

The employer cannot use the cents per mile rule for an automobile if its value when first made available to any employee for personal use is more than an amount determined by the IRS as the "maximum automobile value" for the year. For instance, in the years 2000 and 2001, an employer could not utilize the cents per mile rule for an automobile made available to an employee that year if the value of that automobile at the time was more than $15,400. The cents per mile rule can be utilized, however, if the employer reasonably expects the vehicle to be regularly used in its business during the calender year or if the vehicle meets the mileage test.

The "mileage test" is satisfied if (a) vehicle is driven at least an annual rate of 10,000 miles per year[94] and (b) where the vehicle is used "primarily" during the year by employees. However, use of the vehicle by another individual who is not an employee should not be treated as use by an employee.

Notably, the value of maintenance and insurance for the vehicle are "built in" the cents per mile rate. The rate of any other service provided by the employer to the employee for a vehicle is not included in the cents per mile, and therefore use of the general valuation rule should be utilized to value those services.

THE COMMUTING RULE

The value of this fringe benefit is determined by multiplying each one way commute from home to work or from work to home by $1.50. This value applies to more than one employee irrespective of whether one or more employees ride in the vehicle during the commute. The **commuting rule** is allowed if <u>all</u> of the following requirements are satisfied:

- The employer provides the employee the vehicle for use in the employer's business and the employer requires the employee to commute in the vehicle for bona fide non-compensatory business reasons;[95]
- a written policy is established and implemented whereby the employer does not permit the employee to use a vehicle for personal use other than for commuting or minimal personal use;[96]
- other than de minimus personal use and commuting, the employee does not use the vehicle for personal use;[97]
- if the vehicle used is an automobile, the employee who uses the automobile for commuting must not be a control employee.[98] Rather than using the definition of a control

---

94. For instance, if the vehicle was owned or leased only during a portion of the year, the 10,000 mile requirement is reduced proportionately.

95. As a general rule this requirement is satisfied if the vehicle is used each work day to carry no less than three employees to and from work in a commuting pool sponsored by the employer.

96. Minimal, or de minimus, personal use is considered use of the vehicle for a personal errand either going to and from work or between employee's home and a business delivery.

97. This is the essential difference between commuting rule and the cents per mile rule. Under the cents per mile rule, valuation is determined by taking a snap shot of the miles used for personal miles v. the miles used for work-related business. However, the commuting rule zeroes in simply on the commuting and de minimus personal use, and therefore prohibits significant or more than minimal personal use of the vehicle.

98. A control employee is defined by the Treasury Regulations for the year 2005, as (1) an officer whose pay is equal to or more than $85,000, (2) a director, (3) an employee who makes $170,000 or more, (4) an employee owning 1% interest or more in the employer's business, or (5) an elected official.

employee, an employer may chose to define a control employee as a highly compensated employee.[99]

THE LEASE VALUE RULE

According to the **lease value rule**, the value of an employer-provided automobile is determined by using the automobile's annual lease value. According to the general rule, the lease value of the automobile used by the employee in the employer's business is reduced by the amount excluded from the employee's wages as a working condition fringe benefit. Notably, the employer may choose to include the entire lease value in the employee's wages. The annual lease value of an automobile is determined by first ascertaining the automobile's fair market value on the first day it is available to any employee for personal use. Next, through reference to the Annual Lease Value Table (Exhibit 13.4), the annual lease value is provided by the applicable fair market value of the automobile. Automobiles with a fair market value exceeding $59,999 will have an annual lease value that is equal to 25 percent of the automobile's fair market value plus $500.

$60,000 automobile (25% x $60,000) = $15,000, plus $500= $15,500. Under this example, the annual lease value of a $60,000 vehicle would be $15,500.

EXAMPLE 13.14

As discussed earlier in this section, the fair market value of an automobile is the amount an individual would pay to purchase the automobile in an-arms length transaction from a third party in the geographic area that the same automobile is bought or leased. The fair market value would therefore include an amount for all expenses related to the sale including tax, title and license, sales tax, and applicable fees. Only under these circumstances would a true fair market value be provided.

Importantly, safe harbor provisions apply to the determination of fair market value of an automobile. The safe harbor value may be used for an automobile purchased at arms length by utilizing the employer's costs (including tax, title, license and other purchase expenses) as long as the employer is not the manufacturer of the automobile.

If the automobile is leased, safe harbor value for the lease can be <u>any</u> of the following:
- Invoice price including options and additions of the manufacturer, plus four percent;
- the suggested retail price of the manufacturer, minus eight percent; or
- the nationally recognized retail value of the automobile if that retail value is reasonable for the automobile.

Similar to the commuting rule, the annual lease value in the table provided includes, and has built in, the value of maintenance and insurance on the automobile. The annual lease value should not be reduced by the value of any services that were not provided by the employer. For instance, annual lease value should not be reduced by the value of a maintenance service contract or insurance if the employer did not provide the maintenance or insurance. Conversely, the

---

99.   Under the Treasury Regulations, a highly compensated employee for 2005 is an employee who (1) was a 5% owner at any time during the year or preceding year, or (2) the employee was paid more than $95,000 for the preceding year unless the employee was not also in the top 20% for employee compensation the preceding year.

annual lease value does not include the value of fuel provided to an employee for personal use. The value of the fuel must be included separately in the employee's wages. If any other service other than maintenance and insurance is provided by the employer to the employee for an automobile, the fair market value of that service must be determined based on the fair market value of that service.

The annual lease values that are determined on an automobile may be prorated if an employee was provided an automobile for a period of 30 or more days but less than the entire calender year. The annual lease value is prorated by multiplying the annual lease value by a percentage derived by dividing the number of days of availability by 365 days. Treasury Regulations prohibit use of a prorated annual lease value if the reduction of federal taxes is the main reason the automobile is unavailable during the remainder of the calender year. Nonetheless, if the employer provides an automobile to an employee for a period continuously that is less than 30 days, a daily lease value is assigned. The daily lease value is determined by multiplying the annual lease value by the percentage derived by dividing four times the number of days of availability by 365. The equation is as follows:

$$\text{Daily Lease Value} = \text{Annual Lease Value} \times \frac{(4 \times \text{Number of Days of Availability})}{365}$$

For instance, if the employee used the automobile continuously for 25 days and the annual lease value was $5,100, the daily lease value is calculated as follows.

$$\$5,100 \times \frac{(4 \times 25)}{365} = \$1,397 \text{ Daily Lease Value}$$

ANNUAL LEASE VALUE TABLE

EXHIBIT 13.4

Automobile fair market value	Annual Lease Value
$0 to 999	$ 600
1,000 to 1,999	850
2,000 to 2,999	1,100
3,000 to 3,999	1,350
4,000 to 4,999	1,600
5,000 to 5,999	1,850
6,000 to 6,999	2,100
7,000 to 7,999	2,350
8,000 to 8,999	2,600
9,000 to 9,999	2,850
10,000 to 10,999	3,100
11,000 to 11,999	3,350
12,000 to 12,999	3,600
13,000 to 13,999	3,850
14,000 to 14,999	4,100
15,000 to 15,999	4,350
16,000 to 16,999	4,600
17,000 to 17,999	4,850
18,000 to 18,999	5,100
19,000 to 19,999	5,350
20,000 to 20,999	5,600
21,000 to 21,999	5,850
22,000 to 22,999	6,100
23,000 to 23,999	6,350
24,000 to 24,999	6,600
25,000 to 25,999	6,850
26,000 to 27,999	7,250
28,000 to 29,999	7,750
30,000 to 31,999	8,250
32,000 to 33,999	8,750
34,000 to 35,999	9,250
36,000 to 37,999	9,750
38,000 to 39,999	10,250
40,000 to 41,999	10,750
42,000 to 43,999	11,250
44,000 to 45,999	11,750
46,000 to 47,999	12,250
48,000 to 49,999	12,750
50,000 to 51,999	13,250
52,000 to 53,999	13,750
54,000 to 55,999	14,250
56,000 to 57,999	14,750
58,000 to 59,999	15,250

For vehicles having a fair market value in excess of $59,999, the annual lease value is equal to: (.25 x the fair market value of the car) + $500.

THE UNSAFE CONDITIONS COMMUTING RULE

The **unsafe conditions commuting rule** determines the value of commuting transportation provided by an employer to a qualified employee solely because of unsafe conditions as $1.50 for a one way commute. The unsafe conditions commuting rule requires that a "qualified employee" be provided with the subject commuting transportation. If, however, the employer does not comply with record keeping requirements concerning the wages of the employee, as well as the employee's hours and other conditions and practices, then the employee may not be deemed a qualified employee. For the unsafe conditions commuting rule to apply, the employee must ordinarily walk or use public transportation; the employer must have a written policy against transportation for personal purposes other than commuting because of unsafe conditions; and the employee does not use the transportation for personal reasons beyond commuting due to unsafe conditions.

Quick
Quiz

Highlight the answer to these questions:

1. Employee fringe benefits are generally valued at the fair market value of the benefit provided.
   a. True
   b. False

True.

Finally, whether other "unsafe conditions" exist is determined based on the facts and circumstances of each individual situation. Unsafe conditions exist if a reasonable person would consider it unsafe for the employee to walk or use public transportation at the time of day that the employee is required to commute. Another factor used in determining whether conditions are unsafe is the history of criminal activity in the area surrounding the workplace or home of the employee at the time of day that the employee commutes.

Key Terms

Adoption Assistance Program - An employee-provided program that pays adoption expenses up to $10,390 in 2005. The employee is not taxed on the payments or reimbursements made on his behalf.

Business Premises of the Employer - The employee's place of employment.

Cents per Mile Rule - To determine the value of the personal use of an employer-provided automobile, multiply the standard mileage rate (40.5 cents for 2005) by the total miles the employee drives the vehicle for personal purposes.

Commuting Rule - To determine the value of the personal use of an employer-provided vehicle, multiply each one way commute from the employee's home to work or from work to home by $1.50.

"De Minimus" Fringe Benefit - A benefit of any property or service provided by an employer to an employee that is so small in value that it makes accounting for it unreasonable or administratively impracticable when taking into account the frequency with which similar fringes are provided by the employer to all employees.

Dependent Care Assistance - Assistance that applies to household and dependent care services paid for or provided by the employer to an employee under a dependent care assistance program covering employees. The employee is not taxed on the value of the program or service paid on his behalf under the program (up to $5,000 per year).

Forgone Revenue - The lost revenue or opportunity cost incurred by an employer for providing the fringe benefit to the employee.

Fringe Benefit - A benefit, other than customary taxable wages, provided by an employer to an employee for the employee's performance (in most instances) of services for the employer.

Lease Value Rule - To determine the value of an employer-provided automobile, use the automobile's annual lease value.

No-Additional-Cost Services - Services provided by an employer to an employee that do not cause the employer to incur any substantial additional cost or lost revenue.

On Premises Athletic Facility - A gym or other athletic facility such as a tennis court, pool, or golf course that is operated by the employer, located on the employer's business premises, and "substantially all" of the use of the facility is by employees of the employer, their spouses, or their dependent children. The value of the use of on premises athletic facilities is not taxable to the employee as long as its availability is nondiscriminatory.

Qualified Educational Assistance Program - A plan established and maintained by an employer that provides employees with educational assistance. The employer may exclude $5,250 of benefits from an employee's taxable income.

Key Terms

Qualified Employee Discounts - A discount on the value of property or services offered to an employer's customers in the ordinary course of the employer's business may be excluded from an employee's income (subject to certain limitations).

Qualified Moving Expenses Reimbursement - Qualified moving expenses paid by an employer on behalf of an employee may be excluded from the employee's gross income. This exclusion applies to the reimbursement of moving expenses that the employee could have deducted on his income tax return if the employee had paid, or incurred, the costs without reimbursement.

Qualified Non-Personal Use Vehicle - A vehicle that the employee does not use more than a minimal amount for personal reasons due to the design of the vehicle. The value of a qualified non-personal use vehicle is excluded from an employee's gross income.

Qualified Parking - Parking provided by the employer on or near the employer's business premises. An employee may exclude up to $200 per month (for 2005) from his gross income for employer provided parking.

Qualified Plan Award - An employee achievement award bestowed as part of an established written plan of an employer that does not discriminate in favor of highly compensated employees (within the meaning of Section 414(q)) for eligibility or benefits. The value of an award provided under the plan, up to $400 for a nonqualified award and $1,600 for a qualified award, is excluded from the employee's gross income.

Qualified Tuition Reduction - The amount of any reduction in tuition provided to an employee of an educational organization for education below the graduate level is excluded from the employee's gross income.

Unsafe Conditions Commuting Rule - The value of commuting transportation provided by an employer to a qualified employee solely because of unsafe conditions is $1.50 for each one way commute.

Working Condition Fringe Benefits - Any property or service provided to an employee that enables the employee to perform his work and, if paid for by the employee, is deductible as a trade or business expense (i.e. parking).

DISCUSSION QUESTIONS

1. Describe the term "employee fringe benefits" and identify the types of fringe benefits generally associated with this term.

2. What are the normal tax consequences to the employer and to the employee of employee fringe benefits?

3. Describe the nondiscrimination rules that apply to employee fringe benefit plans.

4. List the requirements necessary for the value of meals provided by an employer to be excluded from the employee's gross income.

5. List the requirements necessary for the value of lodging provided by an employer to an employee to be excluded from the employee's gross income.

6. List the requirements necessary for the value of athletic facilities provided by an employer to an employee to be excluded from the employee's income.

7. List the requirements necessary for the value of an education assistance program provided by an employer to an employee to be excluded from the employee's gross income.

8. Describe the requirements necessary for the value of a dependent care assistance program provided by an employer to an employee to be excluded from the employee's gross income.

9. What are employer provided no-additional-cost services and identify when the value of this fringe benefit may be excluded from an employee's gross income?

10. What are employer-provided qualified employee discounts and identify the requirements for excluding the value of this fringe benefit from an employee's gross income?

11. List the requirements necessary for the value of working condition fringe benefits to be excluded from an employee's gross income.

12. List the requirements necessary for the value of employer provided "de minimus" fringe benefits to be excluded from an employee's gross income.

13. What is an employer provided qualified moving expense reimbursement and what are the requirements for the value of this fringe benefit to be excluded from an employee's gross income?

14. Describe employer provided qualified transportation and parking and identify the requirements for the value of the fringe benefit to be excluded from an employee's gross income.

15. Explain the limitations of excluding the value of employer provided adoption assistance programs to an employee's gross income.

16. Describe the requirements necessary for the value of employer provided awards and prizes to be excluded from an employee's gross income.

17. Describe the requirements necessary for employer-provided qualified tuition reduction plans to be excluded from an employee's income.

18. How are employee fringe benefits generally valued?

19. Describe the cents per mile rule.

20. Describe the commuting rule.

21. Describe the lease value rule.

22. Describe the unsafe conditions commuting rule.

1. Which of the following benefits provided by an employer to its employees is currently taxable to the employee?

   a. Employees of the DEF Department Store are allowed a 15% discount on store merchandise. DEF's normal gross profit percentage is 20%.

   b. On a space available basis, undergraduate tuition is waived by Private University for the dependent children of employees (value of $15,000 per semester).

   c. Fly Airline allows its employees to fly free when there are open seats available on a flight (average value of $200).

   d. Incidental personal use of a company car.

2. Isse Peking is the manager of Airline Highway Motel. Isse lives in Unit 12. He was given the option to live at the motel if he would also look after the night auditing (the value of his reviews is $400 per month) responsibilities. The value of the motel unit on a monthly basis is $800, but Unit 12 rents on a daily basis for $100 per day. How much, if any, does Isse have to include in his gross income for living on the premises of his employer?

   a. $0 lodging for the convenience of the employer.

   b. $400 per month.

   c. $800 per month.

   d. $3,000 per month.

3. Meredith is an employee of a large company. The company has a health facility on its premises for the exclusive use of its employees and their dependents. A comparable private health club membership at a public facility would cost $2,400 per year. How much, if any, must Meredith include in her gross income if her 10-year old daughter uses the facilities for one-half of the year?

   a. $0.

   b. $600.

   c. $1,200.

   d. $2,400.

4. Which of the employee fringe benefits listed below, if provided by the employer, would be included in an employee's gross income?

 1. Business periodical subscriptions.
 2. Season tickets to professional football games.
 3. Free parking provided near its business (value of $90 per month).
 4. The use of an on-premises athletic facilities (value of $180 per month).

   a. 2 only.
   b. 1 and 2.
   c. 1, 2, and 3.
   d. 1, 2, 3, and 4.

5. Kohler Company allows a 25% discount to all nonofficer employees. Officers are allowed a 30% discount on company products. Kohler's gross profit percent is 35%. Which of the following is true?

   a. An officer who takes a 30% discount must include the extra 5% (30%-25%) in his gross income.
   b. Any discounts taken by any employee is includible in the employee's gross income because the plan is discriminatory.
   c. All discounts taken by officers (30%) are includible in their gross income because the plan is discriminatory.
   d. None of the discounts taken by any employee are includible in their gross income because the discount, in all cases, is less than the company's gross profit percentage.

6. Kenny holds two jobs - a full-time job with R Corporation and a part-time job with Z Corporation. Kenny uses his car to drive to work. The mileage is as follows: from Kenny's home to R is 70 miles; from R to Z is 10 miles; and from Z to Kenny's home is 70 miles. Kenny's deductible mileage for each work day is:

   a. 10 miles.
   b. 70 miles.
   c. 80 miles.
   d. 150 miles.

7. Robbin is married to Robert and they have one child Angel, age 14, who is in the 6th grade. Angel is a difficult child and she is cared for in the afternoon by the Sisters of Reformation, a group of Catholic nuns. Robbin pays $6,000 per year for the child care. Robbin's company has a dependent care assistance program. If Robbin makes the maximum use of the dependent care assistance program, how much can she exclude from her income if she files a joint return with Robert?

    a. $0.

    b. $2,500.

    c. $5,000.

    d. $6,000.

8. Professor Stabler has one child, Benson, who is 18 years old and a full-time student at Disc University, a private university where Professor Stabler is the chairman of the Finance Department and a full-time employee. The cost of undergraduate tuition at Disc University is $15,000 per semester, but the children of all full-time employees may attend Disc University for free. Last semester Benson took a Russian history class that was oversubscribed. Twenty-five students were on the waiting list, but Benson was number two. Three students got into the full class. Which of the following are correct?

    1. Professor Stabler has to include the value of the tuition remission in his income for last semester.

    2. In general, there is no dollar limit to the value of no-additional-cost services like undergraduate tuition.

        a. 1 only.

        b. 2 only.

        c. 1 and 2.

        d. Neither 1 or 2.

9. ABC Corp. provides employees with discounts on the flat panel televisions they manufacture. The discounts were established using a length of service and employee status methodology.

Length of Service	Employee Discount	Officer Discount
1 - 5 years	10%	20%
> 5 - 10 years	15%	30%
> 10 years	20%	40%

The gross profit percentage for ABC is 40%.

George is an officer employee who has been with ABC Corp. for 13 years. For Christmas 2004 George bought a 56 inch flat panel television that retails for $8,800 and he received a discount appropriate to the schedule discounts listed above. For 2004, how much, if any, does George have to include in gross income as a result of this transaction?

    a. $0.

    b. $1,760.

    c. $2,640.

    d. $3,520.

10. Baldwin is the president of ZZZ Best Carpet Cleaners. Baldwin has a home with 18,000 square feet of floor space. Every week, Baldwin has the cleaning crew of ZZZ Best Carpet Cleaners clean his carpets. He theorizes that this is good training for the crew. Baldwin's CPA tells him that he can avoid the inclusion of the value of the services in his gross income if he offers to have any employees carpet cleaned at a reduction from retail. Baldwin establishes such a plan and allows a 50% reduction for all employee's including himself. During 2004 the total retail value of the cleaning at Baldwin's house was $20,000, of which he paid $10,000. How much, if any, must Baldwin include in gross income resulting from the discount?

    a. $5,000.

    b. $6,000.

    c. $8,000.

    d. $10,000.

11. Jean works for A&R Law Firm and lives on the west bank of the city. A&R pays (reimburses) Jean $21 per month for riding the river taxi to work. The monthly pass to ride the river taxi is $50. How much does Jean need to include in gross income related to this river taxi pass?

    a. $0.

    b. $21.

    c. $29.

    d. $50.

12. ProLife Inc. has a written adoption assistance program that pays adoption expenses including fees, attorney fees, and other normal expenses. ProLife paid adoption expenses for the following employees during 2005.

Employee and Age	Employee AGI	Adoptee and Age	Amount Paid	Health of Adoptee
Joe (34)	$150,000	Cindylou (18)	$10,630	Excellent
James (34)	$200,000	Randi (6)	$10,630	Excellent
Donna (34)	$80,000	Brooke (3)	$10,630	Excellent
Connie (32)	$100,000	Silky (5)	$10,630	Excellent

Which of the following have income inclusions resulting from the employer adoption plan?

    a. No one, $10,630 is the maximum excludable limit for 2005.

    b. Joe.

    c. James.

    d. Joe and James.

13. Greg is employed by a large corporation with 400 employees. The corporation provides its employees with a no-cost gym membership at a local YMCA. The cost of the membership is $60 per month, which is completely paid for by Greg's employer. How much must Greg include in his yearly gross income related to this no-cost fringe benefit?

    a. $0.

    b. $60.

    c. $600.

    d. $720.

14. Eric moved from Houston to New Orleans. His expenses for the move included $400 for truck rental, $100 for lodging, and $200 of pre-move house-hunting expenses. If Eric's employer reimbursed him $600, how much of the reimbursement is included in his gross income?

    a. $0.

    b. $100.

    c. $200.

    d. $600.

15. Natalie is a secretary at JKL Law Firm. JKL provides her with free sodas at her discretion. Natalie estimates that she drinks $20 worth of sodas per month. How much must Natalie include in her annual gross income related to the sodas?

    a. $0.

    b. $20.

    c. $200.

    d. $240.

Employee Benefits: Group Benefits

14

INTRODUCTION

Most employees value fringe benefits, especially insurance benefits such as medical, life, and disability. With a large number of employees, employers can negotiate lower group insurance rates and better coverage than an individual employee would be able to negotiate in the open market. Thus, where insurance coverage is desired by a large number of employees, the employer may adopt an insurance plan as part of an overall compensation package, which also enables the employer to be more competitive in the labor market. The federal government, in the case of some fringe benefits and insurance plans, also promotes employer insurance arrangements by allowing the employer to pay the premiums for the employees and immediately deduct the cost for income tax purposes without requiring the participant employee to include the premium cost in their taxable income.

Most employer-provided insurance is provided under group insurance coverage that is usually paid, at least in part, by the employer. Any premium amounts paid by the employer are generally deductible by the employer or included in the employee's gross income. It is not a requirement that the employer pay any of the premium of the group insurance; the employee may still benefit through a pretax payment of the insurance premium or through better rates. To receive the potential tax benefits for the employer or the employee, each type of group benefit has specific requirements.

This chapter addresses the following group benefits and details the benefits, requirements, and exemptions of each:
- Group medical plans;
- Group term life insurance;
- Group disability insurance;
- Cafeteria plans used to provide diverse employee groups with a greater selection of employee benefits;
- Flexible benefit plans;
- Medical savings accounts;
- Health savings accounts;

- Voluntary Employee's Beneficiary Association;
- Salary continuation plans;
- Group long-term care insurance;
- Group retirement planning services;
- Business continuation plans;
- Business overhead disability plans;
- Split-dollar life insurance; and
- Key person life insurance.

Know The Numbers

	MSA		HSA	
Established	Before 2006		2004 and Later	
	Single	Family	Single	Family
Health Insurance Deductible	$1,750 - $2,650	$3,500 - $5,250	$1,000	$2,000
Maximum Out-of-Pocket	$3,500	$6,450	$5,100	$10,200
Maximum Contribution	65% of deductible	75% of deductible	100% of deductible limited to $2,650	100% of deductible limited to $5,250
Catch-Up Contribution Available	No		Yes $600 for 2005 $700 for 2006 $800 for 2007 $900 for 2008 $1,000 for 2009 and beyond	

MEDICAL PLANS

There are a number of ways that an employer can provide an employee with benefits for medical expenses due to personal injury or sickness. Many employers use these types of group health insurance plans as a part of the overall compensation package provided to their employees. Included in these health insurance plans are both private insurance plans and self-insurance plans. Any payments made to these plans are deductible for income taxes by the employer and excluded from the employee's gross income.

GROUP MEDICAL INSURANCE

A group accident or health plan is an arrangement that provides benefits for employees, their spouses, and their dependents in the event of personal injury or sickness. The plan may be insured or noninsured and does not need to be in writing. The premiums paid by the employer for health insurance are not includable in the employee's taxable income but are a deductible business expense for the employer. Group medical insurance includes hospitalization coverage, major medical, indemnity coverage, health maintenance organization, preferred provider organizations, point of service plans, and dental and vision plans.

INCOME TAX IMPLICATIONS

The employer can generally exclude the value of accident or health benefits provided to an employee from the employee's gross income. Because the employer cannot treat a two percent shareholder of an S corporation as an employee for this exclusion, the employer must include the value of accident or health benefits it provides to the two percent shareholder in his wages subject to Federal income tax withholding. However, the employer can exclude the value of these benefits (other than payments for specific injuries or illnesses) from the employee's wages subject to Social Security, Medicare, and FUTA taxes.

If the employer's plan is a self-insured medical reimbursement plan that favors highly compensated employees, the employer must include all or part of the amounts the employer pays to these employees in the employee's wages subject to Federal income tax withholding. However, the employer can exclude these amounts (other than payments for specific injuries or illnesses) from the employee's wages subject to Social Security, Medicare, and FUTA taxes.

A **self-insured plan** is a plan that reimburses employees for medical expenses not covered by an accident or health insurance policy. For this exception, a highly compensated employee is any individual who is one of the five highest paid officers of the company or an employee who owns (directly or indirectly) more than 10 percent in value of the employer's stock. In addition, an employee who is among the highest paid 25 percent of all employees (other than those who can be excluded from the plan) is also considered a highly compensated employee for this exception.

Premiums paid by the employer for accident, health, and disability insurance policies are deductible by the employer and excluded from the employee's income. When the insurance benefits are paid, they are includible in the employee's income with the exception of payments received for medical care of the employee, spouse, and dependents; and payments for permanent loss or the loss of the use of a member or function of the body or permanent disfigurement of the employee, spouse, or dependent.

COBRA PROVISIONS

Under the **Combined Omnibus Budget Reconciliation Act of 1986 (COBRA)**, an employer that maintains a group health plan and employs 20 or more people on more than 50 percent of the calendar days in a year is required to continue to provide coverage under the plan to covered employees and qualified beneficiaries following the occurrence of a statutorily defined qualifying event as depicted in the following exhibit.

| EXHIBIT 14.1 | SUMMARY OF **COBRA** PROVISIONS |

Event	Beneficiary (Qualifying)			Period of Coverage
	Worker	Spouse	Dependant	
Normal termination (resigned, laid off, or fired; except gross misconduct)	✓	✓	✓	18 months
Full time to part time	✓	✓	✓	18 months
Qualified Dependent (Child reaches age no longer eligible for plan)			✓	18 months
Disabled employee or dependent (must meet Social Security definition of disabled)	✓	✓	✓	29 months
Death of Employee		✓	✓	36 months
Employee reached Medicare age		✓	✓	36 months
Divorce		✓	✓	36 months
Plan terminates	✓	✓	✓	36 months

COBRA Premiums

The employer may pay for the COBRA coverage either directly or by reimbursing the employee, or the employer may shift the burden of paying for the benefit to the beneficiaries. If the employer pays for the medical coverage, then the exclusion from the employee's income for accident and health benefits applies to amounts the employer pays to maintain medical coverage under COBRA. The exclusion applies regardless of the length of employment, whether the employer pays the premiums directly or reimburses the former employee for premiums paid, and whether the employee's separation is permanent or temporary.

During the statutory COBRA period, the premium cannot exceed 102 percent of the cost to the plan for similarly situated individuals who have not incurred a qualifying event. The 102 percent includes both the portion paid by employees and any portion paid by the employer before the qualifying event plus two percent for administrative costs. If a qualified beneficiary receives the 11 month disability extension of coverage, the premium for the additional 11 months may be increased to 150 percent of the plan's total cost of coverage. COBRA premiums may be increased if the costs to the plan increase, but generally must be fixed in advance of each 12-month premium cycle.

Quick Quiz

Highlight the answer to these questions:

1. The value of health benefits provided to all employees or owners can be excluded from the employee or owner's income.
   a. True
   b. False

2. COBRA premiums paid by the employer on behalf of a former employee can be excluded from the employee's taxable income.
   a. True
   b. False

False, True.

Brandy recently terminated her employment. Her major medical insurance ended on her last day of employment. She will begin work at her new job in two weeks. Should she elect Cobra? Yes, in this instance it is probably a good idea because she does not want to have a period of non-coverage.

EXAMPLE 14.1

Assume the facts above except Brandy is going to take 18 months off to find herself in Africa. Now is Cobra an appropriate election? In this instance, the answer is maybe. On one hand she may find that an individual policy is quite expensive. The risk is that if she elects Cobra, it will end after 18 months. Should she contract a serious disease overseas, then she would become uninsurable and may not be able to get an affordable policy at that time. She may be better off spending the extra money on an individual policy in order to ensure future coverage. Assuming she elects Cobra, she should also purchase a high deductible major medical policy to reduce her overall risk.

EXAMPLE 14.2

GROUP TERM LIFE INSURANCE

Amounts paid by the employer for group term life insurance also receive favorable tax treatment. The employer can deduct the amounts paid for the insurance, and the employee can exclude a portion, if not all, of the value from his income (discussed below). To receive such favorable treatment, the life insurance must provide a general death benefit to a group of employees, and the coverage must provide an amount of insurance to each employee based on a formula that prevents individual selection. This formula must use factors such as the employee's age, years of service, pay, or position.

$ 50,000 coverage tax free

Group term life insurance is pure insurance protection that pays a predetermined sum if the insured dies during a specified period of time (i.e., the term, which may be 1, 5, 10, 20 years or longer). Term insurance generally has no cash value savings or investment component and essentially states, "If you pay x, we will pay y if you die during the term." The protection ceases at the end of the term unless renewed. Term insurance is very inexpensive at young ages (substantially less than whole life). The premium pattern may be level or increasing on an annual or set period basis (i.e., five-year renewable term). The face amount may be level, decreasing, or increasing (i.e., there may be a cost of living provision that increases the face).

Key Concepts

Underline/highlight the answers to these questions as you read:

1. What is required for a life insurance policy to be considered group-term life insurance?

2. What are the tax implications of employer provided group term life insurance?

Group term life insurance is usually renewable on an annual term and does not include the following types of insurance:

- Insurance without general death benefits, such as travel insurance or a policy providing only accidental death benefits;
- Life insurance on the life of the employee's spouse or dependent. However, the employer may be able to exclude the cost of this type of insurance from the employee's wages as a de minimis fringe benefit (as discussed in Chapter 13);
- Permanent life insurance; or
- Life insurance where the employer is the beneficiary of the policy.

DEFINITION OF EMPLOYEE AND REQUIREMENTS

Generally, life insurance provided by the employer is not considered group-term life insurance unless the employer provides it to at least 10 full-time employees at some time during the year. For this purpose, employees are typically defined as current common-law employees, full-time life insurance agents who are current statutory employees, and leased employees who have provided services to the employer on a substantially full-time basis for at least a year (if the services are performed under the employer's primary direction and control).

The employer should count employees who choose not to receive the life insurance unless, to receive the coverage, the employee must pay for benefits other than group-term life insurance. For example, the employer should count an employee who is eligible to benefit from the group term life insurance by paying part of the premium, even if that employee chooses not to receive the life insurance coverage. However, the employer does not count an employee who must pay part or all of the cost of permanent benefits to benefit from the group term life insurance unless that employee chooses to pay the costs and benefit from the life insurance coverage.

If the employer does not meet the general 10-employee-rule, the employer may still be eligible to recognize the benefits of the group term life insurance coverage if the employer's provision of the coverage meets the following three requirements:

1. The employer provides coverage under the plan to all of its full-time employees who provide evidence of insurability.
2. The coverage provided under the plan must be based on either a uniform percentage of pay or a set amount of coverage depending upon age, years of service, compensation, or position.
3. The required evidence of insurability must be limited to a medical questionnaire (completed by the employee) that does not require a physician.

When applying this exception, employers should not consider employees who were denied insurance for any of the following reasons:

1. The employees were 65 or older;
2. The employees customarily work 20 hours or less a week or five months or less in a calendar year; or
3. The employees have not been employed for a waiting period stated in the policy (which cannot exceed six months).

S CORPORATION SHAREHOLDERS

When an employer provides group term life insurance coverage for a more than two percent shareholder of an S Corporation, the cost of the coverage is included in the shareholder's gross income and is subject to Social Security and Medicare taxes. However, the employer does not pay federal unemployment tax (FUTA) on the cost of any group-term life insurance coverage provided to a more than two percent shareholder.

INCOME TAX TREATMENT

Group term life insurance premiums paid by the employer on the first $50,000 of death benefit are deductible by the employer and are excludable from an employee's gross income. The cost, as determined under the Uniform Premium Table provided by the IRS, of any death benefit coverage in excess of $50,000 is taxable to the employee. The monthly cost of the insurance to include in the employee's gross income is determined by multiplying the number of thousands of dollars of insurance coverage over $50,000 (figured to the nearest $100) by the cost shown in the following table. The table corresponds with the employee's age as of the last day of the tax year and the includable amount is reduced by any contribution payments made by the employee.

Quick Quiz

Highlight the answer to these questions:

1. To be considered a group term life insurance policy the employer must have at least 15 employees.
   a. True
   b. False

2. If an employer provides a group term policy with a benefit over $50,000, then the employee must include in income the actual premium cost of the amount over $50,000.
   a. True
   b. False

False, False.

UNIFORM PREMIUM TABLE: COST PER $1,000 OF PROTECTION FOR 1 MONTH

EXHIBIT 14.2

Age	Cost
Under 25	$0.05
25 through 29	$0.06
30 through 34	$0.08
35 through 39	$0.09
40 through 44	$0.10
45 through 49	$0.15
50 through 54	$0.23
55 through 59	$0.43
60 through 64	$0.66
65 through 69	$1.27
70 and older	$2.06

The employee can always receive the first $50,000 of death benefit coverage tax free. Thus, if an employee's death benefit under the employer provided term life insurance is $90,000, the employee will be taxed (as determined above) on $40,000 ($90,000 - $50,000) of the coverage. Also, if an employee pays an amount towards the cost of the taxable death benefit coverage, the taxable amount is decreased by the employee's payment.

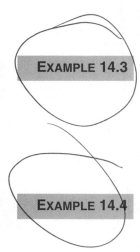

EXAMPLE 14.3

BigBully Corp provides all of its employees with group-term life insurance coverage equal to their salary. Steve earns $40,000 per year and is 40 years old. Steve is not considered a key employee. In this instance, Steve's term policy will provide a death benefit of $40,000. Since the benefit is below the taxable limit, Steve's benefit will be excluded from his income.

EXAMPLE 14.4

BigBully Corp provides all of its employees with group-term life insurance coverage equal to their salary. Steve earns $100,000 per year and is 40 years old. Steve is not considered a key employee. The cost of the insurance that must be included in Steve's compensation is calculated as follows:

Salary	$100,000
Less exclusion	- $50,000
	$50,000
Divided by 1,000	÷ 1,000
	50
Times cost (as provided in table)	X 0.10
	$5.00
Times 12 months	X 12
Yearly inclusion in employee's income (W-2)	$60.00

EXAMPLE 14.5

BigBully Corp provides all of its employees with group-term life insurance coverage equal to their salary. Steve earns $100,000 per year and is 40 years old. Steve is not considered a key employee and pays $50 per year toward the cost of the insurance. The cost of the insurance that must be included in Steve's compensation is calculated as follows:

Salary	$100,000
Less exclusion	- $50,000
	$50,000
Divided by 1,000	÷ 1,000
	50
Times Cost (as provided in table)	X 0.10
	$5.00
Times 12 months	X 12
Yearly premium cost	$60.00
Premium paid by employee	- $50.00
Yearly inclusion in employee's income (W-2)	$10.00

KEY EMPLOYEES

To qualify for favorable tax treatment, a group term life insurance plan must be nondiscriminatory. To be nondiscriminatory, the plan must cover either:

- 70% or more of all eligible employees, or
- 85% of the non-key employees (as defined in Chapter 3).

If the plan does not meet either of the two tests, the plan is considered discriminatory and the key employee must include the greater of either the cost determined in the Uniform Premium Table or the actual cost of the life insurance coverage to the employer in his gross income.

COVERAGE FOR DEPENDENTS

The cost of group-term life insurance coverage paid by the employer for the spouse or dependents of an employee may be excludable from an employee's gross income as a de minimis fringe benefit. The cost of the coverage is determined by the Uniform Premium Table.

GROUP DISABILITY INSURANCE

Disability insurance provides benefits in the form of periodic payments to a person who is unable to work due to sickness or accidental injury. The cost of disability insurance varies depending on occupation, age, and sex of insured, as well as the benefit term, coverage, and the length of the waiting period (elimination period) provided under the policy.

Disability insurance can be provided under a group or individual plan and as either short term (up to two years) or long term coverage (over two years). In any case, the premiums paid by the employer are deductible by the employer and are not included in the employee's gross income. However, when the employer pays the premium and the value is excluded from the employee's gross income, any disability income benefit received by the employee is taxable to the employee. If the employee pays the entire premium with after-tax income or the employer pays the premium and the employee includes the premium payment in income, any benefits received will be considered tax-exempt. As such, many employees choose to include the cost of the premiums in their taxable income even when paid by the employer because any disability benefits paid from such a plan would then be received tax free. If the employer and employee each pay part of the premium, the prorated part of the benefits associated with the employer's contribution is taxable to the employee.

Key Concepts

Underline/highlight the answers to these questions as you read:

1. What are the tax implications of employer provided group disability insurance?

2. What are cafeteria plans, and how are they used?

3. What are the tax implications of employer provided cafeteria plans?

CAFETERIA PLANS

A **cafeteria plan** is a written plan under which the employee may choose to receive cash as compensation or tax-free fringe benefits. Provided the cafeteria plan meets the requirements defined below, the value of the fringe benefit, if chosen by the employee, will be a deductible expense for the employer and will not be included in the employee's gross income. These plans are referred to as Section 125 plans because they are permitted by IRC section 125(d), which requires a cafeteria plan to offer at least one taxable benefit, usually cash, and one qualified nontaxable benefit. The usual nontaxable benefits include group term life insurance in any amount, medical reimbursements or insurance plans, accident and disability benefits, dependent care assistance, and paid vacation.

USES AND APPLICATIONS

A cafeteria plan is appropriate when employee benefit needs vary within the employee group; the employee mix includes young, unmarried people with minimal life insurance and medical benefits needs, as well as older employees with families who need maximum medical and life insurance benefits. A cafeteria plan is also appropriate when employees want to choose the benefit package most suited to their individual needs and when an employer seeks to maximize employee satisfaction with the benefit package, thereby maximizing the employer's benefit from its compensation expenditures. A cafeteria plan is also appropriate when the employer is large enough to afford the expense of such a plan. A cafeteria plan is a way of managing fringe benefit costs to the employer by individually pricing each benefit and providing a total dollar equivalency to each employee to effectively shop for the best mix of benefits for that employee.

Cafeteria plans help give employees an appreciation of the value of their benefit package by allowing them to choose the cash or purchase the benefit. Cafeteria plans can also help control employer costs of providing benefit packages because the employer does not pay for benefits that are not used by the employees. Cafeteria plans are more complex and expensive to design and administer and usually include some insured benefits such as medical and life insurance.

CAFETERIA PLANS

EXHIBIT 14.3

Qualified Benefits	Benefits Not Allowed
• Accident and health benefits (but not medical savings accounts or long-term care insurance). • Adoption assistance. • Dependent care assistance. • Group-term life insurance coverage (including costs that cannot be excluded from wages).	• Archer Medical Savings Accounts (see accident and health benefits). • Athletic facilities. • De minimus (minimal) benefits. • Educational assistance. • Employee discounts. • Lodging on your business premises. • Meals. • Moving expense reimbursements. • No-additional-cost services. • Transportation benefits. • Tuition reduction. • Working condition benefits.

BENEFITS PROVIDED

Qualified benefits include benefits that the employer could provide tax free to the employee except for the items listed above. More specifically, qualified benefits include accident and health insurance benefits (but not medical savings accounts or long-term care insurance), adoption assistance, dependent care assistance, and group-term life insurance coverage (including costs that cannot be excluded from wages). A cafeteria plan cannot include an Archer medical savings accounts, the payment of athletic facilities dues, de minimis (minimal) benefits, educational assistance, employee discounts, lodging on the employer's business premises, meals, moving expense reimbursements, no-additional-cost services, transportation (commuting) benefits, tuition reduction, working condition benefits, and scholarships or fellowships. Generally, a cafeteria plan does not include any plan that offers a benefit that defers an employee's compensation, like a contribution to a retirement plan. However, a cafeteria plan can include a qualified 401(k) plan as an available nontaxable benefit.

The flexible spending account (FSA) is a cafeteria plan funded through employee salary reductions. FSAs are discussed in detail in the next section.

INCOME TAX IMPLICATIONS

Because the employee who benefits from a cafeteria plan has the choice to either receive cash as compensation or use the value to "purchase" fringe benefits tax free within the cash balance pension plan, the cafeteria plan must meet the rules of IRC Section 125. Under this section, the IRC provides the benefits payable from a fringe benefit plan with an exclusion from the constructive receipt rule, which would otherwise require the employee to include the value of the benefits purchased in his taxable income.

A cafeteria plan meets the qualifications of the IRC if the benefits provided under the plan are qualified (as discussed above), the plan does not favor the highly compensated employees, and the nontaxable benefits provided to key employees is less than 25 percent of the total nontaxable benefits provided under the plan to all employees.

When a cafeteria plan meets the requirements of the IRC, the employee will not be taxed on the value of the nontaxable fringe benefits chosen, and the employer can deduct the value of the nontaxable fringe benefits chosen by the employee. In the case where the plan provides a benefit that is not qualified, the value of the benefit will be included in the employee's gross income. Also, in the case where the plan is deemed discriminatory by favoring the highly compensated or providing more than 25 percent of the benefit to the key employees, the value of the nontaxable benefits chosen by the key employees or highly compensated will be included in their gross income.

Quick Quiz

Highlight the answer to these questions:

1. If an employer provides disability insurance to an employee, the benefits received from such a policy will be tax-free.
   a. True
   b. False

2. Cafeteria plans allow an employee to exclude from income the value of the nontaxable fringe benefits selected.
   a. True
   b. False

False, True.

FLEXIBLE SPENDING ACCOUNTS

A **flexible spending account (FSA)** is a cafeteria plan under which employees can choose between receiving cash or deferring income tax free to fund the cost of certain employee selected benefits. Because of the consequences of forfeiture of unused benefits, these are often referred to as "Use It or Lose It" accounts.

A flexible spending account is appropriate in any of the following situations:

1. An employer wants to expand employee benefit choices without significant employer out-of-pocket costs (or possibly realize some actual dollar savings).
2. Many employees have employed spouses with duplicate medical coverage.
3. Employees contribute to health insurance costs.
4. The employer's medical plans have large deductibles or coinsurance (co-pay) provisions.
5. There is a need for benefits that are difficult to provide on a group basis, such as dependent care.
6. The costs of employee benefit plans, such as health insurance, have increased and the employer must impose additional employee cost sharing in the form of increased employee contributions and deductibles.

Key Concepts

Underline/highlight the answers to these questions as you read:

1. What are flexible spending accounts, and when are they appropriate?

2. What are the tax implications of employer provided Flexible Spending Accounts?

The FSA approach minimizes employee outlay since the FSA converts what would have been after-tax employee expenditures for the benefits selected to pretax expenditures. The plan provides employees a degree of choice to receive either cash as compensation or the cash to pay for the costs of certain benefits. The FSA is funded entirely through employee salary reductions, only requiring the employer to bear the administrative costs. Salary reductions elected by employees to fund the nontaxable benefits available under the plan are not subject to income taxes or payroll taxes. There are many nontaxable benefits available from a FSA, which include many benefits that employers might not otherwise provide to their employees such as dependent care, dental, etc.

Using a flexible spending account to pay for dependent care expenses (if provided) may provide more tax savings than utilization of the Child and Dependent Care Credit. In general, it can be said that an employee is better off using an FSA unless his income (AGI) is less than $43,000.

> Sue is a single parent with three children. Sue's income is $25,000 per year. She has $3,000 in child care expenses. In this instance use of the dependant care credit will provide a much greater tax savings. The calculation is as follows:

EXAMPLE 14.6

Dependent Care Credit		Flexible Spending Account	
$3,000	Limit on expenses	$3,000	Expense
X 0.30	Rate for $25,000 of income	X 0.15	Tax bracket
$900	Tax savings (Credit)	$450	Tax savings
		+ 230	7.65 Payroll tax saved by Sue
		$680	Total taxes saved

EXAMPLE 14.7

Assume Sue marries Derek, whose income is $100,000. Sue's income is $25,000 per year and she still has $3,000 in expenses for the three children. In this instance use of the flexible spending account would be more beneficial because of the income tax rate differential on the dependant care credit. The calculation is as follows:

Dependent Care Credit		Flexible Spending Account	
$3,000	Limit on expenses	$3,000	Expense
X 0.20	Rate for $125,000 of income	X 0.28	Tax bracket
$600	Tax savings (Credit)	$840	Tax savings
		+ 230	7.65 Social Security saved by Sue
		$1,070	Total taxes saved

An FSA must meet the nondiscrimination requirements as previously discussed for cafeteria plans. FSAs also require that employees evaluate their personal and family benefit situations and file a timely election form each year indicating their deferral choice. The plan could result in adverse selection that would ultimately raise benefit costs. The employer is at risk for the total annual amount an employee elects to allocate to health benefits under his FSA even if the employee terminates employment before funding the amount used from the plan. In addition, if the employee fails to use all contributed amounts within a certain time period, contributions are forfeited back to the employer (use it or lose it).

INCOME TAX IMPLICATIONS

Employee salary reductions applied to nontaxable benefits are not subject to income taxes or payroll taxes. The employer gets a tax deduction for any amounts it pays under the plan coverage.

Quick Quiz

Highlight the answer to these questions:

1. An employee should consider carefully whether to use a flexible spending account for child care expenses as the FSA is usually more beneficial than the child and dependent care credit.
   a. True
   b. False

2. An employee that contributes to a FSA reduces his taxable income but must still pay payroll taxes on the contributed amount.
   a. True
   b. False

True, False.

Case Study 1

FSA contributions not only affect taxes, but may affect disability benefit calculations. In Brosted v. Unum Life Ins. Co. of America[1], Mr. Daniel Brosted was employed by Dreisilker Electric Motors, Inc., which was also the plan administrator for Dreisilker Electric Motors, Inc. Group Long Term Disability Income Plan, a single-employer employee benefit plan. Mr. Brosted was employed by Dreisilker as a purchasing manager from 1974 until January 3, 2000, and was a member of the Plan from its inception. Another defendant, Unum Life Insurance Company of America, provided the insurance coverage for the Plan. Mr. Brosted sought to recover $22,086.09 for past benefits he felt were wrongfully not paid, as well as an increase of his current benefits by $513.63 per month.

Mr. Brosted was diagnosed with multiple sclerosis at age thirty-two. In 2000, Mr. Brosted was hospitalized for his illness and subsequently was prevented from returning to work by Dreisilker. In June 2000, Mr. Brosted applied for long-term disability benefits under the Plan, and by August 1st, Mr. Brosted reached an agreement with Dreisilker concerning his severance from the company. Shortly thereafter, an Unum accountant reviewed Mr. Brosted's file and discovered that his disability benefits had been improperly calculated. According to the policy, benefits were to be either sixty percent of the claimant's monthly earnings prior to disability or $6,000, whichever was less. The monthly earnings used to calculate the benefit were not to include "pre-tax contributions to a qualified deferred compensation plan, Section 125 plan, or other flexible spending account." Unum's original calculations neglected to take into account Mr. Brosted's pre-tax contributions to his Section 125 flexible spending account and to his deferred compensation plan. As a result, his monthly benefits were reduced by $513.

Mr. Brosted argued that the Plan and Unum were legally prevented from changing his benefit amount and that Unum breached its fiduciary duty to him under ERISA. The Court disagreed, and granted the defendants pretrial motion to dismiss because the pre-tax contributions to his Section 125 flexible spending account and to his deferred compensation plan should not have been included in calculating his disability benefits.

1.Brosted v. Unum Life Ins. Co. of America, 349 F.Supp.2d 1088, 34 Employee Benefits Cas. 1523 (N.D.Ill. 2004).

ARCHER MSAs

The Health Insurance Portability and Accountability Act (HIPAA) established a tax-favored savings account for medical expenses called an **Archer Medical Savings Account (MSA).** The MSAs could be established after 1996 and before 2006 for employers with 50 or less employees and self-employed individuals. Employees could not establish the MSA but could contribute (subject to the limitations discussed below) to the account if their employer established an MSA on their behalf. After 2005, an MSA cannot be established and has been replaced by the Health Savings Account (HSA), which is discussed below. However, the MSAs that were established prior to 2006 are still in existence, may still be maintained, and retain their tax-favored status.

Key Concepts

Underline/highlight the answers to these questions as you read:

1. What are the tax implications of employer provided Archer MSAs, and when can they be established?

2. What are the tax implications of employer provided HSAs, and when can they be established?

3. What are VEBAs, and what are the tax implications of payments made by the employer to the VEBA?

For MSAs to be established, the employer must have provided its employees with a high-deductible health plan with a maximum out-of-pocket cost.[1] A high deductible plan for purposes of meeting the requirements of the MSA is a major medical health insurance plan with a deductible between $1,750 and $2,650 (2005) for individual coverage and between $3,500 and $5,250 for 2005 for family coverage. The maximum out-of-pocket costs for the plan is $3,500 for individual coverage and $6,450 for family coverage. These same limitations apply for self-employed individuals.

Contributions can be made to the MSA by the employee or the employer. Employee contributions are deductible from the employee's gross income. In addition, employer contributions are tax deductible by the employer, not subject to payroll taxes, and not taxable income to the employee. The aggregate contributions to the plan by the employee and the employer cannot exceed 65 percent of the deductible for individual coverage and 75 percent of the deductible for family coverage.

The earnings on the assets within an MSA are tax deferred until a distribution is taken from the account. If a distribution is for qualified medical expenses, the distribution, including any earnings, is not taxable. If the distribution is not for qualified medical expenses, the entire distribution is taxable as ordinary income. In addition, if the distribution is taken before the owner of the account is age 65, the distribution is subject to an additional 15 percent excise penalty tax.

1.IRC Section 220(c)(2)(A); Rev. Proc. 2004-71.

HEALTH SAVINGS ACCOUNTS

The Medicare Act of 2003 created **Health Savings Accounts (HSAs)**, which are very similar to MSAs but less restrictive. Specifically, HSAs can be established by anyone with a high deductible health insurance plan (see below), allow a higher contribution amount, and reduce the penalty for non-medical distributions.

To qualify for an HSA, the individual's health insurance plan's deductible must be at least $1,000 for single coverage and the annual out-of-pocket costs cannot exceed $5,100 for 2005.[2] For family coverage under an HSA, the health insurance plan deductible must be at least $2,000, and the annual out-of-pocket costs cannot exceed $10,200 for 2005.

Contributions to the HSA can be made by the individual or by the individual's employer. In either case, the aggregate contributions cannot exceed the health insurance plan deductible subject to a maximum contribution of $2,650 for individuals and $5,250 for families for 2005. However, individuals between 55 years old and 64 years old can make additional catch-up contributions of $600 over these limits for 2005 ($700 for 2006, $800 for 2007, $900 for 2008, and $1,000 for 2009).[3]

Earnings within the HSA are not taxable, and amounts distributed from an HSA are also not taxable provided the distributions are used to pay for qualified medical expenses. If a distribution is not for qualified medical expenses, the entire distribution is taxable as ordinary income. If the distribution is taken before the owner of the account is 65, the distribution is subject to an additional 10 percent excise penalty tax.

2.IRC Section 223(b) and (c); Rev. Proc. 2004-71.
3.IRC Section 223(b)(3)(B).

EXHIBIT 14.4 COMPARISON OF **MSA** AND **HSA** FOR 2005

	MSA		HSA	
Established	Before 2006		2004 and Later	
Creators	• Employers with less than 50 employees • Self-employed individuals		Any individual	
	Single	**Family**	**Single**	**Family**
Health Insurance Deductible	$1,750 - $2,650	$3,500 - $5,250	$1,000	$2,000
Maximum Out-of-Pocket	$3,500	$6,450	$5,100	$10,200
Maximum Contribution	65% of deductible	75% of deductible	100% of deductible limited to $2,650	100% of deductible limited to $5,250
Catch-Up Contribution Available	No		Yes $600 for 2005 $700 for 2006 $800 for 2007 $900 for 2008 $1,000 for 2009 and beyond	
Penalty for Nonqualified Expenditures	Ordinary income tax on earnings and 15% penalty if owner is < 65		Ordinary income tax on earnings and 10% penalty if owner is < 65	

VOLUNTARY EMPLOYEES BENEFICIARY ASSOCIATION (VEBA)

A **Voluntary Employees' Beneficiary Association (VEBA)** is a welfare benefit plan into which employers deposit funds that will be used to provide specified employee benefits in the future. Technically, the VEBA is either a trust or a corporation set up by an employer to hold funds used to pay benefits under an employer benefit plan. The payments made to the VEBA are deductible by the employer for the year the contributions are made, and the income of the VEBA is income tax exempt provided the VEBA meets the requirements of the IRC.

Application and Benefits

By creating and funding a VEBA, an employer can reduce his income tax burden by accelerating an income tax deduction for the payment of welfare type benefits that would have been funded by the employer in the future. An employer can also potentially reduce his future cash flow and the total cost of the benefits as the earnings within the VEBA are not taxed, which will provide the employer with additional funds to pay the benefit' costs.

VEBAs also provide employees with benefit security, because after the funds are deposited into the VEBA, the funds can only be used for the exclusive benefit of the employees, are beyond the reach of the employer's creditors, and generally cannot revert to the employer.

CONTRIBUTIONS

The level of annual contributions to the VEBA in order to fund benefits is determined actuarially. This amount is paid annually or in more frequent installments if the employer desires and, provided the plan meets the qualification requirements, is fully deductible by the employer in the year of the contribution.

VEBA PROVISIONS

EXHIBIT 14.5

VEBAs Can Provide	VEBAs Cannot Provide
• Life insurance before and after retirement	• Savings
• Other survivor benefits	• Retirement
• Sickness and accident benefits	• Deferred compensation
• Other benefits including vacation and recreation benefits	• Coverage of expenses such as commuting expenses
• Severance benefits paid through a severance pay plan	• Accident or homeowners insurance covering damage to property
• Unemployment and job training benefits	• Other items unrelated to maintenance of the employee's earning power
• Disaster benefits	
• Legal service payment for credits	

SALARY CONTINUATION PLANS

A **salary continuation plan** is an arrangement between an employer and an employee where the employer agrees to continue to pay an employee after his retirement or to the employee's spouse if the employee dies prior to retiring. A salary continuation plan can be provided on a discriminatory basis and provides the benefit of shifting the income to the employee to a period when the tax burden is not as heavy (i.e., retirement).

When the payments are made from the salary continuation plan, the value is included in an employee's gross income, is subjected to payroll tax, and is deductible by the employer. Some employers fund the salary continuation plan through the use of a permanent life insurance policy on the employee. Premiums for this type of insurance are not deductible by the employer, but amounts paid to the employee or to the employee's dependents are deductible by the employer at the time of payment.

GROUP LONG-TERM CARE INSURANCE

The premium payments for qualified group long-term care insurance are tax deductible if paid by the employer and tax-free to the employee (see below for a discussion of self-employed individuals). In addition to the tax advantages, group long-term care insurance generally also provides the following advantages:

- Lower rates than individual policies (generally 30% - 60% less);
- Guaranteed coverage for all employees, even those who might not be insurable under an individual policy;
- Increase eligibility for extended family members including parents, grandparents, and in-laws;
- The policy must be guaranteed renewable;
- The average can be provided in a discriminatory manner; and
- "Qualified" benefits are non-taxable to the recipient of the care.

To be a qualified long-term care insurance plan, the plan must meet the provisions of the IRC, specifically the plan must:

- Only provide long term care insurance coverage;
- Not duplicate benefits paid by Medicare;
- The plan must be guaranteed renewable; and
- Only pay benefits when the employee or beneficiary of the plan is certified by a licensed health care practitioner as chronically ill.

Long-term care premiums cannot be paid for within a cafeteria plan or flexible spending account nor can the premium payment be made with pretax employee salary deferral. If, however, the employee pays the premiums with after-tax dollars, the employee may deduct, as an itemized medical expense deduction, the costs on his income tax return for the year. The deduction limit is the lesser of the premium paid or the amount corresponding to the employee's age in the table below:[4]

ELIGIBLE LONG-TERM CARE PREMIUMS FOR 2005

EXHIBIT 14.6

Age	Maximum Deductible Amount for 2005
≤ 40	$270
41 - 50	$510
51 - 60	$1,020
61 - 70	$2,720
≥ 71	$3,400

Self-Employed Individuals

Self-employed individuals as well as individuals that are considered self employed, including partners of partnerships and members of limited liability companies that are taxed as partnerships, must include the cost of long term care insurance paid by the employer in their gross income. The individual will be eligible for the income tax deduction as discussed above. The premiums paid for by the plan for any other employees who are not considered self-employed will continue to be a deductible business expense for the employer that is not included in the employee's income.

GROUP RETIREMENT PLANNING SERVICES

An employer may exclude from an employee's gross income the value of any retirement planning advice or information he provides to the employee or his or her spouse if the employer maintains a qualified retirement plan. In addition to employer plan advice and information, the services provided may include general advice and information on retirement.

Quick Quiz

Highlight the answer to these questions:

1. A salary continuation plan allows employees to shift income to future years.
   a. True
   b. False

2. Long-term care plans are frequently a benefit option of a cafeteria or FSA plan.
   a. True
   b. False

3. An employer can exclude from an employee's gross income the value of any retirement planning advice provided to an employee whether or not the employer has a retirement plan.
   a. True
   b. False

True, False, False.

4. IRC Section 213(d)(10) adjusted for inflation. See Rev. Proc. 2004-71.

However, the exclusion does not apply to the value of services for tax preparation, accounting, legal, or brokerage services.

EMPLOYER/EMPLOYEE INSURANCE ARRANGEMENTS

BUSINESS CONTINUATION (BUY/SELL) PLANS

In the case of the death of a key employer or business owner, business continuation plans provide the business with funds necessary to sustain the business or provides the surviving business owners the funds to buy the interest of the decedent. Buy/sell agreements are generally funded with insurance, although this is not required, and typically have the following key elements:

- a description of the event that puts them in force;
- a funding arrangement; and
- a predetermined valuation formula or convention.

Premiums on the life insurance policy may be paid by the partners, partnership, stockholders, or corporation that would receive the death benefit, but the premium payments are not tax deductible regardless of the payer. Under an entity plan, the firm is the owner and beneficiary of the policy, but the premiums paid are not tax deductible.

Key Concepts

Underline/highlight the answers to these questions as you read:

1. What are business continuation plans, and what are the income tax consequences associated with such plans?

2. What are the tax implications of business overhead disability plans?

3. What is split-dollar life insurance, and what are the income tax consequences associated with such plans?

4. What is key person insurance, and what are the income tax consequences associated with such plans?

Cross Purchase Life Insurance

Death or disability of a proprietor, partner, or shareholder of a closely-held business may cause serious business problems including liquidation, continuity of management issues, and possible dissolution of the business (proprietorship and partnership). It is appropriate to plan for the sale of the interests of any owner/key person in advance of death or disability with business buy-sell agreements. These agreements can be created without insurance funding, but usually the surviving owners or partners do not have sufficient liquid assets to fund without insurance.

A solid buy-sell agreement will detail the triggering events, such as death or disability; will describe the valuation methodology either by formula or process; and will maintain a funding mechanism. One such funding mechanism is cross purchase life insurance. Under **cross purchase life insurance**, a partner or shareholder purchases a sufficient amount of life insurance on the lives of each other partner or shareholder to assure sufficient liquidity to buy out the deceased or disabled partner or shareholder's interest.

EXAMPLE 14.8

A and B are partners. They conclude that the partnership is worth $500,000. Each partner buys a $250,000 life insurance policy on the other and enters into an agreement binding on the respective heirs to sell the partnership interest to the surviving partner for $250,000 in the event of one of their deaths.

One problem with cross purchase life insurance is that when the number of partners or shareholders increases arithmetically, the number of policies increases geometrically. (Four partners equal twelve policies). The number of policies equals the number of partners times the number of partners minus one [n x (n - 1)]. (Example: 4 partners; 4 x 3 = 12 policies). Another potential problem is the cost difference in funding a policy for older partners or shareholders (more expensive) versus that of funding a policy for younger partners or shareholders (less expensive). The premiums of the policy are not tax deductible, and the death benefit proceeds are usually not included in the recipient's taxable income.

A cross purchase life insurance plan does provide the owners with a new adjusted taxable basis equal to the value set forth in the buy-sell agreement in the interest purchased. It does not change the basis in the interest they owned before the death of the partner or shareholder; it only increases the basis in the new interest.

Entity Insurance

Entity insurance is also referred to as stock redemption if the entity is a corporation. Entity insurance is an alternative to the cross purchase arrangement. The entity itself purchases the life insurance policies on each partner or shareholder. The advantage of entity insurance is that the number of policies is reduced to one policy per partner or shareholder. The life insurance premiums are not tax deductible, and the proceeds are not includible in the entity's taxable income. Because the entity, rather than the surviving owners as individuals, is purchasing the interest from the decedent with entity insurance, the surviving owners do not receive a new adjusted taxable basis in the interest purchased.

BUSINESS DISABILITY PLANS

Disability overhead insurance is designed to cover the expenses that are usual and necessary expenses in the operation of a business should the owner become disabled. Premiums are deductible as a business expense, and benefits payable from the plan are taxable income to the entity. Disability buyout policies are policies to cover the value of an individual's interest in the business should they become disabled.

SPLIT-DOLLAR ARRANGEMENT

A split-dollar arrangement is a discriminatory benefit plan using life insurance. The employer and employee share the cost of a life insurance policy on the employee (usually permanent insurance such as whole life insurance or variable universal life insurance). Such arrangements are typically used by businesses to provide low cost insurance to key employees. A **split-dollar life insurance** arrangement is generally structured in one of either of the two following ways:
  1. The endorsement method, or
  2. The collateral assignment method

The Endorsement Method

Under a split-dollar life insurance plan using the endorsement method, the employer is the owner of the life insurance policy on the employee and the employer pays the premium of the life insurance policy. The employer withholds the right in the plan to be repaid for all of its premium either at the employee's death or the surrender of the life insurance policy. Usually any death benefit or cash surrender value in excess of the employer's refund is paid to the policy beneficiaries.

The Collateral Assignment Method

Under a split-dollar life insurance plan using the collateral assignment method, the employee is the owner of the life insurance policy and the employer makes a loan to the employee to pay the premiums of the policy. In this case, at the death of the employee or at the surrender of the policy, the employer loan will be repaid and any excess will be paid to the policy beneficiaries.

Uses of Split-Dollar Life Insurance

A split-dollar life insurance policy is appropriate when an employer wishes to provide an executive with life insurance benefits at a low cost and low cash outlay to the executive (the premiums are essentially paid for by the employer). Split-dollar life insurance plans are best suited for executives in their 30s, 40s, and early 50s since the plan requires a reasonable duration to build adequate policy cash value and the cost to the executive at later ages is usually prohibitive. Split-dollar life insurance can be used as an alternative to an insurance-financed nonqualified deferred compensation plan or in conjunction with a nonqualified, unfunded, deferred compensation plan. A split-dollar policy is also effective when an employer is seeking a totally selective executive fringe benefit as the nondiscrimination rules do not apply.

A split-dollar plan allows an executive to receive the benefit of current value using employer funds with minimal or no tax cost to the executive. In most types of split-dollar plans, the employer's outlay is at all times fully secured. Upon the employee's death or termination of employment, the employer is reimbursed from policy proceeds for its premium outlays. The net cost to the employer for the plan is merely the loss of the net after-tax income the funds could have earned while the plan was in effect.

Income Taxation Issues

The income tax treatment of split-dollar life insurance arrangements will be determined under one of two sets of rules depending on who owns the policy. If the executive, or someone designated by the executive, owns the life insurance policy, then the loan taxation rules apply. If the employer owns the policy, the economic benefit rules apply.

If the executive owns the policy, the employer's premium payments are treated as below market loans from the employer to the executive. Consequently, unless the executive is required to pay the employer market-rate interest on the loan, the executive will be taxed on the difference between market-rate interest and the actual interest charged.

If the employer is the owner of the policy, the employer's premium payments are treated as providing taxable economic benefits to the executive. The executive recognizes as taxable income the value of life insurance coverage, as well as any increase in equity currently accessible to the executive. By taxing the executive on the increase in equity each year, this arrangement is discouraged.

Death Benefit - Transfer for Value

Death benefits payable from a split-dollar life insurance plan including both the employer's share and the employee's beneficiary's share are generally received income tax free. However, the tax-free nature of the death proceeds is lost if the policy has been transferred for value. The transfer of an insurance policy is exempt from the transfer for value rules and will not cause the loss of the death proceeds' tax-free nature if the transfer is one of the statutorily defined exceptions. Examples of exceptions to the transfer for value rule are:

- A transfer of the policy to the insured.
- A transfer to a partner of the insured or to a partnership of which the insured is a partner.
- A transfer to a corporation of which the insured is a shareholder or officer.
- A transfer in which the transferee's basis is determined, in whole or in part, by reference to the transferor's basis (e.g., a substituted or carryover basis).

Estate Consequences of Split-Dollar Life Insurance

Incidents of ownership will cause inclusion in the gross estate if the decedent retained the ownership or had the right to name or change the beneficiary. Inclusion in the gross estate could result from a policy transferred or assigned with the 3-year period prior to the insured/owner's death.

KEY PERSON LIFE AND DISABILITY INSURANCE

Key person life and disability insurance covers employees who are considered critical to the success of a business and whose death or disability might cause financial loss to the company. The company has an insurable interest in the person. Therefore, the company pays the premiums and is the beneficiary of the insurance policy. The premiums are not deductible, and the benefits are not taxable.

Quick Quiz

Highlight the answer to these questions:

1. The premiums paid for a cross purchase life insurance policy is deductible by the payor.
    a. True
    b. False

2. An entity must include in income any benefits received from a business over-head disability plan.
    a. True
    b. False

3. Key person insurance premiums are not deductible by the employer until the death benefit is paid.
    a. True
    b. False

False, True, False.

Key Terms

Archer Medical Savings Account (MSA) - A medical savings account available for employers with 50 or less employees and self-employed individuals (must have been established by 12/31/05). The account allows participants to make pretax contributions (subject to limitations) to the account and benefit from tax-free earnings provided they are covered under a high deductible health insurance policy. Further, if the funds are utilized for qualified medical expenses, the distributions from the plan will not be taxable.

Cafeteria Plan - A written plan where the employee may choose to receive cash as compensation or, alternatively, the employee may choose from among a range of tax-free fringe benefits.

Combined Omnibus Budget Reconciliation Act of 1986 (COBRA) - Requires an employer that employes 20 or more people in a typical business day and has a health insurance plan to continue to provide health insurance coverage under that health insurance plan to covered employees and qualified dependants following the occurrence of a statutorily defined qualifying event.

Cross Purchase Life Insurance - A partner or shareholder purchases a sufficient amount of life insurance on the lives of each other partner or shareholder to assure sufficient liquidity to buyout a deceased partner or shareholder's interest.

Disability Insurance - Insurance that provides benefits in the form of periodic payments for a person who is unable to work due to sickness or accidental injury.

Disability Overhead Insurance - Insurance that is designed to cover the expenses that are usual and necessary expenses in the operation of a business should the insured owner or key employee become disabled.

Entity Insurance - Insurance in which the entity purchases a life insurance policy on the life of each partner or shareholder that is used for buyouts triggered by death of a shareholder or partner.

Flexible Spending Account (FSA) - A cafeteria plan under which employees can choose between receiving cash or deferring income tax-free to fund the cost of certain employee selected benefits. If the participant does not utilize the money in the account by the end of the year, the participant forfeits the deferred funds.

Group Term Life Insurance - Pure insurance protection purchased as a group that pays a predetermined sum if the insured dies during a specified period of time (i.e., the term, which may be 1, 5, 10, 20 years or longer). The value of the premiums, up to $50,000 of death benefit coverage, provided by an employer may be excluded from an employee's gross income.

Health Savings Accounts (HSAs) - A medical savings account, similar to an MSA but less restrictive, that allows anyone with a high deductible health insurance plan to make pretax contributions (subject to limitations). The earnings within the account and the value of the contributions will not be taxed to the extent they are used to pay for qualifying medical expenses.

Key Terms

Key Person Life and Disability Insurance - Life insurance coverage for employees who are considered critical to the success of a business and whose death might cause financial loss to the company.

Salary Continuation Plan - An arrangement between an employer and an employee where the employer agrees to continue to pay an employee after his retirement or to the employee's spouse if the employee dies prior to retirement.

Self-Insured Plan - A plan that reimburses employees for medical expenses not covered by an accident or health insurance policy.

Split-Dollar Arrangement - A single life insurance policy in which two parties, employer and employee, have an ownership interest. The two parties generally split ownership, premiums, and beneficiaries any way they wish.

Voluntary Employees' Beneficiary Association (VEBA) - A welfare benefit plan into which employers deposit funds that will be used to provide specified employee benefits in the future. The deposits are deductible for the employer at the date of the contribution rather than at the date when the employee benefits are provided.

1. Discuss the tax implications of employer-provided group medical plans.

2. Describe COBRA and discuss the tax implications of employer paid premiums.

3. Describe the requirements for a life insurance policy to be considered group term life insurance.

4. Discuss the tax implications of employer-provided group term life insurance.

5. Discuss the tax implications of employer-provided group disability insurance.

6. Describe cafeteria plans and discuss how are they used to provide employer benefits.

7. Discuss the tax implications of employer-provided cafeteria plans.

8. Describe Flexible Spending Accounts (FSAs).

9. Discuss the tax implications of employer provided Flexible Spending Accounts.

10. Discuss the tax implications of employer provided Archer MSAs and when they can be established.

11. Describe VEBA's and discuss the tax implications of payments made by the employer.

12. Discuss the tax implications of employer provided salary continuation plans.

13. Discuss the tax implications of employer-provided group long-term care insurance.

14. Discuss the tax implications of employer-provided group retirement planning services.

15. Describe business continuation plans and describe the income tax consequences associated with such plans.

16. Discuss the tax implications of business overhead disability plans.

17. Describe split-dollar life insurance and discuss the income tax consequences associated with such plans.

18. Describe key person insurance and discuss the income tax consequences associated with such plans.

1. Medical Trials Inc. has a cafeteria plan. Full-time employees are permitted to select any combination of the benefits listed below, but the total value received by each employee must be $6,500 a year or less.

    1. Group medical and hospitalization insurance for employee only, $3,600 a year.
    2. Group medical and hospitalization insurance for employee's spouse and dependents, $1,200 additional a year.
    3. Child-care payments, actual cost not to exceed $5,000.
    4. Cash required to bring the total of benefits and cash to $6,500.
    5. Universal variable life insurance $1,000.

    Which of the following statements is true? (All employees are full time)

    a. James chooses to receive $6,500 cash because his wife's employer provides medical benefits for him. James has $2,900 of taxable income ($6,500 - $3,600).
    b. Matt chooses 1, 2, 5, and $700 cash. He must include $700 in taxable income.
    c. Randy chooses 1 and 2 and $1,700 in child care. He must include the $1,700 in gross income.
    d. Robin chooses 1 and 2 and $1,700 cash. Robin must include $1,700 in taxable income.

2. Which of the following circumstances suggest the use of a cafeteria plan?

    1. A cafeteria plan is appropriate when the employee mix is comprised only of older employees with families who need maximum medical and life insurance benefits.
    2. A cafeteria plan is appropriate when employers want to choose the benefit package most suited to their employee's individual needs.
    3. A cafeteria plan is appropriate when an employer seeks to maximize employee satisfaction with the benefit package, thereby maximizing the employer's benefit from its compensation expenditures.
    4. A cafeteria plan is appropriate for a small employer who does not have much money to spend on benefits.
    a. 3 only.
    b. 4 only.
    c. 1, 2, and 4.
    d. 1, 2, 3, and 4.

3. Which of the following are advantages of cafeteria plans?

   1. Cafeteria plans help to give employees an appreciation of the value of their benefit package.
   2. The flexibility of a cafeteria benefit package helps to meet varied employee needs.
   3. Cafeteria plans can help control employer costs for the benefit package because the cost of benefits that employees do not need is minimized.
   4. Cafeteria plans are less complex and less expensive to design and administer than general group benefit plans.

      a. 2 only.
      b. 1 and 2.
      c. 1, 2, and 3.
      d. 1, 2, 3, and 4.

4. Jane is covered by a $90,000 group-term life insurance policy, her daughter is the sole beneficiary. Jane's employer pays the entire premium for the policy; the uniform annual premium is $0.60 per $1,000 per month of coverage. How much, if any, is W-2 taxable income to Jane resulting from the insurance?

      a. $0.
      b. $24.
      c. $288.
      d. $648.

5. What is the maximum number of employees that a company with a health plan can have and not be subject to the COBRA rules?

      a. 10.
      b. 15.
      c. 19.
      d. 20.

6. Which of the following premiums for health insurance provided by an employer are excludable from income tax by the employer?

   1. Premiums for the employee if currently employed.
   2. Premiums for the employee's spouse.
   3. Premiums for the employee's dependents other than a spouse.
   4. Premiums for the employee if retired.

      a. 1 only.
      b. 1 and 2.
      c. 1, 2, and 3.
      d. 1, 2, 3, and 4.

7. Employer-sponsored life insurance is usually referred to as group life insurance. Which type of life insurance (offered as group life) is beneficial to both the employer and the employee from a tax standpoint?

   a. Term life insurance.

   b. Ordinary life insurance.

   c. Universal life.

   d. Single premium whole life insurance.

8. Life insurance used to fund a three person partnership buy/sell agreement using a cross purchase technique:

   a. Will have the same number of policies as an entity plan.

   b. Will be paid for with tax-deductible dollars.

   c. Will require three policies.

   d. Will require six policies.

9. Split-dollar life insurance is:

   a. An insurance arrangement in which the employee pays the cost of the premium and the employee names the employer as the beneficiary.

   b. An insurance arrangement in which the employer and the employee share the cost of the life insurance on the employee and the portion of the premium that is paid by the employer is the value of the term life portion of the policy.

   c. An insurance arrangement in which the employee pays the majority of the premium while the employer names the beneficiary.

   d. An insurance arrangement in which the employer is the owner of the policy and is also the beneficiary to the extent of the premiums paid by the employer.

10. The beneficiary of key person life insurance is usually:

    a. The spouse of the employee.

    b. The employee's spouse and dependants.

    c. The company.

    d. The estate of the employee.

11. A business valued at $3,000,000 has 3 partners. Each of the 3 partners buys a $500,000 life insurance policy on each of the other partners. Which of the following is true?

    1. This is an example of an entity purchase plan.

    2. This is an example of a cross purchase plan.

    3. The policies are under funded.

        a. 1 only.

        b. 2 only.

        c. 1 and 3.

        d. 2 and 3.

12. NOTCM partnership has 5 partners who have entered into a binding buy/sell agreement that requires any surviving partners to purchase the partnership interest of any partner to die. The partnership uses an entity approach to fund this arrangement. How many policies are required to satisfy this arrangement?

        a. 1.

        b. 5.

        c. 10.

        d. 20.

13. Wallace and Associates is considering implementing a buy/sell agreement where each partner purchases a life insurance policy on each of the other partners. Which one of the following statements is correct given this information?

        a. The partners are entering into an entity redemption agreement.

        b. Upon the death of an owner, the life insurance proceeds will be used to buy out the decedent's share of the partnership. Those life insurance proceeds are taxable as ordinary income.

        c. The amount of insurance per policy will equal the value of the partnership.

        d. The partners are entering into a cross-purchase agreement.

14. HMO Inc. is paying the premium for long-term care policies for their 250 employees. How are these payments treated for federal income tax purposes?

        a. Payments for group premiums for long-term care are tax deductible to the employer and not taxable income to the employee.

        b. Payments for group premiums for long-term care are tax deductible to the employer but are taxable income to the employee based on the coverage schedule.

        c. Payments for the group premiums for long-term care are not tax deductible to the employer and not taxable income to the employee.

        d. Payments for the group premiums for long-term care are not tax deductible to the employer but are taxable income to the employee based on the coverage schedule.

Glossary

A

Actual Contribution Percentage Test (ACP) - A nondiscrimination test that limits the sum of employee after-tax contributions and employer matching contributions for the HC based on the sum of employee after-tax contributions and employer matching contributions of the NHC.

Actual Deferral Percentage Test (ADP) - A nondiscrimination test that limits employee elective deferrals for the highly compensated employees (HC) based on the elective deferrals of non-highly compensated employees (NHC).

Actuary - An expert professional who makes quantitative calculations and assumptions about inflation, wage increases, life expectancy of the assumed retirees, investment returns on plan assets, mortality rates for retirees, and forfeitures resulting from termination in order to determine funding for a retirement plan.

Adequate Consideration Standard - Fair market value determined in good faith.

Adjusted Gross Income (AGI) - A tax return amount that includes an individual's income less certain deductions, known as "above-the-line" deductions. AGI is calculated before subtracting the standard or itemized deductions and the personal and dependency exemptions. The calculated AGI affects the deductibility of traditional IRA contributions and the ability to make Roth IRA contributions.

Adjusted Taxable Basis - The portion of a distribution that is not subject to income tax. Usually, the return of after-tax contributions or nondeductible contributions.

Adoption Assistance Program - An employee-provided program that pays adoption expenses up to $10,390 in 2005. The employee is not taxed on the payments or reimbursements made on his behalf.

Age-Based Profit Sharing Plan - A qualified profit sharing plan that uses a combination of age and compensation as the basis for allocating the contribution to a participant's account.

AIME (Average Indexed Monthly Earnings) - The adjustment, or index, to a worker's historic earnings to create an equivalent current dollar value.

Alimony - Support payments from one ex-spouse to the other. Alimony received is considered earned income for purposes of making IRA contributions.

Annuity Contracts - While the contracts are not specifically defined in the Internal Revenue Code, an annuity contract must be purchased for the employee from an insurance company and may give a fixed benefit or a variable benefit depending on the performance of the investment. Any contract or certificate that is transferable to a person other than a trustee is not an annuity contract.

Anti-Alienation - An ERISA afforded protection for qualified plans that prohibits any action that may cause a qualified plan's assets to be assigned, garnished, levied, or subject to bankruptcy proceedings. Exceptions to the anti-alienation rule apply for tax levies and QDROs.

Archer Medical Savings Account (MSA) - A medical savings account available for employers with 50 or less employees and self-employed individuals (must have been established by 12/31/05). The account allows participants to make pretax contributions (subject to limitations) to the account and benefit from tax-free earnings provided they are covered under a high deductible health insurance policy. Further, if the funds are utilized for qualified medical expenses, the distributions from the plan will not be taxable.

Average Benefits Percentage Test - One requirement of the average benefits coverage test that requires the average benefit percent of the nonhighly compensated employees to be at least 70 percent of the average benefit percentage of the highly compensated employees.

Average Benefits Test - A qualified plan coverage test that determines whether the plan adequately benefits the nonhighly compensated employees by comparing the benefits received by the nonhighly compensated to the benefits of the highly compensated employees and also determines whether the employee classification is nondiscriminatory. The test consists of the Average Benefits percentage test and the nondiscriminatory classification test.

Beneficiary - The person(s) entitled to receive the death benefit of a life insurance policy or qualified plan at the insured's death.

Benefit Periods - Begins on the first day an individual receives services as a patient in a hospital or skilled nursing facility and ends after 60 consecutive days without further skilled care.

Black Scholes Method - An option valuation model.

Blockage Discount - A reduction in the fair market value of a large block of stock due to the fact that a transfer of a large block of stock is less marketable than smaller amounts of stock.

Business Premises of the Employer - The employee's place of employment.

Cafeteria Plan - A written plan where the employee may choose to receive cash as compensation or, alternatively, the employee may choose from among a range of tax-free fringe benefits.

Capital Gain Property - Property that, when sold, results in either capital gain or Section 1231 gain.

Capital Needs Analysis - The process of calculating the amount of investment capital needed at retirement to maintain the preretirement lifestyle and mitigate the impact of inflation during the retirement years.

Capital Preservation Model (CP) - A capital needs analysis method that assumes that at client's life expectancy, the client has exactly the same account balance as he did at the beginning of retirement.

Cash Balance Pension Plan - A defined benefit pension plan that shares many of the characteristics of defined contribution plans but provides specific defined benefits based on a mandatory contribution and earnings rate.

Cash or Deferred Arrangement (CODA) - Permits an employee to defer a portion of their salary on a pretax basis to a qualified plan or receive the salary as current taxable income.

Cashless Exercise - An exercise of an option where the option holder does not utilize any cash.

Catch-Up Contribution - A contribution that allows those nearing retirement to increase their deferral contributions to improve their financial situation for retirement. An elective contribution for employees 50 and over that allows them to increase their elective deferral limit by up to $4,000 for 2005.

Cents per Mile Rule - To determine the value of the personal use of an employer-provided automobile, multiply the standard mileage rate (40.5 cents for 2005) by the total miles the employee drives the vehicle for personal purposes.

Cliff Vesting Schedule - A vesting schedule that provides the participant's full rights to the plan's assets immediately upon the passage of a certain number of years.

COLA - The cost-of-living adjustments applied to Social Security benefits.

Combined Omnibus Budget Reconciliation Act of 1986 (COBRA) - Requires an employer that employes 20 or more people in a typical business day and has a health insurance plan to continue to provide health insurance coverage under that health insurance plan to covered employees and qualified dependants following the occurrence of a statutorily defined qualifying event.

Commuting Rule - To determine the value of the personal use of an employer-provided vehicle, multiply each one way commute from the employee's home to work or from work to home by $1.50.

Constructive Receipt - An income tax concept that establishes when income is includible by a taxpayer and therefore subject to income tax. Income is constructively received in the taxable year during which it is credited to the employee's account, set apart for him, or otherwise made available so that he may draw upon it at any time or so that he could have drawn upon it during the taxable year if notice of intention to withdraw had been given.

Contributions - Payments to an IRA.

Conversion - When a traditional IRA is converted to a Roth IRA. At the date of conversion, an individual includes the fair market value of the traditional IRA into their adjusted gross income.

Corrective Distribution - A distribution to satisfy the ADP or ACP test that reduces the elective deferrals or contributions of the HC employees by distributing or returning the funds to the HC employees.

Covered Compensation Limit - The maximum employee compensation that may be considered for contributions to qualified plans or the accrual of benefits to a qualified plan. For 2005, the covered compensation limit is $210,000.

Covered Employee - An employee who benefits from a qualified plan during the year.

Credit for Prior Service - To give employees credit for years of service (with the plan sponsor) prior to the establishment of the qualified plan.

Cross Purchase Life Insurance - A partner or shareholder purchases a sufficient amount of life insurance on the lives of each other partner or shareholder to assure sufficient liquidity to buyout a deceased partner or shareholder's interest.

Currently Insured Workers - A worker who has earned at least six quarters of coverage out of the previous 13 quarters for Social Security.

Custodial Accounts - Accounts generally maintained by a bank or other financial institution for the benefit of participants.

Custodians - Brokerage company, bank, or mutual fund company that holds an individual's IRA.

D

Deferred Compensation Arrangements - An arrangement to pay an executive compensation in a future year.

Defined Benefit Plan - A qualified retirement plan that provides its participants with pre-determined formula-based benefits at retirement.

Defined Contribution Plan - A qualified retirement plan that provides its participants the benefit of tax-deferred growth for contributions and earnings in the plan.

"De Minimus" Fringe Benefit - A benefit of any property or service provided by an employer to an employee that is so small in value that it makes accounting for it unreasonable or administratively impracticable when taking into account the frequency with which similar fringes are provided by the employer to all employees.

Department of Labor - Governmental department charged with enforcing the rules governing the conduct of plan managers, investment of plan assets, reporting and disclosure of plan information, enforcement of the fiduciary provisions of the law, and workers' benefit rights as regulated by ERISA.

Dependent Care Assistance - Assistance that applies to household and dependent care services paid for or provided by the employer to an employee under a dependent care assistance program covering employees. The employee is not taxed on the value of the program or service paid on his behalf under the program (up to $5,000 per year).

Determination Letter - A request filed with the IRS requesting a determination on a particular topic. In the case of a retirement plan, they are used when a plan is adopted, amended, or terminated to assure the plan sponsor that the qualified plan complies with applicable provisions.

Dilution - The reduction in the monetary value or voting power of an owner's stock as a result of contributions to stock bonus plans and ESOPs.

Direct Rollover - Occurs when the plan trustee distributes the account balance directly to the trustee of the recipient account.

Disability Benefit - A Social Security benefit available to recipients who have a severe physical or mental impairment that is expected to prevent them from performing "substantial" work for at least a year or result in death. To qualify for these benefits, the recipient must have the sufficient amount of Social Security credits.

Disability Insurance - Insurance that provides benefits in the form of periodic payments for a person who is unable to work due to sickness or accidental injury.

Disability Insurance (DI) Trust Fund - The trust fund that pays benefits to workers with disabilities and their families. It is funded by 0.90 percent of an individual's taxable earnings up to $90,000.

Disability Overhead Insurance - Insurance that is designed to cover the expenses that are usual and necessary expenses in the operation of a business should the insured owner or key employee become disabled.

Discretionary - The choice for a plan sponsor of a profit sharing plan as to the amount and frequency of a contribution.

Disqualifying Disposition - If stock acquired after exercising an ISO is disposed before either two years from the date of the grant or one year from the date of exercise.

Distress Termination - Termination that occurs when the employer is in financial difficulty and is unable to continue with a defined benefit plan.

Diversified Investment Portfolios - An investment portfolio invested in a broad range of investment classes to reduce investment risk.

Early Withdrawal Penalty - A 10 percent penalty on distributions made before the participant attains the age of 59½ (exceptions apply).

Earned Income - Any type of compensation where the individual has performed some level of service for an employer or is considered self-employed.

Economic Benefit Doctrine - An employee will be taxed on funds or property set aside for the employee if the funds or property are unrestricted and nonforfeitable even if the employee was not given a choice to receive the income currently.

Eligible 457 Plans - 457(b) plans for governmental and tax-exempt organizations under 501(c) that allow employees to defer income taxation on savings for retirement into future years. Eligible plans are available to most of an employers employees.

Employee Census - A matrix of information that is used in plan selection and identifies each employee, their age, compensation, number of years of employment, and any ownership interest in the plan sponsor.

Employee Deferral Contributions - Pretax employee contributions to a qualified retirement plan with a CODA. The employee must chose to defer the compensation before earning the compensation.

Employee Plans Compliance Resolution System (EPCRS) - The system provided by the IRS that allows plan sponsors to voluntarily correct any disqualifying actions within two years of the plan year end in which the problem occurred.

Employee Retirement Income and Security Act (ERISA) - An act enacted by Congress in 1974 because of various abuses by plan sponsors to provide protection for an employee's retirement assets, both from creditors and from plan sponsors.

Employee Stock Ownership Plan (ESOP) - A qualified profit sharing plan that utilizes employer contributions to the plan to purchase the stock of the employer's company and allocates the ownership to the plan participants.

Employee Stock Purchase Plan (ESPP) - A plan designed to benefit all or a large portion of an employer's employees that gives employees an incentive to buy employer stock by allowing the employees to purchase the stock at a discounted price and receive favorable tax treatment for any gains if the stock meets certain holding period requirements.

Employer Matching Contributions - Employer provided contributions to a qualified retirement plan, usually a 401(k) plan that are based on the employee contributions.

Entity Insurance - Insurance in which the entity purchases a life insurance policy on the life of each partner or shareholder that is used for buyouts triggered by death of a shareholder or partner.

ERISA Attorney - An attorney who specializes in ERISA law.

Excess Benefit Plans - A type of SERP that is designed solely to provide benefits in excess of the benefits available in qualified plans based on the limits under IRC Section 415.

Fair Market Value - The price that a willing buyer would pay a willing seller, both having reasonable knowledge of the pertinent facts and neither under duress.

Family Benefit - A Social Security benefit available to certain family members of workers eligible for retirement or disability benefits.

FICA (Federal Insurance Contributions Act) - A law allowing Social Security taxes, including Medicare taxes, to be deducted from employee's paychecks.

Fiduciary - An individual that has a special relationship of trust, confidence, and responsibility in certain financial obligations.

15-Year Rule - A special catch-up provision for 403(b) plan participants that have worked for the plan sponsor for 15 years. The catch-up allows them to defer up to an additional $15,000 during the plan year.

50/40 Coverage Test - A coverage test applicable only to a defined benefit pension plans that requires the plan to cover for every day during the plan year the lesser of 50 employees or 40% of all eligible employees.

Final 3-Year Catch-Up Provision - A special catch-up provision for public and private 457(b) plans that allows an individual to defer an additional $14,000 for 2005 ($15,000 for 2006) to the plan in their final three years before the plan's normal retirement age.

Fixed Amortization - The payment is calculated over the participant's life expectancy if single, or the joint life expectancy if married, and the interest rate is reasonable.

Fixed Annuitization - The participant takes distributions of the account over a number of years determined by dividing the account balance by an annuity factor using a reasonable interest rate and mortality table.

Flat Amount Formula - A benefit formula of a defined benefit pension plan that provides each of its participants with an equal dollar benefit at retirement.

Flat Percentage Formula - A benefit formula of a defined benefit pension plan that provides all plan participants with a benefit equal to a fixed percentage of the participant's salary, usually the final salary or an average of the participant's highest salaries.

Flexible Spending Account (FSA) - A cafeteria plan under which employees can choose between receiving cash or deferring income tax-free to fund the cost of certain employee selected benefits. If the participant does not utilize the money in the account by the end of the year, the participant forfeits the deferred funds.

Forfeitures - The percentage or amount of a participant's accrued benefit that was not vested to the employee at the employee's termination from the plan sponsor. The forfeited amount stays in the plan and may be allocated to the other plan participants (defined contribution plan) or reduce future plan costs (defined contribution plan or defined benefit plan).

Forgone Revenue - The lost revenue or opportunity cost incurred by an employer for providing the fringe benefit to the employee.

Form 5304-SIMPLE - The IRS form used to establish a SIMPLE IRA plan when the employees choose the financial institution.

Form 5305-SIMPLE - The IRS form used to establish a SIMPLE IRA plan when the employer chooses the financial institution.

401(k) Wrap Plans - A form of salary reduction plan that enable executives who are subject to salary deferral limitations due to the nondiscrimination rules to contribute higher amounts than otherwise permitted under a 401(k) plan.

457 Plan - A nonqualified deferred compensation plan for employees of state and local government and tax-exempt entities.

Fringe Benefit - A benefit, other than customary taxable wages, provided by an employer to an employee for the employee's performance (in most instances) of services for the employer.

Fully Insured - A worker who has earned 40 quarters of coverage under the Social Security system.

General Safe Harbor Test - A coverage test that requires the employer to cover at least 70% of the nonhighly compensated employees.

Grace Period - If an employer meets the 100 employee limitation in a given year, then the employer will have a two year "grace period" when the employer can exceed the limitation without losing eligibility to maintain the SIMPLE.

Graduated Vesting Schedules - A vesting schedule that provides an employee with full rights to a certain percentage (less than 100%) of benefits after completing a number of years of service and provides the employees with an additional percentage for each additional years of service.

Grant Date - The date of issuance of a stock or option.

Group Term Life Insurance - Pure insurance protection purchased as a group that pays a predetermined sum if the insured dies during a specified period of time (i.e., the term, which may be 1, 5, 10, 20 years or longer). The value of the premiums, up to $50,000 of death benefit coverage, provided by an employer may be excluded from an employee's gross income.

Hardship Distributions - A distribution from a 401(k) plan because the employee has an immediate and heavy financial need and the withdrawal is necessary to satisfy the need. The distribution is taxable and subject to penalties to the extent the participant has other resources to have satisfied the financial need.

Health Savings Accounts (HSAs) - A medical savings account, similar to an MSA but less restrictive, that allows anyone with a high deductible health insurance plan to make pretax contributions (subject to limitations). The earnings within the account and the value of the contributions will not be taxed to the extent they are used to pay for qualifying medical expenses.

Highly Compensated Employee - An employee who is either a more than 5 percent owner at any time during the plan year or preceding plan year, or had compensation in excess of $95,000 for the prior plan year (2005). A special election can be made to count only those employees whose compensation is in excess of $135,000 and are in the top 20% of employees as ranked by compensation.

Hospital Insurance (HI) Trust Fund - The trust fund that pays for services covered under the hospital insurance provisions of Medicare (Part A). It is funded by 1.45 percent of an individual's taxable earnings (no limitation).

I

Incentive Stock Options (ISOs) - A right given to an employee to purchase an employer's common stock at a stated exercise price. If the requirements of IRC Section 422 are met, the employee will not recognize any taxable income at the date of grant. Further, at the date of exercise, the employee will also not be subject to ordinary income tax on the difference between the fair market value of the stock and the exercise price. This difference is a positive adjustment for the alternative minimum tax calculation. When the employee sells the stock subsequent to the exercise, the difference between the sales price of the stock and the original exercise price is considered long-term capital gain and there is a negative adjustment for the alternative minimum tax calculation.

Includible Compensation - An employee's taxable wages and benefits for the most recent year of service.

Indirect Rollover - A distribution to the participant with a subsequent transfer to another qualified account.

Individual Retirement Arrangement (IRA) - Two general types under present law: traditional IRAs, to which both deductible and nondeductible contributions may be made, and Roth IRAs, to which only nondeductible contributions may be made.

Ineligible 457 Plans - 457(f) plans for employees of governmental entities and tax-exempt entities under 501(c)(3). Ineligible plans are only available to highly compensated and management employees.

In-Service Withdrawal - Any withdrawal (from a qualified retirement plan) while the employee is a participant in the plan, not a loan.

Insured - The person whose life is covered by the life insurance contract.

Intangible Property - Stocks, bonds, patents, and copyrights.

Interested Parties - Present employees who are eligible to participate in the plan and present employees who are not eligible for the plan but whose principal place of employment is the same as the principal place of employment of any employee who is eligible to participate.

Involuntary Termination - Termination initiated by the PBGC for a defined benefit plan that is unable to pay benefits from the plan.

IRA Annuity - An annuity contract or endowment contract issued by an insurance company that follows many of the same rules for deductibility of premium payments and the limits for premium payments as a traditional IRA.

IRC Section 83(b) - Elect to include in gross income the difference between the fair market value of restricted stock and its purchase price.

J

Joint Life Expectancy Table - The life expectancy table used to determine a participant's RMD when the participant's sole designated beneficiary is the participant's spouse and that spouse is more than 10 years younger than the participant.

K

Keogh Plan - A qualified plan for a self-employed individual.

Key Employee - Any employee who is a greater than five percent owner, a greater than one percent owner with compensation in excess of $150,000 (not indexed), or an officer with compensation in excess of $135,000 (2005).

Key Person Discount - A reduction in the fair market value of a transferred stock due to an economic reality that the value of the stock will decline if a key person such as the founder, dies or becomes disabled.

Key Person Life and Disability Insurance - Life insurance coverage for employees who are considered critical to the success of a business and whose death might cause financial loss to the company.

L

Lack of Marketability Discount - A reduction in value of transferred asset because the interest is more difficult to sell to the public.

Lease Value Rule - To determine the value of an employer-provided automobile, use the automobile's annual lease value.

Legal Ownership - Possessing legal title to the property.

Lepto-Kurtic - A distribution that appears to be normal but has more area under the two tails than a normal distribution (i.e. fat tails).

Leveraged ESOP - An ESOP that borrows the funds necessary to purchase the employer's stock. The interest and principal repayments on the loan are tax deductible for the employer.

Lump-Sum Death Benefit - A single payment of the life insurance death benefit to a beneficiary.

Lump-Sum Distribution - A complete distribution of a participant's account balance within one taxable year on account of death, disability, attainment of age 59½, or separation from service. Lump-sum distributions from qualified plans are eligible for special taxation options.

M

Mandatory Funding - An amount or percentage that must be contributed to a qualified pension plan by the employer each plan year.

Master Plan - Provides a single trust or custodial account that is jointly used by all adopting employers.

Maximum Family Benefit - The limit on the amount of monthly Social Security benefits that may be paid to a family.

Medicaid - Provides medical assistance for persons with low incomes and resources.

Medicare - A federal health insurance plan for those who have attained full retirement age or have been disabled whether retired or still working.

Minority Discount - A reduction in value of a transferred interest in property because the interest is not a controlling interest.

Modified Adjusted Gross Income (MAGI) (when calculating taxable Social Security) - The sum of an individual's adjusted gross income plus tax exempt interest, including interest earned on savings bonds used for higher education; amounts excluded from the tax payer's income for employer provided adoption assistance; amounts deducted for interest paid for educational loans; amounts deducted as qualified tuition expense; and income earned in a forgone country, a U.S. possession, or Puerto Rico that is excluded from income.

Money Purchase Pension Plan - A defined contribution pension plan that provides for mandatory employer contributions to the plan each year of a fixed percentage of the employees' compensation. The employer does not guarantee a specific retirement benefit.

Monte Carlo Analysis - A mathematical tool used to calculate the success of an individual's retirement portfolio using changing variables.

Net Unrealized Appreciation (NUA) - The appreciation in the value of employer stock after the date of contribution to the plan until the date of distribution.

Net Unrealized Appreciation Treatment - A special taxation treatment for a lump-sum distribution from a qualified plan that treats part of the distribution as capital gain.

New Comparability Plan - A qualified profit sharing plan in which contributions are made to employees' accounts based on their respective classification in the company as defined by the plan sponsor.

No-Additional-Cost Services - Services provided by an employer to an employee that do not cause the employer to incur any substantial additional cost or lost revenue.

Noncontributory Plans - Qualified retirement plans that do not include employee contributions.

Nondiscriminatory - A requirement of all qualified plans. The eligibility rules, coverage requirements, and contributions allocations of a qualified plan cannot discriminate against the rank-and-file employees for the benefit of shareholder, officers, and highly compensated employees.

Nonelective Contributions - Contributions to a qualified plan on behalf of all eligible employees.

Non-Excludable - An employee who must be considered as eligible to participate in a qualified plan.

Nonqualified Deferred Compensation Plan (NQDC) - A contractual arrangement between the employer and an executive whereby the employer promises to pay the executive a predetermined amount of money sometime in the future.

Nonqualified Plans - Plans that do not meet the requirements of the IRC Section 401(a) and therefore do not have the benefits of qualified plans.

Nonqualified Stock Options (NQSOs) - An option that does not meet the requirements of an incentive stock option. The exercise of an NQSO does not receive favorable long-term capital gains treatment but also does not require the holding period associated with ISOs.

Nonrecognition of Gain Treatment - A delay in the recognition of gain available to owners of a company that sell company stock to an ESOP. The transaction must meet the stated requirements of the IRC and the owner must reinvest the proceeds from the sale within 12 months of the sale into qualified domestic replacement securities.

O

Officer - An administrative executive who is in regular and continued service and has the executive authority normally associated with an officer.

Old Age and Survivor Disability Insurance (OASDI) - An inclusive title given to the Social Security benefit system.

Old Age and Survivors Insurance (OASI) - The trust fund that pays retirement and survivors' benefits funded by 5.30 percent of an individual's taxable earnings up to $90,000.

On Premises Athletic Facility - A gym or other athletic facility such as a tennis court, pool, or golf course that is operated by the employer, located on the employer's business premises, and "substantially all" of the use of the facility is by employees of the employer, their spouses, or their dependent children. The value of the use of on premises athletic facilities is not taxable to the employee as long as its availability is nondiscriminatory.

One Year of Service - 1,000 hours of service with an employer within a 12 month period.

Option Price (Exercise Price) - Usually the fair market value at the grant date.

Ordinary Income Property - Property that, when sold, results in recognition of ordinary income.

P

Pass Through Voting - The voting rights of the stock pass through from the ESOP or the stock bonus plan to the participant.

Payroll Taxes - The combination of OASDI and Medicare tax paid by an employee and employer on an employees compensation.

Pension Benefit Guaranty Corporation (PBGC) - Established in 1974 when President Gerald R. Ford signed the Employee Retirement Income Security Act (ERISA) into law. The PBGC guarantees qualified pension benefits. It is a federal corporation that acts as an insurance provider to maintain the benefits promised to employees by their defined benefit pension plans.

Pension Plan - A qualified retirement plan that pays a benefit, usually determined by a formula, to a plan participant for the participant's entire life during retirement. May be defined benefit or defined contribution and requires mandatory funding and allows no in-service withdrawals.

Permitted Disparity (Social Security Integration) - A technique or method of allocating qualified plan contributions to an employee account that provides a higher contribution to those employees whose compensation is in excess of the Social Security wage base ($90,000 for 2005) or selected integration level for the plan year.

Phantom Stock Plan - A nonqualified deferred compensation arrangement where the employer gives fictional shares of stock to a key employee that are initially valued at the time of the grant. The stock is later valued at some terminal point and the executive is then paid in cash the differential value of the stock as compensation.

Phaseout - The AGI range that will affect the deductibility of IRA contributions and an individual's ability to make contributions to a Roth IRA.

PIA (Primary Insurance Amount) - The amount on which a worker's retirement benefit is based; the PIA determines the amount the applicant will receive at his or her full retirement age based on the year in which the retiree turns 62. The PIA is indexed to the Consumer Price Index (CPI) annually.

Plan Entrance Date - The date an eligible employee becomes a participant in a qualified plan.

Plan Freeze - Employer will no longer make any contributions to the plan, but does not want to fully terminate the plan.

Plan Loans - Loans from a qualified plan made available to all participants on an effectively equal basis that are limited in amount, are repaid within a certain time period, bear a reasonable rate of interest, are adequately secured, and require the administrator to maintain a proper accounting.

Pre-1974 Capital Gain Treatment - A special taxation treatment for lump-sum distributions from qualified plans that treats the distribution attributable to pre-1974 participation in the plan as long-term capital gain.

Profit Sharing Plan - A qualified retirement plan established and maintained by an employer where the employer makes deductible contributions on behalf of the employees, the assets grow tax-deferred, and if there is a CODA feature, the employee also makes pretax contributions.

Prohibited Transactions - Transactions between the plan and a disqualified person that are prohibited by law.

Prototype Plan - A prepackaged plan that allows the sponsor to use a check the box approach to plan choices.

Purchasing Power Preservation Model (PPP) - A capital needs analysis method that assumes that at a client's life expectancy, the client will have a capital balance with purchasing power equal to the purchasing power at the beginning of retirement.

Pure Annuity Concept - The basic capital needs analysis approach, which is generally prepared on a pretax basis.

Qualified Distribution - A distribution from a Roth IRA that is made after a five-taxable-year period and on account of the account owner's death, disability, attainment of age 59½, or first-time home purchase.

Qualified Domestic Relations Order (QDRO) - A court order related to divorce, property settlement, or child support that can divide a participant's interest in a qualified plan.

Qualified Educational Assistance Program - A plan established and maintained by an employer that provides employees with educational assistance. The employer may exclude $5,250 of benefits from an employee's taxable income.

Qualified Employee Discounts - A discount on the value of property or services offered to an employer's customers in the ordinary course of the employer's business may be excluded from an employee's income (subject to certain limitations).

Qualified Joint and Survivor Annuity (QJSA) - The QJSA pays a benefit to the participant and spouse as long as either lives; although, at the death of the first spouse, the annuity may be reduced.

Qualified Matching Contribution (QMC) - Additional matching contributions made by the employer to satisfy the ADP or ACP test that increases the ACP or ADP of the NHC employees by who had deferred compensation during the plan year.

Qualified Moving Expenses Reimbursement - Qualified moving expenses paid by an employer on behalf of an employee may be excluded from the employee's gross income. This exclusion applies to the reimbursement of moving expenses that the employee could have deducted on his income tax return if the employee had paid, or incurred, the costs without reimbursement.

Qualified Nonelective Contribution (QNEC) - A contribution made by the employer to satisfy the ADP or ACP test that increases the ADP or ACP of the NHC employees by making additional contributions to all NHC eligible employees without regard to any elective deferral election made by the employees.

Qualified Non-Personal Use Vehicle - A vehicle that the employee does not use more than a minimal amount for personal reasons due to the design of the vehicle. The value of a qualified non-personal use vehicle is excluded from an employee's gross income.

Qualified Parking - Parking provided by the employer on or near the employer's business premises. An employee may exclude up to $200 per month (for 2005) from his gross income for employer provided parking.

Qualified Plan - A retirement plan that meets the qualifications of IRC Section 401(a).

Qualified Plan Award - An employee achievement award bestowed as part of an established written plan of an employer that does not discriminate in favor of highly compensated employees (within the meaning of Section 414(q)) for eligibility or benefits. The value of an award provided under the plan, up to $400 for a nonqualified award and $1,600 for a qualified award, is excluded from the employee's gross income.

Qualified Preretirement Survivor Annuity (QPSA) - Provides a benefit to the surviving spouse if the participant dies before attaining normal retirement age.

Qualified Replacement Securities - Securities in a domestic corporation, including stocks, bonds, debentures, or warrants, which receive no more than 25% of their income from passive investments.

Qualified Trust - A trust established or organized in the U.S. that is maintained by the employer for the exclusive benefit of employees.

Qualified Tuition Reduction - The amount of any reduction in tuition provided to an employee of an educational organization for education below the graduate level is excluded from the employee's gross income.

R

Rabbi Trust - An irrevocable trust that is designed to hold funds and assets for the purpose of paying benefits under a nonqualified deferred compensation arrangement. The assets in a rabbi trust are for the sole purpose of providing benefits to employees and may not be accessed by the employer, but they may be seized and used for the purpose of paying general creditors in the event of a liquidation of the company. Assets within a rabbi trust are not currently taxable to the employee.

Rank-and-File Employees - The non-key, non-highly compensated employees.

Ratio Percentage Test - A coverage test that compares the ratio of nonhighly compensated covered by a retirement plan to the ratio of highly compensated covered by the plan. The comparative ratio must be at least 70%.

Real Property - Land and buildings.

Recharacterization of Deferrals - To change the nature of any excess employee deferrals from pretax employee contributions to after-tax employee contributions.

Recharacterize - Transferring a contribution and its attributable earnings from a traditional IRA to a Roth IRA or vice versa. The recharacterization must occur by the tax return filing date including extensions for the year of the recharacterization.

Remaining Work Life Expectancy (RWLE) - The work period that remains at a given point in time before retirement.

Repurchase Option (Put Option) - An option that allows a terminating employee to receive in cash the fair market value of the employer's stock within a stock bonus plan or ESOP if the employer stock is not readily tradeable on an established market. An option to sell to the employer.

Required Minimum Distribution - A minimum amount that must be withdrawn from a qualified plan each year after the participant attains the age of 70½. The amount is calculated using either the uniform distribution table, the single life expectancy table, or the joint life expectancy tables.

Restricted Stock Plan - An employer provided plan designed to increase retention and compensate employees with a non-cash outflow. The plan pays executives with shares of the employer's stock. The executive does not pay any amount towards the allocation of the stock and, in fact, is restricted by the employer from selling or transferring the stock.

Retirement Benefit - The most familiar Social Security benefit, full retirement benefits are payable at normal retirement age and reduced benefits as early as age 62 to anyone who has obtained at least a minimum (40 quarters) amount of Social Security credits.

Retirement Earnings Limitations Test - A test that may reduce the Social Security benefit paid to an individual based on their other income.

Retirement Life Expectancy (RLE) - The time period beginning at retirement and extending until death; the RLE is the period of retirement that must be funded.

Rollover - To elect to transfer funds from one tax-advantaged account to another tax-advantaged account to continue to defer the recognition of income taxes until the ultimate distribution of the assets.

Roth IRA - An IRA created by the Taxpayer Relief Act of 1997. Contributions to a Roth IRA are nondeductible and qualified distributions are excluded from an individual's taxable income.

S Corporations - Small corporations taxed as pass-through entities that cannot have more than 100 individual shareholders and have only one class of stock.

Safe Harbor 401(k) Plans - A 401(k) plan that satisfies a minimum contribution or matching test and allows the plan sponsor to bypass the ADP test, the ACP test, and the top-heavy tests.

Salary Continuation Plan - An arrangement between an employer and an employee where the employer agrees to continue to pay an employee after his retirement or to the employee's spouse if the employee dies prior to retirement.

Salary Reduction Plans - A nonqualified plan designed to receive deferral contributions from executives to reduce their current taxable income.

Sale - The direct exchange of property with another for a note, money, or property of equal fair market value.

SARSEP - Salary Reduction Simplified Employee Pension. A plan that can no longer be established but allowed employees to elect to defer a portion of their current salary into a SEP-IRA in a similar fashion to a 401(k) plan.

Savings Incentive Match Plans for Employees (SIMPLEs) - Retirement plans for small employers with 100 or fewer employees who earn more than $5,000 in a year. SIMPLEs may be established as SIMPLE 401(k)s or SIMPLE IRAs.

Savings Rate - The average savings amount in the U.S. based on consumption.

Section 501(c)(3) Organizations - Nonprofit tax-exempt organizations that are established under IRC Section 501(c)(3) of the Internal Revenue Code.

Secular Trusts - Irrevocable trusts designed to hold funds and assets for the purpose of paying benefits under a nonqualified deferred compensation arrangement. A secular trust does not create a substantial risk of forfeiture for the employee. Assets set aside in a secular trust results in immediate inclusion of income to the employee.

Self-Insured Plan - A plan that reimburses employees for medical expenses not covered by an accident or health insurance policy.

Sensitivity Analysis - A tool used to understand the range of outcomes for each variable in a retirement plan by rotating each variable toward the undesirable side of the risk to determine the impact of a small change in that variable on an overall plan.

SIMPLE 401(k) - A SIMPLE plan that utilizes a 401(k) plan as the funding vehicle of the plan.

SIMPLE IRA - A SIMPLE plan that utilizes an IRA account as the funding vehicle of the plan

Simplified Employee Pension (SEP) - A practical retirement plan alternative to a qualified plan that can be used by small businesses and sole proprietors. It follows many of the same limits as qualified plans but may require the employer to cover more employees.

Single Life Expectancy Table - Tables used to calculate the required minimum distribution for beneficiaries.

Social Security Integration (Permitted Disparity) - A technique or method of allocating qualified plan contributions to an employee account that provides a higher contribution to those employees whose compensation is in excess of the Social Security wage base ($90,000 for 2005) or selected integration level for the plan year ($90,000 for 2005).

Social Security Statement, Form SSA-7005 - A written report mailed by the Social Security Administration to all workers age 25 and over who are not yet receiving Social Security benefits that provides an estimate of the worker's eventual Social Security benefits and instructions on how to qualify for those benefits.

Split-Dollar Arrangement - A single life insurance policy in which two parties, employer and employee, have an ownership interest. The two parties generally split ownership, premiums, and beneficiaries any way they wish.

Spousal IRA - An IRA created on behalf of a spouse who does not have the necessary earned income to make a contribution to an IRA of their own but can borrow earned income from their spouse.

SSI (Supplemental Security Income) - A program administered by the Social Security Administration and funded by the general Treasury that is available to those at full retirement age or the disabled who have a low income and few assets.

Standard Eligibility Requirements - IRC eligibility rules for participation in a qualified plan. Provides that an employee must be considered eligible to participate in the plan after completing a period of service with the employer extending beyond either the date on which the employee attains the age of 21 or the date on which the employee completes one year of service (1,000 hours of service within 12 months).

Standard Termination - Termination in which the employer has sufficient assets to pay all benefits (liabilities) at the time of final distribution.

Stock Appreciation Rights (SARs) - Rights that grant to the holder cash in an amount equal to the excess of the fair market value of the stock over the exercise price.

Stock Bonus Plan - A qualified profit sharing plan funded solely with employer stock.

Stock Option - A right to buy stock at a specified price for a specified period of time.

Straight Single Life Annuity - An annuity for a term equal to the annuitant's life.

Substantial and Recurring - IRC standard defining the frequency requirement of contributions by employers to profit sharing plans.

Substantial Risk of Forfeiture - An income tax concept that relates to when income is subject to income tax. A substantial risk of forfeiture exists when rights in property that are transferred are conditioned, directly or indirectly, upon the future performance (or refraining from performance) of substantial services by any person, or the occurrence of a condition related to a purpose of the transfer and the possibility of forfeiture is substantial if the condition is not satisfied.

Summary of Material Modifications - Document that provides in plain language the modifications made to a qualified plan.

Summary Plan Description - Document that explains in plain language the details of a retirement plan and how it operates. It provides information on when an employee can begin to participate in the plan, how service and benefits are calculated, when benefits become vested, when and in what form benefits are paid, and how to file a claim for benefits.

Supplemental Executive Retirement Plans (SERP) - Nonqualified deferred compensation arrangements designed to provide additional benefits to an executive during retirement.

Supplementary Medical Insurance (SMI) Trust Fund - The trust fund that pays for services covered under the medical insurance provisions of Medicare, known as Part B. The coverage is funded by general federal tax revenues and monthly medicare premiums paid by enrollees.

Survivors Benefit - Social Security benefit available to surviving family members of a deceased, eligible worker.

T

Tangible Property - Property that is not realty and may be touched.

Target Benefit Pension Plan - A special type of money purchase pension plan that determines the contribution to the participant's account based on the benefit that will be paid from the plan at the participant's retirement rather than on the value of the contribution to the account. Requires an actuary at inception.

Tax Sheltered or Deferred Annuities (403(b) Plans) - Retirement plans for certain qualified non-profit organizations or employees of public educational systems – often called 401(k)s for non-profit organizations.

10-Year Forward Averaging - A method of income tax calculation for certain lump-sum distribution from qualified plans that divides the taxable portion of the lump-sum distribution by 10 and applies the result to the 1986 individual income tax rates. The resulting calculation is then multiplied by 10 to determine the total income tax due on the distribution.

Term Insurance Policy - A life insurance contract which states that if the insured dies within the tern of the contract, the insurance company will pay a stated death benefit.

Third Party Administrator - An organization unrelated to the plan sponsor who is paid to administer the plan sponsor's qualified or other retirement plan.

Thrift Plan - A qualified retirement plan that permits employees to make after-tax contributions to the plan. Although the contributions are taxable before being contributed to the plan, the account still benefits from tax-deferred growth on earnings.

Title I of ERISA - Coverage, participation, funding, and discrimination requirements of ERISA imposed on qualified plans.

Top-Heavy - Rules that were designed to ensure that plans established primarily to benefit the owners and executives of the company also provided some minimum level of benefits for the rank-and-file employees.

Traditional IRA - An IRA that may accept deductible and nondeductible contributions and whose assets grow tax-deferred until distribution.

Trust - A structure that vests legal title (the legal interest) to assets in one party, the trustee, who manages those assets for the benefit of the beneficiaries (who hold the equitable title) of the trust.

Trustee - The individual or entity responsible for managing the trust assets and carrying out the directions of the grantor that are formally expressed in the trust instrument.

Two-Year Eligibility Election - A special election that overrides the standard eligibility requirements and permits the employer to only consider those employees who have two years of service as eligible to participate in a plan. If the employer elects the two year requirement, than the employer must also provide 100% vesting at the completion of two years of service.

Uniform Distribution Table - A table used to calculate the RMD for the plan participant unless the participant's sole designated beneficiary is the participant's spouse and that spouse is more than 10 years younger than the participant.

Unit Credit Formula - A benefit formula of a defined benefit pension plan that utilizes a combination of the participant's years of service and salary to determine the participant's accrued benefit.

Universal Life Insurance - A term insurance policy with a cash accumulation pot attached to it.

Unsafe Conditions Commuting Rule - The value of commuting transportation provided by an employer to a qualified employee solely because of unsafe conditions is $1.50 for each one way commute.

Variable Universal Life Insurance - A universal life insurance policy with investment options available for the cash account.

Vest - To give an employee rights to employer contributions and earnings in their retirement plan benefits.

Voluntary Employees' Beneficiary Association (VEBA) - A welfare benefit plan into which employers deposit funds that will be used to provide specified employee benefits in the future. The deposits are deductible for the employer at the date of the contribution rather than at the date when the employee benefits are provided.

Wage Replacement Ratio (WRR) - An estimate of the percent of income needed at retirement compared to earnings prior to retirement.

Whole Life Insurance Policy - A permanent life insurance policy that guarantees that the policy will remain in force as long as the premium is paid. The life insurance policy has a cash account that grows tax deferred.

Work Life Expectancy (WLE) - The period of time a person is expected to be in the work force, generally 30-40 years.

Working Condition Fringe Benefits - Any property or service provided to an employee that enables the employee to perform his work and, if paid for by the employee, is deductible as a trade or business expense (i.e. parking).

X Dividend Date - The date that the market price of a divided paying stock adjusts for the dividend (i.e., the market price of the stock is reduced approximately by the amount of the dividend).

Year of Service - 1,000 hours of service for an employer within 12 months.

Index

Numerics

U

Uniform Distribution Table 301
Uniform Lifetime Table 301
Unit Credit Formula 148 − 150
Universal Life Insurance 134
Unsafe Conditions Commuting Rule 616, 622

V

VEBA 650, 659, 687
Vesting 85, 225
    Cliff Vesting 85, 87
    Graduated Vesting 85, 87
    Top-Heavy 91
    Years of Service 88
Veterinary Surgical Consultants, P.C. v. C.I.R. 490
Voluntary Employees' Beneficiary Association. See VEBA

W

Wage Replacement Ratio 11, 16, 22 − 23, 26 − 27, 33 − 34, 539 − 540, 554

Adjustments From Preretirement Income to Retirement Income Needs 25
Calculating 22
    Bottom-Up (Budgeting) Approach 23
    Top-Down Approach 22
Sources of Retirement Income 26
    Personal Assets 28
    Social Security 26
The Budgeting Approach 23
The Top-Down Approach 22
Waiting Period 642
Whole Life Insurance 134
Wilhelm v. United States 590
Wilson v. United States 591
Work Life Expectancy 11, 13 − 14, 32 − 33
Working Condition Fringe Benefits 586, 601
Wright v. Oregon Metallurgical Corp. 249

Y

Years of Service 88